ALSO BY ADRIAN GOLDSWORTHY

The Roman Army at War, 100 BC–AD 200

Roman Warfare

The Punic Wars

Cannae: Hannibal's Greatest Victory

The Complete Roman Army

In the Name of Rome: The Men Who Won the Roman Empire

Caesar: Life of a Colossus

How Rome Fell

Antony and Cleopatra

Augustus: First Emperor of Rome

Pax Romana: War, Peace and Conquest in the Roman World

Hadrian's Wall

Philip and Alexander: Kings and Conquerors

The Eagle and the Lion

ATHENS AND SPARTA

THE RIVALRY THAT SHAPED ANCIENT GREECE

ADRIAN GOLDSWORTHY

An Apollo Book

First published in the USA in 2026 by Basic Books,
an imprint of Hachette Book Group, Inc
First published in the UK in 2026 by Head of Zeus Ltd,
part of Bloomsbury Publishing Plc

Copyright © Adrian Goldsworthy, 2026

The moral right of Adrian Goldsworthy to be identified as the author
of this work has been asserted in accordance with the Copyright,
Designs and Patents Act of 1988.

All rights reserved. No part of this publication may be: i) reproduced or transmitted
in any form, electronic or mechanical, including photocopying, recording or by means of any
information storage or retrieval system without prior permission in writing from the publishers;
or ii) used or reproduced in any way for the training, development or operation of artificial
intelligence (AI) technologies, including generative AI technologies. The rights holders expressly
reserve this publication from the text and data mining exception as per Article 4(3)
of the Digital Single Market Directive (EU) 2019/790.

9 7 5 3 1 2 4 6 8

A catalogue record for this book is available from the British Library.

ISBN (HB): 9781800245426 ; ISBN (XTPB): 9781035927272
ISBN (eBook): 9781800245440

Cover design: Jessie Price | Head of Zeus
Text design: Jeff Stiefel
All maps © Jamie Whyte

Printed and bound in Great Britain by Clays Ltd, Elcograf S.p.A.

Bloomsbury Publishing Plc
50 Bedford Square, London, WC1B 3DP, UK
Bloomsbury Publishing Ireland Limited
29 Earlsfort Terrace, Dublin 2, D02 AY28, Ireland

HEAD OF ZEUS LTD
5–8 Hardwick Street
London EC1R 4RG

To find out more about our authors and books
visit www.headofzeus.com
For product safety related questions contact productsafety@bloomsbury.com

ATHENS AND SPARTA

CONTENTS

List of Maps   ix
Acknowledgements   xi

Prologue   1
Introduction   11

PART ONE:
THE RISE OF THE CITIES

1 Greeks   27
2 Land and Cities   43
3 The Lawgiver   59
4 The Great Pronouncement   79
5 The Tyrants   101
6 The People   117
7 The Peers   133
8 The Spearmen   153

PART TWO:
YOKE FELLOWS: THE STRUGGLE WITH THE PERSIAN EMPIRE

9 Great Kings   177
10 The Charge   199
11 The Ships and the Conference   225

CONTENTS

12	The 300—and the 700 and the Rest	245
13	The Wooden Walls	265
14	The Great Battle	285
15	Honour, Prestige, and Empire	305

PART THREE:
GREAT EVILS FOR THE GREEKS

16	Tremors	329
17	Peace, Pride, and Power	355
18	The General	369
19	The Causes and the True Reason	387
20	The Beginning of Great Evils for the Hellenes	405
21	Something Unheard Of	425
22	Fickle Fortune	445
23	Lust for Glory	463
24	'Ships Lost…Don't Know What to Do'	489
25	To the Sound of Flutes and Celebration	509
26	Conclusion	525
	Chronology	537
	Notes	549
	Bibliography	589
	Illustration Credits	605
	Index	607

LIST OF MAPS

1. Lands around the Aegean in the fifth century BC   15
2. Sparta and its conquests in Messenia   91
3. Megara   108
4. The demes of Attica   124
5. Sparta and its villages including later period monuments   140
6. Darius's invasion and Xerxes's advance   203
7. Battle of Marathon   214
8. Battle of Thermopylae   258
9. Battle of Salamis   273
10. The Athenian Empire   320–321
11. Sparta and its Peloponnesian allies   334–335
12. Athens and key monuments in the late fifth century BC   377
13. Pylos and Sphacteria   440
14. Siege of Syracuse   480–481
15. The last battles, 411–405 BC   497

ACKNOWLEDGEMENTS

MY AIM IS TO PROVIDE AN INTRODUCTION TO THE SUBJECT, but one with depth, even though it is impossible to cover everything in equal detail given such a broad theme. The works cited in the notes will help the interested reader go further, each in turn providing references to yet more of the vast array of scholarship out there. As in all my books, I must express my great debt to the many scholars cited and the others whose work has helped my understanding of the period more generally. I will single out three by name, although it could as easily be thirty, and the frequency of references to particular scholars will give some idea of how much I have learned from their work. When it comes to Sparta, the numerous conferences and subsequent volumes organised by the late Anton Powell and his collaborators have been especially inspiring, for the questioning of almost all that the scholarly consensus had concluded about the Spartans. Whether or not the revisionist views convince, this greatly stimulated the debate on so many topics. I should also mention the work of J. E. Lendon on the central role played by honour and perception of status, themes that, as a result, run throughout this book. It has also been my greatest good fortune to turn to this project at a time when Paul Rahe was completing his series on the Grand Strategy of Sparta, surely one of the most ambitious and successful projects in modern classical scholarship.

ACKNOWLEDGEMENTS

At times I may take a different view to that presented by these and other scholars, for that is the nature of the evidence, where certainty is rarely possible, but I never do this lightly. More often, I found that they had anticipated anything I thought might be original, reminding me of a comment by the late Brian Dobson, referring to the study of Hadrian's Wall but just as applicable here: 'Again and again as we strive to express some truth . . . we find that it has already been said, better and clearer. If ever we imagine we glimpse some new truth . . . it is simply because we stand on the shoulders of giants.' At the very least I hope that this book will make a wider audience aware of the wealth of scholarly work that has been—and continues to be—done in the study of the ancient world, much of it often known only to specialists.

Thanks must as always go to my agent, Georgina Capel, for making things happen and creating the circumstances where I can hope to do justice to the topic. Also, many thanks to my editors, Holly Harley and Richard Milbank at Head of Zeus and Lara Heimert at Basic Books, and their respective staffs in London and in New York as they turn the raw manuscript into the handsome volume that one day will arrive through the post. Even after all these years, there is something special about holding a book for the first time. As always, the staff at the Institute of Classical Studies Library in London have been both welcoming and very helpful, as much of my research has relied upon the collection there. More personally, I am once again very grateful to the friends who have spared the time to help. Kevin Powell read and commented on a full draft, doing so in double-quick time and as always very helpfully. My thanks to him. Over the three years or so it has taken to research and write this book, Dorothy King has listened with patience to many of the ideas as they took—very rough—shape in my mind, often improving them or pointing me in directions that have greatly improved the end result. I am very, very grateful.

ATHENS
— AND —
SPARTA

PROLOGUE

SOMETIMES ONE BOOK LEADS TO ANOTHER. A FEW YEARS AGO, while I was writing a biography of Philip II of Macedon and his son Alexander the Great, I kept looking for a fairly recent and accessible history of what had come before—essentially how the Greek world had come to be as it was when Philip was born c. 382 BC. There was only so much space to talk about what the world was like at the beginning of the story, so I hoped to be able to point readers in the direction of one book that would give them a reasonably detailed view of this. I could not find one and do not believe that one has been written since then. There are plenty of books about the Persian Wars, when the Greeks led by the Spartans and Athenians repulsed invasions by the greatest empire of its day, Achaemenid Persia, and there is also a lot of good stuff about the Peloponnesian War fought between Athens and Sparta later in the fifth century BC. Something covering the whole period, rather than just part of it, was lacking, so it seemed a good idea to fill this gap.

This then is that story, the book that I could not find, and, in some ways, it will act as a prequel to the tale of Philip and Alexander. Yet it is meant to be far more than that. Classical Greece is one of the key periods for understanding ancient history, along with Rome in the late republic and early empire. These are eras for which the sources are good—and often for their literary quality and wider influence as well as their historical value—allowing study at a greater depth.

As importantly, these were also times when so much happened that was to have profound consequences for subsequent history and culture. That is not to deny that other eras are also of great interest and importance, but simply to say that these are fundamental. If you wish to gain a deeper understanding of the Greeks and Romans, then you must learn at least something about these periods. That is why they have tended to form the core of ancient history degrees for generations and still should, not least to make sense of any more specific thematic studies. Some framework of events and political developments needs to be there to support any study of narrower topics, for however interesting these may be, they need to be set in a wider context.

Most of my research and writing has been on the Romans, but the influence of Greek ideas and the Greek past on the Romans was so deep that it was always there as background. Yet, in the wider perception of and interest in the ancient world, this is not the case. The Romans tend to get far more coverage in popular culture, and not just in film and drama but in the documentaries shown on television. The last stand of King Leonidas and the 300 Spartans at Thermopylae is an exception, but on the whole most people will recognise the name of Caesar or Nero and have some idea of who they were in a way that they do not for Pericles or Alcibiades. Even Thermopylae tends to be seen in isolation, with little sense of what it was all about. Similarly, the Parthenon, that most recognisable of Greek monuments, has become a symbol rather detached from the reality of fifth century BC Athens. This neglect of Greek history is a shame, and one of my hopes in writing this book is that it will encourage more history enthusiasts to explore and better understand the history and legacy of Classical Greece.

That history is both interesting in its own right and relevant to our own day and age, not least because this era saw the creation of the first consciously democratic systems, as well as the Athenian experiment that gave voters a greater role in day-to-day decision-making than in any state before or since. In the modern world, the Western idea that democracy is the ideal, indeed even the natural, system for any advanced state is so deeply entrenched that it is taken for granted, and the danger is that this makes what happened in the Greek communities seem less remarkable. Often enough, this is accompanied by a level of disappointment, even scorn, that the Greek experiments with democracy did not follow every modern principle, for instance, excluding women from taking part and accepting slavery as natural. Apart from ignoring the context and considering why things were as they were, such a dismissal ignores the basic truths that this was the moment when democracy emerged and that it did so among the Greeks, not to mention just how rare any variation of it has been throughout the world until very recently.

Context matters, and if we are to understand what Greek communities did and why they did it in the Classical period, we must think about the very nature of those communities and of the wider world. Nothing happened in a vacuum or was a question of pure ideas, and not even the Athenians were conducting a theoretical experiment into the ideal constitution and society. Instead, they were trying to work out how their city could become as powerful, prestigious, and rich as possible, competing with other communities when it came to trade and military dominance. The theorising came later, and the reformers who shaped these political systems were concerned with the here and now and with the immediate future, with no real thought for what others might think two and half millennia later. Athenians celebrated their democracy because Athens flourished and became strong under it. In the same way, the Athenians' greatest and most famous monument, the Parthenon, celebrated the glories of their city and its democratic system, not some abstract sense of Hellenic culture. While in design and decoration this monument—at which we still marvel today—drew upon concepts and taste shared with other Greeks, it was meant to parade the glory of the Athenians as greater and better than everyone else.

History must begin with the effort to understand societies that no longer exist and complex events that happened long ago. Only after this is done to the best of our ability can lessons be learned, let alone judgements passed; this book will do little of the first and none of the second, for the task of understanding is big and important enough in itself. Our aim is to glimpse the lives of human beings living in these societies and see how they behaved as individuals and groups, for this helps us better understand ourselves. While much may appear alien to us at first, for instance the ready acceptance of slavery, the frequency of war, the open and unashamed celebration of victory, and the satisfaction at destroying enemies, the Greeks, Persians, and others in this world were not fundamentally different from us. Indeed, even where attitudes and assumptions seem very different, it is often more a matter of degree than anything more profound, and much that we take for granted may be more recent and less fixed in our own societies than we are inclined to think.

Thus, as mentioned earlier, many readily declare that 'Greek' democracy was flawed because many were excluded on the basis of sex or status in a way that would not be considered acceptable in a modern state. The conclusion that this somehow invalidated any claim that Athens or other cities were 'true' democracies is sterile. Which citizens were granted political rights varied from city to city, with only radical democracies like Athens eventually including all male citizens to some degree. Elsewhere the demos—'the people'—might be a smaller group, those owning a decent-sized farm or more than that, but this could still be a substantial enough group to qualify as a democracy, the rule of the people. In other cases, the group was narrower, requiring more wealth and perhaps high birth to qualify, making it an oligarchy or aristocracy, the rule of the few or the best. Monarchy, the rule of one, was rare among Greeks by the sixth century BC.

While these categories of democracy, oligarchy, aristocracy, and monarchy may seem strange and archaic to a modern observer, some of the rationale behind them is not so very different from ideas openly expressed today. Similarly, although the restriction of voting rights to just a section of the population—excluding the poor, women, slaves, and so forth—may appear odd, it is worth remembering that the movement for women's suffrage succeeded not much more than a century ago in most Western countries. Here in the United Kingdom, it is just over fifty years since the voting age was lowered from twenty-one to eighteen, which meant that many of those who fought to defend democracy in World War II were too young to vote. In some circumstances at a local level in Britain, the voting age has been reduced to sixteen, and there is talk of extending this to national elections. At the same time, successive governments have encouraged children to remain in full-time education until the age of eighteen, the same age at which they cease to be considered minors in law. Thus, while few would argue against the principle that all adults should cast a vote of equal validity, there is argument over what counts as an adult for this purpose. Another source of controversy is whether those who have settled in a country from abroad, whether legally or not, can or should gain the right to vote in some or all elections. While there is much talk of principles when such matters are raised, changes to voting rights and procedures, as well as electoral regions, tend to be introduced by those who feel that they will benefit from them the most. There is no reason to think that this was different in the ancient world, even if few Greeks would have understood the willingness of many modern states to grant the franchise to outsiders who came to work and live in their cities.

More importantly, some of the same justifications for restricting the franchise in the fifth century BC have echoes in views expressed today, regardless of the lip service paid to the principle that all votes are equal. Note how media coverage describing a party or a politician as 'popular' is a compliment, whereas saying 'populist' is a condemnation. Demonisation of those who disagree as the wrong people with the wrong ideas is common, especially when such 'wrong people' have the impudence to win an election or other vote. Very readily, when our personal views do not prevail, we seem able to convince ourselves that somehow the winners do not have a proper majority. The impact of technology has helped, since the world of social media allows many to cut themselves off from anyone with opposing views or to abuse them without fear of consequences. It also makes easier declaring the success of an opponent as somehow a failure of the democratic system or even a direct threat to democracy itself. Democracy is readily praised when 'our' side or candidate wins and as readily damned when they do not.

Here in the United Kingdom, these sentiments were particularly common before, during, and after the vote on EU membership that led to Brexit. The Leave vote won, and opponents readily dismissed those who had voted in this way as old, parochial, poorly educated, or all of these things and worse, which, given the overall numbers, was clearly at the very least a gross exaggeration. It really was surprising to hear the frequently expressed view that 'ordinary people'—which essentially meant everyone holding a different opinion to the speaker—were simply too bigoted, ignorant, and unqualified to decide on such an important matter and that they really ought to leave it to their elected representatives, who were naturally wiser and more knowledgeable in every way. The last claim was especially surprising, since enthusiasm for and confidence in parliamentarians are rare sentiments in any other circumstances among those on either side of the debate. Although indirect and largely unconscious, the argument in favour of an oligarchy of right-thinking people was blatant and appears to be a deeply human instinct—what we think must be right and is the only answer. This should help us to understand the arguments and revolutions within Greek states—how readily neighbour could turn on neighbour because of a sense that the wrong people were in charge.

People are and were as emotional and impassioned as ever, and while they can also behave rationally, that reasoning may develop from a range of basic assumptions to lead to very different conclusions about what is right and sensible. For all the modern scorn poured on the Athenians and other Greeks for the limits they imposed on who could vote and stand for office, they would surely have shown matching dismay for many aspects of modern states. In particular, they would not have understood the idea of delegating authority and decision-making to elected officials in the long term, let alone to institutions like permanent courts and judges, who have the right to say that people must do as they are told. Greek city-states possessed elected councillors and magistrates, but their tenures were limited, usually to a year, and they were far more directly accountable to voters, in part because the communities were smaller in the first place. By modern standards an institutionalised state did not exist as something separate from and over the citizens. Those eligible to vote did so regularly and, apart from elections, gathered to decide on other issues and pass laws. The majority of those present decided what was to be done, virtually instantly, with none of the prolonged process of implementation required today. Like everything else, this had good and bad consequences, and at times voters proved themselves irrational and fickle. Law could be changed or created, and only a citizen could take anyone to court, where the case would be heard by fellow citizens and not by a specialist judge or judges. Again, much of this was a legacy of the originally small size of such communities, where once everyone had known everyone else.

Unlike in modern states, where such decision-making is delegated, Greeks assembled to decide whether to start or end a war, and indeed how to fight one, so that both war and politics run through this story. While this may seem strange to modern readers, recent events will make this uncomfortably relevant. For Westerners, inclined to feel that warfare is something consigned to the past, or at least fought at a great distance against technologically inferior opponents, times have changed and, with them, the perception of threats to peace and stability. My last book was finished a few months after the 2022

Russian invasion of Ukraine. That conflict continues to this day, although just possibly peace may be within sight in the form of a compromise giving neither side all that they wanted at the start. At the least, this recent example is a reminder of how plans go awry and how much harder it is to end a war than to start one. It also has shown how difficult achieving a decisive victory on the battlefield can be and how greedily and quickly a full-scale war devours men and matériel. The peace negotiations also emphasise the difficult balance between the practical and the physical—control of land and resources—and the symbols of status, independence, and power.

Hopefully by the time this book is published, almost a year from now, the tensions between India and Pakistan that have flared in recent days will have been calmed without major conflict. What will have happened in Gaza is less easy to predict, while the world pays less attention to other conflicts, such as the one in Sudan. I am writing this prologue on Thursday, 8 May 2025, as my own country and plenty of others mark the eightieth anniversary of VE Day, the end of World War II in Europe. It is good that they do this, remembering far bigger and more costly conflicts. World War II—or at least the way it tends to be remembered—provides an example of a clearly just and truly decisive conflict, which destroyed aggressive political systems in National Socialist Germany, Fascist Italy, and—months later after VJ Day—Imperial Japan.

Like many I am fascinated by World War II, in part because for me it was just one generation away, so that I grew up around so many people who had lived through it, something less and less true for those born later. My late father was serving in the army in Palestine under the British Mandate on VE and VJ Days, while my mother was at school and remembers the celebrations and the sheer relief that it was over at long last. Recently, constant talk of the war and scenes of ruined buildings on the television news have given her bad dreams about the Blitz on Cardiff, which was at its height in the winter of 1940–1941. The memory and fear of bombing raids and cold nights in the air raid shelter remain fresh after so many years. As I have said elsewhere, while I share a deep interest in 'the War', as my parents' generation called it—and indeed have written a novel about it—the historian in me sometimes worries that our simplified popular image of that great conflict makes it harder to understand other wars, most of which lacked such an ideological basis, were less morally clear, and did not prove as decisive. Far more common throughout history has been a pattern of the same states going to war with each other generation after generation and sometimes allying with a traditional enemy against others when it seemed to be of mutual advantage. This was typical in Classical Greece, with each city driven by what it judged most to its advantage. Often these were wars against traditional enemies, where the objective was to gain an advantage for negotiation rather than the opponent's total destruction, and where at times an enemy could become a friend before reverting to being a rival and an enemy once again.

War is still with us, politics is still with us, and the readiness of neighbours to bicker and disagree, even to vilify each other under the conviction that they alone are right, has not dimmed since the fifth century BC. For all the distance in time and attitudes, a good deal about the story of Athens, Sparta, and the other Greek cities still resonates.

INTRODUCTION

Some stories remain famous down the ages because they deserve to be told and retold.

In 480 BC, Xerxes, the great king of Persia, then by far the most powerful empire in the known world, attacked Greece at the head of an immense army drawn from the finest fighting men to live under his rule. Some said that more than a million souls marched to war under the great king. Blocking their path through the narrow pass at Thermopylae was a small force of Greeks led by King Leonidas and his 300 Spartans. For two days the Spartans threw back wave after wave of enemies until the Persians learned about a track that led around behind the pass. Sending most of his force away, Leonidas and the Spartans stayed behind, and on the third day they did not simply defend their position but attacked and for a while drove the invaders back, until the vastly superior numbers told. The Spartan king was killed, and eventually his surviving men retired to a little hill and formed a circle of shields, refusing to surrender. Reluctant to close with them, the Persians shot clouds of arrows at them and kept on shooting until all of them were dead. Later, an inscription set up over their graves bore these famous words: 'Passer-by, go tell the Spartans that here we lie, obedient to their orders.'

Weeks later, the grand fleet that had accompanied the Persian army rowed its galleys into the narrow stretch of sea between the

Athenian coast and the island of Salamis. They were confident, for not only did they have numbers on their side, but false information fed to them by a wily Athenian admiral led them to expect that they need only chase a fleeing enemy. Instead, the Greeks were ready to fight, and Xerxes watched as more and more of his ships were sunk or captured, and the morale of the Persian fleet was permanently broken. A year later, the great king long since returned to his empire, the Spartans, the Athenians, and their allies routed the army he had left behind. The Persian attempt to add the Greeks to the empire had failed and was never repeated. Instead, the Greeks remained independent and free, and the culture that was to have such a deep influence on the world was able to flourish.

It is a remarkable story, and the broad outline is true up to a point, even if the whole truth was a good deal more complicated. Other Greeks apart from the 300 Spartans stayed to the end and fought to the last at Thermopylae. Last stands of the vastly outnumbered are amongst the most dramatic of all stories, and that made by Leonidas and his men has in many ways become the quintessential one. By comparison, the great victory at Salamis is a little less well known, at least these days when the classics have lost their once central role in education in the West. Plataea, the land battle fought in 479 BC, has faded even further from the popular memory, even though it involved the biggest army ever mustered by the ancient Greeks.

Xerxes's grand invasion of Greece failed because of the battles of Salamis and Plataea, and as a result Greece remained free. Yet, in the modern sense, there was no Greece as a country; instead, there were hundreds of distinct and fiercely independent communities. The people of the area spoke the Greek language, shared many beliefs and stories, and competed against each other at festivals such as the Olympic Games, but the sense of being Greek was vague. Far more important was the sense of being a Spartan or Athenian, a Corinthian or a Theban, a Plataean or a Thespian.

INTRODUCTION

These were the communities that mattered, and it was for these that men were willing to fight and die. At the end of it all, just thirty-one communities were recognised as having stayed the course and held firm to an alliance to defend against the Persian threat. Many more Greek communities submitted to Xerxes, and most of these sent men or ships or both to fight as part of the invading horde. Still others stayed aloof throughout the war, and each community acted as it thought best, so in many ways, that as many as thirty-one cooperated to fight against Xerxes was remarkable, and that they bickered, disagreeing about how and where to oppose the invaders, was unsurprising.

The Spartans led the alliance against the Persians, and after them the Athenians won most credit for making the victory possible. None of the other cities involved, not even Corinth, could compare with them when it came to numbers and sheer military strength, making Athens and Sparta the biggest players and the main focus of this story. These two cities were not natural allies and had in the past waged war against each other, while the decades that followed the defeat of the Persians saw tension between them, which in time led once again to open war, most intensively from 431 to 404 BC, a conflict subsequently known as the Peloponnesian War. In itself this may not seem surprising, since these were very different societies, almost polar opposites in the organization and operation of their political and social systems. Yet these conflicts had no ideological basis, and in general these and other Greek communities made alliances and fought wars without too much consideration of such matters. One central theme of this book is that competitiveness lay at the heart of these societies. Within their own communities Greeks vied for prominence, prestige, and power, while collectively they were just as eager to assert their city's status and show its superiority to all the other cities out there. All this came naturally, for the most prominent men in every community tended to be wealthy aristocrats, the same class that met together every four years to compete in the Olympic Games, as well as on other occasions at similar festivals.

CLASSICAL GREECE HAS had a profound influence on the history and culture of the Western world, and two cities and one era stand at the heart of this. Athens and Sparta became the two greatest powers in the Greek world. United, they helped lead the Greeks in defeating the great Persian invasion. Divided, they spread conflict and destruction throughout the eastern Mediterranean, culminating in the horrors of the Peloponnesian War. They were not simply rivals for power but polar opposites in culture and ideology, with Athens the outward looking, radical democracy and maritime empire and Sparta the militaristic, rigidly disciplined, and brutal society. Both were experiments in how to run a state, extremes of the Greek longing to excel.

The roots of these different cultures lay back in a past with Solon at Athens and the semi-mythical Lycurgus in Sparta, but changes late in the sixth century BC exacerbated the differences between them and set them on the path to collision. Yet it need not have been so, and in 510 BC a Spartan army answered a call for help from Athenian aristocrats, allowing them to expel the tyrants ruling Athens. Soon afterwards the Athenians began to take the nascent idea of democracy and push it further than ever before. A generation later, after the Persian invasions had been defeated, Sparta gained huge prestige and then turned in on itself, while the Athenians built on their success at sea to create an empire, predominantly of the many islands in the Aegean. Most communities at first welcomed Athenian protection, then resented it as it became more and more oppressive. The same transition occurred at Sparta, where the Athenians were first praised for protecting the Greeks against future Persian aggression and then seen as arrogant and dangerous rivals. In the meantime Athens developed its own democracy to the extreme, while becoming more and more aggressive and unwilling to grant rights to others.

Beset by plague, farming and trade crippled by war, the two rivals fought themselves to exhaustion. In the greatest irony, the heroes of Greek resistance against Persia went to the current Persian king, and only through his aid and subsidy was the impasse broken. Sparta defeated Athens but was so weakened that her own supremacy was short-lived.

Athens, the aggressive, immensely self-confident, radical democracy, was often brash and even vulgar as well as cruel; yet it also gave the world so many ideas, comedy and drama that moved audiences in ways unlike anything that had come before, and art that has provided inspiration ever since. Spartans did not innovate, while Athenians threw out ideas constantly—some good and some bad. No other major state has allowed thousands to join in debates where anyone could propose a law and see it enacted. This was a society capable of remarkably clear thinking and such pointless savagery as executing Socrates for challenging accepted ideas at a time of general nervousness and political uncertainty.

Sparta and Athens were bigger and more powerful than other Greek cities but also had a lot in common with them. Everywhere there was a striving to excel, to stand out and be accepted as superior to others. Most of the time, men strove peacefully for status and office within their home cities, and similarly cities did everything to assert and prove their strength and valour while stopping short of actual warfare. Yet violence was common enough to be a real possibility in each case, something that could well follow whenever the competition intensified. Revolutions occurred in a high proportion of the hundreds of Greek cities during the period covered by this book, and in a lot of cases the same community experienced several; those that proved stable generation after generation were the exception, while such political struggles tended to be savage, as neighbour slaughtered neighbour with scant sign of reluctance. At the same time Greek communities went to war with each other fairly often, fighting and killing to control land and protect their prestige.

INTRODUCTION

Thus, having fought alongside each other against the might of Persia, Athenians and Spartans became rivals and enemies when they felt it was in their interest to do so. Such changes of attitude were common enough throughout the history of Classical Greece, and indeed much of the history of the wider world. The struggle with Persia had been a great moment for both cities, and for others as well, even if the part these had played was smaller. Spartans were justly proud, and others understandably admiring, of the willingness with which Leonidas and his men sacrificed their lives in the common cause and of their prowess and courage as they bore the brunt of the fight at Plataea. The Athenians had also played a major role in that battle on land—and also, with help from just a single ally, had defeated an earlier Persian invasion at the Battle of Marathon in 490 BC. They had served with distinction on land, but even more importantly, their naval strength and leadership had made the victory at Salamis possible. Even more remarkably, the 200 warships they had provided—well over half the combined fleet—were recently built because the Athenians had decided to turn themselves into a sea power just a few short years earlier. All of those who took part in repulsing the Persian invasion naturally and reasonably celebrated this as among the greatest achievements in their cities' histories. This had been a struggle of the weak against the strong, where the weak had prevailed, and while many communities thrived under Persian rule, it is unlikely that Sparta, let alone Athens, would have done so. Subjects of the great king would not have built the Parthenon to parade their own glory and power.

Repulsing the Persian invasions was a remarkable achievement, long remembered and justly celebrated. Yet, by 431 BC, as war between Athens and Sparta loomed, the Spartan leadership enthusiastically discussed seeking Persian aid to fight against their former allies and fellow Greeks. It did not work out, but later in the war, alliances were made, and it was Persian gold sent to Sparta that allowed the Spartans to create a succession of fleets and win the war. By that stage the Athenians had tried and failed to convince the Persians to switch sides and fund them instead. After the war, allegiances changed at a rapid pace. Athens sided with Corinth and Thebes against Sparta, then with Sparta against Thebes, and all the time the key players did their utmost to get Persian backing. They even agreed to a peace, supposedly guaranteed by the great king, although this did not last, and the Persians did nothing to enforce it. In one sense the empire had won in the end and could claim that the Greeks had submitted, although this never went as far as receiving tribute, let alone imposing direct rule. Ironically, the Persians had turned from a deadly threat to the liberty of the Greeks into a very attractive and rich ally, all in the space of just a couple of generations.

Explaining how this happened is at the heart of this book, and to do that, it will deal with the Persian Wars themselves and the subsequent conflicts between Athens and Sparta, particularly the Peloponnesian War, since these are intimately linked, apart from being dramatic in their own rights. This is the story of Athens and Sparta over more than a century of their history. Each was large and powerful by the standards of the Greek world, but they were very different in terms of their political systems, societies, and economies, all of which were reflected in the way they treated others. The focus is overwhelmingly on politics, diplomacy, and war, which may seem strange to the modern reader. Partly this is because the mental picture that most have of the ancient Greeks emphasises cultural and intellectual sophistication, which in turn, to the modern mindset, is usually held to be incompatible with enthusiasm for violence—or even the acceptance of violence as sometimes necessary. Yet, in many respects, the Greeks were as much a warrior culture as the Romans or Gauls or other races from the ancient world seen as far more warlike. War was frequent and could be brutal, and it was fought between communities living very close together. Even the biggest and most determined rivals lived within easy reach of each other. For instance, in 490 BC a messenger ran from Athens to Sparta, covering almost

INTRODUCTION

140 miles in two days, and a little later 2,000 picked Spartan troops marched the same distance in three days. Events were concentrated in a very small area.

The aim of this book is to explain who the Spartans, Athenians, and other Greeks were, how their communities developed, and why they did what they did. This is a narrative history because this is the best way to understand a period and also because it is how all people live their lives, however confusing each person's personal story may feel. Events occur and follow each other, and a thematic approach all too easily forgets this, turning people into bland groups or categories rather than lots of individuals. This is also mainly a story of politics, empire, revolution, and war. Along the way there are chances to consider other aspects of life, but I had to resist the temptation to dwell too much on art, culture, and society. Such things did not exist in isolation, and concentrating on the thoughts and creativity of the few is dangerously misleading. Most Greeks were not artists, philosophers, or writers, any more than they were Olympic athletes. So much of the evidence for social attitudes comes from Athens and from the perspective of the wealthier citizens that it may not reflect what everyone else felt about such things even in that city, let alone elsewhere.

There is a lot of politics, although, because of the scope, covering well over a century, at times I must skim over the details. From the start it is worth reminding the reader that the Greek cities under discussion were not modern states; instead, they were communities, the largest still very small by modern standards. Each community was made up of citizens—the modern understanding of the term varies and is rarely identical to the fifth century BC concept, but this remains the best word to use. The community was everything. Membership came through the family to legitimate children produced by the marriage of two citizens and was often tied to owning a set level of property. It was very rare for an outsider to move to a settled community and become a citizen, and even those allowed to reside, perhaps for generations, were not granted political rights, especially at Athens.

Alongside politics, there is much about warfare, and here again, this was not waged by institutionalised armies or navies. When a war was fought, it was fought primarily by citizens, serving alongside each other. Risking their lives in this way was the basis of their claim to political rights; it was not a rare or theoretical experience but something that usually occurred more than once in a man's life. Losses from heavy fighting bit deep into the community, in a way reminiscent of the Pals battalions recruited from the same districts in Britain's industrial cities during the Great War. Politics was not an abstract thing; nor was war distant for the Greeks. Some readers may not care for long descriptions of conflicts, but these are essential to understand the events properly.

Much has changed since the fifth century BC, and aspects of politics and war are very different. Yet people have not changed, for all that society shapes aspects of their behaviour, and at its heart the study of history is the study of human beings. Understanding what they did and why relies on the sources, and for the ancient world these always present problems of interpretation and also fail to tell us much that we would wish to know. The only approach is to try to understand them and gauge their reliability, asking questions even if we cannot give firm answers. Frustrating though some find this, for certainty is reassuring however false, my approach is to make clear what is guesswork and how confident the guesses are and also to admit what we do not know. This is the only worthwhile and honest way to study history.

The Athenians were open and liked talking about themselves, whereas the Spartans were secretive, which means that most of the evidence reflects an Athenian perspective. Some of the material was written soon after events, while other authors wrote much later, admittedly with access to earlier works that have not survived. All of them tended to assume that any reader would know a lot in the first place, so that there was no need to explain the commonplace. Surprisingly often, an important aspect of custom or society is attested in a single or at most a handful of passages, some of them very distant in time from what they describe. One great danger of this is that a particular practice mentioned—for instance, this is what the Spartans did—raises many questions that are difficult to answer. The first is whether or not the author himself or his source—most likely in each case an outsider to Sparta—possessed and passed on correct information. Even harder to judge is whether the statement that 'they did something' meant that they did it 'sometimes', 'often', 'nearly all the time', or 'always and without exception'.

All too often scholars make the most of such a nugget of information by assuming a very rigid 'always', which is one reason why it is important to consider everything from a practical point of view and place it in the context of what else we know. An author or the original source may well have assumed that any reader would understand the background, so automatically add a 'sometimes' rather than assuming 'always'. For a modern analogy, we might say that a university student spends three or four years at a particular institution studying a subject to gain a degree. At the same time, we would know that this does not mean that all 365 days of each year were spent in this place doing that and only that. Apart from the other activities of student life, the individual might well work, travel, spend time at home during the vacations, and so forth. Two and a half thousand years later, the same statement might be read as the whole truth, especially if it were the only surviving piece of information for what young people did at that stage of their lives. In approaching history, it is vital always to think of the context, even if this must be inferred, and the practical aspects of any activity.

As is so often the case for the ancient world, the evidence is varied but limited. All types of sources, whether in the form of works written in the ancient world, inscribed texts that have survived, or archaeological exploration of sites from the period, provide different challenges of interpretation. Taken as a whole, very many gaps remain in the evidence for understanding this period. At times, dates are uncertain, even for major events, and further details about what actually happened can be meagre. Inscriptions were set up for a reason, not to provide an unbiased and full explanation for a phenomenon, while the data provided by archaeology, already reduced by chance of survival and excavation, offers only a glimpse of what once was. The literary sources provide the framework for everything, since only they describe events, and at the same time provide different challenges. Two predominate, with Herodotus essential for the Persian Wars and Thucydides for the Peloponnesian War, while both offer significant amounts of other material as well.

Herodotus came from Halicarnassus in Asia Minor, where many Greeks lived as part of the Achaemenid Persian Empire. Later he travelled to Athens and lived there for a while, at a time when a fair number of folk who had taken part in the struggle with Persia were still alive. Dubbed both 'the father of history' and 'the father of lies', he loved a good story and included much that is fanciful because it was entertaining, while his account is full of omens and dreams. In contrast Thucydides served as an Athenian general in the Peloponnesian War until he was exiled for failure, and his style is far more sober, as he attempted to understand how and why things happened. While scholarly opinion changes almost with the tides—or at least with the generations of work done in the field—Thucydides continues to be seen as more inherently reliable than Herodotus, although both have their critics, and no one accepts all of what they say. They are supplemented by Xenophon for the final stages of the Peloponnesian War and its aftermath, and much later by the likes of Diodorus Siculus and Plutarch, who wrote in the Roman period.[1]

The aim here—to understand what happened and why—is best achieved by a narrative structure, dealing with events in turn. Along the way, this offers the chance to explore other aspects of life and society, not least because these help to explain the course of events.

INTRODUCTION

Still, this cannot hope to deal with every aspect of this era in detail, or indeed with every event, so I must skim over much for simple reasons of space. On the whole, I mention names only when they are essential; at other times, I will simply say that a leader, magistrate, or commander did something. This is a question of clarity and keeping the narrative as simple as possible. In the same way I have limited the number of Greek terms and expressions. The sheer beauty of the language and the complexity of meaning of many words make peppering the text with them tempting, but this is intimidating to a reader without a classical background. Instead, I use modern expressions that are close enough, and in the same way I anglicise names, so Achilles rather than Achilleus, Pericles rather than Perikles, Cleon rather than Kleon, and Spartans rather than the variety of terms applied to them, such as the Lacedaemonians. Where appropriate, I discuss points of detail, at least to an extent, but often I cannot cover debates over the specific form of a political institution, the terms of a treaty, or the precise chronology of events, let alone the complex manoeuvres of a battle. Each and every chapter of this book could be given a book-length study of its own, and the references will point the interested reader towards the literature on a topic.

Dates present a different problem. Each Greek community tended to have its own calendar, or sometimes more than one, for instance at Athens, where the political year was divided into ten units, while other systems of measuring time marked festivals and the agricultural seasons. Usually, all calendars were based in some form or other on the lunar cycle and had to be balanced to keep even broadly synchronised with the solar year. More widely the measurement was in Olympiads, the four years between each Olympic Games, but there are doubts about when this system was created and how reliable the attribution of many events to an Olympiad actually was. As a result of all this, precise dating by year is not always possible. Even when it is, the use of lunar calendars and the choice of when a year began tends to mean that the period of a year in the sources does not correspond precisely with the reckoning based on the modern system. Convention expresses this as, for instance, 481/80 BC, where the annual cycle for a community began part way through the modern concept of 481 and ended at the same point early in 480 BC. This is sometimes used, whenever it seemed significant.

This then—after all the caveats—is a history of the relationship between the Spartans and the Athenians from the latter part of the sixth century BC until the early stages of the fourth century—in essence, a long fifth century BC. It is a story of ambition and pride, of diplomacy, politics, and war, but like any history, it matters because it is a story of human beings, produced by very different cultures to those of the modern world but still essentially the same as people today. As with any other civilization and more than most, the story of the Classical Greeks highlights the best and the worst of the human experience.

History is worth understanding in its own right, because it reveals so much about how humans behave, and the distant past is a reminder that the range of possibilities is very broad. Thucydides claimed that his work would always be relevant for this essential reason. There may, as he claimed, be lessons to learn from the ancient past applicable to every age, but first it is vital to try to understand the history on its own terms and in its own context. Complete freedom from bias and preconceptions is an impossible goal, but the aspiration to do this as far as is possible must remain the aim of any serious history.[2]

Part One

THE RISE OF THE CITIES

I

GREEKS

*A people, a language, a real past,
and an imagined past*

c. 1400–800 BC

'SING, OH GODDESS, THE ANGER OF ACHILLES SON OF PELEUS, that brought countless ills upon the Achaeans.' Homer sets the scene quickly in the *Iliad*; then, in twenty-four books—15,693 lines of verse—the poet recounts what followed when Achilles, the greatest warrior in the Greek army outside Troy, felt slighted by Agamemnon, ruler of Mycenae. The first word in the original is the Greek for anger or rage, and because of this insult to his honour and status, Achilles refused to fight and instead waited—some would say sulked—in his tent while successive battles went badly for the Greeks. After a while, his friend Patroclus went in his place, wearing Achilles's armour so that the Trojans would think that their deadliest foe had returned to the fray. The ploy worked, only for Patroclus to get carried away with success, advance too far, and challenge Hector, the Trojan's greatest champion, who promptly killed him. Achilles was plunged into despair, his hatred for Agamemnon switching to Hector. Returning to battle, he carved a swathe through the Trojans until he encountered and slaughtered Hector; he then proceeded to humiliate the corpse, dragging it behind his chariot. Only a plea from King Priam of Troy, Hector's elderly father, at last moved Achilles to pity, his anger and sense of loss spent.[1]

The *Iliad* and the *Odyssey*, which tells of the travails of another of the Greek heroes, Odysseus, who took ten years to return from Troy to his homeland of Ithaca, are the earliest surviving works of literature in Greek, or indeed in any European language. No complete manuscript is preserved of either poem dating to earlier than the Middle Ages, but there are plenty of fragments on papyri from the Greco-Roman world. More importantly, the frequency of quotations from and allusions to Homer's poems in ancient literature and art make clear the central place that they occupied in Greek culture. Like Shakespeare's works, these texts were taught to children and at the same time enthralled and inspired adults, shaping their understanding of the world.[2]

Both poems were attributed to Homer, sometimes dubbed the blind poet, although there was no substantial tradition about him or his life; the songs mattered far more than the singer. Many came to believe that the poems themselves assumed their final form—an authorised or official version, as it were—in Athens in the second half of the sixth century BC and that, before this, there was some variation, albeit minor. Modern scholars estimate that the poems were written down sometime from c. 750 to c. 700 BC, although some push the date a little earlier or up to half a century later. Opinion remains divided over whether one man, whoever he was, composed them both. Clearly, the poems sprang from an older, perhaps far older, tradition of oral poetry, with established set pieces readily adaptable to various characters and situations and formulaic phrases designed to describe people and things crafted to fit the rhythm of a line whenever a name needed to appear.

An extreme position would view the *Iliad* and *Odyssey* as shaped by generations of poets, the text gradually accruing until someone decided to write it down. More convincingly, the power of these poems, not simply for the ancients but to this day, argues in favour of the creativity and voice of a single author shaping the version that was set down. The differences in language and attitudes between the two works are well within the range of one person, while the similarities are far stronger. Still, such judgements are inevitably subjective, making the case impossible to prove either way, and in the end it does not really matter. Most Greeks believed that the same man composed both poems, and, while there was occasional criticism of the stories' content, no one challenged their importance and influence. The Greeks also believed that Homer lived long after the events he described. If the modern estimates are right, then he set down his verses some four or five centuries after the time when the Greeks thought that the Trojan War had been fought. Whether or not the war ever happened or the traditions about it bore even the slightest resemblance to actual people and events, these epic poems were presented from the start as tales of an earlier time rather than the contemporary world. Each reflected some aspects of the real world its audience recognised and much that was strange, more spectacular than the life and times they knew. There is no hint that there was ever a 'Homeric age' when society was exactly mirrored by the poems. The seventh century BC poet Hesiod called that past era an age of heroes, as opposed to the grimmer age of iron in which he lived, when men had to toil to support themselves and their families.[3]

The *Iliad* and *Odyssey* alike look back to a distant past, but whoever wrote them assumed that the audience already knew of Troy and of the kings and heroes who had supposedly fought there. Of the ten-year siege of the city, the *Iliad* deals with a few weeks and focuses primarily on just five days of action. It does not include the story of the death of Achilles, let alone the Trojan Horse and the fall of Troy. The *Odyssey* does deal with these, albeit recounted as a story within the story, as something already history. Similarly, allusions are made to earlier events, but the *Iliad* assumes that everyone already knows about the seduction/abduction of Helen by Paris, of the mustering of the Greek expedition, and indeed the nine years of the war before the story begins. All this is expected to be familiar, a well-established body of tradition and myth, common to all Greek-speaking communities. Homer's poetry became central to this collective sense of identity, but there were many other strands as well, often local. The sense of what it meant to be a Greek was never simple or wholly uniform.

Near the end of the fifth century BC, the historian Thucydides noted that Homer reserved the name Greek—or Hellene, in the Greek language—for just a distinct part of the army outside Troy. When referring to the army collectively, Homer called them Argives, Achaeans, or Danaans, leading Thucydides to the reasonable conclusion that the name Greek/Hellene only became common at a later date. Similarly, Homer did not use the word *barbarian*, the label imposed on everyone who was not Greek, because—in the opinion of Greeks—their speech sounded like gibberish, the repetitive *bar-bar-bar* of a sheep.[4]

Unsurprisingly, attitudes had changed a good deal in the three centuries between Homer's era and Thucydides's day. Yet Homer composed in the Greek language for an audience who understood his words and both understood and accepted the world he portrayed and felt some association with it. Belief could be suspended for heroes to be superhumanly strong and carry absurdly heavy or ornate equipment and for the gods and goddesses to intervene directly and to appear in disguise or in their full majesty. Hesiod presents the Olympians as more responsible and with a stronger sense of justice than Homer, and there was some criticism of both, but most seem to have accepted the poems as stories rather than literal truth, blending a fairly realistic setting with fantastic elements. Thus, for all their might, the heroes experience a gamut of emotions, from fear to jealousy, anger to despair, affection to sorrow, and the rights and wrongs of their behaviour are neither simple nor obvious. Homer does not make it at all clear whether he considers Achilles's emotions and deeds to be admirable or excessive, but he does present them as in keeping with the man's character and, on that basis, understandable.[5]

His heroes are not described as Greeks, but Homer wrote in the Greek language and set the stories in a common cultural heritage that would in time become consciously Greek. The origins of the language are impossible to trace and reach back earlier than even the supposed setting of the poems. Greek is an Indo-European tongue, akin to many ancient and modern European languages as well as to Sanskrit. Opinion remains divided over where and when this ancestor to later languages originated and how and when the people who spoke it spread over such a wide area. The steppes offer a plausible place of origin, and groups of Indo-European speakers may have spread into Europe around 2,000 BC, conquering the groups already there or integrating more peacefully. Plausible cases can be made for and against each of these scenarios, and the spread could have occurred earlier and in different ways.

Whatever language the inhabitants spoke, the lands that would become Greece—Hellas to the Hellenes themselves—had seen a continuous human presence from the end of the last ice age. At first, as throughout the world, these were hunter-gatherers, living in small groups, killing game, and eating fruit and vegetables that they found growing wild. This lifestyle required a large territory to support just a few people, who travelled a considerable distance from season to season, and went on foot, because no animal had yet been domesticated to ride. Food is an essential for life, and the approaches to acquiring it have shaped the development of human society. As people learned the properties of grasses and developed cereal crops, and as they learned to maintain herds of animals for meat, milk, wool, and hides, more food was generated, and communities grew more numerous. The great breakthrough was learning to cultivate crops, for farming supported a far bigger population than any other system. This meant settling down in one place to plant, tend, and harvest and, over time, to develop natural grasses into bigger-yielding cereal crops. All this required moderately good soil, sufficient rainfall, and considerable hard effort.[6]

As more and more little communities began to farm, populations grew, and more and more land was brought under cultivation or used for pasture. Instead of bands of one or two dozen wanderers, there were villages where hundreds lived. These innovations appear to have spread to what would become Greece from the Near East, perhaps in part through settlers and also as ideas were copied and gradually spread from one group to the next. On the whole Greece, let alone the rest of Europe, lagged behind these innovations. Conditions for the first experiments and their development were more favourable elsewhere, for instance in the Fertile Crescent, stretching from the coast of Israel/Palestine through the higher ground of Turkey and Syria into Iraq and the Tigris and Euphrates valleys.

If the first farms developed where there was higher rainfall, the next great jump forward came where rain was less plentiful and instead people worked out how to make better use of river water. The Nile, with its annual inundation, and the Tigris and Euphrates, with their reliable flow, offered opportunities to irrigate the land around. This was more predictable than relying on rain, even though there could still be too much or too little water at critical times. In Mesopotamia and Egypt harvests increased, and larger and more complex societies developed. In the course of the fourth millennium BC, the Sumerians in Mesopotamia created the first real cities, and by 3,000 BC, the first and largest of these, Uruk, may have had a population of something like 60,000. Egypt remained a land primarily of many villages with fewer cities but was united and highly organised, for both agriculture and the construction of major projects. From 2575 to 2520 BC, just three pharaohs presided over the building of the great pyramids, truly gigantic structures, but part of an already well-established tradition.[7]

All societies needed to make collective decisions and resolve internal disputes, to acquire and divide food and resources, and to store and protect those resources from loss, theft, and decay. Means of accomplishing this varied considerably between a band of twenty or so hunter-gatherers and a settled village of a few hundred people, let alone communities of thousands and tens of thousands. At the simplest level, in the smallest communities everyone could know everyone else in a way that was impossible in larger groups. Irrigation systems required considerable amounts of labour to create in the first place and then to maintain, which required large numbers of people to coordinate and work together for long periods. Hierarchies developed in all the early civilizations, in the main concentrating power in the hands of one leader or a small group. These regulated life within the community, controlled the labour force, most of all for grand projects, and gathered and distributed some or all of the food and other produce. Backed by armed men, such rulers imposed their will on others and ideally protected against threats from the outside.

Life remained precarious, nature fickle, adding to the natural human instinct to understand the world and control as much of it as possible. Organised states led to organised religion, whether headed by a priestly class that claimed a special understanding or relationship with the gods and other supernatural forces or by a ruler like a pharaoh who was a divine or semi-divine intermediary living on earth. From such viewpoints, devoting massive resources and effort to building temples or pyramids and making sacrifices was as practical a way of ensuring the next harvest as tilling and watering the fields. Societies that developed writing have left traces of their leaders and beliefs, offering glimpses of their worlds. The Sumerians produced the *Epic of Gilgamesh*, legendary king of Uruk, while the hieroglyphics and later traditions of Egypt offer the names of gods and pharaohs and recount something of the latter's deeds.

Yet most societies from the ancient world have left no written trace. Around 2,500 BC, the great stones that give the place its modern name began to be erected at Stonehenge in southern England, adding to a landscape that had already seen much ritual activity for many generations. No one will ever know who made all this happen, precisely what it meant to all involved, and why changes were made in later phases, for the archaeology on its own cannot reveal such things. Similarly, the stories are lost of the individuals and communities in what would become Greece, whether the hunter-gatherers, the early Stone Age farmers, or the villagers living in larger groups as the Stone Age turned into the Bronze Age. As they were human beings, it is safe to assume that there was ambition and passion, ingenuity and stupidity, kindness and cruelty, energy and sloth, and all the range of good and bad deeds visible in better-recorded societies. The big civilised states of the Bronze Age in the Middle East left more of a trace of their passing. By the middle of the second millennium BC, the biggest powers were New Kingdom Egypt, the Hittite Empire in Anatolia, at times the Middle Assyrian Empire, and a number of smaller kingdoms and states. Among these, second-, third-, or lower-tier powers were the first discernible states to arise in the Aegean.[8]

The earliest were the Minoans on the island of Crete. The name is modern, taken from Minos, the legendary king whose daughter gave birth to the Minotaur, a monster half man and half bull. No one knows what the Minoans called themselves (or whether they had a collective term at all), but the remains of their grand palace complexes have provided a wealth of archaeological material. At its height, the palace of Knossos, the biggest of them all, was truly massive and in places had no fewer than five storeys. This was a literate society, and a large number of clay tablets—accidentally baked hard by fire and so preserved—have been found, inscribed with a language known as Linear A. So far this has proved impossible to decipher, although the almost universal consensus is that it is not a form of Greek. The presence of some pictograms makes clear that most of the texts are lists of produce, and it seems that the palaces were centres for redistribution, provided with ample storage facilities.[9]

Much remains mysterious. There are signs of smaller redistribution centres around the big palaces, but the relationship between the main palaces themselves is unclear. There is very little sign of fortifications at any site, which suggests that no major military threat was anticipated from neighbours, and the imagery of Minoan art, not least in the palace wall paintings, is not overtly martial. Signs of contact with the bigger empires, especially Egypt, are also obvious in this art and in the objects excavated. While much of this contact was peaceful, later tradition, including Thucydides, remembered the kings of Crete for their naval power, and it is unlikely that the society was wholly peaceful. For most of ancient history, the distinction between a formal navy and a pirate fleet was extremely narrow, while trading and raiding were not exclusive. Even so, the destruction of some of the earlier Minoan palaces is more likely to have resulted from earthquake than war, and it is uncertain whether or not the grandeur of Knossos in its later phases represented expansion of its control and changes in the balance of power on Crete.[10]

In Greece itself and on the smaller islands, communities in some areas grew in size during the Minoan era. Several show signs of the emergence of an aristocratic class, distinguished by the greater quantity and cost of grave goods in prominent tombs. Weapons, notably bronze daggers and later swords, are commonly associated with male burials, suggesting a warlike elite. Around 1,400 BC, a number of palace sites appear in what is known today as Mycenaean culture, although, once again, this is a modern term and not the name used by the people themselves. In this case it comes from the nineteenth-century excavations at Mycenae by the maverick archaeologist Heinrich Schliemann, which revealed the first-known example of one of these palaces in mainland Greece.[11]

Like most societies, the Mycenaeans copied the ideas of others, modifying some of them and adding innovations of their own. They were literate and left behind clay tablets written in Linear B, which has been deciphered and is a form of Greek. Many of these documents deal with lists of produce, both agrarian and animal—sheep, goats, and pigs all figure prominently—and there are clear signs that the palace sites acted as storage and distribution centres for the surrounding areas in a broadly similar way to the Minoan centres. Unlike the Minoans, the Mycenaeans appear as overtly warlike, with weapons and images of warfare prominent, while their palaces were positioned with defence in mind and fortified, if not in the initial phases, then subsequently. Several have circuit walls made from very large cut stone, the remains so impressive centuries later that the Greeks called them Cyclopean, as if only giant hands could have fashioned such defences.

The Mycenaean palace centres show every sign of having made war on each other and further afield. On some of the islands, Minoan finds become supplanted by Mycenaean objects around the middle of the fifteenth century BC. The palace complex at Knossos itself was either occupied by Mycenaeans or taken over through alliance by a Mycenaean faction because, when it burned down c. 1,400 BC, the clay tablets preserved in this level were written in Linear B rather than Linear A. Hittite documents mention the land of Ahhiyawa in the west—possibly a garbled version of Achaea—and one text from the Hittite king addresses the ruler of Ahhiyawa as 'brother' and 'great king', epithets common enough in the diplomatic language of the time, but only for the leaders of major powers. A second text included the term 'great king' but crossed it out, and overall Ahhiyawa features far less often than other states. Egyptian sources of this period seem to mention the Minoans in a diplomatic context and also include place names, some of which appear to be Mycenaean centres.

There is more than one way of interpreting this evidence, and some have argued for a powerful Mycenaean state, perhaps wholly or partially united under a single leader, who played a full and active role in the trade, diplomacy, and power struggles of the wider eastern Mediterranean world. The two instances of 'great king' in Hittite correspondence to Ahhiyawa could mean that for a while there was a leader deserving or demanding such shows of respect, who then lost power, died, or was overthrown by weaker kings, rendering these courtesies obsolete.

Caution is needed. Large and impressive though they were, the Mycenaean palaces in Greece lack the sheer scale and grandeur of the Minoan centres. They also vary a good deal in size and probably in function. Judging from the Linear B tablets, each remained the centre for produce from surrounding communities, but there is no hint of a wider, overarching authority suggesting a union between the various centres. Instead, the picture is of rival, sometimes hostile, palace centres each with their own territories. A tablet describing the stationing of groups of men to protect a coastal area does not suggest large numbers of soldiers on the scale mobilised by the Egyptians or Hittites. Equally important, substantial parts of Greece had no palace centres at all, although they were still densely populated by smaller communities with a less obvious hierarchy of sites. Cult and burial practices varied not simply between the regions with and without palaces but between the palace communities themselves. The archaeology does not suggest a unified Mycenaean state, and the Linear B tablets speak only of men with the title *wanax* (pl. *wanakes*), who appear to rule one of the centres, and do not suggest one greater ruler as overlord.[12]

If the Mycenaeans—individually and perhaps sometimes in alliance—took part in the struggle for prominence and power in the eastern Mediterranean, their role was modest. There is no real sign that they were perceived as a serious threat to the big empires, which were able to marshal large and sophisticated armies. Great power conflict did happen—for instance, in 1274 BC, when the Egyptians and Hittites fought each other at Kadesh and both sides claimed victory—although more often there was wary coexistence. Yet, from c. 1,200 to c. 1,000 BC, drastic changes occurred. Egypt, weakened by internal power struggles and less able to deal with threats from outside, shrank to a shadow of its former might. The Hittite Empire collapsed altogether, similarly divided internally but facing more dangerous aggressors from outside. The major and minor states all either vanished or drastically declined in the space of a couple of generations.

The Mycenaean place centres were no exception to this sudden, widespread catastrophe. All were abandoned or replaced by humbler structures, and most show traces of violent destruction. In the centuries that followed, there is every sign of a drastic reduction in the number of settlements in these regions, with the surviving communities smaller in size and less prosperous. Nothing on the scale of the palaces was built for a considerable time. Even more significantly, there is not the slightest trace of the written word being employed anywhere in the Greek world for the next 500 years.

The change was drastic, the impact widespread, even if scholars are less inclined these days to speak of the subsequent era as the Dark Age of Greek history. Why and how all this occurred is unclear, although substantial movements of population, coming as raiders, migrants, and conquerors, play a significant role in all explanations. Egyptian sources speak of wars—and claim victories—against invaders coming from the west and from the sea, groups often lumped together under the modern name of the *sea peoples*. It is possible that Mycenaeans took part in these raids and invasions, always remembering that they were not one united people but many groups sharing the same broad culture. Rivalry between different groups, the *wanakes* of palace centres, most likely led to all-out war and the utter defeat and sack of some places by their near neighbours. Such conflicts then added to the numbers of displaced warriors and leaders, needing to support themselves through violence and plunder, becoming mercenaries or raiders or seeking to take new lands for their own. As more and more communities suffered, and especially as the bigger states declined or collapsed, wider patterns of commerce were disrupted, the impact spreading in ever-widening ripples to all those involved.[13]

Change occurred, and a good deal was violent, but the apparent speed of it all is in some ways an illusion created by the sources. The destruction of the Mycenaean palace centres occurred over the course of several decades at the very least, and the collapse of the greater and lesser powers seems to have taken as long or longer. A decade, let alone fifty years, is not a short period in an individual's lifetime, even if it can appear as such in the excavation levels on a site or when firm dates for events and reigns are few and far between. There were surely many stories, many very different experiences of these dramatic times, but again—like so much of human history— they have not been preserved. There was plenty of time for power struggles within empires and small states, for defeats, and for natural disasters such as poor harvests or earthquakes or epidemics, and for a few of the states and leaders, there were most likely times of success and growth, even if these led eventually to failure. Simple explanations for the process are unlikely to reflect a complex reality.

Something of this is suggested by the archaeology. As noted earlier, in some parts of Greece there is no trace of palaces, the central authority and distribution centres seen as characteristic of the Mycenaeans. In general, those areas without palaces show a far less drastic drop in settlement numbers and prosperity after 1,200 BC than is visible in the lands dominated by the palaces. This could mean that the latter were the focus of conflict and suffered more. Alternatively, the palaces may have been the anomalies, based on ideas copied from elsewhere and in the very long term perhaps not tenable in the conditions of second millennium BC Greece. Much depends on how far the rise and then destruction of the palace societies was part of wider trends beginning in the older civilizations of the Near East. In a sense these may always have been communities on the fringes, benefitting from the prosperity generated by the bigger states but vulnerable when these weakened.[14]

Recovery also came sooner in the Near East than in Greece, as surviving states rebuilt or new ones formed, encouraged by the same conditions that had helped their predecessors to prosper. The end of the second millennium BC and the start of the first saw the transition from the Bronze to the Iron Age. The techniques of working the two metals were different, but while iron required greater heat, it was easier to source and not dependent on the rare commodity of tin essential for turning copper into more useful bronze. Iron tools, especially ploughs, were another significant advance in the ability to grow more and better crops. Thus, after the upheaval of falling empires and states, there was eventually a new growth in population. Among the emerging groups were the Phoenicians, whose cities lay along the coast of what is now Lebanon, and who became the great maritime people of the era, trading—and sometimes raiding—around the Mediterranean and beyond.

Greece was not cut off from this renewal of waterborne trade, although it is fair to say that, as in the past, it lagged behind Egypt and the Near East in the scale and complexity of its communities. Even though the impact of the end of the Mycenaean era meant different things in different regions, overall the population shrank and did not begin to recover and ultimately surpass the earlier period for centuries. Homer appears to have known little about the Mycenaeans, even though his stories were set in that era. He describes palaces as the homes of some of his kings and princes, but they bear little relation to actual Mycenaean ones. Centuries later, historians like Thucydides could find out no more about the past. The impressive ruins of some of the palaces were visible, and there were stories from the age of the heroes but little or no accurate knowledge of the events and societies of those earlier times.

Yet there were some survivals, even if these were largely unconscious and unnoticed. Linear B tablets refer to offerings to Zeus, Hera, Poseidon, and other familiar deities, suggesting that many, if not all, of the Olympian gods and goddesses known to Homer and Hesiod had been revered by the Mycenaeans. That is not to say that there were clear preservation and simple continuity in these cults. Like the Greek language, no doubt beliefs developed over the centuries, with many local variations. When writing returned to Greece in the eighth century BC, it was with a script based on the Phoenician alphabet, the symbols representing sounds. Phoenician was a Semitic language, the vowel sounds not written, but the Greek version added characters for these, greatly increasing its flexibility by creating a true alphabet adaptable to any language. One suggestion is that it was first designed to write down and preserve poetic verse, and certainly it was soon adapted to this purpose and used for far more than record keeping, even if it had actually begun as a means for recording property and transactions.[15]

Poets, including Homer, had a wide audience eager to remember and perform their works. Distinct dialects of Greek developed, but for all the local peculiarities of speech, Greek speakers seem on the whole to have been able to understand each other and to appreciate the same poems. The same gods and goddesses were known, the same stories of heroes and their adventures, even if there were variations of detail and some versions only known in some areas. Homer did not call them Greeks and surely reflected eighth century BC attitudes in this respect, but at the same time he shows the existence of a common language and culture by this time. Aspects of later Greek identity were present, and many of them were clearly not new, but they were still different in many ways to what would follow. Tradition dated the first Olympic Games to 774 BC, but for generations this was a local festival that only later became a Panhellenic event from which non-Greeks were excluded. It is a great leap from the heyday of the Mycenaean palaces to the eighth century BC, when other sources begin to appear to supplement the archaeology. Even then, these offer no more than glimpses of a changing world. Much is still hard to understand about the next centuries, when the cities of Greece took shape, but some trends and developments can be glimpsed, however faintly.

2

LAND AND CITIES

*The rise of the farmers and communities
that became Classical Greece,
c. 800–650 BC*

THE GREEK LANGUAGE AND A COMMON CULTURE SURVIVED the collapse of the Mycenaean palace society, developing and changing over the following centuries. A few of the palace sites would later re-emerge as major cities, notably Thebes and Athens, while others would never again be anything more than local centres or did not reappear at all. In no case was there direct continuity, and the impression is that the palaces were ruined and the sites abandoned for some time. When occupation resumed, even in the cases where the interruption was brief, it was on a far smaller scale and very different in nature. Houses in the following centuries were small, perhaps with stone foundations, but with mud-brick or wattle-and-daub walls and thatched roofs. Communities were also smaller—hamlets rather than villages.[1]

Thucydides claimed that in the past the inhabitants of Greece rarely settled in one place and had no organised system of agriculture. The distinction between farmers and pastoralists was an important one, reflected in Homer and followed down the centuries as a basic Hellenic belief. Primitive peoples lived without agriculture, and also without laws, and dwelt in scattered houses or wandered freely. The more advanced tilled the soil, were governed by law, and lived together in cities, even if these were small in size. This was the hallmark of civilization and became closely interwoven with the Greeks' image of themselves.[2]

Archaeology tells a different story, in yet another indication of how little even learned people in the fifth century BC knew about the distant past. Farming continued after the collapse of Mycenaean civilization, even though it decreased in scale. At the start of the first millennium BC, less land was cultivated by a smaller population, with a greater emphasis on pastoralism than before. Again, there was considerable variation from region to region, with the sharpest decline in the areas where the palace system had dominated, but the picture of decline was more or less true everywhere. This was subsistence farming, allowing small communities to survive from year to year instead of generating the surpluses integral to the Mycenaean system. Rather than wandering, most of the pastoralists lived within the farming communities, grazing their animals locally.[3]

Yet many Greeks later believed that the era after the Trojan War was one of great upheaval and disorder, when whole populations were on the move. A lot of communities maintained that they had been founded by immigrants and conquerors, and the Athenians were unusual in boasting that they had 'sprung from the soil' of Attica rather than arriving from outside. Spartans claimed that their ancestors were part of a great Dorian invasion of the Peloponnese, led by sons of Hercules, the latter the founders of their royal houses. Such traditions were not straightforward, with several contradictory versions coexisting, but they were well established at the latest by the seventh century BC. They helped to explain why different dialects of Greek, such as Dorian and Ionian, were spoken in distinct regions. Even more usefully, claims of conquest justified a community's right to control its territory and dominate neighbours or sections of the population held to be the progeny of the conquered.[4]

The archaeological record does not support the idea of mass migrations, so many scholars believe that stories like the Dorian invasion were later inventions by the Greek communities designed to explain—and validate—the reality of contemporary politics and social hierarchy. Certainly, Greeks and other groups often invoked distant, mythical tales when it was convenient to negotiate alliances or declare war on others. Homer was cited, as were plenty of other traditions, many of them not recorded elsewhere. An extreme case came in the first century BC, when a tribe in central Gaul claimed descent from Trojan refugees, allowing them to become not simply allies but 'brothers' of the Romans, who had their own venerable and surely spurious belief that they were descended from the Trojans. It is always hard to tell how seriously anyone took such claims, and political speeches by Athenian orators in the fourth century BC suggest that ancient politicians could present wildly distorted versions of comparatively recent history without being challenged. Whether this was from general ignorance or a willingness on all sides to accept whatever they chose to believe for the moment is impossible to say, but other eras, and indeed the present day, show that such things are not uncommon.[5]

Homer does tell numerous stories about heroes who establish themselves somewhere else after being forced to flee from their original homes by enemies. Such men bring with them their followers, and it is fair to say that such a migration, not of an entire population but of a leader, his household, and his band of warriors, would be unlikely to leave much of a trace archaeologically. A group numbering in hundreds, let alone a smaller band of several dozen, might well have been strong enough to overwhelm and dominate a village or several villages, even a small city. They would become the overlords, killing, expelling, or incorporating an existing elite, leaving the rest of the population to farm, watch the herds, build, and craft just as they had always done. For all the drastic, even violent, political change, everything appearing in the archaeological remains would be the same, and the same would most likely be true even if the attackers numbered in thousands. Thus there may have been a basis in reality for some of the stories of migration and conquest.

The world presented in Homer's poems has plenty of fantastic, imagined, and exaggerated elements, but at its heart it is plausible and internally consistent. A leader like Agamemnon or Odysseus is a *basileus* (pl. *basileis*), often translated as king or prince and in later centuries applied to Alexander the Great and the Roman emperors. The root appears to be the Mycenaean title *pa-si-re-u*, denoting a regional official/leader, a low- to middle-ranking subordinate of the *wanax*, or high king, who was the true ruler and leader of the palace centre. It is almost as if the collapse of Mycenaean society lopped the top off the hierarchy, leaving only much smaller communities and lesser leaders, the latter turning into local warlords, a scenario that readily fits the archaeological record for the early part of the last millennium BC.[6]

In Homer a *basileus* cannot enforce his will on the wider community or other nobles, so Agamemnon cannot simply order Achilles to return to battle. The *basileus* has a palace, wealth, herds, and fields and receives gifts or produce from the wider community, but he does not own the entire harvest or control it as in one of the old distribution systems. Although there are royal families, there is no simple succession. Agamemnon is king of Mycenae, while his brother Menelaus is simultaneously king of Sparta. Odysseus is *basileus* of the island of Ithaca, even though his father, Laertes, is still alive. When the former fails to return from Troy after twenty years and is presumed dead, his adolescent son Telemachus does not succeed, and instead suitors gather hoping to marry Penelope, Odysseus's wife, and become king through this connection.[7]

Ancestry counted, but a *basileus* had to demonstrate his worth in order to rule, needing to be wise in council and most of all brave, skilful, and successful in battle beyond the mass of men. This being epic poetry, all the heroes are also spectacularly good-looking. They take risks, fighting in the forefront through choice, and this earns them the right to lead but not to command unquestioning followers. Whether at home or encamped on the shore outside Troy, men from the community or the massed army all gather for council. All can speak, but status, reputation, and past actions determined how likely someone was to be asked their opinion and, even more, what weight his words would be granted. On one occasion, Odysseus, acting as marshal at a meeting, told the majority to keep quiet and listen while those braver and more sensible spoke. A man named Thersites ignored him and continued a virulent critique of Agamemnon, until Odysseus turned on him, beating him with a staff of office and driving him away, because of what he said and the way he talked and, more importantly, because he had not earned the right to say such things. Thersites was the 'ugliest man' in the army, lame, hunchbacked, and bald on top, and was worthless in every way for all his ready tongue. The assembled army agreed with Odysseus, judging his silencing of Thersites to be right and proper. A hero and a leader had to stand out and be seen as worthy. The smallest contingent at Troy, carried in only three ships, was led by someone with a distinguished father but himself judged to be a 'weak man', so that very few were willing to follow him.[8]

It seems reasonable to suppose that Homeric society reflects aspects of life in Greece as small communities struggled to survive and grow, albeit presenting everything as bigger and grander. Peace was desirable but often threatened by violence and war. Villages and would-be cities needed to protect themselves when harvests and animals could be stolen and people taken as slaves. Good leaders needed to fight well and inspire others to do the same, guarding against these dangers and perhaps preying on weaker neighbours. Burial patterns reflect this, with prestigious male graves almost always including one or more weapons. This was a dangerous world, and common language and culture did not translate into any reluctance to fight and kill other Greeks. In the *Iliad* the Achaeans band together to attack

Troy without any permanent alliance and friendship between the various leaders and groups.

This was not a world shut off from the outside, for Phoenician traders and raiders appeared, while ships powered by oars and sails feature throughout the stories, and the sea was never far away. Mainland Greece has a long, irregular coastline, with very few places much further than seventy miles away from the coast. The vast majority lay much closer, and, except in those rare cases where there were no natural harbours, most communities could access the sea and be reached by those coming by ship. This was even more true of the islands, which, between them, were home to very many communities in this and later periods. Some islands were tiny, but even so most had more than one settlement on them. Others were large, most notably Euboea to the east of Attica, which is some 110 miles long and varies between a little over 30 and a little under 4 miles across. The strait separating island and mainland is barely 130 feet across at its narrowest point, but Euboea is still an island, and reaching it takes effort. In contrast, the Peloponnese, joined to the rest of Greece by the narrow Isthmus of Corinth, is almost but not quite an island. There were communities several days journey from an accessible shoreline, but these were a minority.

As much as, if not more than, the sea, mountain ranges dominate mainland Greece; there can be very few spots indeed where on a clear day at the very least a hill, and most likely a mountain, is not visible. Mount Olympus is the highest at some 9,500 feet high and even in Homer's day was presented as the home of the gods. Most mountains are lower, and none of the mountain ranges are wholly inaccessible, but they did force travellers along particular routes through the passes and divided the country into many smaller locales. The Greek landscape and the quality and type of soil vary considerably, often over very short distances. The same is true of the climate, which, although broadly of the Mediterranean type—and by all indications, throughout the period covered by the book similar to today—has a huge number of local variations, often very local, affecting small areas. Mountain ranges prompt rain to fall as the clouds reach them, and in general annual rainfall is highest in the north and west of Greece, but again, there are many exceptions, creating a patchwork of highly varied living conditions within the broader hot summers and mild winters.[9]

Central authority had collapsed with the Mycenaean palace system. Whether or not the Mycenaeans had ever come under the rule of one or more overlords, each palace centre had governed a substantial area with a hierarchy of smaller communities and local authorities. None of the communities to survive or emerge in the aftermath operated on anything like this scale. Even so, not all were the same and some were more successful than others. At the start of the last millennium BC, Lefkandi on Euboea was very large by the standards of the day and still had access to many goods from the wider, eastern Mediterranean world. Sometime between 1,000 and 950 BC, a truly grand stone building was raised, rectangular with a semicircular apse at one end, over 150 feet long and quite possibly with more than one storey. This is more than twice the size of any other structure found in Greece in this period, and it would be three centuries before anything on a comparable scale was erected.

It may have been the residence of the local leader but became his tomb, and soon afterwards the whole building was covered by a great earth tumulus. The man was cremated and his remains interred under the building; the goods laid around him included a sword and spears. Four horses were buried nearby, presumably as sacrifice or to accompany him into the afterlife. In addition, a woman was set beside him, her legs and arms both crossed, her outfit ornate and expensive. Two linked golden plates covered her breasts, a rare example of the sort of thing artists and costumiers have so often dreamed up in association with harems. There was also an ivory-handled knife laid beside her shoulder, and the excavators suggested that the woman may also have been a sacrifice, or perhaps a voluntary suttee. However, the idea has not won widespread acceptance, and far too little is known about beliefs in the era to judge whether or not this is likely.[10]

There is no doubt that whoever the man was, and whatever the relationship to the woman buried beside him, his status was sufficient to convince or compel the immense labour and cost to the community of constructing the hall and then turning it into a tomb. The wealth deposited in the graves is also spectacular, and not simply in terms of scale, because a fair few of the items were already old. One piece may be Babylonian and was 500 or even 1,000 years old when it was deposited. The monument is unique—at least so far, and the site of Lefkandi was only revealed in the second half of the twentieth century. Yet, while no one appears to have matched the power, prestige, and wealth of the man interred there, other, more modest burials do contain some expensive and impressive grave goods, as well as weapons, suggesting other leaders and privileged supporters.

Lefkandi was unusually large and successful, perhaps uniquely so. Positioned on the coast of an island, with the strait between it and the mainland offering good, sheltered anchorages, it was well placed to benefit from the steady growth of trade led by the Phoenicians but helped by others. Even so, there is no sign that the city and its ruler dominated all or even most of Euboea, let alone territory on the mainland. Power remained local, and the story of the tenth, ninth, and eighth centuries BC is one of hundreds of small communities dotted around the landscape. Over time more appeared, and many of them grew in size. Sometimes several neighbouring villages expanded until they merged together. Others grew larger and larger and became the main centre for smaller settlements in the area. By the end of the eighth century BC, the vast majority of the major cities of Classical Greece had emerged. Not all were equal, but nearly all of them were more or less autonomous. The pattern remained one of many similar, culturally linked, but politically independent small states, living cheek by jowl with each other.[11]

Underlying everything was a gradual rise in population, eventually far surpassing that during even the heyday of the Mycenaean era. This in turn was made possible by an increase in the amount of food produced. The two are interlinked, since a burgeoning population demanded and also made possible the cultivation of more land. Technology helped, as the growing availability of iron made tools more effective and durable—and simultaneously less likely to survive in the archaeological record, since they also corroded more easily than bronze. Yet the key phase was moving beyond mere subsistence to produce a substantial surplus. This permitted a proportion of the population to devote some or all of their time to craft and other activities, rather than having to focus on generating food. Goods as well as food, whether grain, meat, hides, fruit, or tree crops, could also be traded for products from outside, whether luxuries or essentials.[12]

In the Mycenaean era, organised cultivation and stock rearing had produced surpluses that were centrally gathered and controlled. This pattern was not repeated, as part of the emergence of a very different society. Homer's *basileis* did not own all the land and its produce, although they did enjoy a greater share of everything than anyone else in the community. In battle they had to stand out and take the greatest risks, but even though the poet focuses primarily on their deeds, as one hero encountered another hero from the opposing army, there was no sense that they were alone, even in war. In the *Iliad* large armies mass to face each other, each leader bringing along his followers, such as Achilles and his Myrmidons. These other warriors varied in importance, in equipment, and in the way and skill with which they fought. Now and again, broad descriptions take in the crowds of nameless individuals, before the narrative, Hollywood-like, focuses exclusively on the heroes attacking each other.[13]

Others were there in war and in the councils, where they primarily listened rather than spoke and either approved or disapproved proposals, which meant that their opinion mattered, at least collectively. They were also there in peacetime, and while the development of how land was divided up and cultivated within communities is unclear, significant numbers of men had their own farms. They lacked the influence, prestige, and wealth of the much less numerous *basileis*, while at the same time having greater status and wealth than the majority—and along with these a greater obligation to prove themselves in time of war. Such men held farms that were neither grand estates nor subsistence plots, but something in between. This was not a society whose members felt a driving need to have as many children as possible to help work the land and tend the animals. Farms continued for generations, rather than being divided time and again to provide for several offspring. The owner worked with his own hands, supported by family but relying on slaves, perhaps aided by hired labour. The slave workforce was not a large, anonymous gang but a few individuals working alongside and directed by the owner. They were most likely captives taken in war, whether local or bought from traders, and often unfortunates from distant wars or raiding. The evidence from a little later suggests that a slave might cost a bit less than a mule, and while the slave's life was undoubtedly grim, many other slaves in the ancient world were treated even more poorly.[14]

Farming on this scale introduced many innovations into Greek agriculture, whether copied from abroad or learned by experience. In the early part of the last millennium BC, wild varieties of vines and olive trees were domesticated, largely through the delicate process of grafting, becoming more predictable with better yields. This process took great care and a good deal of time, and only after this did the 'traditional' Mediterranean triad of cereals, olive oil, and wine become a reality in a Greek context. The effort was only worthwhile for people confident of passing on their land to heirs, which in turn requires a reasonably stable community.[15]

Such a farmer cultivated a range of different crops, perhaps combined with keeping some animals as well. Only some of the produce was intended for household consumption, including stored reserves to provide against bad harvests. The rest was always meant to be traded. Olive oil in particular was something of a luxury commodity, as to an extent was wine, and both required considerable processing after harvest. A big advantage of this diversification was that it also spread the most intensive periods of labour over more of the agricultural year, allowing the farmer, slaves, and any other workers to move from one task to the next. It also helped to make best use of the soil, wind, sun, water, and weather characteristic of each little patch of land on the farm, something else that benefitted from knowledge accumulated over the generations.[16]

By the eighth century BC there were significant numbers of these middling-scale farmers throughout Greece, owning land of perhaps four to six hectares (ten to fifteen acres). The figure is a guess, and some would suggest the average was more like ten hectares, but talk of the average or typical in Greece in the ancient world is misleading, since variety was far more characteristic and mere size was not as important as the quality of land and its location. The essence of this class or group was that the farm was large enough to run as a self-sustaining business, producing surpluses to trade, but not so large that the farmer himself was not directly involved in manual labour. He might own oxen to pull a plough—or a waggon when required—or he might hire them. He is unlikely to have owned a horse but might well have had one or more donkeys or mules. There were wealthier men, with bigger farms and the space to keep a horse or two, and the aristocrats including and surrounding the *basileis*, who might own numbers of horses, perhaps even chariot teams, and rarely, if ever, had to stoop to physical work. There were also the less well off, with smaller plots of land, who struggled at a level closer to subsistence and hired themselves or their beast out to others, and those poorer still, who worked for a wage. In addition, there were the slaves, toiling alongside their owners, fed and clothed by them, but still property compelled to do what they were told.[17]

Farming and warfare were closely linked in what remained a dangerous world. The farmers needed to protect their harvests and animals from human predators. This was easier to do at a community level, banding together with neighbours. Those with more to protect were expected to run greater risks and fight harder to defend it. As the population grew, more land was cultivated with more care, so that the class/group of men with medium-sized farms increased faster than the aristocratic classes. At the start of the eighth century BC, the aristocratic culture remained dominant, and a small minority of the population continued to be buried in conspicuous style reflecting their status in life. Feasting, with its attendant vessels and luxuries, was a way of displaying wealth, while competition, in running, riding, or racing a chariot, allowed aristocrats to excel publicly, just like Homer's characters. The Olympic Games and other festivals emerging around this time reflected this ethos. The aristocratic male ideal remained a good-looking, well-tended body, long hair, generosity in gift giving, and conspicuous bravery in war. For centuries most of this would remain the goal of the wealthy, and also of a far broader aspirational class, but as communities grew in size, the numbers and importance of the middle-scale farmers increased correspondingly. By the seventh century BC, burials were more egalitarian, with few standing out for the lavishness of grave goods or the scale of a monument.[18]

While some villages merged into one and others became dependents of a larger community, the way society developed in the Greek-speaking world avoided the emergence of very large states or kingdoms. Instead, there was a proliferation of many small states, each with a central city and the lands around it. The two could not really be separated, since these were communities dominated by farmers. Some of the central places began as protected refuges, often on the high ground of an acropolis, before developing into larger, permanently occupied sites. Yet the people, not the place or the institutions, were important. Greeks were far more likely to speak of the Athenians, Spartans, Thebans, or Megarians as a group than they were to talk of Athens, Sparta, Thebes, or Megara as states. The community was what mattered, and while concepts of Hellenic identity remained vague, individuals strongly identified with their own community. By the fourth century BC, there were around 1,000 such Greek communities or cities. Many were small, and quite a few were not in Greece or on the islands off its shores.

Goods made in Greece, most of all the characteristic pottery that survives so well archaeologically, were being traded in Asia Minor at the start of the first millennium BC. There may have been a community of Greek traders living alongside other local and expatriate groups at the settlement of Al-Mina in western Turkey. At some point—the date and circumstances are obscure—a number of Greek cities were created in the same area of Asia Minor, including Ephesus and Miletus. The eighth and seventh centuries BC saw a good deal of undisputed population movement as Greeks went out and formed new cities in Sicily, Italy, North Africa, southern Gaul, and the Iberian Peninsula to the west. They also pushed along the coast to the north-east of Greece, to the Dardanelles, and—probably a little later—around the shores of the Black Sea.[19]

The Greeks were not alone in this burst of colonization; the Phoenicians were particularly active in the same regions of the western Mediterranean. In both cases colonization followed trade. The Phoenicians had pioneered many of the trade routes, seeking in particular mineral resources, notably tin to make bronze and, as time passed, silver for use as currency. Greek traders operated alongside them, although in each case it is important to remember that neither Greeks nor Phoenicians were part of a united state and instead came from many separate communities. While there may have been rivalry, even conflict, at times, coexistence was more common. The appearance of more merchants, whatever their origin, helped to stimulate the local market, as leaders and groups realised that there was much to be gained by selling a resource, encouraging more to be found or produced. As usual, ceramics leave most trace in the archaeological record, so that details of what was exchanged in different areas are hard to reconstruct. There is good evidence from shipwrecks for the Phoenicians carrying substantial cargoes of wine to the west and probably to Greece as well.[20]

Colonizing parties did not go out into the unknown but went to areas already familiar through long-term trade—and, in some cases, through plundering and raiding. Often accommodation was made with local leaders and communities, although sometimes there was conflict as the existing inhabitants resented the arrival of strangers wanting to seize land. Some colonies failed and the colonists fled or were massacred. The majority appear to have succeeded, whether by force or negotiation or because their presence was seen as advantageous to local leaders. There were colonies primarily concerned with increasing the amount of trade with the area, although even these tended to become self-supporting through farming of the land around. Others from the very start were agricultural communities where trade was secondary, if also one of the goals of the farming activity. While the initial colonists may often have been predominantly, even exclusively, male, at least some women arrived later, and these soon became balanced communities in terms of population. The children of Greek colonists grew up speaking Greek, which implies mothers and some household slaves were fluent in the language, and culturally these settlements were and remained Greek. However distant they were from mainland Greece itself, they were part of Hellas, the Greek world, entitled to take part in Hellenic festivals and competitions.[21]

Many stories were told in later centuries about the foundation of such colonies, but these traditions were heavily adapted or even invented to suit contemporary relationships. Most colonies were held to have been founded by a mother city, and often a relationship was maintained. Some may well have begun as group efforts, with would-be colonists gathered primarily from a single Greek city. Others may have followed a leader or leaders able to organise ships and supplies and with an idea of where they were going. A rising population made so much colonization possible, although the link is not straightforward, and it was not a simple choice between starving in an overcrowded homeland or moving elsewhere. Greece could have supported bigger numbers by dividing farms and existing at something closer to subsistence level, but this did not occur. Going away to take land elsewhere allowed more Greeks to live in the style to which they aspired, many as the middling-level farmers at the heart of the cities of Greece itself. Aspiration rather than necessity was the main driving force. Another factor was conflict, whether between or within communities. Leaders who were defeated, or whose ambitions were frustrated by the strength of rivals, were able to seek fresh opportunity in distant lands. The ambition remained the same as at home: to excel among peers and to prosper, in essence to be a successful Greek within a Greek community wherever it was located.[22]

The Mediterranean made all this possible. Long-established communication and trade around its shores gave the Greeks—and many others—a good sense of a wider world. Colonies were always on or near the coast, just like so many home cities in Greece. In the fourth century BC, Plato wrote that the Greeks dwelt like 'frogs around a pond'. The sea permitted travel and trade far more easily than travel overland. The Greeks were not alone, since the same could have been said about the Phoenicians and many others. Some of the trends seen in Greece in these centuries, such as rising population and the growth of numerous cities, were also reflected in many other areas. Greeks adapted the Phoenician alphabet, and this more flexible creation was then adopted by different groups all around the Mediterranean. In Sicily, Greek and Phoenician colonies coexisted, at least for a few generations, with cities created by the local population, each influencing and being influenced by the others. This was even more true in Italy, with the Etruscans and Latins forming many small states composed of a city and its surrounding territory.[23]

Greek development must be seen within the wider context of the Iron Age in the Mediterranean world. In many regions, people had contact with goods and ideas from far afield and benefitted from trade with distant markets. Each responded in its own way, so that not all cities and societies were the same. At this stage there was no great power directly intervening in the Mediterranean, since Egypt remained weak and prone to civil war. Greeks went there in the seventh century BC as mercenaries, some leaving graffiti on an ancient statue, and were later allowed to create a colony by the pharaoh. The kingdoms of Caria and Lydia bordered on the Greek cities of Asia Minor, but the superpower of the revived Assyrian Empire remained at a distance. Phoenician cities paid tribute to Assyrian kings, as did most of the communities in Asia, without facing direct intervention in their lives.

The Greek cities emerged in a world of very many small and local powers rather than bigger kingdoms, let alone great empires. Most of the trends in society and economy encouraged a degree of localism. Lots of communities developed, culturally close but politically separate. It remained to be seen how they would govern themselves.

3

THE LAWGIVER

*Organising the cities, the emergence of Athens,
and the laws of Solon,
c. 700–570 BC*

HOMER'S HEROES BICKERED AND FOUGHT, WHILE COMMUNIties, much like families, have their jealousies and disputes. To survive, let alone prosper, a community needed to contain such friction, setting limits so that the inhabitants were not always at each other's throats. The threat of outsiders, raiding bands, or neighbouring cities eager to expand their own territory gave an incentive to work together for mutual protection, but more was needed. Over time, each city developed rules to regulate everyone's behaviour, which eventually became codified as laws. So important was this, especially when the rules led to stability and prosperity, that later generations tended to associate their creation with the wisdom and skill of a few individuals, men celebrated as lawgivers and sages. Most were dimly remembered, perhaps even invented, and it is only in Athens, late in this phase of development, that one of them, Solon, appears on the fringes of history.

VIRTUALLY ALL THE cities to play a role in the history of Classical Greece had already appeared by the end of the eighth century BC.

In the next century these communities continued to develop and, in most cases, grow. There is not enough evidence to state with certainty precisely how many there were at any one moment, but a reasonable estimate posits something like 800 cities in mainland Greece and around the Aegean. A main reason it is impossible to be precise is that most were very small indeed, even at their height. An exceptionally thorough modern survey concluded that some 80 per cent of Greek states controlled less than eighty square miles (c. 207 square kilometres) of territory, while more than 30 per cent had less than thirty-eight square miles (100 square kilometres) of land. This was at their height, usually in the fifth or fourth century BC, and in the early days, many may have been even smaller.[1]

By the standards of many periods of history, let alone the modern world, the cities of Greece were small to form independent states. A few, perhaps around 10 per cent of the total, had territory of no more than ten square miles (twenty-five square kilometres) and probably boasted a population of less than 1,000 people, while the overwhelming majority with bigger territories had populations numbering in thousands, and only a few grew larger than this. In each case this was the combined total of those dwelling in the walled city itself and the land around it, since all were part of the same community. Larger states included villages and hamlets in their territory, some of which might be protected by fortifications, but these were not independent, self-governing communities.

In the very small states, the majority lived in the city itself, at least most of the time. Even when the territory was some eighty square miles (207 square kilometres) in extent, the distance from the city to the edge of the state's territory was unlikely to be much more than five miles (eight kilometres), putting it well within easy walking distance. Larger states tended to have a higher proportion of people dwelling in the countryside simply because they needed to be closer to the fields they cultivated. Scholarly opinion remains divided over the question of how many of these folk lived in concentrated villages and hamlets and how many lived on family farms, which may well be less likely to show up in field surveys. Most likely, the pattern varied from region to region and period to period.[2]

Even if there were large numbers of distinct family farmsteads, the scale of everything meant that these were scarcely isolated by any great distance from neighbours, because most of these city territories were so very small, and not even the wealthiest possessed vast estates. Instead, these were all rather small city-states carved into lots of relatively small farms, and in many cases individuals worked several separate plots rather than a single concentrated stretch of land. Neighbours were never far away, even for those living in the territory of a city rather than in the city itself. The same was true at a higher level. With good land in short supply in mainland Greece and the Aegean islands, each small state bordered on one or more others. These were sometimes openly hostile and more often rivals ever ready to exploit an opportunity offered by any sign of weakness, and they were always distinct as not part of the community, even though they spoke the same language and were fellow Greeks.

Greek society as it emerged in the course of the eighth century BC and developed in the following centuries was based around this mass of separate communities, many of them small and all living cheek by jowl. Each community had to find a way for the individuals within it to live in very close proximity to each other, to resolve disputes, and to make as a group the necessary decisions, not least on how to deal with the other states living alongside them. None of this can have been straightforward in a world developing from 'Homeric' society, where violence was common and personal prestige something to be increased and guarded at all costs. There was mutual benefit in coming together with neighbours to form one community, which helped to frighten away or fight off threats from outsiders. At the same time, this had to be balanced against the risk of a stronger neighbour or group of neighbours picking on the weak within this community. The origins of most cities cannot now be known, and scholars are inclined to be sceptical of stories of heroic founders and of ties of kinship among a population. Yet, whatever the truth, communities were created and grew, and as generation after generation lived in the same place and farmed the same lands, the sense of communal identity became very strong. Greeks believed that they had a special, inherited connection with everyone else in their community in a way that they did not with outsiders—even ones living within walking distance. The sense of kinship was immensely powerful.

Yet groups bound by kinship, just like families, can still argue, so that such communities needed to regulate themselves. In Homer's poems even the strongest king or prince was no absolute ruler. Few, if any, of the cities to emerge in this era were ruled by a line of hereditary, sole monarchs, and even those that were overthrew them at an early stage. The real-life equivalents of the Homeric princes, the *basileis*, presided over centres that were little more than villages, and even the smallest city brought together several such communities. From the start, this created a number of prestigious leaders within the city rather than one. Even more numerous were the more distinguished and better equipped warriors supporting these men, in addition to an ever-growing number of farmers able and willing to equip themselves for close combat and, as time passed, even more men to act as archers, javelin men, or stone throwers. An army fielded by one of these cities was more numerous than one of the earlier bands, which meant that a single individual, however brave and deadly, made proportionally less of a contribution to the outcome of any fight.

A Homeric-style hero could no longer dominate so easily either in peace or war because there was too much competition. This did not mean that the ideology of spectacular courage and prowess in battle, of wise words in debate, and of excellence in athletics or simply personal beauty vanished. Instead, it was passed to a significantly larger section of the population. More competitors meant that it was harder to gain supremacy, harder still to keep it, for strength could only come from gaining allies and making sure that no opponent could muster even greater strength. Violence remained an option, but it was in the interest of the community to deter this and to prevent an outbreak turning into an ongoing cycle of violence. The latter would damage a city, perhaps fatally, leaving it vulnerable to attack from outside. Even in the *Iliad* a picture of an idealised city includes a gathering to decide how to make acceptable recompense after a killing.[3]

Alongside life, possessions needed to be protected for communities to function in the long run. The new, more numerous elite gained status through their wealth, particularly land and herds. This was more reliable—and less dangerous—than the Homeric ideal of proving the right to lead through martial excellence, so the natural desire was to pass all this on to successive generations of the family. The same instinct motivated all landowners, however small their farms, all of whom needed to be confident that their land was secure and could be passed on to heirs in due course. Such security benefitted everyone, even those whose property was small. From the start, there was clarity over who had the right to occupy and use each piece of land within a city's territory. In addition, that territory was clearly and definitely defined, not least because neighbouring cities made equally clear what they regarded as their property. A rival community might well challenge another for control of a stretch of land but realise that any attempt is likely to be met with violent resistance.

LITTLE IS DEFINITELY known of the events of the eighth century BC among the Greek communities. There was a memory in later years of a great conflict on the island of Euboea over control of a fertile stretch of land known as the Lelantine plain. This struggle, waged between the cities of Chalkis and Eretria, was later described in almost Homeric terms, with stories of leaders and warriors coming from far afield to join each side. The truth cannot be reconstructed with any confidence, but the significance lies in the memory of conflict fought over the control of farmland. Other wars of the era suggest a similar motive, and all imply conquest—or attempted conquest—of already established communities and their recognised territory. Around the time of the Lelantine War, the site of Lefkandi, which had prospered for so long, was largely abandoned. Most probably, the bulk of the population was absorbed into that of nearby Eretria.[4]

Populations in Greek cities united to fight off attacks on their territory or sometimes to seize more territory, and there was an advantage to having a large number of people within the community. At the same time, the cities developed conventions, rules, and eventually laws to regulate the behaviour and protect the property of their inhabitants. The poet Hesiod talks of a dispute with his brother over the land they inherited from their father and bitterly condemns the corrupt judges who took bribes to favour his sibling. Opinion is divided over whether such poems were truly autobiographical or imagined situations, but in many respects this does not matter. Hesiod's world was one where there were peaceful ways of resolving disputes via arbitration and where who had the right to farm and profit from a plot of land was understood and upheld.[5]

Sources improve a little for the seventh century BC, so that there are more events that can be dated and described with a greater degree of confidence. Cities created magistrates responsible for leading them in peace and war and acting as judges, often supported by a gathering of the community or a selected jury. In the earlier days men may have held a post for life, until the term of office was regulated. By the end of the century, all such offices were usually held for no more than a year, and one of the earliest-known formal Greek inscriptions recorded part of a law regulating how soon a man could seek re-election to the same post. The process of formalising the number and responsibilities of magistrates and who should hold them to account was no doubt gradual and varied in pace and detail from city to city. What emerged in the hundreds of Greek communities was broadly similar rather than identical.[6]

These were not communities of equals. There were slaves with the status of property rather than members of the community, and in most formal senses—except in many aspects of cult and ritual—women were excluded from assemblies, magistracies, and elections, when these started. This was to a great extent because of the ongoing link between participating in the life of the community in peacetime and fighting for the community in war. The best, most aggressive and skilful fighters were felt to deserve a more prominent role in life in general. No community could afford to alienate too many of its most prominent fighting men in the same way that Agamemnon had upset Achilles, for successful war-making in attack or defence depended on having enough of these men. At an even more basic level, such formidable individuals might turn on those around them if not treated with the respect they felt that they deserved.

Wealth and land allowed a man to acquire the best armour and weapons and gave him the time to practice with arms and with such things as horse-riding. This, combined with social expectation, ensured that the wealthier men continued to be prominent in wartime, competing with each other to excel. They were joined by substantial and steadily growing numbers of men farming their own land, able to equip themselves fairly well and highly motivated to prove their worth. Bigger armies were more effective if they worked together as a team. Status in peace relied on importance in war, so that the poorest, who supplied the less decisive, if still useful, missile support in battle, were of comparable significance in everyday life; their opinion mattered, just far less, at least individually. There was a sliding scale of prestige and importance from the wealthiest through successive grades to the very poorest, all tied to a man's military role. All remained individuals, and while all or most men of a similar status might agree on some issues, on others they might not, and there were no parties or permanent blocks of opinion based on class or wealth. In the smallest Greek cities, it was still just about possible for everyone to know everyone else. Even in larger communities, individual personalities and long-standing personal relationships between men and families shaped behaviour. The richest in any city were as likely to be rivals as allies.

It becomes easier to glimpse more of Greek society in the seventh century BC, because this was the era when many Lyric poets began to flourish, even though in most cases their work survives only in fragments. These were poems intended to be sung to musical accompaniment, hence the name, and dealt less with great deeds than with emotions and the challenges of life, ranging from the serious to the frivolous. Sappho is perhaps the only one widely known today, both because of the rarity of female authors in the ancient world and because she sang of love and longing between women. Very little of her poetry survives, which allows a good deal of imaginative reconstruction of her life and world, and it should be noted that some of her verse also dealt with love in the context of marriage. She was celebrated in the ancient world primarily because of the beauty of her poems and their perceived honesty about love. Emphasis on the homosexual element came much later and led in time to the word *lesbian*, since she came from the island of Lesbos.[7]

Sappho was from a wealthy family, one prominent in her home community, and the same was true of the other Lyric poets. They sang of the concerns of their class, although in many cases, especially when it came to love and desire, others shared these concerns as well. Alongside love and straightforward lust, there was sometimes war. Occasionally this echoed very old attitudes—for instance, when Hybrias boasted that his wealth came from his spear and sword and the shield that guarded his body. 'With this I plough, with this, I reap, . . . with this I am called "master of slaves."' Anyone too cowardly to fight had to go down on their knees before him and grovel, calling him 'great *basileus*'. These were sentiments closely akin to the ideals of Homer's heroes, if anything stated even more brazenly—and perhaps deliberately exaggerated.[8]

Other poets sought to inspire men to heroism for the good of the community and were frank about the dangers and terrors of combat.

Nor did they expect to rule by the sword. There were others of influence within the community, some of them seen as corrupt, like the judges condemned by Hesiod. True worth—from family, personal courage, land, and property—did not always get the recognition it deserved in the eyes of several of these poets. Some express disdain for those with newfound wealth, and there is a wider sense of a divide between the 'good' men (the *agathoi*), with superior breeding and inherent virtue, intelligence, and excellence, and the presumptuous 'bad' men (the *kakoi*), who lacked these things, even if they owned farms or had grown wealthy through trade. Obviously the definition of just who fell into each category was a matter of opinion, and the nicknames also varied, not least depending on whether they were applied to self or another. Within each group there were degrees of prestige, and *kakoi* in particular could be applied to a wide swathe of the community by those who considered themselves most assuredly *agathoi*.

Competitive festivals for song and poetry or athletics naturally favoured the well off, who had the time to devote to practice and also possessed the freedom to travel to any events that were not local, something denied those who had to work for their livelihoods. The Olympic Games initially consisted of foot races, notably the 'one stade' of about 200 yards, but over time more sports were added. There were the race run while wearing armour, discus and javelin throwing, boxing, wrestling, and the *pankration*, a brutal fighting sport where almost anything was allowed, apart from the use of weapons; it was later said that in 564 BC a man won the *pankration* posthumously, having died from asphyxiation moments after his opponent signalled that he had given in. This was not the only recorded death. Also important were the horse and chariot races, although as time passed the owner did not necessarily ride the horse or drive the vehicle himself. Raising and training a chariot team made this the most expensive sport of all, so that it was very much the preserve of the wealthiest.[9]

The games were held on a single day every four years, the precise day determined by the lunar calendar, but normally in August. No women were allowed to watch, let alone take part, but by the later eighth century BC, men came from all over the Greek world to compete and spectate. Late in the seventh century BC, several events for boys were introduced, increasing the scale of the festival. A truce was declared to permit those going to and from the games to travel unmolested, and in later periods this lasted for a month. Also on a four-year cycle, but falling between each Olympic Games, were the Pythian Games, which early in the sixth century BC expanded from being predominantly cultural, with an emphasis on music, to include sports as well. Around the same time the Isthmian Games—on the isthmus connecting the Peloponnese with the rest of Greece—expanded in a similar way, as did the Nemean Games. Both of these were held every second year.

As with every aspect of life, religion played a central role. The Olympic Games took place near Elis in the Peloponnese at an established shrine to the Olympian gods and began with a sacrifice to Zeus. The Pythian Games occurred at Delphi, a place sacred to Apollo, home to the most prestigious oracle of the Greek world and a steadily growing complex of temples, shrines, and monuments, all ornamented by gifts from many communities and wealthy individuals. By comparison, the locations of the other festivals were less renowned, but even so the cult element remained prominent. These Panhellenic competitions celebrated the beliefs, as well as the desire to excel and most of all to win, that Greeks felt were the quintessence of their identity as Greeks—most especially as the *agathoi* of high birth, wealth, and excellence. Yet there is no reason to doubt that admiration of Olympic winners spread throughout society, granting them a celebrity status. Greeks saw these competitions as reflections of who they were (or at least aspired to be), while the whole concept emphasised that although they shared similar ideals, they were deeply—almost naturally—divided into many separate communities.

An Olympic victory brought immense prestige, most of all for anyone able to compete and win more than one event. This was all the more valuable to a man who already possessed status, wealth, and reputation in his home community. In 640 BC an Athenian named Cylon was victorious at Olympia. He was clearly one of the 'good', already well connected and influential in his home city and also married to a daughter of the tyrant of Megara to the north-west. A tyrant was a leader able to make himself sole ruler of a city, usually through the use or threat of force. The word appears to have come from Asia Minor and been adopted by the Greeks and was yet to acquire the wholly negative connation it carries today.[10]

Perhaps inspired by his father-in-law's success, Cylon gathered a band of Athenian followers, supplemented them with warriors from Megara, and decided to seize power at Athens. Like many who contemplated a risky venture, he went to Delphi and consulted the Pythian oracle, who advised him to act during the festival of Zeus, which he quite naturally interpreted to mean the Olympic Games. On the day that these were held—presumably in 636 or 632 BC—he gathered his men in Athens and then occupied the Acropolis, the ancient high stronghold of the city, by this time largely given over to temples and cult practice. Presumably he hoped to dictate terms to his fellow Athenians, but, in the event, they were not dismayed by the coup. Instead, they gathered in ever-increasing numbers and blockaded the Acropolis, coming all the quicker because many had assembled for a local festival to Zeus close to the city. Days passed, and charge of the blockade passed to the nine archons, the senior magistrates of the city, from whoever had taken the lead at the start.[11]

Eventually, the despairing band of rebels negotiated to surrender and understood that they were to be spared execution. To make doubly sure, they went to the precinct around the main altar on the Acropolis, where by tradition they were on sacred ground and thus had asylum. They were persuaded to leave, still believing that they had a deal, only to be slaughtered. In 2016, excavators uncovered a mass grave outside Athens dating to the seventh century BC. It contained seventy-nine skeletons, the vast majority young men, with many showing signs of having been bound at the wrists. There were indications that some had suffered injuries, although definite cause of death was not certain from the bone evidence, except in one skeleton with an arrowhead in its chest. These might well be Cylon's men, although it is unlikely that the identification can ever be certain, and perhaps they were war captives, rebellious slaves, or the losers in an unrecorded fight between fellow Athenians.[12]

As the date of Cylon's coup is uncertain, so are many other details, and there is a good chance that the story grew in the telling over the years. In one version, Cylon and his brother escaped, leaving their followers to their fate. The Delphic oracle, whose true meaning is misunderstood, is a common device to explain failures by leaders, making it the sort of detail likely to be invented. Still, Delphi was already very important by this period, drawing pilgrims from all over the Greek world and beyond, and its answers were deliberately cryptic to help uphold its reputation; virtually any course of events could be explained as having been foretold. Thus Cylon may have gone to the oracle and may have felt that he was promised success. Another story claims that the rebels fastened a thread to the main altar on the Acropolis, slowly unwinding it as they were marched away to trial, so that they were still touching it and protected. Unfortunately for them, the thread snapped, and the surrounding mob realised what had happened and killed them.[13]

THE TRADITION ABOUT Cylon contained contradictions and no doubt a good deal of embellishment. Even so, his attempted coup and the subsequent massacre of prisoners definitely happened and is the first—at least roughly—dateable event in Athenian history. Athenians claimed that their city was founded by Theseus, the slayer of the Minotaur, who united all the communities of Attica, an event that they dated to before the Trojan War. Athenians are mentioned once in the list of the Achaean forces in the *Iliad* but are given no prominence and do not appear anywhere else, leading some Greeks to suspect that the lines were later additions to Homer's text, inserted to include Athens in the greatest of all epics.[14]

The archaeology shows that Athens was part of the Mycenaean civilization, probably with a palace on the Acropolis, although later development on the site makes this hard to prove. When the palace system collapsed, Athens appears to have suffered less of a decline compared to other regions. Its recovery was also faster, helped by ready access to the sea, and numerous village sites appeared and grew in the countryside of Attica. Rainfall was low by Greek standards, the soil not especially rich, but while wheat did not flourish except in a few small areas, barley grew well, as did vines and olive trees. There were also mineral resources to exploit, notably iron and silver, and in addition the clay soil proved ideal for making pottery; over time Athenian workshops produced vessels that were traded widely.[15]

Since the Athenians were content to attribute the foundation of their city to Theseus, no other tradition survives as to how the communities of Attica were in fact brought together into one state with the city of Athens at its heart. Once this had occurred, Athens the city was one of the largest urban areas in the Greek world, while Athens the state had the fifth-largest territory, amounting to some 1,000 square miles (2,500 square kilometres). Most of this was densely populated since half or more of the people lived outside the urban area itself. By the fifth century BC, there may have been as many as a quarter million people living in Attica. If not as big in Cylon's time, it was even then one of the largest Greek states in area and population, and Attica probably came under Athenian leadership fairly early on. Certainly there is no trace of a large, rival city in Attica that had to be subdued and absorbed, which suggests that the unification occurred when all the other communities were still small.

Probably the name Athens, with its claim to special favour and protection from the goddess Athena, was also very early.[16]

One consequence of bringing together such a wide area with so many villages and hamlets into a single state was the coexistence of a large number of 'good' men, with lands, wealth, skill at arms, and supporters. Steady growth, the expansion of trade, and the wider prosperity it brought in due course added to their numbers. In much of Greece by the seventh century BC, burial rites were fairly egalitarian, with little to mark out the graves of the wealthy. Athens appears to have broken this trend, with much more lavish treatment given to the elite. The sheer size of the emerging state and the large number of 'good' men may well have made Athens difficult to control and unruly. Cylon's attempted coup was one sign of this, showing both that some of the aristocrats dreamed of supreme power and also that enough others, including rival 'good' men, were willing to fight to stop them.[17]

As is the case with the institutions of other Greek states, it is not known when the post of archon was created. It may originally have been held for life, then perhaps for ten years at a time, but by the later seventh century BC, the post was annual, with the most senior archon giving his name to the year. Another post was the archon *basileus*, an echo of the distant past when a king/prince had led the community. He continued to have a key role in sacrifices and other rites conducted for the good of the state as a whole. There was also the polemarch, the man expected to lead the state's levy in time of war. The remaining six archons did not have any specific title or responsibility, and little is known of how all nine magistrates were appointed or elected, although all were clearly from the established wealthy families—in a sense the 'best', or at least the most powerful, of the 'good'.[18]

The route to creating a stable political system was not straightforward or easy for any Greek city—hence the rise and fall of tyrants in a number of communities. Others managed to avoid this but still faced periods of *stasis*, factionalism often leading to violence, even civil war. Athens seems to have been particularly prone to this. Disturbances occurred, although the details are lost. A year when things were so disrupted that the archons could not be appointed or function, so that there were no formal leaders, was *anarchia*—anarchy. Sometime in the aftermath of Cylon's coup, the Athenians appointed a man named Draco to put together a more effective code of laws. In later years he was famous for his severity—hence the modern word *draconian*—and he is supposed to have instituted the death penalty for almost every crime. There was probably a good deal of exaggeration in the popular memory of his law code, and only part of a single one of his laws survives because it was inscribed on stone when it was reconfirmed at the end of the fifth century BC. This proscribed exile for someone who had unintentionally killed another but also stated who among the victim's family was permitted to negotiate and accept an alternative settlement as recompense from the killer and his family. Homicide was a central issue for Draco, and this law suggests a pattern of vengeance, blood feud, and flight or public reconciliation reminiscent of the world described by Homer.[19]

IN LATER CENTURIES the Greeks remembered a number of lawgivers like Draco, men who singlehandedly created new law codes, even constitutions, for a city. Most of these men were little more than names in the tradition, although the most admired were celebrated for their fairness and wisdom, the most prestigious being remembered as the Seven Sages. One of the latter was another Athenian, Solon, who was active about a generation or so after Draco. For a second time the Athenians chose one man to deal with a crisis, suggesting that any peace and stability provided by Draco's severe laws proved brief. Solon was archon in 594/3 BC, and his reforms may have occurred then or in the following years, but certainty is impossible, and one interpretation places them as late as the 570s BC. He was clearly one of the 'good', from an established, wealthy family, and he may have added to this wealth through successful trading ventures. One tradition claimed that he successfully led the Athenians in a war with Megara over the island of Salamis, but even in the early second century AD, when Plutarch wrote a biography of Solon, he had to confess that the sources about the man's life contained significant contradictions.[20]

This was in spite of the fact that Solon was renowned as a Lyric poet, and many of his poems were widely known in antiquity, even though all that has survived are fragments quoted in other sources. By their nature such snippets are lacking in context, often more tantalising than informative, assuming that the text was not modified to suit the need of whoever was quoting it—a very real danger when his name was invoked in a political context. Solon's laws were preserved at Athens for at least a few centuries, so that later authors had some guide to what he had done. Their language and intent were surely clear, as was appropriate for legislation, but it would be unreasonable to expect the poems to deal with specific issues in the same way, for the genre was very different. When political and social issues are raised, they resemble more a politician's speeches of good intent and boasts about their record rather than anything specific that was actually done. They speak of dreadful problems and Solon's fairness and success in resolving them.[21]

All this means that the precise nature of the crisis facing Athens remains hotly debated by scholars. Broadly, the community was divided along class lines, the rich against the poor, the 'good' against the 'bad' or the 'people' (*demos*), with many of the issues involving land and labour. The balance had shifted too far in favour of the wealthy, placing many in debt to them. Men unable to meet their obligations had found themselves and their families forced into slavery. Some had been sold abroad, while others had fled into voluntary exile to avoid the same fate. Solon's poems talk of greed and imply intimidation and violence on the part of big landowners but do not allow the scale of the problem to be established. A group of small-scale farmers, presumably tenants obliged to give a sixth of their harvest to a landlord, appear to have been suffering in particular.[22]

There is uncertainty over the scope of Solon's reforms, but it is clear that there was a cancellation of existing debts and a ban on anyone making his person, or that of his family, the surety for any debt. Solon did not act against slavery in the wider sense, only against the enslavement of fellow Athenians. There were also changes to the process of legal arbitration, for instance, permitting anyone to take up the case of a fellow Athenian and also permitting appeal against the decision of a judge—an echo of Hesiod's corrupt magistrates. Solon boasted that he had set the 'dark earth' free by rooting up boundary stones, presumably referring to those seizing some or all of the produce to service a debt or perhaps to stretches of land that had been occupied unfairly. Yet he also claimed not to have given way to the 'bad's' hatred of the 'good' and instead to have stood firm like a boundary stone between them. The overall aim appears to have been making clear who rightfully owned and worked each plot of land.[23]

A major reform attributed to him and widely—if not quite universally—accepted by scholars was the division of all male Athenians into four classes. The highest were the '500 measures men' (*pentakosiomedimnoi*). A *medimnos* was a measure of about 52.2 litres, said in later sources to be of either dry food, such as grain, or wet, such as oil or wine, so these were men whose land was expected to yield at least 500 measures each year. Below them were the 'horsemen' (*hippeis*), able to afford and maintain at least one horse and with land producing at least 300 *medimnoi*. Then came the 'yoked men' (*zeugitai*), whose name probably came from their ability to own a pair of oxen for ploughing and who produced at least 200 *medimnoi* each year. Everyone else was included in the remaining class, the *thêtes*, which is harder to translate and perhaps best rendered as 'hired men', who were assessed as having land producing less than 200 *medimnoi* a year. Some owned little or no land, and even those with small farms most likely needed to do some paid work to support themselves and their families. Opinion varies over how large a proportion of society each class represented. Probably this was like a pyramid, with each group becoming more numerous as the requirements for membership grew lower. One estimate suggested that the three higher classes combined formed no more than 20 per cent of the overall Athenian male population, perhaps less, although most scholars believe that the *zeugitai* were significantly more numerous than this would suggest.[24]

Whatever the details, this categorisation, perhaps a modified or more formal version of something already in existence or possibly wholly new, made clear the status, rights, and responsibilities of all free male Athenians. Also, at a basic level, it emphasised to all that all Athenians were part of the same community, reaffirming an old idea. It also determined eligibility for the magistracies, with the archonship probably reserved for the *pentakosiomedimnoi* for the moment, and may also have set how much tax, presumably in the form of produce, was due to meet the modest needs of the state. One tradition claimed that Solon set the standard for coinage, but the archaeological evidence is clear that coins did not come into widespread use in Athens and the other Greek communities until the middle of the sixth century BC. Before this, pieces of silver and other metals were employed as bullion, when exchange of actual goods was not practical. There is talk of other reforms, such as the creation of a council of 400 members, but it is not clear whether this actually happened and, if it did, who was enrolled, for how long, and what collective responsibility it held.

After his reforms, Solon was said to have gone abroad for a decade, both to let the system establish itself and so that he could not be pressured into changing any of it. His measures do appear to have relieved the immediate perceived crisis, and many would remain in force for generations. He was certainly remembered with respect, although in part this was because of stories—many of them invented—about his wider wisdom. Solon's career was in many ways a reflection of challenges facing all Greek communities in this era. As they grew in size and prosperity, more of the male population possessed a degree of wealth and expected to receive status as a result. All were developing a clear idea of who was a true member of the community, someone who was more than simply a resident, inching towards the sort of concepts that would be included in the term *citizenship* in the modern era. Yet circumstances varied from city to city, from the size of the community to the spread of wealth and influence within it. There was no real template to copy or even a uniform system that could be adopted in detail everywhere. Because the sources for Solon and the wider era were set down later, each author had a tendency to anticipate later events and see everything as leading towards an inevitable outcome. Modern scholars have to struggle to resist the same temptation.[25]

Solon, his career, and the Athens he knew remain imperfectly understood. At the very least he helped relieve some serious problems and strengthened the sense that all Athenians belonged to the same community. Wealth was confirmed as deserving greater prominence, honour, and responsibility, but there was an attempt—at the very least an aspiration—to make the justice system fair for all and harder for the influential to manipulate. At the same time, the firm establishment of classes based on property and produce created a clearer path for individuals to rise as they became richer. Over time, a growing proportion of Athenians would prosper through craft and trade, until a substantial minority did not work on the land at all. From the start, Athens, controlling Attica, was far larger than was typical for a Greek state, which meant that creating a stable political and social system for the city was likely to be more complex. Within Solon's lifetime, stability once again broke down, as a more successful tyrant than Cylon emerged.[26]

4

THE GREAT PRONOUNCEMENT

*The Spartans, their origins and early history,
and development of their society,
c. 800–550 BC*

Solon's Athens was unusual by Greek standards for its sheer size. Sparta was also exceptionally large, but very different in many ways, so it is worth thinking about the nature of Athens and Attica before turning to the Spartans. Attica, bounded on three sides by water, covered a large area, was well populated, and provided a range of resources. If the internal problems it faced were common to most Greek communities, the scale on which disputes were conducted was different, and this had important consequences. With such a large population, lasting dominance depended on securing and maintaining the support of a lot of people, something that was inherently harder. A coup such as the one attempted by Cylon would have been far easier to achieve in a small city, and the rivalries in the majority of Greek communities tended to be more quickly decisive because they were disputes between smaller groups. That was one reason why losing factions often chose to migrate and found a colony elsewhere rather than accept the rule of rivals.

The Athenians had not set up any colonies. When Solon brought Athenians back from abroad, these were fugitives from debt or unfortunates sold into slavery. Most Athenians, especially the wealthy and ambitious, wanted to live and succeed at home rather than going abroad. If it was hard for any one leader or group to dominate Attica, because it was large with a large population, it was equally rare to fare so badly compared to rivals that there was no chance of recovering status, if only for a future generation. The advantages of wealth, family reputation, and connections tended to endure, and as Athens continued to grow in prosperity, the value of success only increased. There was also the strong sense of belonging to the community, something common to all Greek states and, if anything, even more pronounced in the larger ones. For all the scepticism of modern scholars, some genuine kinship, however distant, probably existed. Even more important was the long existence of the majority of cities. The same families lived as neighbours and cultivated adjacent patches of land generation after generation. Memory was long and created a deep sense of belonging and shared experience even if kinship itself was not always literal. One reason for the bitterness and savagery of the frequent outbreaks of faction fighting within so many cities was this powerful sense of belonging, indeed of patriotism. It mattered deeply how each community should be run and—especially for aristocrats—who should be in charge.

By the sixth century BC most cities, apart from the newer colonies, were old, far older than living memory. Traditions about their origins were vague, sometimes contradictory, and often embellished or invented to help explain and justify contemporary institutions and society, or for the convenience of current ambitions and policies. None of this diminished the deep belief throughout society that membership of the community of their city marked them out as special, distinct, and usually superior to others, however close by they lived. There is no sign that this passionate conviction was any less in a tiny city of barely 1,000 inhabitants than in one of the exceptionally large states like Athens. Size did have advantages. In Solon's day, Athens faced no immediate threat from a power strong enough to conquer

THE GREAT PRONOUNCEMENT

Attica in just one or a few conflicts. Smaller communities lacked such security, which was one reason why almost all built a wall around the city itself at an early stage in their development. Internal power struggles never appear to have destroyed a city but could weaken it and leave it vulnerable to hostile neighbours. In that sense, a community's quest to create a reasonably stable form of government was not just key to prosperity but vital for success, even survival, in a hostile environment.

Writing around the middle of the fifth century BC, Herodotus claimed that the Spartans had long been one of the worst governed and most divided communities in the Greek world, until drastic reform of their institutions and society transformed them into the most stable and successful state. Much of this he attributed to a man named Lycurgus, like Solon one of the sages and lawgivers celebrated in later centuries. Herodotus's description is brief and uncertain on many details, so that he was unsure whether Lycurgus was inspired by an oracle from Delphi or through direct observation of the workings of communities on Crete or both. Five and a half centuries later, Plutarch wrote a biography of Lycurgus and confessed to an even greater level of uncertainty about who Lycurgus was and when he had lived, even noting that one tradition claimed there were two men of the same name, both important reformers but active at different periods, centuries apart. Like Herodotus, he attributed nearly every aspect of Spartan society to Lycurgus's reforms, with only a few subsequent modifications, and went into considerable detail in his description of many aspects of life at Sparta.[1]

As always, when it comes to the Spartans, the surviving sources are even more difficult to interpret than those for other Greek communities. While the Athenians in later years talked and wrote about themselves at great length, the Spartans did not and were in fact considered to be secretive about their society, customs, and behaviour. Surviving accounts of Spartan life derive almost entirely from the comments of outsiders, sometimes favourably inclined and sometimes very hostile. Either way, they tend to focus on those aspects of Spartan society that seemed peculiar compared to other Greek states: None were inclined to comment on how things were done at Sparta if this seemed no different to anywhere else. Thus the emphasis is on how strange the Spartans were compared to the rest of Greece, and more than anywhere else there is the danger that *often* or even *sometimes* has changed in a source—or in scholars' understandable eagerness to find an answer—into *always*. In the past, Sparta was understood as a uniquely rigid and static society, with the same customs enforced for centuries. Few experts now accept this view, but there is disagreement over almost everything else.[2]

This means that there are few simple and certain answers when it comes to Sparta's history and society. The Peloponnese had witnessed a particular flourishing of Mycenaean palace society and, as was usually the pattern, appears to have suffered especially severely when the system collapsed. In the following centuries there were few settlements, none of them large or showing signs of prosperity. There was nothing like Lefkandi or even early Athens in the Peloponnese. Homer's Menelaus was king of Sparta, but Spartan tradition maintained that their ancestors had arrived much later, as Dorian invaders led by descendants of Hercules who seized the land by force. There is no trace of a Mycenaean centre on the site of what would become Sparta, and although a smaller settlement from that era has been uncovered by archaeologists in recent years several miles away, there is no suggestion of continuity. Spartans claimed to be different to the Achaeans who had lived in Sparta in the heroic age, while at the same time adopting Menelaus and the beautiful Helen in their tradition and creating a cult around them.[3]

For all the scepticism about massed Dorian invasions, by far the most probable interpretation of the evidence is that a group that would become the Spartans in later periods arrived from outside and took by force the territory around what would become Sparta. They may have come from north-eastern Greece, the traditional home of the Dorians, although the prevalence of Dorian dialect in much of the Peloponnese can also be explained in other ways. Precisely who these 'original' Spartans were, their number, and their prior history is impossible to know. They may not have been united at this stage. Several groups of leaders and warriors may well have seized control of patches of land, then fought for dominance before willingly or by compulsion joining together. There is a good chance that along the way, some existing local communities came to terms with the new arrivals and joined them. Perhaps the ethnic makeup of the people later known as the Spartans contained a number of elements, but this did not change their deep sense of shared identity as conquerors, descendants of men who had taken the land by force. Spartans did not believe that they had sprung from the earth like the Athenians.

Conquest runs like a thread through what is visible of early Spartan history. They established themselves in the heartland of Laconia early on, well before the eighth century BC. Elsewhere, the process of several villages merging into one urban centre was common. With the Spartans this was slower and less complete, and the villages retained a measure of separate identity in the long run. Later, in the Hellenistic and especially clearly in the Roman period, there were four of them clustered around the acropolis: Limnai, Pitane, Mesoa, and Kynosoura. At some point a fifth was added, Amyclae, several miles to the south. These five villages effectively became districts of later Sparta and were important much earlier, although it is just possible that other, subsequently forgotten Spartan villages were scattered over an even wider area. No city wall was constructed until well after the period covered in this book, partly because the spread of habitation and the distance of Amyclae from the rest would have required any fortification to be impractically extensive. The Spartans also boasted that the courage and skill of their fighting men was all the defence they needed.[4]

Successful expansion added to Sparta's security, as over time the heartland came to be a long way away from the border with any rival state. This city of villages lay in the valley of the River Eurotas, amid good farmland. Over time the Spartans expanded until they controlled the entire valley, bordered to the south by the sea and to the east and west by mountain ranges, respectively, Taygetus and Parnon. In the north they pushed to the edges of Arcadia, much of which is hill country. In the latter part of the eighth century BC, the Spartans attacked Messenia, beyond the Taygetus range, waging a bitter war against its inhabitants, a struggle remembered as lasting nineteen years. Eventually, the Spartans prevailed, subjugating the Messenian population. Around the middle of the seventh century BC, a widespread rebellion against Spartan rule prompted another hard fight, again lasting for many years, during which the Spartans were also confronted by other opponents. In the end, the Messenians were defeated once again, leaving the Spartans in direct control of a large section of the Peloponnese.

Sparta's conquests occurred over several generations and cannot be traced in detail, but their scale is beyond question. At the beginning, Sparta's heartland on the Eurotas measured around 100 square miles (260 square kilometres). By the end of the seventh century BC, Spartan-controlled territory amounted to some 3,000 square miles (c. 8,000 square kilometres), and much of this was very good agricultural land, for the Peloponnese often combines good soil with benevolent climate by the standards of southern Greece. This was three times the size of Athenian territory and comfortably made Sparta the largest of all Greek communities until the Hellenistic era began in the fourth century BC. As with Athens, sheer size was a powerful defence in itself but did not guarantee success in aggressive wars. The Spartans did not always win, and even successes sometimes came only through prolonged effort. Opponents remained even then. Argos, also a Dorian city, remained an inveterate opponent of Sparta even though it came to be dwarfed in size by its rival's territory. Herodotus also speaks of major defeats at the hands of the Tegeans before the Spartans managed to turn things round.[5]

Tyrtaeus was a Spartan and a Lyric poet whose work was much admired in the wider Greek world and long revered in his homeland, making him a rare exception among a people not generally associated with the arts. His reputation later grew so great that the Athenians concocted a story that he had originally come from Athens and gone to Sparta to enlighten its denizens. Like that of Solon and others, Tyrtaeus's poetry only survives where quoted by later sources, but what does exist often deals with war and battle and clearly drew on personal experience. Modern scholars date his life and work to the middle of the seventh century BC and date the earlier war to conquer Messenia according to a comment that it was conquered by their fathers' fathers—which illustrates just how difficult it is to be precise with events in this era on the basis of such thin evidence.[6]

Tyrtaeus celebrated valour above all things. In one poem he listed many of the most prized aristocratic virtues, such as bodily strength, speed as a runner or skill as a wrestler, good looks, wealth, oratory, and fame, and dismissed them as nothing without the courage to face the fear and stink of battle and slaughter. Homer's heroes understood and overcame fear, going forward among the front fighters in battle, because their exceptional prowess and risk-taking justified their status; they had to be seen to excel. In contrast Tyrtaeus tried to encourage a far larger group of warriors and not simply the aristocrats. He urged the light armed men to throw missiles, but most of all he spoke of the men crouching behind their shields, heads protected by helmets, spears and swords in hand. These he urged to be front fighters, who would close with the enemy, 'setting foot beside foot, resting shield against shield, crest beside crest, helm beside helm', and wound and be wounded without flinching. Victory in one of Tyrtaeus's battles came when the anonymous masses of the *Iliad* pressed forward with as much determination as the aristocrats.[7]

The motivations were also different, and the poet stressed the need to fight to protect the community and its land. Each man was an individual, facing his own fears, but each was to overcome them for the good of all rather than for personal glory. Tyrtaeus spoke of the pathetic fate of a man whose enemies had taken his land, forcing him to wander as a homeless vagabond, trailed by his aged parents, wife, and children. In contrast he depicted the conquered Messenians, toiling like animals so that they could give half of their produce to Spartan overlords. The price of defeat was terrible, which meant that the grim cost of victory had to be paid. Better for a young man to stand his ground and die rather than to flee, for at least he would be remembered in his prime, handsome, admired by men, and desired by women. More shameful still for him to flee and let a stauncher old man die, his entrails spilling onto the ground as he breathed his last breaths.[8]

Tyrtaeus's Spartans faced the terror of battle to protect their lands and to dominate others and enjoy the fruits of their labours. They did this as a group, a community led by descendants of Hercules, so that they and their families could enjoy a good life. Herodotus employed the term *polity* or *political system* (*politeia*) when he wrote of Sparta, the earliest surviving use of this word, and he also implies that by the middle of the sixth century BC, it was widely recognised as the most powerful Greek state. Population is impossible to determine, although modern estimates for the fifth century BC tend to range from 200,000 to 250,000 people. As with Athens, there were numerous nucleated settlements, ranging in size from villages to small cities, but only one political centre. Unlike with Athens, or indeed all other known Greek cities by the seventh century BC, the Spartans were led by kings, hereditary monarchs whose claim to power was from their descent. In contrast to any other known Greek community, there were two royal families at Sparta and always two kings ruling simultaneously, one from each line. This peculiarity may explain why kings survived there and in no other city—kingdoms to the far north, such as Macedonia and Epirus, were questionably Greek in the opinion of communities in the south.[9]

Spartan kings were not absolute monarchs. Plutarch quotes a *rhetra*—a pronouncement, declaration, even law—received from Delphi by Lycurgus that established the basis for the good government so admired by Herodotus. After commanding the creation of some shrines and the division of the community into clans and associations, it decreed a council (the Gerousia) of twenty-eight elders and the two kings, as well as assemblies of the whole people at regular intervals. Plutarch adds that the original text was later expanded to state that the kings and council were to restrain the people and close a meeting of the Assembly before the masses voted for any measure they felt unwise. Not mentioned in the *rhetra* were the ephors, five annually chosen magistrates who acted as executive officers and judges for the state, in many ways comparable to the archons at Athens.[10]

Tyrtaeus wrote a poem praising harmony within the community, and outsiders came to see the Spartan system as unusually, even uniquely, stable because it balanced each element in society against the others. The two kings had equal power and came from two distinct royal lines, most likely a sign of an early merging of two different groups, each with its own leader. The tradition suggests that mutual rivalry meant that each closely watched the other. In turn the council, consisting of men over sixty and generally drawn from the wealthiest, advised and checked the power of the kings. The same was true of the ephors, men who held the position for a year only once in their lives. These had considerable power, but it was temporary. The assembly of the people involved the wider community in decisions in so far as they could approve or reject proposals presented to them. To outsiders everyone had a share in the affairs of the whole community, while no one individual or group dominated.[11]

Yet the truth was more complex, not least because the community of the Spartans represented only a small proportion of the people living in the area they controlled. There were the perioeci—which translates as 'those living around' or even 'neighbours'. These were free and, as the name implies, lived alongside the Spartans, often in distinct villages and small cities, possibly governing their own local affairs. They were obliged to fight in defence of the community under Spartan leadership but were not part of the 'people', the demos, when it assembled to vote, while still being subject to Spartan kings and magistrates.[12]

This was even more true of the third distinct group in society, the helots, whom other Greeks saw as akin to slaves but different. The origin of the name *helot* is unknown, for the ancient suggestion that it was originally linked to the small city of Helos in the southern Peloponnese is clearly wrong. Many other aspects of the status and history of the helots remain almost as obscure, although that could be said about much of Spartan society in general, about almost every aspect of which scholarly debate continues to rage. Later tradition held that the helots were the descendants of the Achaean Greeks conquered by Spartans first in Laconia itself and later in other regions, including Messenia. Helots' status was hereditary, and their fate was to labour for the benefit of their Spartan overlords. When Tyrtaeus spoke of Messenians giving half of their produce to the Spartans, he was emphasising the price paid by the losers in war. Less clear is whether the Messenians were turned fully into helots after the first conflict with the Spartans or this happened after the defeat of the rebellion in the seventh century BC.[13]

Some helots acted as household slaves for Spartan families, preparing food, cleaning, making clothes, and acting as wet nurses, much like the many domestic slaves in any Greek community. There is no reason to doubt that some Spartans also owned slaves that were not helots, but in overall numbers the former were very much a minority. The vast bulk of the helot population worked on the land so that the Spartans did not have to produce their own food. In Messenia, archaeological survey work suggests that the labour force lived in villages, presumably travelling to the fields each day to go about their tasks. In other areas the population may have been more dispersed, with some helots on each individual farm, but far more evidence is needed to answer such questions. There was a distinct helot sense of identity and community, although whether this was a legacy of past independence or developed over many generations of subjection to the Spartans is impossible to say.[14]

There were wealthy aristocrats at Sparta who owned large estates and enjoyed all the influence and prestige this brought in all Greek communities. In the earliest conquests, there is no sense that the conquered territory was allocated equally to all the men who had fought for victory. Things changed as the groups that would become the Spartans grew in number and in the context of the growing size and wider participation in battle occurring more generally throughout the Greek world. Tyrtaeus's poems reflected a Sparta where many fought and all were urged to fight bravely and well for the common good. His verses contain hints of some tension over ensuring fair reward for all who risked their lives, no doubt reflecting a long-term concern. As the Spartan heartland expanded, more and more men were allocated plots of land in newly conquered territory, a process culminating in the permanent conquest of the rich and extensive plains of Messenia.

Inevitably, later tradition attributed all of this to Lycurgus, in a sweeping, one-off reform that established the fixed, unchanging Spartan system. Logic suggests that it was more gradual, as fresh conquests made more land available, and that other leaders introduced reforms. Compared to other Greek states of such large size, the Spartans showed relatively little interest in overseas colonization. Later, it was claimed that they were involved in two successful colonial settlements—one at Tarentum (modern Taranto) in Italy, which emerged in later years as an important state—and also in one or two failed expeditions. In the main, the conquest of neighbouring territory in the Peloponnese satisfied the Spartans' demand for land, hence the sheer size of the Spartan state. Each fresh conquest sufficed to meet the needs of those Spartan men who contributed to the victory even though they possessed little or no property.[15]

Yet the solution was bound to be temporary, to the extent that if the population grew in size, then each generation would require more land. In the sixth century BC, the Spartans sent an army against the city of Tegea, supposedly carrying in the baggage train fetters and measuring rods, the former to enslave—or turn into helots—the Tegeans and the latter to divide the land into farms to reward the victors. Believing that a Delphic oracle had promised them a triumph, the Spartans advanced with supreme confidence—and suffered defeat, so that they ended up wearing the chains and toiling on the land in yet another story where an oracle was wholly accurate and wholly misinterpreted by its recipients. Later, with fresh oracular advice, the Spartans understood where they had gone wrong and procured the giant bones of a hero buried at Tegea—perhaps human or fossils of some prehistoric creature—which allowed them to resume the war with more success.[16]

Captured Spartans became slaves of fellow Greeks as was customary and as such worked at whatever task their new masters chose to set them. In normal times, Spartans did not work for anyone, including themselves. They owned farms, but unlike the substantial class of middling-level farmers doing so much to shape Athens and other Greek cities, the Spartans never worked alongside or even closely supervised their helot labourers. The Spartans were the *homoioi*, a term often translated as 'equals', although perhaps 'peers' is more appropriate and a cumbersome 'those who are alike' even better. They did not work the land or pursue a craft, and neither did they play an active role in commerce. Instead, they were full-time members of the community, the political entity that was Sparta, true citizens of the city-state. Part of this role meant being prepared to fight well alongside fellow citizens whenever there was need for the good of the state. The skill and bravery of the Spartans became, and remain, famous, but to focus solely on this element of their lives is a mistake. They were not professional soldiers, for soldiering was simply one aspect of being a full-time citizen, whose task it was to share in making decisions for the whole community. Perioeci regularly and helots sometimes joined Sparta's armies in the field and fought and

SPARTA AND ITS CONQUESTS IN MESSENIA

died on the state's behalf, in spite of having no say at all in public life. All decisions were made by the *homoioi*, the 'peers', who were expected to demonstrate in every aspect of their lives that they were good citizens, with the best interests of the community at heart. In a sense, they were like a much-enlarged *basileus* class from earlier centuries.[17]

Plutarch claims that Lycurgus divided the land into 9,000 equal plots and allocated one to each adult Spartan male, while 30,000 perioeci were also granted farms at the same time, but knowing so little about the semi-mythical lawgiver, he did not say when this was supposed to have happened; there was a tradition that the initial distribution involved fewer citizens, and two of the kings granted several thousand more at a later date. The full conquest of Messenia most likely offered the greatest opportunity for such a distribution, even if the principle was already well established. Tyrtaeus wrote of Spartans fighting as light armed skirmishers as well as armoured infantrymen who went face to face with the enemy. Later accounts never mention Spartan troops with such light equipment, which suggests that after the victory in the Second Messenian War, all Spartans possessed enough land to afford the more expensive panoply needed for close-in fighting.[18]

The number of 9,000 may come from much later propaganda from the fourth and third centuries BC, when Sparta had shrunk in size and power and rival leaders were inclined to invent stories about the good old days to justify their current plans. Even so, there are reasonable indications that by the later sixth century BC there were as many as 9,000, perhaps even 10,000, adult Spartan males. In the later tradition most fully expressed by Plutarch, whenever a baby boy was born to a married Spartan couple, elders of the tribe (a group not attested in any other source) inspected the infant for signs of physical weakness. Those felt to be sound were accepted into the community and, once adults, granted a plot of land to provide for their own and their family's needs so that they could live free lives, fully contributing to the city. As they grew and throughout their lives, they shared in a rigorous, even brutal regime, training and remaining ready to share in and serve the state.[19]

Later chapters will discuss these aspects of Spartan society in more detail, and the reality was probably a good deal more complex and varied than suggested by later reputation. For the moment suffice it to say that there was probably no single, drastic reform of Spartan society that then endured for centuries. The state developed more gradually, although there were surely several moments when major change occurred, most likely under the leadership of one or more leaders, and perhaps a real Lycurgus played a role at one point. Underlying everything were the demands of a state built on conquest and on maintaining dominance over a large subject population to provide for the needs of the Spartans themselves, who likely never made up more than 10 to 15 per cent of the overall population. Over time, this proportion would decline until it was far, far lower. Spartans were always heavily outnumbered by perioeci, not to mention the more numerous helots.

The Spartan state was large, but the hierarchy was steep. The true Spartans were at the top, seeing themselves as the descendants of conquerors, which gave them the right to command the descendants of the conquered. The helots were at the bottom, in spite of their being far more numerous than their overlords. The evidence is lacking as to whether helots were owned collectively by the state or were considered part of the land on which they worked, so—in practice and perhaps in theory—the property of individual Spartans. In other cities, a Greek owner of a slave was permitted to grant the latter his freedom, but in Sparta only the state could do this. However, a late source asserts that helots could not be sold outside Sparta, which suggests that they could be traded inside. There are good indications that helots had families, raised children, and sometimes lived in stable village communities, although this should be no surprise, since it was sometimes permitted, even encouraged in other, better-recorded forms of slavery. Although it is impossible to be sure, there is no evidence for slaves taken in Spartan wars waged outside their territory becoming helots, unless their homeland was actually conquered. The assumption appears always to have been that the helot population would perpetuate itself naturally and need not be supplemented from abroad. A few other Greek communities, notably in Thessaly to the north and on Crete, had similar subject populations supporting the more privileged citizen body, but they were a distinct minority, and in most Greek states there was no comparable serf-like population.

At Sparta the helots toiled so that the Spartans had the freedom to be proper citizens, protecting and guiding the state and maintaining against threats both external and internal. The role of the perioeci is much harder to pin down, and in many respects they remain an even more shadowy presence in the sources than the helots. At some point—perhaps decreed by Lycurgus as later tradition maintained; perhaps not—Spartans ceased to follow any trade. In the earlier centuries little distinguishes material culture in Sparta from other parts of Greece. There were local styles and preferences, but someone in Sparta produced pottery, whether for domestic use or for ritual dedications, as well as metalwork and the other items most likely to survive in the archaeological record. Spartans may not have been barred from involvement in this manufacturing until comparatively late. After that, the assumption is that the perioeci were responsible for such things, supplemented by craftsmen and traders from abroad. Many, probably most, perioeci were farmers, much like the population of any Greek state. It is not known whether some helots worked on land owned by perioeci or the labour was done solely by more conventional slaves and poorer members of society. Overall, there were substantially larger numbers of perioeci than there were Spartans, and their role in the daily functioning and the overall success of the Spartan state was vital.[20]

Yet the attention of the ancient sources was fixed overwhelmingly on the Spartans, who were clearly at the pinnacle of society, which did not mean that they were truly equals, as some have taken the term *homoioi* to imply. As with other Greeks, perhaps even more than most, competition and the urge to excel dominated the ethos. At some point a picked group of 300 men were marked out as the elite of the army, providing a bodyguard for the kings on campaign. The selection process was bitterly contested, to the extent that men who lost out were inclined to start fistfights with the successful candidates. This unit was called the *hippeis*, or cavalry, even though they fought on foot. Perhaps this was a legacy of an older army where the wealthy could afford horses, just like the similarly named class at Athens. It is clear that for all the supposed egalitarianism of the Spartan system of education and training, wealth and high birth offered significant advantages. As elsewhere in Greece, a man could garner fame and respect by winning at the Olympic Games or other festivals. The better off found it easier to travel and train, and there was a marked fondness among the royal families and aristocracy for horse and chariot racing. Both activities required considerable wealth to raise and school the animals.[21]

Any Spartan was privileged compared to the perioeci and vastly so compared to the helots, even if some Spartans were more privileged than others. In comparison to their counterparts in most other Greek states, Spartan women were granted unusual freedom and independence, not least being allowed to own property in their own right. While the themes of courage and self-sacrifice for the good of the state celebrated by Tyrtaeus are not surprising in a Spartan context, the other Sparta-based poet of this era took up very different themes in his surviving works. Alcman flourished around the same time as Tyrtaeus, or perhaps a little later in the seventh century BC, and composed songs to be sung by choruses of girls and young women. They celebrate love and desire, beauty and marriage in a reminder that Sparta was not solely home to warriors who practiced for and thought exclusively of war. Music, dance, and song were big parts of the lives of the Spartans, not least at the many festivals punctuating the year of a city seen by others—and its own inhabitants—as especially devout in its observance of ritual. Many performances were choral, helping to reinforce that sense of community so important to an elite group dominating a much larger population. Yet, once again, belonging to the community did not mean that all had equal prestige. There were solo parts where individuals could excel and stand out. Alcman praised the grace and beauty of named girls, singling them out from the rest for admiration by the whole community.[22]

Spartans were allowed to be individuals, as long as they were also loyal to the group. A good deal of conformity was enforced by peer pressure and downright competitiveness, the desire to earn and maintain a high reputation and not to be overshadowed by others unless they consistently proved themselves worthy. There was also the shared fear of the vastly greater numbers of helots. Our sources for the sixth and fifth centuries BC attest to only a handful of helot rebellions. Others may have gone unmentioned, especially if they were small in scale, but it is impossible to be certain. We do know that the treatment of the helots by their Spartan overlords was openly repressive, even brutal to the eyes of most external observers. Tyrtaeus presented a pathetic image of Messenians slogging only to give half of all they grew to their masters and then having to mourn publicly when that same oppressive master died. Neither he nor anyone else expected them to like it. Spartan dominance was based on fear, ultimately by maintaining a marked advantage when it came to the use of violent force. Spartans were fewer in number, even when aided by the perioeci, so the state relied on being able to suppress any resistance offered by its helots, but at the same time the treatment of this serf class ensured that they would always be a threat. Later it was claimed that each year the ephors formally declared war on the helots. In a sense the Spartan state was always in conflict with itself.

Wars with neighbouring cities were also common in the seventh and sixth centuries BC, and their long duration suggests that many consisted primarily of raids and counter-raids. Over time, direct conquest ceased to be Sparta's ambition. When the Tegeans were defeated, the war was ended by a treaty, and for all their earlier ambitions, the Spartans did not seize Tegean farmland or turn the population into helot labourers. Instead, Tegea remained independent but became an ally. Their day-to-day affairs remained in the Tegeans' own hands, and they kept their own laws and rituals, so that they were an autonomous community. They simply acknowledged the Spartans as their leaders. One clause of the treaty stipulated that they would refuse to shelter any runaway helots or let them settle in the city and gain rights.[23]

Similar alliances—perhaps with much the same clause about helots—were gradually created with the majority of the remaining independent states in the Peloponnese. Even Corinth, another of the handful of big cities in the Greek world, became an ally of Sparta and treated the Spartans with deference. The biggest exception was Argos, which continued to defy the Spartans. Around 669 BC, the Argives had defeated the Spartans in a major battle and remained enemies in Tyrtaeus's day. Sometime around 545 BC, the two cities supposedly agreed to a strangely ritualised battle, waged not by their entire levies but by 300 picked men on each side. Herodotus reports that 597 were killed, leaving a single Spartan and two Argives. The latter went off to celebrate their success, leaving the Spartan on the field, where he stripped spoils from the enemy dead and went back to the main army announcing that he was victorious. After rancorous negotiation, the full armies fought a battle, and after heavy casualties on both sides, the Spartans won. However, the sole survivor from the Spartan-picked band felt that he could not return home when all his comrades had fallen, so committed suicide.[24]

Herodotus's story, as so often, is fanciful and at best an exaggeration of some attempt at resolving the conflict through a limited fight, not least because so many fatalities without any wounded is implausible. More interesting is the context he provides for the war not as a life-or-death struggle between Argos and Sparta but as a battle for control of territory on the borders of the two states—and in many ways easier for the Argives to access. Direct conquest of an entire community appears no longer to have been a Spartan aim. In part this was because most cities were now larger than they had been in earlier centuries, making it much harder to destroy their power, and even in the earlier period of Spartan expansion, some settlements had been absorbed rather than destroyed. Argos was a substantial city-state, although too small to match Spartan strength and no more able to dream of breaking Spartan power forever than the Spartans could realistically imagine its permanent destruction.

Instead, the Argives could maintain their independence and protect or expand control on the fringes of their state. They were able to avoid becoming an ally of Sparta and accepting Spartan leadership. Yet, even though Sparta controlled far more territory and possessed so many allies, the Spartans in turn made no all-out effort to destroy Argos. More than likely the allies would have been reluctant to assist in the destruction of a Greek city when this was solely in Sparta's interests. At the same time, the need to ensure control of the helots was a greater concern for the Spartans than success elsewhere. The biggest threat to the survival of Sparta came from within.

Thus Sparta in the later sixth century BC was the largest and most powerful Greek state, one created by conquest and based on a permanent distinction between the conquerors and conquered. The true Spartans were an elite class, if a very large one, that had managed to structure all of society to support their continued dominance. In the past, the class had managed to grow as land was conquered and farms and helot labour were made available to support new members of this elite. Conquest and such full exploitation of conquered territory had become rare, changing this dynamic, but for the moment the system functioned well. The *homoioi* and their families were numerous and were granted a comfortable lifestyle by the sweat of others. Much of the land exploited on their behalf was very productive. Tyrtaeus celebrated the plains of Messenia as 'good to sow, good to plough'—both all the greater because the Spartans themselves had to do none of the sowing or ploughing. The *homoioi* remained competitive, and there were distinctions of wealth and lineage, but this competition did not disrupt or destabilise the political system, the *politeia* shared by the Spartan citizens. All understood that it was in their interest to close ranks against threats from elsewhere in the state, most of all the helots.[25]

Herodotus was right to single out the internal stability of Sparta because it contrasted so starkly with the turbulent politics of so many Greek states. Earlier Tyrtaeus had praised harmony (*eunomia*) within the community. The Spartans had managed to achieve this balance of satisfying individual ambition and the desire to excel without risking revolution and faction fighting. They had done this at the expense of the helots, and perhaps in part also the perioeci, whose efforts freed the true Spartan elite from any task other than being good citizens in peace and, especially, in wartime. This was a product of the peculiar history of Sparta and not practical—or even desirable—for other Greek communities. As Sparta emerged as clearly the most powerful of all the Greek states, at least as seen from the outside, the Athenians still struggled to harness the rivalries within their own aristocracy. It is now time to return to this topic.

5

THE TYRANTS

The rule of Pisistratus and his sons at Athens and the revolution that overthrew them, c. 570–509 BC

Spartan society was unusual for its stability compared to other Greek states and was unique for its dual kingship. No other Greek state was led by a king in the sixth century BC, and most had abandoned the institution far earlier than this. There were monarchies in the north, in Macedonia and Epirus, and folk there spoke versions of Greek, but many in the wider Greek world doubted that they were true Hellenes. Society was different there, more akin to the definitely barbarian peoples of neighbouring Thrace and Illyria, and communities did not develop along the lines of the city-states of southern Greece and the islands. When, near the end of the sixth century BC, Alexander, a prince—subsequently king—of Macedonia, wanted to compete at the Olympic Games, there was debate over whether or not he was eligible. Eventually he was admitted, on the grounds that the royal house of Macedonia, the Argeads, descended from exiles from the city of Argos, which implied that simply being Macedonian was not enough to qualify as truly Greek.[1]

Apart from the peculiar Spartans, true Greeks were not ruled by kings, which was not to say that they had no dealings with them.

The Ionian cities on the coast of Asia Minor lived alongside the kingdoms of Lydia and Caria, whose strength had grown as the power of Assyria crumbled, giving a chance for more states to expand. Most of the Ionians came more or less to acknowledge the dominance of the closest kingdom, while retaining self-government. It helped that the ruling dynasties, and probably many in the wider population, showed respect for and interest in many aspects of Greek culture. Styles of art and architecture were copied and often modified to local taste. The kings in particular took an interest in Greek shrines, especially the Pythian oracle at Delphi, sending envoys to seek answers to their questions and lavishing wealth on the shrines as a mark of respect, and no doubt in the hope of securing favourable messages from the gods. King Croesus of Lydia became proverbial throughout the Greek world for his wealth. One story claimed that he sought out Solon for his wisdom, although he was unable at first to appreciate the truth of the latter's words. The process was not all in one direction, and the Greeks also learned much through contact with these eastern kingdoms. It was no coincidence that the beginnings of so many aspects of Greek philosophy and literature came from the Ionian cities of Asia Minor and the closest islands.[2]

Greeks did not have kings, even if major cult sites welcomed the attention and gifts of foreign kings. Yet, in the course of the seventh and sixth centuries BC in particular, many Greek cities came under the rule of tyrants—monarchs by a different name. Cylon, victor in the Olympic Games, had attempted to make himself tyrant at Athens and failed, in spite of assistance from his father-in-law, the tyrant of Megara, who supplied funds and men. Still, the connection with Megara may well have contributed to the swift and hostile reaction of the Athenian population, since the city was always a rival and often an enemy. Outside Athens, more is heard of successful bids for tyranny, of the men who established themselves as rulers at Corinth, Argos, and quite a few smaller cities. Cylon's father-in-law was eventually forced to flee Megara and go into exile, but elsewhere some tyrants stayed in power for a long time, even passing this control on to a son or sons. Even so, tyranny rarely lasted more than a couple of generations.[3]

The word *tyrant* was not originally Greek. There was speculation in later centuries that it might have been Etruscan from Italy, but far more probably it had Asian roots and seems to have been reserved for someone who had seized rather than inherited power. Although the distinction is less clear in Homer, later Greeks differentiated between a king and a tyrant, even though both were monarchs. This was not primarily a judgement on legitimacy or on the quality of their rule. Stereotypes formed of tyrants—and often monarchs—as cruel and capricious, as sexually aggressive and often perverted, preying on decent women and boys, but this was held up as characteristic behaviour for someone with too much power. The term *tyrant* itself lacked the strongly negative associations it has since acquired, and there were believed to be good tyrants. Thucydides connected the rise of tyranny with the growing prosperity of the emerging cities of Greece, while Aristotle claimed that tyrants usually had considerable popular support, especially among the poor. There was likely an element of truth in each explanation, but the reality was more complex: Tyrants emerged from a background of competition for power between rival aristocratic families. Popularity—at least with enough of the community to overawe opponents—was important. So was force.[4]

For centuries Athens had avoided tyranny, although the margin may have been narrow. Cylon's attempt to make himself tyrant had failed, and nothing more is known of him. The massacre of his supporters gives an indication of how frightened some Athenians were and how bitter some of the rivalries among the elite could be. Whatever the details of the breach of faith, from early on these killings were seen as impious, and blame was assigned to one aristocratic family, or perhaps a better word would be *clan*, the Alcmaeonids. A few were arrested and executed, more were exiled or chose to flee, and the rest were considered to some degree cursed. This did not prevent them from remaining an important and influential group at Athens, although their guilt was periodically raked up by their opponents.

Tradition maintained that Solon received an offer or could have chosen to become tyrant but refused. The difference between a man granted the freedom to reform the laws and organisation of a community and one who seized power and imposed reforms could be slim, and several of the lawgivers later celebrated for their wisdom were also tyrants. The stories about Solon maintain that he walked away from power in the hope that the reforms he had introduced would work without his supervision and bring order, even though his verses made clear that he knew many were disappointed in not getting everything they wanted. Rivalry between leading families, including the Alcmaeonids, continued. Within a decade there were two years of anarchy, when no elections deemed legitimate could be held to appoint archons. Then one man managed to hold on to the archonship for more than two years instead of the twelve months allowed. He was deposed by force, a coalition of erstwhile rivals joining together. Such unity proved brief.[5]

Herodotus described two main factions vying for dominance. The 'men of the coast' were led by Megacles of the Alcmaeonids, while the 'men of the plain' were led by another aristocrat, Lycurgus (namesake of the Spartan reformer). A third faction, the 'men from over the hills'—the Greek defies easy translation but does not mean 'men of the hills'—formed around a leader called Pisistratus, who was clearly wealthy, talented, and ambitious but may not have come from the established Athenian aristocracy. He had done well in the ongoing war between Athens and Megara over the territory between the two states, especially Eleusis and the island of Salamis. Victorious in one or more actions, Pisistratus had gained support, even though it is hard to be specific about the identity of his supporters. By the fourth century BC, Aristotle, equating the three main factions to the political ideologies he understood, identified Pisistratus's supporters as extreme democrats, but this probably did not reflect the reality of sixth century BC Athens.[6]

Around 561/60 BC, Pisistratus made his first open bid for power. It was claimed that he faked an attack on himself, appearing in the city bruised and wounded, as if his party and their pack mules had been assaulted. Ancient sources associated this sort of trickery with the wily Odysseus, but at the very least the story suggests that most people believed that political rivalries could—and perhaps often did—turn violent. The community—in what form is unclear—responded by giving Pisistratus the right to a permanent bodyguard. Its members carried clubs, not edged weapons, and may have numbered no more than fifty. Even so, backed by men able to intimidate others as well as to protect him, Pisistratus formally occupied the Acropolis and became tyrant. Yet he was not 'tyrannical' in the modern sense, ruling mildly and upholding the existing laws and customs, which in the main meant the system devised by Solon. Later tradition claimed that the lawgiver was still alive to see what was happening and publicly condemned it, although no one listened and Pisistratus had too much affection and respect for Solon to act against him. While possible, this is probably no more than romantic invention.[7]

Pisistratus's first spell as tyrant did not last long, although just how long and precisely when each event happened is impossible to establish with certainty. Although bitter rivals, Megacles, Lycurgus, and their supporters decided that having someone else reign supreme was intolerable, so they joined forces and expelled Pisistratus. The old quarrels then resumed, and a few years later, around 557 to 555 BC, Megacles decided that he would be better off allying with Pisistratus and making him tyrant once again. In a moment of theatre, they found an unusually tall and good-looking woman, dressed her as Athena, and drove into Athens in a chariot, as if the goddess herself was bringing Pisistratus back. Herodotus expressed his dismay that the famously canny and rational Athenians could have been fooled by such a pageant. No doubt there was more to the return than this, and he does mention that the tyrant married Megacles's daughter.[8]

Many of the stories about Pisistratus have the feel of folklore. In one, an omen, issued by the prestigious oracle at Delphi, was supposed to have warned his father against having a son, not that he paid any attention to the warning. The breakdown of his alliance with Megacles of the Alcmaeonids was explained as a personal dispute. Since he already had sons who were young men, Pisistratus did not want any more children. Therefore, according to Herodotus, he refused to have conventional intercourse with his bride, instead doing something unnatural, if unspecified. Eventually the young woman revealed this to her mother, prompting Megacles's outrage at this offence to the honour of his family and also the spirit of their alliance. The deal fell apart, and Pisistratus fled Athens. At this stage, Megacles appears to have been more influential than Pisistratus, able to make or break the tyranny, even though he could not—or chose not to—take it for himself.[9]

This time Pisistratus was away for longer, perhaps as much as a decade. Aristocrats tended to have connections with aristocrats from other cities in a manner reminiscent of the guest friendships of Homer's heroes. Their wealth gave them the opportunity to travel, whether to visit a shrine or oracle or to compete at a festival, and the desire to grow their wealth also made connections abroad very useful. Many, at least in coastal communities, owned ships, whether as investments or for their own use, and the boundaries between trading and piracy were as slim as ever. The war between Athens and Megara was characterised by naval raiding of the opponent's shoreline, which suggests that Pisistratus had a talent for this activity. He went first to Eretria on Euboea, then further north, eventually spending some time at a settlement on the coast of Thrace. Details are lacking, but the area was rich in silver deposits and in forests providing the timber for building big structures and ships. Over time, he built up the wealth to fund a new bid for power, not through conquest but by making himself a major trading partner of local leaders.¹⁰

Pisistratus needed men as much as silver, if not more. Some of his household and dependents had gone into exile with him, and he was able to recruit from Athenian settlers on the coast of Thrace, folk he may have supported in the past. More help came from his connections in other cities, where he called in favours. The Thebans gave money and men, and an exiled former tyrant from the island of Naxos brought more. At some point, Pisistratus had married the daughter of an Argive nobleman, and Argos supplied one of the strongest contingents for his expedition, whether or not it consisted of 1,000 men as claimed by Herodotus. Mustering at Eretria around 546/5 BC, they crossed to Attica and landed near Marathon (later famous for the victory over the Persians in 490 BC). Some Athenians came to join them, but significant numbers mustered to oppose Pisistratus's return. Once again, the sources tell of an oracle predicting his victory and of his cunning in achieving it. When the two armies faced each other, Pisistratus pretended that he did not plan an immediate attack. His opponents dropped their guard, dispersing to take food and relax. When Pisistratus led his men forward, there was little or no organised resistance as the defending army fell apart and fled. Pisistratus sent his sons riding ahead to tell everyone to go home and that no harm would come to them.¹¹

Pisistratus was once again tyrant of Athens, and this time he and then his sons remained in power for some thirty-six years. Little is preserved in the brief sources about those years, which focus overwhelmingly on the beginning and end of the story and, even then, fail to explain what happened in a convincing way. By the fifth century BC, when Athens was at the height of its imperial power and its democracy was at its most confident, tyranny was anathema to all that the Athenians held dear. Yet, in spite of this, a strong tradition persisted that the rule of Pisistratus was mild, lawful, good for Attica, and even a renewal of the mythical golden age. Acts of repression

against opponents were rare, even if the threat was always there. Thucydides pointed out that under Pisistratus and his sons, Athens waged war effectively against its foreign opponents, religious rituals and sacrifices were properly performed, and the city was improved and ornamented, while levies were light. Attica prospered, and the tyranny did not interfere very much in most Athenians' lives.[12]

There was no formal post or magistracy of tyrant at Athens. Pisistratus may have revived the bodyguard of clubmen originally granted to him or employed a similar force, for the production of painted vases flourished at Athens around this time, and since some show Thracian and Scythian warriors, scholars have conjectured that he may have maintained foreign troops. Equally, this could just represent a taste for images of the exotic and closer commercial connections with Greek communities near the Dardanelles and beyond. Thucydides and others emphasised that existing laws were preserved under Pisistratus. The tyrant made sure that a relative or other reliable connection was among the archons elected each year but otherwise did not interfere in this institution or the courts. On one occasion a charge of murder was made against Pisistratus, and he appeared in court on the day of the trial ready to defend himself just like any other citizen. By this time, his accuser had decided that discretion was the better part of valour and either did not appear or declined to press the charge. Whether true or not, the anecdote highlights the difficulty of pinning down the nature of Pisistratus's regime. On the one hand there is the 'constitutional' tyrant, presenting himself as subject to the same laws as his fellow citizens, and on the other is the intimidating strongman who had seized control by military force and was too dangerous to attack.[13]

Solon had resisted pressure for a major redistribution of land, taking from the big landowners to give farmland to the poorer members of the community. Pisistratus followed Solon's example and did not try anything of this sort, instead offering milder forms of relief. Loans were made readily available to help smaller-scale farmers through difficult patches, when the weather or bad luck had struck them hard. The low level of taxation, presumably in kind, helped. In addition, Pisistratus introduced a system of circuit judges, where magistrates travelled around Attica allowing cases to be settled in the countryside rather than forcing all involved to go to Athens itself. For those who had their hands full working their own farms, this was a major saving in time, apart from the risks that, as relative strangers in the city, they might find little sympathy or understanding of their plight. At the same time, it ensured that the laws and their application were consistent throughout Attica.[14]

At some point, perhaps after Pisistratus's death, his son Hipparchus was credited with setting stone markers along all the major routes, showing the distance to the newly constructed altar of the twelve gods in the Agora (marketplace) in Athens. These stone herms were said to have had a line or so of verse containing words of wisdom on the back, although the only surviving example is too damaged to confirm this. Both judges and markers linked the wider population together as part of the same community centred on Athens. Wherever the trial took place, the judge was appointed in Athens, and the laws were Athenian. Everyone, however rarely they visited the city, was treated as an Athenian. This sense of community was not new, but Pisistratus and his sons helped to make it even stronger.[15]

In many respects this was the story of their regime, confirming and adding to existing trends, as Athens became wealthier and more cohesive as a society. More than anything else, they gave Athens decades of stability and internal peace that encouraged growth. No doubt the public works, both practical when they improved the water supply and pious in the construction of temples, were visible displays of the advantages of being Athenian. The Panathenaea festival was reformed, and every fourth year celebrated on a grander scale, as the Great Panathenaea, with sporting and cultural competitions mirroring those of the Olympic Games but celebrating Athens and its culture rather than Greek culture in general.[16]

Large sections of the population, perhaps even a substantial majority, may have supported Pisistratus enthusiastically, or most Athenians may simply have resigned themselves to accept his dominance as more appealing than the risky option of opposing him. There is no sign of any serious attempt to overthrow him after his third return to power, which meant that the rule of the tyrant gave Athens a time of stability and relief from the bitter, sometimes violent competition of the aristocratic families. The latter were the potential leaders of any opposition, yet chose not to attempt this, suggesting that many were persuaded that there were advantages to remaining quiet. While one of the tyrant's family or partisans was archon each year, the other eight archonships were open to other aristocrats. In later years, the Alcmaeonids claimed that they had gone into exile during the tyranny, only to reappear when Athens needed them. At best this was an exaggeration, and perhaps some of them chose to go abroad for part of the time. However, a fragmentary inscription reveals that Megacles's son Cleisthenes was archon in 525/4 BC, so at least one prominent member of the clan had come to an accommodation with the new regime, and probably such acceptance was common.[17]

Pisistratus died in 528/7 BC, by then an elderly man, so that Cleisthenes held office under his sons. Hippias, the oldest, appears to have led, but since there was not a formal position as tyrant, his brothers shared in what was a family enterprise. Hipparchus, who was probably the next oldest, later had a reputation for his promotion of culture and his wisdom. Around this time, a number of poets and thinkers came to Athens, and the first dramas were written and performed in competition in the city. At some point, the Panathenaea festival came to include recitations of Homer, and some claimed that Pisistratus or his sons were responsible for establishing the final, official version of the poems. Yet, although in later centuries some Greeks made these claims, it is far from clear whether or not they were true, or if they were, whether this was conscious policy on the part of the Pisistratid family.[18]

The same is true of other developments in Athens during these years. Every indication shows a city prospering, with trade booming, but it is impossible to know whether this resulted from the peace and stability offered by the tyrants, from conscious effort on the part of Pisistratus and his sons, or from a mixture of the two. Coinage was not minted in Greece until around the middle of the sixth century BC, although even then not every state chose to produce its own series. At Athens, series of coins bearing distinct symbols first appeared probably under Pisistratus himself. These were not struck in great quantities, and it is always hard to judge how coinage was used in the early days, when a good deal of exchange still occurred by traditional means. While these series of coins may have been meant to pay for specific projects undertaken by the tyrant, or even to pay contingents of troops, these ideas remain conjectural. So little is known about the ambitions and capacity of the tyrants, or indeed about the basic nature of the tyranny at Athens. Hippias and his brothers appear to have continued in much the same style as their father, governing mildly, maintaining the rule of law, and making life tolerable, perhaps even better than that for enough of their fellow Athenians to acquiesce in the regime. Much of the attested building work occurred under Hippias, beautifying the city, honouring the gods, and providing employment for many.[19]

When opposition came, it was not a widespread rising but a conspiracy with very few members, their motives related to private honour. Hipparchus grew attracted to a youth named Harmodius. (In the later tradition of Hipparchus as patron of the arts, a younger brother was made the key player, but this seems unlikely.) Harmodius was already attached to a man named Aristogiton and rebuffed Hipparchus. However, when the youth told him what had happened, Aristogiton became angry and feared the tyrant might use his power to steal Harmodius away. This did not happen, although Hipparchus did try to persuade Harmodius and was refused a second time.[20]

Up to this point, Hipparchus had followed the conventions of aristocratic society, trying to persuade and win over Harmodius, but accepting his refusal and not employing his power to get what he wanted. However, after this second rejection, he decided to take revenge in a way that was both petty and vicious, whether because that was his nature or because of the way the youth had refused him. Harmodius's sister was called to take part in a ritual procession, carrying a basket along with other girls from the city. On the day, she was publicly humiliated by being sent home as unsuited to the honour, which most likely implied doubts about her chastity. This was a slight on the whole family, especially the men who were expected to guard the virtue of their womenfolk.[21]

Aristogiton had already decided to seek revenge for what Hipparchus might have tried but had not actually done. For an aristocrat, the sense that someone could choose to challenge him with overwhelming force was in itself a blow to his pride. Now, after the slight to his family, Harmodius was just as eager for revenge, so the two formed a conspiracy with a small group of friends, fearing that including too many people risked the secret being revealed. All involved appear to have been from aristocratic families or their close associates. Another reason for keeping the numbers small may well have been a strong desire to gain the lion's share of the glory and perhaps a sense that few others had a particularly pressing reason to strike against the tyrants.

In 514/3 BC, the Great Panathenaea was celebrated, and its grand public procession offered the perfect chance to get close to Hippias and Hipparchus, for the aim was to kill both brothers—and perhaps their other close relatives—and overthrow the regime. Hippias, as the older and senior, was the principal target, until Aristogiton and Harmodius saw one of their fellow conspirators chatting to the tyrant as the column was forming. Fearing betrayal, the pair panicked and ran back to where Hipparchus was. Pulling out daggers concealed in their clothes, they stabbed him to death. Harmodius was himself killed moments later by the tyrant's guards. Aristogiton was captured and, before dying under torture, named many of his confederates. Arrests were made, and executions followed.

Later, Athenians celebrated Harmodius and Aristogiton as the martyred heroes who had brought down the tyranny. In fact, Hippias continued to rule Athens for another four years. Frightened and angered by the murder of his brother, he did become suspicious and harsher in his treatment of others. The sources are poor and hint at occasional exiles, and perhaps a few common murders, in the first three decades of the tyranny. It is assumed that the killing of any prominent aristocrat was ordered—or at the very least condoned—by Pisistratus or his sons, since anyone seen as too prominent and powerful was bound to be perceived as a potential rival. One Athenian Olympic victor around this time took care to attribute his victory to Pisistratus's family, although this did not prevent his eventual violent death. After the assassination of Hipparchus, there were more executions, and the tyrant came to be resented far more. Even so, the Athenian aristocracy did not join forces to expel him, whether from fear of his power or inability to cooperate.[22]

Having collaborated with and prospered under the Pisistratids, the Alcmaeonid family may have suffered more in these later years of the regime, and perhaps at this point Cleisthenes and other leading members were forced or chose to go into exile, whether that meant leaving Attica altogether or retreating to its fringes where they had land and supporters. Like many aristocrats, they had developed connections with leaders in other cities and also began to make major donations to the cult site at Delphi. Herodotus also claims that there was a direct bribe to the Pythian priestess who delivered the famous oracles. By this or other means, she was persuaded to tack on to the end of any answer given to a Spartan request that they should free the Athenians.[23]

In the main the Spartans had not been hostile to Pisistratus and his sons, largely because they had far more pressing concerns and Athens was distant and presented no immediate threat. Vague friendship and an avoidance of interfering in each other's affairs were mutually beneficial to the Pisistratids and the leaders of Sparta. Around 519 BC, the city of Plataea, which lay close to the border of Attica, appealed to Sparta for help against Thebes, on the basis that the Spartans had a high military reputation and were unlikely to be intimidated by the Thebans. However, for the moment the Spartans saw few advantages in close alliance with the distant and modest-sized Plataea and instead advised the Plataeans to seek Athenian aid. Allegedly this was less from any goodwill towards the Plataeans than from a vague desire to cause trouble for the Thebans. Hippias proved much more welcoming and gave direct military assistance to the Plataeans, helping them to inflict a sharp defeat on the Thebans. It was the beginning of the particularly close alliance between Athens and Plataea that long outlasted any personal connection with the Pisistratid family.[24]

For whatever reason, by 511/10 BC King Cleomenes of Sparta favoured intervention, although the first effort was on a limited scale and more in the nature of backing free enterprise. A leading Spartan gathered a force of men and ships and landed in Attica. News of the attempt had spread, so that Hippias was ready and met them with an army of his own. This included Thessalian cavalry, provided by an allied king in Thessaly, and these so harried the invaders that their army collapsed and the survivors fled back to their ships. The whole episode has the feel of many attempted coups, of the sort led in the past by Cylon or Pisistratus himself, since it relied to a great extent on allies, mercenaries, and freebooters rather than 'national' armies.[25]

The next attempt was different, when in 510/9 BC Cleomenes led a substantial Spartan army and marched overland to Attica, presumably having arranged passage with the states in between. Better organised, better trained, and better led, the Spartans brushed aside the Thessalian cavalry, who then appear to have returned home. Hippias and his supporters holed up in a fort they had constructed beside the Acropolis. Some Athenians joined the besieging Spartans, but there is no sense of a massed rising to overthrow the tyrant with the aid of the foreign army. So far Cleisthenes and his family do not appear to have returned, although they were soon to do so. Hippias was well prepared to resist, and the Spartans were not eager to press the siege beyond a loose blockade. The Pisistratids tried to sneak most of their younger members out of Attica to a safe stronghold overseas, and by chance the group was intercepted and taken prisoner. Negotiations followed, with Hippias agreeing to leave Attica within five days in exchange for the return of the hostages.[26]

The tyranny was at an end. Later generations liked to celebrate and sing of Harmodius and Aristogiton, whose love and sense of honour had inspired them to take a stand against the rulers of the city, even though it cost them their lives. Yet, in truth, their plot failed, and the Pisistratids were only expelled by the intervention of a Spartan king and his army. Athens was 'freed' by foreigners—indeed, Dorian Greeks from a city that would in time become Athens's greatest rival and enemy—and not by the courage or skill of the Athenians themselves. Like many uncomfortable truths, over time most Athenians chose to forget all about it and preferred the dramatic story of the tyrannicides, which offered a simple, dramatic, and homegrown explanation for the revolution.

6

THE PEOPLE

*Athens, Cleisthenes, and the new democracy,
c. 510–500 BC*

King Cleomenes did not stay long in Athens. Keeping a substantial force of troops together in the field required effort and no longer appeared necessary. The Spartan king had come in obedience to the Delphic oracle's commands and presumably because he felt that deposing Hippias was in his own and Sparta's interest. At the very least, the successful intervention in the affairs of a state as large as Athens had demonstrated Spartan strength, making up for the failure of the first attempt. In the past, Pisistratus and his sons had maintained good relations with the Spartans, but subsequent events make clear that Cleomenes expected the new regime at Athens to be even more favourably inclined and duly deferential towards Sparta. He and, presumably, other Spartans were now eager to extend their influence well beyond the Peloponnese, but there was no question of direct rule of a community as large as Athens.[1]

At Athens, no one had any appetite for replacing one tyrant with another, and instead the aristocracy seized the chance to resume the traditional competition for honours, office, and power, at last free of the restrictions on this imposed by the Pisistratids. Cleisthenes, the son of Megacles, emerged as one of the key figures, helped by his recent exile and open opposition to Hippias. Almost nothing is known about his main rival, Isagoras, other than that he had developed a close political friendship with King Cleomenes. They became guest friends, that long-established tradition by which aristocrats formed bonds with leaders from other cities, exchanging gifts, hospitality, and favours in a way that would have been familiar to Homer's warrior princes. Rumour claimed that Isagoras was such a generous host that he turned a blind eye when the visiting Cleomenes slept with his wife.[2]

In 508/7 BC Isagoras won the senior archonship, defeating a candidate backed by Cleisthenes, who had served as archon already so could not stand for the office again. Disappointed, Cleisthenes broadened his support by appealing to 'the people'. What followed fundamentally changed Athens, making the difficulty of tracing precisely what happened in the sources all the more frustrating. 'The people' meant significant numbers of Athenians from outside its aristocracy as well as those attached to them by pre-existing ties of loyalty. It may primarily refer to the third class established by Solon, the *zeugitai*, or 'yoked-men', most of them owners of moderate-sized farms, but it is possible that some of the fourth class, the *thêtes*, joined in the cause, perhaps particularly those at the upper end in terms of property. Attica's already large population had grown during the course of the sixth century BC, and levels of prosperity had grown with it. More land was exploited, harvests increased, and trade in agricultural and other products blossomed. Since Solon had based membership of his classes on assessment of wealth, economic growth added to the numbers in each group. One inscription proudly recorded a man's rise from the fourth to second category through his own efforts. New additions to the higher classes may not easily have fitted into traditional relationships tying them to the aristocracy, and most likely resented this exclusion.[3]

Because there were more Athenians, and because overall Attica had prospered, helped by the stability created by the tyrants, more Athenians had at least a degree of wealth. Even if Cleisthenes found support only among the *zeugitai*, by 508 BC these likely represented a substantial number of men, enough to alter a balance of power resting on long-established loyalty to aristocratic families, including his own. There is a good chance that he picked up on, rather than created, an existing and widespread sense of dissatisfaction with the way public life had functioned in the past. Perhaps an opportunist, a sincere convert, or a mixture of both, Cleisthenes became the leader of a broad movement demanding at least some political involvement for a significantly greater section of society.

Unable to match the enthusiasm and numbers of his rival, Isagoras appealed to King Cleomenes for support. At first the Spartan ruler contented himself with reminding the Athenians of the curse associated with the Alcmaeonids, Cleisthenes's family. The latter and his immediate family withdrew from the city and perhaps from Attica altogether. Then in 507 BC Cleomenes arrived in person at the head of a small body of troops. Isagoras ordered the expulsion of more opponents—allegedly some 700 households—and these also obeyed and left. Next, accompanied by his Spartan allies, he went to dismiss the council (*boule*). Isagoras had some 300 supporters of his own and may have wanted to create a new council composed of these men.[4]

The *boule* he ordered to disperse may have been the one created by Solon—assuming that the lawgiver actually did create this body—or something introduced by Cleisthenes and his popular faction. Either way its members refused to be intimidated, and this act of resistance began to draw an ever-growing crowd. Isagoras and Cleomenes did not feel able to overcome this opposition and withdrew to the Acropolis. Soon they were besieged, but unlike Hippias, they had not prepared for this and within three days ran short of supplies. Negotiations followed, and the king and his troops were allowed to go back to Sparta. Less clear is the fate of their Athenian allies. Isagoras went into exile, but although one tradition claims that his men were also allowed to go, another version maintains that they were executed and their property confiscated or destroyed. Either way, the 'popular party' had triumphed. There is no information concerning who had led them in these critical days or explaining whether the resistance was spontaneous or planned. Presumably the crowds who mustered to back up the council were men from the city or close by, since the brief conflict did not give much time for news to spread and others to join them from further afield. Only in the aftermath were Cleisthenes and the other exiles recalled.[5]

Cleomenes had not given up, and in 506 BC he tried to coordinate a triple attack on Athens intended to crush opposition and install Isagoras as tyrant. While allied forces from Thebes and Chalkis on Euboea each launched a separate invasion, perhaps essentially a grand raid, Cleomenes and his fellow king, Demaratus, led the main army of Spartans and Peloponnesian allies. At first all went well, and the two kings advanced on Eleusis, but there the campaign began to unravel. The Corinthians had provided a substantial contingent but now complained about the objective. They claimed that placing a tyrant over any Greek community was wrong and was especially shameful for the Spartans, who had acquired a reputation as foes of tyranny. The Corinthians left the army, and soon afterwards Demaratus also decided that he did not believe in his royal colleague's objective and turned back. All or most of the other allies followed him. With numbers and general enthusiasm so depleted, Cleomenes gave in and marched home with the rump of the army.[6]

The biggest threat was gone, and the Athenians put together a field force to deal with the other attacks. Moving quickly, they routed the Thebans and then caught and defeated the Chalcidians before the two groups of invaders could join together. Each time they captured a large number of prisoners and later celebrated the stunning success by erecting a monument on the Acropolis of a bronze four-horse chariot, partly decorated with the chains they had used to secure the captives. Greeks rarely showed any reluctance when it came to enslaving fellow Greeks, but in this case most were released on payment of a ransom, a mutually satisfactory outcome for both sides. However, the Athenians had greater demands when it came to Chalkis, for they had followed up the victory by crossing to Euboea. A large swathe of Chalcidian land was confiscated from the big landowners so that it could be allocated as farms to 4,000 Athenians. The latter remained members of Athens's community, which apart from anything else boosted the numbers qualifying as *zeugitai*, or perhaps higher if they already owned property. Some settled on their new farms, while others may have preferred to stay in Attica as absentee landlords.[7]

The Athenians' victory against the odds was spectacular, perhaps as surprising to them as to everyone else. For the moment the Spartan threat was gone, and the leaders of the popular movement were exultant. Later tradition attributed the reforms that followed to Cleisthenes, and his role was surely central, even if plenty of others assisted, advised, and supported him. It is notable that he held no formal office at this time and, unlike Solon, does not appear to have been invested with any special powers as a lawgiver. Instead, Cleisthenes presented his proposals to an Assembly of the People, which approved each of them in turn. In the process the basis of the Athenian political system for the best part of two centuries was established, placing the people—the demos—at the centre of public life as the ultimate authority. This was democracy (*demokratia*), the rule of the people, or at least so it would be remembered and called by later generations proud of what Athens went on to achieve.

For some Cleisthenes was the founder of democracy, while others praised him for reviving it on the questionable basis that, from Solon onwards, Athens had really been democratic apart from the interval of the tyranny. How Cleisthenes was remembered makes establishing what he actually did difficult, particularly as the sources preserve very few details about his life, and there is no equivalent for him of the fragments of Solon's poetry. This means that his intentions and aims have to be deduced from what he did, but this becomes more complicated because what he did and what others added later is not always clear. By the fourth century BC many Athenians believed that the political system they knew was in every respect the same as when first created. Yet there is some evidence for changes to details of the constitution in the decades that followed, and it is perfectly possible that more significant alterations occurred without being recorded in the surviving sources. In the same way, there may have been phases of experimentation and modification in the earliest stages, as the reformer and those around him tried to put their ideas into practice. Many of the details of the system attributed to Cleisthenes are only firmly attested as late as the fourth century BC. Yet there is little to suggest that such alterations were profound, and even the later version reflected at the very least the essence of the reforms introduced by Cleisthenes and his associates.[8]

At the heart of everything was a new way of organising the Athenian population—or at least its free, adult males. Traditionally there were four tribes, a common system for Ionian Greeks, in contrast to the typical three tribes of Dorian communities. These old tribes were not abolished and continued to play a role, most of all in preserving long-established ritual and sacrifice, but they were supplanted in importance by ten new tribes, intended to be approximately equal in the numbers enrolled in each. The basic building block was the deme, which was a clear geographical area. In the countryside this was often a central, village-like settlement, perhaps with smaller hamlets as well as individual farms included with it. In the city itself, it encompassed a district. Demes varied in area and population. By the fourth century BC, there were 139 of them, and this was possibly the original number.

Cleisthenes then divided Attica as a whole into three large districts: the city, the coast, and the plain. Within each of these, demes were grouped together so that each group had a broadly similar total population, the group being known as a *trittys* (pl. *trittyes*). Often these groups were physically adjacent, but there were exceptions where one deme formed an enclave or island surrounded by demes belonging to a different group. Every tribe was allocated three of these groups of demes, one each from the city, the coast, and the plain. In most cases the three components were not contiguous. Within each deme were existing communities and long-established relationships linking neighbours to each other and to aristocratic families. The reform did nothing to change this. Instead, the aim in creating tribal groups including villages and districts from different parts of Attica was to bring together individuals and groups who would not otherwise have met and acted together. One result was the reduction of aristocratic influence. A family might be able to dominate a small region and perhaps wield strong influence in a regionally based tribe but would struggle to do the same thing in a majority of the ten tribes.[9]

More importantly, the new tribal system defined who was an Athenian and what that meant. To be a citizen a man had to be registered in a deme. He was encouraged to refer to himself by name and as the son of his father and also by his deme, and although this practice never became universal, it was widely adopted, at least in certain circumstances. Membership of a deme was—or became—hereditary, so that over time many Athenians no longer lived in their deme, although they and any sons had to be registered there and remained members of both deme and tribe. The Athenians allocated land in Euboea, and those given land on Salamis, which by now was firmly under Athenian control, were from the start registered in a deme in Attica, marking this out as different from colonization overseas, where the settlers became citizens of a new community and no longer members of the old one. Instead, the settlers remained Athenians, which meant that they belonged to a deme and its tribe in Attica, wherever they actually lived.[10]

However close the association had been in the past, Cleisthenes's tribal system made clear that Attica and Athens were one inseparable

whole. Everyone was a citizen, and everyone had his place in tribe and deme; all were Athenians. Being enrolled in a deme conferred membership of the community, full citizenship, and Cleisthenes included large numbers of resident foreigners and freed slaves in the initial reorganisation, something never to be repeated on such a scale. All were now Athenians, whatever their ancestry, and whether or not they ever visited the city itself, the sense was greatly enhanced that they were all part of the same community, all sprung from the soil of Attica spiritually if not literally. Backed by the authority of the Pythian priestess at Delphi, Cleisthenes named each of the new tribes after a mythical hero associated with Attica, with the exception of Ajax, who in the *Iliad* led a contingent from Salamis, which sailed alongside the Athenians on the way to Troy. It was surely no coincidence that Theseus, the quintessentially Athenian hero whose exploits rivalled those of Hercules and who was supposed to have united the Athenians, became particularly prominent in art in the late sixth century BC.[11]

Cleisthenes encouraged, but did not create from thin air, this sense of shared heritage and identity. The system he introduced brought together the free population of Attica as Athenian citizens, men with a shared sense of belonging to the same community, and there were a lot of them. By the middle of the fifth century, there were some 40,000 to 50,000 adult male Athenians, with perhaps a total population for Attica, including women, children, resident foreigners, and slaves, of 150,000 to 250,000. No other Greek state, with the possible exception of Syracuse in Sicily by the end of the fifth century BC, had such a large citizen population. Sparta possessed land, much of it very fertile, that was significantly bigger in area than Attica but had far fewer citizens. Even if the Athens of Cleisthenes had yet to reach this peak of population, it emerged from his reforms as the largest community of citizens in Greece.

Little is known about how the Athenians organised themselves for war before this point, and there is a fair chance that aristocrats were responsible for forming and leading bands of dependents and neighbours in the traditional, almost Homeric style. A good deal of warfare involved maritime raiding, where it was easier for the wealthy to provide the ships needed to transport fighters. Pisistratus and his sons took control of war-making, but how they managed this is not described, so that it is unknown how far they relied on foreign, allied, or mercenary soldiers and how great a role Athenians played. After Cleisthenes, each of the ten tribes mustered as a regiment, which would fight as a unit in battle under the command of a general (strategos) elected by his fellow tribesmen. The latter were often from the established aristocratic families, but this change altered the relationship between leader and led, again emphasising that all were Athenians and fellow citizens rather than a *basileus* and his dependents. The *zeugitai* fought in the main battle-line, their property allowing them to afford the weapons and armour required, and their sheer numbers ensured that they were a—if not the—critical element of strength in a tribal regiment.[12]

In wartime the men of a tribe served alongside each other. In peacetime the tribes also played a prominent role in leading the state. Cleisthenes created the *Boule*, a council consisting of 500 members, with each tribe providing a delegation of 50. Based on its population size, each deme within the group provided a set number of delegates every year. Thus, the share in authority of each individual deme varied considerably; by the fourth century BC, one urban deme sent twenty-two delegates, whereas several tiny demes in rural areas contributed just one apiece. Even so, the system ensured that men were drawn from every part of Attica. Delegates were originally elected, which most likely favoured the aristocracy and those they backed. This method was replaced with selection by lot and the stipulation that no one should serve on the *Boule* more than twice in his lifetime—and not in consecutive years. The minimum age for eligibility was thirty, and the *zeugitai* were probably eligible from the very start, for the numbers required by the process were considerable.

This meant that as the years passed, a significant number of Athenians served in this council.

The sources do not say how frequently the entire *Boule* assembled in the early years. Each tribe's delegation of fifty led the council for a tenth of the year, during which time they were charged with preparing business for wider debate and decision. Eventually, a purpose-built hall, the *bouleuterion*, was constructed, some 100 feet square on the edge of the Agora, and some would date this as early as c. 500 BC. In its eventual form it included rooms where some of the fifty-man delegation in charge (*prytany*) could sleep, so that there was always someone on hand in case an emergency faced the state. The *Boule* could not pass laws but presented proposals and set the agenda for meetings of the People's Assembly (*Ecclesia*). Since it represented a broader range of opinions and interests compared to the past, there was a good chance that its recommendations would pass. The new tribal system and the wider enrolment when it was created meant that a lot of Athenians could chose to attend meetings of the Assembly, even if work and distance prevented many.[13]

Cleisthenes created ostracism as a new method of curbing aristocratic rivalries before they became violent and disturbed the state. Every year, on taking over the *Boule*, the sixth group of fifty, or *prytany*, asked the People's Assembly whether they wished to consider the banishment of an individual. If they did, then, at a meeting attended by at least 6,000 Athenians, each cast a ballot with the name of a man on it. The one with the most votes was expelled from Attica for ten years but did not lose property or other rights. Plenty of these clay ballots, or ostraca, have been found, naming many of the leading politicians of the fifth century. However, the process was rare, and only nine ostracisms are definitely attested. The threat itself—that anyone who became distrusted or simply disliked by too many of his fellow citizens could be banished for a decade—was enough to restrain most leaders most of the time. That 6,000 attendees were required indicates what was considered a reasonable attendance at the meetings of the Assembly. The Pnyx hill soon became reserved for the Assembly and had the space to accommodate these sorts of numbers, albeit perhaps slightly fewer in its earliest phase, before it was developed to suit this purpose.[14]

Aristocrats retained their wealth, connections, and opportunities to parade their achievements but now had to take more care to win over a larger section of the population both to ensure their success and compete with rivals doing the same thing. For the moment, the archons continued to be elected and to have considerable executive power, the 'eponymous archon' giving his name to the year, while the Areopagus composed of former archons retained its prestige. It had jurisdiction in homicide cases and internal attacks on the state. Yet, for all the prestige of the magistracy itself and the Areopagus, which continued to be restricted to the highest of the Solonian classes, the Areopagus operated in a very different environment, where the *Boule* council of 500 and the People's Assembly were more significant and assertive.

The council was a constant presence, with a *prytany* of fifty members sent by a tribe marked down as responsible at any one time. They decided what needed to be done on behalf of the state, sought approval from the Assembly, and then supervised the magistrates or whoever else was tasked with turning any decision into action. Whether or not this was stated in law, the precedent was soon established that even the archons were subject to its scrutiny, and behind the *Boule* lay the tribal system based around the demes. Within a generation of Cleisthenes, a change was made so that archons were no longer elected and instead chosen by lot from a list prepared by the tribes. This diminished the status of this ancient magistracy, especially since, in contrast, the generals (strategoi) were always appointed through election, presumably on the basis that warfare required particular talents and its supervision was best not left to chance. Not only were they elected each year whether or not there was actual warfare to be waged, but no limit was placed on the number of times anyone could hold the post, so that soon this became a far more attractive option for the ambitious. Inevitably most were aristocrats, whose wealth freed them from the need to work for a living, allowing them to devote themselves to politics. Old families like the Alcmaeonids continued to figure heavily in public life, but the big difference was that now success relied on winning over voters to get elected and then being able to sway the Assembly when it mattered.

From the start, the *thêtes* were able to attend and vote in the Assembly. Whereas in the past pebbles had been used to count the votes, the greater numbers attending meant that voting was done by a show of hands or acclamation. Membership of a deme, and by extension a tribe, marked a man as a citizen and thus eligible to take part, but Athenians voted not as tribes but as individuals. At first the Assembly probably met once in each of the ten-month periods of the council. Over time the frequency increased, so that by the fourth century BC, there were often some forty meetings in a year. Cleisthenes sowed the seeds for an ever more active participation in public life on the part of all Athenian citizens. In due course *thêtes* were eligible for service in the council, and later they could become jurors in the courts. The process was slow, and at first it may have been difficult for such men to take time away from work, especially if they lived a day or two's journey from Athens. Only later were they given a salary for public service so that it was less of a burden.

In almost every aspect of public life, the trend was for the people and their representatives to assert themselves more and more. The Assembly could pass a resolution on any matter, with modified and wholly new proposals emerging during the course of a debate. These were genuine discussions of a range of viewpoints, successive speakers being called upon to express their opinion, especially if the mass made clear that they wanted the presiding officials to pick someone. Once again, the aristocrat able to devote himself to training in oratory had a marked advantage in addition to his fame and connections, but he still had to compete with others like himself, as well as anyone else with the passion and charisma to sway the crowd. Leaders, whether those holding formal office or those wanting to influence the decisions of the Assembly, had to persuade their fellow Athenians of all classes. They could not compel them to obey.

Underlying the tribal reorganisation at the heart of Cleisthenes's reforms was this emphasis on belonging to the community. This marked Athenians out as different to everyone else in the world. Their home was Attica, whether Athens itself or the countryside, and this was shown by enrolment in one of the demes. A man who was a member of one of these little communities was an Athenian citizen, a privilege granted to no one else. This was a large community, far more united than in the past, and it was also exclusive, as over time, it became more and more difficult for anyone not born to Athenian parents to gain enrolment in a deme. There were Athenians, and then there were other Greeks, outsiders, even if they were not mere barbarians. Being an Athenian made a man special, hugely reinforcing that Greek sense that belonging to any city was a unique privilege. Nationalism was at the heart of the democratic system at Athens, with a clear and simple dividing line between who was a citizen and part of the community and who was not.

Athenians were registered by their class, which depended on wealth and could change for an individual or over generations. All, even the *thêtes*, played an active role in the life of the community. They could vote in the Assembly, where their vote carried as much weight as that of any fellow citizen—for numbers mattered, not the amount of property each owned—whether to approve a law or ostracise an unpopular politician. From the start, a significant proportion of the citizens could be called upon to serve in public office, and over time this was extended to include everyone, at least for some responsibilities. All were required to fight in wartime and risk their lives, serving in a capacity commensurate with their wealth, commanded by leaders they had collectively elected.

Democracy as Greek thinkers came to define it varied considerably, since a lot depended on how the people—the demos—were counted. In many Greek cities, 'the people' considered worthy of political responsibility consisted of those possessing some property, usually in the form of an independent farm. This was a wider group than a narrow aristocracy of wealthy, established families but still excluded many of the less well off. Property owners fought for their community because it was in their interest to defend their own property, an incentive felt to be lacking for the poor. The combination of Solon's class structure and the mass tribal enrolment under Cleisthenes produced something very different at Athens. Regardless of property, all men considered to be Athenian had a role to play, with rights and obligations unmatched anywhere else, at least for the moment. The scope and extent of participation steadily increased in Athens and was never matched by any state as large and powerful.

Cleisthenes vanishes from the surviving sources after his reforms. Later Athenians remembered him with reverence as playing a crucial role in shaping the democracy they felt lay behind their success. The idea was expressed by Herodotus, who lived in Athens for some time around the middle of the fifth century BC. Before Cleisthenes, the Athenians had been divided and weak or subject to tyranny. After the restructuring of the state, Athens and the Athenians flourished and in an incredibly short time became one of the major powers of the Greek world. This was all because of the internal harmony brought by the new system. Aristocratic rivalries were controlled, the energy previously devoted to this competition now channelled into a quest to serve the state in the most distinguished way possible. It would be almost a century before Athenians turned on each other again and factionalism and revolution recurred.[15]

Athens had created internal stability, that elusive ambition for the vast majority of Greek states. Sparta had done the same by excluding the vast majority of the population and the entire labour force from public life. 'The people' who had a say in public life at Sparta were the full citizens, the fairly narrow top of a high and wide pyramid. Self-interest in preserving this dominance restrained them from turning on each other. In contrast, Athens after Cleisthenes included all Athenian men—a substantial minority in the overall population of Attica—within the system. Everyone had a role, everyone had a share, everyone was a citizen, and this was the basis for harmony at Athens.

7

THE PEERS

*Sparta's citizen warriors
and the helot serfs who fed them,
c. 700–500 BC*

Sparta's stability and rise to power came much earlier than the remarkably swift change in Athens's fortunes, but Cleomenes's interventions had given the Athenians and Spartans reason to treat each other with suspicion. During one of his visits to Athens, the king had learned how the Alcmaeonids had convinced the Delphic oracle to deceive the Spartans into overthrowing Hippias. Having failed to establish Isagoras as a friendly leader, the king and other senior Spartans sent envoys to Hippias, who had fled to a family stronghold on the Asian coast of the Dardanelles. A plan was agreed upon to bring the tyrant back, returning victoriously from exile, just like his father before him, and use force to impose him on the Athenians. Once again, the Corinthians demurred, arguing that it was wrong to set a tyrant over a free Greek people, and the rest of the Peloponnesians followed their lead. Without backing from their allies, the leadership declined to act, and the plot came to nothing.[1]

Cleomenes and his fellow king, Demaratus, may never have got on well, and the latter's decision to abandon the expedition on behalf of Isagoras soured relations even further. The Spartan system required the kings to balance each other's power and did not need them to cooperate all the time. Even so, it was decided, in the light of the abortive campaign, that from then on only one king should accompany and command a field army to avoid such divided counsel. Demaratus and Cleomenes did their best to weaken and thwart each other, aided by supporters—or men who simply disliked the other king. Taking a leaf from Cleisthenes and the Alcmaeonids, King Cleomenes lavished gifts on the Delphic shrine in the hope of 'guiding' the words of the priestess at a critical moment.

Demaratus had been born early, well before his mother had completed her full ninth month of pregnancy (or tenth for the ancients who tended to count inclusively), leading to rumours about his true paternity, since his parents had also been married less than nine months. A charge was made, the Pythian priestess was consulted to end speculation once and for all, and she obligingly announced that Demaratus was not the son of a king and therefore had no right to rule. He was stripped of office, and after a brief period of public mockery, he went into voluntary exile. The deception was subsequently revealed and the Pythian priestess also sacked, but by then it was too late to change things.[2]

Demaratus was replaced as king by his main accuser, who then disgraced himself by accepting bribes while leading a campaign in Thessaly. Put on trial, he was deposed and exiled. Cleomenes also fell afoul of public opinion, his behaviour becoming increasingly erratic, although his taste for trickery was undiminished. In 494 BC he massacred some Argives after defeating them in battle. Many were burned alive in a building deliberately set on fire, which was felt to violate a truce, and his actions were compounded by the subsequent mistreatment of a priest who had defied him. There were also rumours of bribery, but for a while he campaigned with a force based around troops personally loyal to him rather than a formal Spartan army. Fighting alongside Scythian allies was supposed to have set him on the path of heavy drinking, seen as characteristic of such barbarians. For all his odd behaviour and stories of insanity, he continued to rule until 490/89 BC, when he came to a violent end, possibly through suicide while not of right mind or murder now that he had become a liability. Herodotus's version has him locked in something like wooden stocks to prevent him from harming himself. Only one helot guarded him, and the king persuaded the man to pass him a knife. With this Cleomenes stabbed and cut at his own thighs and stomach until the wounds were fatal. Whatever really happened, and although some of Cleomenes's deeds may have damaged Sparta's reputation, his career had not significantly weakened Spartan power. To outsiders—and to most Greeks—Sparta remained the pre-eminent state in Greece, its military might unsurpassed.[3]

That was not to say that the Spartans' strength was overwhelming or their victory certain, as the Athenians had shown when they weathered the storm of Spartan hostility. Luck played a part, and the Athenians were helped by Cleomenes's failure to convince his co-ruler and Sparta's Peloponnesian allies that imposing an aristocratic or tyrannical faction on Athens was a good idea. The Athenians themselves routed the invaders from Thebes and Chalkis once they were able to concentrate on these lesser threats. A few years later, they would defeat the Thebans once again, and for Herodotus the clearest sign of the changes resulting from Cleisthenes's new system was that the Athenians waged war with great success from then on. Their citizen population expanded and united, the Athenians were able to field large numbers of highly motivated warriors, while their wealth and maritime experience in due course allowed them to create a powerful navy.

The change was remarkable not only for its scale but for its sheer speed. Up until this point, the Athenians had often struggled to win against modest-sized states like Megara. Suddenly—no doubt shockingly quickly from the point of view of other states—Athens emerged as one of the major powers in the Greek world. No one knew how long this might last, and it took time for everyone, including the Athenians, to accept that their internal stability and the strength it gave would endure. For the moment, other Greeks had to adapt to a world where Athens was a significant force.

This did little or nothing to dent Spartan military supremacy, which was already well established. Athens had fended off Spartan aggression, but so had Argos, which lay much closer to Sparta. The Argives stubbornly maintained their independence, refusing to be drawn into Sparta's network of allies. At the same time, they lacked the numbers and power to stand the remotest chance of overrunning Sparta. The Athenian position appeared similar. Remarkably quickly, for such was—and often is—the nature of politics, the Spartans, including Cleomenes, found that seeking friendly relations with the Athenians was useful. The failure to install Isagoras and then restore Hippias did not lead to a state of permanent hostility between Spartans and Athenians. Each state had too many other, far more immediate concerns to waste energy and resources in direct rivalry with the other.

The Spartans, just like everyone else, shifted their perceptions to accommodate Athens as a significant player in interstate affairs. Everyone—not least themselves—still 'knew' that Sparta was the most militarily powerful Greek state. At the heart of this was the belief that Spartan armies were superior to those of other communities. That superiority was based around the Spartans themselves, who formed the heart of each field army and provided the commanders, even if allied contingents formed a significant proportion of the troops. Spartans prepared for war far more thoroughly than any other Greeks.

To outsiders, and especially to later generations of Greeks and Romans, life for a Spartan was extremely tough—hence the use of the adjective today to mean austere—and effectively a constant preparation to be a soldier who fought with skill and did not give up. A composite picture of life as a full Spartan citizen, one of 'the peers' or 'those who are similar', has often been assembled by drawing together sources written centuries apart and assuming that they are essentially accurate and also describe the same long-lived and unchanging system. Neither assumption is guaranteed, although we must temper scepticism with the simple truth that rejecting this evidence leaves us with only conjecture and far more questions than can possibly be answered. Thus this generic picture is worth repeating, for at the very least it does show what many others thought the Spartans did. Equally interesting are the many aspects of life not discussed at all in any of the sources.

As mentioned in Chapter 4, Plutarch claims that soon after birth, a male baby born to Spartan parents underwent inspection by the 'elders of the tribes'. Only those judged healthy and robust were accepted and their families permitted to raise them, while the rejected were left to die. The exposure of unwanted infants was practiced in a fair few ancient societies, and others, including the Roman aristocracy in later centuries, also waited a few days before formally examining and accepting a child, so in itself this was not uncommon. As with many things, the perception was that Spartan standards were higher and their judgements harsher than those of other societies. Nothing is said of the treatment of infant girls at Sparta.[4]

The raising of all Spartan children occurred in the home until age seven and was entirely the responsibility of the family and especially the mother. In his seventh year, a boy began to take part in communal education, overseen by an official appointed from the former magistrates. There was considerable emphasis on physical fitness and the ability to endure hardship. Boys went barefoot to toughen the feet, helping them as adults to march, run, and climb more readily than men who had grown up wearing shoes. A single cloak was permitted, to be worn in all seasons over a tunic, which presumably could be chosen according to the weather. Food was deliberately kept meagre, one source explaining that too much encouraged plumpness, whereas less was likely to make a boy taller. The boys were expected to learn to cope with hunger, something useful when, as adults, they might face short rations on campaign.[5]

They were also allowed to steal food to supplement what they were given, and the only crime was to be caught, which earned both shame and a beating. Plutarch tells a story of a boy hiding a captured fox inside his tunic to prevent an adult from discovering that he and his friends had stolen it. As the animal bit and clawed in its attempts to escape, the lad remained silent, only to die of the injuries he suffered. Older boys competed at an annual festival in the Temple of Orthia, trying to steal a cheese defended by men carrying whips. Outsiders tended to see this Spartan encouragement of theft as shameful. Xenophon, an Athenian who spent time in Sparta in the fourth century BC and knew many Spartans, rationalised it as good training for war. It taught boys how to stay awake at night, because darkness was the best cover for theft, and at the same time they learned how to scout for food worth taking and how to plan together to seize it.[6]

Xenophon provides the earliest detailed account of how Spartan boys were raised, and there was a later tradition that his own sons underwent at least some of the system. Around the age of twelve—or perhaps fourteen—the boys' status changed, and their training intensified. Age was important in Spartan society, as it was in many Greek cities. At twenty the boys ceased to be children but did not become fully adult until a decade had passed. They were expected to go to war if required, and the regular, probably annual, selection of 300 of them to serve as the *hippeis*, the elite unit of the army, was fiercely competitive. At the same time, they were not permitted to visit the marketplace and had to ask older men to go on their behalf and purchase anything they wanted. Boys kept their hair cut short, while adult men wore theirs long, cultivated beards, and shaved the upper lip so that they did not have a moustache, a style that required a good deal of care. Boys were expected to be unkempt, even dirty. Young men in their twenties held an intermediate place and may well have still worn their hair short. They were expected to be modest, most of all in public and in the company of their elders, looking demurely down as they walked. The expectations for proper behaviour were clear, and adherence to them shaped someone's reputation.[7]

A tough upbringing was expected to produce tough adults. Boys were encouraged to fight each other, individually and in groups, as well as to compete in athletic competitions. Yet there were limits to rivalries, and there was always someone with authority to restrain excessive or improper behaviour. The supervisor was aided by whip bearers, while leaders were appointed from among each group of boys, and if no official was present, any adult Spartan man was entitled and expected to take charge, inflicting punishment if he felt this appropriate. When a man beat or flogged another man's child, the boy's own father was expected to repeat the punishment as soon as it was reported to him. The wider community was ever present, watching and judging. Toughness and the desire to win were valued but were always subordinate to the harmony of the community. Young men who failed to gain selection to the ranks of the *hippeis* watched the successful, criticising any misbehaviour, sometimes even provoking fights with them. Yet these were not allowed to go too far, and any full citizen was able to command them to stop. The opinion of the wider community mattered, including not simply boys of the same age group who had grown up together but members from every generation, with particular reverence for the older and more experienced. A far better attitude was represented by the often-told story of a man who had not been admitted to the *hippeis* and expressed his pleasure that they had managed to find 300 young men better qualified than himself, since this was good for the community.[8]

Irony was valued as part of the clipped, well-chosen comment that was the Spartan ideal, hence the word *laconic*. One of the most famous examples is the story that in the early stages of the Persian war, the Spartans were told that the enemy's arrows would fill the sky, prompting the response 'Then we shall fight in the shade.' The knack

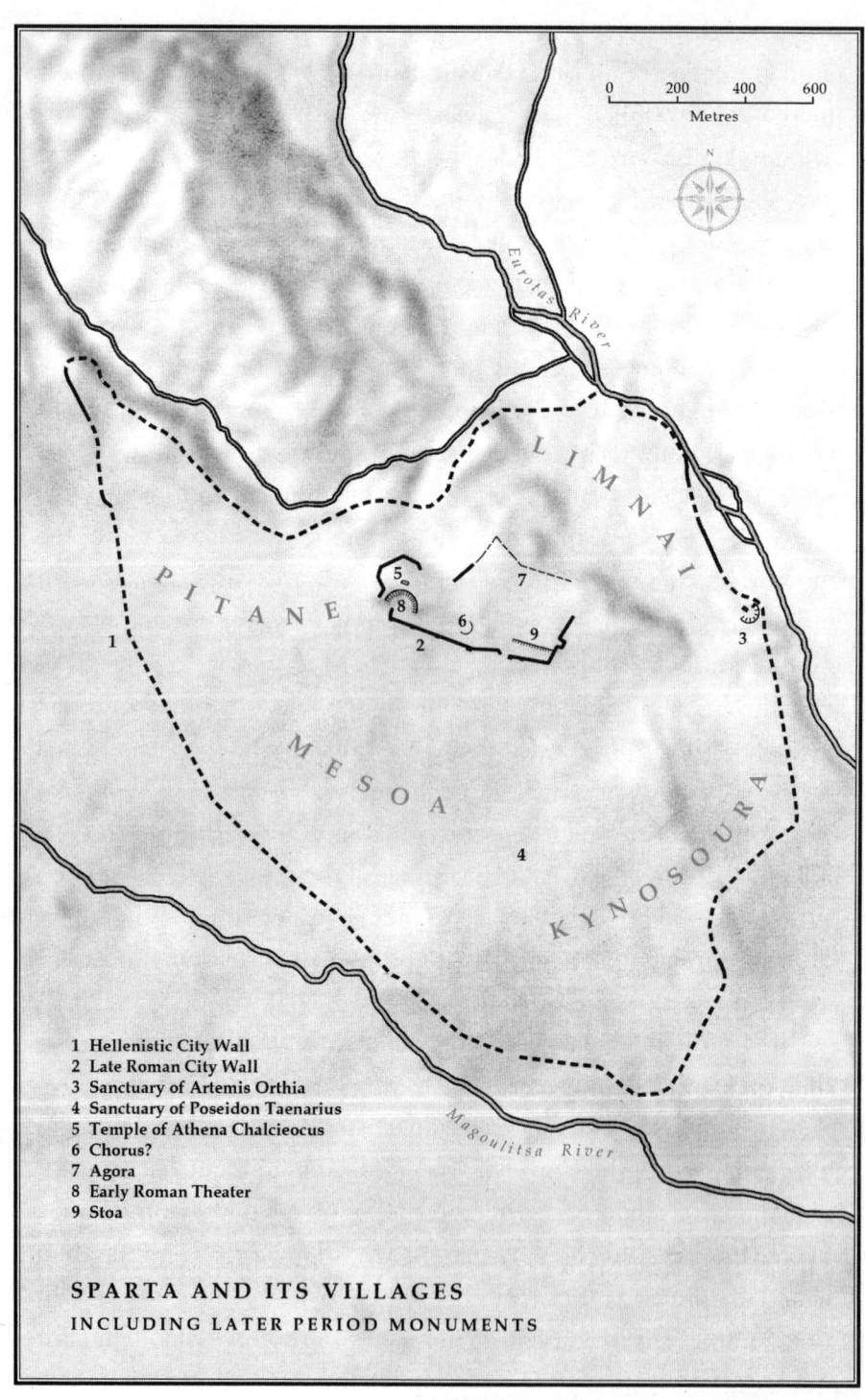

SPARTA AND ITS VILLAGES
INCLUDING LATER PERIOD MONUMENTS

1 Hellenistic City Wall
2 Late Roman City Wall
3 Sanctuary of Artemis Orthia
4 Sanctuary of Poseidon Taenarius
5 Temple of Athena Chalcieocus
6 Chorus?
7 Agora
8 Early Roman Theater
9 Stoa

was developed over time, through practice and through listening to others. A Spartan was expected to joke about his comrades, whether these were boys, youths, or adults, and in turn to take the jokes made at his expense. There were acceptable limits to this mockery, which had to be learned over time, and like so much of Spartan society, the arbiter was the opinion of fellow Spartans, especially those whose age, deeds, and reputation gave weight to their judgement.[9]

When a boy was a teenager, in the second stage of his education according to Xenophon's categories, an older man, often in his twenties, would choose to become his mentor. In describing this, outsiders used the language of love, widely employed among other Greeks, with the older lover (*erastēs*) winning the affections of the younger beloved (*erōmenos*) and guiding him. Such relations appear common in the Greek world, at least among the aristocratic classes, and most sources assume that the sexual element was important, perhaps even paramount, although by normal—which often means really Athenian—standards, this was considered improper once the boy's beard began to sprout. Myths included many stories of gods loving male youths as well as girls and women, and one of the principal Spartan festivals, the Hyacinthia, was associated with Apollo's love for a boy. Although it was not a feature of Homer, the majority of surviving sources accept such a relationship as fairly common and often admirable, whereas little or nothing is said about homosexual affairs between two adult males.

Modern scholars have tended to follow this tradition and assume that there was a sexual element to the relationship between lover and beloved and also that every Spartan teenager was taken on by an older partner. In contrast, Xenophon maintained that Spartans would have considered any relationship motivated first and foremost by physical desire as shameful. Instead, he claimed, it was about character. Older men effectively became foster fathers—or an additional parent—to teach and shape the character of the young. Honour was the key. A man of good reputation was expected to pass on his wisdom to the next generation, so that the state continued to have fresh citizens who knew how to behave properly and for the common good. In one story a well-respected man was criticised for failing to pick a boy to mentor. The character-building element was also part of the ideal relationship between lover and beloved in Athens and elsewhere, so none of this was wholly foreign to Greek ideals, even for those who saw physical passion as central.[10]

Xenophon's tone suggests that he did not expect to convince people that sex was not equally important in the Spartan system, and it is fair to say that his philosophical background encouraged him to believe that the most admirable relationships were based on an intellectual rather than physical bond. However, he had a far better knowledge of Sparta than any other surviving source, so his opinion should not be dismissed lightly. Attempts to draw parallels with pederastic relationships studied by anthropologists in more recent eras do not convince, not least because the scale and type of community is very different. Unless the argument is made that sexuality is entirely the construct of each society, it is unconvincing that every Spartan man felt physical desire for boys. Xenophon's fervent denial that the relationship between the mentor and the youth he chose ever had a physical element most likely exaggerates. Judging from attitudes among other Greeks, a sexual element may sometimes have played a role, depending on the inclinations of the older partner. Perhaps this was only the case for a minority, even a very small minority. As so often, the judgement over what was acceptable came from the wider community of fellow Spartans.

There were expectations about how a lover should behave and how the beloved should respond. The former was to set a high standard for the latter to emulate. In this sense Xenophon was surely right to emphasise that the mentoring was far more important than anything else. Effectively the boy was given a personal tutor to further his training and also a guide to introduce him to the world of adults. Whether or not there was ever a physical element, the 'love' between the pair carried on throughout their lives. Each was expected to take an interest in the other and share some responsibility for their behaviour. This was not a replacement for the family, and the mentor did not supplant a youth's father. Instead, this was an extension of those relationships, a way of broadening someone's connections beyond simple blood. Boys from wealthier, aristocratic families were often chosen by mentors from a similar background, cementing or creating useful political connections. There is not enough evidence to say whether the system was always universal and that every boy was chosen by someone, just as it is unclear how much time the pair were expected to spend in each other's company. As always, the Spartan sense of what was appropriate guided behaviour, which means that its nuances cannot be reconstructed.

The communal element was a strong feature of the raising of Spartan boys, and also of girls, although there is far less information about this in surviving sources. Both were trained to be good members of society and to be physically healthy, not least because this was thought to promote the physical health of future generations. Boys were supervised by an appointed official; they could be instructed, rebuked, or even beaten by any Spartan male who happened to be present; and some or all were guided by an older mentor/lover. They were raised to understand the privileges and responsibilities of being a Spartan and to know that those around them constantly scrutinised how they lived their lives. Men in their twenties were said to undergo a routine inspection at the gymnasium, stripping naked to show how well they were maintaining their body.[11]

The community, guided by magistrates and elders, watched, judged, and rewarded or rebuked. Such things happened in some other Greek cities, but the Spartans were believed to take everything much further, and this naturally drew the attention of the sources. Yet none of this meant that the family was excluded from the process. When boys began their corporate education at the age of seven, they continued to live at home, assembling for their instruction each morning—or as often as group training and education were conducted. Later tradition emphasised the close bond between a Spartan and his mother, even when he was an adult. Less was written about his relationship with his father, but this was also important. At twelve, Plutarch suggests, boys sometimes slept as a group, probably in the open air, but there is no evidence for the idea that they were separated from their families for the entire year, or even the greater part of it. This does seem to have occurred in their twenties, when they underwent something akin to full-time military service, or at least were kept available for service at very short notice, and lived in barracks. No such buildings have been identified, although it should be noted that there is no real indication of what they may have looked like.[12]

Men in their twenties had already developed a close bond with their families and especially their parents. Some of their education in the years before this seems to have occurred in the context of home and family. Although outsiders sometimes mocked Spartans for their rudimentary education and cultural ignorance, Spartans could certainly read and write to a reasonable level and were numerate, not least to allow the state and, on campaign, the army to function. All were familiar with a repertoire of poems and songs, notably Tyrtaeus, and a good number seem to have known Homer and other widely admired works. None of the sources record anything about how this knowledge was acquired, which implies that in these respects Spartans did things much like other Greeks. While there may have been some group classes in literacy and numeracy, they likely learned much of this at home. Who provided the actual instruction is impossible to say. Xenophon and other moralists contrasted the willingness of other Greeks to rely on slaves to teach children with the Spartan reliance on fellow citizens, but the distinction may have been one of degree, at least in the household context. As elsewhere, wealthier families could afford more thorough tuition. The royal families, or at least the boys marked out as prospective heirs, did not follow the public education system in any formal way, although they were still expected to match or excel against those who did.[13]

At thirty a Spartan was old enough to become a full citizen, his upbringing and education—almost an apprenticeship—complete. Yet the change in status was not automatic and hinged on gaining admission to a communal mess. This depended in the first place on the consent of existing members and relied on his ability to contribute resources for meals they all shared. The ingredients for the monthly contributions—barley for bread rather than wheat, cheese, wine, figs, and small amounts of meat or fish—were basic in their nature while at the same time substantial in quantity. In order to provide them, as well as to feed his own family and household, a man needed to possess a moderately sized farm, not least because the helots also needed to survive in order to keep working in the fields. Land allotted to every citizen was sufficient to do this, although it is unclear whether there was one or more than one distribution—the reform attributed to Lycurgus.[14]

The drawback was that once the Spartans ceased to conquer new territory and new subject populations to become helots, the amount of available land could not be increased, limiting the maximum number of citizens it could support. A fair proportion of land belonged to the wealthy, established elite, whose estates offered them far more than the basic requirements of belonging to a communal mess. Even so, there were limits over the generations to how often such an estate could be divided to provide for more than one male heir and also for daughters. For those with only the basic plot of land, the problem was far more acute. The impression is that a son who went through the education system successfully would normally inherit his father's land. Less clear is whether one farm could support both father and son as members of a mess at the same time or what happened when more than one son reached manhood. Land became available when a man died without a son to take it over, but there were no incentives to have large families. Richer citizens paid for poorer boys to go through the education when their families were unable to do so, and at least some in time gained land and were able to become full citizens. Yet the trend in the fifth and early fourth centuries BC was an inexorable decline in the number of 'peers' because, in the longer run, the system was unsustainable.[15]

All this took time, but the desire to pass on land to heirs, though not to too many heirs, led to a number of peculiarities in Spartan society, at least as far as other Greeks were concerned. One that attracted particular attention was the freedom given to Spartan women to own and bequeath property. Another was the practice of brothers sharing a wife—or at least more than one man making love to the wife of one of them to provide a healthy heir. Most Spartans married, usually after the age of thirty. A man who married in his twenties faced restrictions on the time he could cohabit with his wife, having to sneak away to visit her in secret before returning to spend the rest of the night with his comrades in the 'barracks'. Plutarch records the custom of cutting a bride's hair short and dressing her like a boy before the groom came to her on their wedding night, everything taking place in a darkened room. Outsiders then, and plenty of modern scholars since, have interpreted this as a means of easing the man from his supposed past experience of sex with other males as beloved and later lover, even though this is a lot to rest on a custom that may have had other origins, assuming that there is any truth in it at all.[16]

It was supposedly considered bad form for even a man in his thirties to be seen going into or coming from his wife's chamber in their house, although presumably this only meant that he should not be observed by guests rather than the rest of the household. Plutarch and other sources assert that every night every man between thirty and sixty—the age at which his obligation to military service came to an end—dined with his fellows in the communal mess, returning home without the aid of lamp or torch to light his path. The only valid excuses for his absence from these meals were hunting expeditions, the marking of a private festival in peacetime, or active service in wartime, although, even then, some or all of a mess often served together and no doubt camped and ate together.[17]

A mess consisted of around fifteen members, which, not coincidentally, was the ideal number for a drinking party in Athens and other cities. Yet there were very important differences. Drinking parties occurred in the host's house, whereas a Spartan mess convened in a room set aside for this purpose in a public building (although, once again, none have been identified, and it is unclear what such a site would look like archaeologically). Drinking to excess, often competitively, boasting, and the presence of musical entertainers and sex workers—often one and the same—were common features of a drinking party, which by its nature tended to be staged by those with money in other cities. In a Spartan mess, each man ate and drank what he had provided for the meal, served by the youngest member or sometimes a boy brought along by his mentor. No limit was placed on how much he ate or drank, except the opinion of his fellows, which encouraged moderation, but everything was plain—most of all the notorious 'black broth', a form of stew. Later in the evening, extra treats—game provided by a hunting expedition and anything donated by wealthier members—were shared, giving the chance for individuals to show off their prowess as hunters or their riches. Members of each mess ran the whole gamut of ages, which was another moderating influence, making the tone very different from a gathering of young aristocrats in another city. The Spartans had clear conventions about proper conduct. Arguments were never to escalate into violence, which the training in making jokes and accepting mockery helped to prevent, as did the expectation that no one should get too drunk. There are stories of helots being made to drink to excess in public and to wear ridiculous costumes to reinforce Spartans' sense of their own superiority and also to remind them of their duty to behave with more dignity.[18]

Scholars generally accept the presumption that all Spartans attended the communal meal every night of the year, apart from the exceptions noted previously. There is no real indication of how many private rituals excused a man or how frequently the majority chose to go hunting or how far they went on these excursions. In addition, it is widely accepted that all of the messes were centrally located in Sparta itself, along the Hyacinthian Way, which meant that Spartans all spent the vast majority of the year in or close by the city. To return to their houses after the communal meal in these circumstances meant that they had to live within, at the most, a couple of hours' walking—or just possibly riding—distance. This would mean that unlike the Athenian population, where many lived some distance from the city itself and rarely visited the place, the Spartans were overwhelmingly concentrated in a small area. One advantage of this would have been that every citizen could play an active role in society, not simply taking part in assemblies but living their lives visibly in the manner appropriate for a Spartan, keeping physically fit and well trained.

Some of the implications of this interpretation are rarely explored. There is no evidence for permanent Spartan garrisons in Messenia, although it seems reasonable to suggest that something of the sort existed, since otherwise getting across the mountains would delay any military response to rebellion. If the assumption that all Spartans lived close to Sparta itself is correct, then Messenia rarely saw a Spartan. Men with farms and helots in Laconia may have visited them frequently or, in the case of those near the city itself, lived on them, but those Spartans with land in Messenia rarely if ever saw these fields or met their labour force. While possible, this requires explanation of how overlordship of Messenian helots was maintained if there was little or no direct contact between Spartans and the helots working for them, and various theories involving privileged helot overseers or perioeci have been proposed.[19]

There is another possibility, which would make Sparta more like other large Greek communities, where a significant part of the population lived outside the city itself. Although there is no direct evidence for this, perhaps Spartans with land in Messenia and some of the other more distant regions spent some of the year there. They might return to Sparta for major events, notably the festivals, perhaps even live there the majority of the time. This need not necessarily have meant that conventions such as the communal meal in the mess needed to lapse, since, as on campaign, the group—or a temporary group of men from different messes—could still have met together. No source explicitly states that all the messes convened in Sparta. Wealthier men, especially the horse- and chariot-racing aristocracy, surely wanted to spend time training and observing their stock, and horses need space to be healthy—especially space where they can run without damaging crops. Hunting expeditions offered another opportunity to wander and perhaps visit property, not least because if everyone hunted close to Sparta and only there, then the game was bound to suffer and the returns of each trip diminish. Convention dictated that any Spartan could make use of another's property if needed, including that person's helots. With hunting dogs, the courtesy was to invite the owner on an expedition. If he declined, then it was proper to borrow his hounds.[20]

Spartans may have moved around more than scholars tend to assume. While physical and military training was important and a major concern throughout adult life, no athlete can train at full pace every day of the year. Little is known of how most Spartans spent most of their time. Such activities as loafing, talking with others, and practicing their wit account for only so much time to add to the training. Men may well have spent far more of each day with their families than is usually assumed, and perhaps also on their farms, even if they did not deign to work the land. It may be better to think of Spartans not as training full-time, dining communally every night, and always living in or near Sparta until they were called away to war. Instead, perhaps they did all of these things to a degree seen as exceptional by the standards of other Greeks, which led them to behave differently to the people of other cities. The Spartans were far better trained and prepared for war than others and spent far more time in each other's company—dining, singing, dancing, and being good citizens—than was normal, but this was not their entire life. They also had homes, families, and other concerns, and private as well as communal lives. There is a great danger in taking sources highlighting the unusual as telling the full story.

In part because of their secretive habits, little survives to show what Spartans did for most of their days. Presumably those who failed to secure sufficient land to pay their way as a member of a mess became lesser members of society akin to the perioeci, but their lives are even more shadowy in the evidence. There is also the question of the boys who were injured or became weakened, even crippled, by disease during the course of their education. The same risks applied to adults, who faced the added danger of suffering injuries in battle, and there is no indication that they were excluded from society. For all the hardships of their upbringing, and for all the pressure to conform and live up to the standards of the wider community, not every Spartan was able to cope fully with the fear of combat. Most extreme were the 'tremblers', men considered to have been proven cowards and pushed to the fringes of society. They suffered many humiliations, tending to be excluded from sports and other activities and even beaten on a whim, while still remaining Spartan citizens, albeit perhaps with reduced rights.[21]

For all the rigours of the system, Spartans were not identical automata but individuals. Boys learned and men sang Tyrtaeus's songs, which urged them on to face the horrors of battle and never suggested that this was an easy thing to do. Spartans were just as prone to ambition, jealousy, rivalries, and hatreds as other Greeks, but their upbringing and the constant emphasis on belonging to a community imposed limits on how these played out. There were constant reminders that as Spartans they were special, privileged, and overlords of a far more numerous helot population. Plutarch told a story that Lycurgus was struck in the face with a stick and blinded in one eye by a young man who resented being forced to dine in a common mess. The reformer took the man under his tutelage, employing him as a personal attendant until he became a model citizen. While the story is surely a later invention, partly to explain why Spartans did not carry staffs when they attended public meetings, the moral reinforced the importance of restraint. Spartans mocked each other, competed for honours and in sport, and craved a good reputation for courage, wisdom, and proper behaviour, but this competition was only permitted to go so far and was never to weaken the essential unity of 'the peers'. The common messes brought the rich and the less well off into regular contact, which emphasised what they had in common and their dependence on each other.

Fear of the helot majority reinforced this sense of needing each other. Helots were humiliated and despised at the same time as they were essential to permit Spartans to live as they did. Considerable effort was taken to maintain Spartan dominance, and the longevity of the system shows that these were highly effective. One institution that attracts a good deal of attention, even though the ancient sources are meagre, was the *Crypteia*, or 'secret service'. As part of their upbringing, some or all of the younger men spent time away from the rest of society, when they were to keep out of sight, forage for and steal food, and sleep under the stars. This was meant to promote stamina, self-confidence, independence, and stealth. A small number were selected to take this further and given the task of operating under cover of darkness. They were to spy on the helots and to kill any they saw too boldly wandering and mixing with others. Plutarch describes the *Crypteia* but could not bring himself to believe that the revered Lycurgus could possibly have designed something so savage, so suggested that it was a later innovation. Given the widespread secretiveness of the Spartans, it is unsurprising that something they considered especially secret is poorly documented. Other sources speak of occasional mass killings of helots seen as likely leaders of resistance, often using subterfuge to lull the victims to their deaths. The coherence and relative unity of Spartan citizens came at the expense of the mass of the population, and dominance was only maintained through constant effort. Aristotle claimed that every year the ephors formally declared war against the helots as a reminder to all of this constant state of siege and also to legitimise the killing of any helots, should such killings occur.[22]

8

THE SPEARMEN

Greek warfare, the rise of the hoplite spearman, and the massed phalanx, c. 750–500 BC

CENTRAL TO THE SPARTANS' SENSE OF THEIR OWN IDENTITY was the belief that they were conquerors, and regardless of the true origins of their community, the absorption of Messenia and other lands in more recent times was visible proof of this. They—or at least their ancestors—had won control of this territory 'by the spear', victory showing that they were braver, more skilful, and more favoured by the gods than the conquered. This same courage, prowess, and piety in the current generation of Spartan citizens justified their rule over the far more numerous helot population. Whether or not it was always the custom to make a formal declaration of war on the helots, as Aristotle claimed, control of their subject people ultimately rested on the Spartans' ability to use violence to quell opposition. Other means and compromises were employed to convince the helots that it was better to accept their lot rather than to rebel or flee, but without the threat of force, none of this would have sufficed. The Spartans were the conquerors, the helots the conquered, and as far as the Spartans were concerned, that relationship would never change, at least for the vast majority of the helot population. Helots were not expected to like this truth, but it was assumed that they and everyone else would accept it.

In much the same way, the rise of Sparta to dominate so much of the Peloponnese was based on successful war-making. Some peoples were conquered and absorbed; others became allies because this act in itself demonstrated acknowledgement of the military might of Sparta. The relationship was not one of equals but offered advantages to both sides above the practical aspects of aiding each other. That the Spartans were willing to negotiate and form a tie of friendship with another community, such as Corinth or Tegea, demonstrated to all that this other city deserved to be treated with respect. At the same time, it confirmed Spartan might, as more and more cities showed that they felt it was wise, advantageous, and simply safer to accept the terms offered to them. By the last decades of the sixth century BC, Sparta was widely acknowledged as the most powerful city in the Greek world. That did not mean that there were no other significant powers or that the Spartans could not be defeated, as the Athenians demonstrated when they thwarted King Cleomenes. Far more often than not, the Spartans won, whether through direct military victory or by convincing the other side to back down. Sparta's pre-eminence rested on its prowess in warfare, which gave proof of the Spartans' worth and of the need for everyone else to respect, even fear, them.

War figures heavily in Greek art and literature. The *Iliad* is set during a great war and punctuated with battles, and while the theme of the *Odyssey* is different, raiding and violence are always there on the edge of the story. Yet the frequency of warfare in real life is much harder to judge before the fifth century BC. That warfare was fairly common is implied by the truce between Greeks declared every four years for the Olympic Games. This ran on either side of the festival, allowing the competitors and spectators to travel to the Peloponnese without being molested by enemies. The problem is that the sense that warfare was readily imaginable does not show how frequent it actually was. There are plenty of references to conflict, from the Lelantine War to victories attributed to Solon and Pisistratus during the long-running struggle between Athens and Megara over Salamis and other territory. Thus, there were certainly wars fought between communities, but so few details are preserved that little can be said with confidence about the scale and nature of the fighting. Disputes over land appear common, and perhaps this was the most frequent cause of conflict, even if it was not the only one.[1]

The Spartans were treated with respect because they were believed to be good at waging war. In one sense this was a reflection of the attitudes in Homer, where Achilles and the other heroes are honoured and enjoy the best of things because of their skill and courage in battle, which reinforced the wisdom of their words because it proved their inherent worth. The same idea shaped the development of Greek communities during the early centuries of the last millennium BC. The *basileus* class of wealthy aristocrats led in peace because they went first and counted for more in battle, which in turn meant taking the greatest risks. As settled communities began to flourish once again and populations grew, there were more men able to afford the weapons and armour needed to fight in the forefront of battle. For all the resistance of established elites to admitting new members, any community able to field more good fighters than its neighbours had an obvious advantage; other things being equal, numbers were likely to tell. Those who fought in a manner that was both dangerous and contributed significantly to the outcome of any battle or fight deserved honour. Over time, their own and others' sense of their worth tended to convert into greater status and rights within their community.[2]

The end result of this process is far easier to see than the process itself. By the fifth century BC, the overwhelming majority of Greek cities relied on their own citizens to provide the bulk and most important part of their military manpower. Men with sufficient property were expected to furnish themselves with a shield, spear, probably a sword, and—given the high risks of close combat—additional protection in the form of a helmet, cuirass, and often greaves. This was the panoply of a hoplite, and the vast majority of these men were farmers owning their own land. They were neither wealthy nor poor, and in most cities they were never a majority of the population but could be a substantial minority. Small cities fielded hundreds of hoplites, while larger ones could field thousands. Numbers mattered, and when hoplites fought, they fought in a massed formation described as a phalanx, which was usually at least eight ranks deep and sometimes deeper still. These hoplite-farmers acted together to protect their city and its interests and prestige because they were citizens. Some cities by this time were democracies, and even the most limited definition of 'the people' included all those required to serve as hoplites. Other communities continued to be dominated by smaller aristocratic elites, but even in these cases the hoplite class enjoyed considerable rights. Aristotle saw a direct relationship between importance in battle and political rights in peacetime.[3]

One mark of the importance of these farmer-soldiers as a group was that the aristocrats in all cities fought in the phalanx alongside everyone else. Battles between Greek cities were decided by a massed clash of phalanxes, not by the conspicuous daring of individual heroes, while those who fought on horseback or as skirmishers were relegated to supporting roles. Herodotus made a Persian commander mock the folly and simplicity of the Greeks, claiming that they fought without any guile or plan, simply choosing a flat piece of ground, so that two phalanxes could charge each other, causing horrendous casualties even for the victor. Passages like this exaggerated and simplified, while later generations of Greeks were inclined to romanticise warfare in the 'good old days', when the rivals willingly sought open battle, clashed once, and then accepted the outcome as deciding the war.[4]

Things were never quite so simple or indeed uniform, but that did not mean a considerable basis of truth did not lie behind all the exaggeration. Greece and the Greek islands are not noted for their open spaces and gently rolling plains, making it odd that they placed such emphasis on the phalanx, which needed reasonably open and even ground. Over the centuries, battles tended to recur on or close to the same spots, simply because these were the areas between states where there was enough space for the armies to deploy and fight. There was a common rhythm to many wars, beginning when one city mustered an army that marched into the territory of another city—a journey of no more than a few days and sometimes less—and then settled down and began to 'devastate' the land. In response, the defenders mustered their own army and moved to confront the invader. The two phalanxes faced each other with a fair degree of mutual consent, since if one positioned itself on high ground, or indeed anywhere else offering a significant advantage, then the other army was very unlikely to attack. Instead, they formed on either side of open ground, and then one or both advanced. The two massed formations met, fought, and eventually one broke and fled, at which point it tended to suffer heavy losses as the victors struck at the backs of the fleeing men, a dreadful peril spoken of by the Spartan poet Tyrtaeus. Slaughter was savage but brief, for there was rarely any concerted pursuit, not least because these armies made little use of fresh troops in reserve or of cavalry. The winner occupied the field, erecting a trophy to mark the success, and in due course the loser came to ask permission to retrieve and bury their dead. By doing so they accepted that they had lost and negotiated a peace with the victor on that basis.[5]

The heart and main strength of a city's army was its citizen hoplites, the vast majority of whom were farmers led usually by commanders they had elected. They were amateurs as fighting men, reluctant to spend too much time away from running their farms, so that waging war had to fit into the agricultural cycle rather than supplant it. A brief campaign was convenient, especially if it led to a quick and clear decision in the form of a pitched battle. Farms and fields were prime targets of an invading army, since a direct attack on the walled city at the centre of the enemy state was unlikely to succeed and would very probably be costly, while a prolonged siege was equally uncertain of outcome and meant spending weeks, probably months, away from home.[6]

Yet the scale of damage it was possible to inflict on the agriculture of an enemy in just a few days was small. Most of a state's territory would not be harmed simply because of time constraints, while crops like vines were very difficult to damage, and harvests were only vulnerable to fire or to being gathered by the invader for a short period. Individual farmers suffered, and, as in any small business, the margin between prospering, surviving, and suffering year on year was narrow and easily unbalanced, but there was no prospect of the devastation caused by a hoplite invasion permanently crippling the agricultural economy of a Greek state. The attacks on crops, herds, and property were gestures, statements of hostility and a challenge to the defenders. To stay snug behind the city walls and watch as villages and farms burned would imply that they were too frightened to face the invader in battle. Brave men, men of worth, did not accept such a humiliation. Those who did lost prestige and respect, so that there was no reason for others to treat them with honour in disputes or disagreements; they were weak and could be scorned or attacked by anyone.[7]

In the main, the defenders came out from behind their walls to fight in the open, unless the attackers had an overwhelming advantage in numbers—after all, even the heroes of the *Iliad* were allowed to show discretion when the odds were heavily against them. The defenders did this not because the alternative risked starvation but because they were unwilling to be humiliated and, in the main, confident that they could win. The attackers gave up their efforts at laying waste the countryside and moved to meet them at a likely spot. Delays after this were rare, no more than a day or two, before the phalanxes formed, sacrifices were made on each side, and the armies advanced and charged each other. On average the victor suffered some 5 per cent fatalities and the loser two or three times more. Then the war was over, peace was arranged, and the attackers went home to their farms. The weeks before the grain harvest were a common time to fight because, while the crops were most vulnerable, more importantly the whole business could be settled and everyone could get back to their own farms in time for the harvest itself, the most labour-intensive period of the farmer's year.[8]

Hoplite warfare was not subtle. Campaigns were short, the battles brief and brutal, their outcomes hard to predict since there was little or no manoeuvring beforehand or any room for subtle tactics, but they were decisive. One phalanx eventually collapsed, and since there were no reserves, that decided the battle without the need for any more fighting. Whatever issue had prompted the war, whether control of disputed land or some other cause, was resolved, at least for the immediate future, but the loser was not permanently crippled, still less destroyed. Many treaties specified a set number of years of peace between the parties involved. In practice these sometimes lasted even longer, but more often they were broken once it was convenient for one of the sides, since the original grudge that had provoked the war in the first place tended to endure while new ones emerged. Rivalries and simple enmity between communities tended to become ingrained. A brief campaign culminating in a clash between phalanxes resolved a war quickly, at least in the short term. In the longer run there was a very good chance that the cities involved would go to war with each other again and again.

For states whose principal military strength came from their farmers, the conventions were useful. No one was kept too long away from work, not least because fighting as a hoplite did not require long hours of practice and drill. Bodily strength helped, as did the determination to close with the enemy and fight, especially to stand with fellow citizens and ideally work as a group. Armies of amateurs fought against other armies of amateurs who behaved in much the same way and obeyed the same conventions because they were of mutual convenience to each side. Much as the heroes of Homeric society had maintained their pre-eminence by ensuring that they were the decisive element in a battle, the massed hoplite class did the same, since they formed the heart of a phalanx and phalanxes decided battles. Many scholars argue that these conflicts had a ritualised nature, with wars limited in scope and the way they were fought because this suited the dominant class in Greek cities. This develops the idea expressed by later Greeks that wars between fellow Hellenes used to be conducted according to an unwritten but understood set of rules and were simpler, more honourable, and less devastating than the conflicts of the later fifth and fourth centuries BC.[9]

The equipment characteristic of a Greek hoplite first appeared in the second half of the eighth century BC. The name *hoplite* derived from the shield (sometimes called a *hoplon* but more often an *aspis*) or rather the other equipment associated with it. This shield was round, about three feet in diameter, and markedly concave apart from a flat edge or lip. It was made from wood, and while most shields were faced with a thin layer of bronze, this was more about decoration and added only a little to its effectiveness in stopping a blow. Such a shield was heavy, although scholars debate about just how heavy, with estimates ranging from fifteen pounds to less than half that. Inevitably reconstructions vary and must remain conjectural, since only a few traces of wood are left of surviving examples. Others had used round shields in the past, notably many Assyrian infantrymen, but such shields were held by a single handgrip near the centre, sometimes aided by a shoulder strap. The Greek shield was different: a man grasped a handle near the edge (*porpax*) with his left hand, having first thrust his arm through a central loop (*antilabe*), which rested by the elbow. This spread the burden of the shield across the arm rather than concentrating it on the wrist, at the cost of restricting ease of movement. In addition, the lip of the shield allowed a man to rest it on his left shoulder, spreading the weight even more.[10]

The shape was unusual, making the shield more complex to manufacture than most other types. Herodotus claimed that the design came originally from Caria along with other aspects of the fighting style adopted by the Greeks. While this is possible, there is no other evidence to support the assertion, and most scholars are sceptical, preferring another tradition that came to refer to it as the Argive shield, created—or at least first made popular—at Argos. The typical hoplite was unlikely to have been a tall man by modern Western standards, although estimates of the average height in the sixth and fifth centuries BC vary from 5'4" to 5'7". This meant that most men were able to shelter more than half their body behind the shield, the fighting pose putting the left shoulder forward, with the rest of the body at an oblique angle. In the main they held it rigid, relying on its sheer size to block incoming blows rather than shifting it to parry. As well as offering protection, the shield was also used to buffet, shove, and unbalance an enemy, giving it an offensive as well as defensive role.[11]

A shield could not do much to protect the head, and the next most important piece of defensive armour was the helmet. This was bronze and enclosed most of the head; for instance, the famous 'Corinthian' style left only a small gap for the mouth and holes for the eyes. This reduced the arc of vision, and since there were no holes for the ears, a man's hearing was badly impaired. Such a helmet was heavy, although the Corinthian type could be pushed back and worn on top of the head until the last moment before battle—a style very familiar from images of the goddess Pallas Athene. Even heavier and more cumbersome was bronze body armour, the bell cuirass covering back and front and offering even greater protection should a spear get past or through the shield. Greaves, also made from bronze and using the metal's flexibility to clip onto the leg without the need for straps, guarded the calves, which the shield could not cover. At times, especially in the earlier periods, at least some men supplemented this with arm guards, thigh guards, and ankle guards.[12]

In comparison to his protective gear, a hoplite's offensive weapons were comparatively light and simple. By the fifth century BC at the latest, his main weapon was a spear, with a shaft some eight to eight feet, six inches long and a metal head, usually of iron but sometimes of bronze. On the other end it carried a small spike, often bronze, nicknamed the lizard killer. This may have had some use as a weapon, and some have interpreted the holes in armour dedicated as spoils of victory as made by these points when jabbed down to finish off a wounded opponent. However, more prosaically even if more practically, its primary purpose was to allow the spear to be thrust upright into the ground until needed. The spear was backed up by a sword, generally short and either straight bladed or curved rather like the Gurkha kukri with the edge on the inside. Especially in the seventh century BC and before, hoplites are depicted carrying two shafted weapons, with at least one of these being a javelin intended to be thrown before contact rather than used in hand-to-hand combat.[13]

All in all, the full panoply of a hoplite has been estimated to weigh as much as fifty to seventy pounds, although once again other scholars offer significantly lower figures. Its cost was significant, hence the need for hoplites to own some property. In the later fifth and especially the fourth centuries BC, armies grew larger, many adopting simpler and cheaper helmets that did not enclose the head. Even before this, some preferred stiff linen or leather armour to the bronze cuirass, and by the later period a good few dispensed with body armour altogether. The bell cuirass may never have been universal, and in the finds of dedications of spoils found at Delphi and other temple sites, helmets outnumber it ten to one. Another means of lightening the overall burden and reducing the cost was to wear just a left greave, since the left leg was usually forward and at greater risk than the right. Wearing the full panoply gave very good protection, especially to the front, while even a man with shield and helmet was fairly well protected from attacks to the front. The hoplites around him also offered added support.[14]

In its later form the phalanx was a close order formation. Hoplites stood side by side and with more men behind them, but just how close together is a subject of debate. The majority of scholars suggest a frontage of around three feet per man, although a minority would increase this up to six feet, and a few argue that it could be even narrower, at least at times. A depth of eight ranks was common, although in larger armies the contingents formed by different groups, especially allied communities, formed up separately and might choose a different depth from the rest. There is a good chance that men with the full panoply tended to be at the front where the risk was greatest and that the less well off and less heavily equipped filled the centre and rear of the phalanx. Thucydides noted that every man felt himself less protected on the right than on the left, since he carried his shield in his left arm. Thus they tended to edge to the right to get closer to their neighbour and his shield, which cumulatively made the whole phalanx drift to the right as it advanced. He also described the Spartans as unusual, because they went forward slowly, marching in step to the accompaniment of flutes in order to keep the phalanx in order. Other armies, less well drilled and all eager to get the dreadful clash over with as soon as possible, went faster and tended to break into a running charge, yelling out a war cry that was often an ululation. No one could stay in neat ranks and files while running, so this made the formation loosen out as it went.[15]

At times one side or the other flinched at the last minute, turning to flee before a blow was struck, sometimes dubbed a 'tearless battle'. More often their resolution held. Some individuals kept running and tried to drive a spear through or past the opponent's shield or knock him over. Others may have slowed down and approached with more care before they struck. Either way the noise was enormous, especially for men living in a pre-gunpowder, pre-industrial age. Spears broke, shields shattered, and men grunted and screamed as they fought and were struck. The rest of the phalanx closed up behind the first rank. A spear was long enough for men in the second rank to reach the enemy, especially if one theory is right and it was balanced to be held nearer the butt end, so that two-thirds of its length reached forward. The others could not fight unless men fell ahead of them and they stepped forward to take their place in the first or second rank. The rest of the time they waited, deluged with noise as far as their restrictive helmets allowed them to hear, seeing only what was just ahead of them, the backs and bobbing helmet crests of the ranks in front. Battles may have lasted an hour, perhaps longer, although only if there were lulls in the fighting as the front ranks caught their breath. Everyone knew that a collapse could come suddenly, anywhere along the line, and that it would spread until the whole phalanx was in rout. They also knew that those most likely to die as the elated enemy came forward were the ones who waited too long to flee. Even the hoplites not actually fighting were gripped by a permanent state of tension.[16]

Later Greek military theorists argued that it was best to divide the bravest men in the phalanx into two groups, the first to make up the front couple of ranks and give the formation its cutting edge. The other group was stationed at the back to prevent any faint hearts from retreating. Sheer numbers and depth in a phalanx had this advantage in morale. Not only did the men at the front feel encouraged by the presence of those behind them, but simply by being there and standing firm, the men in the centre and rear ranks made it impossible for those in front to run away. Many scholars take this further and give an active role to those in the rear. The sources talk of the 'shoving of shields' and of a phalanx 'shoving' or 'pushing' an enemy back into defeat, and it is argued that this should be taken literally. No one would doubt that the hoplite shield could be used to barge at an opponent, unbalancing him or driving him back, but this theory asserts that the men in the ranks behind the first pushed as well. The peculiar design of the shield meant that a man rested it on his left shoulder and leaned against the back of the hoplite in front, physically forcing him forward. This made the clash of phalanxes a giant shoving contest, and the stronger, better co-ordinated team eventually rolled the opposition back until their phalanx fell apart and they fled. The sources also make clear that the men in the opposing front ranks wielded their spears and sometimes swords effectively during a battle, which would not have been possible if they were being pushed by those behind. For advocates of massed shoving, the battle developed in phases, first fighting and then pushing.[17]

One consequence of this interpretation is to add to the belief that the Greek style of battle was unusual, perhaps even unique in history, and that the equipment of a hoplite was intimately linked to this type of fighting, especially in the case of the double-grip shield. Thus, for some, the appearance of the shield, the Corinthian and similar enclosed helmets, and the bronze body armour implies the introduction of the phalanx and its associated style of warfare as early as the end of eighth and beginning of the seventh centuries BC. The invention of this superior tactic meant that armies needed to be bigger than before, so that states led by aristocratic elites had to recruit the less well off, leading to the hoplite class eventually receiving more and more rights. From this point of view, warfare drove the social and political change to create the Greek city-state, which is a considerable weight to rest on the technological developments of new shields and armour.[18]

An alternative is to see the tendency towards massed fighting as developing more gradually, the tactics of the phalanx evolving as communities grew larger and stronger. Equipment was then adopted or adapted to suit them. Rising populations led to the more effective exploitation of more land, creating a nascent class of hoplite-farmers for whom the simple and quick nature of phalanx battles was ideal. This leads to a debate over precisely when the style of phalanx battle seen later actually emerged as the dominant form of land warfare between Greeks, with some arguing that this was not until the fifth century BC itself. Much depends on just how distinct the phalanx was from other mass infantry formations. The Assyrians deployed large numbers of heavily armoured infantrymen, as had other Near Eastern powers, but the little evidence that exists for their tactical use does not suggest battles involving aggressive close-formation clashes in the hoplite model. More than anything else, an emphasis on the bow as primary weapon suggests far more fighting at a distance than a rush to close to hand-to-hand fighting.[19]

Homer's battle narratives raise far more questions than they can answer, even without the uncertainty over whether they give a fair impression of actual battles at the time they were set down or earlier. In the *Iliad* large armies appear and are marshalled, and sometimes the Achaeans or Trojans or groups of heroes take position side by side, in something like a mass formation, shoulder to shoulder, plumes touching. Later Greek authors could see phalanxes in Homer even if the poet only used the term a few times. Yet the bulk of his battle scenes consist of heroes fighting heroes, and much of this fighting is at a distance. More heroes fall to missiles, usually a javelin or spear, than to a spear thrust or the cut of a sword. Obviously, there are chariots, which did not appear on the battlefield by the sixth century BC and had probably fallen out of use much earlier, even if a wealthy man might choose to travel to the battle in one as a mark of his status. In a loose sense, the crested helmet, shield, sword, and spear or spears of the hoplite panoply could be the equipment of one of Homer's heroes, but then the descriptions could also apply to very different gear.[20]

Art is of little help, not least because it was extraordinarily difficult to depict ordered phalanxes of hundreds, even thousands, of men fighting each other. Along with an ongoing interest in mythological or Homeric scenes of heroes facing each other, it was far easier to portray individual duels than battle between masses. The few surviving attempts at showing formations, or even organised groups, of hoplites are never easy to interpret. The seventh century

BC Chigi vase—which, like so many Greek works, was found in Italy—shows lines of hoplites advancing towards each other and has often been seen as the clearest evidence for phalanx fighting as the well-established form by c. 650 BC at the latest. The hoplites have the double-grip shield emblazoned with individual devices and stand very close together. Behind one front rank a piper plays, which many link to Thucydides's description of the Spartan advance and implies the importance of order. Each hoplite wears a bell cuirass and has a high-crested Corinthian-style helmet, and the two front ranks wield their spears overarm, the commonest blow depicted in art.

They also carry a second spear, gripped in the left hand, which the *porpax* made easy. Behind one army, some hoplites are still preparing for battle and donning their armour, with a pair of spears thrust into the ground beside each man. Each spear clearly has a leather thong as a throwing loop attached to the shaft. This imparted a spin to a thrown missile, making it fly faster and with greater accuracy. Pairs of spears with throwing loops, one shaft shorter than the other, are common in art in the eighth and seventh centuries BC and sometimes appear later. All this suggests that at least one was intended to be thrown before contact, with an exchange of thrown missiles preceding any hand-to-hand fighting. Perhaps both were—or at least could be—used in this way or held back to stab. Another interpretation of the piper would be that he sounds the call to arms, warning the hoplites to get ready to face the sudden enemy onslaught, and it is important to note that Thucydides represents the Spartan practice of marching in step to music as highly unusual and probably unique. The ranks of figures on the Chigi vase stand some way apart, not close together, one behind the other, as a proper phalanx ought to be, raising the question of whether this is simply artistic licence or deliberate depiction of a more fluid type of combat with waves going forward to throw their spears or javelins.[21]

The poetry of Tyrtaeus can similarly be interpreted in more than one way. His encouragement for men to close with the enemy 'shield to shield, chest to chest' and stand their ground strikes some as the epitome of fighting in a phalanx, which required dogged aggression against an enemy fighting with similar determination. On the other hand, he does not appear to talk about the men in the rear or suggest clear ranks behind the first. At the same time, he implies that each warrior faced a choice of whether to go forward among the 'front fighters' or to hang back, something familiar from Homer but not an option for a man standing in a massed phalanx, who must go forward if everyone else pressed on. Talk of archers and skirmishers fighting in their own way, covered by the warrior's shield, might be figurative, with the light troops operating on the flanks of the phalanx, or literal, the various types of men intermingled in one loose crowd, again reminiscent of the *Iliad*.[22]

Such ambiguity has allowed other reconstructions of Greek warfare to emerge, which argue for a more open, looser battle formation. This sees a direct line with the Homeric-style battles, where masses of less well-equipped and less motivated followers support and shelter small numbers of heroes. From the second half of the eighth century BC, the aristocratic warriors adopt some or all of the hoplite panoply without fundamentally changing the style of fighting, where missiles predominate. Over time, developments in society increase the number of men with the wealth to afford such gear, and a growing proportion of warriors become 'front fighters'. Eventually armies raised by communities were larger and became dominated by men with the hoplite panoply, while other troops were pushed to the margins. Advocates of this model tend to favour a fairly open phalanx, with six feet or so per man, even in its developed stage, which obviously would rule out any suggestion of massed shoving. They also argue that the double-grip shield, Corinthian helmet, and bell cuirass were neither so heavy nor so cumbersome as to prevent their effective use in open combat and individual duels. This meant that the gear could have been adopted before phalanx tactics—especially in any close order form—were employed. Those who see the phalanx as very close order from the start deny this and judge the hoplite panoply dangerously clumsy for a man not supported by hoplites on either side.[23]

Further complication comes from considering the broader range of organised violence in the Greek world in the wider era, over and above the clear model of war between two or more Greek states being decided by a quick campaign culminating in a phalanx battle. Greeks colonizing the Mediterranean world and beyond took hoplite equipment with them but faced many opponents with a wide range of military cultures, who were often unwilling to meet them in a simple, decisive battle in an open field. Sometimes colonies were wiped out, but the majority found ways to defeat local enemies, which meant that they learned how to fight effectively in the local conditions. Raiding, especially by sea, always seems to have been part of warfare, especially in colonial expeditions, and there were skirmishes and smaller-scale fights. Occasionally, if rarely, cities were captured by assault, siege, or treachery, so that the apparent restraints encouraging everyone to conform to the simple rules of war as just an encounter of phalanxes did not always apply.[24]

As so often, there is a tendency here for academic debates to polarise, and both sides make valid points. The comparatively rapid adoption of hoplite equipment in the later eighth century BC does suggest that it could be used by men who fought in open order as individuals. Judging from artistic depictions of warriors, the double-grip shield was not used by everyone, and for several generations a substantial minority of men carried the Boeotian shield, combining it with the bell cuirass and Corinthian helmet. Oval, but with scalloped sides that made it lighter to carry, this shield usually had a single grip and was probably made from leather and/or wood, which would explain why no physical examples survive. Thus, plenty of hoplites did not carry the quintessential hoplite shield and instead used a lighter one. The hoplite panoply was not useless for any type of fighting other than a close order phalanx, even though it was probably better suited to the latter than to anything else. Emergence of the phalanx in its final form required other things to be in place.[25]

Perhaps it happened that over time more and more men went to battle with heavier equipment. As for Homer's heroes, the primary weapon remained the throwing spear, but they could choose to close the distance and fight hand to hand. Such men discovered that they did better if they grouped together. One incident in the *Iliad* noted that the Greeks suffered fewer losses in a hard fight because they stood close together and were able to help and protect each other. The hoplite shield gave best protection to attacks from the front. When men stood in line, they presented a wall of shields, perhaps overlapping, which was good at warding off javelins and other missiles. Even small groups—of ten and twenty—did better as a group in practical terms but also encouraged each other by their simple presence. Over time, as the numbers of men armed as hoplites increased even more, such groups got bigger, taking on an ever more important role in the fighting, until there were enough of them to create a large phalanx that became the battle-line, relegating other fighters to the flanks. Along the way, men realised that if a close-formed group—a phalanx large or small—charged home on the enemy, then there was a good chance that the opposition would flinch or be beaten down, especially if they tended to rely mainly on javelins to fight at a distance. If a man carried only a spear, and one too heavy to throw very far, he had a big incentive to close to fight hand to hand. Armies with more hoplites did better against those with fewer, and even better when they formed up to support each other and acted aggressively, charging the enemy.[26]

This is conjectural but fits the evidence, even if it cannot pin down when these changes occurred. Key was the rise of enough men able and willing to fight for the community in this manner, which is tied to social and political developments. It is possible that the experiences of the many Greeks who fought as mercenaries in Egypt and the Near East influenced what happened in their home communities, at least in terms of the advantages of working together as a team and perhaps also in tactics. Yet, for almost every city, mustering a large army meant calling out its citizens, most of whom were farmers first and fighters very much second. There is no evidence of regular training sessions as a phalanx or individually. Exercising in the gymnasium was seen as good for strength and physical health, which transferred as advantages to the battlefield. Yet only the rich could afford to do this very often, for the less well off were too busy working. Hoplites were amateurs, and since in most cities a citizen was expected to serve in time of war from the age of around twenty to sixty or even older, they were bound to vary a good deal in physical strength and ability.[27]

Other types of fighting, such as raiding and piracy by sea, favoured the wealthy, usually aristocrats and those with enough time to train, not least to learn to sail and row a ship. As a result, numbers were bound to be relatively small, far too few for them to challenge a muster of a whole city—at least a city of any size. When a community called out its citizens to attack a neighbour or defend against invasion, those citizens came with their own gear, their own supplies of food, and their slaves or servants to carry both as they marched out to fight. This did not require training, although over time most men would have grown up with some sense of how to do all of this, passed on from earlier generations. Fathers and sons served in the same army, probably close to each other. The enemy army was a mirror image, clumsy and slow moving but wanting a quick result. Equipment was only donned at the last moment because it was awkward and heavy. The ploy of attacking when the enemy had decided that there would not be a battle on that day worked for both Pisistratus and Cleomenes because of this delay before the opposition got ready.

The clash of phalanxes suited many citizens because it was quick and decisive. In other societies, many, perhaps most of a community, provided themselves with weapons to fight on behalf of the group, and many, especially in later centuries, formed up to do so in fairly dense formations—Julius Caesar described both Gallic and Germanic armies as phalanxes. Yet few if any tribesmen in such armies were able to afford anywhere near as much defensive equipment as a hoplite, especially in terms of bronze helmets, which encouraged the Greeks to close more readily than others, confident in being well protected. In that respect at least, hoplite battle was unlike warfare in much of the rest of the world, especially when it first appeared. It did not exclude other types of fighting altogether, but probably for generations it was by far the most important. Too much raiding against a neighbour risked provoking that neighbour into mustering an army and coming to challenge the community held responsible. Then the latter had the choice of fighting, which was risky, or avoiding battle, which was humiliating. Hoplite battles did not have to occur too often for them to act as a powerful deterrent. Escalate any dispute too far, and the challenge would come to face the opponent's massed phalanx. Yet, as with all such systems of deterrence, especially those where honour and reputation matters, it was often difficult to judge just what would provoke a rival too far.[28]

By the sixth century BC, at least a form of phalanx fighting was the normal method of waging war for a Greek state. Larger states with more citizens were able to muster bigger armies than smaller ones, although balance could be restored by finding allies. War was important, most of all in establishing a community's status and reputation, where perceived weakness was dangerous since it invited attacks. Thus, the reorganisation of the Athenian army on the basis of a regiment for each of the new tribes was a significant aspect of Cleisthenes's reforms. The expansion of citizenship at the same time meant that the Athenians were able to muster an unusually large army, even if they did not call out every eligible citizen. Herodotus may also have been right to see the Athenians' newfound confidence in this new regime as spilling over into good morale during a war.

The Spartans were different. Their citizen numbers were large, if not as large as those of Athens and a handful of other big cities.

However, the Spartans were landowners who did not work with their own hands and instead had more in common with aristocrats elsewhere, having the free time for other pursuits. Their upbringing and the communal messes made clear what society expected of them, and learning and singing the inspiring verses of Tyrtaeus acted as a reminder. They exercised in the gymnasium to maintain a high level of physical fitness. In most states there were dances, notably the Pyrrhic dance performed in armour and carrying weapons, while the Olympics and other festivals had added a race run in hoplite armour. These things were common throughout the Greek world, but they were practiced more often and more rigorously at Sparta. Little is known about other more specifically military training at Sparta and how often it took place. The key difference between the Spartans and citizens of other states was that the former did train and prepare for war, whereas on the whole the latter did not.[29]

When the Spartans went to war with another Greek state, they went to fight as a phalanx like anyone else, using the same equipment and the same simple tactics. The difference was that they did these things far better than anyone else. Their army was divided into a series of subunits beneath the basic tribal regiments, down to a platoon-sized formation of thirty of so. Each unit had its appointed commander, and the whole force had a clear hierarchy. Everything they did, they did with greater control and order. Marching in step, something others could not emulate because it took practice, was a visible sign of this.

A hoplite could fight in a phalanx with no real preparation or training because the basics required of him were simple, but the Spartans were clear proof that preparation and training still gave a marked advantage. Through their drill, they were able to approach the enemy in far better order than their opponents. Physically fit, they had the strength to fight harder for longer as individuals in the front rank, and the nature of their society made them less likely to give in during a fight. Added confidence came from the many past successes of Spartan armies, which in turn was bound to daunt opponents. The sheer sight of a Spartan phalanx, moving slowly and steadily to the music of the flutes, the men silent as they listened for orders, was intimidating in itself, even before the two sides clashed. The Spartans' reputation for might and the difficulty of beating them in battle was to endure throughout the fifth century BC, almost, but not quite, unstained.

PART TWO

YOKE FELLOWS

The Struggle with the Persian Empire

9

GREAT KINGS

The wider world, the great empires of the East, the rise of Persia, and the origins of conflict between Persians and Greeks, c. 800–494 BC

As frogs living around the Mediterranean pond, the Greeks had never been cut off from the outside world, even in the generations following the collapse of Mycenaean society. As populations rose and more and more communities appeared and flourished from the eighth century BC onwards, this engagement with others only increased. Goods, ideas, and people moved around, often over considerable distances. The wider world came to Greek communities most often as traders or as slaves, and even Sparta, for all its famed exclusivity, offered a market for a wide range of goods while selling produce from its own territory. Underlying the development of all Greek cities was the ability of a significant section of society to produce an agricultural surplus.

At the same time the Greeks had spread widely around the shores of the sea, as large groups establishing colonies and as individuals and smaller groups trading or seeking resources to use or sell. Others went as mercenaries, hiring out their sword arms for profit, for adventure, or because they had fled from their homes. Many went to fight for Egypt or the kingdoms of Asia Minor, but others went much further. There was a fair chance that in any major conflict Greek soldiers of fortune found themselves fighting against Greek mercenaries hired by the other side, but since Greek cities routinely waged war on each other, this is unlikely to have prompted any deep soul-searching.

In mainland Greece and the Aegean islands, as a rule Greek cities only had land borders with other Greek communities. By contrast, Greeks elsewhere, whether living in long-established cities or newer colonies, often lived alongside non-Greek peoples—Iberians, Gauls, Carthaginians, Thracians, Scythians, and many others. Rarely were the Greeks able to dominate through numbers or military prowess, at least beyond the territory they physically occupied. These cities survived by combining a willingness and capacity to defend themselves with an even greater willingness to come to terms with nearby powers. In many cases the latter were stronger, the dominant partner in any alliance. In others, especially in the more loosely organised tribal societies, there was scope for playing one group off against others. Even so, a significant minority of Greek colonies failed, and a few were wiped out altogether by local resistance. The majority survived, more or less willingly submitting whenever they faced a neighbour stronger than themselves. Others remained heavily dependent on support from their home city to maintain themselves.

For much of the period discussed so far in this book, as the Greek cities emerged, the Assyrian Empire was by far the greatest power in the world known to the Greeks. Its heartland was some way to the east (in what is now northern Iraq and Syria), and it only directly impinged on the cities of Ionia and Cyprus, although there was some diplomatic contact further afield. In the early seventh century BC, one Assyrian king boasted of receiving tribute from 'kings' in Greece, but since he also claimed the same about Spain, this was probably more propaganda than reality. The reach of the Assyrian Empire in its periods of greatest strength was long, but not that long. Its army was truly formidable and highly organised, even if the bulk of the men appear to have been part-time soldiers. Consisting of chariots, cavalry, and infantry, the bulk of them archers, it was very effective in open warfare and displayed especially high levels of engineering skill and sheer determination when it came to sieges. Opponents trusting to the strength of their city walls were crushed time and again, and the price of defeat was often appalling. In earlier centuries in particular, royal pronouncements boast of flaying, impaling, or burning enemy leaders and large numbers of captives. Later the mass of a population more commonly suffered deportation to a distant settlement where they would labour on behalf of the Assyrian king.[1]

Yet, for all their talent in war, the Assyrians were unable to eradicate all their rivals, and by the end of the seventh century BC, Nineveh and all of their key cities had fallen to an alliance of enemies. In the aftermath, as mentioned in Chapter 1, no single power was able to maintain a comparable dominance. Egypt, Babylonia, and Elam to the east, as well as the increasingly strong Medes, were the biggest players, but others also had room to flourish and expand, and for the Greeks of Ionia, the kingdoms of Caria and Lydia were their immediate neighbours. Each was stronger than any one Greek city, and the Ionian Greeks displayed no more enthusiasm for working together than the communities of Greece itself. The relationship between the cities and the kingdoms was generally amicable, with goods and ideas passing in both directions, each group accepting innovations from outside without losing their own distinct identity, but there was never any doubt that the kingdoms were the stronger partners, and the Greek communities treated them as such.[2]

In the sixth century BC, Lydia reached the height of its power during the reign of King Croesus (c. 560–546 BC), its territory expanding to include most of Anatolia. The Ionian Greek cities accepted this reality and became his allies, their subordination marked by the payment of tribute. The burden does not appear to have been too heavy and was all the easier to bear because of the king's respect for Hellenic culture and because the Lydians, like the Carians, were familiar, so significantly less alien than other foreigners. Greeks believed that the Lydians were the first to mint gold coins, and the wealth of Croesus became famous, aided by the fact that he made lavish gifts to a number of Greek shrines, including Delphi, whose oracle he consulted.[3]

Around 550 BC the balance of power in the wider region started to shift very rapidly, with the sudden rise of the Persian leader Cyrus II, whose advance brought him to the borders of Lydia. Croesus, determined to protect and, if possible, expand his own kingdom, sent envoys to Delphi to seek guidance. Herodotus says that the priestess of Apollo informed him that if he went to war with the Persians, then a great empire would fall. Encouraged, Croesus attacked and was soundly beaten in the first battle. Then, to the Lydian king's great surprise, Cyrus did not stop waging war over the winter months as was usual and instead struck fast to exploit his advantage. Lydian resistance collapsed and a great empire—that of King Croesus—did indeed fall. Traditions regarding Croesus's fate vary from execution to imprisonment, mass suicide alongside his family, or escape. Whatever happened to its king, Lydia's power was broken in a few short campaigns, and it became a region of Cyrus's empire, governed by his satrap, who resided in Croesus's old capital at Sardis.[4]

The speed and scale of Cyrus's conquests were staggering. His people, the Persians, had once been nomadic before settling on the Iranian plateau—the name of modern Fars province derives from the name *Persian* (*Parsū*). They lived on the borders of the kingdom of Elam and the developing society of the Medes but were not politically united and were of no more than marginal importance for many centuries. Cyrus described himself and his royal ancestors as kings of Anshan and rarely if ever used the name *Persian*. The process may well have begun earlier, but he was able to unite the different Persian groups under his rule. In the last few generations, Media had turned itself into a great power, acting with the Elamites to overthrow Assyria, absorbing much of the former Assyrian Empire, and also pushing eastwards and subjecting the Persians to their rule. Cyrus came to the throne of Anshan in 559 BC, and by 550 BC he had overthrown the last of the kings of Media, having persuaded significant sections of the Median nobility to defect to his cause. He became king of both Medes and Persians, with the new regime absorbing much of the culture and administration, even the dress and symbols of power, of the old Median kingdom. Greeks far more often spoke of Medes than of Persians, so that in a sense they saw Cyrus's new empire as a continuation of the old, more familiar Media.[5]

In 550 BC Cyrus followed up this early success with his rapid conquest of Lydia. Before the confrontation with Croesus, Persian envoys went to the cities of Ionia in the hope of persuading the Greeks to change sides. On the whole this failed, and the Ionians fought alongside the Lydians and were defeated with them. In the aftermath, each city in turn was compelled to submit by threats or direct force. Herodotus says that the Greek communities asked Cyrus to grant them similar terms to the ones they had enjoyed under Lydian rule, only to be told that they had missed their opportunity to be treated as his friends. Miletus was shown more favour than the other cities and may have been more welcoming to his envoys from the start.[6]

In 539 BC Cyrus added Babylonia to his conquests, bringing under his control all of the major Asian powers of the post-Assyrian era. Once again, some communities and leaders changed sides to join him, and the military campaign was rapid, highly efficient, and spectacularly successful. Discontent with the rule of the last Babylonian king, some political and some provoked by his religious policies, was exploited, as was any hostility to the old regime. Cyrus was welcomed by the substantial population descended from the Jewish captives transported to Babylonia by Nebuchadrezzar from Jerusalem. Cyrus received even more praise when he granted this captive community permission to return home and begin the restoration of the temple central to their faith.[7]

Cyrus's regime did not try to make all the conquered peoples Persian. Just as he had respected Median traditions, in most cases each community was allowed to continue with its own religions and its own laws. All had a strong tradition of obedience to central authority and of organised taxation and administration, and these continued, each region either under local leaders or a Persian satrap governing the district. Those individuals or groups who had welcomed or aided Cyrus did best, followed by those who had remained more or less neutral, but even those who had fought were kept on a fairly loose rein as long as they did not rebel. Tribute was paid to the great king, as Cyrus now styled himself, or sometimes king of kings or king of the whole world, and a central bureaucracy was created to regulate the financial affairs of the empire and control in detail the movement and support of royal officials and troops. Some land was confiscated in conquered territory and given to Persians, who in return were obliged to perform military service, but most regional elites came to terms with the new empire. In the Greek cities along the Ionian coast, Persian-backed tyrants emerged. The great king was a good friend to those he favoured and permitted considerable local autonomy.[8]

Cyrus spent some time expanding to the east, although very little is known about his activities there, and one tradition maintained that he suffered a defeat. Whatever the circumstances, he died in 530 BC and was succeeded by his son, Cambyses, who four years later conquered Egypt, the last remaining of the great powers. The pattern was similar to his father's campaigns, with key defections preparing the way for the rapid advance of the army. Traditions about Cambyses are confused, with some sources depicting him as dangerously insane. There may well have been a disaster when a column was sent into the Western Desert wholly unprepared for the conditions and was entirely lost, and there is a tradition that he mistreated and killed the sacred Apis bull, but caution is needed. Egypt was absorbed into the empire, and indeed the Persians pushed some way to the west along the African coast and held onto this territory as well, while significant groups within the elite of the two kingdoms of Egypt accepted Persian rule, at least for the moment.[9]

GREAT KINGS

With the addition of Egypt, the empire founded by Cyrus and passed on to his son now included all of the big players in the post-Assyrian world. In sheer size it was the largest empire yet to emerge in the wider region, a superpower without a significant rival. At its height it covered almost as large an area geographically as the Roman Empire in the second century AD, although the population was far smaller. It did not last as long as the Roman Empire, for some 200 years later, Alexander the Great would bring it to an abrupt end and push even further into territory never held by the Persians. While not quite as rapid as Alexander's, the scale and speed of conquests under Cyrus and Cambyses were certainly in the same league and have rarely been matched in human history. Cyrus was also styled 'the great', but compared to Alexander very little is preserved about what he did and how he achieved it, which is one of the main reasons why he is less often thought of as one of the most successful leaders of all time. Another difference with Alexander is that Cyrus appears to have devoted more effort to consolidation, which was one reason why the Macedonian's great empire fell apart when he died young and without a viable heir.

Something similar almost happened in 522 BC, when Cambyses also died suddenly. A brother, Bardylis, succeeded him, although the story spread that this man was actually an imposter, because Cambyses had had his sibling killed in secret some time before. Whoever he was, he was murdered in a conspiracy led by Darius, who claimed descent, albeit at some distance, from common ancestors of Cyrus and his family. The odds are that plenty of others had better claims, but Darius displayed much of the talent of Cyrus when it came to politics, intrigue, and war. He soon made official the claim that Bardylis was not who he claimed to be and was instead one of the magi from Media who resembled the murdered son of Cyrus.[10]

Darius had to fight rivals among the Persians and then faced a series of rebellions in almost every region of the empire, some probably backing rival claimants to the throne and even more attempts to regain independence. All failed, and one by one Darius and his generals defeated all the challenges, disposing of challengers and convincing each region that it was wiser and safer to accept his rule. The methods were often brutal in a manner reminiscent of the Assyrians and, indeed, of most of the great powers of the past. In one inscription Darius boasted that a captive enemy leader was mutilated, having his nose and ears cut off, his tongue cut out, and one of his eyes blinded. The captive was chained and put on public display outside a royal palace until Darius decided that his exhibition had served its purpose and had him impaled on a stake. This was rarely immediately fatal, so that the victim died a slow death, often lasting several days, in a terrible warning to others.[11]

Far more than Cyrus, Darius styled himself a Persian. He also presented himself as the favoured one of Ahura Mazda, for at least some Zoroastrians the greatest god of their pantheon, and he may well have represented a different style of the religion. A relief depicts the god giving his blessing to Darius as the king triumphs over his earthly opponents. Ahura Mazda represented and protected the Truth, as opposed to the Lie propagated by devils in the spiritual world and evil-doers on earth. The king's duty was to do the same in the physical world. Herodotus states that all Persian boys were raised to excel at three things: shooting a bow, riding a horse—Darius boasted that he was a good horseman and a good bowman on horse or on foot—and telling the truth. This likely became far more pronounced under Darius, who, from sincere belief or to justify his rule, pushed a more focused interpretation of existing beliefs. To oppose his rule was to oppose the Truth and all that was good, and thus deserved punishment.[12]

Once he had beaten down all of his opponents, this attitude did not make his rule any harsher, as long as no one challenged it, and there was no effort to make the population of the entire empire abandon their traditional religion and convert to Zoroastrianism in any form. Local communities continued to enjoy considerable autonomy in their day-to-day affairs, not least because any close supervision by the king and his court would have been impractical given the immense size of the empire. Several royal centres were created, notably Pasargadae, where Cyrus was buried, Persepolis, and Susa. Even when the great king was not on campaign or touring the empire, the royal court moved, partly to avoid less comfortable extremes of weather as the seasons changed and also to oversee administration over a wider area.

The satraps were the king's representatives, with over twenty satrapies being created. Each satrap had an army at his disposal and possessed the authority to deal with all but the largest problems within his province. This was an organised empire, with silver currency to facilitate taxation and trade, an extensive system of record keeping dealing with accounts, reports, and orders, and a developed road system, most notably the great royal road eventually reaching from the western coast to the royal cities and beyond. Yet the sheer distances meant that nothing and no one could travel quickly even on the most urgent royal duties. Much had to be left for the man on the spot, whether satrap, local dynast, or official, to deal with because it was simply impossible for the king to respond quickly and handle every issue. These were limits imposed by the technology of the times, and the Achaemenid Persian Empire managed them as well as or better than any other power before or for a good while later.

This empire emerged very suddenly and expanded rapidly. If Cambyses was possibly unbalanced and certainly a less gifted ruler than his father, then the empire survived as a unit, and when Darius seized the throne, he was able to beat off all opponents and once again unite the empire. Soon he began to expand it even further, its strength rapidly recovering from the chaos that had followed his seizure of power. Unfortunately, the meagre evidence makes it impossible to trace or understand fully who created the structure of the empire and how. Herodotus says that men remembered Cyrus as a father, Cambyses as a tyrant, and Darius as a shopkeeper or merchant (or even huckster). Perhaps the latter was more concerned with revenue and regulation, although this may have simply reflected the transition from conquest to a more stable and permanent empire.[13]

The Ionian Greek cities were part of this empire from early on, and due to the frequent trade and other contact between these communities and the Aegean islands and the mainland of Greece itself, the wider Greek world was aware of the new empire from the start. Around 547 BC representatives from some of the Ionian Greek cities went to Sparta and asked for assistance or support from the Spartans. Herodotus claims that the Spartans sent an envoy to the great king asking that he do no harm to the Ionian Greeks unless he wished to face retribution. Cyrus—bemused, disdainful, or perhaps both—after asking advisors who the Spartans were, was not impressed and simply got on with arranging matters as he saw fit. He declared that nothing was to be feared of men like the Greeks, who had a marketplace at the centre of every town where they could cheat and swear falsely to each other. The story may be apocryphal, but even if it is garbled or untrue, his ignorance and unconcern likely do reflect reality. There was no reason for a man who had absorbed Elam, Media, and Lydia to worry overmuch about the feelings of even the largest and most militarily formidable state in mainland Greece.[14]

The new empire was a greater concern for the Spartans and other Greeks than they were for Cyrus. Mainland Greece was some 2,000 miles away from the royal cities and the heartland of the Persian Empire, a journey of many weeks. In contrast, the coast of Asia Minor was only a comparatively short sea voyage away from Attica or the Peloponnese. For many of the Aegean islands, the Achaemenid Empire was within fairly easy reach and sometimes literally within sight, so that Persian presence and influence was there from the beginning. Even for those further afield, the Persians encroached on the Greeks far more than the Assyrians or other powers of Asia ever had, and as time passed the new empire moved ever closer. Some Ionians and islanders left their cities rather than live within the empire, perhaps because they resented Persian rule, since the Persians were a good deal stranger and more alien than the familiar Lydians. Other migrants may have been the leaders and their supporters who had lost out to rivals given power under the new regime. More Ionians remained than left, but significant numbers departed, some to settle eventually in Italy alongside the numerous existing Greek colonies.[15]

If Ionian representatives did in fact go to the Spartans asking them to speak on their behalf to Cyrus, this was an open recognition of the Spartans' prestige and strength as greater than those of the cities making the appeal. Links between communities and especially between prominent individuals, guest friendships akin to those between many of Homer's heroes, were a main method of formal interaction between Greek states. Many aristocrats had such friendships with leading men elsewhere, adding to their status and sometimes offering more tangible benefits. Tyrants, would-be and successful, relied on such connections, for instance between Cylon and Megara and between the Pisistratids and Eretria and other cities. An association with a colony, or one of the less formal settlements overseas, was especially valuable. Pisistratus built up the wealth and resources to mount his final and most successful bid for control at Athens by exploiting such a connection with settlers in Thrace.

The coast of Macedonia, Thrace, and the Dardanelles, with the Black Sea beyond them, gave access to many valuable resources, such as timber for shipbuilding, precious metals, and grain. As Athens grew in size it far outstripped the capacity of Attica to feed the population from its own produce. This gave a particular incentive to establish outposts in and forge alliances with the region. The Athenians came late to colonization but over time devoted ever more energy to such projects, underpinning their society and urban life with basic resources drawn from far afield. Accomplished, at least at the start, through the personal activities and energy of individual aristocrats, over time these evolved into more corporate enterprises controlled by the democratic state.

A prominent man might spend many years abroad without severing his ties with or losing his property in his home city. Pisistratus did this, and under his and his sons' rule, others also went abroad, perhaps to avoid being in Athens under a tyranny. The Elder Cimon, the nobleman who won a series of chariot races at Olympia and sensibly dedicated the last victory to Pisistratus to demonstrate his devotion to the tyrant, had a brother who was the strongman, warlord, or tyrant of a community in the Gallipoli Peninsula. The population was not Greek but had seen in a Greek leader and his entourage a means of protection against local enemies, a task he performed with great success. The connection with Athens was not severed, trade prospered, and cordial communication went back and forth with Pisistratus and his sons. On request, they despatched one of Cimon's sons to assist and succeed his uncle. When both were dead, the older man from age and the nephew having been murdered, the tyrants of Athens sent out Cimon's other son, Miltiades, to take over, giving him a warship and escort. The relationship was not a simple one: Athens did not control this outpost by the Dardanelles and instead had friendly relations with its leader. Giving opportunities to members of other aristocratic houses, whether in the form of magistracies and honours at home or opportunities abroad, helped to keep the tyrants' potential rivals contented. No doubt there was wariness on all sides, and the murder of the Elder Cimon—officially unsolved but generally laid at the door of Hippias and Hipparchus—as well as the assassination of Hipparchus and eventual overthrow of Hippias, showed that the relationship between tyrants and nobility was never fully stable.[16]

Miltiades ruled his own little state for decades. During that time, he does not appear to have ever returned to Athens but did not lose his status as an Athenian. He acted as a regional warlord and married a wife from the royal house of one of the tribes. Other Greek aristocrats turned tyrants or warlords acted in much the same way, leading cities along the north coast of Asia Minor, in the Dardanelles, and on the Thracian coast. Under Darius the Persians absorbed all of these areas, adding to the number of Greeks—or at least Greek-led communities—owing loyalty to the empire. The Thracian tribes submitted, as did the kingdom of Macedonia, and even if Darius had less success in an expedition beyond the Danube against the Scythians, it did not weaken his control of the other areas, whether they were ruled directly by a satrap or by local kings, as in Macedonia.[17]

The Macedonians spoke Greek, albeit in an outlandish dialect, and opinion remained uncertain about whether or not they were fellow Hellenes. Regardless of this, they were now allies of Persia, giving the great king a land border with Thessaly, where the inhabitants were most definitely Greek. The last years of the sixth century BC and the early years of the fifth saw the ongoing expansion of Persia, coming ever closer to the cities of southern Greece. There was no obvious reason why the empire should stop. Soon after he had put down rivals and rebellions, Darius sent out an exploratory expedition, which learned about the coastlines of Greece and even sailed as far as southern Italy. Royal propaganda bolstered the impression that this was an empire set on further conquest, and this can only have been obvious to close neighbours like the Greeks.[18]

The Spartans do not appear to have reacted directly to the rebuff from Cyrus, assuming the incident is historical. Given that Persian rule was relatively mild and respected local customs, perhaps this was considered sufficient. More importantly, they could do little, at least in making any sort of direct challenge, for they were not a maritime power, and the peculiar nature of Spartan society ensured that there was a deep reluctance to send too many Spartans far away for any length of time. Yet there are signs that leading Spartans viewed the ever-closer advance of Persia with concern and that it became an additional factor in their decision-making.

A tyrant named Polycrates had come to control the large island of Samos sometime around the middle of the sixth century BC. Piracy was something of a tradition on the island, as was tyranny, and under

Polycrates the Samians were very well organised and became particularly energetic marauders. They do not appear ever to have been too fussy about the identity of their victims, at least as far as extortion and theft were concerned. In earlier years a Spartan embassy going to Croesus and an Egyptian embassy heading for Sparta were both relieved of valuable gifts that they were carrying to oil the wheels of diplomacy. Other envoys may have suffered, to say nothing of traders and communities on vulnerable coastlines. There are signs that when Cyrus conquered Lydia, Polycrates fiercely asserted his independence and may have fought against the invaders, even though leaders of communities on other islands soon made peace with the Persians. At the start, the Persians had no navy, but as their hold over the Ionian cities was confirmed and the Phoenicians were forced to submit, they gained the significant naval assets of these subordinate allies. Polycrates allied with the Egyptian pharaoh, although the alliance broke down before Cambyses conquered Egypt. The Persians had already taken Cyprus, a venture made possible now that they controlled a strong navy, and Polycrates sniffed the wind and decided that there was more future in supporting the great king of Persia rather than the pharaoh of Egypt. Hoping that his past behaviour would be forgotten, he became a subordinate ally of the great king.[19]

In 525 BC a group of Samian aristocrats came to Sparta after being expelled for opposing Polycrates and asked for aid to return home and depose the tyrant. In one sense this was a familiar-enough story in the Greek world, as the losers in competition within one state sought help from outside. Unprecedented was the willingness of Sparta's leaders to send an army against Polycrates. Her ally, Corinth, provided ships, for the Spartans had none, and a joint Spartan-Corinthian expedition sailed to Samos. This was a major extension of the Spartans' ambition, taking them not only beyond the Peloponnese and beyond mainland Greece but to an island close to the shore of Asia.

It began well, as they were able to land on Samos in spite of Polycrates's fleet, and laid siege to the city of Samos itself, perhaps having won victories on sea and land to achieve this. Yet an operation of this sort was wholly new to those involved, and the Spartan system did not lend itself to long sieges of strongly walled cities, let alone protracted operations at such a distance from home. After forty days the expedition abandoned the siege and returned home. Herodotus recounts a rumour, which he claims was false, that Polycrates had bribed some of the Spartan leaders, fooling them by paying in lead coins concealed by a thin layer of gold. A few years later the trickster was himself fooled. The local satrap, remembering the former hostility of Polycrates and unwilling to trust someone so unscrupulous, ordered him to report in person. As soon as the tyrant arrived, he was arrested and crucified—or perhaps impaled—on the coast itself, within sight of Samos across the straits.[20]

The satrap who had killed Polycrates grew ambitious in the aftermath of Cambyses's death and the murder of Bardylis, taking over several satrapies beyond his own. His success was brief, and he in turn was executed by Darius. A newly appointed satrap was instructed to install Polycrates's younger brother, a man of proven loyalty to the empire, to rule Samos. This succeeded, chasing away the tyrant who had seized power in the meantime. The latter went to Sparta, where through pleas and offers of bribes to King Cleomenes, he tried to arrange for a second Spartan intervention. No one was convinced, and there was a wariness about attempting another overseas adventure, so the former tyrant was expelled and told to leave the Peloponnese altogether.[21]

In the meantime, the Athenians under Pisistratus and his family appear to have had cordial enough relations with Persia, although there is little sign of anything closer. Men like Miltiades accepted their place within the Persian Empire, and he was one of many Greek leaders from Ionia and further north to take part in Persian campaigns, notably the expedition across the Danube. Miltiades was an Athenian, but his actions in no way committed his home city to any close association with Darius and his empire. While the sense that

Hippias was too well disposed to the Persians may have helped convince Cleomenes to depose him, this was at most a minor factor. The earlier cooperation in the attempt to overthrow Polycrates contributed to Corinthian reluctance to act against Athens once the tyrant had gone.

Hippias moved to Asia Minor following his expulsion, exploiting existing links with communities overseas and willingly accepting life in Darius's empire. When Cleomenes began organising his grand attack on Athens in 506 BC, with the army of Spartans and allies coming from the west, while forces from Thebes and Chalkis advanced independently, the threat was so great that the Athenians voted to send envoys to the Persians. They were received at Sardis by the satrap, who happened to be one of Darius's brothers, who asked them to make a symbolic offering of earth and water to receive Persian protection. This clear mark of submission was a regular feature of Persian diplomacy, bringing a community into the empire's sphere of influence if not automatically under its direct rule. The Athenians readily agreed, accepting this as the price for preserving their new democratic system. In the event, no Persian assistance was given, largely because by the time the ambassadors returned to Attica, none was needed. Cleomenes's army had turned about, with the Corinthians again playing a significant role, and the Athenians had trounced the Thebans and Chalcidians.[22]

With the crisis over, the Athenian Popular Assembly may have repudiated the actions of their ambassadors, as Herodotus claims, or may simply have rebuked them and then felt that the whole thing would simply lapse. The Persian attitude, that of an empire led by a king divinely sanctioned to defend truth from the lie, was inevitably different. Hippias went to the satrap and found favour. It was common enough for the empire to appoint an approved ruler or tyrant to govern a city or small state on its behalf, and the Athenians were instructed to accept the exiled Hippias back as their leader. They refused, which violated the submission conveyed when they gave earth and water, but for the moment nothing more was done about this. Darius ruled a vast empire, and responding to an insult from one small state, however large by Greek standards, was not a major priority. Any response could wait for a more convenient time, so Hippias lived on as a well-treated and honoured guest of the Persians, and the Athenians were left alone for the moment.[23]

Cleomenes of Sparta had tried and failed to convince his countrymen and their allies to restore Hippias, but as noted in an earlier chapter, in later years his attitude to the new regime at Athens mellowed. The inhabitants of the island of Aegina were long-time enemies of Athens, habitual raiders of the shores of Attica, and also allies of Sparta. When leaders there made submission to Persia, as more and more Aegean communities proved willing to do, Cleomenes supported the Athenians against them. Given the confusing traditions about the king and his irascible, perhaps unbalanced, personality, it is difficult to be certain, but it is more than possible that growing concern about the threat posed by Persia did a lot to guide his actions and that other leading Spartans shared his fears. The story that Cleomenes began his decline into alcoholism through feasting with Scythian envoys also fits with interest in another region where Darius was expanding. Once again, a suspicion the empire was most likely one aspect influencing Cleomenes and prominent Spartans makes sense. Yet, when the opportunity came for direct action against Persia, neither the king nor anyone else proved keen.[24]

THE SPARK THAT would lead to the Persian invasions of Greece was lit around 500 BC, although no one could have guessed that this would happen at the time, for in the beginning it was a local matter involving Greeks living in or near the Achaemenid Empire. Exiles from the island of Naxos approached Aristagoras, the Persian-backed tyrant of Miletus in Ionia, asking him to support them against the opponents who had expelled them from their home. Aristagoras was enthusiastic and went to Sardis to propose a major expedition. The satrap was also keen, and the idea was passed up to Darius, who gave it his backing. In 499 BC a large fleet was assembled carrying a sizeable army. This set out from Miletus but took a roundabout route as part of a deception plan, before eventually landing on Naxos. Long before this, Aristagoras and the Persian admiral had begun bickering over their respective seniority. The defenders were well prepared, and after a siege lasting four months, the project was abandoned amid rumours that someone, possibly the admiral, had treacherously warned the Naxians.[25]

Few leaders have ever been ready to embrace their responsibility for failure, and since Aristagoras had begun the whole project and promised success and profit, he understandably expected to bear the brunt of the great king's disappointment. His uncle Histaeus had been tyrant at Miletus before him, until he was summoned to live with the royal court, a high honour that at the same time suggested doubts about his reliability. This was a sign that he could in turn be replaced and led Aristagoras to decide that a brighter future lay in throwing off imperial rule. Herodotus claims that his uncle was part of the conspiracy, on one occasion shaving a slave's head, tattooing a message on the skin of his scalp, waiting for the hair to regrow, and then sending him to Miletus with this message. This is one of the Historian's most entertaining and least convincing moments, although later events suggest that Histaeus was involved, even if he was playing a game of his own.[26]

Aristagoras had the advantage that communication and decision-making took so long in the Persian Empire and also that plenty of others within the Ionian cities were restless under imperial rule. Too little is known to judge how oppressive taxation and other burdens actually were, although, to some extent, this may be the wrong question; throughout history rebellions have broken out because enough people *felt* that the current situation was intolerable even if, in strict economic terms, conditions were not excessively bad by the standards of the day. When the revolt did break out in Ionia, one of the first acts was to depose the tyrants in many cities, which might mean that these men were especially hated, perhaps with justice. On the other hand, the rebel leaders may have been the aristocrats who had lost out in local competition to rivals and sought any excuse to reverse the situation and overthrow these local enemies.[27]

Before the rising began, Aristagoras travelled to Sparta, revealing his plans and seeking support. At first Cleomenes showed interest, apparently contemplating sending troops. However, when the visitor displayed a map or chart and revealed that Darius's heartland lay more than three months' journey from the coast, any enthusiasm died. The expedition to Samos had stretched Sparta's military system and failed, making anything on this far bigger scale utterly unthinkable. Aristagoras was told to leave, so went to Athens, where he was allowed to make his proposals to a gathering of the Assembly. This time the reception was enthusiastic, everyone eager to embrace the links of kinship with fellow Ionians, and the demos voted to send ships and men to aid the rebels. Herodotus rather tartly commented that this proved how much harder it was to dupe one man than a crowd of 30,000.[28]

When the revolt began, the Athenians sent twenty warships, joined by ten from Eretria on Euboea, an ally of Pisistratus that had maintained good relations with the new regime in Athens. Together with a force of Ionians, some of the crews from these ships marched inland and attacked Sardis itself. The satrap was wrong-footed, his army either not yet assembled or in the wrong place, and he could do no more than hole up on the very strong acropolis. The city itself was overrun, and, accidentally according to Herodotus, much of it was set on fire, destroying several temples. Unable to capture the citadel, the attackers withdrew but were harried during the retreat by newly arrived Persian troops and suffered badly.

After this chastening experience, the Athenians and Eretrians went home and took no further part in the war, but since they were little more than a token force, this made little or no difference to the course of events. The rebellion quickly spread to Caria and Cyprus. Between them, the rebels drew away most of the naval strength available to the Persians, with the exception of the Phoenicians and Egyptians. For a while this gave them an advantage at sea, and they operated north along the Asian coast, convincing other communities to join them. On land, the advantage always lay with the Persians, and the rebels failed to assemble any strong field armies. In spite of victories at sea, Persian troops steadily recovered Cyprus, taking by siege any city that refused to surrender. The Carians were beaten in battle, then suffered another defeat even though they had been joined by Ionian reinforcements. In the aftermath, the Carians managed to mount a nighttime ambush of the victorious Persians, killing the satrap and a number of his senior officers, but this only gave a brief check to the Persian advance.

The last great hope was at sea, and in 494 BC an enormous fleet of more than 300 warships was assembled to protect Miletus. More than two-thirds of these were sent by Lesbos, Chios, and Samos, the three biggest islands close to the Asian shore. Even so, the Persian fleet was larger still, with 600 vessels according to Herodotus, although this is likely an imprecise phrase meaning no more than 'a very large fleet'. It was an indication that, while slow to gather momentum, the sheer size of the Achaemenid Empire gave it huge resources and a long-term advantage whenever a war escalated. The two fleets confronted each other off the island of Lade, until the ships from Samos and most of the ones from Lesbos deserted the allied cause and fled. Even so, the fighting was long and bitter before the Persians shattered the Ionian fleet.[29]

On land, the Persians demonstrated skill and determination at siege-craft reminiscent of the Assyrians and the other major powers of Asia. One by one, the Ionian cities were taken, their walls undermined or overwhelmed by ramps. Miletus resisted but eventually fell. Persian rule was in many ways mild, but Persian vengeance on those who had broken faith, who had defied the Truth, was savage. Many men were killed, the women and children enslaved. As in other cities, the better-looking and higher-born girls were reserved for the royal harem, and the boys were castrated as eunuchs for the royal court. Although it had taken years, the Ionian rebellion was thoroughly crushed by the satraps and generals sent to deal with the problem. Darius had never needed to take charge in person.[30]

10

THE CHARGE

*The first Persian invasion of Greece
and the Athenian victory at the Battle of Marathon,
494–490 BC*

By the end of 494 BC, the Ionian revolt was wholly crushed, as were the rebellions by other peoples in the wider area. Aristagoras had abandoned the cause long before the end, ultimately getting killed in Thrace. His uncle Histaeus had proclaimed his loyalty to Darius and been sent back to help suppress the rising, but his subsequent actions made him distrusted by all sides. The Persians eventually arrested and impaled him. Other leaders fled or were killed, and new leaders were appointed to each community, replacing the ones who had proved unreliable. Rather than installing tyrants in the Ionian cities, Darius imposed a system where a broader aristocracy shared power, which in many ways was more in keeping with trends in the wider Greek world. The satrap would settle disputes between the cities rather than letting rivalries spill over into conflict. This was a curb to their freedom and sense of reputation and, at the same time, a sensible measure likely to foster peace, which in turn encouraged stability and prosperity. There were punishments, and more land was confiscated to reward Persian soldiers and leaders, but fairly quickly the region started to recover. Even Miletus, for all the horrors of the sack and the conspicuous reprisals against the leaders and their families, was not eradicated and in time would thrive once more.[1]

At Athens, a new play, *The Fall of Miletus*, was written and performed, but only once. Horrified as the actors presented the grim final moments of a once proud city, the audience was so shocked that citizens assembled and voted to ban the work from ever being performed again, fining the playwright for good measure. Sorrow for the fate of the Milesians was reinforced by the knowledge that the Athenians had angered the great king whose soldiers had stormed Miletus. Perhaps there was guilt at the thought that the Athenians had done nothing to aid Miletus and the other Ionians, at least after their early, brief involvement. More to the point, seeing that the same fate might befall Athens did not require any real imagination.[2]

Herodotus says that Darius asked about the Athenians, after hearing that they had taken part in the destruction of the temples at Sardis. The great king took an arrow and shot it high into the air, pledging to inflict the punishment that this sacrilege deserved. He gave orders that three times during dinner, one of his servants should whisper into his ear to 'remember the Athenians'. The story may be an invention, for while it rightly illustrates that, for the ruler of a vast empire, Athens was a very minor concern indeed, it still gives the Greeks and the Athenians in particular considerable importance. Herodotus does not state specifically that the crimes of the Athenians at Sardis were all the worse because of the earlier offering of earth and water, from the Persian perspective making them rebels, but this was surely the case. Yet, for all that, Athens was just one city, and Darius's plans were far greater in scale.[3]

In 493 BC, Persian control of Thrace and Macedonia was confirmed, as has already been described, and the edge of the empire reached northern Greece. There was no reason for the Greeks to expect expansion to halt, or for Darius and the Persians not to continue. Greece was a well-populated, increasingly prosperous region, well worth adding to the empire. At some point in the next year or two, Persian envoys visited many Greek cities, asking that they offer earth and water to the great king. The Spartans killed the envoys by throwing them down a well, while the Athenians voted to execute them and hurl them over a cliff into a pit reserved for bodies of criminals. Eretria and Plataea merely rejected the appeal. Otherwise, most cities performed the ritual and submitted to Darius or at least gave a respectful and noncommittal reply.

Doing violence to emissaries violated normal behaviour, although Herodotus was not sure whether the Athenians ever really paid a price for this. Cleomenes was probably still a king when the envoys came to Sparta, and such a violent outburst was well in keeping with the stories about him, although no source claims that he was involved. A few years later, the Spartans became worried about the propriety of the action and made some attempt to avert divine punishment for it, but they do not appear to have regretted it in any other respect. Conventions of behaviour may well have been looser when it came to dealing with outsiders rather than fellow Greeks, and whether or not the Spartans and Athenians committed an impiety in killing the envoys, the message of defiance was clear.[4]

For the Athenians, the choice followed on from their earlier willingness to aid the Ionians against Persia, and the same was true of the Eretrians. Plataea, encouraged by Cleomenes to seek protection from the Thebans by alliance with Athens, may simply have chosen to stand with its ally. For the Spartans, this was the first open hostility to Persia, even if suspicion of the empire had played a role in decision-making for some time. Sparta's status as the pre-eminent military power in the Greek world was the reason why Aristagoras had appealed to them before the Ionian revolt. For the Spartans to have accepted a subordinate relationship with any state, even one as mighty as the Persian Empire, would have meant a loss of prestige, diminishing their own self-esteem and the awe in which others held them. This was presumably too high a price in the view of Sparta's kings, magistrates, and citizens. A range of opinions may have been expressed at Sparta and at Athens, but Herodotus does not suggest prolonged debate before a decision was made. If the brutal rejection of Persian overtures was not necessarily the universal opinion of all Athenians or Spartans, it does appear to have reflected the mood of the overwhelming majority.

Still, a feature of the Persians' expansion from the very start had been their ability to convince significant groups and individuals to defect and join them. The Athenians had had more contact with Persia than the Spartans and also had recent memory of tyranny and civil war. Their democracy was still new, the future unknown. Hippias was a favoured guest of the Persians along with his close followers, while relatives of the Pisistratids and even more of their former supporters still lived within the citizen community of Athens. The wealthy and well-connected aristocratic families who had dominated public life for generations remained rich and influential, the rivalries between them potential fault lines of the sort exploited so well by the Persians in the past.

A fairly recent returnee to Athens was Miltiades, elected archon under the Pisistratids and then sent off to the Gallipoli Peninsula with their blessing and support to succeed his uncle and brother as local warlord. A subject of the Achaemenid Empire for some years, he had joined the rebellion against it, only to show little interest in the wider cause of the Ionian cities. Instead, he saw a chance to expand his own little empire, taking Imbros and Lemnos, although he handed over control of the latter to the Athenians. Later, everything turned sour, as the Scythians attacked his territory; even worse, as the revolt was crushed, Darius began to deal with those who had opposed him. Miltiades fled, narrowly escaping his Persian pursuers. One of his sons was less fortunate, or perhaps felt that his best interests lay elsewhere, and let himself be caught. Welcomed at the imperial court, he was given both land and a Persian wife.[5]

Miltiades himself made it to Athens around 493 BC, only to be put on trial within a year for tyranny and perhaps for other charges,

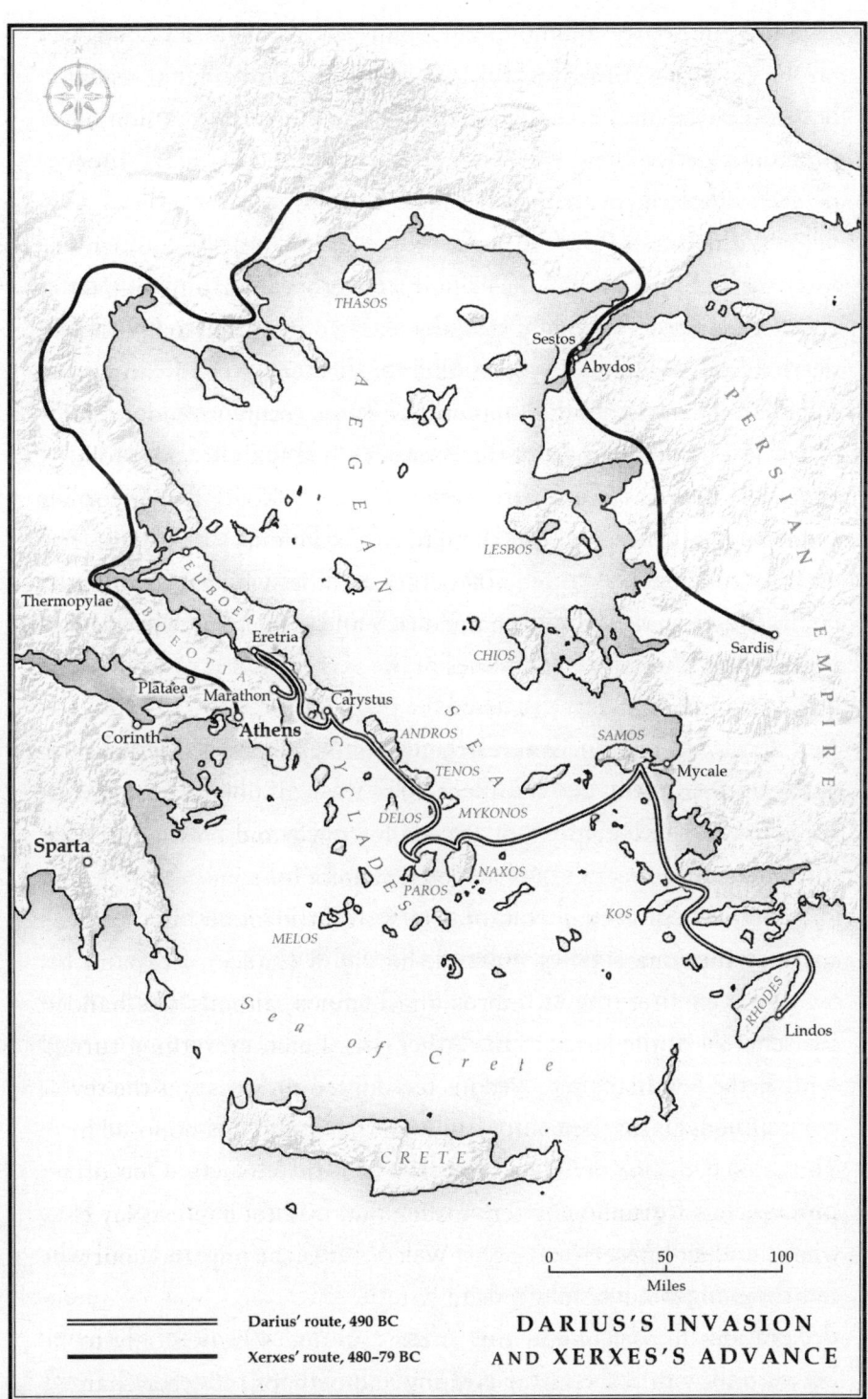

although the courts commonly threw any questionable deed at a man on the basis that it revealed his true character, so there may not have been other specific accusations. Tyranny, or supporting tyranny, had been outlawed in the early days of the new democracy, but Miltiades defended himself on the basis that he had not ruled at Athens, over fellow Athenians or indeed fellow Greeks, but instead commanded foreigners in a distant land. The defence worked, aided by assurances that he was a true Athenian. Herodotus tells a story that many suspect derived from Miltiades's protestations at this time. In 513 BC, he and other Greeks under the dominion of the Persian Empire had taken part in Darius's expedition across the Danube. In the main, they provided ships and crews, and a small group of them were left behind at the bridge of boats used to cross the great river. The king had not returned with his army at the end of sixty days as he had planned. Miltiades claimed that at this point, or perhaps sooner, he had proposed that they destroy the bridge and leave Darius stranded in hostile territory. The other Greek leaders discussed the plan, until caution won out and they decided to remain loyal. The bridge remained intact, Darius eventually rejoined them, and the alleged plot was never betrayed, so either the secret was well guarded or the whole story was invented or embellished to suit Miltiades's needs twenty years later.[6]

Miltiades survived this legal attack and soon began to adapt to the very different style of politics under a democracy created while he was away from the city. In 490 BC he was elected as one of the ten generals (strategoi) at a time when the Athenians were threatened with Persian retribution. Darius had issued orders for the coastal communities to prepare ships and the satraps to muster an army at Tarsus on the coast of Cilicia (later the birthplace of Saint Paul). This process took time and could not be carried out in secret. Apart from that, the impending threat was a way of putting pressure on all who felt they might have incurred his wrath, since there was no public declaration of objective at this stage. Command was to be shared between the son of the satrap and Datis the Mede, a commander with considerable experience in the wider region. Among their entourage was Hippias, by now a very elderly man.

Herodotus reports that the fleet gathered in 490 BC consisted of 600 ships, although, once again, this number may be a convention meaning no more than 'very big'. Ancient warships, especially the trireme, the pinnacle of technology at the time, required very large crews in proportion to their size, so that 600 triremes would suggest something like 120,000 crewmen, a truly vast number to water and feed. This was not a royal expedition, so such a big total in addition to the army seems much too large. The figure of 600 ships may mean nothing at all or include a significant proportion of other vessels to transport soldiers and supplies. Herodotus mentions that some boats were converted to carry horses for the cavalry. At no point does he give any figure for the size of the land forces, for although rowers from warships could and did disembark and fight on land, they tended to do so as light troops rather than forming in the main line of battle. A few far-later sources give unconvincingly large numbers, and this seems no more than the well-established Greco-Roman convention that all Persian armies were immense, adding to the glory of victories won over them. Modern scholars have proposed a wide range of estimates, with many opting for some 20,000 to 25,000 troops. While plausible, this remains conjectural.[7]

The Athenians, Spartans, and citizens of other Greek cities who had rebuffed Darius's envoys were aware of the Persian preparations but, for the moment, could do little more than wait. The expedition might possibly have a different purpose, and more importantly, until it set out, they had little idea of when and where it would strike first. None of the cities were great naval powers at this stage, and the successors to the great fleet assembled at Lade in 494 BC were now serving on the Persian side. If invasion came, it must be met on land, but for armies whose strength lay in their hoplites, there could be no question of raising an army and keeping it waiting until it was needed. Citizen soldiers simply could not spend weeks, let alone months, away from daily life and work, devoting themselves to training and preparing for war or drilling as an army. Nor was there any real need for such measures, and there ought to be time to react if and when the Persians landed, by which time the nature and location of the threat would be clearer. Thus the Greeks waited, the normal life of the cities continuing. Perhaps the election of Miltiades and the elections in general showed that the Athenians' minds were heavily concerned with impending war, but this is not necessarily the case, since much about him was likely to appeal to voters at any time.

Once embarked, the Persian fleet sailed north to Samos, which might suggest that it planned to continue in that direction and follow the European coast around to Greece. After all, the Persians had mounted large-scale operations in Thrace just a few years before, so knew the region and had allies there. Yet, in 493 BC they had also suffered heavy losses when a storm devastated a fleet sailing near Mount Athos. That was a warning that the seas in that region were unpredictable and dangerous, and the initial move to the north may have been a ploy from the very beginning, since after a landing on Rhodes, the Persians struck south-west at Naxos, achieving surprise, unlike the previous attack masterminded by Aristagoras. Unprepared, the Naxians abandoned their city and hid in the hills. Naxos and its sanctuaries were looted and set on fire, after which the Persians re-embarked.[8]

Next the Persians went to Delos, famous for its sanctuaries, to which the Athenians under Pisistratus had made generous gifts. The inhabitants fled, only to be reassured by the Persian leadership. Here, as always when not directly opposed, the Persians showed great respect to established cults and their sacred sites. Datis made an offering of a necklace at the shrine and, together with his colleague and the army as a whole, presented a gift of a large supply of incense. The message of the expedition so far was a familiar one: Darius treated his friends with respect and generosity, but being his enemy was unwise. As the fleet continued its progress along the islands of the

Cyclades, most of the communities submitted immediately or after brief resistance. Many had already offered earth and water in earlier rounds of Persian diplomacy. On islands where there was resistance, the Persians spread out in a cordon, sweeping along the land to catch any fugitives, a tactic likened to using a net to catch fish.[9]

The summer of 490 BC was well advanced by the time the fleet landed on the southern end of Euboea. The city of Carystus refused to admit them, so the Persian army surrounded it and began to build siege mounds, sending out parties to devastate the farmland. Sensing that defeat was only a matter of time, the citizens of Carystus surrendered. The Eretrians, understanding that they were bound to be the invader's main target on the island and having a little time to prepare, set to work repairing and strengthening the city walls. They also sent word to Athens asking for assistance, and the Athenians despatched the citizens given land taken from Chalkis, some 4,000 according to Herodotus. However, when these arrived, they discovered that the Eretrians were arguing with each other about the best course of action, some wanting to hold the city and others to take their valuables and flee. Seeing this indecision, the Athenian force promptly turned around and went back to Attica.[10]

Most of the Eretrians opted to defend their city. The Persians came by sea, sailing along the coast to land at three separate beaches in case they were opposed. There were no defenders on the shoreline, so the bulk of the army, including the cavalry, disembarked behind the advance guards. They then proceeded to besiege Eretria, doing so with all their usual skill and determination. For six days the defenders resisted staunchly, making it hard for the attackers to approach the walls and begin their siegeworks. The following night two Eretrian aristocrats betrayed the rest of the community, opening the gates to admit the attackers. The sack that followed was as grim as the one at Miletus or anywhere else deemed to deserve conspicuous punishment for opposing the king. Temple sanctuaries were burned and large numbers of prominent citizens arrested for deportation, with good-looking youngsters chosen as recruits for the harem or royal eunuchs. Presumably the turncoats were spared and rewarded with power, and the worst of the reprisals focused on the upper- and middle-class citizens who had formed the heart of the resistance.

The strait between Euboea and Attica is very narrow, and the Athenians realised that they were next and that the attack could come within days. There was debate over the best course of action, since, after all, debate and collective decision-making were at the core of the young democracy. Some argued that it was best to let the Persians come to them and defend the city itself, while others believed that it was better to muster an army and meet the enemy in the open field. There is not enough evidence to make clear the state and strength of Athens's city walls in 490 BC or how practical it would have been to store sufficient food to supply the people if they sheltered inside the defences for any length of time. Apart from that, the Persians had repeatedly demonstrated their prowess at taking walled cities. Miltiades was among the voices arguing that a siege could only end one way and that it was far better to fight in the open, and this view prevailed. When the invaders came, the Athenians were determined to confront them in battle.[11]

THE PERSIANS ARRIVED almost at the end of summer, in late August or early September 490 BC by the modern calendar. They landed at Marathon, guided there by Hippias, who had disembarked there in 546 BC, fifty-six years earlier, with his father at the start of the victorious campaign that saw Pisistratus firmly established as tyrant. Herodotus says that the spot was chosen because it was the shortest route from Eretria and also offered the best open country where cavalry could operate effectively. While neither point is strictly speaking true, it offered the best balance between the two. More importantly, Hippias was able to provide them with plenty of information about the lay of the land, even if his knowledge was a little dated.[12]

Marathon was a deme in the system created by Cleisthenes, an area of farmland around a small central village. The size of the latter in 490 BC is unknown, as is the exact coastline and the extent of the marshy area or lake near the northern headland. Some twenty-five miles or so from Athens itself—the precise distance depending on the location of the village—it was separated from the city by a line of mountains, forcing travellers to take slightly longer routes to travel between the two. For an active individual it was a journey of six or seven hours. Larger groups and armies tend to move more slowly, especially when forced to follow one main path, but it is fair to say that Athens was readily accessible for an invading army, potentially within a day's march. Landing there rather than immediately outside the city itself made a good deal of sense and reflected similar concerns over an opposed landing shown by the Persians at Eretria. No Athenians were waiting to confront them at Marathon, so they were able to land unmolested and begin the laborious process of getting horses and gear ashore.[13]

News reached Athens quickly, carried by runners or signals or both, and within the day the Athenians knew that the Persians had arrived. A messenger named Philipiddes (or, in some sources, Pheidippides) was sent to Sparta asking for assistance. Preparations to muster the army may already have been underway in expectation of the Persians' imminent arrival. Citizens assembled to vote, approving a proposal by Miltiades to grant freedom to slaves willing to fight against the invader and confirming the decision to meet the enemy in battle. Throughout Attica, men readied their own armour, helmets, shields, and weapons, gathered up food and drink to take along, and set out. Many had one or more slave attendants to carry the gear, and often the wealthy rode horses rather than having to walk all the way. Much of the army gathered at Athens and marched out in a body under the command of Callimachus, the polemarch, or military archon, for the year, and the generals for each of the ten tribal regiments. Sacrifices were made and oaths sworn to defend their country and to treat properly with the Plataeans and Spartans in the future. It is usually assumed that the entire army gathered and marched together, leading to debate over which of the two most likely routes were followed, but this may be imposing modern ideas of regularity on the fifth century BC. There is no reason why large groups may not have followed both routes as well as others, and men coming from their homes likely joined the others on the march and perhaps were still coming in over the next day or two.[14]

The Athenians moved to Marathon and made camp near the precinct of Hercules, the precise location of which has not been established. The army probably settled down on the slopes of Mount Agrieliki and was soon joined by the contingent from Plataea. How soon the Persians realised that the defenders were coming is uncertain, for there is no evidence for what degree of patrolling and scouting was considered normal, but at the very least the dust thrown up by so many feet would have given early warning. The invaders were busy organising themselves on shore and made no effort to intervene. Ancient armies often lumbered towards each other, settling down for some time before actually joining battle.

Depending on how the sources are understood, most agree that there were 1,000 Plataeans and 9,000 to 10,000 Athenians, although opinion is divided over whether this was the entire army or simply the hoplites, the men of status who mattered in society because they played the key role in fighting. Most Greek armies included some lighter armed troops, throwing javelins or rocks, who supported the heavily armed infantrymen. None are mentioned in the accounts of the subsequent battle, but this is common enough since these were drawn from the poor, perhaps even from non-citizens, so were unlikely to be described unless they did something truly exceptional. It does not mean that none were present. There is no evidence for how many slaves were granted their freedom to fight at the battle, let alone any indication of whether they were given a basic hoplite panoply to join the phalanx or fought as light troops.

The Chigi vase (*c.* 650–640 BC) offers a rare depiction of formations of hoplites in battle, as two lines of men fight at close quarters, while others come up to support them. Note that each man appears to have two spears, one in reserve and one held overarm to thrust or throw.

Battles were hard for sculptors to depict, so this shows individuals fighting rather than formations clashing. On the fourth-century BC Nereid Monument, two hoplites clash while the one on the left is supported by an archer.

This close-up of a hoplite on the Nereid Monument shows the unique design of the Greek *aspis*, or shield, whose considerable weight was supported by a double grip. The arm was thrust through a strap near the centre, the *antilabe*, while the hand gripped the *porpax* near the rim.

Greek armies did not develop sophisticated siege techniques, which meant that even a fairly basic wall was enough to fend off most Greek opponents; direct assaults like this were very rare. Almost every Greek city was surrounded by a defensive wall, although the sprawling community of Sparta was not.

This bronze statuette (*c.* sixth century BC) is believed to depict a Spartan wearing a helmet and swathed in a cloak, with his long, carefully plaited hair clearly shown. The transverse crest is unusual, so this man may have been an officer.

In earlier periods, the Athenian Acropolis was the inner stronghold and sanctuary for its citizens, although it swiftly fell to the Persians in 480 BC. Later generations turned it into a monumental and sacred celebration of the glories of their city, epitomised by the Parthenon.

Little trace of fifth-century BC Sparta is visible today, proving Thucydides's claim that future visitors would struggle to understand just how powerful and important the city was from the remains it left behind. Those visible here date from the Roman period, when Sparta was virtually a museum of no political or military significance.

The Spartans were unusual among the Greek communities for the freedom given to their women, and especially the daughters and wives of the well off. They were famous for their choral singing and dancing as well as their athleticism. This bronze statuette most likely depicts a girl competing in a race, although others prefer to see her as dancing.

Athenians of later generations greatly revered Aristogiton (bearded on the far left) and his younger lover Harmodius (on the right) for murdering the tyrant Hipparchus (centre). Yet the truth was that their act did not end the tyranny, and Hipparchus's brother was only expelled years later with Spartan military assistance.

Athenian democracy placed 'the people' at the heart of decision-making as well as elections. Here, on the Pnyx Hill, a substantial proportion of male citizens assembled on multiple occasions throughout the year to debate and decide all significant—and many minor—issues facing the community.

For Athens this was a genuine existential crisis, for defeat would mean, at the very least, the end of its democracy, even if the city might be allowed to continue under the command of Hippias and as a subject of Persia. In the circumstances, it made sense to field and equip as many fighting men as possible. It is reasonable to suppose that men not formally obliged to serve as hoplites did their best to find sufficient equipment to take their place in the ranks with shield, spear, knife, and a basic helmet or leather cap. Not every Athenian man was present, for some were surely ill, infirm, or too old to go with the army, and some men may have been stationed elsewhere, for instance, remaining in Athens itself in case the Persians managed to march—or sail—past the main force. Nothing more is heard of the 4,000 men allocated land in Euboea, and although many assume that they joined the main army, the sources simply do not say.[15]

Herodotus presents the army as jointly led by the ten generals, presided over rather than commanded by Callimachus. The Historian was probably wrong to assert that the polemarch was chosen by lot, since at this stage the position was still elected and the transition to allocating archons randomly to specific posts 'by the bean' was introduced sometime after 490 BC. Miltiades had served under Darius, so had some experience of how the Persians waged war, and he had also fought campaigns on his own behalf as warlord of his little principality. Quite a few Athenians had also played a role in their own state's comparatively recent wars—for instance, in the victory over Chalkis and the two defeats inflicted on the Thebans. Plenty of men, probably including Callimachus and at least some of the generals, had fought and won before, so that by Greek standards this was a fairly experienced army. Like all Greek armies it was mixed, most of all in age, with teenagers standing shoulder to shoulder with men in their sixties, and the presence of newly freed slaves made it even more varied than usual, with aristocrats, farmers, former slaves, and better-off craftsmen. Aeschylus, already making a name for himself as a playwright, was there, ready to fight in the phalanx, as was his brother. This was an army of neighbours and kinsmen, although since Attica and its population were large, everyone did not know everyone else. Yet the communities were there, with the demes and tribes.[16]

Many of the Athenians were veterans of earlier wars, but none of them had fought a Persian army in the open field. It is also quite possible that the Persians had never before faced an army dominated by hoplites. Ionian Greeks and Carians employed hoplite equipment, but whether the main strength of their field forces during the Ionian revolt lay in hoplites or other troops is not at all clear. Regardless of the details, the Persians had won every major land battle during that conflict, so had plenty of reasons to feel confident. That really was the point. The Athenians and Plataeans faced an army sent by the greatest power in the known world, an army used to crushing all opponents, so it was natural to be intimidated.

Herodotus and the other sources imply or claim that the Persian army was also a lot larger than the Greek force, so that numbers were against them as well. Many of the modern estimates for the opposing sides suggest that the Greeks were outnumbered by at least two to one, not counting the sailors of the Persian fleet, who added to the impression of a vast horde even if their battlefield capacity was limited. Caution is needed, since all the estimates of numbers on each side are highly conjectural, and throughout history many armies have often believed that they were outnumbered when this was not really true. A high proportion of the Persian army were bowmen and very good ones, whereas there were few if any archers among the Greeks, certainly not enough to play a significant tactical role. While wealthier Athenians and Plataeans most likely rode to Marathon, they would take their place on foot in the phalanx for the battle itself, and the Greek army had no cavalry with it. In contrast the Persians had gone to great effort to bring horses, and Herodotus gives the suitability of the country for horsemen as one of the appeals of landing at Marathon. Estimates of the number of cavalrymen in the expeditionary force at Marathon vary from a couple of hundred to around 1,000, although, as usual, these are guesses.

The Persians camped near the shore were a very different opponent from any the Athenians and their allies had ever faced in the past. Numbers were—or at the very least seemed to be—strongly against them, and this was enough to give pause to the leaders of the Greek army. However, there was lively expectation of Spartan assistance, and the fame of the Spartans as fighting men surpassed that of any other Greeks, so it made sense to wait for their reinforcement before seeking battle. Philipiddes had gone to Sparta to report the Persians' arrival. A well-trained athlete and trusted messenger, he ran the 140 or so miles from Athens to Sparta in two days. The route was not easy, and en route it was claimed that he encountered the god Pan, who asked why the Athenians did so little to revere him when he was so well disposed to them.[17]

When they received the request for aid, the Spartans similarly expressed themselves as well disposed but explained that they were in the middle of a religious festival—identified as the nine-day Carneia—and were forbidden by solemn law from setting out for war before the next full moon, which brought the rituals to an end. In the fourth century BC Plato was sceptical of this explanation and claimed that the Spartans were actually busy suppressing a rising among the helots, not specifically mentioned anywhere else. The balance of probability favours Herodotus, and the implication is that the Athenians were unaware of this custom, which casts some doubt on suggestions that the Persians, informed by Hippias, had deliberately chosen to land at a time when the Spartans were preoccupied. Either way, the Spartans were not coming for a while, and within a few days Philipiddes had brought the disappointing news to Athens, from where it was conveyed to the commanders at Marathon.[18]

The two armies had already spent at least four or five days watching each other, just a couple of miles apart. Herodotus does not say so, but there is a good chance that, on most or all of these days, each

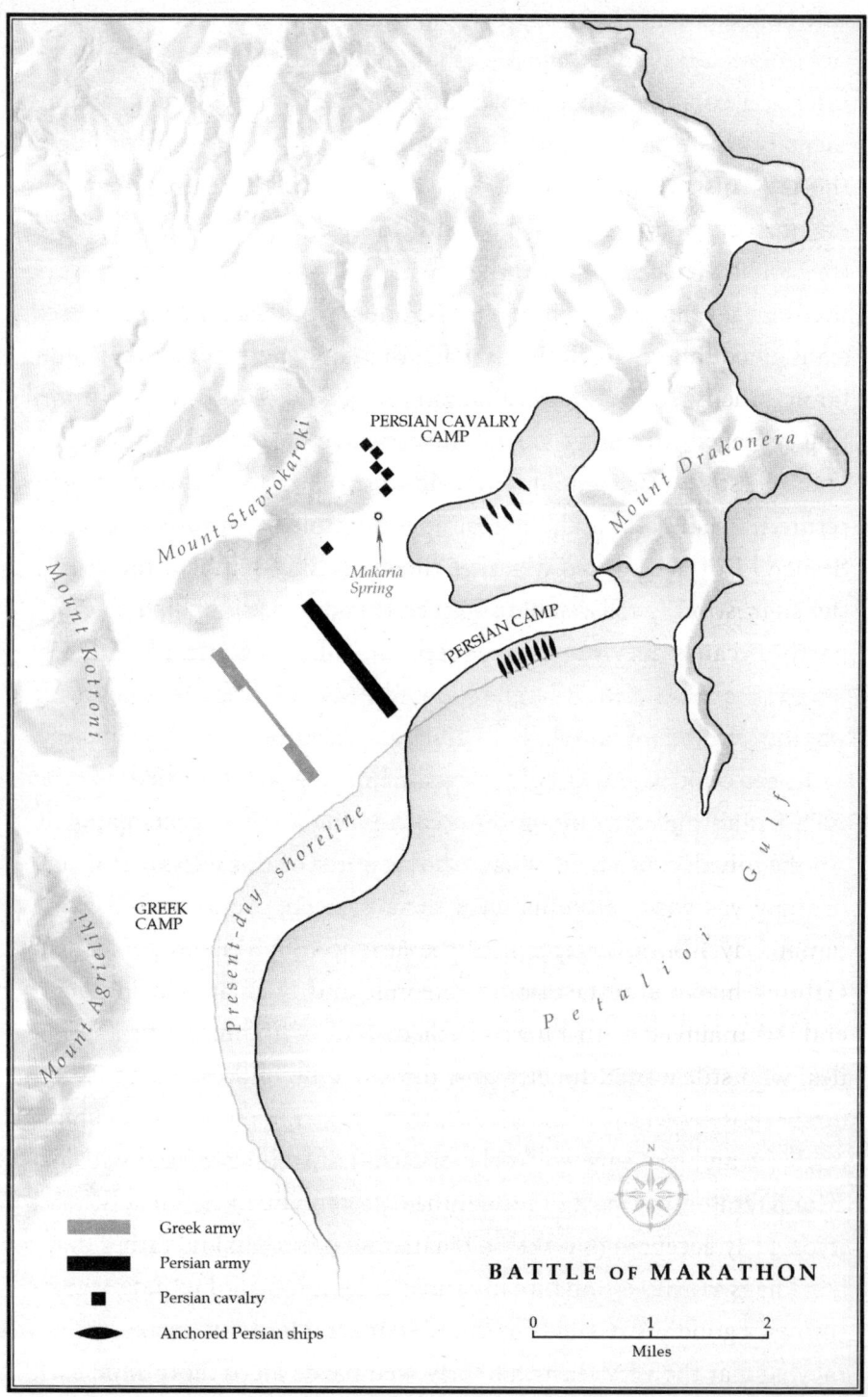

side formed up in battle order, challenging the other to advance and fight. The Greeks were on higher ground, and even a slight slope offered a considerable advantage in battle. They were reluctant to sacrifice this edge and move down onto the more open plain, and the Persians in turn did not wish to attack up a hill. Commanders on each side were able to assure their men that the enemy was too frightened of them to fight, while each became more used to the strange appearance of the opposition. Hippias was with the Persians, encouraging them in the belief that his family remained popular at Athens, so that defections were likely. Herodotus tells a story that the aged former tyrant dreamt of having sex with his mother and at first saw this as a sign that his homeland would welcome his return as leader. Then he fell on landing ashore, lost a tooth, and despaired of his hopes. Whether there was any truth in the story, the suggestion is reasonable that the Persians were willing to wait partly because they hoped that Athenian unity would collapse. A later source does claim that heralds were sent in attempts to negotiate with the Athenians.[19]

In Herodotus's version of events, Miltiades saw the need for the army to advance and attack the enemy, but the ten generals were equally divided between those who agreed and those who still felt caution was wiser. Command of the army supposedly passed from day to day from one general to the next until Miltiades persuaded Callimachus to give the casting vote in favour of an attack. The generals who agreed with him gave their days of command to Miltiades, who still waited for his own day of command to act. Scholars doubt most of this, for the idea of such shared command does seem unlikely, and see some sort of alternation of responsibility as senior administrator, a sort of officer of the day, as more likely. In addition, it is widely accepted that the polemarch was in command rather than serving as little more than a chairman. Still, it is hard to judge what seemed a good way to do things in a young and self-confident democracy, and at the very least they may well have placed more emphasis on debate and corporate decision-making than more formal armies of later eras.[20]

The Battle of Marathon proved a great victory, one that became an important and much celebrated moment for the Athenians, but Herodotus's account leaves many unanswered questions, and the meagre other sources are late and of dubious reliability. Thus, the many attempts to reconstruct what happened vary over almost every detail. Certainty is impossible, and it would take many pages even to survey the main points of controversy, so that the account that follows will do its best to stick to the essence and only address some aspects where the issue is truly fundamental.[21]

Days, at least five and perhaps seven or even ten, passed with the two armies in close proximity but neither willing to force an action. During that time the men on both sides had to eat and drink. Since they were within Attica, family members or slaves could have walked to the camp to bring the Athenians and their allies supplies once the initial rations began to run out. The Persians presumably brought the bulk of their food with them by ship and foraged to supplement this. During the Roman period, visitors to Marathon were shown troughs supposedly used to water the Persian horses. Feeding men and animals for days on end required organisation and effort, as did the disposal of waste, both human and animal, to minimise the risk of disease. These factors tended to limit just how long armies were willing to face off against each other before one either forced battle or moved away. There is no indication that this limit had been reached at Marathon, but it is a factor to bear in mind.[22]

The central question is why the Athenians and their allies waited for so many days and then decided to attack, and did so aggressively and quickly. Herodotus simply states that Miltiades wanted to fight a battle all along and waited for the day when it was his turn to be the senior general. Most scholars assume that something must have changed on that day, offering an opportunity not present before. One theory, which rests in part on the explanation of a Greek phrase given in a late Roman textbook written fifteen centuries after the battle—hence closer to today than to 490 BC—claims that the Persians had decided against pushing their way through the Athenians. Instead, they would re-embark and use the mobility offered by their ships to land further down the coast. Miltiades realised that the enemy cavalry horses had gone back on board the transports, removing this dangerous part of Persian army, so decided to attack—hence the fact that Herodotus makes no mention at all of the cavalry in his account of the fighting. While it is true that he does not, he also fails to mention lots of things about the battle. Later tradition claimed that the neighing of ghostly horses could be heard at Marathon centuries later, and a grand painting of the battle made at Athens a few decades afterward does appear to have shown at least one Persian horseman. All in all, the re-embarkation of the Persian cavalry rests on no good evidence but has proved surprisingly persistent in modern accounts of the battle.[23]

More plausible are variations arguing that the Persian horsemen were present but not in their proper place to play a significant role in the fighting. Horses need care and attention, and in the fourth century BC Xenophon states that the Persian custom was to hobble them at night far enough away from the enemy that there was no risk of the animals falling prey to a surprise attack. Thus it is suggested that the mounts were taken each night well beyond the Persian camp on the side furthest from the Greeks. Each morning, the Persians formed up and advanced towards, but not too close to, the Athenians to offer battle without forcing the issue. On this morning, the Persian infantry were ready in position, but the cavalry were late, delayed for some reason—one theory is that the moon set unexpectedly late. Spotting this, Miltiades—or Callimachus—gave the order to attack before the horsemen could join the main force. An alternative theory shifts the battle nearer to sunset than sunrise and suggests that the Greeks realised that the Persian cavalry were quitting the battle-line earlier each day, giving them an opportunity. Such ideas are interesting, definitely plausible, and impossible to prove one way or the other.[24]

For whatever reason, the Athenians and Plataeans decided to attack. Herodotus's account more naturally suggests this occurred at the start of the day but is not explicit. They came down onto the level ground and formed the ten regiments of Athenians in a line with the Plataeans on their left. About a mile away the Persians were forming their own battle-line—or had done so often enough for its length and structure to be clear. They may have been wrong-footed because the enemy had suddenly decided to advance far further than before but do not appear to have been in serious disarray. The centre comprised Persians and Saka, who were nomads from the north-eastern borders of the empire, famous as cavalry, particularly horse archers, but in this case perhaps fighting on foot. Herodotus says nothing about the ethnic composition of the rest of the line. To match the frontage of the enemy army, Miltiades made the phalanx shallower in the centre. Scholars often assume that the hoplites were in four ranks there and eight ranks on the wings, but once again this is conjecture. It does suggest a desire to avoid being outflanked and, given what happened, some forward planning to cope should the centre prove too thin and give way.[25]

Once formed up, the Athenians and Plataeans charged. In later tradition Miltiades shouts out a simple 'Rush at them!' Herodotus says that they were the first Greeks to attack at a run and claims that the Persians were surprised to see them coming on 'without cavalry or archers'. He gives the distance as eight stades, which is roughly a mile and a very long way to run, especially wearing helmet and armour, carrying a shield and spear, and needing enough energy to fight afterwards. Understandably, most scholars have been sceptical of this, although debate continues about just how far hoplites *could* have run, while it is hard to gauge the validity of modern experiments, given doubts about the actual weight of equipment, let alone the differences between modern Westerners and fifth century BC Greeks. Probably they began at a brisk walk, advancing with considerable determination markedly in contrast with the reluctance to engage shown so far. The walk speeded up, turning into a jog and finally a running charge, perhaps over the last couple of hundred yards.[26]

The Persians do not appear to have advanced to meet them. After all, they were strong in archers, so the usual tactic was to wait and deluge the enemy as he approached. Past experience for the Persians was in the main against opponents who fought in a similar way, edging forward by slow steps and pausing regularly to shoot their own missiles. Persian cavalry relied on javelins and bows to harass and wear an enemy down, only charging, spear or sword in hand, once the enemy was wavering. If there were horsemen in place in the battle-line, any move forward to start weakening the Greeks with missiles would quickly have pulled back. It was simply not the job of the cavalry to meet well-armoured infantry head-on, but usually battles were slower affairs and there was time for the missile-armed troops to do their work. As importantly, after months at sea, periodically landing on Euboea and elsewhere, the horses were not likely in a very good state, limiting the performance of the cavalry.

The Greeks did not pause but kept on coming. Perhaps some hoplites were still carrying throwing spears, but in this case they either did not throw them at all or, less probably, scarcely checked before surging forward. Arrows began to fill the air. Persian archers were good and used sophisticated composite bows that could send an arrow 300 yards or more, although they were more effective at 200 yards or less. A storm of arrows made a lot of noise, and instinct would encourage men with shields to cluster together and crouch behind this protection—especially when backed by archers of their own able to reply.

Yet the Greeks did not stop. No doubt some fell, mostly wounded rather than killed, for hoplite equipment offered good protection against a fatal strike from the bronze-headed arrows favoured by the Persians. Scholars largely agree that the Athenians and Plataeans ran the last 200 yards or so, moving as fast as they could through the most intense killing zone of the enemy archers, a recognised tactic in later periods. Whether they were ordered to do this or were propelled by instinct and the enthusiasm of a great crowd of kinsmen and neighbours rushing on to drive invaders off their land does not really matter. The price of going fast was an inevitable loss of order and formation, and charging faster and further than usual exacerbated this. Whatever view is taken of the density of a phalanx in normal conditions, at Marathon the Greeks reached the Persian lines far more as a loose crowd than as neat ranks and files. There is often a reluctance to think in such terms, but apart from the gleaming bronze, there was probably little difference between this attack and the onslaughts of many tribal armies, for instance, the Gauls or, for that matter, the Highland charge at Culloden. The Greeks came on fast, yelling war cries, usually an ululation, and facing this oncoming horde would test the nerves of any defender.

The Persians did not break. Their arrows had not slowed, let alone stopped, the enemy, and this was not the way they expected battles to work, but the soldiers of the great king held firm. Men in the front rank or ranks had short spears and carried large shields. How many had armour, especially metal body armour, is hard to say, and metallic helmets appear to have been very rare. Overall, the Persians were less well protected than the Greeks, for their shields were wicker and leather rather than wood, designed to stop arrows rather than spear thrusts delivered at close range. In turn the Persian spears were markedly shorter than those carried by hoplites.

Some Greeks may have turned their pelting charge into an immediate attack, slamming into the defending line and trying to put all the momentum behind their spear thrusts. More probably the pace slackened at the last moment, when it was clear that the Persians were not about to flee. Men slowed down, groups forming so that they could support each other. Once they felt ready, they stepped across the last few paces to jab at the Persians. Herodotus states that the fighting went on 'for a long time', which begs the question of just what this meant. At the least it suggests that the struggle was considered hard fought. For all that their equipment put them at a disadvantage against the Greeks, the Persians did not give way easily. In the centre, where the Athenian line was shallowest and the Persians were the elite of the army, the Greeks began to step back, giving ground. After a while, some gave way and fled, pursued by the enemy.[27]

On the two wings the story was different. The Greeks were in greater numbers there, and the Persians gave way, routing back towards their camp. Some of the hoplites may have obeyed their instincts and followed, but many, perhaps most, did something truly remarkable. They rallied, re-formed into some sort of order facing towards the victorious Persian centre, and routed them in turn. While likely part of a plan, this still speaks very highly of the leadership of Miltiades, Callimachus, and many other unnamed men who made it happen in the chaos of a battle. The move left the whole Persian army in retreat and much of it in rout. Fighting continued as the Greeks chased them, with lots of scrappy little encounters between small groups. Some of the Persians got caught in the salt marshes and were slaughtered. Greeks reached some of the beached or moored ships, most likely an outlying group of vessels. Callimachus was killed trying to capture them. Aeschylus's brother grabbed hold of the stern of one vessel, only to have his arm cut off. He died because they were unable to stop the flow of blood.[28]

Seven ships were captured, but the remainder got away, carrying the substantial number of survivors from the Persian army. This suggests that exhaustion brought the pursuit to an end and that the bulk of the camp and anchorage was at the far end of the plain and not reached by any organised attack. There was time for the Persians to escape and apparently re-embark in some sort of order. Herodotus states that the Greeks counted some 6,400 Persian corpses in the aftermath of the fighting, and there is no convincing reason not to accept this as broadly accurate. The Athenians collected 192 of their own dead, burned the bodies, and interred them on the field, eventually piling up a burial mound (*soros*) visible to this day. The Plataeans and the freed slaves who fell were buried separately, and although a burial site has been associated with this, not everyone is convinced, and it does not provide a definite total for their losses. Hoplite armour gave good protection, suggesting that there were at least several times more injured men needing care than there were fatalities.[29]

The battle was won, and clearly won, but the campaign was not quite over. Herodotus tells us that a shield was raised as some sort of signal, presumably from a 'fifth column' in Attica favouring the Persians. He says that afterwards some blamed the Alcmaeonid family, but he did not believe this himself and could find no real explanation of the incident. Whether in response to this or simply still hoping for victory, the Persian fleet gathered itself and then set sail towards Athens. Worried that their home might fall, nine of the Athenian tribal regiments wearily gathered everyone fit to move and began the march back to the city, while the other tenth remained to deal with casualties and secure the battlefield. The Athenians won the race, helped by the shape of the coast and the prevailing winds, which meant that the Persians came more slowly. Whether or not the Persian commanders had genuinely hoped to take the city and were deterred by the sight of defending forces mustering, no attempt was made. Instead the Persian fleet turned about and sailed away. The first Persian invasion of mainland Greece was over.[30]

In later years a story grew up of a runner, variously named, who preceded the Athenian main force on the march back to Athens. His job was to carry the news of the triumph, both to reassure the families of the men who had fought and to deter anyone who might wonder whether the time had come to switch sides. So that he did not appear to be a straggler fleeing disaster, he carried his arms, forcing the pace to arrive as soon as he could. The strain was so much that, barely having had time to gasp the good news, he dropped dead from exhaustion. It is a good story and helped inspire the modern marathon race, but Herodotus does not mention it, and since he dearly loved a good story, this strongly suggests a later invention.³¹

Herodotus does describe the arrival of the Spartan reinforcements too late to take part in the fighting. They numbered 2,000, no doubt with servants and helots in support, and had completed the march in three days, a very quick time for a formed body rather than an individual runner. This suggests that they were younger men, fit even by Spartan standards, judged capable of getting to Attica quickly. If not the entire Spartan army, it was a significant contribution to the war, and there is no hint that they arrived late by design. Inspecting the battlefield and the Persian dead, they praised the Athenians and Plataeans for their victory before going home. This time the Spartans had missed out on the glory.³²

11

THE SHIPS AND THE CONFERENCE

Greece between the two Persian invasions, the creation of the Athenian navy, and the Spartan call for unity, 490–480 BC

THE BATTLE OF MARATHON HAS OFTEN ASSUMED IMMENSE importance—for instance, becoming the first encounter included in Edward Creasey's 1851 *Decisive Battles of the World: From Marathon to Waterloo*, which enjoyed such wide popularity that it was republished with a frequency rivalling Charles Darwin's *On the Origin of Species*. Both had a theme of development as the success of those deserving success, a sentiment appealing to confident Victorian society. John Stuart Mill famously felt that Marathon had had a greater impact on Victorian Englishmen than the Battle of Hastings in 1066. Greek, and specifically Athenian, culture was rightly seen as highly influential on the unfolding of subsequent history, most of all the development of Western societies, and Marathon was felt to have saved that culture when it was only just beginning to flourish. If the Athenians had been beaten, the assumption was, Athens would have become a subject state of Persia ruled by Hippias and his successors, the light of democracy would have failed, and without it, the explosion of ideas, of art and architecture, drama and comedy, philosophy and history, all focused in and around that city, would not have occurred.[1]

Since the Athenians and Plataeans won the day, it is impossible to know precisely what would have happened if the outcome had been different, and considering the what-ifs of history always warrants caution. The hoplites won the battle, and Athenian democracy flourished, surviving the far greater threat of a second Persian invasion a decade later. It is doubtful that everything would have occurred in exactly the same way if they had lost, but extending this to make all events of the next two and half millennia wholly dependent on the clash on the plain at Marathon is at best a gross simplification. Hindsight is always an obstacle to understanding history, and a sense—right or wrong—that a moment was especially pivotal only makes the task harder. As far as is possible, the aim must be to understand the significance of an event at the time and in the immediate aftermath for people who did not know what the future held.

The Spartan contingent had arrived too late to fight, which was surely a disappointment, especially as the battle had gone so well. The lion's share of the glory went to the Athenians, and most of what was left, to the Plataeans, and according to Herodotus the Spartans were generous in their praise. His narrative suggests that they felt a need to explain why they were too late but at the same time shows that they could take pride in their willingness to stand with the handful of states actively opposing the Persians. In the event, the Spartan contribution proved essentially moral, adding to the resolve of the others. The key thing was that the war was won, and the Persian expeditionary force had retreated. No Persian garrison was left on mainland Greece, or on Euboea, or even at Eretria itself. The forces of the great king had attacked and been repulsed, suffering casualties that would have crippled any Greek city for a generation. So late in the year, there was no real prospect of the Persians returning, and the defeat they had suffered might prove enough to deter them forever.[2]

Herodotus, knowing that this was not true and that a second invasion would follow in 480 BC, depicted Darius as outraged at the defeat and determined to exact revenge. In his narrative, planning and preparation for a much grander expedition to Greece was the central concern of the Persian Empire for the next ten years, and he gives few details of other events. This was natural enough. The struggle with Persia was of fundamental importance to Greeks and a source of immense pride, making it natural for them to assume that it was just as important for their opponents, forgetting the sheer size and strength of the Achaemenid Empire. Marathon was a defeat at the end of a highly successful campaign. A succession of island communities had submitted from the start, while those that offered resistance had been beaten. A visible proof of success came in the form of the captives from Eretria, settled at the king's pleasure deep within his empire. Although Athens remained unpunished, the campaign could readily be presented as a mostly successful operation against savage and unsophisticated peoples on the fringes of the empire.[3]

Cyrus, Cambyses, and Darius had all suffered some military failures, without these diminishing the overwhelmingly successful record of their armies. Only seven ships had been lost, far fewer than had sunk in the storm just three years earlier off Mount Athos. Casualties were higher, but not on a scale that seriously diminished the military might of the empire. The Athenians and the Spartans, and still more the Plataeans, remained little peoples, no more than very local powers, which in no way represented a major threat to the prosperity, let alone survival, of the Persian Empire. From Darius's perspective, the repulse of his expedition was disappointing, but the mainland Greeks remained an irritant rather than a major concern. They deserved punishment for the burning of Sardis and the killing of his envoys and now for the defeat at Marathon. At the same time, expansion and conquest were natural for a divinely approved great king and protector of the Truth, and Greece was a region worth conquering, not least because it would facilitate control of the communities in Ionia and on the islands already part of the empire.

There is no reason to believe that Athens, Sparta, and the Greeks in general were not of some concern to Darius, and in turn to his son and successor, Xerxes, but this remained one issue among very many others. Similarly, although the ideology of rule over the world and a divine mission on earth encouraged expansion, this did not compel the Persians to unrelenting wars of conquest. Herodotus tells us almost nothing about Darius's activities in the years immediately after Marathon, which means no more than that the great king was occupied with tasks not directly involving the Greeks. He does mention a rebellion in Egypt in around 486 BC, although he gives very little information about it. As Egypt had been a great power and was a large province rich in resources, reasserting control there was a priority demanding the attention of the great king and the allocation of considerable troops and supplies. By comparison, any dealings with the Athenians and Spartans were very minor affairs.

The revolt in Egypt was put down, although Darius died before this was complete. Xerxes was not his eldest son but had the advantage of being the child of Atossa, daughter of Cyrus the Great. He seems to have been marked as successor during his father's lifetime, and his siblings offered no challenge. Even more strikingly, none of his family was executed on his accession to the throne, making this wholly bloodless transition of power unique in Achaemenid history. This was a mark of the stability created by Darius and most likely also of Xerxes's own considerable ability as a politician and administrator. Around the time that the rebellion in Egypt was suppressed, there was a revolt in Babylonia, which again took a couple of years to defeat. Taken together, the internal revolts, the succession, and the establishment of a new regime under a great king who appears to have had a particular interest in reforming the administration and structure of the empire kept Darius, Xerxes, and their senior advisors very busy for much of the decade after Marathon. Given the poverty of the sources, there may quite possibly have also been other matters to preoccupy them during the 480s BC. For the moment, settling scores with Athens and Sparta was neither urgent nor sufficiently important.[4]

UNDERSTANDABLY, THE ATHENIAN perception of Marathon was wholly different. An invading army sent by the greatest empire in existence had landed in Attica and had been routed. This was a spectacular victory, seen from the very start as miraculous, and the gods were believed to have fought on the side of the Athenians and Plataeans. Before the battle, a vow was made to sacrifice to Artemis one goat for every enemy slain. Since the Persian death toll was estimated at over 6,000, this caused a practical problem; it was decided that the goddess would be content with 500 animals but that the offering would be repeated every year. Pan received more honours in response to the message brought by Philipiddes, and there was talk of local deities and heroes appearing during the battle itself, including one wielding a plough stave as a club. Herodotus also tells a story of a supernatural being fighting for the Persians. An Athenian was supposed to have seen this massive hoplite coming at him. The apparition killed the man standing beside him, but the sight was so terrifying that the Athenian became blind and never recovered—perhaps a psychological response to the trauma of combat.[5]

If the Persians had had divine aid, then it had proved weaker than the gods and heroes on the Greek side, proving that the latter's cause was pleasing to the heavens. Ritual and religion intertwined with every aspect of life in the ancient world, so that it was natural to honour the gods as the source of success. Since the victory was so immense—as well as surprising—the Athenians were especially eager to parade this divine support. At the same time, they celebrated the humans involved. Their honoured dead were interred on the battlefield under the great mound, whereas in the past the norm appears to have been to bring the remains back to Athens whenever possible. Monuments and memorials were erected on the field and at Athens on the Acropolis. Callimachus received praise, but Miltiades got much of the credit and was given a monument at Marathon. In addition, when trophies were sent to be dedicated at Delphi and at the shrine of Zeus at Olympia, Miltiades was permitted to make a dedication on his own behalf at Olympia, and a helmet inscribed with his name was excavated at the site. It is a Corinthian-style helmet, so perhaps the one he wore during the battle, unless it was taken from an Ionian or Carian fighting on the other side.[6]

The victory at Marathon was seen as yet another vindication of the democratic system and one far greater than the successes over Thebans and Euboeans. Better yet, it was a battle won by citizens of good standing, the men who brought their own equipment to charge and fight as hoplites in the phalanx. If the poorest were there and did their best to fight in support of the heavy infantry, then they did not warrant inclusion in the accounts or the subsequent artistic depictions of the fighting. Perhaps the story of a hero fighting with a piece of a plough hints at the involvement of labourers using improvised weapons alongside the men of substance, but that is the closest to a mention of anyone who was not a hoplite during the fighting. The hoplites included the rich, fighting alongside thousands of others of middling income and some with comparatively little property. There is a good chance that some of the fighters were *thêtes* from the upper levels of that lowest economic class, with enough property to acquire the basics of hoplite equipment—at least a shield and spear—and there were also the freed slaves.

The people, the demos, had fought together, shoulder to shoulder, and won together. Later tradition maintained that the poet Aeschylus wrote his own epitaph and spoke only of fighting at Marathon, ignoring his immense contribution to the arts. What mattered was that he had gone as a citizen of status to face and defeat the 'Mede'. One story claimed that Miltiades asked for the right to wear a wreath as a mark of his leading role in the victory. This was declined, and someone commented that if he ever won a battle on his own, only then would he be entitled to such an honour. Marathon was a victory of the Athenians acting together and, most of all, of the men of property—even small amounts of property—fighting to protect their community. For the ideology of the still-young democracy, it was the right sort of victory.[7]

Triumphant over the Persians and the elderly tyrant who had accompanied them, the Athenians had preserved their right to live as free citizens, competing, debating, and arguing. Rumours circulated that some of the Alcmaeonid family were responsible for the shield signal made after the battle, with the implication that they were in league with Hippias and his supporters and hoped for a return of the tyranny. Herodotus did not believe the charge, but in all the euphoria of victory, there was clearly a return to bitter rivalries between prominent men. Miltiades failed to get all the honours he wanted but was able to persuade his fellow citizens to appoint him to command an expedition to the islands so recently overrun by the Persians. Details are obscure, for Herodotus's account is confusing and not very plausible, which probably reflects accusations and rumour flourishing after the events.[8]

In 479 BC Miltiades led an expedition of some seventy ships, apparently enjoying minor successes before landing on the island of Paros and besieging the city. The attempt failed, as sieges so often did, since most Greek armies lacked the skill, organization, and determination necessary to capture a walled city. At some point Miltiades was injured in the leg, and the wound became infected. Returning to Athens, he was charged with misleading the people about his intentions or betraying them in some other way, crimes punishable by death. By now he was dying of gangrene and unable to stand, let alone appear at the trial to defend himself in person. The Athenians still found him guilty, although there was sufficient memory of his past services and consideration for his condition to impose a fine instead of executing him. Miltiades lived long enough to know the verdict, but the sum of fifty silver talents* was paid by his remaining

---

* The standard for a talent weight varied, but later the Attic talent weighed about fifty-seven pounds (twenty-six kilograms) and, if silver, was equivalent to 6,000 drachmas.

son, Cimon, whose brother lived out his life in the Achaemenid Empire. This was a huge amount and testifies to the wealth Miltiades had managed to bring back to Athens with him and, just possibly, to extortion in the recent campaign. Cimon was still young, and the extent of family wealth and property was such that even after paying this fine, he was able in due course to emerge as one of the leading men in Athens.[9]

MILTIADES'S DEATH REMOVED one of the most prestigious men from Athenian public life, shifting the balance between those left who were seeking office and honour. Wealth and family mattered in public life at Athens, but more important was winning and retaining the favour of the people, especially those able and willing to attend meetings of the Assembly. Late in 487 BC, for the first time, a majority of the citizens met and voted to ostracise a fellow citizen, removing one of the leading figures in public life. The chosen victim was Hipparchus, a relative of Pisistratus and leader of many former supporters of the tyrant and his sons. Aristotle felt that it was a sign of the inherent mildness of the Athenians that many such men had been accepted as members of the community for so long after the fall of the tyranny. In both 486 and 485 BC the people again voted to send a man into ten-year exile; Aristotle claimed that these men were connected to the Pisistratids and implied that this was the chief motivation for their ostracism. He viewed the vote to ostracise a man named Xanthippus in 484 BC as different, not in any way connected with tyranny, and implies that the same was true of ostracisms in subsequent years.[10]

Cleisthenes is said to have instituted ostracism, but the first attested use of the process was not until 487 BC, leading some scholars to argue that it was actually created in that year. This is just one of many puzzles about the process and, in particular, its frequent use in the 480s BC. Aristotle wrote in the fourth century BC, long after the events, and the vagueness of his wording has led to speculation over whether he meant tyranny in the specific context of association with Pisistratus and his sons, even though Hippias was by this time very old, if he was still alive at all. It seems improbable that there were significant numbers of Athenians eager for the return of such a geriatric leader, and no specific heir to the line is ever mentioned in the sources. For some, it was not the Pisistratids but their Persian backers who were feared, and the tyranny could be taken to refer directly to the rule of the Achaemenid Empire, so that the first ostracisms happened because of suspicion—justified or not—that the men involved were sympathetic to or even partisans of the Persians.

This would not explain subsequent ostracisms, and great care is needed, for it is hard to judge how much the Athenians knew about Persian actions and activities or indeed the extent to which there was active consideration of and preparation for a renewed attack on Greece. The decade can be seen as dominated by an ongoing threat from Persia, but there simply is not the evidence to prove the case one way or the other. Surviving ostraca, the fragments of pottery on which a name was written to cast a vote, do occasionally include accusations of sympathy for the 'Medes' and in one case even a crude sketch of the man dressed as a Persian. However, although initially dated to the 480s BC, the find containing these is now generally considered to come from a decade or so later. Nor is it certain that a single factor such as this was decisive in any individual ostracism, even if it formed part of the accusations and insults bandied around at the time. The broader context was certainly of competition to lead the state, mainly between the wealthy and aristocratic, where personality mixed with policies and arguments made in the public debates and with perceptions of a man's character and ambitions, as well as his actual conduct while holding office.[11]

Such rivalry was characteristic of most Greek cities most of the time, as men struggled to prove that they were the best, most worthy of office and respect. The democracy did not change this drive to excel but instead made the people the ultimate arbiter. Gathered together, the majority approved or rejected proposals made to the Assembly and, if they voted in sufficient numbers against an individual, to ostracise him. Whatever the context, each individual ostracism was a collective decision, requiring 6,000 citizens to approve it—or possibly just the casting of 6,000 votes in total. The will of the demos, the people, was sovereign, and the process itself reminded all taking part of this truth. All were members of the community, and anyone angering a sufficiently large proportion of that citizen community faced a ten-year expulsion. The risk came only once each year, and the penalty could fall on only one man in a year, but this was a way of relieving tensions that in other cities might have led to violence. In each case the ostracised accepted their fate and went into exile, no doubt helped by the knowledge that they lost no property and would be permitted to return at the end of the decade.[12]

More than 10,000 ostraca have been excavated, apparently dumped after being counted. Although a single find dominates—the one now dated to the 470s BC—nearly all the men known to have been sent into exile are attested. Handwriting evidence indicates that those targeting a particular opponent often had quantities made up beforehand with the name written on them, ready for distribution to anyone unable or simply disinclined to provide and inscribe his own token. Most names appear on numerous surviving ostraca, although some are attested only once or twice, suggesting that individual citizens expressed their own grudges regardless of the wider mood, even though attention was generally focused on a small number of prominent men.[13]

QUITE A FEW Athenians voted to ostracise Themistocles during the 480s BC, though never enough for him to top the ballot and actually be sent into exile at this time. He was obviously a man of wealth but appears to have come from outside the established aristocracy of the city. His mother may not have been an Athenian, and the family lands were in rural Attica, while tradition maintained that he was ambitious from a very young age, practising oratory and argument. In 493/2 BC he was eponymous archon—the one who gave his name to the year officially—and began the process of building a proper port at the Piraeus some three miles south of Athens itself. Up until this point, Athens had relied on the natural harbour at Phaleron, but the new development provided docks, buildings for storage, and ship construction and maintenance. There may have been a military element and a sense that a city of the size and prestige of Athens, situated so comparatively near but not on the shore, ought to develop greater naval power. As important was the simple fact that Attica had long ceased to be self-supporting when it came to food and relied on substantial quantities of staples, such as wheat and barley, from abroad.[14]

According to Plutarch, Themistocles was elected as general by his tribe in 490 BC and positioned with his fellow tribesmen near the centre of the line at Marathon. He was probably about thirty at the time. After that, nothing is heard of him for the next seven years, although the ostraca bearing his name suggest that he was sufficiently well known to be disliked by a significant minority of Athenians. In 483/2 BC a plentiful new seam of silver deposits was discovered in the long-established mines at Laurium in Attica. These were publicly owned, assets of the city, and the custom in such circumstances appears to have been to share the profit equally among citizens. Themistocles proposed something different: that instead the state should use the silver to construct a fleet of triremes, the largest and most up-to-date warships in existence, and he convinced the majority of his fellow citizens to vote in favour. Herodotus says that the fleet was to be of 200 triremes, whereas Aristotle and others say that 100 were to be constructed. Either way, this represented an unprecedented expansion of Athenian naval strength, in both quality and quantity.[15]

As already mentioned, the boundary between trade and piracy or warfare was slim, and for many centuries this was reflected in ship design, with most vessels being suitable for both. Homer's warriors travelled to Troy in ships, as they did to other areas where they would raid or fight, and planned to go home the same way, although this would prove difficult for Odysseus. Much of the action in the *Iliad* describes Trojan attempts to reach and destroy the beached and anchored ships and the Achaeans' desperate and ultimately successful efforts to repulse them. Homer never mentions battles at sea, with the crews of ships fighting each other, and the use of ships in war in his poems is entirely a matter of transport. A vessel was designed to carry warriors and crew—the two largely the same—and men like Odysseus were accomplished helmsmen. It also needed space for supplies and to accommodate the loot and captives anticipated from a successful war. In trading ships the emphasis was more on cargo, but it was some while before a distinctive type of merchant ship appeared. This was fairly short and broad, hence the later name of 'round ships', and was handled by a small crew, relying as much or more on sailing than rowing.[16]

Ships meant for war were longer and slimmer and would later sometimes be called 'long ships'. By the eighth century BC, most common were the triaconter, with thirty oars, and especially the penteconter, with fifty oars. Neither had a deck, except probably a small platform at bow and stern. They had the option of raising a mast and sail when the wind was favourable but were primarily powered by rowing, and the design was an ancient one in most respects. Homer clearly imagined the ships in his stories as much like these, and the basic design dominated for centuries. Probably sometime in the eighth century BC, someone came up with the idea of fitting a ram to the prow of a penteconter, so that it could attack an enemy ship directly. This suggests that fighting ship to ship was now felt to be a real possibility, and presumably there were battles and skirmishes at sea, even if the primary role of these oared ships remained taking warriors to and bringing them back from where they fought on land.

The profound change came with the development of the trireme, far bigger in size and with a crew four times larger than the fifty rowers of a penteconter. This was a warship primarily designed to fight other ships, with no provision to carry substantial cargo or passengers, unless the number of oarsmen was drastically reduced, with a commensurate reduction in its fighting effectiveness. It completely outclassed a penteconter, relegating these to the fringes of any battle, in much the same way as ships of the line outclassed frigates in Lord Nelson's day. Like the latter and most other big warships throughout the ages, from dreadnoughts to aircraft carriers, the trireme was expensive to make and to operate, requiring a large and skilful crew. It is not certain who came up with the idea of building such a ship and why, although perhaps the adoption of rams on penteconters made people think more about the best way to fight at sea. The most likely candidates for inventing the trireme are the Phoenicians, probably near the end of the eighth century BC. Other sources credit the idea to the Corinthians, so perhaps they were the first Greeks to make and operate such ships.[17]

The name *trireme* means 'a three', and for generations a scholarly debate raged over just what this signified, with suggestions ranging from a ship with three banks of oars, each rowed by one man, to a ship with a single bank of oars, each rowed by three men, to various ideas of two banks of oars, the top one rowed by two men and the bottom one by a single oarsman. The question was resolved to—almost—universal satisfaction by the building and testing of the *Olympias*, a full-scale trireme, relying on educated deduction and guesswork to fill the many gaps in the primary sources. This was surely the most ambitious and successful exercise in experimental archaeology ever attempted. The reconstructed ship is some 121 feet (36.9 meters) long and 18 feet (5.5 meters) in the beam and has three rows of oars each rowed by one man. Thus, the name came from the size of a team of rowers on all three levels on one side of the ship. The crew consisted of 170 oarsmen and 30 deck crew and marines. Far more will be said about the findings of these experiments in later chapters, for triremes played a vital role in the power struggles of the fifth century BC, but for the moment it is worth emphasising that a trireme had a very large crew for its size. Operating a fully manned fleet of 200 vessels required 40,000 personnel, which shows the scale of the commitment the Athenians had voted to support.[18]

The Athenians had sent just twenty ships to assist the Ionians in 498 BC. In 489 BC they had put Miltiades in charge of a fleet of seventy vessels. In neither case is it clear whether any or all of the ships were triremes. Some probably were, and the Pisistratids had sent Miltiades off to the Dardanelles in a trireme, the earliest specific mention of such a ship in Athenian service. A few years before Themistocles's successful proposal, Athens had purchased twenty triremes from the Corinthians for use in their conflict with the island of Aegina. The Corinthians, sympathetic to the cause, gave them each vessel at a nominal price of just five silver drachma coins. Thus, it seems that the Athenians possessed some triremes before 483 BC, which may have led to the confusion in the sources. The decision may have been not to build 200 triremes but to create a fleet of 200 including existing ships. Even if Aristotle's figure of 100 new ships is correct, this still at least doubled the Athenians' naval power.[19]

In the past, ships appear to have been supplied by individuals, wealthy men who funded and maintained ships and crews and placed both them and themselves at the city's disposal in time of war. Equipping a penteconter was affordable for a significant number of aristocrats; these smaller ships could be used for trade as well as war and were valuable assets for those with connections overseas. A trireme was far more expensive, out of reach for more than a handful of the very wealthiest, and could only be used for war. Themistocles used state money to make ships that were then owned by the state, although the details of how this was managed are unclear. Aristotle claims that well-to-do citizens were given a talent of silver apiece and tasked with having a ship made and then equipping it. Similarity with the system in the later fifth and fourth centuries BC makes it possible that this is an anachronism, but it is hard to see how the city could conjure up an administrative structure to supervise such a huge project of fleet building so quickly. Probably the task was delegated to individuals, and this was well in keeping with the democratic ethos, entrusting tasks and funding to citizens to get the job done. Much of the material needed to come from abroad, most of all the timber, much of which was bought from Macedonia with silver from the new finds at Laurium.[20]

Themistocles presented his plan as necessary to deal with the Aeginetans, for a lot of the fighting with the islanders had gone badly. It is important to remember that before 480 BC, the Athenians had no great reputation for skill in naval warfare. Thucydides felt that privately Themistocles also had the Persian threat in mind and was surely right in this, although it is harder to say how far such a concern influenced the voters. While Herodotus's claim that the Persians were bent on a second invasion of Greece throughout the decade exaggerates, for an Athenian or Spartan to consider the possibility that they might return cannot have required great imagination. Similarly, if vengeance on Athens and the rest was not the primary concern for Darius and then Xerxes, it was an ambition, if and when it became possible. For Herodotus, the project became feasible once the Egyptian rebellion was stamped out, and active preparations for a new expedition to Greece filled the next four years. Given the sheer size of the Achaemenid Empire, organising and preparing for a major operation would require time, and if taken to mean that the project was under consideration and that plans were made and some preparations begun, then this focus is likely to be broadly true. This did not mean that Xerxes committed himself to the decision at such an early stage, only that he gave himself the option.[21]

Scholarly opinion is divided between those who see the Greek cities and the Persians as very well informed about what the other was doing and those who see both sides, especially the Greeks, as very ill informed, even uninterested. The truth likely lies somewhere between the two, and given the contact and trade across the Aegean, it is more reasonable to assume a fair degree of knowledge on both sides. From a Persian perspective, it was neither practical nor desirable to hide major preparations for war and better to parade the immense power of the great king's forces. The Athenians' decision to create the biggest and most modern fleet of any Greek state is unlikely to have gone unnoticed and was surely provocative from a Persian point of view, as a fairly recent enemy armed at an alarming rate.[22]

Little is known of Spartan affairs in the 480s BC, making it hard to know how far Persia entered into the thinking of its leaders during these years. Cleomenes may have still been alive at the time of Marathon but certainly did not live much longer. He was replaced by his half-brother, Leonidas, who was married to Cleomenes's daughter Gorgo. Such marriages of close kin appear intended to keep the lines of the two royal houses narrow and to prevent too many other men from having some claim to royalty. Gorgo is one of the few Greek women of the fifth century BC to appear in the surviving sources, advising both her father and her husband, always wisely.[23]

Herodotus does record that many Spartans became worried about the killing of the Persian envoys before Marathon, not because they regretted the rejection of the demand for earth and water but because it was an impiety. A community that prized a scrupulous honouring of the gods felt that this violation of the respect normally awarded to ambassadors might weaken their special relationship with the gods. After some discussion, two volunteers came forward and pledged to go to the great king and accept whatever punishment he chose to inflict on them. In this way, two would suffer and the rest be absolved of responsibility. When they finally arrived at the Persian court, Xerxes was impressed by their courage and willingness to sacrifice themselves on behalf of their fellow citizens. Instead of being executed, the men were lavishly entertained, praised, and sent home by the great king.[24]

By 481 BC, if not earlier, Xerxes was engaged in active diplomacy with the communities of the islands and mainland Greece. Once again, envoys arrived requesting earth and water, although this time none went to Sparta or Athens. If the incident with the two scapegoats dates to around this time and actually happened, he may have wanted to show the Spartans that he could be magnanimous and a good friend. This diplomacy, combined with a programme of shipbuilding, the gathering of contingents of soldiers, and the massing and moving of vast quantities of food and other supplies, made obvious that Xerxes was preparing for an expedition to Greece. Demaratus, the former king of Sparta and rival to Cleomenes, had long since ended up as a favoured guest at the Persian royal court, where he advised the great king about Greek customs and strengths. According to Herodotus, he also warned his former countrymen that Xerxes planned an invasion. In a story reminiscent of the message tattooed on a slave's scalp, the exiled king wrote on the wood of wax tablets and then had them covered with clean wax to hide the writing. Gorgo is credited with working out that a delivery of blank writing tablets must be a ploy of some sort and uncovering the hidden messages, but as always it is hard to know whether this is simply a good tale or contains any truth.[25]

However the Spartans learned of Xerxes's intentions, by 481 BC they were convinced that an invasion of Greece was likely, perhaps even inevitable, and asked other cities to send representatives to them for a conference, probably held in Sparta itself, although a second meeting was to be held at the Isthmus of Corinth. A fair few complied and sent a delegation, and the fact that most communities had already sent men to Delphi to seek the wisdom of the oracle shows a sense of the wider concern about what was expected to happen. This was traditional, an almost automatic response to any big decision, and apart from its hallowed and ancient reputation, the Pythian oracle at Delphi got things right—or at least could be interpreted to have been more or less accurate—often enough to maintain respect. It does appear to have relied upon gathering sufficient information to aid its predictions.

In this case, the messages were bleak and appeared based on an assessment of the overwhelming strength of the Persian Empire. The Athenians were told to flee when first they consulted the oracle. Advice from a local aristocrat moved them to try a second time and led to a second verse, still bleak, telling them to trust in the 'wooden walls' and suggesting that the island of Salamis would prove important, although not in a way that was clear or necessarily positive; only hindsight gave the explanation that the 'wooden walls' were the ships of the newly constructed fleet that would face and beat the enemy off Salamis. Around the same time the Spartans were given an answer telling them that either the state would fall or a king die. The death of a king, like the mention of Salamis, foreshadowed real events, leading some scholars to see both oracles as fabrications from after the war. Even so, the answers given seem to have been grim. Guided by Apollo or by shrewd gathering of information, the pronouncements issued did not encourage anyone to resist by promising divine aid or assurance of victory and instead suggested impending disaster.[26]

This may well have reflected the judgement of many communities, especially those that had no history of conflict with Persia and saw no reason to pay for the follies of the Athenians and Spartans. Some watched and waited; some gave earth and water, or at least a friendly response, to the Persian envoys, which did not mean that at this stage they were not also willing to send a deputation to the Spartan-organised council. How many states sent representatives is unclear. After the war, only thirty-one Greek cities were felt to have joined together to resist and defeat the Persians, although some others had given less support or had changed sides after their homelands were overrun. Sparta's allies attended, including Corinth, as did Athens, Plataea, and other cities from outside the Peloponnese. At this stage many were hedging their bets. The Aeginetans attended, even though they had given earth and water before 490 BC and were long-term enemies of Athens. Argos, the even more inveterate foe of Sparta, did not sent a delegation.

If anything, that so many Greek states sent envoys and that some chose to work together is more surprising than that the majority remained neutral or in time sided with the Persians. The Greeks accepted a kinship and broad cultural identity, but there was no 'Greece' in any political sense. Sparta, Athens, and then Corinth were the three biggest states involved, and many of the others were much smaller. Athens had the prestige of Marathon and, more tangibly, its new fleet, but Sparta had the longer-standing status as the pre-eminent Greek community when it came to waging war. Sending out the appeal for delegations to come and staging the meeting in the Peloponnese confirmed this. The excellence of the Spartans in war was acknowledged by all.

A new alliance was formed, distinct from the existing network of allies created by the Spartans, and the cities involved all agreed to join forces to oppose the Persians. The Spartans would lead, providing men to head the forces both on land and at sea, but they would not command. States kept their independence; decisions would be reached only after debate and required approval by all. In the meantime, all wars between the allies would cease, which most notably brought to an end the conflict between Athens and Aegina. Old enmities were to be set aside, ideally permanently, to face the common danger. Communities who sided with the Persians were to be punished with loss of territory. The Athenians also did their best to heal rifts within the community, recalling the ostracised.[27]

All of this was far more ambitious and larger in scale than the pledges of support exchanged between Sparta, Athens, Plataea, and Eretria before the first Persian invasion in 490 BC. Not everything was to turn out as planned; many communities did not join the alliance, and some fell away, while after the war no fines appear to have been imposed, and the goal of stopping warfare between Greek communities proved elusive. Even so, the decision of a significant number of states to join together under Spartan leadership and face the daunting prospect of Persian attack represented an unprecedented willingness to unite for a common purpose. States were agreeing a mutual defence, committing citizens to fight away from their own lands. The Athenians possessed far more triremes than anyone else and agreed to serve in a combined fleet led by a Spartan. There was enough fellow feeling and pragmatic leadership in several states to make this happen.

The council also agreed to appeal to others for aid. Argos wavered, asking to be put in charge of the war effort, perhaps because it believed that Sparta would never agree to such a provision. In the event Argos did not join and played no active part in the war. The cities of Cyprus gave a quicker answer, inspired by a particularly pessimistic response from Delphi, and refused to join. Syracuse in Sicily was well on its way to becoming the largest Greek city in the world, and envoys were sent to ask its tyrant for help. Like the Argives, he negotiated, offering substantial numbers of troops and warships on the condition that he be appointed to overall command. Again, the provision may have been meant to provide a convenient excuse to refuse, as inevitably it too was rejected. No help was to come to the new allies from outside, and the Syracusans would have their hands full repelling an attack by the Carthaginians, so probably would not have been in any position to assist.[28]

The Spartans, the Athenians, and the rest would have to rely on their own resources and resolve. None of them had any experience of waging war as a coalition on this scale and against such a formidable opponent. By the beginning of 480 BC, it was clear that a grand expedition led by Xerxes himself would soon be launched. No one could really have known what to expect, but nothing had changed in the fundamental balance of power since the gloomy forecasts of the Pythian oracle. The Spartans, the Athenians, and the rest were about to face the full might of the greatest empire in the world.

12

THE 300—AND THE 700 AND THE REST

Xerxes's great invasion and the defence of Thermopylae, 481 to summer 480 BC

ANOTHER DECISION OF THE MEETING CALLED BY SPARTA WAS to send spies to Asia to discover as much as they could about Xerxes's forces and his intentions. These men were captured, but rather than having them tortured and executed, the great king gave orders for them to be given a tour of the army's camps. They were then allowed to go back to Greece to tell of what they had seen. Xerxes wanted the peoples in the path of his advance to hear of the sheer size and might of his army and navy. This desire to parade rather than conceal ran through all the Persian preparations for war. Everything was done openly and on the grandest scale, which makes it possible that Herodotus's talk of four years of preparations was close to the truth. Xerxes wanted the world to believe that he was undertaking a project so vast in scope that only he and his empire could even dream of doing it.[1]

The Persians had no permanent standing navy and themselves were not a people with a long seafaring tradition. Their subjects on the Mediterranean coast had some warships, but Xerxes wanted far more and instructed them to build more and arranged the resources to achieve this. On a far bigger scale than Themistocles's expansion of the Athenian fleet, Phoenician, Egyptian, Carian, and Ionian communities, among others, all set to work making triremes and then finding and training the bulk of the crews to man them. Greek sources claim that when the squadrons of ships were all brought together, the combined fleet consisted of no fewer than 1,207 triremes and thousands of supply and transport ships—double the size given for the fleet at Lade and then for the Marathon campaign. To avoid any repeat of the storm that had wrecked so many ships in 493 BC off Mount Athos, a canal was dug cutting through the peninsula.[2]

The army was said to have been even larger than the navy, and Herodotus offered a long description of the many different contingents drawn from all parts of the immense Achaemenid Empire. He claimed that there were to be something like 1.7 million fighting men attended by camp followers and accompanied by the royal court, all of them needing pack and draught animals to carry food and equipment. This would be the first time that camels set foot in western Europe, at least in any quantity. To help with supplies, vast quantities of food were gathered and then stockpiled in supply dumps set up in Asia, Thrace, and Macedonia, for much of the route was to pass through territories already part of the empire. Unlike in 490 BC, this army would not travel in ships and would instead walk or ride to Greece. Rather than being ferried across the Dardanelles, older ships were gathered and two pontoon-style bridges set across the strait. Each one required over 300 ships as well as great quantities of cordage, and the design allowed sections to be uncoupled and drawn back so that ships could pass through.[3]

There was no need for such engineering marvels, and it would have been perfectly possible to ferry men, animals, and supplies across the Dardanelles. Similarly, the canal dug by Xerxes's engineers and labourers to avoid rounding the cape off Mount Athos appears to have been abandoned within a year, rapidly silting up because everyone else was content to watch the weather and choose their moment to sail around. In practical terms, the time, effort, and resources devoted to the bridges and canal were excessive, almost wasteful. For Greek observers, especially those commenting after the war, these were marks of the inflated, almost deranged, vanity of a foreign king. When the bridges broke in a storm, Xerxes ordered the chief engineer executed, the sea punished by flogging and having fetters dropped into it, and new bridges made to replace the old ones. Few acts better epitomised irrational, excessive human pride (or *hybris*), which inevitably led to divine retribution.[4]

This missed the point, and there was a logic behind all of this, even if it made little sense to the Greeks. In the past, Persian expeditions had defied nature, building bigger bridges or other projects than anyone had done before. Xerxes went further, sending a message that there was nothing the armies of the great king could not do and nowhere they could not go. He was the 'king of the world', protector of the Truth, appointed by Ahura Mazda. The storm that wrecked the bridges challenged these claims, so must represent an aspect of the Lie. Ritual punishment confirmed that the weather had committed an impiety, and that the new bridges remained in place and the army was able to walk across the Dardanelles was proof that the proper order had been restored. The workmen even scattered earth over the planking to help reassure the animals and to emphasise that the sea had been turned into land.[5]

The sheer scale of everything sent a clear message of overwhelming might. Xerxes ruled the greatest empire ever known and had at his disposal soldiers, ships, and other resources on a scale dwarfing those available to anyone else. Every successful Persian war had seen widespread defections, and those who did this or surrendered quickly were treated well by the great king. Everyone else was beaten down in the end, and the great king's retribution was often terrible. Grand projects, even if not strictly necessary, illustrated what the Persians could do and were meant to convey the empire's irresistible force. Greek sources had every reason to exaggerate enemy numbers and add to the glory of subsequent victory, but there is a good chance that some of the stories came originally from Persian boasts about their strength, which deliberately exaggerated in order to intimidate. The great king wanted victory and did not require that victory to come through battle and destruction unless it was unavoidable. The more enemies who could be terrified into submission the better, so that Persian reverence for the Truth could be set aside to make advantages in numbers and power even greater than they really were.

In the early spring of 480 BC, Xerxes marched out from Sardis, for the great king would accompany the expedition, which meant that most of the royal court also went. Wherever he was in the empire, the great king was the great king and needed to correspond with his satraps, other deputies, and leaders in all the provinces, dealing with problems that arose. Ceremony surrounded him at every stage. Soldiers from various provinces and a substantial part of the baggage train set out first, probably in sections over several days or more. Xerxes himself was surrounded by Persians, with the royal guard of 1,000 horse and 1,000 foot as close escort. Ahead of the great king went a sacred chariot, drawn by the finest Nisean horses, a breed the Persians considered the best in the world. The chariot's car was empty, symbolising the divine presence. After this came Ahura Mazda's representative himself, Xerxes, riding in another magnificent chariot, although after the formal departure he often switched to a carriage instead. Either way he was followed by more picked Persian troops, including a unit of 10,000 infantrymen the Greeks knew as 'the Immortals'. Achaemenid organisation was based on groups known as thousands and ten thousands. As with a lot of military orders of battle throughout history, actual numbers may not have matched the theoretical strength, but it seems that effort was made to keep the Immortals as close to this as possible.[6]

As the army processed out of Sardis, Herodotus says that they passed a grisly symbol of the wrath of the great king. A local nobleman had energetically contributed to the war effort, so much so that

Xerxes had offered to grant any favour. Having brought all his sons to go with the expedition, the man asked that the oldest, his heir, be excused, so that his line was secured. Enraged, Xerxes released all the other brothers but had the eldest killed and his corpse cut in two, so that half could be placed on each side of the road, for nothing less than absolute commitment to the king's war was acceptable. Unlike his father or grandfather, Xerxes had not fought his way to the throne, and the expedition to Greece was intended to give him a reputation as a great conqueror and fitting successor to such able war leaders. For all the desire to overawe potential enemies, the direct involvement of Xerxes, given his limited military experience, does seem to have made the arrangements even more gargantuan than necessary to intimidate the communities in the path of his advance.[7]

Xerxes's army was large by any standard and gigantic by the standards of the communities of Greece. It was likely the largest army up to this point ever to operate in Europe, and its size would rarely, if ever, be surpassed until the nineteenth century. On this much scholars generally agree, and similarly all reject Herodotus's claim for over a million men. Even if Xerxes had been able to muster so many soldiers, feeding them would have been impossible. Beyond this, opinions vary, and estimates of the total of fighting men range from 60,000 to 300,000, to which must be added servants and households for the nobility as well as the royal court. One estimate, offered by a retired British general who had gained detailed knowledge of the region during and after World War I, took into account the availability of water along the route and opted for a little over 200,000 people maximum, including any non-combatants. This is plausible but at best offers an upper limit. Xerxes's army might have pushed to the very limits what was possible or might have been significantly smaller while still seeming vast to the Greeks.[8]

The Achaemenid Empire was wealthy and well organised, meaning that it was capable of massing and supplying forces on a scale impossible for any other state in the known world. It could bridge the Dardanelles and cut a canal to bypass the cape off Mount Athos, and there is no reason to doubt that supply dumps were prepared and established along the projected route. An additional problem in estimating numbers comes from the uncertainty over what proportion of the total was concentrated in the main field force and how many were detached to work on these projects or to guard, maintain, and operate the supply depots. For much of the time, even the main field army appears to have split into distinct columns, only concentrating when needed.

The same is likely to have been true of the fleet. More scholars have been inclined to accept the figure of just over 1,200 triremes for Persian strength at the start of the war, although in some cases they have suggested that not all were fully crewed and some were employed as transports. The total is less impossible than the numbers given for the army, even if it still suggests immense manpower. If fully manned, so many triremes would have required some 240,000 rowers, sailors, and marines, all needing water and food. Once again, if the figures from the sources are rejected, any alternative estimate can never be more than conjectural, and it is safe only to say that the combined Persian fleet greatly outnumbered anything the Greek allies were able to muster.[9]

Army and fleet were meant to support each other, not fight wholly separate campaigns, so that whenever practical the land forces would stay near the coast and keep in touch with the navy. Often the geography rendered this impossible, which necessitated arranging to rendezvous at a later stage. The fleet offered the option of transporting significant numbers of troops and landing them further down the coast, although the idea is not mentioned in any source, and this does not appear ever to have happened. However, for the first months of the campaign, none of this really mattered, and any plans were academic, since the Persians were marching through friendly territory. Herodotus says that it took seven days and nights of constant movement for the army with all its animals to cross the bridges over the Dardanelles. While an unbroken column would only have been a recipe for appalling traffic jams whenever the path became difficult or narrowed, a week for the crossing is plausible enough. Most likely the force was broken up into smaller columns with baggage, all following routes at substantial intervals, since this was far more efficient. They faced no opposition, and food awaited them at the supply dumps to supplement and replenish the stocks carried in the baggage train. They did not hurry, partly because this was impractical and more because it was unnecessary. Xerxes's great army came on slowly and steadily, giving plenty of time for those in its path to think about what would happen when they arrived.[10]

The Spartans and their new allies gathered again for a conference at the precinct of Poseidon on the Isthmus of Corinth, the site of the Isthmian Games. Representatives from the cities of Thessaly in northern Greece attended, asking for aid, and it was decided to send an army of some 10,000 men, mostly hoplites, and to place a Spartan officer in overall charge. This force, comparable in size to the army that had won at Marathon, took station in the pass at Tempe, a naturally strong position that was narrow enough to prevent the Persians from overwhelming them with sheer numbers. As it turned out, the vanguard of Xerxes's army was nowhere in sight and, as soon became clear, would not arrive for weeks. Alexander I of Macedon had long-standing connections with the Athenians, and probably leaders in other states as well, and sent word of the location of the invading army and its immense size and strength. At the same time, talking to the locals, the leaders of the expeditionary force discovered that the pass was easily outflanked.[11]

Greek plans had fallen apart. There were no Persians to fight, at least not yet and not for some time. This expedition was larger in scale and had gone further than anything ever before attempted by a group of Greek communities, and, unlike the Persians, the Spartans, the Athenians, and the rest were simply not prepared to maintain and supply such a big army in the field for a prolonged campaign.

Waiting in place was not a viable option, especially now that they understood that the position was untenable without significant reinforcements to hold the other routes around the pass. After just a few days, the army withdrew, its contingents splitting up to go home, and the first effort of defence mounted by Sparta and the allies was over. Sometime later, the Persians arrived, and all of Thessaly submitted, offering earth and water. Xerxes praised their wisdom, showing how kind the great king was to all who acknowledged his might and majesty. He took time to meet the leaders of the communities, to do some sightseeing, and even to stage horse races, for the Thessalian aristocrats were keen horsemen and breeders of horses. No doubt to the great king's satisfaction, the Nisaeans of his own men triumphed over the local horses in nearly every event.[12]

So far the campaign was going very well for the Persians, the advance a stately progression that had not involved any actual fighting. Probably men and animals had been lost to disease and accident, and perhaps also to desertion. Herodotus claimed that wolves took a heavy toll on the pack camels, seemingly drawn to this new prey, but although he talks of rivers being drunk dry, even he does not suggest that the Persian supply arrangements on the whole were failing. The Thessalians had defected, and as the advance continued, surely more communities would follow suit and 'medize', as the Greeks later called it. The Spartans and their coalition of allies had achieved nothing of practical value, beyond the—admittedly remarkable—feat of getting numbers of cities to agree to work together. A natural instinct for all concerned was the desire to protect their own cities and farms, and to have persuaded Peloponnesians and Athenians alike to send troops to fight in Thessaly, even if they achieved nothing before coming home, was quite something.[13]

Late in the summer of 480 BC, as Xerxes's forces approached southern Greece, it was agreed to send out another field force to block the Persians' progress. As before, the plan was to rely on the topography to counter the enemy's greater numbers, and the location chosen was Thermopylae (the Hot Gates), named for its springs, in Boeotia. The route ran between the shore and mountains through three main passes, all of them narrow. Across the strait was Euboea, and because of the shape of the coastline, the sea was to the north and the mountains to the south. King Leonidas of Sparta was put in charge of an army of Peloponnesians, joined by Thespians, Phocians, and Thebans, among others, on the march to Thermopylae. The Athenians contributed no soldiers but provided by far the largest contingent in a fleet of 271 triremes based at Artemisium on Euboea, some forty miles from Thermopylae. Themistocles led the Athenians, but overall command was, as usual, given to a Spartan, Eurybiades. Not from the royal family, perhaps not even from among the leading families, he was presumably an experienced military man judged to be capable. Whether he had any extensive knowledge of the sea and ships is not known.[14]

The Spartans were in charge just as the coalition had agreed, but for the moment their contribution remained small in terms of manpower. Leonidas had a force usually estimated at from 5,000 to 7,000 men, which included just 300 Spartan 'peers', for, as in 490 BC, the Persians appeared during the Carneia. The Spartans promised to send more men once the festival was over; how they justified sending Leonidas and his men straightaway is not clear. Although a unit of 300 at first sight suggests the *hippeis*, in this case Leonidas selected the men individually, choosing mature citizens who had one or more sons, which perhaps meant that each family still had male representation at the festival. Claims that the whole expedition was a forlorn hope and that the Spartans and their king expected to die do not convince, even with the supposed Delphic oracle about the death of a king. Although smaller than the force sent to Tempe, this remained a reasonably large army by Greek standards and, more importantly, was supported by the considerably more numerous fleet, which reinforcements would eventually increase to more than 300 ships. The objective was to block the Persian advance at Thermopylae, where quality and close-in fighting would count rather than quantity, and the Greek ships could try to counter any attempt by the Persian fleet to outflank the position. No one could be too sure what would happen, but when the Carneia ended, more troops would be available, and the coalition could decide what to do next.[15]

Thermopylae has changed drastically since 480 BC, adding to the challenges of reconstructing the fighting and separating myth from history. Geological survey suggests that the modern ground level is some sixty-six feet (twenty meters) higher than that of fifth century BC, while the shoreline has advanced by a couple of miles, so that the pass is nowhere near the sea. Most of the fighting on the first two days occurred at the Middle Gate, where there was perhaps sixty to seventy feet of open space from the steep slopes of the mountain to the marshy shoreline. Judging from surviving remains, the already ancient Phocian wall, which the Greeks hastily repaired, did not cross the track, as so often imagined on modern maps, but ran at an angle, channelling any attacker along a particularly narrow approach. This was not the only way that Xerxes could reach Attica and ultimately the Peloponnese, but if the Persians changed their minds and took one of the alternative routes, there would be plenty of time to learn of this and withdraw.[16]

The pass at Thermopylae gave Leonidas the chance to defend a narrow front, but in war, even more than life in general, rarely are things perfect. Soon after he reached the position, he learned from the Phocians of a route running around the pass. It was just a path, suitable for goats and men, very difficult for horses, and impossible for waggons, and it was not easy to find, even if locals knew it and, if threatened or bribed, might well tell the Persians all about it. Leonidas sent the contingent of 1,000 Phocians back to occupy the last strong position from which to halt any sizeable body of men coming along this route. He and the other allied leaders could do nothing else about this risk, and if they could hold until the Carneia was complete and more forces available, then the whole situation would change.[17]

Xerxes's army reached Thermopylae after the Spartans and the others were firmly ensconced in the pass. Scouts reported seeing men exercising in the nude, as was the Hellenic custom, while others were combing their long hair. Demaratus explained to Xerxes that these men were the Spartans, as good as any fighting men individually and far superior fighting together, that it was their custom to look their best for a battle, and that they would fight and never give in. For several days the Persian army camped in front of the pass and waited, not due to fear but because the fleet had not yet appeared. On top of that, while it is convenient to speak of the Persian army arriving at a place, all this normally meant was that some advance units had reached the spot. The bulk of the army was hours or days further back, and there was little point concentrating everyone together until needed. A substantial part of the troops did close up on the advance guard, and with them was the royal court, so that Xerxes could observe and supervise, even though command was left to subordinates.[18]

The Persian navy was late, an indication of how difficult it was to coordinate separate forces in the ancient world. Morale was buoyed when a squadron of Persian ships caught sight of three Greek triremes acting as scouts near the island of Sciathos. Two were captured, and the third—an Athenian ship—ran itself aground, allowing the crew to escape and trek home. Herodotus reports that the crews of the two captured ships were inspected by their captors. From the marines, men from the hoplite class who fought on the deck, the most handsome was selected and sacrificed by having this throat cut. This was supposed to bring good fortune for the campaign, not least because the man chosen happened to be named Leon (lion), although the custom may have owed more to one of the allied contingents than the Persians themselves. Either way, luck proved to be in short supply when a storm lasting several days battered the Persian fleet while at anchor. Herodotus claimed that 400 warships were wrecked along with many supply ships. The Greeks, better placed at Artemisium and far better informed about local weather and tides, celebrated the destruction as sent by the gods. They were still heavily outnumbered and were learning that in general the enemy warships were faster than theirs, whether through construction or the skill of their crews or both, but the destruction caused by the storm was encouraging.[19]

Eventually Xerxes ordered an attack into the pass at Thermopylae, sending forward a force of Persian soldiers. Throughout the war, Persians, Medes, and other Central Asian and Iranian soldiers, who were clearly the pick of the army, bore the brunt of the fighting. The Spartans were the first to hold the pass, presumably forming up as a small phalanx across the narrow stretch of open ground. Archers first and foremost, the Persians likely did their best to wear down the defenders with missiles before closing. It is from Thermopylae, after all, that the famous story comes of the Spartan, informed that the enemy would shoot so many arrows that they would blot out the sun, replying that this was good, since it would mean they could fight in the shade. Yet these were not favourable conditions for massed archery. To be effective, the archers needed to get within 200 yards, and the narrow ground meant that only fairly small numbers could get into position. Even with the ranks behind the first joining in, this still meant that compared to an open battle, relatively few could shoot, and most would be shooting blind, unable to see the target. At the same time a couple hundred yards was an easy distance for the hoplites to charge.

Most of the fighting was hand to hand, and, just as at Marathon, the Spartans and their allies had better arms and armour for such close-in fighting, as well as a fondness for it. Herodotus claimed that the Spartans fooled the enemy by pretending to withdraw, luring the Persians into a rash pursuit. Then the hoplites halted, formed up again, and turned on their pursuers. There were lulls in the fighting, which was a series of attacks rather than a continuous onslaught. As the Spartans tired, they withdrew and allies took their place, so that each attack of fresh troops could be met by equally fresh defenders. The Persians made no headway, so as the day drew on, Xerxes committed the Immortals to the attack, but these did no better than the rest as all the advantages still lay with the defenders. There were losses on both sides, but the Persians suffered far greater casualties and inevitably had difficulty bringing back their wounded. The Greeks were better protected by their shields, helmets, and armour and, since they held their ground, could evacuate their own injured. The first day of attacks ended in utter failure for Xerxes's men, and the second day went no better than the first. Leonidas and his men were being worn down, but only slowly and at dreadful cost. At this rate they could hold out for many days.[20]

The situation was no better at sea, where actions were fought at the same time as the attacks on land. Inspired by Themistocles, the Greek fleet had gone out to meet the enemy, but before the Persians got close, the Greek triremes formed themselves into a large, defensive circle. As on land, the idea was to negate the enemy's superior numbers. At the same time, it denied the chance for the nimbler enemy ships to pass through a line of triremes, swinging round to ram the stern or side. The Persians do not appear to have expected this and were unable to improvise an effective counter. As ships tried to find a weak spot, sometimes the Persians grew careless and became separated, allowing bold Greek captains to surge forward and ram them, retreating before other Persian ships could catch them. As at the pass, the Greeks did not win the encounters, but nor were they defeated, and they won lots of small successes, inflicting far heavier losses than they suffered.[21]

On the second night, a local man named Ephialtes went to the Persian camp and told them of the path around the passes. In the aftermath, others were also blamed for this, and no one was quite clear whether the informants wanted reward or felt that their communities would have to accept Persian rule so might as well gain favour. A large detachment of the Immortals was sent to follow the goat track,

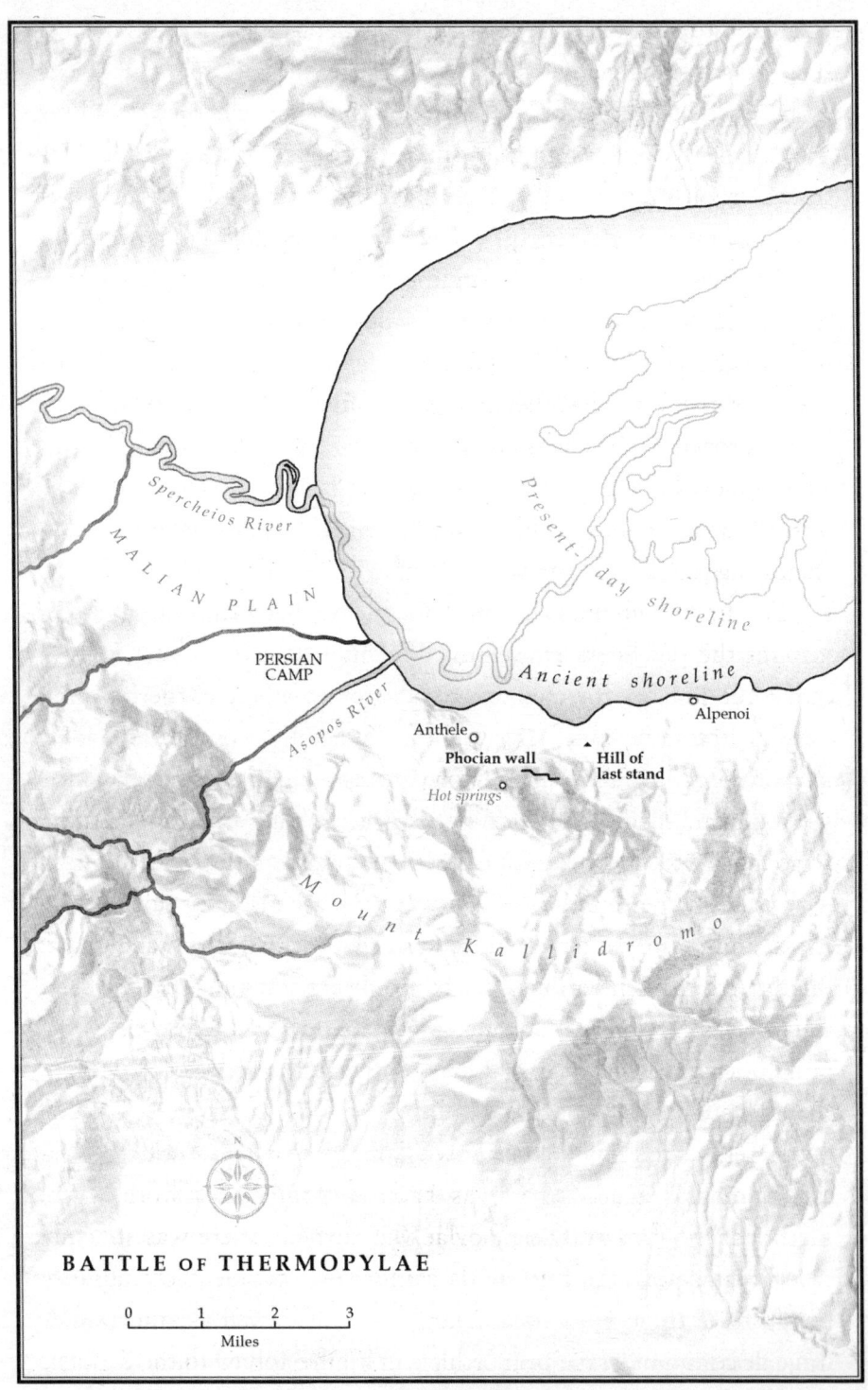

BATTLE OF THERMOPYLAE

guided by Ephialtes. Days before this and on his own initiative, the Persian admiral had sent ships to go all the way around Euboea and come up the strait from the south, so that the Greek fleet would be taken from two sides and trapped. Fortunately for the Spartan admiral at Artemisium, a Greek serving with the Persian fleet slipped away and informed them of what was happening. This man was known as a great swimmer, and later tradition differed over whether he had swum, partly under water, or used a small boat for the journey. Still, travelling around the long island of Euboea was bound to take the Persians a long time, so Greek observers were stationed to watch for the approach of the enemy squadron. Once again, the weather came to the aid of the Greeks, for a high wind blew up and drove most of the squadron onto the shore of Euboea, wrecking the ships and removing the threat of being surrounded.[22]

The Immortals reached the Phocian position around dawn and caught the defenders by surprise. Perhaps after watching for two days, the Phocians had relaxed and decided that the enemy would not find out about the path. These were not professional soldiers but farmers willingly fighting for their community, and for all their enthusiasm, such men could be naive when it came to campaigning, much like the men surprised by Pisistratus and Cleomenes in the past. To their credit, they did not panic when they saw the Persians and the first arrows started to land; instead they withdrew to higher ground where they formed up in a phalanx ready to defend themselves. The Persians were trained soldiers and led by men with a broader understanding of war. Some may have stayed to hold the Phocians in check, while the bulk of the force continued along the path so that they could come down behind the main Greek army.[23]

Leonidas learned what was happening and sent word to the fleet that the pass at Thermopylae was turned. There was still time to retreat before the Immortals came down behind them, and the majority of the Greek troops marched away. Leonidas and the contingent commanders appear to have mutually agreed to the decision.

The Spartan king stayed where he was, along with what remained of his 300 Spartans, the 700 Thespians, and the 400 Thebans. There may also have been men from the eighty-or-so-strong contingent sent by the city of Mycenae, and there were helots serving as light infantrymen. How many men from all of these groups were still on their feet is not recorded, given that there had been two days of heavy fighting. Two Spartans were absent, stricken with eye infections, and another had been sent away to carry a message. One of the sick men ordered a helot to lead him back to the main force, and he would fight and die with Leonidas. Herodotus claimed that Leonidas, suspicious of their commitment to the cause, forced the Thebans to stay against their will, but this is likely an invention based on the knowledge that Thebes did join the Persians after the battle. Perhaps somewhere from 1,000 to 1,500 men stayed at Thermopylae and twice as many withdrew. There was plenty of time, because the detachment of Immortals was still a fair few hours away from cutting the main route, and Xerxes deliberately delayed any attack through the pass to give them time to arrive.[24]

None of the sources say why Leonidas chose to stay, since he probably could have left with the others, although Herodotus speculated that he felt it dishonourable to retreat and was aware of the oracle from Delphi, which spoke of the death of one of Sparta's kings. Whether the Spartans and the rest would have had enough of a head start to avoid being caught by pursuing cavalry is much harder to say. A logical explanation for the decision to keep some troops blocking the pass was to act as a rearguard, delaying the Persians so that the other Greeks would have more time to put some distance between them and any pursuit. While this makes sense, it can never be more than conjecture. Herodotus implies that the Spartans were bound by a strict code of behaviour not to abandon a position, and plenty of scholars have accepted this. The difficulty is that this belief relies very heavily on what happened at Thermopylae, and too little is known of earlier Spartan campaigns to be sure that such a code existed.

Cleomenes had surrendered and withdrawn from the Acropolis at Athens just a generation earlier, which at the very least suggests there were circumstances when Spartans felt able to retreat and were not blamed for this by their fellow citizens. Ultimately, as with so many of the most dramatic moments in history, the precise motives of those involved will never be known.[25]

None of this in any way detracts from the courage of the men who stayed behind at Thermopylae. In later tradition, Leonidas led a daring attack on the Persian camp, trying to reach Xerxes's tent and kill the great king, but this was supposed to have happened under cover of darkness, and it is hard to see how there was time to mount such an attack. Herodotus wrote much closer to the events, and his narrative makes more sense. The Greeks waited as dawn came and waited more hours as the Persians failed to attack. If the objective was to give the others more chance to get away, then this was all to the good.[26]

When the sun was already high and the Persians had failed to advance, Leonidas formed his men and led them towards the main enemy army. For the first time, they pushed beyond the narrowest section of the pass, which meant that they would fight on a wider frontage, and more of the Greeks could be in the main line. There was still not enough space for all the Persians to reach them, so the numbers able to fight hand to hand were roughly equal. The Spartans and the other Greeks attacked, probably at a steady pace rather than in the wild charge like the one at Marathon. Either way the advance was surely unnerving to the Persians, but the Persians were good soldiers and formed deep, meaning that the presence of all the ranks behind made retreat difficult for those in front. Herodotus claimed that officers stood at the back of Persian units, whipping the reluctant men forward, but this is probably a slander invented by the Greeks. Even so, close combat was a traumatic experience, and it is to the credit of both sides that they did stay to face the enemy.[27]

For all their lack of overall numbers, the Greeks came on boldly, and through determination and with the advantage of equipment better suited to such encounters, they seem to have made some headway, pushing the Persians back. Leonidas fell in the thick of the fighting, for if his costume did not mark him out as the king, by now he was surely well known to many Persians. A bitter fight broke out over the Spartan king's body, a struggle bound to remind Greeks of the similar fights in the *Iliad*. Several times the Spartans drove the enemy back, only to be pushed back in turn—Herodotus describes this as a 'shove'. In the end the Spartans retrieved their king and his gear, but by this time they and their allies were close to exhaustion. Most of their spears had broken, and some had lost even their swords, so that they fought with their hands or knives. They pulled back, and the Persians let them. By now the Immortals had closed the pass behind them, so the Greeks clustered together in defensive circles, perhaps one for each contingent or with the Thespians and Spartans in one and the Thebans some distance apart. Rather than risk their lives facing such desperate and still determined men, massed Persian archers deluged the Greeks with volley after volley of arrows. One by one the Thespians and the Spartans—and the remaining helots—were killed or crippled. Only when the heaps of bodies were still, did the Persians go forward to give the coup de grâce to those still breathing. Those Thebans still on their feet after the previous days of fighting and the attack on the last day surrendered.

Herodotus says that 4,000 Greeks died in the three days of fighting at Thermopylae, but only after killing five times as many Persians. As always, it is difficult to know how reliable such figures are, since the total for the Greek army at the start of the battle is unclear. Herodotus notes that there were many helots among the dead, who may not have been included in the numbers given for the initial forces. Most or all of the Phocians got away, as did the main Peloponnesian contingents, with the exception of those killed or wounded and unable to travel from the fighting on the first and second days. Xerxes invited representatives from his fleet to view the battlefield and the corpses, although he allegedly first had many of the fallen Persians buried to conceal their numbers. Leonidas's corpse was found and beheaded, and the severed head was then mounted on a stake as symbolic punishment of all the Spartans for opposing the great king. The other bodies were treated with respect. Herodotus says that some Thebans were killed while trying to surrender and that Xerxes ordered others branded as runaway slaves, since their city had earlier offered fire and water.[28]

On the last day of fighting, the fleets clashed once again, with losses on both sides but no clear advantage to either. At sea the Greeks had held their own, inflicting enough loss to permit them to retire unmolested, now that there was no army to support. Before they went, Themistocles and the Athenians seized substantial numbers of Euboean sheep and cattle, slaughtering some in a great feast and sacrifice and carrying off what they could, so that the enemy was denied this resource. He also had men go to the best anchorages, especially those with ready access to fresh water, and paint or scratch messages for the Ionians in the Greek fleet, telling them that they were on the wrong side. His thinking was that he might just convince some of them to desert, for one or two had already done so. Even if this did not happen, he felt that it would sow doubts over the Ionians' reliability in the mind of Xerxes and the senior Persian officers.[29]

With this trick worthy of Odysseus, the Athenians departed. Although they had taken some losses, they had inflicted more damage on the enemy. More importantly, the majority of the Athenian ships were intact or could readily be repaired, and the same was true for the other, smaller contingents. The first Greek army to take the field and meet the Persians was dispersed, captured, or dead, but the fleet remained strong and had grown in confidence from its encounters with the enemy. In terms of numbers the Greek allies were able to muster and man some 300 triremes. It remained to be seen how—or indeed whether—there was the will to use them and continue the war.

13

THE WOODEN WALLS

*The evacuation of Athens, the sack of the city,
the Athenian fleet, and the great victory at Salamis,
late summer to winter 480 BC*

I<small>T IS ALL TOO EASY TO FORGET THAT</small> T<small>HERMOPYLAE WAS A</small> Persian victory, for the focus naturally remains fixed on the final stand of Leonidas and his men. They fought to the last, with skill and courage, against overwhelming numbers. In later years memorials were raised, claiming, for instance, that 4,000 Peloponnesians had fought against 300,000 Medes. Most famous was the epitaph given to the king and his 300 Spartans: 'Passer-by, go tell the Spartans that here we lie, obedient to their orders.' In Western culture, the last stand of the '300 Spartans' has become the archetype of heroic last stands, simplified to the point where it does not matter that there were no longer 300 of them by the time it happened and that helots, Thespians, and perhaps Mycenaeans stood and died with them. At the time, the courage of Leonidas was praised as the only good thing to come out of the affair. Of the two Spartans sick with eye infections, one was led back to the pass and died, while the other went home to be scorned by his fellow citizens, although not excluded from society. His decision was put in a worse light when the man sent as a messenger, therefore absent for an unquestionably justified reason, hanged himself for surviving. As a community, the Spartans took pride in the determination with which their fellow citizens had held the pass and then resisted to the death.[1]

Yet Thermopylae remained a Persian success. Xerxes's great army had been delayed and, as at Marathon, had struggled to match Greek hoplites in hand-to-hand combat and suffered much higher losses than the enemy. In spite of this, the position had been outflanked and taken, and all the enemies who had not fled were killed or captured. On top of that, one of Sparta's kings was dead, which was an important symbolic punishment of his state, the greatest military power in Greece and the leader of the alliance opposing Persia. At sea, the advantage was less clear, and there had been losses to bad weather in addition to ships captured or sunk in the fighting. From the Persian perspective, Artemisium was not a defeat, and in the end the Greeks had withdrawn. As importantly, if the Greek alliance still possessed a lot of warships, the Persians had far more.

The big question was whether the alliance between the great king's enemies would hold together. In the aftermath of Thermopylae, many more communities made their submission to Xerxes, feeling they had little choice in the matter since their territories had already been overrun or now lay open to the invaders. While the rest of Boeotia medized, the Plataeans continued to stand with Athens, which meant abandoning their city and lands, which the Persians promptly sacked and burned. Thespiae suffered the same fate, as did Euboea. A column approached Delphi but turned back, and stories circulated of a landslide sent by the gods to protect the sacred site. More likely the Persians saw no reason to strike at this famous cult centre. The Phocians refused to submit, and most abandoned their city and settlements to hide in the mountains. Herodotus was inclined to think that they did this from old rivalry with and hatred of the Thessalians, being simply unwilling to be on the same side as this traditional enemy. Some of the Phocians were caught by Persian troops devastating their land, and a grim tale tells of captive women being raped so many times that they died from the experience. Whether ordered or not, the wrath of the great king was appalling, just as his generosity and kindness were lavish for those who submitted. From a practical point of view, the Persians were also able to draw supplies and troops from the states that switched sides.[2]

Attica lay open, and like the Plataeans, Thespians, and others, the people decided to flee rather than submit. Indeed, there is a good chance that this choice had been made before Thermopylae. An inscription set up some 200 years later, but purporting to record a decree passed by the Assembly in 480 BC—or even earlier, in 481 BC—states that before the fleet was despatched to Artemisium, Attica's entire population was to evacuate, taking with them all that could be moved. Debate continues to rage over the reliability of the text, whether it was partly or wholly fabricated long after the events or is genuine. At the very least it means that there was a tradition holding that the Athenians collectively were willing to abandon their homes rather than submit to the Persians and made this choice very early, before Attica was actually under threat. The bleak messages from Delphi encouraged this, as did other omens. A giant snake was supposed to dwell in the Temple of Athena on the Acropolis, although, since only the priestess and attendants could see it and had the task of feeding it, everyone else had to take their word for it. Now the priestess announced that the beast had gone, signifying that the goddess had departed because this was not the time and place to fight.[3]

In a major effort almost the entire remaining population of Attica was evacuated, something over 150,000 souls and perhaps substantially more, including women and children, the elderly, citizens, foreigners, and slaves. Tens of thousands of adult men were already serving with the fleet, and these helped the move. Some of the women and children went to Troezen, a city on the coast of the Peloponnese, others to Aegina—the former enemy and newfound ally. More went to Salamis, the island just a short distance across the Saronic Gulf from Athens and part of the Athenian state. Other refugees may have joined them or headed for the Peloponnese. Although the distances involved were fairly small, the scale of this operation should not be underestimated. In addition to the transport of goods and people, everyone needed to be fed for as long as necessary. Apart from anything else, the efficiency with which all this was achieved does suggest that the Athenians had time to plan and prepare, which does much to support the idea that the decision was made in principle at a very early stage. Debate and disagreement were natural in a democracy, but in this case the mood was unanimous. There is no talk of secret signals or suspicions about leading men as there had been at the time of Marathon. As a mark of conciliation, another provision recorded on the same inscription permitted all those ostracised to return home, just as Herodotus claimed.[4]

When the Persians advanced into Attica, they found the farms, villages, and Athens itself almost abandoned. A few stray folk were killed or captured, the ones too stubborn, infirm, or old to leave. The only organised group holed up on the Acropolis, determined to defend it in the desperate and unwise belief that the barricades they raised were the 'wooden walls' spoken of by the Pythian oracle. It was the closest thing to a siege in the entire invasion campaign and was a very modest affair. Persian archers used fire arrows to set the barricade ablaze. For a while, the attackers could find no way to climb the cliffs, but eventually some men managed to ascend and get into the position. Resistance collapsed, and the defenders gave way and were massacred or jumped to their deaths. The city was set on fire, with particular devastation inflicted on the shrines atop the Acropolis, the damage so thorough that archaeologists have been unable to give a precise picture of its layout before 480 BC. The defenders had been overrun within a matter of days, demonstrating why no other Greeks attempted to defend a city against Persian assault.[5]

Sparta had been beaten in a battle, and one of its kings was dead. Attica was overrun, and Athens itself sacked and its temples destroyed. It was now September, with the end of the campaigning season approaching, and Xerxes's expedition had already inflicted severe punishment on the two most important states opposing him. Plenty of other Greeks had switched sides and submitted to the Persians, reducing the number of his active opponents to just thirty-one, only twenty-two of which could contribute ships to the fleet, albeit in some cases just one or two vessels. When the news of Thermopylae spread, the Spartans and their allies from the Peloponnese mustered a large army and sent it to the Isthmus of Corinth, where they began work on a rampart to defend its narrowest point. The Carneia was over, freeing the Spartans to make a much larger contribution. The fleet, following a suggestion of Themistocles, had rallied at Salamis. This meant that the ships could assist with and protect the evacuation of Attica but at the same time ensured that the island was even more crowded. Once again, the supply system appears to have coped, at least in the short term, but the allies had yet to agree on a new plan of what to do, now that their first one had fallen apart.[6]

Eurybiades, the Spartan commander of the combined fleet, summoned the leaders of all the different contingents to a council to decide what they were to do next. Themistocles wanted to stay where they were, so that they could fight the Persian fleet between Salamis and the shore of Attica, where space was limited and the Persians' greater numbers would come less into play. Instead, the voices of the many Peloponnesians carried the day, arguing that the fleet should pull back and take up a new position, supporting the army at the isthmus.

After some time to think and consult, Themistocles persuaded the Spartan admiral to reconvene the meeting. He reinforced his argument by saying that they were already closer to the army than they had been to Leonidas when they were at Artemisium and that the Athenian triremes were heavier than Persian ships, which would give them an advantage in the restricted space, where speed and manoeuvrability mattered less than they would in the open waters off the isthmus. Plenty of commanders, especially the Corinthian leader, remained unconvinced, wondering why they should fight here rather than protect their own homes. After all, Attica was lost, and nothing could be done about that, so the Athenians were essentially a people without a city of their own. Themistocles countered by saying that the Athenians' city came in the form of their 200 triremes, and if no one would stand by them, then they might as well take all their people and sail off to Italy and settle there.[7]

The threat worked. Without the Athenians, the fleet had no hope at all, wherever it chose to fight. Reluctantly, the council reversed its earlier decision and voted to stay at Salamis. The sources are unclear about how many ships the fleet had, although reinforcements meant there were more than had been at Artemisium. There were pentecontors as well as triremes, but the triremes were what mattered. A plausible modern estimate suggests 368 ships in total, perhaps more, for Corcyra (modern Corfu) had promised to send a powerful squadron, but it did not arrive. More than likely the Corcyraeans were reluctant to commit to a potentially doomed cause, so hedged their bets and delayed their journey to join the fleet. Even if they had arrived, the Greeks would still have been heavily outnumbered, although the actual size of the Persian fleet is disputed and impossible to know. Some 600 to 700 warships is a convincing guess, but still a guess.[8]

The Persian fleet had come back into close contact with the main force of the army when it settled at Phaleron, the bay that had served as Athens's main anchorage until the development of the Piraeus. Xerxes inspected his fleet and held a council of war with his commanders, although Herodotus's account of the discussion that followed may owe much to his imagination based on what happened afterwards. The invaders had achieved a lot, and autumn was approaching, when it would become even harder to feed all the soldiers, sailors, and camp followers, especially if they were concentrated. If Xerxes were to use either the fleet or the army or both in a major operation that year, then he needed to do so soon. One option was to concentrate the army and attack the Greeks on the isthmus. Whatever fortification the defenders had thrown up was bound to be fairly basic, and although there would be far more Greeks, especially Spartans, it ought also to be easier to make use of the Persians' superior numbers and perhaps their cavalry. The alternative was to move against the Greek fleet and try to beat it at sea, doing enough damage to convince more of their home cities to submit. Removing the Greek fleet from the equation would make it easier to force the isthmus by landing troops on the shores of the Peloponnese. However, until the Greek fleet was no longer a factor, the Persian army and navy could not operate together against the isthmus, because the navy risked attack by the Greek ships.

Xerxes decided to deal with the Greek fleet. His own navy set out from Phaleron bay, sailed around the headland, and arrayed itself in the open water outside the Saronic Gulf. The Greeks refused to come out to meet them, however, so the Persians went back to the anchorage. Oarsmen could not be expected to stay in their cramped seats overnight unless this was unavoidable, so it was better to moor again and disembark to rest, eat, and wash. No doubt their commanders assured them that the enemy was too frightened to face them in battle. Work may already have begun, or at least plans been drawn up, to construct a mole linking Attica and Salamis, which would have allowed the might of the Persian army to play a more direct role.[9]

In truth the confidence of many Greeks was ebbing away, and the old divisions resurfaced between those who wanted to pull back and defend the isthmus and those who wanted to stay where they were. Themistocles decided on a desperate ruse, one that was much celebrated in the years to come and appealed to Greeks who had grown up revelling in the cunning of Odysseus, the man who got the Achaeans inside the walls of Troy when all the direct heroism had failed. Themistocles sent a man from his household, his children's attendant or tutor, in a small boat across to the Persian camp with a message. He told the Persians that the Greek fleet had decided to retreat from Salamis. He also said that his master, Themistocles, the creator and leader of the Athenian navy, was inclined to switch sides and bring his fellow citizens over to submit to the great king. Given the breakup of the Ionian fleet before Lade and the recent retreat from Artemisium—a series of fights that could easily be seen as an overall success by the Persians—talk of a fresh withdrawal was convincing and unsurprising. Similarly, Persian campaigns usually saw major defections from the enemy, and so many Greeks had already accepted that Persian victory was inevitable. All in all, the information was plausible and very welcome, and the messenger was not only treated well but permitted to depart.[10]

The Greeks were leaving, and if the Persians could stop them, then that might well hasten the end of the war as many or all of them changed sides. Setting out under cover of darkness to get into position before the Greeks realised what was happening and had a chance to slip away, Xerxes ordered his fleet to cover the main entrance to the Saronic Gulf and the western channel between Salamis and the shore. Themistocles had stirred the Persians into action, but his ruse was not yet complete, for he had to break the news to the other Greeks and stiffen their resolve rather than shatter it. Given his reputation for wiliness—some would say as an unscrupulous and shifty rascal—he doubted that he would be believed if he brought the news that the enemy fleet was at sea and on its way to seal off the exits to the gulf.

Fortunately, another Athenian was at hand, Aristides the Just, recently returned from ostracism and known not simply as a determined rival and adversary of Themistocles in Athenian public life but as a man of high character and impeccable honesty. A story was later told that on the day of the vote for ostracism, an illiterate citizen unaware of who he was approached and asked him to write 'Aristides' on the pottery shard to be cast as a ballot. When asked the reason for his hostility, the man replied that he knew nothing of Aristides but was simply sick of hearing him called 'the just'. Aristides

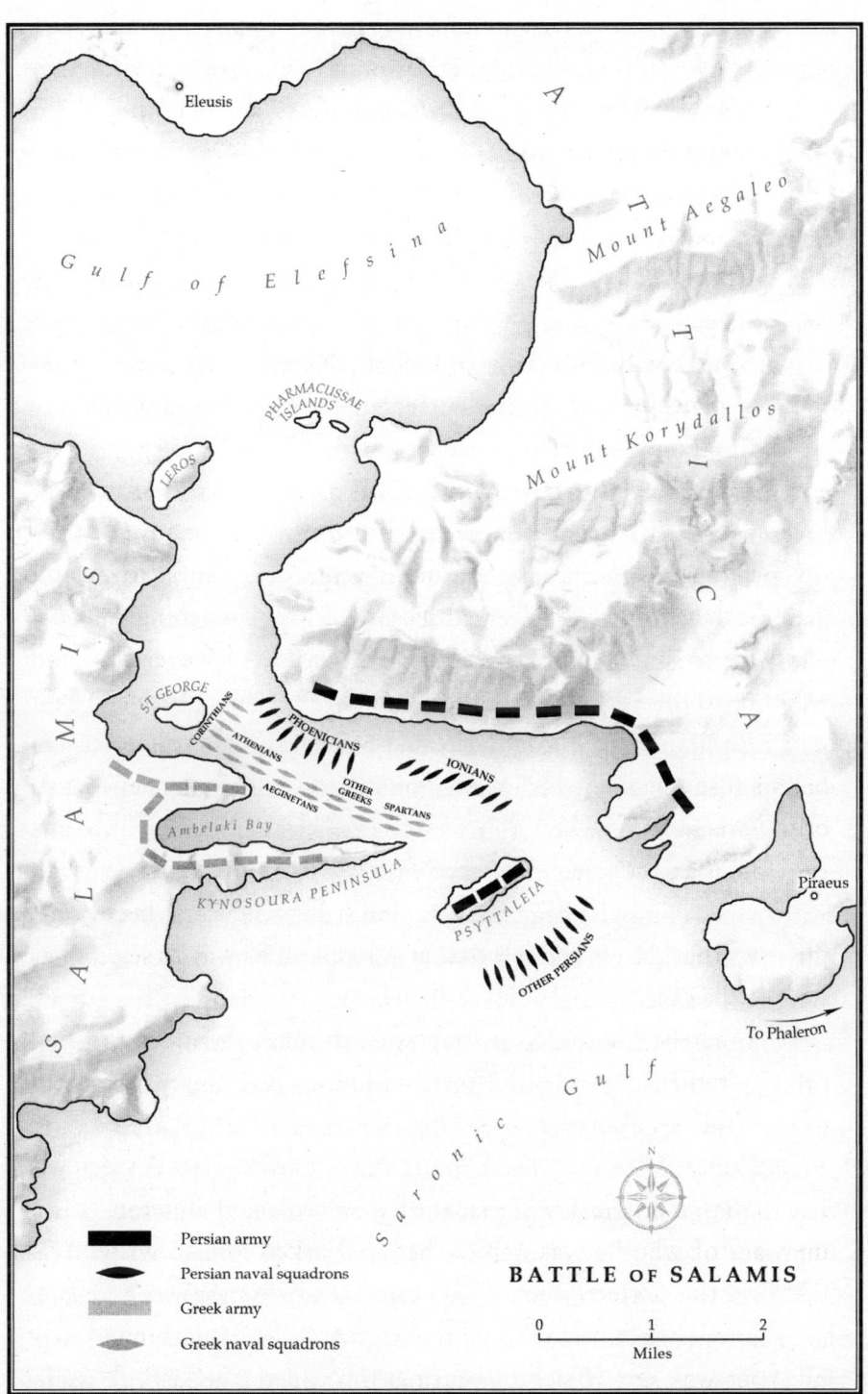

273

the Just duly wrote his own name and gave the man the ballot, not bothering to reveal his identity. True or not, such a story does appear to reflect the widespread respect felt for him. When he reported that the Persian fleet was on the way, everyone was soon convinced. They also resolved to fight, at least if the Persians did push into the Saronic Gulf, where—as Themistocles had been assuring them for days—their advantage in numbers would matter less and conditions should favour the Greeks.[11]

Naval battles did not happen quickly. It took time to man ships and prepare to fight; after that nothing could happen faster than the speed of the vessels, which in itself depended a lot on tide and wind. Triremes and the other oared warships of this era did not fight under sail, since the wind was too unreliable and their performance under sail unsuited to the basic tactics of ramming or coming alongside and boarding. Such ships relied on rowing, and whenever possible before battle, the main mast was not only lowered but taken off and stored on shore to reduce unnecessary weight. One story held that the Corinthian ships hoisted sails and headed off towards the western channel. This may be a slur spread by the Athenians when, half a century later, the two cities were bitter enemies, or just possibly it was another ploy, meant to convince the Persians that the Greeks really were running. Themistocles's plan required the enemy to come into the Saronic Gulf and not simply mass outside it, so such a deception made sense. It is also clear that in the aftermath of the battle, everyone on the Greek side accepted that the Corinthians had played a full role in the fighting and suffered losses accordingly, so at that point no one accused them of fleeing. A trireme usually had a second, smaller sail, and it may be that the Corinthian ships used these if they did feign a retreat and that their main sails and masts were not onboard.[12]

Oar power was what mattered, which was why triremes had such large crews considering their slim shape. A Greek trireme had space for 170 rowers and 30 deck crew, or at least there is good evidence to suggest that this was the standard crew for an Athenian trireme in the later fifth and fourth centuries BC. Such a ship was the model for the reconstructed *Olympias* and reflected a state-funded and -controlled navy with a standard design and specifications for its basic warship at a time when Athenian naval power was at its height. This was the warship of a navy that had built a lot of ships and gained a lot of experience in design and handling over several generations. Themistocles's triremes came at the start of this process, which means that it is hard to be sure how closely the ships of this first great Athenian fleet resembled the later ones, particularly when it came to details. Beyond the report that they were heavier but slower than most Persian triremes, few details are given. This does suggest that the plan from the start was to rely on ramming rather than boarding, since the weight added to the force of a strike. The Persian tactic was the opposite, and while they had the same number of rowers, they carried sixty deck crew, with twice as many marines as a Greek ship. Many were archers, so this allowed the Persians to employ on sea one of their greatest advantages on land and shoot at the deck crew of enemy vessels before they boarded.

Battles at sea involved a lot of people because of the essential part played by the rowers on each side. At full estimated strength, 368 triremes, each with 170 rowers, meant 62,560 men toiling at the oars and 11,040 deck crew, and allowing for the Persians as well, the figures climb to 200,000 or more combatants at the Battle of Salamis. Caution is needed, for the proportion of pentecontars and smaller ships may have been higher than the sources appear to suggest. On top of this, the numbers given and reflected in the reconstructed *Olympias* may well represent the pinnacle of trireme development, and some triremes may have been smaller, while still having three tiers of oars and being able to fight in the main battle. It is inherently unlikely that ships made by a range of Greek states, let alone those produced by subject communities in Egypt, Phoenicia, and elsewhere for the Persians, were identical in design and dimensions.

Considerable variation within the basic class of ship was far more likely, influenced by different concepts of what was best and the availability of materials.

On top of this, armed forces throughout history have had great trouble maintaining units or crews at their ideal size. The Persian fleet had come a long way, and there were bound to have been losses to disease, accident, and desertion, apart from casualties in the fighting at Artemisium. Some replacements may have been found, although there was then the task of integrating them into rowing teams, but there is also the strong possibility that many vessels did not have their full complement even at the opening of the campaign. The great king had commanded his subjects to provide ships, no doubt a set number for each leader or community, and such things were easily counted and checked, whereas counting every single crewman was less likely, as long as the ships had sufficient manpower to operate with reasonable efficiency. One scholar has even suggested that many Persian vessels were deliberately provided with the minimum number of crewmen to leave space for them to act as transports for men or stores when necessary and that some were even seen as reserves to replace ships lost in battle.[13]

The Greek situation was no doubt similar. A fleet of 200 Athenian ships required total crews equal to or larger than the entire male citizen population, which included a significant proportion of men too old to serve. The naval effort was the central commitment of the Athenians to the war effort, with all classes taking part. At some point in 480 BC, Cimon, the son of Miltiades, is supposed to have gathered a group of his friends, all young aristocrats with the proper qualification and knowledge to serve not simply as hoplites but as cavalry when necessary. Making a great show of it, these noblemen went to the Acropolis and formally dedicated their bridles to Athena. Cimon instead took down a shield hanging as a trophy in the temple, and then he and the rest walked to the Piraeus, signifying to all that they would serve at sea. When they did so, they would fight as deck crew, throwing missiles at the enemy and repulsing any attempt at boarding—or when the opportunity presented, fighting their way onto the deck of an enemy vessel. The hoplite had a role to play in a naval battle, but rarely did this mean pulling an oar. In addition, the Athenians had found at most 9,000 men to serve as hoplites at Marathon, whereas a decade later manning the fleet required three or four times as many men, even after some ships were loaned to the Plataeans and others, who provided crews.[14]

The same inscription recording the decision to evacuate Athens also describes the commitment of the Athenian fleet, with part of it to go to Artemisium, and stipulates how each ship was to be manned—for instance, that the marines were to be aged between twenty and thirty. Given that the deck offered a precarious platform—with men having to sit much of the time to keep the ship trimmed, then having to stand and fight and keep their balance under the terrific impact of ramming or being rammed—having younger, fitter men may have been an advantage. The rowers were to be provided not simply by citizens but by foreigners as well, which also makes sense given the sheer numbers required. In later years poorer citizens served alongside non-citizens and sometimes slaves, all of whom were paid. Significantly, each ship appears to be allocated just 100 rowers, and this does suggest that a vessel could still be effective without its maximum compliment of oarsmen. During the trials of the *Olympias*, on several occasions only the middle and upper tiers of the trireme were manned and the lower tier was not, without drastic reduction in performance.*[15]

---

* One complication is that the lowest tier of rowers generally failed to perform as well as expected in the trials of the *Olympias*, and the team behind the project planned to alter the design to improve this if ever a second reconstruction should be made. Modern rowers are significantly taller than their fifth century BC counterparts, so that in most cases only female rowers were short enough to fit into the space for the lowest tier, but they still felt their rowing movements were restricted. This may mean that the difference between fully manned with all three tiers of rowers and just having two might in reality have been far greater. It should always be remembered that the project was trying to deduce and replicate the lessons learned over generations by the Athenians. This only makes the success of the project all the more remarkable.

Perhaps this all means that there were situations when it was felt better to have perhaps 100 triremes with 75 per cent of their full crew than 75 at full complement, or 90 with two-thirds' crew rather than 60 fully manned. There would inevitably be some reduction in the power generated by a smaller crew, while careful arrangements would have to be made to balance the ship, since the bodies of the rowers provided the main ballast in a trireme. Other factors—most of all the level of training and coordination in rowing and the ability of the deck crew, especially the helmsmen, to steer, so that the best was brought out of the ship—were at least as important in making the ship effective, and probably more so. As with anything crafted by hand, even when the design is essentially the same, each vessel would behave in a unique way depending on conditions, and its performance in battle was the product of this and the ability of the crew at all levels. Thus, there is a high probability that triremes varied in size and even more in the number of men serving on them. This has implications for the total figures proposed for the men serving in a fleet, which, since the numbers are so big, means that reduction of a tenth, a quarter, or a third would be considerable, with implications for such matters as supply. Even so, the fleets would still be enormous and operated by very large numbers of people, just not quite as many as some estimates suggest.[16]

Salamis was a very big battle as well as an important one, although, as is usually the way with the ancient sources, it is hard to reconstruct what happened in detail. As the sun rose, the main part of the Persian fleet approached the mouth of the Saronic Gulf. Much of the army was formed on the shore of Attica to observe, and a grand viewing platform topped by a throne was ready for Xerxes. A detachment of Persian soldiers landed on the little island of Psytalleia, which lay near the middle of the channel, providing a secure refuge for any sailors who ended up in the sea and could swim that far.[17]

The Persian ships rowed into the channel, perhaps—or perhaps not—encouraged by the sight of forty or so Corinthian vessels sailing away. Yet they soon realised that the Greek fleet, rather than fleeing, was ready and waiting for them. The Greeks had had plenty of time to prepare, to issue orders and make sacrifices before they embarked. A grim tradition later circulated that Themistocles agreed to the sacrifice of three captured Persian noblemen alongside the usual animal sacrifice. The first indication that the Greeks were waiting and not inclined to run was the raising of the paean, the savage, shouting chant sung before battle, this time by far more voices than at Marathon. That at least is the story told by Aeschylus, the veteran of the 490 BC battle who was surely present at Salamis and whose play *The Persae* tells of how news of the battle dismayed the Persian court.[18]

Still, naval battles occurred at a slow pace of their own, and the great battle chant did not precede a jogging charge as it had at Marathon. The Persians pressed on, more and more of them following the leading squadrons into the waters between Salamis and the shore of Attica. At first the Greeks may have advanced, forming a line of ships, or more probably at least two lines, stretching for a couple of miles. Then they backed water, slowly pulling away from the enemy, whether to tidy up their formation or to lure the Persians further into the gulf. Admirals in an ancient naval battle could do little to influence the fighting once the fleets had deployed, for only the most rudimentary signals could be sent, and even then, there was no guarantee that everyone would hear or see them, let alone pay attention. For all the hundreds of ships involved, the fighting quickly broke down into contests of one against one, two against three, and the like.

Later there was an argument over how the fighting actually started, and rival claims put forward that it was an Athenian ship or one from Aegina whose captain spontaneously surged forward and rammed an enemy vessel. Other ships closed in, and more combats were fought. It is probably best to imagine an ancient naval battle along the lines of a massed dogfight between fighter aircraft in World War I or II—albeit without the third dimension of height. If ships tried to ram each other bow to bow, the result was mutually devastating. Perhaps the heavy Athenian triremes were capable of this, but it seems unlikely; not until late in the century did the Corinthians start to design ships strong enough to do this. Ironically enough, long before that time and probably soon after 480 BC, the Athenians switched to building lighter, faster, and more manoeuvrable triremes (like the *Olympias*), probably because the quality of their crews had improved substantially.[19]

At Salamis head-to-head clashes were to be avoided, even for the heavier Athenian ships, and the aim was to get around to the flank or rear of an enemy vessel. Striking against the stern was best or, failing that, at the rear sections of the hull. The aim was to come in at an angle, for attacking at something like ninety degrees risked driving the ram so deeply into the enemy hull that it could not be withdrawn. The *Olympias* trials consistently registered speeds of 7.5 to 8 knots for bursts lasting a few minutes, equivalent to ramming attacks or close manoeuvres in battle, and also showed considerable agility—for instance, making very tight turns. Fighting was very much a team effort, although the captain/helmsman more than anyone else was vital to success. It took careful judgement to time and direct an attack, always communicating with the rowing master to ensure that the right amount of power came at the right moment or that oars were pulled in whenever there was a danger that they might be struck by the ram or hull of an enemy ship.[20]

Even more than with the battles on land, there is a good chance that no one was ever able to offer a clear account of Salamis, for the simple reason that no one was in a position to see all that was happening and make sense of the confusion. Observers from the shore were too far away, and those in the fight too preoccupied, as well as limited in their view because triremes were fairly low vessels, and other ships blocked line of sight. So did wrecks. When a trireme was rammed by another, the hole made by the ram was not especially large—something like a foot square. Water came in, but did not flood in that quickly, which meant that apart from anyone injured by the strike, most of the crew had plenty of time to abandon ship. As the rowers, sailors, and marines jumped overboard—assuming that the ones on deck had not been knocked off by the impact—the ship was relieved of their combined weight. A disabled trireme tended to float rather than sink, because effectively its ballast had been removed. Some turned over, and Aeschylus wrote of the hulls of ships turned turtle.[21]

The fighting lasted for most of the day, although there were lulls and pauses when individual ships had a chance to rest. From the start, the Greeks did well, sinking far more ships than they lost. Sometimes, in spite of Persian archery and their stronger contingents of marines, they were also able to board and capture ships. Themistocles's promises panned out, and the conditions—perhaps including wind and tide—favoured the Greeks and especially the Athenians with their heavy triremes, their hulls seen as the 'wooden walls' of the oracle. Other Greek contingents also did extremely well, presumably using ships built in a range of different styles. Over time, the advantage shifted even more heavily in favour of the Greeks, perhaps because too many Persian ships had followed the advance elements too closely and crowded into the space, making it hard to manoeuvre or escape. Aristides led a party of hoplites by ship from Salamis to storm the island of Psytalleia, massacring the little Persian garrison and then killing any enemy sailor who swam there for refuge. Greeks who ended up in the sea had a good chance of swimming or floating to safety, whereas only those few Persians able to reach Attica avoided being speared or clubbed to death by Greeks in no mood to take prisoners.[22]

There are plenty of stories of individual exploits during the battle—for instance, of the captain of a trireme from Aegina ramming a fleeing Persian vessel being pursued by Themistocles and jubilantly yelling to the Athenians about what they thought of Aegina's attitude to Persia now. Probably most famous is the tale Herodotus tells of Queen Artemisia, who led from the deck of one of her warships. When the battle was going badly, she tried to flee, only for one of her own Carian warships to block her path. Making a snap decision, she rammed the friendly vessel, crippling it or overturning it, and was able to escape. Xerxes witnessed the action, recognising Artemisia's ship but mistaking her victim for a Greek warship, and sulkily commented that his women had become men, but his men had become women.[23]

There is no reason to doubt the courage of the Persian fleet at Salamis, for even the Greeks remembered that the enemy had fought hard and with skill. Yet the invaders did not have the incentive of fighting to protect their homes and were a less homogenous force than their opponents. The Phoenicians fought particularly well, as, it seems, did the Egyptians, both nations with strong maritime traditions. However, it is worth noting that only a minority on either side had much experience of a big battle at sea, apart from the recent fights off Artemisium. The Persians opted to give battle in a situation that favoured the Greeks and paid the price for this. Much of the credit must go to Themistocles, not simply for doing so much to create the Athenian fleet, without which the Greeks simply would not have had the strength to match the Persians under any condition. More than this, he helped guide the strategy of the war at sea, and by argument and guile not only kept the Greek fleet at Salamis but caused the battle to happen. In the aftermath he won the accolade as the man most responsible for the victory, although only because every leader voted for himself first but Themistocles second.[24]

Salamis was a Greek victory and a Persian defeat. It did not win the war, but like many a pivotal battle throughout history, it kept the Greeks in the fight and encouraged them. Herodotus does not record the losses on both sides, although a later source claims that 200 Persian ships were sunk and more captured, while the Greeks lost 40, with many more damaged. There is no way of knowing how accurate these numbers are, and since there is no certainty about the size of the fleets in the first place, the scale of losses is hard to judge. The

Persians' fleet was not destroyed, and there is a fair chance that after the battle they still had as many ships as the Greeks, if not more. Morale was another matter, and in this respect the advantage now lay overwhelmingly with the Greeks.[25]

Xerxes discussed with his senior commanders what to do, although, again, it is hard to know whether Herodotus based his account on any reliable information or simply deduced what seemed likely. The campaigning season was spent, so that a major offensive against the Peloponnese that year was not practical. For the moment, his fleet was not fit to play a major role with any likelihood of success, and all those sailors and rowers still needed to be fed. Salamis was an embarrassing failure, but this did not alter the fact that most of Greece outside the Peloponnese had surrendered or been overrun, Athens was in ruins, and the head of the Spartan king had been impaled on a spike.[26]

The great king decided to return to Asia and leave the rest of the war to his army commander, Mardonius, who would keep the pick of the troops to complete the job. He would win the conflict on land, so that the fleet, so burdensome to maintain, was sent back, and for the moment the land contingent withdrew to Thessaly. Mardonius and his troops were to remain there, the task of feeding them made easier by the support of the cities of the region that had submitted and by closer proximity to whatever resources remained in the supply dumps established before the campaign. Xerxes kept going, escorted by a large army. The sources talk of hunger and breakdown of discipline in this force, and while retreating armies commonly fall apart, the sources most likely exaggerated. A storm had destroyed the bridges across the Hellespont, so this time the great king had to use a boat, and he, his court, and his army were easily ferried across the strait.[27]

Themistocles had suggested that the Greek fleet should hasten to the Dardanelles, destroy the bridges, and trap Xerxes and his soldiers, but the idea got no support from the other leaders, most of whom were eager to see the back of the great king and had no desire for him to remain in Europe. Instead, elements of the fleet started to operate in the islands of the Aegean, liberating unwilling subjects of Persia and attacking communities more ardent in their loyalty to Xerxes.[28]

Mardonius had withdrawn, which meant that the Athenian refugees could return home, at least for the moment, and see what havoc had been wrought on their homes and lands. That this big Persian army planned to stay in Greece was soon clear; come the spring of 479 BC, it was bound to march south again, and there was nothing to stop it from overrunning Attica for a second time. Salamis had kept the alliance led by Sparta backed by Athens in the fight, at least for the moment. The war had still to be won, and there was every possibility that it could still be lost.

14

THE GREAT BATTLE

The Persian army in Greece and the campaign and Battle of Plataea, late 480–479 BC

THE GREEKS HAD WON AT SALAMIS, AND THE PERSIANS HAD lost, although the scale of the success came as a surprise to everyone and the Greek leaders most of all. Herodotus is clear that the Greeks were preparing and fully expected to fight another fleet action on the day after Salamis. After all, Artemisium had gone on for days, and even if they had sunk far more Persian ships this time, there were still plenty left. The rapid withdrawal of the Persian fleet and then the Persian army at first stunned and then elated them; because it was so unexpected, the victory seemed all the more miraculous. It was natural to thank the gods, but as the scale of the success became apparent, the dedications locally and at the Panhellenic shrines like Delphi grew particularly lavish. The pronouncements of the oracle also soon became a good deal more optimistic, as the chances of successful resistance were revived.[1]

A strong hint of improvisation in the Greek's reaction to the withdrawal divided the counsels even more than usual. In addition, it is vital to remember that absolutely no one on the Greek side had any experience of waging war on this scale. Never before had any group of Greek states gathered so many warships in one place, and even these had only operated together for a matter of weeks, stretching the cities' ability to supply them almost to the limit. Waging war in this way and for so long required a good deal of invention and improvisation, adding to the difficulty in judging what was practical for them to do in the aftermath of Salamis, as well as what was desirable. As mentioned in the last chapter, the Greek fleet failed to catch the Persians and instead tried to coerce and persuade some of the island communities into joining the alliance, with limited success. Autumn, a season when bad weather was likely and naval operations difficult and often dangerous, soon ended the campaign, and the fleet dispersed.[2]

Themistocles was later accused of trying to extort money for his own enrichment from the islanders, and whether he tried to get more than was needed to pay and supply the fleet is impossible to know. For the moment his reputation still rode high, at least with the allies. Apart from being awarded the prize for leading the victory, he was invited to Sparta, where he was praised and presented with a wreath of olive leaves. The *hippeis*, the pick of Spartan citizens under arms, escorted him on the start of his journey back to Attica, an honour never before accorded to a foreigner and never repeated. Yet Themistocles's popularity with his fellow Athenians soon plummeted, perhaps increased by a wider mood of sorrow and anger as they saw what the Persians had done to their homes. Athens had suffered especially badly, with the deliberate destruction of the sacred sites on the Acropolis and less focused but still widespread destruction elsewhere. The Persians had not been in Attica all that long, so the amount of damage to the villages and farms varied, but even when it was small, these were communities of farmers, where land had often been in the same family for generations. All will have felt something like the anger, almost a sense of violation, experienced by anyone whose house has been burgled, just magnified many times.[3]

Perhaps the Athenians were unhappy and angry and needed to vent their rage on someone. Perhaps they felt that the navy and the sea would be less important in the next year than they had been in 480 BC. Or perhaps, now that the immediate danger had been removed for a few months, relief allowed the normal competitiveness of a vibrant democracy simply to resume. Whatever the cause, Themistocles was not included amongst the ten generals, the strategoi, chosen for the next year and does not appear in the accounts of 479 BC. Presumably he served as a hoplite, for the Athenians eventually mobilised most of those who were eligible, but he was not entrusted with any position of authority.

Salamis and the subsequent retreat of the Persians had come as a surprise. A far less pleasant surprise came when Mardonius and his army settled down to pass the winter in Thessaly, for this made clear that the war was far from over, even if Xerxes had gone. An army remained, as large or larger than any force the Greeks might hope to assemble and including substantial numbers of cavalry. Although Leonidas's stand at Thermopylae had demonstrated that Greek hoplites could more than hold their own in a head-to-head confrontation in the narrow pass, this offered little reassurance that the Persians could be defeated in open country.

No one could campaign in any strength during the winter, and even when spring and summer came, the Greeks could not muster a large army and then keep it in the field for a prolonged campaign of manoeuvre. No one wanted to be away from home—and for most hoplites, from their farms—for weeks on end. Even the Spartans were reluctant to leave for a long time, given the peculiar nature of their regime. Apart from that, gathering and transporting enough food to supply a large force for long was very difficult. Any campaign needed to be brief, and ideally decisive, since once an army dispersed, re-forming it at a later date would be hard. This meant that the initiative lay with the Persians, so the Greeks had to wait to see what Mardonius did before they could decide on a response.[4]

Before any military action, the Persian commander did what any self-respecting Persian commander would do and embarked on a programme of diplomacy. None of the mainland Greek communities to submit to the Persians in 480 BC had broken away from them, and most were to send troops to fight under Persian command once the campaign began. In addition some of the Phocians had given in and joined the invaders, although others stayed in the mountains and managed to evade the enemy and survive the winter. Persian envoys and gifts went out to other communities, especially as the campaigning season approached and the threat of the Persian army became more immediate.[5]

Mardonius sent Alexander I of Macedon to Athens as his envoy, for the king was known to have connections with the city, no doubt including ties of friendship with individual aristocrats. As someone who had competed at Olympia, Alexander was at once a reliable agent from the Persian perspective and someone able to understand Greek aristocrats. There is no evidence to suggest that he had visited Athens before or seen its democracy at work, although Athenian activity around the Dardanelles and on the European coast near Macedonia ensured that he had negotiated with Athenians often enough. As noted, the ships of the Athenian fleet, the ones that had made Salamis possible, were built largely from timber brought from Macedonia.[6]

The terms carried by Alexander were generous by Persian standards, promising autonomy if the Athenians submitted to Xerxes and demanding no more punishment than had already been exacted. Whether or not the threat was overt or so obvious that the words need not be said, the alternative was a fresh invasion by an army far bigger than the Athenians could hope to resist on their own. To have the slightest chance of facing off against Mardonius on land, the Athenians needed the help of allies, most of all the Spartans and other Peloponnesians. Less clear was whether either would be willing to send the greater part of their citizens to defend Attica, whether on the spot or to confront the Persians further north in Boeotia. In 480 BC the first instinct of most Peloponnesians was to defend the isthmus, the only land route to their own territory, and there was little indication that this mood had changed.

Themistocles was remembered as the wily manipulator, but he was far from the only Athenian to admire and emulate Odysseus. Alexander I was entertained but not given a chance to speak for many days, so that there was time for the news of his arrival to reach the Spartans, who duly sent envoys to Athens. None of the sources suggest that the Athenians were considering defecting, and the presence of the envoy was meant to remind their allies in the Peloponnese that they needed the Athenians as much as the Athenians needed them. Had the Athenians decided to cooperate with the invaders, then their fleet would have rendered the Isthmus of Corinth indefensible. At long last, Alexander was allowed to present his proposals, emphasising to the Spartans that it would be very easy for the Athenians to switch sides. Fear of this had added to Spartan assurances of their continued willingness to stand together, so, having emphasised the point, the Athenians bluntly refused Mardonius's offer.[7]

Diplomacy is rarely about the permanent and rests on the assumption that attitudes and circumstances can change. The rejection did not in any way sour the Athenians link to Alexander I, and Mardonius would try to persuade them to submit once again, after he had advanced. Yet, when the Athenians met to debate this renewed Persian offer, only one man suggested considering it, prompting his neighbours and fellow citizens to stone him to death. Perhaps a crowd of women was waiting near the meeting to find out what would happen, for when the news spread, a large group of them went and murdered the man's wife and children. The Athenians were determined to fight, and this determination appears never to have wavered. They just needed to cajole and convince their allies to stand by them and not simply protect the Peloponnese.[8]

Even so, the allies had difficulty agreeing on a detailed strategy for the coming campaign until when and how Mardonius would attack was absolutely clear. For many Spartans and Peloponnesians, the defence of their homelands, still unsullied by the invaders, seemed more important than protecting Attica, already sacked by the enemy.

There was a desire to follow up the success at sea by attacking the islands nearer the Ionian coast, keeping the Persian fleet busy there and unable to return to Greece. In 480 BC the Spartans had sent an otherwise unknown man to command the combined fleet, but this year one of the kings would go. The other, the son of Leonidas, was no more than a boy, so a regent was appointed to act on his behalf. The first choice fell on one of Leonidas's brothers, but this man died during the winter of 480–479 BC, and he was replaced by his son (and thus Leonidas's nephew), Pausanias.[9]

A willingness to commit a king to the naval effort showed that the Spartans were taking this aspect of the war seriously, although they remained incapable of providing a significant number of ships. Altogether, a fleet of around 110 triremes was assembled at Aegina, but to turn this into a major force capable of taking on the Persians required the Athenians to take part, and they were hesitating, wanting more assurances that their allies were not simply concerned with the Peloponnese. An offer to give shelter to Athenian non-combatants for the duration of the fighting failed to convince them, as long as the isthmus was planned as the main line of resistance, which continued work on the wall across it made clear.[10]

In late spring or early summer, Mardonius marched from Thessaly into Boeotia and then on to Attica, striking before the Athenians had a chance to begin the harvest. For a second time, the population was evacuated to Salamis, safe behind even this narrow stretch of water because the Persian fleet was still at Samos on the other side of the Aegean and showed no signs of heading west. Yet evacuations, however well conducted, did nothing to evict the invaders. An Athenian delegation hurried to Sparta, including two of the ten elected generals and perhaps also Cimon, the son of Miltiades. Aristides may have joined them at some point.[11]

The Spartans were busy with one of their many festivals, the Hyacinthia dedicated to a boy lover of Apollo. This did little to speed up the negotiations, but more important was a deep reluctance to fight outside the Peloponnese. Days passed, then weeks, without Sparta's leading men showing a willingness to bend and without any real plan emerging. The Athenians grew ever more frustrated, until they made plain that if their allies were unwilling to defend Attica, then they would have no choice but to accede to the Persian demands. That would have meant handing over to Mardonius a fleet almost double the size of the one mustered under command of Sparta's king, opening up the Peloponnese to invasion. The threat clinched the matter and was more important than the added pleas of states like Plataea. Even so, the Spartans were not about to be seen as giving in to pressure and secretly sent out orders to muster a large army.[12]

Five thousand men, some two-thirds of the total number of male citizens, and perhaps more if estimates of the overall population are too large, armed themselves and marched out under cover of darkness, led by Pausanias. Herodotus claimed that seven helots accompanied each Spartan, carrying supplies and also ready to fight. The next day the stunned ambassadors learned that the Spartan army was already on the march and would shortly be reinforced by another 5,000 hoplites provided by the perioeci, those citizens of lesser communities forming part of the Spartan state. Now that the Spartans had finally given a lead, other states rapidly mustered their forces and sent them to join the army as it paused at the Isthmus of Corinth. The Athenians fielded 8,000 hoplites backed by 600 more from Plataea, as well as sending ships to the navy, more than doubling its strength. Corinth sent 5,000 hoplites, Megara and Sicyon 3,000 each, and other states provided contingents of 1,000 or fewer. Altogether there were some 38,700 hoplites and perhaps a similar number of servants and light infantrymen. Many scholars are reluctant to accept Herodotus's figure of seven helots for every Spartan, but if this is correct, then the total for the army would have been over 100,000, an immense, perhaps impossible, number for the allied states to have fed. This has led some to suggest that a high proportion of the helots were not with the army and instead tasked with bringing convoys of supplies to support the campaign.[13]

Argos sent no men to join the allies and instead despatched a messenger to Mardonius, warning him that a Greek army was on the way. Suitably warned, the Persian commander withdrew from Attica into Boeotia, judging that the terrain around Athens was not well suited to his cavalry. As importantly, there is a good chance that only some columns had gone to ravage Attica. Pulling back allowed Mardonius to concentrate more of his main force and also put everyone nearer to the supplies offered by his allies at Thebes and elsewhere, as well as to whatever stockpiles remained in Thessaly and Macedonia. Part of the Persian army under another commander remained at some distance from the main force and never in fact joined up. Even so, Mardonius had a big army, with at least parity in overall numbers to the Greeks and possibly a significant advantage. A substantial part of his force was Greek, from Boeotia and Thessaly, with even a Phocian contingent joining, which meant that there were hoplites on both sides. Contingents from Thessaly and Thebes also added to the already strong force of horsemen at Mardonius's disposal.[14]

Mardonius came from an important aristocratic family, with connections to the royal family and generations of service in senior posts. He had served under Darius, notably commanding the operations securing Thrace and Macedonia in 493 BC, a campaign blemished by the loss of much of his fleet in the storm off Mount Athos. This failure probably led to his exclusion from the 490 BC expedition, but any loss of favour was temporary, and he was Xerxes's most senior subordinate with the army in 480 BC. He was by then a mature man, with a lot of military, diplomatic, and administrative experience, although saying anything too specific about his talent for command is impossible. He may never have commanded such a large army in battle.[15]

This was certainly true of his opposite number, Pausanias, who was only in his twenties and may never have fought on campaign at all. He had never commanded an army; indeed, no Greek leader had ever commanded an army as big as this one because such an army had never before gathered in one place. No Greek had ever before had to coordinate the movements of so many men, let alone feed them. It helped that everyone spoke the same language, whatever their dialect, and that they fought in essentially the same way; on the other hand, these were not formally disciplined armies but groups of citizens, many of them used to discussion rather than automatic obedience to orders. There was plenty of enthusiasm, for these men were voluntarily fighting to protect their homes and families and standing alongside neighbours and relatives whose esteem mattered, but they did not comprise a sophisticated army, speedy and supple in its movements.[16]

The Greeks needed to make Mardonius and the Persians quit Greece, which meant that they needed to defeat them in battle, since they were unlikely to want to go otherwise. At the same time, the army was truly immense by Greek standards and could not stay in the field for very long, certainly for no more than a month and probably less, for food would run short, and men would need to return home to work. Yet this was also the only army the Greeks would ever be able to muster. If it was defeated in battle and suffered heavy losses, then apart from the devastating blow to morale, the casualties simply could not be replaced until the next generation had grown to maturity. All this meant that Pausanias really needed to fight a big battle but had to be very careful when and where he did so, since if things went badly, he could lose the entire war in a matter of hours.

Mardonius's problems were different. He was in charge of an army formed by an empire very good at organisation, consisting of soldiers who—at least for the duration of the war—were full-time fighting men who did not need to return home for the harvest. His Greek allies were different, but their role was secondary to the main fighting force of high-quality, mostly Iranian soldiers. Even so, supplying the army took a great deal of effort, for Greece was not the easiest place to support a large army, particularly one with a lot of horses. The task, though less challenging for him than for his opponents, was still difficult, especially as he needed to take care not to drain the lands of his allies of resources. At the same time, while winning a big battle and smashing the enemy army was attractive, it was not the only way for the Persians to win. The threat of force was less risky than its actual use and might persuade one or two or more of the Greek states to defect. The more communities that changed sides, the weaker the alliance against the great king became, and in turn the greater the chance that others would also decide that further resistance was hopeless. Mardonius held the initiative and could afford to fight a long war, at least as long as Xerxes let him retain his command. No servant of the great king could afford too many mistakes or disappointments.

As the two armies closed near Plataea, neither side was keen to rush into battle, and instead they settled down to watch each other, waiting for the right opportunity. Pausanias's Greek army arrayed itself on high ground as protection from the Persian cavalry, and as before Marathon, both sides watched the other, neither willing to attack at a perceived disadvantage. Day followed day, and Mardonius sent forward some of his horsemen to probe the Greek position. They found a weak spot where the Megarians were stationed and the slope offered less real advantage to a defender. Squadrons of cavalry started to come closer, rushing in to shoot arrows or throw javelins and then wheeling away and withdrawing. Pausanias's army did not stand for hours on end in formation, ready to fight, for that was not how Greek armies worked, and hoplite equipment was too heavy for this. Presumably a detachment stood to arms to cover the rest, and some of the light infantry supported them.

However it was managed, the Megarians began to suffer from the nibbling attacks of the horsemen and were unable to drive them off. They asked for aid, specifically Athenian aid, at least according to an anecdote that may well have an Athenian origin. Three hundred

Athenian hoplites, probably the men able to stand to arms the fastest or perhaps a special unit kept at the disposal of the overall Athenian commander, were sent. With them came some archers, perhaps mercenaries hired and normally employed on Athenian warships, and the longer range of their weapons changed the balance of the fight. Chance played a role, for one of the arrows brought down the horse of the commander of this division of cavalry, who was thrown to the ground. Horses tend to kick up a lot of dust on dry ground, and this, combined with the standard tactic of surging forward, loosing missiles, and then galloping away, meant that his squadron did not notice and left him behind.

The Greeks did see what had happened and surged forward to surround the prostrate man. Repeating blows failed to do much damage, for underneath his colourful outer tunic, the Persian general wore armour of gilded plates. Eventually someone stabbed him in the eye, according to Plutarch, using the butt end spike of a spear. By this time his absence had been noted, and the Persian cavalry charged, no longer by squadrons but en masse, to rescue their commander, or at least retrieve his corpse. The Athenians had already requested aid, and growing numbers of their fellow citizens and allies arrived, until the Persians had been repulsed in a hard-fought skirmish. This was encouraging, because it demonstrated that Persian cavalry could be defeated in the right circumstances. More worrying was the damage the Persians had been able to inflict on the Megarians in the first place, as well as the central role played by the Athenian archers, who were relatively few in number and could have far less influence on a full-scale battle.[17]

After this little victory, the Greek army moved forward to another line of high ground, closer to Plataea and, even more importantly, with better access to water from a stream. Mardonius shifted his own army to take up a similarly strong position facing the new Greek line, and once again both sides settled down to watch each other, neither willing to attack the enemy. So far both armies were managing to feed their men, although the task was getting harder as day followed day. The Greeks bickered about precedence in the battle-line, the Athenians successfully convincing a majority of the army that they deserved to be on the left wing, the second place of honour after the right wing. After eight days, Mardonius, guided by his Theban allies, sent out a force of cavalry under cover of darkness to conceal themselves near the mouth of a pass through which the Greeks were bringing supply convoys. Next morning, one of the convoys arrived, and the Persians emerged from ambush, killing or capturing the slaves guarding it, as well as some of the draft animals, and hauling off the remaining waggons to their own camp. Mardonius also sent his cavalry to harass Greeks whenever they went to the stream to fetch water, and after two days this became too dangerous to attempt even in daylight.[18]

Pausanias's army faced running out of food and water, but no one seems to have known what to do, and a couple more days passed. Herodotus says that during the next night, a lone horseman rode up to the sector where the Athenians were camped and declared himself to be their friend, Alexander I of Macedon. He warned them that Mardonius planned a full-scale assault. Perhaps this happened, even if the rider was a messenger rather than the king himself, or perhaps this was a good story that Alexander was happy to spread after the war was over. Far less plausible is the claim that as a result the Spartans and Athenians swapped positions, since the latter had experience of beating the Persians at Marathon, but that both returned to their original sectors before anything else happened. Still, the story may reflect the indecision within the high command of the Greek army.[19]

Mardonius did not launch an all-out attack straightaway and instead continued to wear down the Greeks' ability to resist. A cavalry column was sent around behind the Greek position and spoiled the water in, or somehow blocked, the fresh spring that had become the Greeks' main water source once access to the stream was cut off.

Pausanias met with the leaders of each contingent, and they agreed that their current position was untenable. Instead, under cover of darkness, the army was to withdraw to another position, dubbed 'the island' by Herodotus, which had little streams on two sides, offering protection and water, as well as a safer approach for supplies coming from further afield. The need to pull back was reinforced as the Persian cavalry probed and harassed different sectors of their front throughout the day. With so few good archers in the army, there was no way of defending against such attacks all along the line.[20]

When night fell, the Greeks moved off, but marching a large army in the dark is difficult, and these were not trained soldiers used to such things. Confusion was inevitable, with columns getting lost or breaking up. One contingent overshot its destination by a mile or so accidentally. Uniquely, Spartans did practice travelling at night, at least as individuals and possibly in groups, so ought to have had fewer problems, save that one of their officers refused to obey the order to move. The details may have become garbled, so that it is hard to know whether the man in question felt it dishonourable to retreat at all or something about the young Pausanias provoked his resentment. The regent went to give his orders in person, leading to an angry exchange witnessed by some Athenians sent over to find out what was going on.

The man in question adamantly refused to obey, and Pausanias ordered the rest of his men to hold their original positions. Only at dawn did he begin to move off, perhaps hoping that the recalcitrant officer would finally back down and follow. The main Spartan force marched for more than a mile before halting and giving an opportunity for the isolated unit to join them. Around this time, the Persian cavalry began to move forward, planning to resume their harassing attacks of the past two days. They saw the isolated Spartan unit, which finally began to move back, and it quickly became apparent that the other Greeks had retreated. A messenger galloped back to report the news, while the cavalry commanders followed the enemy.

The Spartans and their allies from Tegea had gone the shortest distance and were quickly located.[21]

Mardonius saw an opportunity to strike at a disordered enemy, already retreating and surely dispirited, and seized the chance with both hands. Mustering his army, he led it out to follow the cavalry. None of this happened quickly, but within a few hours the main strength of the Persian army was advancing with orders to attack any Greeks they encountered. At some point, Mardonius and his commanders began to realise that the Greeks were not panicking, as they willingly turned around, ready to fight, and even advanced to contact. By then it was too late to halt the attack, even if the Persians had wanted to, and they probably still felt confident. Thus, the great Battle of Plataea happened largely by accident. Neither army was concentrated, and this was not a simple clash between two ordered battle-lines but a series of encounters, really of smaller battles, fought over a wide area with little or no contact and coordination between the leaders of each distinct clash.

Herodotus and the later sources focus on the Athenians and the Spartans, plus those allies in close support of them and say little about the fighting elsewhere, so that even by the standards of other ancient battles, much remains obscure and is unlikely ever to be known. The Athenians and Plataeans were on the left, the second-highest post of honour after the right wing—the shield-less side and the side of the spear for an individual, so associated with the offensive. They had been allocated this after a dispute with Tegea, and won on the basis of Marathon, helped by the fact that after the Spartans and perioeci, they were the largest contingent with the army. Facing them were the Thebans and others from Boeotia, so that here this was a clash of hoplite against hoplite, Greek against Greek—and also, as was common, of old enemies. Phalanxes formed up, advanced, and clashed, and the Athenians and their allies won, driving the medizing Greeks back.

Pausanias was on the right of the army with the Spartans, perioeci, helots, and Tegeans, and facing them was the pick of the Persian infantry, supported by cavalry, all under the direct command of Mardonius. The horsemen were in the lead, harassing the Spartans as they formed up, but Pausanias probably only realised that this skirmish was turning into a battle when the Persian infantry came up. Hastily the Spartans began the rituals necessary before battle, as Mardonius's men formed into a line facing them, at most a couple of hundred yards away. Both sides performed sacrifices and waited, although the Persian archers were in range and began to shoot arrows. There may have been a covering force, but most of the Spartans sat down in their units, each man sheltering as well as he could behind his round shield, which, with helmet, cuirass, and in some cases greaves, protected him well—well, but not perfectly. One man, widely acknowledged as the handsomest man in the army, was mortally wounded by an arrow that found a gap in his protection.[22]

The Spartans waited because the omens provided by the sacrificed animals were not favourable for battle. Animal after animal was killed, and perhaps this failure to see favourable signs was the genuine opinion of the priest or perhaps a reflection of Pausanias's continuing reluctance to commit to battle. He had sent a rider to the Athenians asking them to move to support him or, if they were held in their position, then at least to send him their archers. Pausanias may have felt that the situation was out of control and that his army risked being defeated in detail. By the time the messenger reached the Athenians, they were already heavily engaged and could not send help, but for the moment the Spartan regent did not know this, and it is unlikely that he could see much of what was happening in the rest of the battlefield. He waited, and his men endured the barrage. There were probably few other fatalities, but a wound to the arm or leg usually took a man out of the battle. The risk was there, made worse because the hoplites could not strike back, for the javelins and stones available to the helots and other light infantry were badly outranged. Pausanias began to pray to Hera.

The hoplites from Tegea were stationed next to the Spartans, but lacked their training and upbringing and, it seemed, their patience.

They stood, shuffled into rough formation, and began to advance, quickening their pace to get through the storm of arrows as fast as they could, just as the Athenians had done at Marathon. Then, through the perceived will of the gods or the sense that the regent had made up his mind, the next sacrifice offered a clear sign of divine favour. Pausanias ordered the rest of his men to attack as well. They went in better order, so that the Tegeans reached the enemy first.

The Persian infantry had adopted their usual formation, the men of the front rank planting their rectangular shields into the ground to form a barrier. They and perhaps the next rank or so had spears, and behind them were archers, shooting up over the heads of the front ranks. Such missiles were hard to aim, and the idea was to deluge the enemy with a cloud of arrows. Once the Greeks closed up with the Persian shield wall, it became difficult for the archers to drop their arrows onto them, and close fighting developed. If anything, the hand-thrown javelins and rocks lobbed by the helots from behind the lines of the phalanx were more suited to this short range. The Persians were brave and determined, and there was a stiff fight before the Greeks battered their way through the line of shields. As at Marathon, hoplite equipment was better suited to this close-in fighting, the armour protecting men well, while their spears had a longer reach than those of the enemy.

Yet, just as at Marathon, in spite of this the Persians fought hard and did not give in quickly. This was remembered as a bitter combat and lasted for a long time, although, as always, just how long is hard to know. Herodotus said that it came to 'shoving', like the contest over Leonidas's corpse. This was a large engagement, with some 11,500 hoplites squaring off against as many or more Persians in and around the precinct of a sanctuary of Demeter, and the odds are that the combat swayed back and forth in different parts of the line, with lulls and surges in each direction. Steadily, the Spartans and their allies kept pushing forward. Mardonius was close to the fighting, urging his men on, and was brought down by a missile—apparently

THE GREAT BATTLE

a stone picked up and thrown by a Spartan, something straight out of the *Iliad*. The blow or the fall killed the Persian commander, and this, combined with the continued pressure from the Greeks, led to the collapse of the Persian line.

Both wings of the Persian army were in rout, and in the central sector the Persians either did not come into serious contact or were likewise defeated. None of this was due to any great tactical sophistication on either side, and neither Pausanias nor Mardonius was able to influence events other than those immediately around them. Everywhere the Persians seemed to be in retreat, while the Greeks advanced, not always in very good order. A large group of men from Megara and other cities, hurrying in pursuit and straggling in a loose mass, had the misfortune to encounter Theban cavalry, still fairly fresh and under control. The horsemen rode down the scattered infantry, killing some 600 men and pursuing them for a mile or more, emphasising the scattered and open nature of the fighting.

This was the heaviest loss suffered by the Greek army anywhere on the battlefield. Otherwise, Herodotus said that the Athenians lost fifty-two men, the Tegeans sixteen, and the Spartans ninety-one. All of these numbers are likely to include only hoplites and to exclude any helots and light infantry to fall. Although relatively modest in total, this was testament to the effectiveness of a hoplite's shield and body armour, which made it difficult to inflict a fatal wound with the weaponry available to the Persians. The wounded probably outnumbered the dead by a large margin, perhaps by as much as five or even ten times. Among the Spartan dead was the last survivor of the 300 at Thermopylae, who fought with such spectacular courage in a desire to prove himself that other Spartans judged him unworthy of being recognised as the best warrior on the field. That accolade was reserved for a man who had done a better of job of staying in formation with his comrades and shown excellence in a more disciplined and less reckless way.[23]

Persian losses were much heavier, as was always the case when a side broke while in close contact with the enemy. The pursuit was limited, not least because the Greeks possessed no significant force of horsemen, while much of the Persian cavalry was still in some sort of order. Once the Greeks reached the Persian camp, they lost interest in chasing fleeing soldiers and instead focused their attention on this palisaded position. There was some fighting, and the Athenians subsequently boasted that the Spartans had to wait for them to arrive before they could force a way inside. When the Greeks did break in, they ran amok, slaughtering soldiers and camp followers alike amid the tents full of luxuries. Pausanias protected and freed an Ionian Greek woman who was there as mistress of one of the commanders. Others were less fortunate and were taken as slaves, although the Spartan regent is supposed to have restricted looting. Select items were taken to be dedicated to the gods, and the Greeks soon turned to proper burial of their dead, who were interred in a series of tombs on the battlefield.[24]

The loss of the camp probably meant the loss of most remaining supplies with the field army, but as the surviving troops re-formed, they made no attempt to recapture it. The spirit of the Persian army was broken, from the highest levels down, and none of the remaining senior officers appear to have thought of anything else but retreat. This extended to the commander of the other corps, which had not been involved in the battle and had operated independently of Mardonius's main force. The remnants of Mardonius's men joined these troops, and then all began the long march back to the Dardanelles. No one was to remain in Greece, and the allies of the great king there were left to their own devices beyond whatever protection his name offered. That this was diminishing was illustrated when former allies, including the Macedonians, chose to harry the retreating Persian army, although the damage they managed to inflict was probably inflated in later years.[25]

A second severe blow to Xerxes's war on the Greeks was delivered around the same time as Plataea, and tradition claimed it actually fell on the same day. The Greek fleet had become a viable force once the Athenians had contributed ships and more than doubled the total available to some 250. For a long time it waited, since the Persian fleet, reduced to barely 300 ships, many not properly manned, stayed on Samos and made no aggressive move, content by its mere presence to overawe the Ionian communities. Eventually the Spartan King commanding the fleet decided to attack, crossing the Aegean to Samos. Such was the poor state and even poorer morale of the Persians that they refused to face the enemy at sea, and instead they crossed to the Asian shore and drew up most of their vessels near Mount Mycale, surrounding them with a rampart. The Greeks landed down the coast and marched on the position. Appeals were made to the Samians and other Ionian Greeks serving with the Persians to remember their true loyalties, prompting nervous commanders to have these men disarmed. There appears to have been little will to resist in any quarter, and there may have been too few men to guard the long perimeter necessary to enclose the ships. The Greeks stormed the position and slaughtered the Persians, looting the camp and burning the warships.[26]

The whole campaign demonstrated the overwhelming dominance of the Greeks at sea, which makes it all the more important to remember that the Athenian fleet was a very recent creation. The victory at Mycale, following on from the hard-fought triumph at Salamis, meant that any naval supremacy the Persians had possessed in the eastern Mediterranean was shattered, at least as long as the main Greek states were willing to work together. There is every sign that by 479 BC the Persian high command had lost interest in the war at sea, and one reason for the lacklustre performance of the Persian fleet was that substantial numbers of men had been allowed to return to their home communities.

Plataea was the critical battle, for on land the Persians had not given up. Luck played a big role in the outcome, for until the final battle, the balance in the campaign was favouring Mardonius and slowly weakening the Greek army. Somehow, throughout the year, the alliance between the Greek states led by Sparta had held together, and they had eventually decided to act, forming an army and confronting the Persians. None of this came easily, and at any stage it could all have fallen apart. If Mardonius had not attacked the apparently retreating enemy, then the campaign might well have gone on without such a decisive outcome. One or both sides would soon have been forced to disengage in order to supply themselves. The Greek army had already been in the field for several weeks, and how long it could have remained together in any position before being forced to disperse is far from clear. If it had dispersed, whether it could have mustered again later in the year is equally uncertain. Disunity was never far from the surface in the alliance opposing Persia, and, more importantly, the harvest had to be brought in. No Greek state, not even Sparta, was suited at this stage to waging all-out war for months on end.

Events prevented them from having to do this. The battle was fought by the Greeks, scattered and in separate contingents but still united as one huge army with the same purpose. Each of the main encounters played more to the strengths of the Greeks than the Persians, so that chance brought on almost the ideal battle for them to fight. Unity survived, and the assembled hoplites of more than two dozen states fought as they best knew how, and won. Like Marathon, this was a victory for hoplites, making it all the more satisfying to the better-off citizens of each community compared to Salamis, where the poor and non-citizens had provided the rowers on whom success depended. Salamis had stalled the Persian invasion and kept the Greeks in the fight. Plataea, confirmed by Mycale, had driven the invaders from Greece.

15

HONOUR, PRESTIGE, AND EMPIRE

*Adding to the Greek victory,
the new alliance led by Athens, 479–c. 470 BC*

IN 479 BC THE GREEK STATES THAT HAD RALLIED UNDER SPARtan leadership won a great victory, soon made all the greater when the Persians evacuated their remaining troops from Greece without leaving a single garrison behind. Xerxes's invasion had been defeated, and this was a serious blow to the great king's reputation. Although he could boast that Athens was in ruins and one of Sparta's kings was dead, so that his most prominent enemies in mainland Greece had paid a price for their past conduct, the defeats at Salamis and Plataea damaged his prestige. Even Mycale, which was much smaller in scale, was embarrassing as a defeat inflicted on the mainland of Asia itself that, for the moment, effectively broke Persian naval power.

Xerxes had accompanied the invasion, intent on making clear that the anticipated triumph was a personal one and proof that he was a worthy successor to Darius and Cyrus. This meant that some of the stigma of failure was bound to attach itself to him, even if he had made his departure after Salamis, so had not been present at Plataea. Great kings had suffered defeats before, some of them serious, and had continued to rule, managing the administration of the empire well and parading other, non-military achievements. Heavy though the losses were in ships and men in 480–479 BC, they did not cripple the military might of the still vast Achaemenid Empire, at least in the longer term. There was no prospect of the Spartans or any of their allies striking at the heartland of the empire, which remained as many weeks' march from the coast as it had been when Sparta's leaders had quickly rejected any thought of an attack in the early days of the Ionian rebellion. After 479 BC the Persians were in no position to amass a fresh grand army or fleet quickly, for apart from recovering from the recent defeats, mobilising the strength of the empire always took a long time. Yet the basis of their strength, most of all the huge reserves of manpower and wealth, remained in place. The Achaemenid Empire remained the greatest power in the known world.[1]

Xerxes's personal reputation was damaged, as was faith in his rule, but in neither case was this fatal, for the great king was expected to play other roles, and Greece was distant and vaguely known by most of his subjects. The sources say little of his remaining years, other than a lurid tale of lust, deception, and sadistic cruelty within the royal family recounted by Herodotus. This is akin to similar stories of murderous passions within many other dynasties of the ancient world, including Rome's emperors, and, as always, distinguishing truth from malicious gossip is hard. Xerxes, the man who had ascended the throne without bloodshed, was eventually murdered in a palace coup and ultimately replaced by one of his sons, Artaxerxes, in 465 BC. There is a good chance that the heavy losses in Greece and the limited achievements of the expedition weakened Xerxes's reputation and that he was unable to restore it fully. Perhaps his own sense of frustration at the failure of the expedition preyed upon his mind, making him feel less secure and rendering him ever more suspicious of family and courtiers, so that he became a poorer leader, but this cannot be more than speculation. Some thirteen years passed between the defeat of the expedition to Greece and Xerxes's assassination, which means that any connection between the two was limited. Other factors, incidents, perceived failures, and grievances were surely more important in Xerxes's eventual fall. His reign was certainly not a period of serious decline for the empire as a whole, and Artaxerxes took over a regime that continued to control a vast swathe of territory and command immense resources.[2]

In 490 BC the Persians lost at Marathon and withdrew, only to return in far, far greater strength ten years later. In the aftermath of Plataea, no one knew that the same thing would not happen again, as soon as the Persians had had time to recover and were free of other challenges. Achaemenid Persia was an empire far too large for any alliance of Greek states to overthrow. Its soldiers had left Greece, but garrisons along the coast of Thrace, thus in Europe itself, acted as reminders that another great host could one day come by land and advance on Attica and the Peloponnese. At sea, the allies were dominant for the moment, but the Aegean was relatively small, and the threat of a resurgence of Persian naval power would always be there.

After Plataea the Greeks gave thanks and—in a manner natural for societies whose aristocrats competed regularly at the Olympic and other games—decided who deserved the greatest admiration for their prowess. Hoplites from Mantineia and Elis in the Peloponnese arrived after the battle was over, too late to take part, and Pausanias publicly rebuked them, seeing their tardiness as deliberate. The previous year, Corcyra had sent a squadron of ships that similarly dallied and failed to join the fleet in time for Salamis, and those who had shared in the dangers and the glory long remembered this reluctance to commit to the wider cause. In contrast to such public shaming, Pausanias formally restored the Plataeans to their home, the city having been devastated by the Persians, and tasked them with guarding the monuments and tombs of those who had died in the battle fought on their lands.[3]

Other Greeks had not only failed to devote themselves to the war effort but had joined the invaders. Even if the Persians had left, these communities remained allies of the Achaemenids, at least in theory.

Only a handful of Boeotian cities had, like Plataea, abandoned their homes to continue the fight, and the rest had more or less willingly medized. Therefore, Pausanias kept a substantial part of the coalition army together for a few more weeks and advanced on Thebes, by far the largest and most important of the cities to collaborate with the invaders and some eight to ten miles away. The Spartan regent demanded that the Thebans hand over the leaders responsible, and when they refused, he began to lay waste the fields around the city in the classic provocation of Greek warfare. The Thebans, who had fought and taken losses at Plataea, lacked the numbers or will to risk another open battle and handed the men over, apart from one who managed to slip away. A little later, Pausanias took them to Corinth and executed them without trial, out of sight of most of the collation army, which by this time had dispersed.[4]

By now it was autumn, and the army, the largest ever assembled by Greek cities acting together, had already been in the field for a long time, even if some contingents had gone home. With the campaigning season over and no urgent threat facing them, all the remaining troops now dispersed and went home. Never before had so many citizens been absent from their states for such a long time, even if smaller expeditions had sometimes lasted longer. Even for Sparta, whose citizens did not work, the absence of the vast majority of adult men, accompanied by a substantial number of allies and helots who actually did labour in the fields and at crafts, caused a degree of dislocation in normal life. For the Plataeans, Athenians, and others who had evacuated their entire populations to places of safety, this entailed a complete suspension of activity, and now they were eager to bring everyone back home and begin the task of restoring their homes, their workplaces, and, most of all, their farms. This was no easy task, but it was vital if the community was to recover and thrive again.

Later tradition held that at several stages the Greeks uniting under Spartan leadership had sworn solemn oaths not only to remain staunch during the fighting but to behave in certain ways after it was over. For instance, before Plataea the Athenians were supposed to have persuaded everyone to pledge not to repair the temples destroyed by the invaders and instead to leave the ruins as a memorial to the danger the Greeks had faced and the impious savagery of their enemy. It does look as if this rule was followed at Athens, at least for a couple of decades, so that the buildings on the Acropolis remained largely ruined for this time.[5]

The Spartans are said to have wanted Greek cities to do without defensive walls, perhaps on the basis that the pledge to end wars between communities rendered them unnecessary. After all, no one had felt confident enough to stand behind such walls and face the Persians, so their value in the face of any fresh invasion could be seen as negligible. At the same time, the Spartans and plenty of other Peloponnesians had toiled to build a wall across the Isthmus of Corinth and had clearly assumed that this would have been defensible. The city of Sparta itself sprawled over a wide area and had no fortifications. Cynics at the time, and certainly more recently, have viewed their resistance to other cities being protected by walls as meant to ensure that every state was vulnerable to an attack by Sparta's hoplites, who were so formidable in the open field but lacked the skill and patience for a prolonged siege.[6]

In 479 BC, the Athenians were the only ones for whom this became an immediate issue, since the Persians had slighted their existing city walls. Alongside rebuilding homes and resuming the cultivation of crops, they were eager to restore the fortifications around their city, but according to Thucydides, the Spartans opposed this. With the Persian threat diminished for the moment, Athens still possessed a fleet larger than anything Sparta's allies, let alone Sparta itself, could hope to gather. Possessed of this naval might and sheltered behind city walls from the threat of the Spartan phalanx, the Athenians were in a strong position should they decide to oppose the Spartans. In Thucydides's telling, Themistocles, a man deeply honoured at Sparta for the role he had played before the war with Persia and most of all at Salamis, was sent as the head of a delegation to discuss the matter with the Spartans. He feigned a willingness to be convinced by his Spartan hosts that Athens had no need to restore its fortifications and kept them talking for days, delaying any decision to take action. In the meantime, a concerted effort by all able-bodied Athenians, using any material at hand, repaired all the breaches made in the walls by the Persians. Finally Themistocles presented his hosts with the news that Athens once again was securely fortified.[7]

Some scholars dismiss the story altogether, while many question whether at this point the Spartans were willing even to consider compelling the Athenians to obey their instructions, by force if necessary. It does seem improbable that the situation came close to an actual conflict so soon after the exhausting struggle with Persia. Yet it remains impossible to know, or indeed to judge the mood of the times. The Persian invasion in 480 BC, even more than the attack ten years earlier, was unlike anything the communities of Greece had ever experienced in the past. Led by Sparta and with Athens playing a key role, a group of them had worked together, setting aside past disputes, coordinating their efforts, and waging war on an unprecedented scale. The initial alliance and subsequent behaviour during the fighting had all assumed that this cooperation was more than temporary expediency and would last. Everything was new, from the nature of the Persian attack to the question of what to do once the Persians had retreated.[8]

That tensions developed among the allies was unsurprising. Each community was first and foremost concerned to protect its own territory. Thus many Peloponnesians had wanted to wait until the invaders came close to them before doing battle, whereas the Thessalians were reluctant to fight without aid, and most of Boeotia had submitted once the Persians overran their territory. The Athenians were unique in contributing so much to the common war effort even when their own country had been taken by the enemy, and without them

Salamis—and the wider war—could not have been won. The Plataeans and others similarly fled their homes rather than submitting to the enemy but lacked the numbers and the naval strength of the Athenians.

Dozens of Greek communities accepted Spartan leadership and common goals, and even if only thirty-one stayed the course to the end, this level of unity was remarkable. Yet they remained Greeks, and the instincts of individual aristocrats and entire communities remained highly competitive, which added an edge to natural self-interest. Leaders and communities wished to be treated with a respect commensurate with their worth, something that all, even minor aristocrats and small communities, were inclined to set at the highest level. Honour and reputation mattered. The Spartans were accepted as leaders of the coalition because of their military prowess. They in turn were expected to treat their allies with dignity and respect, which in each case reflected individual status. In essence the relationship mirrored how Homer represented the Greek army in the *Iliad* as a collection of individuals who chose to fight alongside one another. They had a leader in Agamemnon, but he could not command, let alone force, anyone to obey him, and he was expected to treat each man in accordance with perceived worth based on current and former deeds as well as birth. This was not a minutely defined or rigid system, for it depended both on someone's sense of his own value and the opinions of everyone else about this. For a hero or a community in the fifth century BC to accept treatment below the standard they felt was deserved quickly led to an actual loss of status.

Thus the Spartans led but did not issue orders that had to be obeyed. Athens and Tegea bickered over who deserved the second place of honour in the battle-line just as Homer's heroes competed for distinction. Before Salamis, debate raged over how to continue the war, and not simply the logic of each argument but the reputation of the speaker and the community he represented influenced the decisions made at each meeting, just as they did in the build-up to the campaign in the following year. The Athenians possessed their fleet, without which the allies could not hope to match the Persians at sea. They were also able to field more hoplites than any of the other communities apart from Sparta (if the perioeci are included) and also had the unique distinction of having faced and defeated the Persians at Marathon. All this enhanced their status, but such things were never fixed and were instead subject to constant renegotiation, hence the comments about their lack of a physical city. Most of the Peloponnesians naturally wanted to protect their own homelands, so wanted the Athenians to join them and fight in the way they deemed best to do this, but they could not make the Athenians do this. Just as Achilles at Troy had withdrawn from battle because he felt that Agamemnon had failed to treat him in accordance with his own proven and superlative worth, the Athenians had every right to walk away from the war with Persia, whether to go off to Italy or to make peace.

The alliance that had turned back the Persian invasion in 480–479 BC worked not as a clear and rigid hierarchy but through persuasion and accommodation of each of the allies' sense of their own value. Greeks fought well because they wanted to justify their status in the minds of the other states involved, just as citizens of the same state fought to keep the good opinion of their kin and neighbours. The same factors applied now that the immediate threat of Persian forces in mainland Greece had gone, for the war was not over even if its nature had changed.

The decades that followed are poorly recorded in the surviving sources. Thucydides gives the fullest account of the almost fifty years that passed between the repulse of Xerxes's invasion and the outbreak in 431 BC of the all-out conflict between Athens and Sparta known today as the Peloponnesian War—or more precisely the Second Peloponnesian War, since there was a briefer, less intense conflict somewhat earlier. Yet his narrative is fairly brief, effectively an introduction to his main theme, and focuses on the events that he felt were most important in shaping what subsequently happened. Other sources add additional information, although judging its reliability can be hard. All in all the events of the period remain very difficult to pin down and even to date with any precision, leaving considerable doubt over the precise sequence of events and hence the relationship between them. This means that any reconstruction involves a considerable degree of conjecture, not least when it comes to explaining the aims, intentions, and motivations of all involved.

In the spring of 478 BC, the allies put together a fleet to operate against the Persians and Persian allies. As before, command was given to a Spartan, although Pausanias the regent was entrusted with the naval command, replacing King Leotychidas, the victor at Mycale. Thucydides speaks of a 'multitude' of ships, but the effort in this year was clearly on a far smaller scale than in the previous two years. Athens contributed thirty triremes, the Peloponnesian allies of Sparta just twenty, although a later source gives the number as fifty. Since Mycale, there had been no grand Persian fleet, which meant that there was no prospect of fighting a major battle at sea, and many of the ships involved probably carried fewer rowers and more men able to fight as hoplites. More importantly, each of the allies needed time to recover from the immense exertions of 480–479 BC. The Athenians in particular needed to rebuild their homes and restore the agricultural and economic basis of their society, so were reluctant to commit too high a proportion of their manpower to waging war, now that the question was no longer sheer survival. Even so, a squadron of thirty ships was the biggest contingent sent by any single state to the joint effort. They were led by Cimon, son of Miltiades, who was still comparatively young. He was a man rising to prominence, rather than an established figure, which similarly suggests the commitment of substantial but much less than full effort.[9]

The combined fleet went first to Cyprus, sweeping it free of any Persian garrisons and mounting a show of force to reassure those Greek communities on the island inclined towards sympathy with

Sparta and the allies. There does not appear to have been much serious resistance, suggesting that Persian troops were few and swiftly fled, surrendered, or were defeated, so that Pausanias soon decided to move on. No garrisons were left behind, and the fleet headed north to the Dardanelles and the coast of Thrace. Here, the Persians did have garrisons under determined commanders, and there was serious fighting as the Greeks blockaded a number of walled cities. One Persian commander ordered his family and household killed before committing suicide by leaping onto their funeral pyre.[10]

Pausanias captured Byzantium on the European side of the Bosporus (later famous as Constantinople, the capital of Rome's eastern empire). However, in the aftermath of this and other victories he became deeply unpopular with many of the leaders serving under him. They complained of his arrogance, high-handedness, and enthusiasm for inflicting punishment and claimed that he was becoming seduced by the luxuries and culture of the Persian Empire. After accusations were made at Sparta of secret communications with the nearest satrap and an alleged desire to medize, he was recalled. The Spartans sent an officer to replace him as commander of the fleet, only to discover that the mood of most of the allied leaders meant that they were unwilling to accept any Spartan as their leader. Instead, they preferred that Athens take the lead.[11]

There was a logic to this. Persian losses meant that no fresh invasion was likely for a considerable time, while the Greeks did not have the resources or the will to fight a major land war in Asia against them. Therefore, the conflict would likely be fought in and around the islands and coasts of the Aegean and would be reliant on sea power. The task was to remove Persian influence from this area, taking advantage of the superiority at sea gained at Salamis and Mycale and with the longer-term aim of hindering and ideally deterring any future Persian attack on Greece. The Spartans had no significant fleet of their own and no great interest in or enthusiasm for creating one or even committing large numbers of citizen soldiers to expeditions abroad. In contrast the Athenians—and only the Athenians—had created the largest and most powerful navy currently in the wider region and had already produced leaders who clearly understood how to employ this force to greatest effect. Everyone acknowledged that Salamis and Mycale had been primarily Athenian victories and could see that in any significant expeditionary force, the Athenian contingent was bound to be the largest. Without Athenian participation, the allies could hope to achieve very little.

Thucydides reported that the allied communities urged the Athenians to take over command of the war at sea. For Herodotus and Aristotle, the initiative came more from the Athenians, eager to add to the prestige and power of their city, but all sources suggest widespread enthusiasm and a belief that the Athenians were better suited and more interested in prosecuting this new phase of the war. Already representatives from the Ionian Greeks along the coast of Asia Minor had asked for help in securing their independence from the empire. The Spartans had considered this and proposed transplanting the Ionian communities to mainland Greece, settling them on land that was unused or taken from states that had medized during the war. How serious a proposal this was, let alone its practicality, is difficult to say, but it ignored the deep attachment of communities to their homes. The Ionians wanted protection and to keep their lands, wealth, and trading connections and were enthusiastic supporters of the Athenians, who seemed inclined to offer them this.[12]

In 477 BC a new alliance was formed to prosecute the war and avenge the harm the Persians had done to the Greeks, the formal agreement marked by an established ritual where lumps of metal were dropped into the sea to symbolise that the promises were to hold until the metal floated to the surface. Scholars have dubbed this alliance the Delian League, for in the early stages representatives from all those states involved met on Delos, and the treasury of the alliance was kept there. Everyone was obliged to provide fighting men to serve in operations, but naval power was central, which meant that the alliance needed a powerful fleet. Ships were expensive to build, more expensive still to crew and maintain, and everyone was expected to assist in this. Larger states provided triremes, with the communities on big islands like Lesbos, Chios, and Samos sending squadrons of ships, while smaller states provided just one or two vessels.

However, many of the 100, perhaps even 150 or so, allied communities who joined at the start or in the early years were so small that they were incapable of offering even a single warship, so instead they paid a sum of money each year into the common treasury. Aristides the Just was appointed to assess the wealth of each member and to set the level of this annual contribution. Thucydides claimed that the total was 460 talents of silver at the beginning, although scholars have questioned whether this is accurate and, if so, what it actually meant. It is unclear whether those contributing ships were assessed at a level of monetary contribution even though they did not pay anything and instead provided one or more triremes. The money was employed to support the war effort, with most going to build and pay for the crewing and maintenance of warships. These triremes were constructed at Athens and operated by the Athenians, for all intents and purposes becoming part of the Athenian navy.[13]

The new alliance did not dissolve the agreement reached in 481 BC to oppose the Persians under Spartan leadership, and Athens and some others were part of both agreements. On the whole Peloponnesian states did not join the new alliance; nor did the island of Aegina, perhaps because of its past history of hostility to the Athenians. The majority of members of the Delian League were Ionians in language, although there were exceptions, and most came from the eastern coasts of Greece, the coast of Asia Minor, and in particular the islands of the Aegean. Decisions were made jointly, with every state having the right to speak and casting an equal vote, even if such equality was illusory, at least where Athens was concerned. Without the Athenian fleet, now bolstered and supported by contributions from the allies, the Delian League could not hope to achieve anything worthwhile. No member state came close to Athens in its military might, population, or wealth, making it natural for Athenians to supervise and organise the group war effort. For the Athenians this was no more than common sense, combined with a proper acknowledgement of their contribution and essential worth.

Whoever had originally pushed the idea that Athens should lead the war for the foreseeable future, the Athenians accepted this role with enthusiasm. The attitude at Sparta is less clear, and probably its leaders held a range of opinions. Yet the essential truth was that they could contribute little in concrete terms to campaigns waged largely through naval expeditions. Sparta did not abandon the struggle with Persia, and at some point in the decade after 479 BC, King Leotychidas took a force of Spartans and Peloponnesian allies to attack leaders in Thessaly seen as enthusiastic medizers during the invasion. Land operations of this sort were far more suited to Spartan strengths, unlike expeditions to the far shores of the Aegean. However, after initial success, the campaign bogged down amid suspicion that the king had accepted bribes in another story of a Spartan apparently losing all self-control once away from home. Leotychidas was deposed, and the army returned home.

There was inevitably a change in the balance of prestige compared to the time when Sparta had led based on acceptance that she had the best and most important fighters. Cimon would later speak of the Spartans as the Athenians' 'yoke fellows', the two leaders and main strengths in the conflict with Persia. Because Athens had gained prestige, inevitably Sparta's light seemed a little less bright than before, and this was not ideal. Still, the sense of standing together as allies in resisting Persian encroachment held strong. Remaining free, rather than submitting to a foreign empire, also ensured the freedom to compete for reputation. The Athenians' achievements in naval warfare deserved admiration and did not directly challenge the Spartans' proven record in battle on land.[14]

One of the earliest actions of the new alliance was the capture of Eion, another Persian garrison on the coast near Thrace and Macedonia. Cimon was again in charge and enslaved the remaining inhabitants, who were not Greeks. The site was a good one, at the mouth of the River Strymon, which in turn led towards a region rich in mineral deposits, so a colony was established. Many of the settlers were Athenian, although others probably came from other states within the Delian League. Subsequently, more colonists came out from Athens and attempted to expand the colony or add a new one further inland, but this came to a bloody end when they were annihilated by Thracian tribes.[15]

There is a good chance that the forces of the League operated somewhere in every year during the 470s and 460s BC, even though the sources mention only a few incidents. Cimon's next-known success was taking the island of Scyros. Once again, the population was not considered to be Greek, although the only mention of support for Persia during the invasion claims that one of them had helped the Persians to mark and avoid a dangerous reef. The locals may have engaged in piracy or shown hostility to members of the Delian League, but no real details are preserved. They were enslaved, and once again the Athenians established a colony on the island. Tradition maintained that Theseus, mythical founder of Athens, had been killed and buried there, and Cimon duly claimed to have discovered his remains and returned home with parts of an immense skeleton and ancient weapons.[16]

From the perspective of an ongoing struggle against Persia, the capture of Eion was understandable, helping to remove the Persian presence in Europe. Scyros was a less obvious target, although it was well placed to guard or hinder ships travelling from the Black Sea to Greece. Athens had come more and more to rely on grain and other resources from that region, so that controlling the sea route was very attractive to the Athenians. The Delian League needed a strong Athens in order to be effective, so this could be presented as a good thing for the other allies as well, whether or not they had any direct benefit from it. The colony on the island and the one at Eion appear to have been considered Athenian, even if others were included among the settlers. It was also proper that the Athenians should be rewarded in accordance with their central role in making each victory possible, just as the most important of Homer's heroes expected a greater share of the spoils.

The stated element of revenge on Persia should not be ignored. Vengeance came from hurting an enemy, and one of the clearest ways to do this was to take plunder or land from that enemy. At the same time, each victory added to the reputation of the alliance, and the more formidable a state or group of states—or indeed an individual—was perceived to be, the more it intimidated past or potential enemies. An appearance of strength was a powerful deterrent in the international relations of the era.

The city of Carystus lay at the southern end of Euboea and in 490 BC had resisted the Persians only to succumb to a siege. It had not joined the Spartan-led resistance in 480 BC; nor had it signed up for the Delian League, so at some point the Athenians led an expedition and, after some fighting, forced the Carystians to become part of the alliance. This was reasonable enough as an action to strengthen the League's dominance of the Aegean and at the same time further improved the Athenians' control of the main sea route from Athens to the Thracian coast and the Black Sea. Still, it was the first time a Greek community was compelled to join the alliance. At some point the moderately sized island state of Naxos, which had been part of the Delian League from the start, decided that it wished to leave. Thucydides does not explain why the Naxians' leaders reached this decision, reporting simply that the Athenians and allies sent a fleet, blockaded the island, and forced its surrender. No one was permitted to break the pledges made when they joined the Delian League. The Naxians were punished—Thucydides speaks figuratively of enslavement—and were now lower-status members, quite possibly contributing money rather than ships as in the past.[17]

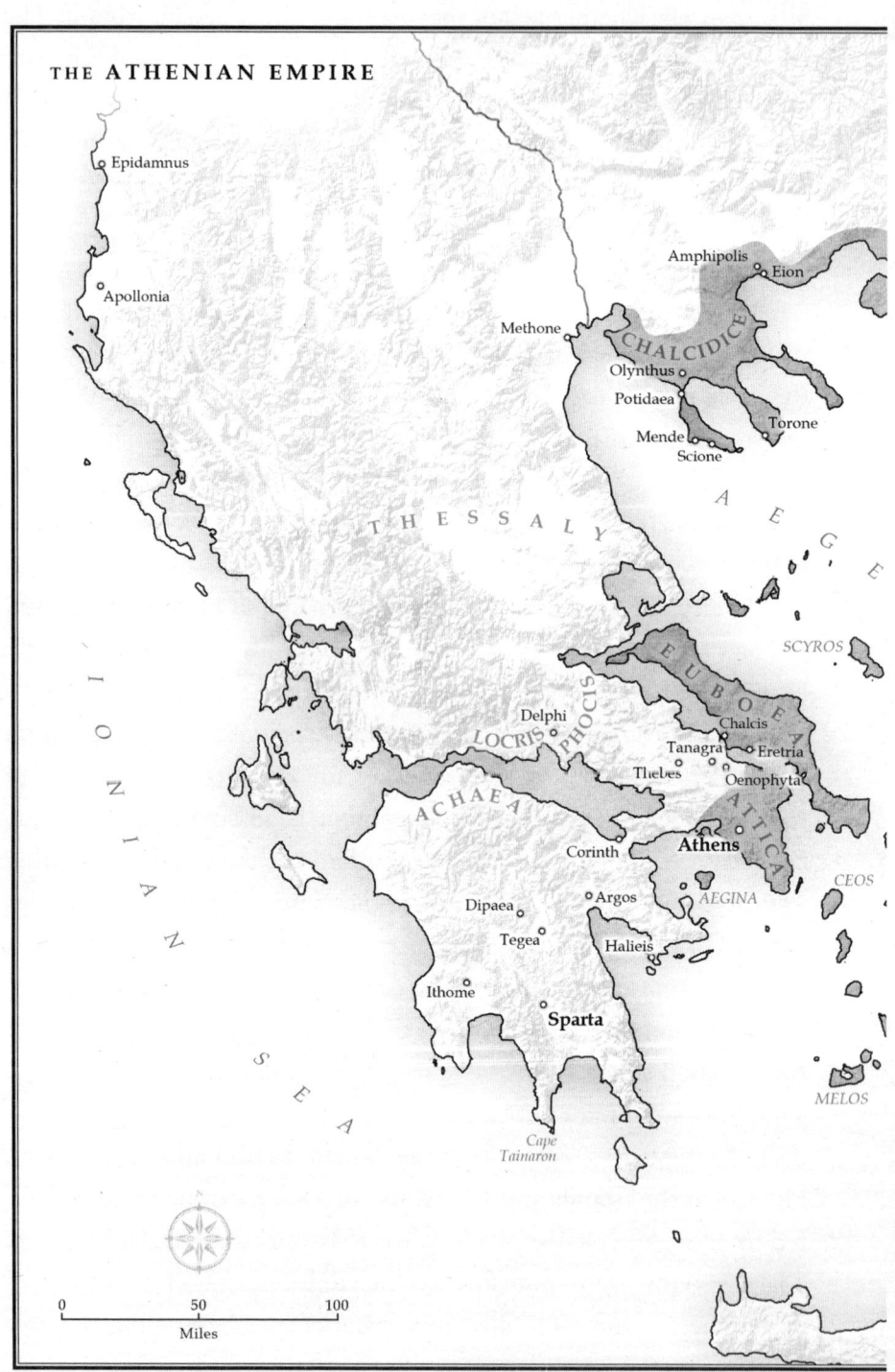

The Persian threat remained, which was a strong reason for preserving solidarity at all costs. After all, the Persians had always been very good at weakening opponents through defections. They were also rebuilding the forces available to deal with, what was for them, the Greek threat, and it looks as if more and more of the coastal cities of Asia Minor had allied with Athens. A large Persian fleet—200 triremes according to Thucydides and more in later sources—was constructed and brought together, prompting the League to muster a larger-than-usual force to deal with it. Cimon commanded, and in the first major sea battle since Salamis, he met the Persian fleet not far from the mouth of the River Eurymedon. Not only did he smash the enemy squadrons at sea, but he then followed up by landing and storming the Persian camp. It was a spectacular double victory, as well as a reminder of the strength of the Achaemenid Empire and also the might of the alliance brought together and led by Athens. In the following years, Cimon was again active against the Persians and their local allies in Thrace.[18]

Yet not everyone was happy to be part of the Athenian-led alliance or remained willing to devote considerable resources every year to the conflict. The island of Thasos lay in the northern Aegean close to the Thracian coast and had long benefitted from commerce with the wider region, controlling a trading post on the continent with good access to, perhaps even control of, gold and other minerals mined there. Thucydides reported that the Athenians wanted to take over this territory and trade, and resentment over Athenian incursions and other grievances prompted the Thasians to rebel and to ask for Spartan aid. He claimed that Sparta's leaders were sympathetic, whether to the cause or because they felt that the Athenians were becoming too powerful and too domineering. A secret agreement was reached promising aid, perhaps in the form of sending an army into Attica as they had done under Cleomenes, before another, far more urgent crisis brought on by a natural disaster prevented the Spartans from actually doing anything. Whatever the truth of this—and judging something supposedly planned but never implemented is always particularly hard—the Thasians rebelled. Even without Spartan assistance, the Athenians and their allies took three campaigning seasons to defeat them. Their city wall was slighted or completely demolished, making it far easier to capture the place should they rebel a second time. In addition, all the Thasians' warships were confiscated, and presumably they were forbidden from replacing them. The Thasians also had to pay a large fine and from then on contribute to the Delian League's fund every year at a rate set by Athens. The Athenians also took over the trading posts and the mining areas, bringing in more colonists to control them.[19]

Athens was always and inevitably bound to dominate the Delian League, because none of the other members came remotely close to matching her strength—which became all the more true as the collective resources of the allies came to augment and support Athenian naval power. Everyone benefitted from the protection the alliance offered, but the Athenians benefitted most of all and grew in power. Human nature tends to resent a burden all the more when it is imposed in response to a threat perceived to be distant. Thucydides suggests that from quite early on many communities were reluctant to send the money or resources required by the League or were slow in meeting their promised commitments. As time passed and the memory of the Persian invasion began to fade, enthusiasm declined even more, while resentment increased. There is a good chance that quite a few states preferred to pay rather than build, maintain, and operate warships to serve with the combined fleet, and after a while only Lesbos, Chios, and Samos continued to provide triremes. While this meant that others paid to supplement the Athenian navy, this initiative may well often have come from the allies rather than the Athenians. Since 480 BC, first Sparta and the allies, then Athens at the head of the Delian League, had prosecuted warfare on a far larger scale and of a far larger duration than was normal for Greek communities. Many grew weary of so prolonged and considerable a commitment.[20]

The Athenians remained firmly committed to the cause, not least because they profited from it financially, while their role gave them immense prestige, adding to the sense that their democratic city was truly remarkable, inherently superior to others. Their great sense of their own worth turned into a growing arrogance in their treatment of everyone, including their allies, which in time added still more to the latter's distaste for the burdens placed upon them. Greeks, and especially the aristocrats who provided their leaders, were naturally competitive and often inclined to flaunt their success as proof of their own great worth. Although the Athenians were highly successful, after a while they became widely disliked. Yet, set against this was the willingness of Athenian citizens year after year to volunteer to serve and fight in operations far from Attica. A significant number died while doing so, their names recorded by tribe on memorials in Athens for their sacrifice on behalf of the community. The pre-eminence of Athens came at a price in blood as well as treasure.

Most allies and outsiders soon realised that the alliance was unequal, that Athens made all the key decisions, and that the allies were clearly subordinate to her wishes and interests; over time this became ever more blatant. The communal treasury was moved from Delos to Athens, and either at this point or before, a sixtieth of each contribution was taken for the cult of the city's patron goddess, Athena. This was a fortunate development for historians, as fragments of inscribed lists of these donations have been discovered, adding to the understanding of how the wider tribute system worked. Everything was under even closer Athenian control, at the same time as funding the Athenian fleet and later other Athenian projects. Legal disputes involving an Athenian and any ally were decided by Athenian laws in Athenian courts, and there was gradual encroachment in many domestic matters as well. If the need to stand together in the long term in the face of the Persian threat might have justified all this, that did not make it any easier to accept.[21]

Athens had played a critical role in defeating the Persian invasions, winning at Marathon with only the aid of Plataea, playing the principal part in the victories at Salamis and Mycale, and providing key support, second only to the Spartans, at Plataea. In the years that followed, the Athenians took the lead and became the main power in the Aegean. They also increased their influence in Greece itself, if not the Peloponnese. After a while, old enemies and rivals, including Aegina, were attacked and forced to join the League as subordinate allies. There was a good deal of truth in Herodotus's claim that the establishment of their democratic system energised the Athenians, making possible the creation of a fleet and the acquisition of an empire, which is what the Delian League became in less than a generation. Athens was without doubt the biggest winner of the Persian war and its aftermath.[22]

YET THERE WAS a deep irony that two of the leaders in the great victories of 480–479 BC did not do anywhere near as well. Pausanias was regent, never destined to be king, and after his first recall from Byzantium was criticised for his conduct but found innocent on the charge of medizing. He subsequently returned to Byzantium and again came under suspicion of excessive ambition and plans to defect to the Persians or otherwise betray his country to the enemy. He was recalled again but then accused of stirring unrest among the helots. Similar accusations had been made against Cleomenes, and these men possibly saw personal advantage and perhaps great benefits for the community as a whole in some form of drastic social reform. If so, this was anathema to their fellow citizens, who saw their own privileged status as the greatest achievement of their society. Yet perhaps this was just routine invective in the rivalries surrounding members of the royal families. It is striking that almost all the Spartan kings and their relatives whose careers are recorded in any detail at all appear to have encountered bitter opposition and in several cases been deposed. Pausanias was threatened with arrest, so took refuge in a shrine, prompting the ephors to have him walled up inside. Deprived of food and water and exposed to the elements because the roof had been removed, he slowly starved. When he was at death's door, part of the wall was demolished so that he could be dragged out to expire without polluting the sacred place.[23]

Themistocles fared better, at least for a while, once again becoming a prominent and fairly popular figure in the Athenian Assembly. He returned to earlier projects—for instance, convincing his fellow citizens to complete fortification of the Piraeus begun during his archonship. However, late in the 470s, the man who had so often attracted a significant minority of votes during the ostracism process finally upset enough of his fellow citizens to be ostracised. He went first to Argos in the Peloponnese, Sparta's bitterest enemy, and may have travelled more widely in the region, for there is a sign that several formerly staunch allies of Sparta were wavering in their loyalty. Perhaps he hoped to weaken Sparta and as a result further enhance Athens's status before returning at the end of the decade. However, the Spartans complained to the Athenians, claiming that Themistocles had been in touch with Pausanias and was plotting with the former regent in the interests of Persia. A connection is certainly possible, since the men knew each other, and if Pausanias had planned to free or improve the lot of the helots, this could well have tied in with Themistocles's desire to undermine Sparta's military dominance.[24]

Whatever the truth, enough influential Athenians disliked or distrusted the wily and rapacious Themistocles to condemn him in his absence. He fled from Greece, eventually going to Persia, where he received a warm welcome at the royal court. Artaxerxes made him governor of the city of Magnesia and provided generously for him and his family. Thus the victor at Salamis lived out his last days as a privileged subject of the great king.[25]

Part Three
GREAT EVILS FOR THE GREEKS

16

TREMORS

The earthquakes that devastated Sparta and the growing fractures in the alliance against Persia, c. 470–457 BC

XERXES'S GREAT INVASION HAD TOUCHED THE LIVES OF VIRtually everyone living in the communities of mainland Greece, whether or not Persian troops actually reached their homes. Nothing like this had happened to them before, and this conflict was different in nature and sheer scale to those waged in the past with Greek neighbours. Dealing with the challenge had meant doing new things, be it working together with other communities for longer; abandoning homes to the enemy, as did the Athenians and Plataeans; or submitting en masse to the invaders, like the Thessalians and Boeotians. To the surprise of almost everyone, not least the priests at Delphi, the Spartan-led alliance won, and this victory created a world that was in many ways just as new and strange.

The three or four decades after the Persian invasions are very poorly documented and difficult to understand. Hindsight lends an inevitability to the big trends, from the emergence of Athens as supreme leader of the Delian League, to the gradual transition of this alliance into something resembling an Athenian empire, and then to the confrontation with Sparta culminating in the bitter and costly

Peloponnesian War. That story is, after all, the main focus of this book. This very familiarity makes it all too easy, however, to interpret the meagre and confusing sources for these decades solely within this framework, where the key players anticipate the future rather than reacting to the past and trying to succeed in the uncertain present. So much was new, for there had never been alliances quite like the ones formed by the Spartans in 481 BC or the Athenians in 478 BC, both apparently meant to last a long time, perhaps forever, and designed as a response to the threat of Persia. No one knew how such arrangements would fare in the long run; nor could communities be too sure where they fitted into this novel, still emerging pattern or how far their record during the war would determine their prominence from then on. At one point the Spartans wanted to expel from the Amphictyonic League, the council supervising the cult at Delphi, all of the member states that had submitted to the Persians. The Athenians successfully opposed the move, partly by pointing out that this would have meant excluding the majority of the traditional members of the council.

Well-established status still mattered and had not simply vanished because of decisions made and actions taken in the last few years. Thebes and Argos were large cities capable of fielding substantial numbers of hoplites and had long records of military prowess as well as the prestige of association with many myths and traditions important to all Greeks. That the first had fought alongside the Persians and the second had remained neutral dented their reputations but did not change the fact that they were still large and powerful states. They were also famed in story—far more so in this respect than Athens, let alone many medium-sized and small cities. Even during the Persian invasion, Greek cities continued to jockey for prominence and respect as they had always done—for instance, arguing over the positions of honour in the battle-line at Plataea.

After the Persian retreat, there was even less reason for restraint in such competition, and the deep-seated urge to excel was granted full rein. Thus, it is hard to say whether respect for tradition or fear that the change might add to Spartan influence was the chief motive for the Athenians when they blocked the attempt to expel the medizers from their role at Delphi, and it may have been a mixture of both. Fundamental to such competition was the need for an audience and acclaim. The truest excellence and greatest worth in an individual or a state was demonstrated when everyone else acknowledged it, however grudgingly, and the more participants there were, the more success mattered. Such attitudes encouraged rivalries, disputes, and conflict, while imposing at least some limits on behaviour, for the wider audience was watching and judging, willing to be impressed or not. In turn the value of these opinions, individually and collectively, rested on the status of each community. For all the big or medium-sized Greek cities, there were far more small ones. The vast majority of the states belonging to the Delian League were tiny, their contribution to its war effort or funds only of significance because they were part of this big alliance. Yet, even the smallest communities were jealous of their reputation, and in most of them individuals vied with each other for local prominence—because this was what Greeks did. Free men wanted the respect of their fellow citizens, and ideally their admiration, and at the same time also wanted the equivalent reputation for their community as a whole. Big events did not change this deeply engrained behaviour, even though they might offer unusual opportunities for winning such prestige.

The struggle with Persia had confirmed the Spartans' military pre-eminence. They had led because others had answered their call to join together, and they had then led the alliance to victory, giving proof of why those others had been willing to follow their lead in the first place. Alongside this, the Athenians had demonstrated the new-found might of their city, on land at Marathon and Plataea and most of all at sea at Salamis and Mycale. Their naval pre-eminence was a fact that simply could not be ignored as everyone tried to work out the current balance of prestige and power—in a sense the pecking order—in the Greek world. Just where Athens and Sparta stood in relation to each other provided the background to this era, but this was merely the biggest uncertainty as everyone sought to understand where power, both real and as imagined by others, now lay. Conduct during the war counted for a lot but was not everything.

Ongoing reassessment of prestige and worth continued because this was natural for these societies. In the same way, however much the great war had disrupted normal life, it resumed as soon as possible, as seen, for instance, in the urgency with which the Athenians and Plataeans rebuilt their homes and resumed farming their lands. As in any pre-industrial society, more people laboured to produce food than at any other work. The agricultural year brought times of intense activity, alongside a near-constant list of tasks to perform. Spartan 'peers' were unusual in that they did not toil in the fields, but even they, like the aristocrats of other cities, enjoyed this privilege because others worked their land for them. Their society rested on production of a satisfactory harvest every year. At the same time Athens was in the process of becoming a community where a significantly lower proportion of people were involved in agriculture than anywhere else, feeding its burgeoning population from imports, but even there a link remained between owning farmland and playing a role in public life, including fighting for the state. In Greek communities, the citizens who mattered were landowners.

Greeks lived close to nature, far closer than it is perhaps easy to imagine from a modern perspective. Generations of accumulated knowledge meant that farmers usually knew the local conditions extremely well and how to get the best from them, but knowledge did not mean control, and risk was ever present. Too much or too little sun, wind, or rain at the wrong moment—perhaps only by a matter of days—could ruin a crop, while beasts, like the humans who laboured to make it all work, could become injured, sick, or lame when they were most needed. Each year brought a farmer no guarantees, save that he would have to do it all over again the next year and the next. The profit from any surplus could fluctuate, and like craftsmen and traders, farmers wanting to sell some or all of their produce were subject to the uncertainties of supply and demand, and the margin between success and ruin was often very narrow. The sea was never far away and helped trade to flourish, while adding the perils of storm. Even without war, which was frequent enough, infant mortality was high, and treatment for disease or infection very limited.

There is a danger of being too bleak in estimates of life expectancy or productivity from the land. Significantly more people succeeded than failed, and the common pattern among the Greek communities continued to be a growth in overall population and in prosperity, at least for some. Yet it was much harder for Greeks in the fifth century BC than for many people in the modern world to maintain the illusion of control over their lives, although there were practical ways of managing the risks. Farmers diversified in the hope that at least some crops would do well each year. Experience and skill helped them to manage this, traders to understand their markets, and sailors to avoid or cope with bad weather, while the growth of Athenian naval power offered protection for the Athenians and their allies. More often than not these factors were enough, and sometimes more than enough, to permit the vast majority to survive and many to prosper, but no one enjoyed absolute security. Misfortune, even utter disaster, could strike at any time.

In Homer's poems the gods intervened in the activities of men, often with drastic and sometimes cruel effect. Hesiod sang with reverence of the gods and goddesses and the need for mankind to honour them. A few philosophers, at first mainly from Asia Minor, began to try to explain the world through laws of nature, and some minimised or excluded the role of the divine, especially in day-to-day events, but these very much remained minority views. Most Greeks, like most people for the bulk of human history, accepted the existence of supernatural powers, and most of all gods, as an obvious truth. These were forces far greater than humanity but understandable

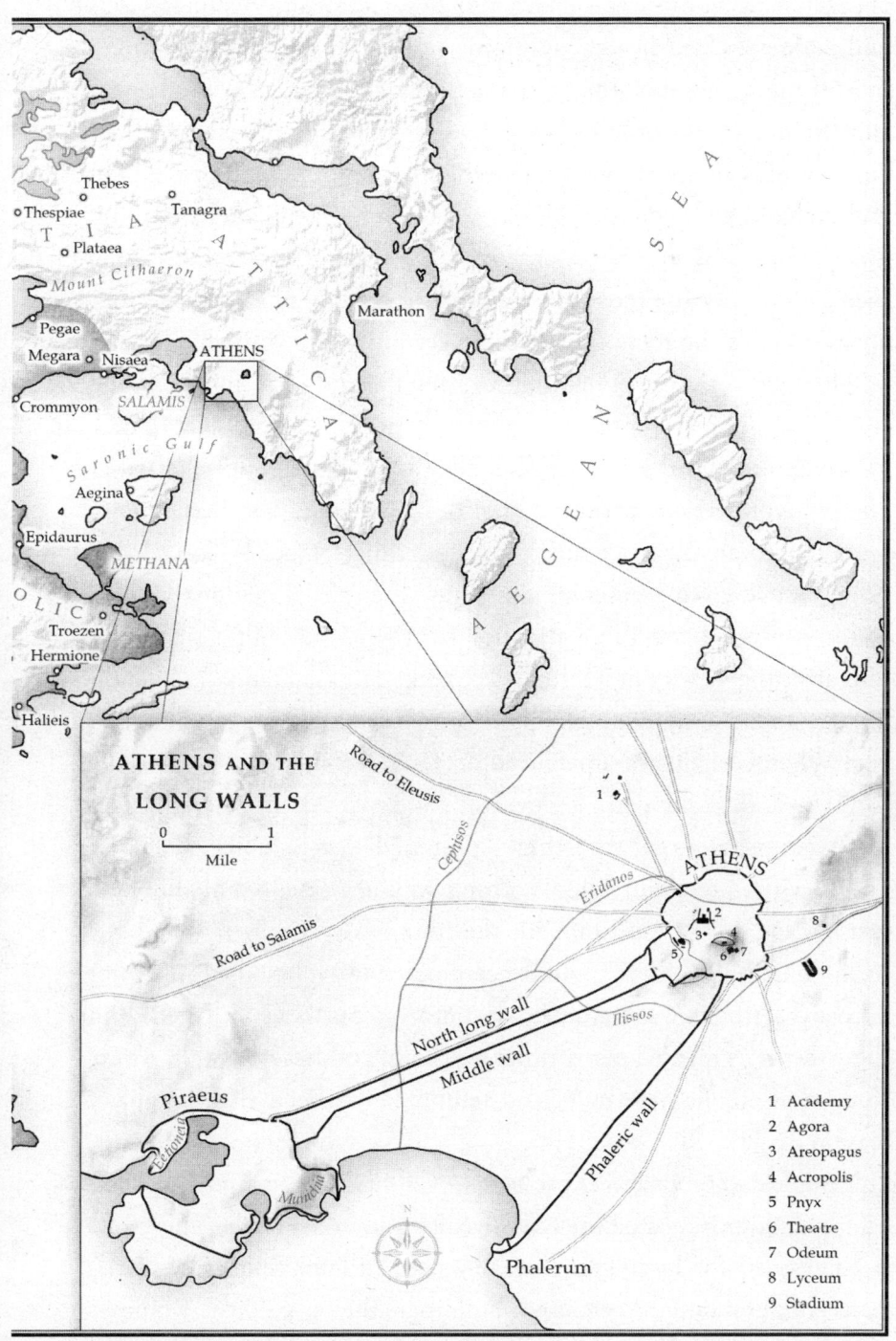

because they had human characteristics, likes, and dislikes. Gods and goddesses had beauty, wisdom, and power beyond anything a mortal might possess, thus deserved an even greater level of reverence than mortals with such attributes. Oracles gave a sense of the balance of feelings towards an individual, a community, or a plan and hence suggested whether success or failure was likely, without giving clear and simple predictions of events in detail. Consulting them, especially the most prestigious, such as Delphi, offered guidance and gave confidence rather than certainty of outcome.

More generally, most felt that revering the gods was only common sense and natural. Ritual and religious practices were everywhere in Greek communities, as indeed they were throughout the wider ancient world. Long-standing tradition, the older the better, gave authority to any practice, although new things could be introduced or a practice given greater emphasis, as when the Athenians decided to recognise the god Pan's affection for them and built a shrine for him after the victory at Marathon. Greeks took part in cults as individuals and especially as groups—for instance, of family, tribe, and city. When Cleisthenes introduced his ten new tribes and made them fundamental to his new democratic system at Athens, he still kept the existing tribes so that these continued long-established rituals and sacrifices to ensure that nothing was neglected or abandoned, just in case it was important for the community. Every city had one or more deities as its particular patron, but the relationship was not exclusive. Athena was naturally of central importance at Athens, but the Athenians revered many other gods and goddesses as well. At the same time, there were cults and temples to Athena elsewhere, not least at Sparta.

Temples were visible expressions of a city's piety, and their size and splendour indicated the city's wealth and importance. They were not designed for large gatherings. When, in later centuries, Christians sought a design for church buildings, they copied the Romans' hall-like civil basilicas rather than their temples. Temples were symbolic homes for the gods, places to make offerings, although animal sacrifice was usually performed in the precinct outside, and they were waypoints for the processions often held during a festival, such as the Panathenaea at Athens. Most Greek communities had such celebrations, held at various times through the year, when the community came together. These were acts of worship, as well as holidays from work and celebrations of belonging to the same city. All took part according to their status and the dictates of tradition, which gave particular roles on the basis of age or gender. The elite were prominent, often funding aspects of the ceremonies with the aim of showing off their wealth and commitment to their fellow citizens through the lavishness and style with which they performed their allotted tasks. None of this meant that the festival itself, and the reverence it showed for one deity or several, was not important. A good relationship with the divine was seen as literally vital, especially with those gods believed to have a particular affection for the community, thus to be responsible for its life and success up to the present day. Famous events drew large numbers of visitors from outside to witness and in some cases take part, just as the Panhellenic games were staged in religious settings, accompanied by sacrifice and ritual.

The Greeks were a religious people, and the Spartans were seen as particularly scrupulous in their observation of rituals even by Greek standards. Famously, the need to observe a festival made the Spartans too late to fight at Marathon and led them to send to Thermopylae only 300 Spartiates (the 'peers' who were the only full citizens). Scholars may speculate over whether these were excuses to conceal deliberate and cynical policy, but the essential point is that they expected the given explanation to be plausible to others. There were lots of festivals at Sparta, many involving the choral singing and dancing for which the Spartans were renowned, especially Spartan women and girls. As elsewhere, ceremonies combined reverence for the gods with celebration of the worth and achievements of the Spartans themselves. Sparta was the greatest power in the Peloponnese, acknowledged as supreme in warfare throughout the Greek world. Exceptional success and exceptional diligence in honouring the gods went naturally together, proof coming once again in the defeat of the Persian invasion. The Spartans led and merited the honour from others because of their own worth, conduct, and piety.[1]

Reality tended to be less neat, the Spartans' behaviour less than perfect—hence eventual worries about the killing of the Persian ambassadors or the rather messy effort to prevent Pausanias's polluting the shrine where he had been imprisoned and starved by pulling him out so that he took his last breaths outside. In the 470s BC, the veneer of Spartan strength began to weaken, so that her dominance of the Peloponnese became less certain. Part of the reason was that Argos's male citizen population had revived after the devastating losses to its hoplites inflicted by King Cleomenes. There were more Argives of military age once more, so that these inveterate opponents of Sparta were willing to risk aggression and not simply defend their homeland.

Elsewhere, especially in Arcadia in the north of the Peloponnese, attitudes to Sparta shifted, probably as part of changes within the communities there, most likely linked to a growth in the population and especially prosperity. Several smaller cities and towns merged politically to form one city-state at Elis, creating a new regime more democratic than aristocratic, suggesting that substantial numbers of men there owned some property and demanded to be given a significant role in public life. Perhaps the humiliation of arriving too late for Plataea in 479 BC had discredited some of the previous leaders of these communities, although the Elaeans were named among the allies in the monument erected at Delphi, an honour denied to the similarly tardy Mantineans. Still, several communities similarly came together into one city-state at Mantineia, probably some years after the change at Elis. Scholars speculate that Themistocles, living for a while in Argos and travelling more widely, may have encouraged these developments, although he is unlikely to have created the trends behind them.[2]

Very little is known about events in the Peloponnese in these years, even less than is recorded about the Athenians. Herodotus, describing the career of a renowned Spartan seer, responsible for interpreting sacrifices and other omens, lists two battles apparently fought in the later 470s or early 460s BC. Both were Spartan victories, but the conflicts' precise dates, scale, and causes can only be conjectured. The first was fought near Tegea against the Tegeans and the Argives. At Plataea the Tegeans had fought alongside the Spartans, after losing out to the Athenians in their bid to be stationed on the left wing, the second place of honour after the right wing of the army. In 479 BC the Tegeans had nevertheless fought well and with great success in the sector Herodotus presented as most critical to the outcome. Perhaps they felt that the Spartans had not supported them sufficiently in the claim over the Athenians or given them fitting praise for their part in the fighting, or perhaps political changes, the coming together into one community rather than a loose alliance of separate ones, altered their attitudes to themselves and to the Spartans as dominant allies.

Their neighbours may have shared similar sentiments, with or without Themistocles's urgings, for the second battle won by the Spartans was over all of the Arcadian cities apart from Mantineia, which had not joined the alliance against them. Later tradition claimed that this victory was all the more remarkable because the enemy heavily outnumbered the Spartans and their allies, so that they had to make their formation very shallow. For all the prowess and indomitable spirit of the Spartan 'peers', success in any major war relied very much on the extra manpower provided by perioeci and especially the allied communities. When the latter turned against them, not only did they make formidable opponents, but they also significantly reduced the number of men the Spartans could muster for a field army. Nor could the Spartans be everywhere. Argos inflicted a serious defeat on Mycenae during these years, another sign that its strength was resurgent.[3]

Spartan dominance of the Peloponnese was reduced but far from broken, at least for the moment, but for the Spartans victories abroad could never take away the permanent threat represented by the helots at home. Pausanias was suspected of having encouraged some of this serf population to hope for better things, a similar charge to those levelled at Cleomenes. At some point around this time, some helots openly resisted or rebelled in some way and took sanctuary in a temple of Poseidon. They were promised their lives if they surrendered and came out, but this deal was soon broken, and all were executed in an incident reminiscent of the massacre of Cylon's followers at Athens and the subsequent curse associated with the Alcmaeonid family. Like that earlier incident, this one assumed more significance with hindsight, because sometime around 465–464 BC a dreadful series of earthquakes struck Sparta.[4]

THE GREEKS WERE familiar enough with earth tremors, for the region was subject to them, and usually saw them as bad omens, often associated with Poseidon, whom they gave such epithets as the 'earth shaker'. This time the concentrated succession of shocks was exceptionally severe, with widespread devastation and considerable loss of life. Most of the details come from later sources, such as the claim that only five houses remained standing, presumably from the old village districts making up Sparta itself. Plutarch tells a story about two age groups exercising in the same hall. The younger ones spotted a hare and all ran off to chase it moments before the earthquake struck and buried the older group, those aged around eighteen to twenty, beneath the ruins. He claimed that the monument to the latter was still visible in his day, more than 500 years later. Whatever the truth of the story—for instance, whether this was supposed to have happened to all boys of that age or just some—it is a reminder of how sheer chance determined who lived and who died in such a disaster.[5]

The centre of the earthquake was around Sparta itself and Laconia, although it is probable that lesser tremors were felt in Messenia and beyond. There were many deaths, and the survivors were naturally intent on recovering their remains and finding survivors, as well as retrieving valued and essential possessions from the ruins, but Plutarch wrote that King Archidamus quickly ordered the alarm sounded, calling the Spartans to arms in case of trouble from the helots. Whether or not this story is true, many helots did see the chaos as an opportunity to win their freedom and turned on their Spartan overlords. The revolt spread widely, most of all to Messenia, and even more worryingly, at least two whole communities of perioeci (one certainly and the other possibly in Messenia) took up arms alongside the rebels. Thucydides stated that it took ten years for the Spartans to stamp out the uprising, and even those scholars who are sceptical of the claim suggest that the war lasted at least five or so years. This was not a war decided by two phalanxes facing each other in the open, not least because the helots did not have the equipment or ethos for such fighting. Instead, it was a war of raids and skirmishes, where the rebels made best use of terrain less suited to hoplites. Herodotus claims that a detachment of 300 Spartans—the same size as the one sent to Thermopylae—was annihilated. Messenia became the heart of the resistance, and for years the main force of rebels along with their families held Mount Ithome against all attempts to dislodge them.[6]

There is much debate and no certainty about the details and consequences of the earthquake and its aftermath, and, as ever, reliable information about what went on in secretive Sparta is meagre. Thucydides offered few details but clearly believed the earthquake to have been a catastrophe and the rebellion that followed a dire emergency for the Spartans. There is no reliable way of estimating the loss of life as a result of the tremors, let alone judging whether it fell evenly on Spartans of all ages, on both men and women, and how many perioeci and helots suffered and in what proportions. Diodorus claimed that 20,000 perished, but there is a good chance that this was simply a round figure with little basis, and even if accurate, it gives no indication of whom the total included. As noted earlier, far too little is known of where the Spartans and others lived and how and where they spent their time in general, let alone where most were when the earthquake struck. Speculation that more women may have died than men—on the basis that the former spent more time indoors, so were more likely to perish when a house collapsed—has not convinced everyone, not least because Spartan women are believed to have lived far more active lives than women elsewhere.[7]

There is no way of knowing how many Spartans were killed by vengeful helots in the aftermath of the initial disaster or during the course of the long war that followed. In the initial stages, families were bound to have been vulnerable to the helots in the household or those working the fields close by, should these have chosen to attack them. Over time, the risk shifted overwhelmingly to the men of fighting age seeking to put down the rebellion. In 479 BC the Spartans had sent 5,000 'peers' to fight at Plataea, in spite of losing 300 the year before. After the earthquake and rebellion, they struggled to field half as many, and in most cases sent fewer than that, while by the early fourth century BC, sending some 1,200 or so hoplites to war represented a maximum effort. Over several generations, the number of Spartiates drastically declined in a way that the military manpower of other cities did not. Few scholars would doubt that the earthquake and subsequent helot rebellion played a role in this process, although opinions are divided over whether it was a main—perhaps even *the* main—cause or simply accelerated an existing trend due to fundamental weaknesses in Sparta's social and economic structure.[8]

Significant numbers of Spartans died in the earthquake and subsequent war against the helots, and a casualty total for adult males numbering in thousands is more than possible. Inevitably this loss of life disrupted the system of landholding, which permitted the Spartiates their privileged status. More to the point, many helots may well have died during the earthquake, while far more were killed during the rebellion, and others, having rebelled, were certainly not toiling away in the fields on behalf of their masters. Some Spartans 'owned' farms that provided them with no produce for years on end, perhaps even a decade, as Sparta's system of landownership and cultivation was severely dislocated. Even when the rebellion was over, there were fewer adult Spartans to manage and benefit from the land and fewer helots to do the actual work, at least in the short to medium term. There is a good chance that in the meantime, many Spartans came to possess bigger estates than in the past, since the state would not likely have permitted helots to go on farming simply for their own benefit without giving much of the produce to a citizen. Human nature made the owners/overseers of such enlarged estates inclined to keep what they had and pass it on, which may have resulted in reluctance to have too many male heirs, leading to careful marriages and women owning more property in their own right, as families attempted to maintain and grow their possessions. Deep down, most Greeks associated landowning with status and naturally wanted to own as much as they could. Sparta steadily became a state with a smaller and smaller class of ever more privileged citizens.[9]

Such trends developed in the longer term, but in the immediate aftermath of the earthquake, the Spartans prioritized survival and restoring control. Thucydides claims that only this emergency prevented them from following their promise to the envoys from Thasos and intervening on the island's behalf in its war with the Athenians. He never explains how or when the wider world, including the Athenians, learned of the agreement, but his narrative implies that this was not until sometime later. There was no sign of immediate ill will on either side, for as the helot rebellion developed, the Athenians were one of a number of allies asked for military help. The basis for the appeal was the treaty agreed in 481 BC to oppose Xerxes's invasion, to refrain from wars against fellow Greeks, and to aid each other should the latter develop. Plataea sent one-third of its hoplites to fight alongside the Spartans against their serfs. Aegina also sent a force, as did Mantineia and most likely a number of other states. Given the long duration of the war and the relatively short distances involved, various allies most likely sent troops more than once, each contingent staying for some or all of a campaigning season before returning home. Plutarch claimed that Cimon, the son of Miltiades and the most prominent and successful Athenian leading expeditions on behalf of the Delian League, went to help early on in the crisis and again later. Given that active men could walk from Athens to Sparta in three days, this is certainly possible.[10]

Around 462–461 BC the Spartans asked for Athenian aid in particular. By this time, the Messenian helots had holed up on Mount Ithome, and the Spartans were unable to make much progress in their attacks. The Athenians were deemed more experienced at this sort of 'siege' warfare, presumably on the basis that in recent years they had blockaded into submission several coastal and island cities, rather than simply because they had been the first to break into the Persian camp at Plataea. The matter was brought before the Assembly at Athens, where a man named Ephialtes was the most prominent opponent of sending the requested aid. His argument rested less on direct hostility to Sparta than on the belief that anything that weakened a major Greek city, in this case the most distinguished of all, was bound to help raise the prestige of Athens. Cimon opposed him, arguing that if Sparta collapsed, Athens would lose 'a yoke fellow' and Greece 'one of the two legs' carrying it. He was a great admirer of the Spartans, even naming one of his sons Lacedaemonius, but his arguments also struck a chord with the majority of his fellow citizens gathered to make the decision. This was the case of one great and prestigious city calling upon another for aid. The Greeks as a whole were better off led by two strong cities—Sparta and Athens—serving side by side as equals, or something close to it.[11]

The Athenians voted to aid their Spartan allies and sent Cimon at the head of a substantial army to join the Spartans and other allies around Mount Ithome. Together, they pressed the assault but, even so, were unable to make swift progress, which was surely a tribute to both the strength of the helots' positions and their determination in defence. At this point, the Spartan attitude changed. Thucydides claimed that they grew concerned about the boldness of the Athenians, perhaps as much in thought as action, and worried that they might even switch sides and support the helots. For so many outsiders from other cities to be in the heart of Sparta at the same time, and for them to see the Spartans as they behaved in their homeland, albeit in exceptional circumstances, was certainly rare. Friction was unsurprising, and the Athenians were perhaps especially sensitive about their treatment by the hosts they had come to aid. Whatever the details, Cimon and his men were informed that their services were no longer required. The other allies were to stay and continue the fight, but the Athenians were sent home. The insult was clear, especially since this openly demonstrated that the Spartans were unwilling to consider the Athenians as their equals.[12]

Cimon had been one of the most prominent Athenian leaders for well over a decade. In many ways an aristocrat of the old school, he nevertheless had adapted well to public life in a democracy. The family wealth had recovered from the immense fine imposed on his father in 489 BC, largely through the marriage of Cimon's sister to one of the wealthiest men in the city. Cimon was famed for his generosity, good looks, and skill as a war leader, fifth century BC manifestations of virtues familiar in Homer's poems. Probably he was elected as general, or strategos, on multiple occasions and given important commands. However, there was sometimes criticism, and after the subjugation of Thasos, he was put on trial, accused of taking bribes from the king of Macedon. Cimon was exonerated, but simply having to defend against an accusation of this sort was damaging, and worse was to come. After the Spartans sent the Athenians home in such a humiliating fashion, his fellow citizens voted to ostracize him.[13]

The anger felt at Athens was deep and soon expressed, perhaps reinforced if they had learned of the Spartan promise to aid Thasos. The veracity of the tale did not matter if the Athenians believed it to be true. Rejecting the 481 BC treaty to stand alongside the Spartans against the Persian threat, but not abandoning the war against Persia, the Athenians severed their link with Sparta and instead allied themselves with Argos. This was followed by further alliances with communities in Thessaly long hostile to the Spartans. The mood in the city had changed, and one tradition claimed that Ephialtes had used the absence of Cimon and his expeditionary force sent to Messenia to introduce a widespread reform. Details are few, but the overall trend was to increase the influence and direct power of the demos. In particular, powers were taken from the Areopagus, the old council of former archons, which seem to have included the right to conduct all but a handful of trials and also to scrutinise candidates for office and the performance of officials when they stepped down. Even though the archonship had long been filled by lot from a pool of elected men, they still tended to come from the aristocratic families, making this magistracy and the Areopagus as a body inclined to protect entrenched influence. Ephialtes is a shadowy figure, who appeared abruptly as a leading figure and had only a brief prominence before being assassinated. Although the man who wielded the knife was identified as an outsider from Tanagra, no one ever seems to have confirmed in public who gave the order to the killer or why. The murder did not lead to any political upheaval or reversal of the changes associated with him.[14]

ON THE WHOLE, the Athenians continued to display the immense self-confidence they had shown since the defeat of Xerxes's invasion. A large expedition was sent to Cyprus, only to receive a request for aid from Inaros, a Libyan prince who claimed a connection with the pharaonic royal line and had invaded Persian-occupied Egypt. He had already won some victories, and perhaps significant numbers of Egyptians saw him as a better alternative to the truly alien Persians. The Athenians voted to assist him, sending a fleet perhaps as large as 200 triremes that brushed aside the Persian squadrons operating in the area and then assisted in the fighting on land.[15]

As always, it took a while for Achaemenid Persia to muster a large field army and deal with a serious problem on the edge of the empire. In the meantime, an ambassador travelled to Sparta, which, like Athens, was still at war with the Persians. Presumably the latter were aware of the recent bad blood between Athenians and Spartans, so viewed this as a minor inconvenience and suggested that the Spartans launch an invasion of Attica. The ambassador was generous with his gifts to influential men, no doubt hinting at even greater generosity if they decided to go to war with Athens. The gifts were taken, but no public debate or action followed, and eventually the ambassador went on his way. For the moment, with the ongoing helot rebellion and other challenges, the Spartans had more pressing concerns. Still, it is nice to believe that they were still very reluctant to take Persia's part against the Athenians. No doubt they were also confident that, in spite of all their misfortunes, their reputation as the foremost and strongest state in the Greek world remained unmatched. At a basic level, and however clumsily, they had dismissed their Athenian allies from Ithome because they could.[16]

The sources, albeit some very late, hint that some Athenians joined an Argive campaign against Spartan allies around this time and may even have defeated the Spartans in a small encounter that was celebrated as a far grander affair than it really was. At some point the Spartans despaired of capturing by force the last helot stronghold on Mount Ithome. Spartan lives were always valuable, and the losses suffered in recent years surely made them more than usually reluctant to pay the cost of storming this last nest of resistance. Instead, a convenient prophecy issued—or 'remembered'—from Delphi was interpreted as meaning that Zeus offered some protection to the 'suppliant of Ithome'. Negotiations followed, and an armistice was arranged, by which the helot defenders and their families were allowed to leave unmolested. It was a remarkable victory for the rebels, even if the numbers involved were small compared to the overall population of Messenia and helots elsewhere. Provocatively, an Athenian squadron of ships that 'just happened' to be off the coast carried the rebels away and settled them in the allied city of Naupactus, on the northern shores of the Gulf of Corinth.[17]

Other Athenian actions were less direct challenges or insults to Sparta than to Spartan allies. At some point, perhaps around 460–459 BC, Megara and Corinth became involved in a dispute over border territory, that most common cause of friction between Greek states. Both were long-time allies of Sparta, and in the past, admittedly a couple of generations before, Megara had fought against Athens over control of land—including the island of Salamis. Now the Megarians abandoned their agreement with the Spartans and instead sought alliance with the Athenians, who readily accepted. An Athenian expedition went to Megara and laboured to construct lines of fortification linking the main city with its port, so that the Megarians could be supplied with food and anything else they needed, even if enemies blockaded them on land. The Corinthians, who in the past had aided or favoured the Athenians, selling them warships cheaply or turning back from the Spartan-led invasion of Attica under Cleomenes, were outraged. The bad feeling on both sides that grew from this probably explains Herodotus's tall tale about the Corinthians fleeing at Salamis.[18]

Anger swiftly turned to open hostility. An Athenian force landed at Haleis on the coast but was driven off by Corinthians. However, the Athenians and their allies defeated a fleet of ships from Corinth and a number of other Peloponnesian cities. These operations seem to have occurred at the same time as the large-scale Athenian expedition to Egypt and demonstrate the resources of Athens and her allies. In each case, allied communities were still providing a significant proportion of ships at this stage, while more allies seem to have served for pay onboard Athenian ships as crew or marines and probably as hoplites for land operations. This victory was followed up by an invasion of the island of Aegina, long-time rival of Athens, but for the last two decades an ally against Persia. The Aeginetans, who had fought so well at Salamis, met the Athenians at sea, only to be overwhelmed by numbers or perhaps by skill, for the Athenians and their allies had more experience of recent naval operations than anyone else. The Athenians captured seventy ships and were able to land and surround Aegina with a blockade.

A significant number of the Aeginetans' best hoplites were very likely still serving with the Spartans in the war against the helots. However, the Corinthians managed to get a few hundred of their own men into Aegina in spite of the Athenian blockade. They then mustered a larger army of their own and allied hoplites and advanced against Megara. Perhaps they hoped that the Athenians were currently overstretched and either would be unable to help their new-found allies at Megara or could only do so by withdrawing from Aegina. Instead, Athens mustered another army, composed—probably in part rather than solely—of boys in their late teens and men over fifty, who were normally only expected to serve in direct defence of the city itself. The campaign that followed may have been tentative, but after some indecisive fighting, the surprised Corinthians retreated. Ashamed to have fled from such a ragtag opponent, they advanced again twelve days later to claim victory by setting up a monument, only to be chased away by the Athenians. One small detachment strayed from the proper route, became hemmed in between ditches and their pursuers, and were stoned to death.[19]

Sparta and Athens had not clashed directly in any of these encounters, and Sparta's allies were just that, allies with the right to conduct their own affairs when these did not clash with those of Sparta. The Athenians had taken risks, choosing to support Megara, raid the Peloponnese, and invade Aegina at the same time as they were fighting a major war against the Persians in and around Egypt. Every year the city's ten tribes each set up a memorial listing all of their members who had died in the service of the state during the year, and one that survives almost intact makes most sense if it refers to this year of intense fighting. Just one tribe lost more than 185 men in Cyprus, Egypt, and Phoenicia (perhaps referring to sea fighting against the Persian fleet or raids on the coast), at Haleis and Aegina, and in the territory of Megara. Only Haleis had been a setback, so overall this was the price of a spectacular run of victories in only one year, admittedly one with a lot of fighting in different theatres. Sadly, only a fragment of a monument from one of the other nine tribes survives for the same year, making it impossible to tell whether this one suffered a fairly typical proportion of casualties in these operations or had been especially unfortunate—or, less probably, especially fortunate—in that particular year. Overall citizen losses were bound to have been higher than those of just a single tribe, to which must be added the cost in lives of the allied contingents serving alongside the Athenians, except in the force sent to Megara. Prominence and power came at a price in blood.[20]

Linking inland Megara to its port with a fortification proved successful, for all Greek states struggled to capture strong walls as long as such walls were manned by defenders. Perhaps some Athenians were already wondering about doing something similar for their own city, or perhaps the work at Megara inspired them, but at some point during these years a major project began. The Piraeus had been developed as a harbour for trade and to support warships and then fortified by Themistocles. Now a wall was constructed linking it to the city wall of Athens itself, while a second wall stretched from the city to the older harbour at Phaleron. Each wall was some 3.5 to 4 miles long, made from large blocks of stone to strengthen it. Together, they effectively turned this section of Attica into a triangular island. Once completed, they represented a formidable challenge to any attacking army, since the Athenians had the option of staying behind their walls rather than fighting in the open, secure in the knowledge that food could be brought in by sea in the quantities sufficient to outlast the resources of any blockading force. From a Spartan perspective, this was even less welcome than the repair of Athens's city walls after the Persian occupation.[21]

Even so, direct confrontation between Athens and Sparta came by a roundabout route sometime around 458–457 BC. Phocis, an ally of Athens, attacked Doris in central Greece, taking at least one of its four main cities. The Phocians may also have threatened or even occupied Delphi. The Spartans and most of the other Peloponnesian communities were Dorians and claimed that their ancestors originally came from the region of Doris, giving them an interest in the fate of its inhabitants. They decided to intervene, and a regent was sent at the head of an army of some 11,500 men to set things right. Sparta provided only 1,500 of these, and many or most of them were perioeci rather than 'peers', for apart from the losses to the earthquake, the war with the helots was still ongoing. Even so, this was a large army, demonstrating that for all the defections, the bulk of Sparta's allies remained loyal.

The Phocians were expelled, and the regent may well have taken the opportunity to aid friends elsewhere, for there is a tradition that his support helped Thebes to reassert itself as the dominant city in Boeotia. Perhaps it was now led by different men from those who had fought for Xerxes with such determination at Plataea. A messenger also arrived from a faction of Athenians displeased with the way public life had developed in their city under the leadership of men like Ephialtes. Whoever they were, they were willing to call on the Spartans to help them mount a revolution at home, and there are signs of nervousness about this possibility among the wider Athenian population.

No Greek army, especially one of this substantial size, could stay in the field for months on end, so the regent faced the problem of leading his army back home before the end of the campaigning season. Yet Megara was hostile, and the Athenians had troops there, making the most natural route difficult and perhaps impossible. In the meantime, the Spartan-led army appears to have marched to Tanagra close to the border with Attica. The Athenians mustered an army of 14,000 hoplites, including 1,000 from Argos and supported by cavalry from Thessaly as well as contingents from other allies. The presence of these additional troops suggests a degree of advanced planning, at least for the possibility of having to confront this Spartan expedition. Plutarch recounts a story that the ostracised Cimon presented himself and asked to serve with the army but was refused. Instead, he urged his friends and associates in the ranks to fight with all their strength, keen to demonstrate that he and they had no sympathy with anyone plotting a coup with Spartan aid.

Little is known of the short campaign that followed, but any attempts at negotiation failed. A battle, or perhaps several engagements, was fought over two days and may have resembled the rather confused fighting seen at Plataea more than a single, simple clash between two massed phalanxes. At some point the Thessalians switched allegiances and joined the Spartans. Losses were heavy on all sides, perhaps especially for the Argive contingent and among Cimon's friends, who fought hard to prove their own and his loyalty. In the end the Spartans and their allies were left in control of the battlefield, and the Athenians pulled back. This was a Spartan victory by the standards of the day, and Diodorus claims that a four-month truce was agreed, during which time the army marched back to the Peloponnese unmolested. Yet, if there had ever been a serious prospect of Spartan-backed revolution at Athens, it came to nothing, and in the meantime work on the long walls linking Athens to its ports moved towards completion.[22]

At best this was a limited victory, confirming Sparta's reputation for military might and rounding off a locally successful campaign. It did nothing to relieve the pressure on Aegina, if this had been an intention, for the siege remained unbroken. After some nine months the city surrendered, and Aegina was compelled at this point to join the Delian League. Before this happened, the Athenians sent a strong force to Boeotia, winning a battle—perhaps more than one—against opponents there. Phocis was restored to its former strength and Athenian dominance established over the whole area. The Athenians had confronted the Spartans in battle at Tanagra and lost, but that failure was more than balanced by so many successes.[23]

17

PEACE, PRIDE, AND POWER

Disaster in Egypt and subsequent recovery as the Delian League becomes effectively the Athenian Empire, c. 457–444 BC

THE DECADES AFTER THE REPULSE OF XERXES'S INVASION SAW the Athenians becoming bolder and bolder, as success followed success. Failures were rare and did little to slow the momentum of expanding power. Defeat at Tanagra was followed by victory in Aegina and Boeotia. The list of allies, both forced and more willing, continued to grow. All of them contributed to maintaining a navy the like of which had never been seen before. Xerxes had assembled many more warships for the expedition to Greece, but this fleet, like other Persian fleets, had never been intended to remain in permanent existence. In contrast, every year, as decade followed decade, the Athenians and their allies operated with powerful squadrons of warships, backed by still more ships and experienced crews who could be called upon whenever needed. They ranged seemingly at will, striking at the Peloponnese and the western coast of Greece or sailing to the Dardanelles and Black Sea beyond. Any place readily reached by sea lay open to the Athenians. Allies, including the Messenian rebels, were established in cities on the north coast of the Gulf of Corinth, sometimes backed by Athenian garrisons. There was also an Athenian presence in Boeotia, supporting the regimes convinced to accept Athenian power, and others may well have been dotted around the territories forming the League. Reasonably enough, by the early 450s BC the Athenians were becoming used to success, expecting it in even the boldest enterprise.

Then things began to go wrong, although the precise dating of events is uncertain. The Persian Empire moved slowly but retained immense strength, and after some four years a field army was gathered and sent to Egypt to deal with the rebellion there. Inaros, the Libyan prince and self-proclaimed pharaoh, along with his Athenian allies, became blockaded, and all were eventually forced to surrender. He was executed in the manner traditional for rebels who had challenged the great king; Thucydides says that few of the Athenians ever made it home and that most were killed. To add to the disaster, a squadron of reinforcements, as many as forty triremes, arrived, blissfully unaware of what was going on, and was annihilated. Some scholars believe that the fleet of 200 ships originally sent to support Inaros had stayed there throughout the four years of conflict, so suggest total losses of perhaps 40,000, making this one of the worst catastrophes ever suffered by Athens or any comparable state.[1]

That it was felt to be a major disaster is clear, but almost nothing else is certain, and such interpretations rely on a very rigid reading of Thucydides as well as other questionable assumptions—for instance, that every ship possessed its maximum crew. An expedition to Egypt was a major enterprise, but once there, the fleet was not impossibly far away, forcing it to remain there throughout the seasons and years until the task was done. It is hard to see what role so many warships and their crews could have played in operations that appear after the early stages to have been fought on land. Some operations in the Nile delta and the river beyond occurred but inevitably on a limited scale. As importantly, this was a fleet raised from Athenians and allies and sent by a state with annually elected generals and an Assembly playing an active and frequent role in decision-making. The Athenians and their allies supported Inaros and remained committed to him until his utter defeat. That did not mean that the level of actual support physically present in Egypt stayed constant throughout the four years, and contingents may well have come and gone, depending on what was deemed to be useful in the short-term future. The arrival of the fresh squadron at the last minute suggests such a pattern. On balance, losses numbering in thousands rather than tens of thousands are far more likely, but even so their severity must not be underestimated. By the scale of Greek warfare, so many killed or enslaved represented an appalling blow, even to a state with the population of Athens and its allies. These men were fellow citizens, serving because they were citizens. If the majority of crewmen on a ship were *thêtes*, these were still Athenians with families and neighbours able to vote. Many, like the allies and hired men serving alongside them, were also experienced and skilful, making them a valuable asset to lose.

The Egyptian campaign ended in a major disaster, even though the casualties were probably far fewer in number than many modern estimates. This was a blow to the reputation of Athens and her allies as the dominant force in the eastern Mediterranean, and the losses were serious. Yet Athens was an exceptionally large state by Greek standards, its allies were numerous, and big states tend to be resilient. Forty years later, the Athenians were not broken by the even more serious losses suffered in their disastrous expedition to Sicily—a defeat described in far more detail by Thucydides, if with similar language. Just as the Roman Republic—an enormous entity by the standards of city-states—could endure appalling numbers of deaths in the struggle with Carthage in the third century BC, the Athenians and their allies soon began to rebuild their strength.

There are signs of concerns in the short term. After all, a Persian army had crushed the expedition to Egypt, and the League had been formed to confront the Persians. Even though the great king gave no immediate sign of assembling a navy strong enough to challenge the Athenians at sea, they had every reason to fear that he might and certainly could do this. The original alliance forming the League had been made on Delos, and the communal treasury was kept there. The island was sacred to Apollo, and in 490 BC the Persian commander had treated its sanctuary and the islanders with respect, but this only emphasised the point that, as an island, it was vulnerable to a hostile navy. In 454/3 BC, in the aftermath of the defeat in Egypt, the League's treasury was moved permanently to Athens, where it would be more secure—and more directly under Athenian control.[2]

Cimon, the victor of Eurymedon and other campaigns against the Persians and their allies, was due to return from his ostracism by 451 BC at the latest. One tradition claimed that the Athenians voted to recall him sooner, and whether or not this happened, he did enjoy considerable popular support on his return. He may well have helped negotiate a five-year truce with Sparta, which was of mutual benefit since both sides had other priorities far more urgent than waging sporadic war against each other. Sparta was still dealing with the consequences of the earthquake and helot rebellion and working to restore some of its past dominance of most of the Peloponnese. Around this time, Tegea once again became a Spartan ally. With its citizen manpower reduced and destined never to recover, the Spartan reliance on allied hoplites to give weight to its field armies became all the more important. At the same time, Sparta had little to gain if Athenian power crumbled and the Persians once again became a force in the Aegean. There were concessions, and the Athenians appear to have ended their alliance, or at least active cooperation, with Argos.[3]

Cimon was put in charge of a major expedition to Cyprus, surely meant to provoke a Persian response and restore Athenian dominance after the failure in Egypt. Details are confused, the accounts poor and conflicting, although it was clearly a great success. Some ships were sent to Egypt, where a rebel leader was maintaining himself in a wide area of the marshy delta. On Cyprus itself, cities surrendered or were blockaded into submission, while at sea a Persian-led and predominantly Phoenician fleet was trounced. There may also have been a victory over the Persians on land, unless the sources invented this to make the campaign seem more like Eurymedon. The expedition was Cimon's last victory, even if he did not live to see it, for at some point he died, perhaps from disease or a wound turned bad. One story claimed that he ordered his death kept a secret, whether to encourage his own forces or dismay the enemy, and the other Athenian commanders may well have led the critical fighting.[4]

This was the last big confrontation between the Athenians and the Persians, and by the fourth century BC several Athenians claimed that this was because the two sides had agreed to a treaty in 449 BC. Known as the Peace of Callias after Cimon's brother-in-law, who negotiated it, it was remembered as a great success, by which the Persians accepted the right of Ionian and Lydian cities to ally with Athens and promised not to send forces into a coastal strip of territory, measured as the distance a rider could cover in one or three days, depending on the tradition. Most of the sources contrasted this agreement, presented as negotiated by the Athenians from a position of strength, with what they saw as the weakness, from a Greek perspective, of subsequent deals made with the Persians.

Yet there are problems, the most serious being that no fifth century BC source mentions the treaty at all. Herodotus does tell a story about Callias visiting the court of Artaxerxes, but his main concern was what happened to representatives of Argos who were there at the same time. Thucydides does not mention the treaty at all, although a later passage may imply that some sort of arrangement had been reached with the Persians, effectively ending hostilities. Even in the fourth century BC, not everyone was convinced, and one author argued that the inscribed text at Athens purporting to be the treaty was not genuine but set up considerably later. Other traditions add more confusion, claiming that there were earlier negotiations and a peace agreed between Athens and Persia after the Battle of Eurymedon, and perhaps subsequently as well, preceding the treaty in 449 BC.[5]

Nothing is certain, and the scholarly debate has failed to produce a consensus. Still, from c. 450 BC onwards, the Athenians launched no more attacks on the Persians, most of the coastal communities of Asia Minor were allied to the Athenians, and the Persians made no attempt to intervene in the Aegean. Some form of negotiated agreement between the two sides is the most natural explanation for this, be it the Peace of Callias or something less formal. Either way, the great king would have presented any arrangement as fully in keeping with his divinely sanctioned power, with Persia as the dominant partner, even if the Athenian view differed.[6]

Formal or not, there was peace, and it proved enduring. This has tempted many scholars to assume that the war with Persia was over, and with it, the central, publicly stated purpose of the Delian League. Treaties between Greek communities rarely led to a permanent end to hostilities, while those specifying so many years of peace not only implied that these could well resume in due course but rarely lasted for the full duration. Both sides understood this and knew that the only long-term security came from remaining—and, as importantly, being perceived as—strong. Former enemies naturally took advantage of any weakness when no other greater commitments occupied them. Thus the end of active fighting and an agreement to coexist for the moment on particular terms did not mean that the Athenians and their allies, on one side, and the Persians, on the other, were determined never to go to war again. If it suited them, they would do so with little qualm, and a pretext for conflict was easy enough to find. In the meantime, both had other concerns and saw no immediate advantage in continuing the fight, but such factors could change as time passed.

Perhaps some of Athens's allies felt that, the danger having lessened, the burdens of contributing to the fleet grew heavier, but no source makes such a claim. Perhaps also the Athenians became less considerate in their treatment of their allies and more demanding around the middle of the century, and there is evidence for substantial numbers of Athenian citizens being granted land in allied territory. These were cleruchies, like the ones established in Euboea in the early days of the democracy, where Athenians, most of them poor, were granted farms and as a result owned more property, so rose in class. Most went to the lands in question and farmed them directly, although others may have been absentee landlords. Either way, they remained full citizens of Athens and did not join the other community or form new colonies of their own. Details are lacking—for instance, whether the land came with some obligation for existing occupants to provide labour and, more importantly, precisely when and on what scale these cleruchies became more common and in what circumstances. Cities that rebelled and attempted to leave the alliance often suffered some confiscation of land, but whether other communities that had not challenged the Athenians in this way were also expected to give land to Athenian cleruchs is uncertain. There are cases where an ally's contribution to the League dropped significantly, perhaps in reward for voluntarily giving land to cleruchs.[7]

Yet the difficulty of dating many events makes understanding cause and effect especially problematic for these years. One inscription, recorded in the nineteenth century but subsequently lost, deals with the aftermath of the rebellion of Erythrae in Ionia and may date to the late 450s BC. The constitution of the city was changed to something close to the Athenian model, including the democratic organs of the *Boule* and the Assembly. Members of the *Boule* were to swear to act as well and as justly as they could on behalf of the Erythraean people and the Athenians and their allies. They were not to rebel against Athens and its allies, whether on their own initiative or through persuasion by fellow citizens. Particular concern in this respect was made clear about a group of Erythraeans who had fled to take sanctuary with the Persians, none of whom were to be allowed to return to the city without Athenian permission. The commander of the Athenian garrison established in the city and inspectors sent out from Athens were to supervise both this and the functioning of the new constitution.[8]

The decree reveals the extent of intervention in the domestic affairs of one allied city, with the imposition of Athenian ways of doing things and the assumption that the interests of Athens and its allies were—at the very least—of equal importance to a citizen's loyalty to Erythrae itself. Similar terms were imposed on other defeated rebels and, as in this case, empowered a demos drawn from a wider section of the population than just the aristocracy. Less clear is whether the Athenians intervened in the internal affairs of cities that did not rebel. Fourth century BC evidence shows wide resentment of the confiscation of land for cleruchies, while constitutions of the sort imposed at Erythrae were clearly attacks on the freedom of citizens to determine their own affairs.[9]

At the same time, the decree attests to rival factions within the city's population, and to view everything as a simple acceptance or rejection of the alliance with Athens, let alone to assume that all citizens in any community were unanimous in their opinions and attitudes, is a mistake. These were Greek communities, and joining the Athenian alliance—as indeed allying with Sparta—did not mean that internal competition for office and prestige ceased. Some individuals and groups benefitted from the alliance and, as a result, tended to embrace it. If it ceased to be advantageous to them, then they might well consider other options. For their rivals, the men who were not doing so well as things stood, a revolution was always tempting and likely to mean a repudiation of the link with Athens. Whenever there is any detail describing a rising against the Athenians, there are traces of more than one group within the community involved, and it is safe to assume that such glimpses of local disputes were merely the tip of the iceberg. The rise of Athens to dominate the seas was a factor no one could ignore but remained just one element in ongoing competition within and between the cities of the Greek world.

AROUND 448 BC, the Spartans intervened at Delphi for a second time, expelling the Phocians who had once again taken over the region and the cult centre. Not long after the Spartans returned home, the Athenians sent a force and reimposed Phocian control. In spite of this success, in barely a year their hold on Phocis and Boeotia began to collapse. Exiles from several cities, including Orchomenus, managed to return home and seize power, presumably with at least some support from the mass of the population. These men, forced out during the Athenian takeover a decade earlier, were joined by other exiles from Euboea, Locri, and especially Thebes. Athens responded by sending a general at the head of an army, who enjoyed some early successes until he walked into ambush at Coronea. The Athenian commander died, along with many of his men.

This was followed by the rebellion of four major cities on Euboea, again led by exiles. Athens gave up the contest in Boeotia and central Greece, perhaps even reaching an agreement with the new leaders of the main communities there, for Euboea was both closer and far more important. Another army was mustered and command given to Pericles, the son of Xanthippus, a man who had been ostracised at the urging of Themistocles and recalled at the time of the Persian invasion. By the time he had crossed the narrow strait to Euboea, news arrived of another coup, this time at Megara, where yet another group of exiles had returned home backed by allies from Corinth and several other cities. Sympathisers admitted them into the city, and they quickly took over, massacring the Athenian garrison, apart from a few who managed to escape to the fortified harbours. The new regime controlling the city swiftly made an alliance with Sparta. Athens recalled Pericles from Euboea, but, even before this, the Athenians seem to have sent troops to Megara in an attempt to regain control.

Events overtook them, for the Spartans mustered a large field army of their own citizens and allies and were freely admitted by the Megarians on their way to invade Attica. The Athenian force included elements of at least three tribal regiments but was greatly overmatched. Guided by a local man, Pythion, whose grave memorial survives, the Athenians managed to dodge the enemy and make their way back home by a roundabout route. The inscription boasts that Pythion killed 'seven men, and broke his spears in their bodies', so there may well have been some fighting, unless this referred to his previous exploits. Whether or not this manoeuvring delayed the Spartan advance, when King Pleistonax led his men into Attica itself, he was confronted by Pericles and his army. There was no battle, and after some posturing and negotiation, the Spartans turned about and withdrew. Rumours quickly spread that the Spartan king had been bribed, so that Pleistonax joined the growing list of Spartan monarchs to be discredited and dethroned by his own countryman after an adventure abroad. When it came to accounting for his own conduct in office, Pericles joked about a sum spent on something like 'miscellaneous expenses' and was happy to be seen as a wily operator in the best traditions of Themistocles or Odysseus.[10]

There was surely more to it than this. Battles were risky and likely to be costly in lives, a possibility of even greater concern for the Spartans now than in the past. Athens gave up any efforts to regain control of Megara, which returned to the Spartan fold. This alone meant that, in future, it would be easier for a Sparta-led army to reach Attica whenever it wished, passing through allied rather than hostile territory. For the moment, the Athenians were relieved of the need to fend off such an invasion and instead sent their army back to Euboea, where it subdued the rebel cities one by one. One city, Hestaia, was singled out for harsh treatment on the grounds that its men had executed Athenian prisoners. The population—or at least its wealthier members—were sent into exile en masse and their land allocated to Athenian cleruchs. Other cities may have suffered smaller confiscations of territory, and all had a new constitution imposed upon them. A surviving text from Chalkis was similar to the decree for Erythrae, although the citizens pledged loyalty to the Athenians alone, rather than to them and their allies. Perhaps this revealed the changing nature of the Delian League, as alliance turned to empire, assuming that the Erythrae decree really is earlier. On the other hand, Euboea was a lot closer to Attica, and the Athenians had long-established involvement on the island, predating the anti-Persian alliance. The people of Chalkis were also forced to submit some legal disputes to Athenian courts, and this does appear to have become more and more common as time passed. Juries of Athenians naturally gave judgement on the basis of their own standards of what was right, which inevitably tended to mean that the interests of Athens itself were always a major consideration.[11]

The defeat in Egypt and the loss of control in Boeotia and Megara did not much diminish Athenians' pride and sense of their own worth. Plutarch claims that sometime around 447 BC, Pericles inspired Athens to send out envoys all around the Greek world, inviting delegates from each city to attend a conference where they could discuss how to proceed in the years to come, now that the Persian threat was less immediate. Once again, Thucydides makes no mention of this move, but the stipulations for the selection of and tasks for the ambassadors, outlined in Plutarch's text, have the ring of a decree of the Assembly. Much about this is reminiscent of the Spartan organised council in 481 BC to discuss the threat posed by Xerxes. Then Sparta sent out the call, and many attended because they were willing to acknowledge the Spartans' supreme reputation in war. For the Athenians to send out a similar invitation was an assertion of status, a bold claim to have earned the right to be treated as a leader in the same way. At its root were assertions of honour and power, the latter based on the fleet, its record in war, and the remarkable qualities of the city leading the alliance that made it all possible. This was supposed to have earned Athens the right to be held in comparable esteem to Sparta.[12]

That, at least, was the Athenian claim, but the Athenians could not compel everyone to accept it. The Spartans declined the Athenian invitation, as did many other cities, so that the proposed conference came to nothing, which might well explain why Thucydides did not bother to mention it in his brief account of this period. Sparta had no wish to acknowledge any other state as its equal, let alone as its superior. On the other hand, it also had no desire for open confrontation with the Athenians for the moment. Around 446/5 BC, the two cities agreed to a thirty-year peace. As part of this Athens gave up its control of the fortified anchorages of Megara, as well as a couple of coastal cities in the Peloponnese seized in the last decade or so, although it retained Aegina. Each side agreed not to attack the other unless a dispute arose and the other city refused to submit to arbitration by another state. There also appears to have been recognition of each other's wider alliance, whether or not this was stated formally. At the very least the treaty was a mark of respect on each side, although the Athenians and Spartans no doubt saw the relationship differently. After a five-year truce had broken down, two powerful cities had pledged themselves to one lasting thirty years. That did not mean either had abandoned its suspicion of the other or its ambitions, but the truce gave them the freedom to concentrate on other matters, as the Spartans reasserted themselves and continued to reconstruct their society and economy and the Athenians consolidated their own power.[13]

Ultimately the basis of Athens's might was the fleet, which allowed it to hold together such a far-flung alliance; at the same time that fleet was partly funded and manned by those very allies. Little is recorded of the activities of the navy in the years following the peace with Sparta, other than its ability to range wherever it wished. Activity on the Thracian coast, around the Dardanelles, and in the Black Sea continued, protecting and expanding access to the resources, particularly grain, on which Athens depended. At the same time, the Athenians looked to the west, establishing a large new colony at Thurii in

Italy in 443 BC. Only a minority of the colonists were Athenian, the remainder being from other Greek cities, and there was an element of prestige in taking the lead in a Panhellenic enterprise, as well as a sense that the fleet gave Athens a very long reach overseas. Athenians did not lack ambition.[14]

18

THE GENERAL

*Athens at its height and the
pre-eminence of Pericles, c. 445–430 BC*

THE NAME OF PERICLES FEATURES HEAVILY IN THE SURVIVING ancient accounts of these years and even more heavily in most modern histories, as scholars try to weave a fuller narrative around the meagre evidence. He was presented as rival to Cimon, then to others, until in c. 443 BC his only remaining influential opponent was ostracised. No other adversaries are named in subsequent years, which often leads to the presentation of any action taken by Athens as solely planned and implemented by Pericles. This must be an exaggeration, for other men were active and influential in public life, and they surely had different opinions. Still, from around 445 BC, Pericles was elected strategos, or general, for fifteen consecutive years, and later Thucydides wrote that what the Athenians believed to be democracy was in truth the rule of one man. He is unlikely to have meant this literally. Pericles was famous as an orator, his record in warfare competent enough but not nearly as spectacular as Cimon's. He got his way by persuading the Assembly to vote for what he wanted, not by commanding them. His agility with words surpassed anyone else's. His rival, the man ostracised in 443 BC, famed as a wrestler and a victor in the Olympic Games, was said to have complained that whenever he put Pericles on the ground in a debate, the latter was able to convince everyone that this had not actually happened and that he had 'really' won.[1]

Wrestling, like the other activities of the gymnasium and competitive sport, was very much a nobleman's pursuit. Pericles, hailing from this aristocratic class, was a member of the Alcmaeonid family, with a father prominent enough to have been ostracised in the 480s BC. Yet his lifestyle broke from many of the traditions of the elite. He does not appear to have vied with others in sport as an adult and shunned the drinking parties (*symposia*) that were such a central feature of well-to-do society. Instead, he associated with philosophers from abroad, some of whom expressed highly unconventional ideas. One of them was noted as saying that proving whether or not the gods existed was impossible. There is no suggestion that Pericles himself espoused such wild thoughts, and if he did, he did so in private. He is supposed to have enjoyed long discussions with such thinkers, often on fairly abstract topics. The example mentioned by Plutarch concerned a hypothetical case of a javelin going wildly astray during a games and killing a spectator. The question concerned who or what was to blame: the javelin itself, the man who threw it so wildly, or the organiser for letting the situation arise.[2]

While Pericles enjoyed the stimulating, even challenging company of free thinkers and artists in private, he did not fill his public appearances and speeches, aimed at his audience, with eccentric and theoretical ideas. His lifestyle was austere, overly so for his sons as they grew to adulthood. Some criticised his manner as too distant, reminiscent of a tyrant, an impression reinforced by claims that he looked a lot like Pisistratus. This was probably a concern more for other aristocrats, whereas to most of his fellow citizens he came across as a sober and wise counsellor. Even so, concerned that he might irritate them if he spoke too often in meetings of the Assembly, Pericles used to employ friends and allies to voice his opinion there.

Such concerns reinforce the sense that there were far more debate and opposition than a simple narrative of Periclean Athens suggests. Pericles succeeded for so long because he managed to reflect and promote attitudes and desires shared by a substantial majority of his fellow citizens, and stark oppositions between him and Cimon or others are artificial. Many of the policies he promoted built on things done in the past and proposed by others, pushing them towards a logical goal.[3]

AT THIS POINT it is worth pausing to consider Athens in the middle years of the fifth century BC. It continued to grow in terms of population, boosted by its role as head of such a grand alliance, and over time the city also became more splendid. The Athenians had deliberately left the shrines on the Acropolis in ruins as a reminder of what the Persians had done, whether or not they and others had formally sworn an oath to do so before the Battle of Plataea. Yet, after essential rebuilding within the city, such as houses and the defensive circuit walls, some grander monuments were constructed, especially as the profits from successful war-making came in. Cimon constructed a stoa, a long-roofed meeting place, open on one side, on the edge of the Agora, or marketplace. Its inner wall was decorated with grand paintings depicting scenes of mythological battles alongside Marathon, all done by some of the most famous artists of the day. In time it became known as the 'Painted Stoa', and it combined beauty with practicality, offering shelter from the wind and shade from the high summer sun. As importantly, it was open to all, a monument to be used by citizens, with reminders of both distant and recent Athenian glory.[4]

Spoils from the victory at Marathon, presumably kept safe and separate ever since, funded wholly or in part another great artwork, this time a statue of Athena Promachos (the front fighter). Some thirty feet tall and covered in bronze, this was set up on the Acropolis, with work beginning soon after the victory at Eurymedon, although it may have marked victories over the Persians more generally rather than any specific battle. Such a tall statue in a high place became a landmark and remained so even when the Acropolis was redeveloped in grand style. Sailors rounding Cape Sounion some forty miles away were said to take their bearings on seeing the statue, or perhaps the glint of the sun striking the bronze.[5]

The Athenians never rebuilt the temples on the Acropolis destroyed by the Persians, but from around 447 BC, they did start to set up new monuments, carefully respecting the existing foundations and integrating the new projects with them. Pericles was associated with this grand building program, although doubtless others were also involved, and there was a general enthusiasm for making Athens look as magnificent as possible. From the start the designs and materials showed immense aspiration and ambition. Other cities had their monuments—for instance, the great temple to Aphaia built on high ground above the strait separating Aegina from Attica—and there were the complexes around major cult sites, such as Delphi. The Athenians were competing with the wider Greek world in this respect as they did in so many others.

Work first began with what would become known as the Parthenon, surely the most famous and instantly recognisable Greek monument to survive to this day. The name only came later, taken from the colossal statue of Athena housed within it, and there is no evidence as to what it was called in the first place. This statue, made in sections fastened onto an inner wooden frame, depicted the goddess as Athena Parthenos (the maiden/virgin) with her helmet pushed well back on her head and her shield and spear at rest. The skin was made from ivory, and her hair, robes, other garb, and equipment from gold, decorated in places with gems. In times of need, the gold plate and other valuables could be turned into coin or otherwise spent for the good of the city. The statue was designed and made—or at least supervised—by Pheidas, who had already produced the bronze

Athena Promachos and was also one of the main architects of the entire building. He was long remembered as one of the greatest of all Greek sculptors.[6]

The Parthenon was designed like a temple but intended to be grand. Situated on the southern edge of the Acropolis hill, it towered over the city below and was visible from afar. Its base measured some 228 by 101 feet (69.5 by 30.7 meters), and the outside had forty-six columns, each some 34 feet high. While many temples were decorated with some marble, the Athenians built the outside entirely from marble blocks, quarried and shaped some eight miles outside the city and then conveyed to the building site. Inside was the main rectangular structure, divided into two halls, one housing the statue, and these walls were ashlar. Decorations of finely sculpted and painted scenes ran around the top of the outside wall of the chamber, and more scenes ran above the columns on the main structure. Themes included mythological battles against centaurs and amazons as well as the Trojan War. All of these celebrated the triumph of the civilised Greeks over barbaric outsiders, even if Homer and the tradition in general actually said little about any Athenian role at Troy. Other sculptures harked back to the foundation of Athens, while the friezes on the inner chamber showed a procession, perhaps an idealised version of the Panathenaea festival. The fine artistry of these works stood out, as did their quantity and size. Less obvious at first glance was the ingenuity of angle and dimensions of the entire building. To the human eye, a large building that is perfectly square, straight, and symmetrical looks wrong. The Parthenon's columns, walls, and joins were angled to appear perfectly aligned even though they were not. A Roman architect writing centuries later mentions texts written by the architects explaining how this was all done, but sadly these have not survived.[7]

Eventually the great monument became called the Parthenon after the goddess whose statue stood inside. It resembled the design of a temple; yet that it was one is less certain, at least as the term is usually understood. No altar was ever associated with the building, and there is no trace of a priestess or a cult attached to it. In addition to the gold of the statue, the Parthenon was from the start used to house the treasury of the city, making it a public building, albeit a sacred one. Not far away, a column was erected and listed year by year the sixtieth share devoted to Athena taken from the contribution of each ally to the common fund—the tribute lists that provide scholars with so much evidence about the Delian League. Pericles's opponent, the man who was ostracised, criticised him for using the resources of the allies to 'tart up Athens like some brazen woman', but whether money from the allies went directly to building projects in Athens and Attica is unclear. At the very least, the contributions helped to pay for the fleet, allowing the Athenians to stay so strong militarily and still have funds to spare for other things such as grand monuments.[8]

The Parthenon was only the first of a number of big projects. The Propylaea is in some ways temple-like—for instance, in its use of columns and the same marble as the Parthenon—but it was simply, if that is the right word, a gateway through which any visitor, including the processions of the Panathenaea, would reach the top of the steps and enter the Acropolis. Essentially an entrance, it was made on a scale to inspire awe in anyone who saw it and served no other practical purpose. Adjacent to it was a temple to Athena Nike (the victorious), and other shrines would follow as the Acropolis became a celebration of Athens and the deities believed to favour the city above all others. Other parts of the city also received monuments. Built on the edge of the Agora, the Hephaisteion may well be earlier than the Parthenon and today is one of the best-preserved temples in Greece. It celebrated the lame craftsman of the Olympian gods, so was associated with many of the tradesmen and artisans who had set up workshops in the city. At the same time, myth claimed that one of Athens's first kings was his child, sired accidentally on mother earth after Hephaestus's failed attempt to ravish Athena. Sculptures depicted the labours of

Hercules on one side of the building and the feats of Theseus on the other, setting the demigod renowned throughout the Greek world for his triumphs alongside—so in a sense equivalent to—the less famous but truly Athenian hero. Nearer the Acropolis, Pericles persuaded the Athenians to construct a roofed concert hall, the Odeion. This was huge and supposedly inspired by the tent of Xerxes, which was in fact a complex of tents, meant to replicate the feel and organisation of a royal palace. The Athenian version was square with a high roof that was either peaked or conical in shape and supported by row upon row of pillars. Visibility and acoustics may not have been ideal, but no other city had such a large covered area with permanent seating reserved for musical performances. To make best use of it, the Panathenaea added competitions in music and singing.[9]

The building programme ornamented the city, and fresh projects would be added in the decades to come. They very publicly proclaimed Athenians' sense of their city's grandeur and status. Some were functional as well as decorative once complete, and all were expensive while at the same time sources of good employment. Inscribed records reveal citizens, resident foreigners, or metics, and slaves working side by side for the same pay—some or all of which, in the slave's case, may have gone to the owner. Plutarch claimed that providing employment was one of Pericles's motives for encouraging the building programme, and although some scholars are inclined to see this as the reasoning of a man used to the actions of Roman emperors, on some level it was true. Apart from the construction workers and craftsmen on the site, others worked in the marble quarries or provided other materials, so that a lot of people profited from the projects, and many honed their skills, which were then available for hire for less grand enterprises.[10]

EPHIALTES HAD REDUCED the role of the Areopagus—for instance, taking from the council of former archons the responsibility for conducting most trials. Instead, judgement was delivered by juries of citizens, often numbering hundreds and sometimes even some 2,000, depending on the nature of the case. Pericles may well have cooperated or at least supported Ephialtes, and Plutarch did not believe the claim that he was responsible for the latter's subsequent murder. Pericles was certainly enthusiastic to see more and more of his fellow citizens paid to perform public services. Jurors received a wage for every day they were active, and all male citizens were eligible to serve. Similarly, anyone undergoing military service was paid, including the rowers, while more and more officials or garrisons were required to spend time in allied communities. A doubtless apocryphal story claimed that in his early career, Pericles had wondered how to match the largesse Cimon gave from his personal wealth. The answer, the advice he received, was to give the people their own money—to use state funds to pay citizens.[11]

Athens had considerable resources aside from the contributions of its allies. The silver mines at Laurium, which had allowed Themistocles to fund the first big naval expansion, continued to provide a rich yield. They were the basis for coinage, and from the middle of the century each coin had the head of Athena on the face and her symbol of an owl on the reverse. Known as a result as 'owls', they were minted in exceptionally large quantities by the standards of the day and became widely used throughout the Greek world. This was partly a recognition of their quality and also reflects Athenians' insistence that more and more trade within the network of allies, let alone in Athens itself, employ Athenian weights, measures, and often currency. Standardisation did foster exchange, removing the confusion of every city having its own system of measurement, so there was a wider benefit to this. At the same time, it confirmed and emphasised Athens as the centre of it all and came most naturally to Athenians.[12]

Athens played an ever-increasing role in the lives of its allies. Attempts to break away from the alliance provoked a military response and the installation of a new regime and constitution that

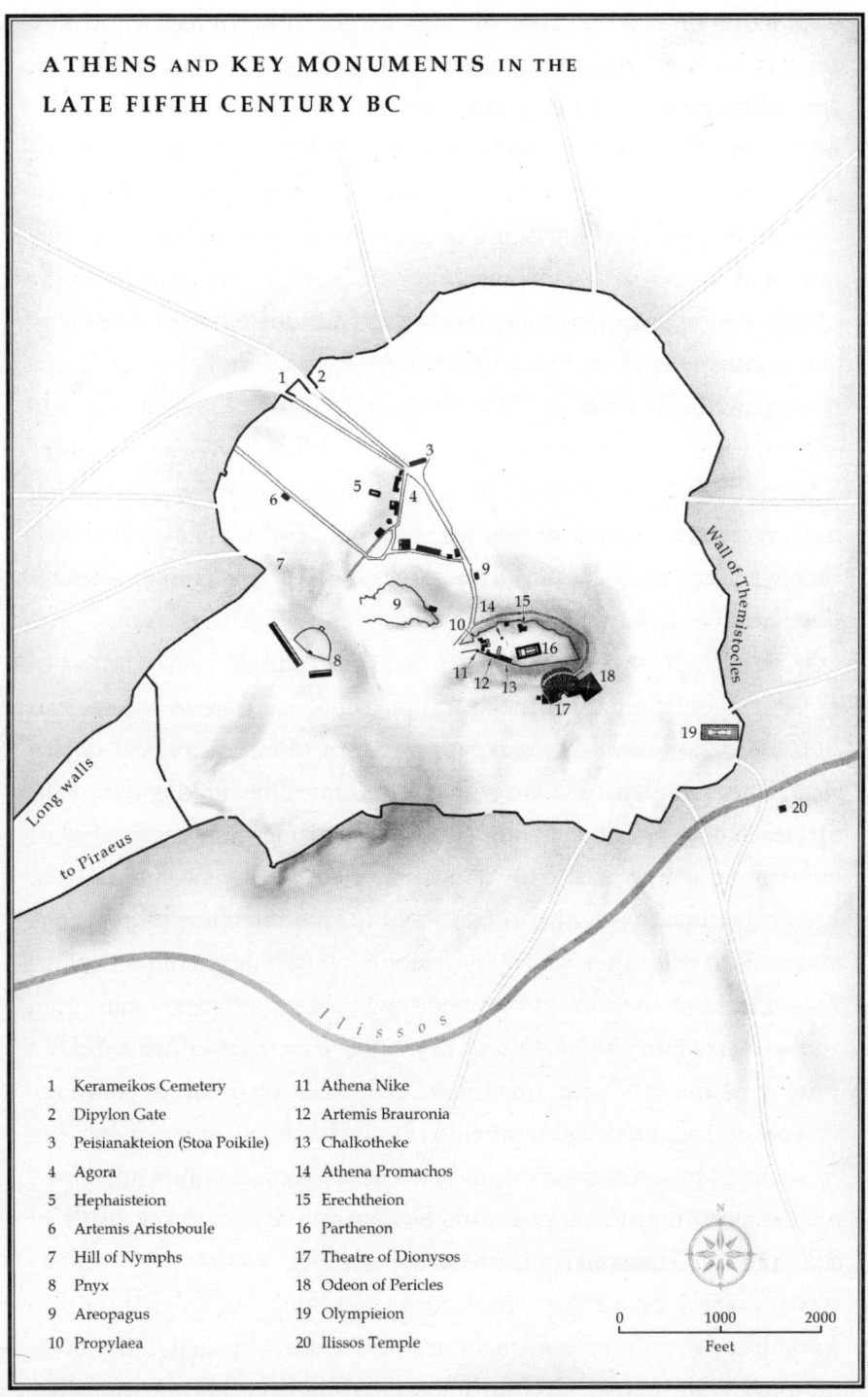

ATHENS AND KEY MONUMENTS IN THE LATE FIFTH CENTURY BC

1 Kerameikos Cemetery
2 Dipylon Gate
3 Peisianakteion (Stoa Poikile)
4 Agora
5 Hephaisteion
6 Artemis Aristoboule
7 Hill of Nymphs
8 Pnyx
9 Areopagus
10 Propylaea
11 Athena Nike
12 Artemis Brauronia
13 Chalkotheke
14 Athena Promachos
15 Erechtheion
16 Parthenon
17 Theatre of Dionysos
18 Odeon of Pericles
19 Olympieion
20 Ilissos Temple

gave loyalty to the Athenians equal weight to loyalty to fellow citizens. How much this impinged on daily life is hard to say, and in the main, those most affected were the politically active, who tended to be the wealthier and aristocratic. Communities that did not rebel—and these were always the vast majority, even if many were tiny cities—probably had less sense of an Athenian presence, unless Athens had a garrison or cleruchies on their land. How often Athenian officials—for instance, men tasked with administering the funds of the alliance—appeared and the extent to which they interfered in a community's affairs most likely varied a great deal. Each ally contributed to the common military effort, in the main in money, although a few still sent fully crewed warships. In each case the whole community shared the cost of this contribution. The many allied citizens who went and took service in the Athenian fleet are assumed to have done so voluntarily and as individuals, although their home cities may possibly have sometimes sent them as groups.[13]

Allies contributed to the common fund, a share of which was donated to the cult of Athena, at least after the treasury had shifted from Delos to Athens. Before that, the share may have gone to the Delian cult of Apollo. The inscriptions recording this suggest that no contributions were made for one whole year, perhaps c. 447 BC and possibly coinciding with Pericles's call for a conference of all Greek states. Whatever the reason, the tribute, as scholars tend to call it, resumed. Both the carved lists and the literary accounts suggest that some states were late or did not pay every year. In itself, this did not provoke automatic and immediate Athenian retribution, although prolonged failure to deliver the due funds likely prompted a forceful response. The amounts delivered sometimes varied, and a good case can be made that this was sometimes due to the imposition of Athenian cleruchies, which took land from an allied community, reducing its communal income and therefore the amount deemed fair for it to pay. Other fluctuations in the amount delivered by individual allies may reflect particular circumstances, such as poor harvests or other problems, and there is no reason to believe that the Athenian officials overseeing the tribute were rigid and uncompromising. For practical purposes alone, it was good for Athens to keep her allies willing and able to contribute in the long term.

It was also important that the allies treated the Athenians with clear and open respect, since they were the leaders and the ones who made the alliance strong and paid a price in sweat and blood to maintain this. A symbolic reminder of the bond with Athens came each year when every allied state was expected to send a sacrificial cow and an ornate military panoply as offerings to Athena during the Athenaea festival. The relationship was clear, showing respect to the goddess of the city that led the alliance and whose citizens were the mainstay of its fighting force. There was no reciprocal equivalent, where the Athenians made a regular offering to a cult of an allied state, but then, none of the allies came remotely close to the sheer size, power, or prestige of Athens.[14]

FESTIVALS, LIKE THE annual procession to honour Athena and the grander version, the Panathenaea, held every fourth year, brought Athenians together to celebrate the glories of their city. Important for generations, their scale and lavishness grew with Athens's wealth and power. Pisistratus and his sons had added to them, creating the Great Panathenaea, and the democracy that followed did the same. Pericles included musical competitions in the games associated with them and had the Odeion made as a spectacular venue for these. New mixed with the old. Central to the procession was the transport of a new robe to replace that on a truly ancient statue of Athena—smaller and less ornate and spectacular than the newer ones but hallowed by tradition and saved from the Persians during the occupation. On its route to the Acropolis the robe was carried in a sacred boat, the origins of this ritual far, far older than the emergence of Athens as a naval power. After that, the party walked up the carved stairs and—once it was finished—passed through the grand entrance of the Propylaea and entered the

Acropolis itself. Over time, and in contrast to the modern impression of a wide, open space apart from the grand Parthenon, other buildings were erected, and statues and other symbols and trophies testified to the piety of the Athenians and the greatness of their city.[15]

A little less fervently patriotic—but only a little—was the Dionysia festival, also held each year in honour of the god of wine and ecstasy. Alongside a procession and sacrifices, this became an occasion for dramatic performances. As the celebrants were Greeks, these were competitions, and the type of presentation developed from recitations to an actor and then actors interacting with a chorus. A set of plays, all written by one man, was presented by a *choregos*—effectively a producer. The latter was a citizen, naturally one of wealth and status. Prominent men seeking the job competed to be granted the role by an archon, and then did their best to make their offering the one chosen as the best. As a comparatively young man, Pericles had been the producer for Aeschylus with the triad of performances including the *Persae*, which successfully broke with tradition by treating recent events rather than presenting a version of ancient myth. This was a good way for ambitious men to become better known, since their own money went to fund entertainment offered to their fellow citizens. Politics sometimes intervened in the judgements; after one victory Cimon was called upon to judge the competition and favoured the plays of the younger Sophocles over Aeschylus. In time, as the new form of comedy developed and was included, performances ruthlessly satirised prominent figures in public life, and Pericles, who was more prominent that anyone else, was a frequent target.[16]

Aeschylus, Sophocles, Aristophanes, Euripides: The names remain famous to this day, even though only a fraction of their work survives, and even those who find little to admire about the history of Athens in this era still marvel at the artistic achievement seen on the stage as well as the magnificence of the new monuments. Athenians may well have taken all this almost for granted, and it is notable that when Thucydides has Pericles tell his fellow citizens of the greatness of Athens, he makes next to no mention of the cultural aspects so admired in the modern era. Instead, he praises them for their quality, their worth, their courage, their individuality yet willingness to come together for the good of the state, their active involvement in public affairs, and, most of all, their prowess in war and the greatness of their power. Perhaps Pericles, and Thucydides, took the other glories of Athens as natural, since her military might and political stability made them possible.[17]

Because of their sheer quality and humour, which so often remains funny to this day—though admittedly modern audiences cannot match the Athenian appetite for jokes about bottoms and sodomy—there is a temptation to exaggerate the influence of the playwrights and, indeed, to interpret their works as simply presenting the ideas and attitudes actually held rather than as intending to entertain. Apart from that, the performances came only at the annual festival, as the authors, performers, and producers competed with each other. Many Athenians may never have seen a play performed, and even those who were enthusiastic did not get to see one very often, although they might subsequently learn some or all of the texts. The stage was still simply one aspect of life and certainly not a dominant one. As mentioned earlier, Aeschylus was said to have stressed his valour at Marathon in his epitaph rather than his creative works. Sophocles served as a strategos, and even if less is known of the others' lives, they were most likely active as citizens as well as playwrights. Being a citizen at Athens meant taking part in the communal life of the city, serving in peace and war as necessary. Pericles is supposed to have reproved Sophocles during a campaign for getting distracted from his duties by the sight of a good-looking youth. Even if there is truth in these anecdotes, Sophocles was elected to command and did serve his city in an active capacity.[18]

MANY OF THE stories told of Pericles may well have their origins in jokes from such performances, as well as criticism from rivals, and may be wholly fictional or at best a heavily distorted version of the truth. He married and fathered two sons before divorcing his wife. That none of the sources appear to mention her name is often seen as symptomatic of the status of women in Athens, suggesting that on the whole they mattered as daughters, wives, and mothers of important men rather than in their own right. More recently, one scholar has made a case for identifying Pericles's wife as a woman named Deinomache, and if this is correct, she was his first cousin, but the lack of certainty shows how little importance was attached to so many aristocratic women.[19]

Pericles did not get on well with his sons, who felt that he was too strict and rather mean in his provision for them from the profits of the family estates. One of the young men supposedly told the story about Pericles and his philosophical friends spending so long discussing the hypothetical incident about the javelin accidentally killing a spectator. The same son also supposedly accused Pericles of carrying on an affair with his young wife. Pericles did have a reputation as a womaniser, somewhat at odds with his otherwise austere public image. Unlike with Sophocles and a fair few other prominent Athenians, there are no stories suggesting he had an interest in boys. Nor does his interest appear to have been solely in obtaining sex, which would have been readily accessible in a slave-owning society. Instead, he was said to be a seducer of free women, especially other men's wives. One story alleged that Pheidas assisted, persuading women to come to private viewings of his latest sculptures and paintings so that his friend Pericles could have time with them alone.[20]

Whatever the truth of such stories, Pericles without doubt had a long affair with Aspasia, a woman from Miletus in Ionia. Whether this began before or after his divorce, it continued to the end of Pericles's life, and they had a son together, whom he openly acknowledged. There are many stories about Aspasia, but sifting through the slanders to find the truth is almost impossible. It is safe to say that she was both intelligent and highly educated, with a keen political mind. Pericles discussed public affairs with her and was believed to pay great attention to her views. She is depicted sometimes as little more than a whore or an owner of prostitutes and sometimes as the more sophisticated companion, or *hetaira*—perhaps *courtesan* gives the best sense, even if there was no court as such. Such a woman had to be won over with gifts and persuaded rather than commanded. On the other hand, they may have married, even though she was not an Athenian citizen. As she was foreign, with the added association of luxury and decadence attached to the Ionian cities of Asia Minor, the connection was at the very least controversial, and Aspasia was the butt of jokes, satire, and simple abuse.[21]

Even more than his other alleged affairs, Pericles's very public relationship with Aspasia made him vulnerable to criticism, even legal attacks, and the fact that he continued it anyway suggests how important it was to him. In a sense it may also have been a reminder that he was from an aristocratic family. He may well have adapted his political style to the context of a democracy, while retaining a strong sense that he could do what he wanted in the way he wanted because of who he was. The slanders about Cimon, his sister, and their lifestyle never appear to have caused serious political damage and, in a way, show a similar self-assurance from a member of the elite. Cruel personal abuse is common in the surviving political speeches from fourth century BC Athens, and there is no reason to believe that this was anything new or to assume that everyone believed such stories.

Pheidas figured in a number of wild tales, apart from the one claiming he helped Pericles have sex with women in his workshop by or actually within the precinct of the Parthenon. Plutarch reported that he was also accused of another impiety, as people thought they recognised his likeness and that of Pericles in the figures on the shield of the statue of Athena Parthenos. Supposedly this, together with accusations of pocketing some of the gold and other precious materials bought for the work, led to his being placed on trial. Aspasia and other associates of Pericles were similarly said to have faced prosecution as indirect attacks on Pericles. The vast majority of scholars dismiss these stories, and if anything did happen, it did not prevent Pericles's unprecedented and never repeated success in being elected strategos each year. In spite of one tradition, Pheidas did not end his career in the Athenian jail, for he is mentioned as some years later working on a colossal statue of Zeus at Olympia. One source does claim that he was again accused of stealing materials in this project. Probably scholars are right to discard this detail as an invention repeating the earlier, quite probably untrue, but established story concerning his time at Athens, unless he genuinely was either very poor at accounting for the materials entrusted to him or was actually stealing.[22]

The cost of great statues, let alone the grand buildings to house and surround them, was considerable, if not as vast as the cumulative and ongoing expenditure on maintaining the fleet, from the triremes themselves to their crews and the shipyards to support them. The navy represented the central purpose of the alliance between Athens and the other communities, and those who did not choose to send ships sent silver instead. When the treasury of the alliance was at Delos, this common fund went without question to support the war effort, even if the Athenians administered it. After the move to Athens, the distinction between the city's own treasury and the funds gathered to support the alliance may have blurred. Pericles was accused of using money from the allies in his building projects, but since his accuser was ostracised, this would suggest either that his fellow citizens did not mind or that the charge carried no truth. Direct evidence is lacking for any use of substantial funds provided by allies for solely Athenian projects. The sixtieth share given to the cult of Athena is the only certain case of tribute being allocated to a non-military and expressly Athenian purpose.

ATHENS POSSESSED CONSIDERABLE resources of its own, hence the widespread use of and faith in its currency. In a sense the contributions from the allies helped to underwrite the immense cost of maintaining the fleet, so allowed the Athenians to spend a higher proportion of their own revenue on other things. Athens benefited from the alliance in so many respects that it boosted its own prosperity in the first place. Allied money built and equipped large numbers of warships, the work being done in Athens by Athenian contractors. The ships were then crewed by Athenians—alongside allies, it is true—paid while in service from the contributions of the allies to serve on their behalf. Led by and largely composed of Athenians, this unprecedented naval power brought plunder from its frequent and generally successful operations. The greater part of such profits naturally went to the Athenians since they supplied the greater part of the men who risked their lives. Sometimes successful war-making allowed colonies to be established, giving lands to settlers and getting better access to profits from the resources of a region.

At the same time, being granted cleruchies in allied territory enabled some Athenians to move to a higher class and status. Trade flourished under the protection of the navy, facilitated by standardisation of measures and currency, and the Athenians were best placed to profit most from this. Athens itself drew merchants and skilled craftsmen because it was so large and offered such a big market. Athenians served in a warlike capacity and also as jurors and in other official roles, including eventually in the *Boule*, where they were paid in coin for their time. Compared to other Greek communities, the proportion of Athenians relying predominantly on working the land to meet all their own and their families' needs grew smaller—if never small. More people engaged in craft and trade, while others, partly or in full, supported themselves through public service, and there was a lot more money around to exchange for commodities and less bartering of goods.

Directly or indirectly, this prosperity rested on Athens's position as leader of such a large alliance, especially since, in size and strength, it dwarfed all of its individual allies. This was different to Sparta's network of allies in the Peloponnese, which included Corinth, a large, renowned, and populous and prosperous city in its own right. There was no equivalent member of the Athenian alliance, a state far too big to be compelled to do anything. Even the largest Athenian allies were small and weak by comparison, outmatched by the military resources of Athens, and many member states were very small indeed. Added to this, and unlike on the Peloponnese, there was no geographical coherence. Without the Athenians, and really without the might of the Athenian fleet, there was absolutely no reason for or likelihood of all the member states working together. For the little states, alliance with Athens made them a part—even if a small one—of something very large and powerful and offered greater security from local threats apart from Persia than they could ever have found on their own.

There were also some benefits from trade and sharing the prizes of victory, which made it easier to accept the dominance of Athens—something the Athenians constantly paraded. Resentment tended to grow stronger in some of the bigger allies, which, ironically enough, probably benefitted more and at the same time resented having to defer to the Athenians. There were fewer such states, far fewer, but they were the most likely to attempt to break free of the connection to Athens. The vast majority of the allies never tried, largely because they were so vastly outmatched in military resources. When a state was even a little bigger, the balance between the advantages of alliance with Athens and the cost to a sense of self-esteem tended to shift.

19

THE CAUSES AND THE TRUE REASON

The growing hostility between Spartans and Athenians and the outbreak of the Peloponnesian War, c. 450–431 BC

Around 446/5 BC the Spartans and Athenians had agreed to keep peace with each other for thirty years, showing at least a desire to be seen as more serious about ending hostilities than when they had agreed on the earlier, five-year truce. Each acknowledged that the other party had allies and pledged not to suborn or attack these out of respect for their leader. Effectively each accepted that the other was the head of a coalition or even empire, in the original sense of having the power to dominate over others. The Spartans secured some promise on the part of the Athenians to treat the people of Aegina with consideration but accepted that the island now formed part of the Athenian-led alliance.[1]

Like so many Greek treaties, the Thirty Years' Peace did not last for its full term, and just fourteen years later, in 431 BC, the two cities actually went to war, striking the first blows in a conflict that would escalate in scale and intensity and itself last the best part of thirty years. The conventional name for the conflict, the Peloponnesian War, assumes an Athenian perspective, and no doubt for the Spartans and their allies this was the Athenian War. Either way, it proved appallingly costly for all caught up in it, and during this time far more Greeks died at the hands of other Greeks than had been slain in the Persian Wars. Thucydides proclaimed that he felt moved to write a history of this conflict because nothing comparable had ever happened before. As it turned out, he did not live long enough to complete the task, his narrative stopping abruptly several years before the war finally did end in the total defeat of his native Athens.[2]

Although he did not describe the end, Thucydides devoted considerable space to explaining how the great war began in the first place. In his view several incidents had escalated and led to friction between the Athenians and the Spartans, underlaid by the truest reason or cause: the Spartans' fear of Athens's growing power. Scholars have analysed his account ever since, following, modifying, or rejecting it and dissecting his phrases in an effort to define with absolute precision what he was trying to say and why. Opinions remain divided, often fiercely so, and there seems little prospect of a consensus emerging on this important question. Before discussing this, it will help to deal, as far as the evidence permits, with the main events of the fourteen years when the peace actually held.[3]

In 440 BC the island of Samos and the city of Miletus on the Ionian coast came into conflict over the much smaller community at Priene, also on the Ionian coast. Its territory bordered that of Miletus and also Samian-held land on the mainland. All three communities were allies of Athens, but even so, Miletus and Samos went to war with each other over which should be allowed to dominate Priene. Samos was one of the few allied states still providing fully manned ships to the common cause rather than money, so was the more powerful in its own right. The original oath of the alliance spoke of its members having the same friends and enemies, but in this case the Athenians initially did nothing to enforce this. There was some fighting, and the Milesians had the worst of it, at which point they appealed to Athens for support, joined by a faction from within Samos eager for constitutional change towards a more democratic form. That Pericles's mistress, Aspasia, came from Miletus fuelled rumour, if nothing else, but for whatever reason the Athenian Assembly voted to send forty triremes to deal with the problem. Samos was made into more of a democracy, an Athenian garrison installed, hostages taken from leading families, and the dispute resolved in favour of Miletus.[4]

Some Samians had benefitted from this—the men eager for democracy were naturally those who felt that they would do well in the new political system. Others were less pleased, and some who felt they were now worse off refused to give up and banded together to change things back. A delegation went to the Persian satrap in Sardis and persuaded him to provide support, which allowed them to raise a force of 700 mercenaries. With these and their own forces, they crossed by night to Samos and achieved complete surprise, seizing control and taking prisoner most of the leading democrats as well as the Athenian garrison. They followed up this success by retrieving their hostages, sent to Lemnos by the Athenians. Firmly established in control, accepted more or less willingly by a good part of the population, they assembled seventy triremes and a strong force of soldiers and prepared to settle matters with Miletus. The Athenian prisoners were handed over to the Persian satrap, in the hope of securing more assistance from him and also as a clear break from the alliance with Athens. Thucydides does not explain why, but the city of Byzantium decided to quit the Delian League at the same time and allied with the Samians.

The Athenians responded as they were bound to do in the face of such provocation and sent sixty triremes. Both Pericles and Sophocles were generals in this year and accompanied the expedition. The former may have been in overall charge, and at the very least his reputation and force of character meant that he had considerable influence. There was some dispersal of the force, as rumours arrived that Phoenician warships were on the way to join the rebels, and also a gradual realisation that the situation was more serious than at first thought. Athens sent out more triremes and summoned others from Lesbos and Chios. Before these reached the fleet, the Athenians won a sea battle and began to blockade Samos itself. Walls were constructed by the besiegers to surround the city on its three landward sides, while patrolling ships tried to cut off anyone coming in or out by sea.[5]

A fresh report arrived that a Phoenician fleet was on the way, prompting Pericles to draw off the majority of his warships and head south to intercept them. While they were away, the Samians came out and broke the blockade at sea, until Pericles returned about two weeks later and reinstated it. There is no indication that he had met any Phoenician warships, and in the end the Persians gave no more practical aid to the Samians. More Athenian and allied reinforcements arrived, and the stranglehold around Samos became ever more secure. After nine months the Samian leaders capitulated, giving hostages, handing over all their warships, and pulling down the city's walls. Most likely a new constitution was introduced, emphasising the importance of loyalty to Athens. From then on, Samos contributed money rather than crewed triremes to the alliance and, rubbing salt into the wound, also agreed to pay the Athenians money equivalent to the cost of mounting the campaign to suppress them. Byzantium surrendered around the same time and seems to have been accepted back into the alliance without heavy penalties imposed on its people.[6]

On one level the episode reflects the belief that the Delian League gradually turned into an Athenian empire, as the Athenians intervened more often in their allies' internal affairs and at the same time reduced the number of allies maintaining their own navies, preferring that everyone pay tribute to fund the Athenian navy. While containing a degree of truth, such a summary obscures far more than it explains and implies that the initiative lay always with Athens, which was clearly not the case, since local factors played such an important role. The Persians also took part, although only after the faction of Samians approached them. Given the distances involved and the likely timescale, the satrap acted on his own, without direction from the great king. He gave the rebels money to hire mercenaries to use against their own city, accepted Athenian prisoners into his care, and promised naval aid. In the event, the Phoenician ships were either too few in number or had been ordered not to push on and confront the Athenian fleet. All in all, this still appears as a clear violation of the terms of the Peace of Callias from 449 BC—if such a formal arrangement had actually been agreed—or a breach of some more tacit ceasefire if that was what had happened. It is the only such incident preserved in the sources, and the Athenians did not respond with a renewal of more direct attacks on the Persians, so the peace continued. Perhaps the lack of involvement of the great king allowed this to be seen as a temporary aberration. Still, it serves as a reminder that even apparently secure peace agreements between states in the fifth century BC might be broken whenever one party saw an advantage in doing so. On the whole, both the Persians and the Athenians do not appear to have scented such an opportunity in the next few decades, so avoided confrontation.

The whole incident started not with the big players but with two Athenian allies arguing over a third, even smaller allied community. Bigger, more prosperous, and more populous than the majority of the allies, Samos and Miletus had a long tradition as independent and locally powerful states in their own right, before first the Persians and then the Athenians arrived in the area. A dispute over control of a smaller neighbour was nothing new, and threats and then conflict were traditional ways of resolving such disputes. This is the only such confrontation recorded involving Athenian allies on both sides, making it hard to know whether similar friction had not appeared elsewhere or the Athenians actively restricted such things.

Alongside such old-fashioned rivalry between states, there was equally traditional rivalry within a state. The Milesians were backed by a faction of Samians who wanted constitutional change within their city and were happy to have this imposed by an outside force. Once this had been achieved, another faction was equally willing to seek Persian aid to achieve a counter-revolution. There is no sense that the origins of this lay in definite pro- or anti-Athenian sentiment or, for that matter, in pro- or anti-Persian sentiment. Local issues and ambitions were the root of everything, and subsequent actions were all about how best to prevail. After that, the larger players reacted in their own interest. For whatever reason, the Athenians chose to back the claims of Miletus and the Samian democrats, other Samians refused to accept this, and the situation escalated even further until this became the largest-scale Athenian and allied naval campaign since Cimon's final expedition in 451 BC. While the war was one-sided, and the Samians had no real prospect of achieving military victory, to prevail the Athenians still had to commit around 190 to 200 warships and considerable numbers of troops for the best part of a year.

In his narrative of the conflict, Thucydides makes no mention of what the Spartans and their allies thought about it, but later he claims that they took a direct interest. Summoning their allies, presumably after deciding that they might need or wish to do something, the matter was debated and considerable enthusiasm expressed for intervention, most likely in the form of an invasion of Attica to distract the Athenians. However, the Corinthian delegation argued against this on the basis that how Athens interacted with its allies was her business, just as the internal affairs of the Spartans' alliance were theirs. This persuaded the others, and no action was taken, for which the Corinthians would later argue they deserved gratitude and consideration from the Athenians. As always when nothing actually happened, the truth of the story is hard to know. At the least it serves as a further reminder that most Greeks felt that any peace treaty had a good chance of being broken when it suited one side.[7]

In the years after the assertion of Athenian control over Samos, there were also additions to the list of Athenian allies. In 437/6 BC a colony was founded on the River Strymon in Thrace, the same region that had seen earlier, failed attempts at Athenian settlement.

This time a mix of settlers, only a minority of them actually Athenian, succeeded, naming their new city Amphipolis. The location was good, hence the previous efforts and the determined resistance of local leaders, and the settlement soon began to prosper through the ready access to the many resources of the region. Athens had an almost insatiable demand for timber for shipbuilding and other construction, and apart from this, nearby mines yielded gold and other valuable minerals. This time the local leaders were persuaded or intimidated into accepting the presence of the colony. Pericles led a sizeable fleet on a voyage to the Black Sea around this time, confirming alliances and making new ones, without apparently having to fight anyone. Athenian power was paraded and confirmed, and access to vital grain supplies made more secure, which would remain true for generations.[8]

THEN, AROUND 436/5 BC, the domestic politics in the minor Greek city of Epidamnus turned violent. Founded in the seventh century BC by colonists from Corcyra (the modern island of Corfu), led by a citizen of Corinth and probably accompanied by other Corinthians, this coastal community would become known in the Roman period as Dyrrachium. Located in the north-west (today's Albania) on the fringes of the Illyrian tribes and the kingdom of Epirus, it lay beyond the regions frequented by the Athenian navy. It was not an ally of Athens; nor is there any sign of particular contact between Epidamnus and Athens in the past. Corcyra considered Epidamnus its colony and expected to be treated with deference as the mother city. At the same time, Corcyra was originally a Corinthian colony, so Corinth in turn felt that she deserved respect, even deference, from the islanders on Corcyra. Apart from anything else, Corinth, one of the biggest Greek cities, was a highly successful trading power, helped by the significant strength and proven prowess of its war fleet. She was by far the most important single state among Sparta's network of

Peloponnesian allies. Yet, by the second half of the fifth century BC, Corcyra was a very large and prosperous state by Greek standards, boasting a fleet of 120 triremes. All of this meant that many Corcyraeans were not inclined to see themselves as mere colonists of another city. They neglected traditional honours and issued some deliberate insults to make this point, and while this was all symbolic, such symbolism was important.[9]

None of this mattered at first to the people of Epidamnus, and instead it provided the context for events as internal power struggles created ripples that spread far more widely. For Thucydides it began with a revolution, expelling a previously dominant group of aristocrats and creating a more democratic form of government. The exiles, as was so often the case, were not inclined to quit. They allied with Illyrian leaders and led raids against their home city on land and preyed on their ships at sea. The new regime in Epidamnus appealed to Corcyra for help and, not getting what it wanted, mooted the idea of turning to Corinth instead and asking for Corinthian protection.[10]

First though, a delegation went to Delphi to ask whether they should do this. The oracle—well informed and well disposed towards Sparta and Corinth, among other things—approved, and the Corinthians proved very obliging. Thucydides claimed that this owed partly to their dislike of the disrespectful Corcyraeans and also to a sense that, as the founder of Corcyra and part founder of Epidamnus, their assuming the full and prestigious mantle of mother city was right and proper. They acted quickly, sending a force of their own and allied citizens to settle in and help protect Epidamnus. The exiles in turn went to an enraged Corcyra, which readily agreed to support them. Threats were made, and when these failed, the Corcyraeans began to blockade Epidamnus. Undeterred, the Corinthians decided to reinforce the men already sent there and make the city firmly and clearly a new colony of their own. Both to secure eager participants and to involve more states in the project, they took volunteers from even more communities, promising everyone land and full citizenship. Plenty responded, and in the hope that this would deter the Corcyraeans from trying to stop them, the expedition included ships from other Peloponnesian communities, including Megara, as well as the main contingent of Corinthians. Corcyra protested to Corinth, the envoys accompanied by Spartan and other representatives as witnesses, demanding the withdrawal of the garrison already sent and that any Corinthian claim be submitted to outside arbitration after guidance from Delphi.

Demand and counter-demand led nowhere, and around 434 BC the Corinthians declared war on Corcyra. The fleets clashed near the Bay of Actium—later famous for the defeat of Antony and Cleopatra in 31 BC—and the Corcyraeans won a clear victory. Around the same time, the city of Epidamnus surrendered to them under terms that sacrificed the foreigners sent there by Corinth. All save the Corinthian citizens were sold as slaves, while the former were held captive for the moment as a bargaining counter. Similar distinction sealed the fate of the prisoners taken in the naval battle, with all save the Corinthians being executed. For months Corcyraean ships dominated the west coast of Greece, raiding communities allied to Corinth. Eventually the Corinthians assembled another fleet, which returned to Actium and prompted a standoff, neither side willing to risk a battle, until the summer ended and everyone went home.

Fearing that wealthy Corinth might outmatch them in resources, the Corcyraeans turned to Athens and asked to become her ally, assuring the Athenians that this was in Athens's best interest. They argued that their island was well positioned, especially with regard to Italy and Sicily, and that their navy was powerful. Should Athens find itself at war with Sparta and the Peloponnese, then their warships would reinforce Athenian naval supremacy. On the other hand, should Corcyra and its fleet fall under Corinthian control, the combined forces might well challenge that supremacy. Against this, a Corinthian delegation sent to argue their city's case claimed that they had a better claim to Athenian friendship and emphasised that the thirty-year treaty with Sparta offered protection to each side's existing allies.

For two days the Assembly debated, before settling on a compromise of a limited alliance with Corcyra, pledging that each would defend the other against direct attack. A mere ten Athenian ships were sent, albeit with Cimon's son, 'the Spartan', as one of the commanders and with strict orders not to engage in any aggressive action and to respond only to an actual attack on Corcyraean ships. If meant as a gesture to deter the Corinthians, it failed, and the two fleets fought a great battle, 110 Corcyraean triremes against 150 Corinthian ones, both sides trying to get close and board the enemy. Thucydides dismissed such tactics as crude and old-fashioned, for by this time the Athenians were masters of speed and manoeuvre and always tried to strike from the rear or flank rather than take the enemy head-on.[11]

At first the Athenians held apart and did not fight, until things began to go so badly for their allies that they joined in. Even so, the Corinthians sank or took more ships than they lost, and only the sighting of a fresh squadron approaching made them disengage. These were twenty more Athenian ships, presumably sent because the Assembly had decided that greater force might be useful, and the Corinthians could not know that this was the total force and not simply the vanguard. Having driven the enemy back, the Corinthians were able to tow away captured vessels and massacre the enemy sailors swimming beside or clinging to wreckage. Both sides claimed victory, and tactically the Corinthians were right to do so, while Corcyra could count this as a strategic success, for the island was spared invasion. Peace between Athens and Sparta held, in spite of the provocation, and Spartan interests had so far not been directly involved. For the moment, the grievances were between Corinth and Athens.

Among Athens's numerous allies was Potidaea on the Chalcidice—the headlands including Mount Athos where Mardonius's Persian fleet had suffered so badly due to storms in 493 BC. It was also a

Corinthian colony and on rather better terms with the mother city than Corcyra had been. Distrusting this relationship, the Athenians instructed Potidaea to expel the magistrates traditionally sent to her from Corinth and also to pull down her city walls. Naturally, the Potidaeans asked the Athenians to reconsider. At the same time, they began to explore their range of options, beginning tacit negotiations with their closest neighbours, including King Perdiccas of Macedonia, and also with both Corinth and Sparta. They received a good deal of sympathy and some promises of support. Perdiccas had been an ally of Athens, until the Athenians decided that his brothers might prove more useful if one overthrew him. Admittedly, he had changed sides quite a few times, making such a plan as understandable as his reaction was predictable. The Corinthians were active in their support for their colony as well as already hostile to Athens, and Thucydides claims that the Spartans agreed to invade Attica should Potidaea come under siege.[12]

The Athenians had already prepared a force of 1,000 hoplites and thirty triremes to go against Macedonia in 431 BC and felt that these could show the flag and, if necessary, subdue the Potidaeans. However, by the time they arrived, not only Potidaea but several other allied cities in the area were in open revolt. News went back to Athens, prompting it to send reinforcements, and in the meantime the Corinthians also raised a force consisting of a few citizens and rather more mercenaries hired in the Peloponnese. As each contingent arrived, the fighting escalated, and the Athenians and the Corinthian-led force fought a confused battle before the Athenians began to blockade Potidaea by land and sea.

In spite of their earlier pledge, the Spartans did not join the war at this stage. However, at the request of the Corinthians, representatives from all the allies were invited to Sparta to discuss the matter. Anyone else with a grudge against the Athenians was asked to state the grievance. Representatives from Aegina—no longer a Spartan but an Athenian ally, so attending in secret—complained of interference in their domestic affairs in alleged violation of the Thirty Years' Peace. Megara had an even clearer complaint, for the Athenians had banned them formally from using Athenian and allied harbours or marketplaces.[13]

The Megarian Decree, as this measure is known to modern scholars, is poorly understood, not least because Thucydides only alludes to it and does not describe or explain it with any clarity. The date is unknown, as is how it worked, and the meagre sources say that it was imposed to punish the Megarians for cultivating sacred land and giving refuge to runaway slaves. (There were also jokes in Athenian comedy about Pericles using the decree to distract his fellow citizens from other matters or advocating it to please Aspasia because Megarians had abducted three prostitutes from her brothel, but these were likely no more than jokes.) Whatever prompted the action, whether it caused serious food or other shortages for the Megarians is both hotly debated and impossible to answer. Such situations tend to impact some more than others, and in any commercial enterprise even a slight change can prove catastrophic. Some citizens of Megara suffered, and more were annoyed by this treatment, so that it felt serious. To see things in stark terms of survival or starvation is a mistake, for the withdrawal even of luxuries can feel like a very serious deprivation.[14]

The Spartans listened to all the complaints and opinions and discussed the matter at length. Thucydides claims that Athenians present on other business were also allowed to address the Assembly. For him, the Corinthians and the Aeginetans were the keenest advocates for war, with the former citing the growth of the Athenians' power and their lack of restraint in intervening wherever and whenever the mood took them. One of Sparta's kings was a minor, so the other, an older man named Archidamus, urged caution, only to be contradicted by an ephor who convinced the gathered citizens that they must stand up for allies like Corinth. A deputation went to Athens for at least one and probably several rounds of negotiation. The repeal of the Megarian Decree was a key Spartan demand, making the scant attention paid to it by Thucydides all the stranger, and the Athenian Assembly debated each of the proposals in succession. Pericles argued fluently for war with Sparta and her allies as both logical and winnable. For him, any compromise or concession would simply be interpreted as weakness, so result in more and greater demands. He and many others felt that the Spartans had promised few definite compromises on major issues and instead made vague expressions of willingness in this regard. Demands also increased, and apart from Athenian withdrawal from Potidaea, the Spartans also wanted full independence for Aegina.[15]

In the negotiations, neither side shifted its position to any extent or came up with proposals that satisfied the other. The Spartans felt that Athenian actions were unreasonable and contrary to the spirit and perhaps terms of the peace treaty, while the Athenians in turn felt that they were being asked to make concessions that were neither in their interests nor appropriate given their power. As part of the bargaining and sabre-rattling, the Spartans reminded the Athenians of the curse on the Alcmaeonid family for the killing of Cylon's followers almost two centuries earlier. Pericles came from the family but had no intention of going into exile. Instead, the Athenians suggested that the Spartans deal with two curses they had suffered after starving Pausanias to death on sacred ground and executing the helots taken from Poseidon's temple. Neither side was willing to back down even when it came to accusations of ritual pollution and divine enmity.[16]

Sparta sent a delegation to Delphi to ask about its prospects should it go to war, and the oracle answered favourably, promising the aid of Apollo and victory—as long as the Spartans waged war with their full effort. Once again, representatives from her Peloponnesian allies were called to a council at Sparta, and there was more debate, with the voices urging peace and even caution now significantly fewer. Another embassy went to Athens, and again the

Assembly debated—and rejected—the Spartan demands. The Athenians offered only a promise to submit to outside arbitration as long as this was conducted fairly and appropriately, because they were unwilling to submit to demands out of keeping with the prestige of their city. In essence, they were demanding the right to be treated as the Spartans' equals. With this answer the Spartans went home and sent no more formal embassies, both sides having concluded that the peace was at an end and both apparently very confident in their own military strength and the advantages they possessed. By the end of 432 BC, both sides accepted that they would soon be at war, but neither was inclined to start, let alone prosecute, this war, which they did not actually begin to wage against each other until the spring of 431 BC. The Athenians continued to blockade Potidaea, but the Corinthians and the others made no more attempts to break the siege or give any direct assistance. The difficulty of campaigning in the autumn and winter months can partly explain this inactivity, and perhaps some still hoped the other side would back down. Yet most on both sides did not hesitate at the prospect of war itself.[17]

THUCYDIDES'S NARRATIVE HAS a clear logic, showing how domestic rivalry at Epidamnus drew in ever more and larger outside aid, prompting conflict between Corinth and Athens, which in turn spread to Potidaea and the surrounding region. These were the sparks that ignited the blaze. His deeper or truer explanation—the author's meaning in the original Greek evades exact translation—that the Spartans feared the growth of Athenian power has prompted a wide range of reactions. For instance, a good case can be made that by 431 BC, Athens was actually weaker and Sparta stronger than twenty or so years earlier, when the Athenians dominated Boeotia and the Spartans were still living with the immediate aftermath of the earthquake and subsequent revolt. This suggests that the Spartans had less cause to fear the Athenians when the war actually broke out, leading scholars to put forward alternatives to Thucydides's interpretation. Often the debate becomes more about blaming either the Spartans or the Athenians as chiefly responsible for the war. Sometimes Pericles, rather than the Athenians as a whole, is presented as the prime mover, and more often than not theories come from an individual's attitude to each side and the statesman. Admirers of Athenian democracy tend to depict the Spartans as mainly to blame, while critics of Athenian 'imperialism' stress Athens's aggressiveness.[18]

Almost all of the evidence comes from Thucydides, and whatever view one takes of his explanation, there is no reason to doubt that he accurately reflects the immense confidence of both sides in their own strength and prowess. Neither side offered to make any significant concessions during the negotiations, and neither side appeared at all reluctant to go to war when it actually broke out. After all, they were ending a peace less than halfway through its term; that peace had been negotiated after a period of open war, which had not been the first time Athens and Sparta had come to blows. Greek states went to war with each other remarkably readily, and if hindsight makes clear that this war was to be unprecedented in scale and devastation, no one knew that then. Each side expected to win, and both the Athenians and Spartans felt collectively that the likely consequences of not fighting the war outweighed those of fighting it.

Why they felt like this is complex and owes as much or more to perception than to tangible strengths and weaknesses. Wholly dismissing the part played by fear and suspicion would be rash, and even if the Athenians were less strong in real terms than they had been in the past, that does not mean that many Spartans did not view their power and the very nature of the Athenian state as dangerous. Athens had been able to expand in power and prestige to head a very large alliance of states. The Athenians were immensely strong and relentlessly ambitious, with the greatest navy anyone had ever known. Even if weaker now than two or three decades before, they showed no sign that their might was crumbling or would not grow even greater in the future. Athenians and Spartans had in the past been allies for a while and sometimes enemies, but they were always rivals for prestige.

Spartan security rested on the practical might of the armies it led and the allies who acknowledged its supremacy, which underwrote its unique society and economy. Controlling the helots and maintaining the network of allies rested in part on enough people believing that to placate the Spartans was better than to risk fighting them. A perception of Sparta's worth, that it deserved to lead by proven prowess in war, had to be maintained. Similarly, Athens's dominance was built on the number of its ships and the warriors they carried, but also on a sense that antagonizing the Athenians was dangerous. This was less about winning every battle than convincing potential opponents that, in the long run, fighting the Spartans or the Athenians was hopeless. Those who chose to fight either power were bound to lose in the end, and the consequences of defeat would likely be terrible. Maintaining this sense of respect or fear was important for each state, as indeed, to a lesser degree, it was for every Greek community. The same competition and jealousy over adding to and protecting prestige that had fuelled so many conflicts for centuries was just as present in the build-up to 431 BC. It was never just about Athens and Sparta, even though they were the biggest players.[19]

The rise of Athens to become so great a naval power and head of such a large alliance represented the greatest shift in the balance of prestige, respect, and fear—as well as practical power—in Greece and the wider Aegean in living memory. The Athenians were proud of what they had become and determined to make others accept them as a power different from Sparta, but on the same level when it came to reputation and martial prowess. At home and abroad they laid claim to status of this sort in big things and in small. Sparta resisted, refusing to accept this, and so did many other states. Any change to a world where just about everyone, even enemies like Argos, saw the Spartans as *the* great military power was bound to be seen as a

The Parthenon—the name coming from Athena Parthenos or the Virgin, whose grand statue was housed within it—is today one of the most potent symbols of Classical Greek culture and achievement. Yet it was meant as a monument to the glory of Athens and the Athenians to show that they were pre-eminent among all fellow Hellenes. It was built in the fifth century BC.

Grand in its size and design, the Parthenon was rendered all the more spectacular by the quality and quantity of its decoration. Scholars continue to debate just what is depicted, but the prominence in the procession of young horsemen emphasised the continuing importance of the aristocracy in the democratic system.

As well as a procession of some sort in contemporary Athens, the sculptures showed the gods and scenes from early legends. One theme is a fight against predatory centaurs, such as the one shown here abducting a woman. This sculpture glorified the defeat of outsiders/barbarians, evoking the Athenians' role in the defeat of the Persians.

The owl, the symbol of Athena, marked the silver coinage minted at Athens. Because of their high quality, and also the emergence of Athens as an imperial power dominating the Aegean, they became widely used by other communities as well.

The Persian great king lived his life surrounded by ceremony as a constant reminder of his power and of his subjects' duty to obey and revere him. Here a seated Darius is attended by Xerxes. So secure was the position of both of them that when Xerxes succeeded to the throne on his father's death, the transition was entirely bloodless.

The heart of the Persian armies always consisted of soldiers from Persia and Media. They wielded spears and were excellent archers but compared to Greek hoplites were less well-protected and less-well equipped for close combat.

Olympias, the reconstructed Athenian trireme, seen at sea. The trireme became the dominant type of warship in the fifth century BC, using sails for long journeys but powered by teams of rowers in battle.

Themistocles convinced his fellow Athenians to invest a windfall from the silver mines to build an unprecedentedly large fleet of triremes in 483/2 BC. The existence of this fleet made possible the defeat of Xerxes's invasion as well as Athens's subsequent rise to imperial power. In spite of this, the wily Themistocles was exiled by his fellow citizens and died as a subject of the Persian king.

Pericles (*c.* 495–429 BC) was an aristocrat who, by persuasion, won election year after year and became the dominant figure in public life during the height of Athenian power. The malicious claimed that he liked to be depicted wearing a helmet because it concealed the peculiar shape of his head.

Athens's democracy sought to diffuse rivalry between politicians before it turned violent, but allowed for one man to be exiled or ostracised each year if sufficient citizens voted against him. Votes were cast by writing the man's name on a fragment of pottery like these—the top one against Aristides and the bottom one against Themistocles.

The island of Sphacteria is small, and the number of Spartans who defended it and were captured by the Athenians in 425 BC was also small compared to the major battles of the era, but the consequences were out of proportion to its size. Luck favoured the Athenians when a cooking fire spread and burned away much of the scrub covering the island.

This unusually well-decorated Corinthian helmet was typical of the types worn by the majority of hoplites until the later fifth century BC. It offered excellent protection to the wearer, at the cost of restricting his vision and hearing.

This Spartan shield was captured by the Athenians at Pylos in 425 BC and dedicated as a trophy of victory. The wooden parts have decayed, now showing the bronze covering. The surrender of the Spartans on Sphacteria turned this minor campaign into a great success for the Athenians.

diminishing of status. This was a blow to pride, as well as dangerous. Past events had shown that neither the Spartans nor the Athenians were universally popular with their allies. Perceived weakness was inherently hazardous.[20]

Underlying factors in wider Greek society and the particular histories of Athens and Sparta certainly made confrontation between them likely, but that does not mean war was inevitable. Sparks were needed to start the blaze, and the local rivalry at Epidamnus could have developed differently and not drawn in Corinth and then Athens. There is much to be said in favour of Thucydides's view that immediate points of confrontation and an underlying problem encouraged those involved to act in the way they did. Again, it is worth emphasising that in his account neither side displayed much hesitation. For him, the Spartans believed in the strength of their army and their allies on land, while the Athenians were equally certain of the power of their navy backed by their allies. The land power and the sea power each believed that it was superior, with Sparta determined to fight to preserve its status and Athens wanting to prove its claim to comparable prestige. The conflict was to be a clash of very different societies and very different military systems, but at its heart lay a particularly Greek desire to excel—and be seen to excel.

20

THE BEGINNING OF GREAT EVILS FOR THE HELLENES

The opening rounds of the Peloponnesian War and its rapid escalation in scale and savagery, 431–429/8 BC

BY THE WINTER OF 432–431 BC, ALMOST EVERYONE BELIEVED that war between Sparta and her allies, on one side, and Athens and her allies, on the other, was inevitable. Yet for the moment there was no formal declaration of war, and the Thirty Years' Peace continued as the Spartans had not formally rejected the Athenians' offer to submit to outside arbitration. Greek states, and most other states and communities in the wider world, went to war readily, breaking treaties whenever it was convenient, but at the same time they liked to present their actions as justified, reasonable, and proper. The Athenians continued to besiege the Corinthian colony of Potidaea, but no more aid went from the Peloponnese to the defenders.

Thus, for the moment, they planned how to fight a war that had not yet begun. For the Spartans, this was more a question of detail than devising innovative strategy. Their strength lay in war on land, and most of all in battle on land, decided by phalanxes of hoplites. This was the traditional and by far the most prestigious way to fight and win a war, and the Spartan 'peers' were accepted as the finest hoplites of all—not least in their own estimation. The earthquake, the helot rebellion, and a low birth rate meant that the generation of full citizens preparing to face the Athenians was significantly smaller in number than their ancestors who had faced Xerxes's invasion. The Spartan contingent at any battle in the late fifth century BC never numbered as many as the 5,000 'peers' who had fought at Plataea in 479 BC, and it was exceptionally rare even for half as many to take the field. While there were fewer of them, the Spartans' reputation as warriors remained as strong as ever, and most enemies were likely already half beaten as soon as they realised that they were facing a Spartan phalanx.[1]

Everyone knew the Spartans were different and was intimidated by them. Their numbers were also supplemented, as in the past, by perioeci—and perhaps by some poorer Spartans not qualified to be full citizens, which makes it harder to work out how many actual 'peers' were in a total number of men sent out by the Spartans at any time. Probably at least half, and usually more, of any force, let alone the contingent sent to a field army by Sparta, consisted of men who were not peers. Opinion is divided over whether these men fought in separate and distinct units or in the same units on the battlefield as 'the peers'. Either way, if they could not match the disciplined skill of the full citizens, they seem always to have fought very well. More importantly, the Spartans had allies, whose own hoplites were also considered good, if not in quite the same league as 'the peers'. In 431 BC, they could call on a high proportion of the Peloponnesian states and also much of Boeotia to join them and invade Attica. In most cases, the Spartans asked for each ally to send two-thirds of its military manpower, which produced joint armies numbering in the tens of thousands. The one formed in the first summer of the war was probably the largest host they were to assemble throughout the years of conflict. The Boeotian allies were especially useful because they brought with them hundreds—perhaps even 1,000 or more—cavalry, for the Peloponnesians could muster few horsemen and the Spartans none at all.[2]

Sparta's greatest asset was this ability to raise a very large and rather good army. Apart from 'the peers', these men did not wage war as their principal occupation, so that each army would be bound by the familiar restrictions of Greek warfare. They were willing to fight, to risk their lives, and to march into enemy territory, but only for a while, because they needed to go home and get back to work, in most cases farming their own land. Traditional restrictions encouraged the Spartans to adopt a very traditional plan for their war. Once it had begun, they would wait for the spring to mature and with it the crops that were their targets. Then they called their allies to muster in one great force and to advance on Athens. With Megara as an ally, the route would be entirely through friendly territory. On arrival in Attica, they would begin to devastate the farms, destroying or consuming the crops and herds. Ideally, this provocation would prompt the Athenians to call their citizens to arms and march out to confront them in open battle—which the Spartans and their allies were confident of winning. Such a victory might well resolve the conflict in a day. If the Athenians were not willing to come out and fight, then more of their lands would be ravaged, and they would be shown to the world to be timid and weak. Athens was a big city and Attica an extensive state by Greek standards, which meant that a single invasion might not do them sufficient damage and insult before the army needed to return to the Peloponnese and disperse. If the Athenians did not give in during the first year, then the exercise could be repeated in the following year, and so on. Most Spartans—and plenty of outside observers—believed that it would take at most three such annual invasions before the Athenians risked battle and were defeated or refused battle and were humiliated enough to sue for peace.[3]

Sparta's main war effort was to be highly traditional, if on a truly grand scale. Yet, from the start there was discussion of other ways to put pressure on the Athenians. The Spartans themselves had hardly any warships, and their small naval dockyard was some distance from Sparta itself and had already proved vulnerable to Athenian attack in the earlier conflict. It did not have the space to build and house a large fleet; nor did Spartan society have the capacity to pay for one or find sufficient men to crew it. Their allies were a little better off, although only the Corinthians possessed a substantial fleet. Appeals were made to more distant allies in Sicily and Italy to construct triremes, just as the Spartan-led alliance had requested military and naval support from Syracuse in 481 BC. That earlier appeal had produced nothing, and a fresh request in 431 BC for 200 warships fared no better. The sources make no hint that a single ship was ever built, let alone delivered to the Spartans. Grand talk of massing a fleet of 500 triremes seems to have been only that, and a Corinthian suggestion to take treasure from Delphi and other shrines to hire rowers does not appear to have been followed up. If silver and gold were borrowed from any of the major shrines, it was done on a small scale.[4]

In contrast, Athens already had plenty of ships and substantial funds. Something like 300 triremes were in acceptable condition. A minority were ready or could be fitted out and crewed quickly, while preparation of the rest needed more time. In addition, a few of the allies, including the new ally Corcyra, were able to provide more on request. Sparta and her allies simply could not match these numbers, even before the quality of ships and crews was taken into account. Dreams of contesting the seas with the Athenians remained just that for the foreseeable future. When it came to financial resources, the Athenians also had a clear advantage, since their alliance was designed to generate funds in a way that Spartan alliances were not. At the start of the war, the Athenian treasury in the Parthenon contained 6,000 talents of silver, apart from other reserves such as the gold on the statue. Around 600 talents came in each year from the allies who did not provide ships, supplemented by other sources of income, notably the silver mines at Laurium. This wealth allowed the city to pay men to go on long campaigns, whether as hoplites or ship crew. The willingness even in peacetime to spend silver and send squadrons of triremes to sea ensured a large pool of experience at all levels, from the trierarchs who supervised the fitting out of each ship to the captains and deck crew who operated them and the men who rowed them. This was expensive, and relying on a powerful fleet to prosecute the coming war was very, very expensive. Sending all 300 triremes to sea fully crewed would consume the 6,000 talents of the reserve in about twenty months. Athenian funds and income were substantial but not inexhaustible.[5]

By Greek standards Attica covered a large area, and the Athenian population was considerable and prosperous. Thucydides states that 13,000 Athenian citizens qualified to serve as hoplites and were in the prime of life. Some of these men had experience of campaigning and combat, although this was less true than in earlier generations. Thucydides also noted that so many men on both sides were eager for war because very few of the younger men had actually fought in one before, so had little idea of what it was actually like. Those Athenians with experience would mostly have got it serving as marines on board ship and in seaborne campaigns of raid and blockade directed against communities near the shore. Only a handful had participated in a major clash of hoplite phalanxes, for Tanagra had been fought more than a quarter century before and even the smaller and scrappier Battle of Coronea had occurred seventeen years previously.[6]

Experience was rare on all sides at the start of the war, and the Athenians were numerous and very confident. In addition, they were supported by another 16,000 men who could serve as hoplites if needed. These included several thousand resident foreigners, or metics, many of whom dwelt in Athens and were an important part of the community, even if they were excluded from formal politics. The rest were those who were too young or too old to be called upon for the sort of distant and often prolonged campaigns that were typical, but who were fit enough to serve in defence of the city. Altogether, Athens had the capacity to muster a very large army in Attica itself.

In addition, allied communities had their own hoplites and could be called upon to support the Athenians. However, in contrast to the Spartan situation, most of Athens's allies were distant, too far away to be summoned to defend Attica and have much chance of arriving before a campaign was over.

On their own, the Athenians were strong enough to form a large army and challenge a Spartan-led invasion of Attica, just as Pericles had done when King Pleistonax had attacked, although in that case no battle had resulted. It seemed unlikely that another Spartan army would withdraw so readily, and in any case, Pericles had no intention of going out in force to meet a fresh invasion. Since that earlier incident, the long walls connecting Athens to the Piraeus and the old harbour had long since been completed. They had also been made even stronger by an additional wall, close behind the one running down to the Piraeus. Thus, should an enemy be bold enough to land on the coast between the two ports, they would still need to break through this inner wall to sever the connection between the city and its main military and civil harbour at the Piraeus.[7]

Greek armies were not good at taking serious fortifications, as witnessed by the Athenians' slow progress at Potidaea. Therefore Pericles planned to abandon the fields of Attica and bring the rural population into the city itself. The Spartans might do their best to ravage the fields, but in the meantime more than sufficient supplies of food would be brought in by sea to feed the entire population. Already formidable, the city walls and the long walls were to be strongly defended by the large numbers of hoplites available. This was a plan with an early genesis, for not only had the outer defences been constructed at considerable cost and effort, but other provisions were made to fight a very different sort of war. Alongside their hoplites, the Athenians had created a force of 1,000 cavalrymen, far more than in the past. Some were aristocrats from the higher classes, especially younger men, drawn once again to this way of fighting, at least in some circumstances. Fighting as a hoplite in the phalanx was still seen as more dangerous and therefore more honourable, but in this case no such fighting was likely to happen. There were also 200 horse archers, some perhaps hired from abroad and the rest citizens of lower social status than the other horsemen. The corps of archers created to serve the fleet at the time of the Persian Wars had also been expanded to number 1,600.[8]

Pericles convinced the Athenians that the best way to deal with a Spartan attack was to refuse the challenge to battle and let the people remain protected behind the walls. The cavalry, supported by light troops, offered a means of striking back, watching and harassing the invaders and making it more difficult for them to wander freely, destroying at will. This was a small consolation for the loss of honour and deep humiliation entailed in letting an enemy wander at will over the farmland owned by citizens. Yet Athens possessed its mighty fleet, crewed for the most part by the poorer citizens, who tended to be city residents. With this, they were able to strike back at the enemy. Pericles cautioned everyone against getting distracted and seeking to add to Athenian power by subduing states unconnected with the alliance facing them. They must focus on the main enemy and remain resolute. Athens was wealthy enough to pay for the needed food and to maintain a fleet far stronger than anything the Spartans could muster. Let the Spartans lead their grand alliance into Athens and see what good it did them—an invading army would soon be forced to return home and disperse. It might come again the next summer and the next, but to no more purpose. As long as the Athenians refused to come out and fight a battle, and as long as they refused to submit to negotiations on the enemy's terms, then eventually the Spartans would accept the futility of their efforts and give in. Athens had its superb and highly experienced fleet and the money to support a long war fought in this way. The Athenians just needed the patience to stay the course and stick to Pericles's strategy.

More than a few modern observers have criticised both sides for devising strategies that failed to strike at the true strength of their opponents and aimed at not losing the war rather than decisively winning it. This is to miss the point and ignore the central importance of honour and status. The Spartans spoke of fighting for the freedom of the Greeks, only to make very little effort to encourage rebellion among Athens's allies. The Spartan war was first and foremost intended to protect Sparta's status as the most powerful state in Greece, which in turn ensured the continuing dominance of its small elite of full citizens. Athens at the very least wanted acceptance by the Spartans, and more widely by others, as Sparta's equal and as greater than any other Greek city. Neither wanted to destroy the other, and both may well have realised that to do so was beyond their capacity. The Athenians did not want to free all the helots and cripple Sparta any more than the Spartans wanted to free all the slaves in Attica. Even if each had a different view of the other's status, both were very big and powerful communities. Small cities might be eradicated or have their citizen population replaced, but no one could remember such a fate befalling a really big state. Few Greeks are likely to have considered such an event possible, and fewer to think it desirable. This was a war over honour and status. In that sense, if the Spartans were able to humble the Athenians and make clear to all their inferior status, then they would offer 'freedom' to the Greeks because Athenian allies would be more confident and capable of seceding from the great power.[9]

BOTH SIDES HAD plans for how to wage a war not yet declared, but as is often the way throughout history, an unexpected event led to the killing starting early. Unsurprisingly in a fifth century BC Greek context, it all began with local ambition and rivalries within a community. Plataea had proved a staunch ally of Athens since the Spartans had recommended that they seek Athenian friendship back in the previous century. Then, the Plataeans had wanted protection from Thebes, a much larger and ambitious Boeotian city that lay a little more than eight miles away. However, early in 431 BC, a group of Plataeans became dissatisfied with the status quo within their community and decided that they should become its leaders. Like so often in such circumstances, they looked for outside aid and decided to approach Thebes. The Thebans were keen and calculated that if they could seize the place before the war began, then a treaty would be far less likely to require them to return it at the end of the conflict. One night the conspirators opened one of the city gates to admit a band of 300 or 400 Theban hoplites into Plataea, the advance guard of a full army. Surprise was complete, but to the dismay of the Plataean faction, the Thebans refused to embark on an immediate purge of their opponents. Instead, the force occupied the marketplace and proclaimed that all citizens were welcome to join them and become allies of the Thebans, who were fellow Boeotians and thus kin, unlike the Ionian Athenians.[10]

There was sense for the Thebans in trying to secure lasting support within Plataea, but they had badly misjudged the mood of the city. After the initial shock, with dawn approaching, the Plataeans began to realise how few enemies there were. Knocking holes through the mud brick walls of their houses, they passed from one to another to communicate and plan how to expel the invaders. When ready, they attacked, the men armed and fighting in the streets, women and slaves climbing onto the roofs and hurling tiles—large and heavy missiles—onto the Thebans. Almost all were killed or captured, along with the faction who had invited them in. The main Theban army had got lost on the march to Plataea and was too late to save them. It was very hard to take a city by storm, and as importantly, the Plataeans held Theban citizens as prisoners. After some negotiation, the main army withdrew, the Thebans believing that this guaranteed the lives of the captives, although the Plataeans subsequently denied that any promise had been made or oath sworn about this. They had sent a messenger to Athens, reporting what was happening, and the Athenians—probably the *Boule* council rather than a meeting of the

Assembly—sent word back to hold the prisoners as hostages. It was too late. Before the Athenian message arrived, the Plataeans had executed all of the captives.

For the Spartans, this was highly embarrassing. The Thebans were their allies, and they had launched an unprovoked attack on an Athenian ally before war had been declared and had not even had the skill to succeed. In later years, many Spartans would worry that this breach of proper behaviour was impious, earning their side the disfavour of the gods in the subsequent war. Yet the same drives to conflict remained, and in the summer they and their allies mustered their grand army. It was led by King Archidamus, an older man and a voice of caution, who had argued that the time was not right to confront the Athenians and that the Spartans should wait until they were better prepared. Some then, as well as more recently, believed that his leadership of the campaign reflected this lack of enthusiasm, but this is likely unfair. The army moved slowly because big armies tend to move slowly, and by Greek standards this was a very large army. Probably he hoped that the display of immense force might be enough to bring the Athenians to their senses, and he sent heralds to Athens in the hope of opening negotiations. Pericles had these turned away without having a chance to deliver their offer.[11]

Archidamus pushed on. He spent some time in a failed attempt to capture Oenoe, a very small walled settlement that acted as a border fortress, if a tiny one. The inability to take even such a small stronghold illustrates the very limited capacity of Greek armies in siege craft. Hoplites were simply unwilling to accept the casualties likely in direct assault. Archidamus gave up and pushed on, and the determination of the Athenians became clear, for the land was empty. In the main, the flocks and herds had been taken to Euboea, presumably with plenty of slaves and some citizens to care for them. Everyone else had abandoned their homes, just as their ancestors had done in the face of the Persian invaders, and taken refuge either behind the long walls or in Athens itself. Athenian cavalry, as well as some horsemen sent from Thessaly by allies there, appeared to harass the parties that spread out to lay the land waste, but Archidamus had his own cavalry, mainly provided by the Thebans and other Boeotians. The Athenians could not stop the invaders from going where they wished, and this meant only that the Spartans and their allies had to move in force and protect the men actually labouring. Some crops were gathered or destroyed, some olive and fig trees chopped down, but 1,000 or more were left untouched for every one that was harmed, for Attica was large, and this sort of farming involved immense numbers of trees.[12]

The scale of the damage mattered less than the ability of the Spartans to inflict it. A minority of farmers suffered badly, more suffered a little, and the majority incurred no tangible loss at all. Pericles, concerned that Archidamus, with whom he had a relationship of guest friendship, might spare his estates to suggest collusion, announced that if his lands were not touched at all, then he would donate them to the city. All Greeks understood the rules of war, and the Athenians were no exception. To stand idle while an enemy did what he liked on your land was humiliating, an open admission that you were too afraid to risk meeting him in battle. Because plenty of Athenians felt this deeply and wanted to go out and fight, Pericles prevented any meetings of the Assembly during the course of the actual invasion. Presumably this was only possible because enough influential men, magistrates, and councillors agreed with his strategy. After about a month, Archidamus and his great host marched away, this time going home via Boeotia. They had paraded their own strength and the Athenians' impotence to protect their own lands, which had been the goal from the start. It is hard to see how a more aggressive commander could have achieved any more in the circumstances.[13]

Attica could not be protected, but soon after the invasion began, the Athenians sent 100 triremes, subsequently joined by 50 more from Corcyra, and raided the coasts of the Peloponnese. A Spartan officer called Brasidas thwarted an attempt to capture the small city of Methone; this was the first appearance of a man who would make a name for himself in the years to come. Elsewhere the landing parties were more successful, ravaging the fields of Elis and pulling out before the locals could muster to meet them in force. Sollium, a port controlled by the Corinthians, was taken and presented to its neighbours, while the island of Zakynthos willingly joined the war on Athens's side. Around this time, Aegina's population was expelled and replaced by Athenian settlers, confirming control of the island. There were operations elsewhere, and the siege of Potidaea continued, but the biggest effort came at the end of the summer when Pericles led 13,000 hoplites and other troops into Megara and laid waste to the Megarians' fields. There was no prospect of Sparta's allies mustering a second time in the year, and since Megara bordered on Attica, there was also little time for any response. The Athenians did what they wished while the Megarians stayed behind their walls and did not dare to face the numerically far superior enemy.[14]

The first year of the war was over, and there are signs that more people were starting to realise that this struggle would likely be long; a depressing prophecy circulated at Athens that the war would last three times nine years. More practically, the Assembly approved a law stipulating that 1,000 talents from the treasury be set aside and used only if the city came under direct attack. Alongside this, 100 triremes in good condition were also to be kept back, so they could be fitted out using this money and form the nucleus of a powerful fleet. Thus the Athenians prepared for a long conflict. As always, the Spartans moved more cautiously, reluctant to rush to change their strategy. The Spartans had done what they planned to do, inflicting a humiliation on the Athenians. The latter had responded by doing the same thing on a smaller scale in the attacks launched by the fleet and then the advance against Megara. Nowhere had one phalanx of hoplites confronted another; nor had there been a major clash at sea. So no one incurred either the glory of victory or the shame of defeat from these most honourable forms of warfare. Late in the year, Pericles was chosen to deliver the annual oration made to honour Athens's war dead. Thucydides, who probably was present, made him emphasise the virtue of Athenians, the superiority of their lifestyle, and the courage it created compared to the Spartans and promise them ultimate victory. For the moment at least, the war was going according to his plan.[15]

In the summer of 430 BC, King Archidamus led another army into Attica. This was a smaller force than in the first year, but still very large. This time he stayed longer, for no less than forty days, advancing much closer to the city and reaching the mines at Laurium, not that there was much prospect of doing serious damage to the workings there. Once again, the Athenians retreated behind their walls and fought down the instinctive urge to throw the invaders off their land. Pericles formed a fleet of 150 triremes, a third of them from Lesbos and Chios, carrying 4,000 hoplites supported by cavalry, the horses carried in triremes converted into transports. They raided the southern and eastern shores of the Peloponnese and made a few deeper incursions. There were successes and minor failures, but more of the former, and the Athenians demonstrated that they could strike the lands of Sparta's allies even if they could not defend their own. In each case the damage was limited, far short of pushing any community to the brink of starvation or inflicting crippling economic damage.[16]

Then something happened that no one, including Pericles, had anticipated. At some point during the summer, a disease broke out at Athens and spread rapidly. It seems to have originated in Africa, spreading to Egypt and from there to the rest of the Persian Empire, whose many densely populated cities proved very vulnerable. Eventually the epidemic reached Athens, most likely through the crews or passengers of the many ships landing there. Diseases change over time, mutating and sometimes dying out, and no virus or bacterial infection known to modern science quite matches the description of the Athenian plague. Thucydides caught it fairly early on and managed to survive and recover. He described how apparently healthy men suddenly developed a high fever, inflammation of the eyes and throat, and foul breath, followed by bouts of sneezing and a wracking cough. Then came vomiting, diarrhoea, renewed high temperature, and desperate thirst. Many died within seven to nine days, others later, and there seemed little pattern in who succumbed and who did not. Athens itself, and the land between the long walls, was crowded with refugees brought in from the countryside, who camped in every available space, including temple precincts and public buildings, with an inevitable impact on sanitation and hygiene. All this helped spread the disease, and as more and more died, the problem of disposing of the dead made the conditions even more insanitary.

Thucydides deals with the plague in one long passage, mentioning several outbreaks over the course of three or four years. It may have been seasonal, made worse when the rural population came in to take shelter, and whether the death toll was spread evenly or was heavier at certain points is not clear, but the latter seems likely. After Pericles brought the fleet back from raiding the Peloponnese, it was sent north to help prosecute the siege of Potidaea, but the men took the disease with them. A quarter of the 4,000 hoplites serving with the expedition died within a matter of weeks—and Potidaea still held out. The fatalities were on a similar scale for the entire population by the final end of the epidemic. Thucydides noted that going from the official lists of citizens, 4,400 qualified as hoplites and 300 qualified to serve as cavalry died, and a similar proportion of between a quarter and a third of other sections of the population can be assumed to have perished. At the worst moments, social conventions broke down. Corpses—usually treated with great respect by all Greeks—were left where they fell or sometimes tipped onto a pyre meant for someone else. Some despaired and quickly succumbed, while others went on hedonistic sprees, flouting every moral convention; plenty of both groups died. Thucydides seems to have recovered without side effects, but others were crippled and so many simply perished, regardless of their age and general health. Pericles lost both sons from his marriage, each an adult by this time. Special legislation was passed to allow his son with Aspasia to become a citizen in spite of the law he had himself brought in some time before. His sister also died, and Pericles himself—the rational man who chose philosophers as his friends—took to wearing a lucky charm that he believed would ward off the disease.[17]

Surrounded by so much death, people unsurprisingly searched for any explanation and any promise of safety. For Greeks it was natural to seek a divine cause, and many turned to either traditional cults or new beliefs. Apollo was associated with plagues; he had sent his arrows into the camp of the Achaeans at Troy to punish them, and the Delphic oracle sacred to the god had promised aid to the Spartans. As it turned out, the plague did not spread throughout all of Greece, and the Peloponnese was barely touched at all. King Archidamus may have hurried his withdrawal from Attica once the extent of the pestilence became apparent but does not appear to have suffered any losses from it and had probably already reached the limit of his ability to remain in the field. Afterwards, the Athenians began to doubt everything and turned against Pericles, the Assembly voting to strip him of his office as strategos. In this desperate moment, envoys were sent to Sparta asking for peace, but whatever terms the Spartans offered proved far too harsh even to consider. Some encouragement came when Potidaea surrendered on terms near the end of 430 BC. Its citizens were allowed to take basic requirements and leave, along with their families. This was generous by Greek standards and may reflect both the Athenians' low spirits and their desperation to get the siege over and done with. It had been an expensive operation: Paying for so many men to serve for so long had cost some 2,000 talents—a third of the pre-war reserve.[18]

This was a victory, but the war continued, as did the basic strategies on each side. Pericles was elected as strategos again, but his magic charm failed him, and he died of the plague late in 429 BC. During that year the main Spartan field force did not attack Attica and instead marched on Plataea. Most of the city had been evacuated and the population given shelter at Athens, a kind gesture even if it turned out to be dangerous. Whether anyone stayed to tend the fields is not clear, but if so, they fled as the enemy approached. The small city was left effectively as a fortress, with just 600 souls inside: 400 Plataean fighting men, 80 Athenians, and 120 women—perhaps slaves—to cook and care for them. The Spartan-led army numbered in the tens of thousands at the very least but, despite this overwhelming advantage in numbers, was reluctant to mount a direct attack. At first, the army attempted to persuade the defenders to surrender, offering them alliance or freedom and a pledge to care for their farms during the war and return them afterwards. With their families and many fellow citizens in Athens, the Plataeans had little room to negotiate, even had they been inclined to do so.[19]

A siege began that was to last a very long time, even though the attackers were initially more aggressive than usual. The Spartans and their allies made an effort to prepare the way for an assault, constructing a siege mound to approach the walls and start to weaken some of the stones with battering rams. The Plataeans responded with equal, perhaps greater ingenuity. They increased the height of their walls with timber parapets and towers, adding in places a second wall behind the first to block any breach, and later began to hinder the besiegers' efforts more directly. They dug a tunnel underneath the mound so that they could remove soil from it during the night, and for a while the attackers were baffled as to why they were making so little progress. After this, the attackers piled combustible material between the mound and the wall and set it on fire, hoping to burn the timber additions to the city walls, until a heavy rainstorm put an end to that plan. Eventually the Spartans and Thebans surrounded Plataea with two walls, one facing inwards and one facing outwards, and settled down to blockade the little city into submission. Sufficient men were left to continue the siege, as the rest of the army went home.[20]

While Plataea was blockaded, the Athenians sent encouragement but no actual help. Unwilling to face a big Spartan army in the open in Attica, they were no more eager to send an army to the relief of an allied city and fight a pitched battle there. For the moment the essence of the Periclean strategy continued, even if the man himself was dead. During the year, small forces went by sea to raid and attack Spartan allies. If the numbers involved were smaller and the operations more limited, it is still striking that so much was done in this era of plague. In the Gulf of Corinth, a man named Phormio operated with a squadron of just twenty triremes, protecting friendly cities, especially Naupactus with its population of former helots.

Phormio appears to have been a very gifted commander, and he and his crews demonstrated all the hard-earned experience of Athenian sailors. A Corinthian-led expedition of forty-seven triremes, admittedly many carrying troops rather than prepared for battle, tried and failed to slip past him. Instead they took up a dense, defensive formation, most likely a circle similar to the one employed at Artemisium in 480 BC, with a handful of picked ships in the centre as reserve. Phormio, knowing the waters, sailed around them and waited for the wind to change and drive the enemy warships together. When they were too confused to respond, his ships pounced, darting in to sink a number of vessels and capture a dozen more.[21]

This was a humiliating defeat given the odds, even if it was not a major battle, and the Spartans sent two observers, including Brasidas, to stiffen the resolve of the local commanders. At the same time more ships arrived, so that even after the defeat the Corinthians had fifty-seven triremes to send against Phormio. The latter sent word to Athens asking for reinforcement, and the Assembly approved the sending of twenty ships, but gave this force a mission to do first, sending them to Crete in response to what proved a wildly over-optimistic appeal from a local nobleman. Long before they arrived, a threat to Naupactus forced Phormio into narrows where there was less room for manoeuvre and his main advantages were lost. Ten triremes were able to pull back, but nine Athenian ships were captured, and one more, slower than the others, was hotly pursued. Though slower than the rest, the vessel was still made and crewed by the Athenians. It continued to flee, stretching out the pursuers as each ship went as fast as skill and design permitted and abandoned any thought of keeping in formation. Seeing a merchantman, higher in the water and under sail, the Athenian captain dodged behind the trading ship, becoming temporarily invisible to his pursuers. Instead of continuing to flee, he changed course, looped back around the merchant ship, and rammed the leading enemy ship. The others panicked, stopping or turning to flee, and the remaining Athenian vessels turned about and raced at them. They retook all save one of their own vessels and captured six more from the enemy. Both sides set up one of the captured vessels—the only one they still held in the case of the Peloponnesians—on shore as a trophy to claim victory, but once again the superiority of the experienced Athenian navy was obvious, as Pericles had promised it would prove before the war began. Sparta and its allies could not hope to win the war with 'victories' like this.[22]

In the aftermath of this second, even more embarrassing failure, Brasidas helped to inspire a plan to raid Athens by sea, striking at the Piraeus late in 429 or very early in 428 BC. Caution and weather conspired to reduce this ambition to an attack on Salamis, which went surprisingly well, while the mere rumour of a threat to Athens caused panic and chaos until everyone realised that the enemy was not actually on the way. If the raid achieved little in practical terms, it was at least encouraging, and there were signs that many Spartans were beginning to wonder whether more was needed to win the war. There had been talk of seeking aid from the Persian great king in the build-up to the war. In 430 BC, Athenian allies among the Thracians intercepted a Spartan delegation travelling overland on its way to the court of Artaxerxes. They were arrested, sent to Athens, and promptly executed, but other envoys did manage to get through. Later in the war, the Athenians captured a Persian on his way to Sparta carrying letters in which the great king expressed his bewilderment, because the Spartans kept asking him for different things and he did not know what to make of it. Perhaps the Spartans wanted money, perhaps something more, although it was difficult for them to proclaim the liberty of the Greeks if at the same time they wanted the Persians to attack Athens's allies in Asia. Nothing tangible came from all of this during Artaxerxes's life, and following his death a period of confusion and civil war left the Persians too preoccupied to concern themselves with Greece.[23]

By the end of 429 BC, three years into the war, the expected Athenian capitulation had not come as a result of three massed invasions, at least not on any terms that the Spartans were offering them. Athens, still being devastated by the plague, had already lost many of its citizens and would lose more before the disease finally burned itself out. There is no indication of how long Pericles expected the avoidance of battle on land and the harassing of the enemy from the sea to take to persuade the Spartans to negotiate in a way that made clear their acceptance of Athenian status and might. For the moment this strategy was still in place, even though it was proving very expensive.

Wars tend to be easier to begin than to end, especially when both sides are determined and have plenty of resources. There was still restraint, for this was not a total war but one waged over status that assumed the enemy would still exist afterwards and accept the new order. That did not mean that from the start there was not a good deal of savagery. The Spartans and their allies sent out ships to attack merchantmen and stray warships, even though they could not face the might of the Athenian navy. All their captives, fellow Greeks and sometimes from neutral states, were routinely executed, presumably on the assumption that they were doing business with the enemy. The Plataeans had slaughtered their Theban captives, while the Athenians had killed the Spartan ambassadors caught in Thrace, not bothering with any trial or granting them proper burial. Thucydides wrote that the start of the war was the beginning of a great many evils for the Hellenes. Many more were still to come.[24]

21

SOMETHING UNHEARD OF

War, plague, victories, and defeats, 428–425 BC

IN 428 BC, KING ARCHIDAMUS ONCE AGAIN MARCHED INTO Attica to spread devastation. The siege of Plataea continued, and there was no need for more troops there, so the main effort was to be against the Athenian heartland. In response, the Athenians planned another naval raid on the Peloponnese, until reports arrived from Lesbos, one of only two major allies still to contribute ships rather than paying tribute. The leadership of Mytilene, the largest city on the island, was unhappy, as were the leaders in all save one other community, all judging that Athens was weaker than in the past and might be defied. They reached out to Sparta, because Athens was still not toothless. In the meantime, the Athenians had acted on the reports and sent ships, hoping to surprise and take control of Mytilene during a local festival. This failed, and a truce followed, with another delegation sent from the city, supposedly to go to Athens, although in fact they went instead to Sparta. This was an Olympic year, and the envoys were publicly received and paraded by the Spartans attending the games, a confident if unsubtle gesture that the Spartans accepted them as allies for all to see, including those Athenians competing or present as spectators.[1]

The Olympics had brought their usual truce to permit this participation, and Archidamus and his army had withdrawn from Attica before it began. By the time the festival was over, the summer was nearing its end. The Spartans had promised the Mytilenians to launch a second invasion, but in the event this proved impossible. The hoplites of most states were busy on their farms and unwilling to go on campaign twice in one year, and the Athenians were raiding again, with ships partly rowed by men who would normally have served as hoplites, such was the shortage of manpower. No distraction could be staged on behalf of Mytilene, and by this time Athenian reinforcements were on their way to Lesbos. The Spartans began to put together a force of some forty triremes under a Spartan named Alcidas to help them, but organizing this took time, allowing the Athenians to begin the siege of Mytilene. In 427 BC the Spartans once again invaded Attica by land, which represented more positive aid to the rebels, although it failed to reduce the Athenian pressure on Lesbos.[2]

Yet, as usual, capturing a city by blockade was a slow process, even if the movements of the Spartan fleet in 427 BC proved even slower. Alcidas took a very roundabout route and indulged himself in raiding and capturing merchant ships. Even by the grim standards of warfare at sea, he proved especially eager to slaughter any captives, concentrating on these depredations rather than the main purpose of his mission. He appears to have lacked any great talent as a naval commander, but this also reflected the psychological dominance established by the Athenian navy over their Peloponnesian opponents. A lone Spartan officer did manage to get to Lesbos and sneak through the lines into Mytilene, where he effectively assumed military command, for such was the prestige of the Spartans as fighters. This was encouraging to the defenders, but as the winter turned into spring and summer and food supplies ran low, his assurances that Alcidas and the relief force would arrive soon wore thin.

Mytilene's leaders were a relatively small aristocratic group, and much of the population had no access to proper weapons. The Spartan ordered hoplite equipment issued to these poorer citizens, hoping to increase his fighting strength. Instead, the newly armed men accused the ruling group of withholding hoarded grain and other food from them and threatened to surrender the city if they did not hand this over. Whether or not there really were hidden supplies, Mytilene surrendered, and the rebellion soon ended, as the other communities also submitted. Alcidas had begun to edge a little closer, until he found out that Mytilene had fallen a week earlier, at which point he turned for home, ignoring the suggestions of subordinates that a sudden attack on Lesbos might catch the Athenians by surprise and win back the island. Returning to what he knew best, he took some more prisoners and was about to have them killed before being persuaded that slaughtering potential allies made little sense.[3]

Frightened people can readily turn to savagery. The Spartan officer who had led the defence was sent to Athens and executed, in spite of his claim that he could persuade his countrymen to abandon the siege of Plataea. Angry at the perceived betrayal of the rebels on Lesbos, the Athenians were in no mood for mercy when the Assembly met to debate how to punish the people of Mytilene. Around 1,000 seen as the ringleaders and most prominent members of the regime that had sought Spartan aid had already been arrested and brought over to Athens, but for the moment one Mytilenean looked much like another to many Athenians. Thucydides claimed that the poorer citizens had always been inclined towards keeping the alliance with Athens but had had no choice in the matter until they were armed. Pleas of this sort made little impression, and before the day was out, the Assembly voted to execute every man and sell all the women and children as slaves. Orders were sent to the commander on Lesbos to carry out these instructions.

This sort of thing had been done before, but rarely in the case of a moderately large city with such clear divisions among its citizens. It was a mark of the rage felt by most Athenians at rebellion on the part of a trusted and prestigious ally. Overnight tempers cooled, and an obvious mood of strong regret compelled the Assembly to meet again the next day to review the decision. Thucydides describes this second session in much more detail, mainly through opposing speeches, the first defending and the second condemning the harshness of the earlier judgement. The advocate for utter ruthlessness was Cleon, a leading supporter of the proposal the day before. For him the Mytileneans had no excuse for rebellion, for they had enjoyed much greater independence than most of Athens's allies, possessing their own warships and strong fortifications. Such ingratitude demanded punishment, lest it inspire less favoured allies to believe that revolt carried little risk. Only stern and terrible penalties would serve the interest of Athens; anything milder was sentimental folly.

Thucydides loathed and despised Cleon, seeing him as the epitome of the inferior leaders who came after Pericles and led Athens to disaster. Yet, like Pericles, Cleon had a talent for convincing fellow citizens in public meetings. Thucydides dubs him a 'leader of the people', or demagogue, a very early use of the term. Cleon was not a member of one of the old aristocratic families, although he was clearly a man of some inherited wealth, for his father had served as a producer at a dramatic festival, a task only allocated to the well off. Playwrights like Aristophanes mocked him as nouveau riche, his money coming from owning one or more tanneries, and presented him as a wild fool, jumping to conclusions and making speeches accordingly. There is no evidence that he had held the post of strategos or performed any distinguished military service at this stage in his career, a big contrast to Pericles. For all that, Cleon had carried the day in the first debate and still had considerable support.

His opponent argued for restraint, stating that rushing to a decision and letting emotion play too great a role was unwise. Yet the main thrust of his argument was pragmatic—as Cleon had claimed was also true of his view. Extending mercy to those least involved would best maintain Athenian dominance. Even when some leading men turned against Athens, the wider population was generally well disposed, and keeping it that way would be worthwhile. More importantly, if a revolt should break out—and the pattern of politics in Greek cities made the emergence of factions wanting change fairly likely—then those who came to realise that rebellion was doomed should have scope to act. If everyone knew that all would perish whatever they did, then surely any rebels, however reluctant or repentant, must fight to the bitter end. From the Athenians' perspective, it was far better that a rebel community surrender and seek terms early on than that a long and expensive campaign be needed to beat them down. Instead of slaughtering everyone irrespective of their level of guilt, shrewd expediency would punish the ringleaders and show clemency to everyone else.

A lot of people continued to side with Cleon, but the other side won the vote narrowly. A second ship sailed with new orders to cancel the mass execution and enslavement, and the Mytilenean envoys in Athens gave its crew gifts and supplies of extra rations. The captain drove them as fast as he could, the rowers sometimes eating food as they sat in their rowing benches, and they made good time. It was not good enough to reach Lesbos before the first ship, but the message was delivered to the Athenian commander before he had begun the killing. A more familiar form of settlement was imposed instead: city walls slighted, a new constitution imposed, and large swathes of land given to Athenians, although the locals would work them for their new landlords, much like Spartan helots. Thus the bulk of the population was spared the very worst of Athenian vengeance. In contrast all the ringleaders were executed, the mass killing done by hand as was always the case in the ancient world, so that the exercise took a lot of time.[4]

The Athenians were frightened, but it is striking that they could still be persuaded by argument and equally notable that the opposing speeches as given by Thucydides both based their cases on a rational presentation of what the respective speaker deemed the community's best interests. Pragmatism rather than morality and the best means to win the war and preserve Athenian power were central to each argument. Pericles had not planned for the devastation caused by the plague, and perhaps not for the struggle with Sparta to take this long. Potidaea was a very expensive and prolonged operation to capture a modestly sized city, and the eventual success there did not convince other cities in the region to submit. Athens's substantial resources at the start of the war were eroding faster than they could be replaced. As a result, the Athenians increased the levels of tribute required from their allies and made efforts to ensure all allies paid their due. This did not always go well. A tax-collecting expedition to Lycia, the southernmost region included within Athens's empire and also close to Persian territory, ended in the massacre of the generals and troops sent to conduct it. Yet, for all the concerns about funds, there was also ambition, and a force was sent to intervene in power struggles in Sicily.[5]

CORCYRA HAD BEEN one of the key flashpoints leading to the conflict in the first place, and in 431 BC the Corcyraeans had sent fifty triremes to join the Athenian fleet raiding the coasts of the Peloponnese. After this, Thucydides does not mention any more direct support coming from the island and a little later explains why. The first appeal for alliance with Athens had come from a regime at Corcyra engaged in a power struggle elsewhere. At some point, an internal struggle broke out in Corcyra itself, led on one side by men taken prisoner by the Corinthians in the naval battle back in 434 BC. During their captivity at Corinth, these men were treated well, and on their eventual release, they displayed a fondness for their former captors and a deep antipathy towards the regime that had caused the war in the first place. Debate and argument turned to violence, leading to an attack on the council chamber and slaughter of unarmed opponents. Reprisal led to reprisal, the savagery increasing with every turn. The Spartans and Corinthians sent a squadron to intervene, hoping to exploit the situation. In response the Athenians sent their own ships and forced the enemy away but then stood by as the Corcyraeans slaughtered each other; Thucydides's description concentrates on the slide into viciousness and cruelty as neighbour turned on neighbour. He saw this as reflecting a broader collapse in proper behaviour brought on by the wider conflict. For most of the war, this kept the Corcyraeans too busy to make any significant contribution to the Athenian war effort. Yet the size of the island and the strength of its fleet meant that both sides had to bear the Corcyraeans in mind. A sudden revolution, installing a regime inclining towards them, was a potential prize for the Peloponnesians and a threat to the Athenians. Both were obliged to keep a wary eye on the events of this unstable community, and as things turned out, it remained under loose Athenian influence without contributing anything much to the wider war.[6]

As civil strife continued to rage at Corcyra, the siege of Plataea came to an end. Back in the winter of 428–427 BC, the defenders had staged a breakout, described in wonderful detail by Thucydides. Preparations were careful, lots of men spending time counting the bricks in the besiegers' wall, the result then averaged to give the best chance of accurate calculation and allowing them to make ladders of the right height to scale it. They waited for their moment, choosing a stormy, moonless night, each man keeping one foot bare to help grip the damp ground. It started well, until a noisy fall raised the alarm and led to fighting, with some of the defenders giving up on attempts to escape. Even so, more than 200 did get through the siege lines and headed straight towards Thebes, figuring that this was the last direction the besiegers would expect. The ploy worked, and once the pursuers had lost their trail, they doubled back and made it to Attica.[7]

Those left behind kept up the defence, but with food supplies and hope steadily dwindling, until in the summer of 427 BC, they decided to surrender, hoping for decent terms since they had not forced the enemy to continue to the very bitter end. Their representatives now, as they had before the siege, reminded the Spartans of the Plataeans' past services to them. After all, the Greek alliance had smashed the army of Mardonius on their land in 479 BC, Pausanias himself entrusting them with care of the monuments to the dead heroes of that struggle and making the Greeks swear to protect Plataea in future. Plataeans had fought in that battle, as they had at Artemisium, and more recently as willing allies of Sparta during the helot rebellion. None of this helped. The Spartans asked each prisoner in turn whether he had done anything to help Sparta in the current war. Since the only honest answer was no, each man made this response and was led away to execution. The women were sold as slaves, which they may—or may not—have been in the first place.[8]

Perhaps the Spartans intended this as an object lesson to deter anyone they might besiege in the future, or perhaps they felt obliged to indulge their Theban allies' long-standing hatred of the Plataeans. Whatever the reason, they refused to show any clemency. For a while Theban settlers occupied Plataea, before the decision was made to abandon the site, probably because it was vulnerable. Thus an old city, if a fairly small one, ceased to exist. The Athenians had done nothing to break the siege but had sheltered the bulk of the population and presumably any herds they had managed to bring away. Now they took the powerful step of enrolling the remaining Plataeans as full citizens of Athens. This was a big gesture—especially for the Athenians, who thought themselves very special—and in a small way helped to boost the citizen population at a time when there was a fresh outbreak of plague.[9]

In 427 BC neither side made much progress in damaging the other in pride or power to the extent that they were willing to seek peace. The Spartan invasion of Attica proved briefer than usual, for a spate of earthquakes, seen as bad omens by all sides, soon spurred retreat. Perhaps late in the year or early in the next, the Spartans recalled King Pleistonax from exile, encouraged by the pronouncements of the Delphic oracle, likely enough influenced by his generosity to the shrine. Still, he was not given a command for the moment, and there were surely differing opinions at Sparta, even if the details are not preserved, as to how best to prosecute the war. For the moment, no one had devised any drastic change of strategy or, if they had, managed to gather support for it. Spartan military thinking remained cautious and conservative, in part because the approach had served the city well in the past.[10]

By contrast the Athenians were hasty in making decisions and turning them into action and were able to reach far and fast, courtesy of their dominance at sea. In 426 BC they sent an expedition to Melos, which, although some distance out in the Aegean, was a Dorian city that each year received a Spartan magistrate. The Athenian commander, Nicias, ravaged the island but was unable to take the city itself and soon headed off to the east coast of Greece, landing in Boeotia. A force from Thebes and Tanagra was defeated in what was essentially a grand skirmish, and some damage was done to farmland before the Athenians returned to their ships and sailed home. In the meantime, another force had gone to the west coast above the Gulf of Corinth, an area that had seen frequent Athenian interventions before and during the war.[11]

The two commanders, Demosthenes and Procles, tried to bring the hill country of Aetolia under control. The Aetolians, Greeks in speech and culture, were herdsmen as much as, or more than, farmers and tended to live in small villages, so lacked a major centre. Also, unlike most Greeks, they did not fight as hoplites but operated instead as fast-moving skirmishers. Abandoned by most of its allies, the little Athenian army got into trouble against an enemy that knew the land well and did not fight by the normal rules. For a while, the contingent of archers kept the harassing enemy at bay, until too many of them were hit and most of their arrows had been used. The more numerous enemy did not run out of javelins or stones and fled whenever the Athenian hoplites charged, only to return and nibble away at them with missiles. After a long time, the Athenians could take no more and broke, fleeing back towards the coast. Procles was killed, along with 120 of the 300 hoplites, and the Athenians admitted that they had lost when they asked the enemy for permission to recover the corpses. Thucydides, who perhaps knew a number of these men, implies that many were of a similar age and dubbed the fallen the best men lost by Athens in the entire conflict.[12]

Demosthenes survived and sent the remnants of the expedition home while staying in Naupactus, afraid that his fellow citizens would be angry with him for this failure. Then, encouraged by the Aetolians, a Spartan general led 3,000 Peloponnesian hoplites in an attempt to surprise and take Naupactus. This failed, and instead they marched into Acarnania, allying with some of the neighbouring Ambraciots. Troops from the nearest Athenian naval squadron joined the local allies, and all accepted the command of Demosthenes. A small battle was fought, with phalanxes on either side, but Demosthenes had concealed 400 men in cover behind where he knew the enemy would deploy. When they emerged from ambush, the enemy army, until now victorious, panicked and fled. Heavy losses included the Spartan commander. His deputy conceded defeat and asked permission to march home. Demosthenes agreed, but only for the Peloponnesians, who promptly abandoned their local allies. The fate of the latter was made even worse when a second force of Ambraciots approached, totally unaware of what had happened. Demosthenes marched against them, the former helots from Naupactus taking the lead and calling out in Dorian-accented Greek that they were friends. The camped Ambraciots, not expecting to meet an enemy, were taken completely by surprise in what became a massacre more than a battle. Thucydides believed that Ambracia lost a higher proportion of its male citizens in these few days than any other city during the long war.[13]

Another campaigning season had passed, and men had died and farms been laid waste without any drastic shift in the fortunes of the two sides. Demosthenes's reputation was restored, but otherwise little had changed. As in almost every year, the Spartans had invaded Attica and failed to provoke a battle, and the Athenians had raided Megara. The latest outbreak of the plague was especially bad, and as part of a desperate longing for some end to it, the Athenians decided that the island of Delos, sacred to Apollo, needed attention. Generations before Pisistratus had acted to 'purify' the island, and now the Athenians went further, carefully removing every known grave on the island for reburial elsewhere and declaring that from then on, no one should be born or die on Delos, effectively reducing it to a place for ceremonies, although before long the impracticality of this became obvious, and the restriction was dropped.[14]

IN THE SPRING, King Agis, successor to the now dead Archidamus, led the attack on Attica. As usual the Athenians refused to offer battle, so the invaders did what damage they could and then marched home. In response, continuing the pattern of Athenian expeditions setting out after the Spartan invasion, two generals led a fleet heading west around the Peloponnese. With them went Demosthenes, not holding any formal office, although he may have already been elected strategos and been due to take up the post later in the year, when the new archons assumed office along with other magistrates. He lobbied hard on behalf of a plan to set up a fortified base at a chosen spot on the coast of Messenia, an out-of-the-way headland called Pylos. No one was inclined to listen, until the weather took a hand and a storm forced them to land there. Even then, according to Thucydides, only boredom convinced the sailors to start building ramparts to wall off the tip of the headland, and eventually, once the storm had relented, Demosthenes was left behind with five ships and their crews to hold the outpost. Word of this reached Sparta, once again, at a time of festival, and nothing was done. In contrast, when the report reached Agis, his army hurried straight back from Attica, after spending just fifteen days there, achieving even less than usual in some unseasonably wet weather. Very quickly, Sparta's leaders came to see this tiny outpost as a major threat, not least because it raised the prospect of the helots of the wider area deserting to the enemy or openly rebelling.[15]

There were few helots close to Pylos, for this was a barren area unsuitable for intensive cultivation, so hardly any people lived there. The headland itself was small, and south of it was a wide bay, known today as the Bay of Navarino, where in 1827 the last great battle of the age of wooden sailing ships was fought. On the western side, most of the bay was closed off by Sphacteria, a slim, rugged island some three miles long. The gap between its northern tip and Pylos was narrow, the open water to the south much wider, if still restricted. Agis had returned to Sparta with his army, but apart from the Spartans, the rest had gone home, having already fulfilled their obligation to serve on campaign. Requests were sent to all the allies to raise fresh contingents, while the Spartans set off for Pylos, some forty-five miles away across the mountains. At the same time the Corinthians and other cities that possessed warships were instructed to assemble a squadron.

Demosthenes had been reinforced by a couple of small ships from Naupactus, which were also carrying supplies of wicker shields, and he issued these to as many of his sailors as possible. To defend their position, the Athenians had built two walls, relying on the natural cliffs and rocks elsewhere. A spring provided water, but there was little in the way of food apart from what they had brought with them. As the first Spartans arrived on land, Demosthenes sent two of his triremes to summon aid from the main squadron, leaving him with some 400 to 600 men, or perhaps a few more, depending on how large the crews were in the first place. He had at least 120 hoplites and a few dozen archers. Yet, as throughout the war, even a comparatively small force behind rudimentary fortifications tended to make a Greek commander think twice before attacking. The Spartans waited for their fleet to arrive, which it did, having managed to avoid the Athenians on the way. For the moment numbers overwhelmingly favoured the attackers, and the Spartans first ferried more than 400 hoplites, along with helot servants, to the island of Sphacteria. This force could do nothing to strike against the position at Pylos, but it reinforced the sense that the Athenians were surrounded and prevented the latter from making another fort there. The island was bleak and normally uninhabited, much of it overgrown with scrub, so every day or two the Spartans replaced the men there with a fresh contingent to share out this dull and uncomfortable task.[16]

After days spent in preparation, the Spartans simultaneously launched an attack on the main land wall built across the peninsula and another by sea. Demosthenes felt that the latter was the biggest threat and went himself with sixty hoplites and twenty archers to meet it, guessing correctly that the enemy had to land on one narrow stretch of beach. Some of the attackers were cautious, for it meant driving a ship onto the shore or rowing in backwards to beach stern first. Brasidas was on one ship and as usual pressed on when others were slow to act. He led his men ashore but was wounded several times and eventually fainted, his shield lost in the waves, although he was carried back by his men. The attack failed, as did the one against the landward wall, and the Spartans began to prepare for a longer siege.[17]

Then the Athenian ships arrived, and everything changed. The Spartans might have defended the entrances to the bay, but instead their commanders dithered. After a day to consider the situation, the Athenian triremes rowed in unopposed, and only once they were inside the sheltered bay did some Spartan ships come out to face them. These were quickly defeated, and the Athenians even captured and drew away some of the vessels moored by the shore in another demonstration not simply of their skill but of the timidity and fragile morale of the Peloponnesian crews and captains when opposed to them. From then on, a constant patrol of Athenian triremes sailed round and round Sphacteria. Instead of the Athenians being besieged, the 420 hoplites were now stranded on the island. A little less than half of these men were 'peers', and a fair few came from important and well-connected families. Rich reward was promised to any helot willing to cross to the island under cover of darkness carrying food. Some swam, some rowed little boats, and a fair few succeeded, but this obviously would not suffice in the long run, while there was no prospect of assembling another fleet confident and capable enough to drive off the Athenians. Not wanting to lose so many full citizens, the Spartans were willing to talk.[18]

A truce was agreed on the spot, with set amounts of food being permitted to go across to Sphacteria, while the guard was maintained and all the remaining Peloponnesian triremes in the wider area were handed over to the Athenians as a surety of goodwill. In the meantime, an Athenian ship took Spartan envoys to Athens to propose an end to the conflict between their two cities. In essence the Spartans were willing to grant the Athenians the equality they craved, making an alliance between the two on that basis, which also respected each side's right to have allies. The terms were good, and only a few years earlier the Athenians had vainly sought a peace less advantageous to them. Yet the Spartan eagerness fed the excitement at Athens brought about by this change of fortune. Cleon was a prominent voice calling for the enemy to give more and suggested that the men on Sphacteria should surrender straightaway as a sign of the Spartans' sincere longing for an end to the war. Uncomfortable discussing matters in the raucous and volatile setting of the Athenian Assembly, the ambassadors asked that the details be hammered out first in private. Cleon claimed that this was a sure sign that they were up to no good. Plenty of other citizens were eager for peace, and the debate was fierce, but in the end the majority voted to reject the Spartan offer.[19]

The envoys went home empty-handed, and the Athenians claimed a technical breach of the truce as an excuse to keep the triremes given over to them. Yet, while they had the Spartans trapped on Sphacteria, they were no nearer to capturing them, and the summer was coming to an end. At the moment, the fleet could rest on another island, a little out to sea, since there was neither the space nor the water for them at Pylos, but eventually the weather would worsen, and staying there would become difficult, even dangerous. The successful defence of the position at Pylos offered a reminder that storming a position held even by a few hundred men was no easy thing. Sphacteria lacked walls, apart from a small refuge that the Spartans had built on a high point, but the island was rocky, with few landing places, and the dense scrub and woodland gave the enemy plenty of cover, while making it difficult to coordinate any attacking force.

A month passed with the island still firmly held, and many at Athens began to wonder whether they had missed a great opportunity. Cleon was criticised but remained unrepentant, declaring that the island could be taken and its little garrison killed or captured. Nicias, one of the generals and acting as spokesman for the rest, called his bluff, volunteering to step aside and give Cleon the command if he was so sure of how victory was to be achieved. Many in the crowd, scenting blood, supported the suggestion, so that a reluctant Cleon, backed into a corner, was forced to accept. His rivals felt that they would win either way, whether he succeeded, or went off and got killed, or at least failed so publicly that he would be discredited. That at least is Thucydides's version, and many scholars have been sceptical, feeling that his loathing of the popular leader led him to distort the truth. That in itself would not mean that he and others at the time did not believe what he reports. Still, there is a lot to be said in favour of the idea that Cleon and Demosthenes had been in contact for some time—after all, most leading Athenians knew each other well. There were newly hired contingents of light infantry and archers at Athens, apparently requested by Demosthenes, and when Cleon set sail, he took these troops with him. Before he left, he promised the Assembly that he would achieve total victory and return in just twenty days.[20]

Luck was on his side. Around this time an Athenian ship landed in a quiet bay on Sphacteria so that the men could cook some food. A little over 400 hoplites could not hope to control every foot of a

PYLOS AND SPHACTERIA

three-mile-long island, and the covering of vegetation meant that the landing party went unobserved—and no doubt had taken precautions to defend themselves or flee if necessary. They were less careful about their cooking fires, which set the grass alight, and the flames rapidly spreading until a large swathe of the island was burned clear of vegetation. With Cleon and his reinforcements, Demosthenes began carefully planning his attack. He landed at night, not wanting to see a repeat of his own success in defending a narrow beach with just a small force against far more numerous invaders. As it happened, the closest Spartan outpost was keeping a poor watch. The Athenians found them all fast asleep and killed them. More troops were landed behind them as a beachhead was formed. Demosthenes had some hoplites and thousands of light armed troops, some archers, and some enthusiastic sailors. They split into groups and began to comb the island, now substantially bare. Remembering his own bad experience in Aetolia, he ordered his men to give way whenever the Spartan hoplites charged, avoiding any close combat.

The tactics worked, although it was a slow business, and the Spartans and the perioeci fighting with them showed all the stubborn courage for which they were famous. Time and again they charged, but the attackers followed Demosthenes's orders and withdrew, closing again once the charge was spent. The defending hoplites were heavily outnumbered, allowing the light troops to slip around their flanks and rear, bombarding them with arrows, javelins, and stones. One by one, men fell, some dead, some wounded, and the net around the surviving groups closed ever tighter. It was a hot day in late summer, and charging repeatedly, manoeuvring out of encirclement, and simply keeping a shield upright to fend off missiles was tiring work, especially with so much ash and dust in the air from the recent fire. Hardly any Athenian troops were killed, and more lightly equipped and far more numerous, they were able to stay fresher.

Eventually the remaining defenders retired to the little redoubt they had built, its back to slopes so sheer that they seemed impassable cliffs, until a contingent led by men from Naupactus found a way up. These emerged behind the last group of hoplites, who were now surrounded and under missile attack from all sides, just like the last of Leonidas's men at Thermopylae. Their commander was dead, his badly wounded successor had been left somewhere on the field and was also presumed dead, and 128 other hoplites were also dead or mortally wounded. The Athenians could have shot the rest all down, but Demosthenes and Cleon realised that prisoners would be of far more value than corpses. They paused the attack and asked the Spartans to lay down their arms. Permission was granted for them to send an emissary across the bay to the far shore to ask the senior commanders what they should do. The reply was vague, telling them to make up their own minds but to avoid dishonour.

The survivors discussed the matter, for they were Greeks, and this was the natural thing for them to do. Then they laid down their arms and surrendered, so that after some two and half months, the Pylos campaign was over, the barren headland and the rocky little island both now firmly under Athenian control. Although often bitter, the fighting had always been on a rather modest scale, and apart from on the beach at Pylos, hoplite had not fought hoplite. Yet the consequences were out of proportion to the scale of the campaign. The Athenians had taken 292 captives, 120 of them Spartan 'peers' and the remaining 172 perioeci—it is doubtful that Thucydides bothered to count any helots or other servants taken with them. The news stunned the wider Greek world, for no one could remember anything like this having happened before, and most had believed the tales that no hardship or fear of death could ever break a Spartan's resolve to keep fighting. A Spartan officer might be forced to give in when a city fell, as had happened at Mytilene, but here the men had had the option of resisting to the very last, like the 300 at Thermopylae, and had made a different choice. Sparta's reputation for raising the finest fighting men in the world was tarnished, if only a little, and that mattered in terms of prestige. The difficulty of getting to the truth of Spartan culture makes it hard to know just what was expected of their men in such a situation, where death was certain and there were no real prospects of demonstrating their courage and skill because the enemy would not let them close. When taunted by his captors that the fallen were better men than the ones who had given in, one Sparta prisoner retorted that it would be a remarkable arrow—he used the word *spindle*, a women's tool, to show his contempt for all missile weapons—that could pick out only the brave as a target.[21]

Cleon was back in Athens with his victory and his prisoners within the promised twenty days. Once again, it is worth remembering that the distances involved were not vast. Still, he had taken a gamble with his credibility, but the preparations made by Demosthenes had made it a calculated risk. Soon there was more good news for the Athenians. A large force, bigger than the total ever engaged at Pylos, had set out and raided Corinthian territory. Altogether the Athenians sent out 2,000 hoplites, supported by more from their allies, and 200 cavalrymen. The efforts involved in transporting even this number of horses show the increasing importance of more mobile supporting arms in warfare. Hoplites were still the heart of an army, both in terms of their social status and fighting power, but they found operating on their own more difficult. When the Corinthians reacted and sent out troops to meet the invaders, the Athenian cavalry played a key role in a victory that left 200 Corinthians dead compared to 50 Athenians.[22]

As the year came to an end, the Athenians could feel well satisfied with recent events and, for the first time in a while, could also feel more optimistic about the prospects of victory. A force remained at Pylos, and in the months and years to come, a few helot runaways would seek refuge there. Exactly what Demosthenes had hoped for when he came up with the plan in the first place is impossible to know, although it is certain that he cannot have anticipated all that had happened. Establishing a permanent stronghold on Spartan soil was of value in itself, even if it was a tiny fort in an out-of-the-way part of the land, since it showed that the Spartans were too weak to prevent it. The escalation of the campaign, the naval success, and the isolation of the men on Sphacteria brought new dangers for both sides and could have ended in Athenian failure and humiliation. Skill, good leadership, and luck dictated otherwise, turning it into a spectacular success. Much of this was symbolic, raising Athenian prestige as it damaged that of Sparta, but it also brought the tangible prize of 120 Spartan prisoners, and no one suggested executing them or the allies captured with them.

In the aftermath of the surrender, the Spartans from the shore had formally admitted defeat, asking and being granted permission to retrieve their dead from Sphacteria and give them proper burial. Later a succession of delegations went from Sparta to Athens to negotiate an end to the war and return of the prisoners. Thucydides does not provide details of the proposals they made because they came to nothing. The Athenians were riding high, and enough of them were like Cleon and willing to press their luck further in the hope of an even greater victory. The war continued.

22

FICKLE FORTUNE

Negotiations, peace, and two great battles,
424–418 BC

IN 424 BC THE SPARTANS DID NOT SUMMON THEIR ALLIES TO muster as a big army and march into Attica to lay waste to the land. The Athenians had threatened to execute the Spartan prisoners if this happened, and the warning was sufficient deterrent. This did not prevent the Athenians from landing raiding parties on Spartan territory, and in one encounter they defeated a Spartan-led and partly Spartan-composed force in a skirmish, setting up a trophy to mark their victory. Thucydides claimed that morale among Sparta's leaders and citizens sank to a very low ebb and that to get them to give in and accept whatever humiliation the Athenians imposed as the price for peace would not have taken much. He may have exaggerated, because their leaders did decide to mount an expedition to the north-east, selecting as its leader Brasidas, now recovered from his wounds. The only 'peer', or just possibly one of a few other officers, involved in this enterprise, he began to raise more than 1,000 mercenaries and 700 helot volunteers, who were given hoplite equipment and the promise of freedom at the end of their service. It was a way of finding manpower in a state whose shrinking citizen population had been highlighted by the losses of dead and captured in 425 BC. Better yet, this was expendable manpower and removed bolder spirits—and perhaps potential rebels—from the helot population. Thucydides claims that at some point, an appeal for volunteers to fight was made to the helots, and the 2,000 who came forward were praised, crowned with garlands, and then taken off, one by one, to be murdered in secret. He gives no indication of a date for this episode, and some scholars are sceptical of its truth, which does not mean that keeping control of the helots was not always a major concern for all Spartans.[1]

Brasidas's expedition was the only major offensive enterprise planned by the Spartans at this time. Otherwise, their thoughts were defensive, and considerable numbers of Spartan and allied troops were dispersed in mobile columns or as garrisons around the Peloponnese in the hope of fending off Athenian incursions. In contrast, the Athenians were even more aggressive than usual, buoyed by success and because the plague had burnt itself out, and would not in fact return in the future. As so often, the internal politics of a city offered an opportunity when a faction within Megara appealed for Athenian aid and offered a new alliance with Athens. This was a great prize, for Megara lay on the land route from the Peloponnese to Attica. If it came back into the Athenian sphere, this would not make an attack impossible, since the only way to stop a big, Spartan-led army was to confront it with a similarly large army. However, it would make the Spartans' task harder, for the invaders would have to spend more time in hostile territory. Effectively, it would advance the main boundary between Athenian and Spartan power further to the west.[2]

Demosthenes and another general—who happened to be Pericles's nephew—took charge and carefully made and agreed on a plan with the conspirators at Megara. The first step was to take the long walls connecting the city to its port, the predecessors of the bigger defences at Athens. In order to do this, the conspirators went out each night through one of the gates, carrying a boat and assuring the guards that they were off to raid Attica, which was just a short trip across the water. Each time they returned before dawn, until the guards were so used to this that they thought no more of it. Then one night the men turned on the guards and killed them, holding the gate open to admit an advance party of Athenians who had sneaked undetected into Megarian territory. Attempts to follow up this success by infiltrating the fortified port and Megara itself failed, but Athenian reinforcements of 4,000 hoplites and 600 cavalrymen arrived on time, and the long walls themselves were secured. This army had been waiting at Eleusis, just across the border, emphasising—like the Theban attack on Plataea—just how small the distances separating enemies often were.

The Athenians demanded the surrender of the port and, when this was refused, built walls to isolate it and place it under blockade. After two days, the garrison surrendered, handing over the few Spartans and other Peloponnesians who were there. At this point Brasidas appeared, having a knack of being in the right place at the right time and never dithering. Initially he had the army that he was organising for his northern expedition; allies hastily summoned from Corinth and other neighbouring communities joined this force until he had numbers to match the Athenian hoplites, at which point he marched to confront the Athenians. When he arrived outside their city, the Megarians were cautious, for the moment refusing to admit either side. The rival armies stared at each other and postured, but as time passed more reinforcements reached Brasidas, including contingents from Boeotia, while encounters between cavalry and light troops went against the Athenians. Brasidas advanced and formed his army up for battle in plain sight of the enemy. He had numbers on his side, and the Athenian commanders declined to risk a clash of phalanxes and instead withdrew to Attica. Brasidas did not try to force a battle, partly because this was the convention and partly because he did not need to, for the Athenians had visibly shown that they were unwilling to fight him. Seeing this, Megara promptly opened its gates to the

Spartan general and renewed its alliance with Sparta. Men seen as implicated in the conspiracy were executed or fled.³

The attempt to bring Megara over to their side had failed, but the Athenians had still taken control of its port, rendering the long walls irrelevant, so there were some lasting benefits. For the moment, the Athenians had something even more ambitious in mind: a double advance into Boeotia, with Demosthenes coming from the west and a general named Hippocrates advancing from the south-east. Once again, factions within some of the cities encouraged this, claiming that the wider population could readily be persuaded to switch sides. In the event, ambition outreached actual capacity and luck, and the two forces failed to coordinate their actions. Demosthenes got there first, well ahead of the other army, and found himself confronted by a large Boeotian army, for word of the Athenian plans had slipped out. He withdrew, having achieved nothing.⁴

Not knowing of this, Hippocrates proceeded with his part of the plan, marching towards Tanagra and seizing the shrine at Delium, which he and his men proceeded to fortify. This done, most of the light infantry started back on the march to Attica, while the main force camped just over a mile away from the newly built fort, planning to follow soon afterwards. By this time the Boeotians had mustered another army at Tanagra, since the one that had confronted Demosthenes had already dispersed home in the usual way. This time they had managed to assemble 7,000 hoplites, 1,000 cavalry, 500 peltasts (well-armed skirmishers), and some 10,000 less well-equipped and -trained light infantrymen. Hippocrates had a similar force of hoplites, as well as some cavalry, but most of his light armed foot soldiers had already left.⁵

The Boeotian army did not have a single leader in 424 BC but a number of elected magistrates from the various cities, and for a while they were uncertain what to do, until one of them, a Theban named Pagondas, stirred them to action. He argued that it was a humiliation for an enemy to march into their lands and leave unchallenged and that the Athenians' having set up their fort was an even greater shame and provocation, especially as they had done this on sacred land. Spurred on, the Boeotians marched forwards before halting behind a hill that hid them from the enemy's view. Concealed, they formed their battle-line. Pagondas's fellow citizens, the Thebans, took the place of honour on the right of the line, where they deployed in an unusually deep phalanx of twenty-five ranks. Hoplites from other Boeotian cities were stationed in the centre, and the contingents from Orchomenus, Tanagra, and Thespiae were on the left wing, the second place of honour. None of these formations appear to have been as deep as the Theban phalanx, and the deployment meant that more men were concentrated on the right on a fairly narrow frontage.

Hippocrates had been away from the army, organising things at Delium over a mile away, when reports came in that the enemy was approaching. A messenger went to the army, ordering it to prepare for battle, while the commander followed as quickly as he could. The Athenian hoplites formed up eight deep, probably in a line of tribal regiments rather than a single solid block. Their cavalry were on the wings, apart from some detached earlier to support the garrison at Delium, and there were fairly few light troops in support. Everything had to be done in haste, and when Hippocrates arrived, he began to go along the line, encouraging each sector at a time. He had not covered even half the army before the Boeotians came over the high ground and attacked.

Delium is one of a handful of hoplite battles described in any real detail, which means that it is often used to portray a 'typical' such encounter. This is misleading, since it was brought on rather more hastily than many other battles and saw an advance over a longer-than-usual distance as both sides rushed towards each other. Pagondas's decision to halt some distance away and deploy out of sight may partly explain the exceptional depth of the Thebans. A deep formation will naturally have a narrower frontage, allowing it to move quicker and over a greater distance without losing its order and breaking up. The Thebans were in this way able to surge forward and still keep together in a dense array as they pushed on. There was open ground where the armies met, but there were also gullies, streams, and other obstacles restricting the space for fighting. The extreme wings, including the Athenian cavalry and many of the Boeotian counterparts, did not really get into the fighting at all.

Other Greeks saw Boeotians as tough fighters, not as famous as the Spartans and some of their Peloponnesian neighbours but still among the better hoplites. Still, no one on either side had much experience of a battle on this scale, for it was the first major land encounter in the entire war. The Athenians had beaten the Thebans at Plataea back in 479 BC, and then had beaten them again and subsequently been defeated by them in 457 and 449 BC. On the Athenian left and the Theban right, both sides came on confidently, charging at a run. The Thebans had the advantage of coming downhill, at least in the beginning, and their deep formation helped them to keep together as they advanced. Yet the Athenians did not break in the face of their charge; still less were they bowled over. Probably both sides checked at the last minute, realising that the other was determined, and then began to fight, spear against spear, shields both protecting and being used to barge. The Thebans had the edge, helped by the ground and their formation, and step by step the Athenians gave back, still fighting.

Elsewhere the story was different. The other Boeotians were not deployed so deeply and perhaps had not had the time or capacity to form up in as orderly a way at the start, before the advance inevitably shook out their formations. Here the Athenians had the advantage, and the enemy began to give way. Most of the Boeotian formations collapsed into flight, apart from the Thespians, whose forbears had stayed and died with the Spartans at Thermopylae. They kept together and kept on fighting but were soon surrounded by masses—or perhaps still rough formations—of Athenians attacking from the flanks. They were cut down, and such was the confusion of the situation, with men having lost their sense of direction and no national uniforms to tell one hoplite from another, that Athenians for a while started fighting their fellow citizens, mistaking them for the enemy.

Thucydides says that Pagondas saw his left and centre collapsing, which implies that he was not fighting in the front rank as many leaders chose to do. He ordered two groups of cavalry, who had been kept in reserve and were still waiting behind the hill out of sight, to loop around and help the remnants of his left. When they approached, the Athenians thought that they were the vanguard of a fresh army, coming against them when they were tired and disordered after the fight. The rumour spread swiftly and with it panic, as more and more men turned and fled. About the same time, perhaps independently of this or hastened by ripples of confusion from it, the Athenian left wing stopped giving way grudgingly and collapsed into rout, so that the entire army was in flight. The Boeotians pursued, their horsemen leading the way, killing freely amid the mob of fugitives. Men who gave up and fled were easy targets, while those who kept their heads did better. The philosopher Socrates proved as determined in battle as he was in debate and remained ready to defend himself, leading out others who clustered around him and were willing to present a bold face to the enemy. The battle had begun late in the day, so before long darkness brought an end to the pursuit.[6]

For the first time in the war, the Athenians had fought a large land battle, that most prestigious type of warfare against which Pericles had cautioned them, and they had been utterly defeated. Something like 1,000 Athenians were dead, along with their commander, compared to half that number of Boeotians, the majority of them Thespians. Pagondas's men were left in unchallenged control of the battlefield, where they erected a trophy to display their triumph. A few of the Athenians made it into the fort at Delium, the rest heading by land or sea back to Attica. After a while, representatives returned to ask for permission to recover and honour their dead, but at first the Boeotians refused, accusing the Athenians of polluting the shrine at Delium by turning sacred ground into a military stronghold. The bold assertion that the site was now formally Athenian since they had claimed it prompted scorn: The Athenians were welcome to come and try to take the land by force if they dared. They did not, and no aid went to the little outpost. Someone among the Boeotian army devised a crude and cumbersome but effective flame projector, setting fire to the timber walls at Delium and burning out the defenders, all of whom were killed or captured. The site was re-consecrated, and only at this stage, some seventeen days after the battle, were the Athenians allowed to come for their dead. Inevitably, given that this was at the height of the hot summer, the remains had badly decayed, making this task even grimmer than usual.[7]

Fortune had turned sharply against the Athenians, and more was to come. After his successful intervention at Megara, Brasidas had completed his preparations and led his army north. They went by land, for travelling by sea was too risky in the face of Athenian naval power. He bluffed his way through Thessaly, a region with plenty of Athenian allies, and always kept moving, giving no one time to think too deeply about what he was doing, eventually reaching Macedonia. King Perdiccas had already agreed to aid the Spartan expedition, which meant that they were on friendly territory. Brasidas advanced on Acanthus in the Chalcidice, encouraged by a faction within the city. Not everyone was convinced, but they allowed the Spartan officer to come into the city on his own and speak to them.[8]

Brasidas was an extremely gifted military leader and in so many ways an even more unusual Spartan, for he had a way with words. Where most senior Spartans tried to bully others, especially anyone who was not Spartan, Brasidas treated them with respect and courtesy. Now he spoke of Sparta's promise to bring liberty to the Greeks, assuring them that any state to side with him against Athens would have full self-government and autonomy after the war—they were not facing a choice between Spartan or Athenian domination. Persuaded by his words and manner, the citizens of Acanthus voted to join him and admit his army. It was the first of a number of successes won by his confidence and apparently open and straightforward nature. Alongside this, Brasidas was a master of guile and surprise attack. City after city was captured through speed and stealth or convinced to join him. The greatest prize was Amphipolis, where he arrived after force-marching through a snowy night and convinced the inhabitants to defect to him. The Athenian commander in the area, Thucydides himself, failed to arrive in time to prevent this, although he did manage to secure a smaller community nearby. For this failure he was exiled and in time felt the urge to record the history of the war.[9]

The loss of Amphipolis shocked Athens, for the colony, established after so much previous effort and failure, was a mark of its success as well as so valuable for controlling access to the resources of the area. Following on from the defeat at Delium, which took a heavy toll in lives and at the same time struck a major blow to their pride, the Athenians were more willing to negotiate with the Spartans and in 423 BC agreed to a suspension of hostilities. This was to last for a year, during which the parties expected to hammer out a more enduring peace, which the Spartans hoped would at long last secure the return of the men taken on Sphacteria. Both sides were weary and despondent, hence willing to make fewer demands on the other, and at the very least the Athenians wished to bring a halt to Brasidas's run of successes. In this they were to be disappointed.[10]

After his first campaign, Brasidas had sent a message back to Sparta asking for more men and resources. He had few friends among the leaders at the time and perhaps had even been sent so far afield because many viewed his eager aggression and successful record with suspicion and jealousy. Only modest support came, but this did not deter Brasidas. Before news arrived of the armistice, he had convinced the city of Scione to break with Athens and join him, soon followed by the defection of nearby Mende. The Spartan general argued artfully that this did not violate the agreement between Athens and Sparta and put small garrisons into both, refusing to give them up. For a while, he focused his attention elsewhere, taking his main force to join Perdiccas in an expedition against some of the Illyrian tribes. This went badly, with the Macedonian king's local allies dispersing, and Perdiccas himself followed them, abandoning Brasidas and his men, who had to fight their way to safety. While Brasidas was away on this fruitless enterprise, Mende had seen a revolution, with a different faction turning against the new regime and letting the Athenians in. In this way one city was lost, although Athenian attempts to capture Scione failed.[11]

The year ended, and with it the suspension of hostilities, for the two sides had failed to reach a more permanent agreement. Even so, in 422 BC, almost all the main action occurred in the north-east, and neither side seems to have mounted a major operation anywhere else. The Spartans had decided to send more reinforcements to Brasidas, but as usual they moved slowly, far slower than the Athenians. Cleon once again received a military command, being sent to take charge of the troops already facing Brasidas. In addition, he was given thirty triremes and a force of 1,200 hoplites and 300 cavalry. There is no evidence that he had gained any more military experience since Sphacteria, but things started well when he captured the city of Torone with a sudden attack from the sea. By this time, Brasidas and King Perdiccas were openly hostile to each other, and some help came from the Macedonians, while both sides enlisted as many Thracian allies as they could.[12]

As always, Amphipolis was the great prize, and Cleon marched there, only to balk when he realised that Brasidas and his main army were in the city, having raced him to get there. The Athenians made a demonstration of force outside the walls, coming close in considerable strength even though Cleon had no intention of risking an actual assault. Brasidas formed his men up in columns, on the roads behind the two main gates, and waited. After a while, the Athenians began to withdraw clumsily, reflecting Cleon's ignorance of large-scale manoeuvres and also the low standards of drill and training in all Greek armies apart from the Spartans. As they began to shamble away, the gates opened, and the columns charged out, Brasidas in the lead of one of them at the head of a band of 150 hoplites. The fight was brief and one-sided, as the Athenians, caught off guard and unprepared for combat, collapsed into rout. Some 600 were killed, many struck in the back as they fled, allegedly the fate of Cleon. Yet some fought back, if only for a while, and the Spartans lost seven men, including Brasidas, who took a mortal wound and lived just long enough to see his victory. The people of Amphipolis, rejecting their Athenian founder, honoured the dead Spartan with the cult of a hero and revered him as the new founder of their city.[13]

Different in so many ways, Brasidas and Cleon were alike in their determination to overcome the enemy and win the war. Without them, both sides more easily reached an agreement early in 421 BC, although negotiations went back and forth a good deal before it was settled and the war declared to be over. The treaty is known as the Peace of Nicias, since he led the Athenian side of the talks. By it each side pledged to return any places captured since 431 BC, when the Peloponnesian War had started, and prisoners were released, so that, after four years, the men captured on Sphacteria were allowed to go home. As Thucydides presents it, recovering these men had been Sparta's principal goal since their capture, and to achieve this the Spartans were clearly content to sacrifice the desires of their allies. Corinth, Thebes, and others got little from this settlement, other than a reminder that they were less important than Sparta, for it was essentially a unilateral deal between Sparta and Athens. This added to the confusion in the months and years that followed, as some aspects of the agreement were honoured and some were not. Brasidas's subordinate refused to hand over Amphipolis, honouring his predecessor's promise that communities should be autonomous. Reluctantly, the Athenians were forced to accept this for the moment, although in generations to come they would make several unsuccessful attempts to retake the city. In reply they kept the outpost at Pylos as a bargaining tool. A little later the Athenians and Spartans agreed to a fifty-year peace, again between themselves, further upsetting Sparta's allies.[14]

The Spartans were all the more eager for peace because the thirty-year peace treaty agreed with Argos was coming to the end of its term. During the struggle with Athens, the Argives had remained neutral, trading with both sides, but such an attitude could not be taken for granted indefinitely. On the whole, once the agreement was made with Athens, the Spartans were more concerned with the Peloponnese than with the wider world. Several communities of their allies were restless, eager to expand their own power at the expense of their neighbours and disenchanted with Spartan leadership after a decade of hard warfare had brought such little gain. There were also problems closer to home—for instance, how to treat the returned prisoners. The public shaming associated with the 'tremblers' did not seem practical in the case of 120 citizens, many of them from important families. At first, they were denied full citizen rights, but before long these were restored.[15]

For the Athenians the Peace of Nicias represented a victory of sorts, although perhaps it did not seem such a great one, given the heavy cost of the war, the devastation wrought by the plague, and the raised expectations in the moments of highest success. The Spartans were now willing to treat them as equals and accept that Athens was a great power, and with their other concerns they had concluded a defensive alliance with the Athenians, each pledging to come to the other's aid if attacked. Whether all this merited such a high cost was another matter, but most felt immense relief that the war seemed at last to be over. Over time, dissatisfaction grew, and neither side fulfilled all of its obligations. Just as Amphipolis and other cities in the region were not forced back into the Athenian alliance, Pylos continued to be held by a small Athenian garrison, although for a while they did remove any helots or men from Naupactus from the fort and pledged not to accept any more helot fugitives. In the north, the Athenian siege of Scione continued until the city was taken and its population killed or enslaved. Although major direct conflict between Athens and Sparta had ceased, there was never a full peace, and any trust that briefly existed soon began to erode. Thucydides argued that the war continued, simply at a lower level, until all-out conflict resumed.[16]

There was also much bitterness towards the Spartans on the part of many of their allies, who felt that Sparta had neglected them in the settlement and, more generally, restricted them from pursuing their own best interests. Argos offered an alternative as a powerful and prestigious city, and negotiations began, leading Mantineia, Elis, and Corinth to join a new coalition led by the Argives. Many of the Boeotians, feeling equally abandoned by Sparta, were tempted to join but for the moment held back. Everyone was looking for the best deal, and the Boeotians coerced the Spartans into making an alliance with them akin to the one the Spartans had concluded with the Athenians—and almost certainly in violation of the latter, not that either side formally objected at first. This made the Argives nervous and prompted them to negotiate for a new alliance with Sparta, until some Athenians encouraged them to go to Athens instead.[17]

Most prominent among this group, at least according to Thucydides, was a young aristocrat named Alcibiades, who had grown up in the household of Pericles after his father had fallen at Coronea. Hearing that Argos was sending ambassadors to Athens, Alcibiades is supposed to have manipulated the Spartans into delivering a message that he felt the Assembly was bound to reject, although this may have been no more than rumour, and added confusion came when an earth tremor caused the suspension of public business. Yet it soon became clear that neither side was willing to satisfy the other. Instead, the Athenians now made an alliance with Argos, Mantineia, and Elis, although not Corinth, even though the Corinthians maintained their separate alliance with Argos. They seem to have felt that Athens was always too dangerous to their interests to befriend, even under these circumstances, and gradually drifted closer to Sparta once again. The Boeotians decided to distance themselves from what was going on, pulling away from the recent agreement with Sparta.[18]

Four years had passed since the last Olympic festival, so the games were held again in 420 BC, and since Elis controlled the sanctuary, its leaders advertised their newfound allegiance by banning the Spartans from taking part. In 419 BC, the Athenians elected Alcibiades as strategos and sent him with a force into the Peloponnese to engage in minor operations. The Argives mustered an army and attacked a Corinthian ally, the city of Epidaurus, but although the Spartans sent King Agis with an army to deal with them, he decided against risking battle and withdrew. The public reason was that the omens from the pre-battle sacrifices were bad, and given the deep-seated Spartan reverence for proper ritual, this might have been true. The year ended with negotiations that led nowhere and an ongoing siege of Epidaurus by the Argives and their allies.[19]

In 418 BC, King Agis took the field with a bigger army, outmanoeuvred the enemy, and was about to challenge them to battle when the Argives proposed a truce. Neither side was really in much mood to negotiate, so little came of this, although the king had already withdrawn. Once back in Sparta he was attacked for his performance and threatened with a fine and even the demolition of his house. Eventually the ephors decided to send a board of ten advisors with him, expressly to prevent a premature end to the next campaign. Soon another army was raised and Agis placed in command, for the allies had attacked Tegea, still loyal to Sparta, in part because of its hostility to Elis and Mantineia. This time Agis was too aggressive, ordering his men to advance and attack the enemy in a strong position where they had the high ground. In a fascinating display of Spartan society, an experienced 'peer' called out to him that this was folly, and the king took his advice and ordered a halt. No one objected to this, and the account implies that the man was not an officer, at least not a senior one, and was simply respected as a veteran and for speaking wise words.[20]

The following day, as the Spartans marched near Mantineia, they found the concentrated allied army waiting ahead of them, and this time there was a battle. Numbers favoured the Spartans just a little, and most estimates suggest that each side had something like 10,000 to 11,000 hoplites, plus cavalry and supporting troops, making this the largest battle fought during the entire Peloponnesian War in terms of the phalanxes. Indeed, this was the only genuinely big pitched battle other than Delium fought on land during the conflict. There were 1,000 Athenian hoplites present, as well as 300 cavalry, and the size of the force may reflect caution in being seen to have broken the Peace of Nicias fully. Alternatively, they may simply have expected this to be another prolonged campaign of smaller operations, and this modest force was easier to spare and supply for a longer period. Consequently, in neither battle did the main strength of the Spartans face the main strength of the Athenians in the traditional clash of phalanxes. At Delium the Athenians were present in great strength but fought the Boeotians not the Spartans, and at Mantineia in 418 BC, the vast majority of the army facing the Spartans came from the Peloponnese.

The Mantineians stood on the right of the allied army, granted the place of honour because the battle was being fought in their territory. Beside them were Arcadian contingents, then 1,000 picked Argives, men paid and kept in training at the state's expense, and to their right the rest of Argos's hoplites. More Peloponnesians stood beside them, and the Athenians held the left flank, their cavalry beside them. Facing them were men from Tegea, who seem to have held this honour as a tradition, and beside them were the Arcadians allied to Sparta. The Spartans, some 3,000 of them in total, were in the centre, opposed to the Argives, with the left held by the helots who had served under

Brasidas and won their freedom and also the Sciritae, a Tegean people, who were granted this position by custom. Such points of pride and prestige were important for motivating Greek citizen soldiers. Leaders went along the lines, encouraging their men with promises of victory and the benefits it would bring.

Both sides advanced, the Argives and their allies cheering themselves on and breaking into a run. In contrast the Spartans, who had already sung together to stir up their courage—no doubt the old verses of Tyrtaeus, among other battle-songs—went slowly and silently, apart from the music of pipes that set the rhythm as they marched in step, keeping very good order. In spite of this, both armies were veering to the right, and in the passage describing this—alone in all Greek literature—Thucydides states that hoplites always did this because each man felt that his right side was poorly protected, so unconsciously edged ever closer to the shield of the man on his right side. Agis became worried that the Mantineians were outflanking his left, while his own right was drifting too far beyond the enemy left to be useful. To deal with this, he ordered his left wing to shift to line up with the enemy, while two units of Spartans were to pull out of their position nearer the centre and march over to plug the gap this created. The officers (polemarchs) commanding these units refused to obey the order and stayed where they were on the basis that it was too late for such fiddling around. How close the enemy was at this stage is hard to say, and obviously formation changes at the last minute ran the risk of creating disorder. Instead, Agis sent messengers to tell the left wing to close back up with the rest of the army, although this re-ordering was not complete when the armies met.

King Agis was in the centre of the line, leading the 300 *hippeis*—the young warriors chosen each year amid fierce competition—with the other Spartan units arrayed around them. Their uncannily disciplined and steady advance, combined with the realisation that these were the Spartans, the most famous fighting men of all the Greeks, so unnerved most of their opponents that many broke before contact,

Argives, some Athenians, and other allies streaming off the field in panic. Some stayed to fight, among them many of the Athenians on their wing. On the Spartan left there was more stubborn fighting, but the Sciritae and Brasidas's men were badly positioned and outflanked. The gap that had opened between them and the rest of the army's line was still there, and many Mantineians and the picked force of Argives surged through, some getting as far as the Spartan baggage train, where they killed the elderly men left to guard it.

The remaining Athenians were in trouble, steadily being outflanked by the Tegeans and closest Spartans, although their horsemen were managing to slow this down for a while. Fortunately for them, Agis saw the breakthrough of his own line as the most serious threat and shifted his army to deal with this. It was a tribute to Spartan discipline and the ease of the victory over so much of the enemy line, which meant that much of his army was still fairly fresh and in good order, that he was able to re-form his units and turn them round to face the exultant Mantineians. Some were caught, but most saw the re-formed Spartans approaching and fled. While this was happening, the Athenians were able to pull back in reasonable order and escape.[21]

Setting up a trophy to mark their victory, the Spartans and their allies found that they had lost about 300 dead, the enemy something like 1,100, of whom 200 were Athenian, including both the generals who had been present. The two Spartan officers who had disobeyed the king's order were charged with cowardice and exiled. There seems to have been no formal charge or even concept of insubordination at Sparta, so they were assumed to have been too frightened to obey, while everyone could see that the gap in the line had created the greatest crisis of the battle. Nevertheless, the Spartans had won decisively in a pitched battle where none of the defeated could pretend that they had lost through ill chance or some unfair stratagem on the part of the enemy. The Argives and their allies had chosen the battle site; the Spartans had accepted the challenge and come on openly and then thrashed them.

After the battle, the Spartan army dispersed, as was usual, the Spartans themselves returning home to celebrate the Carneia festival, which had fallen due. There were some more small-scale operations, but by the end of the year the Argives clearly wanted peace. A treaty was agreed, creating a strong alliance between Argos and Sparta, which only lasted a short time before a shift in the balance of power at Argos led to its rejection. Such long-standing hostility had deep roots, and the Argives began work on their own long walls to link the city to its port on the coast some five miles distant. Still, the prospects for reviving an Argive-led alliance were poor, and Sparta's old enemy was not an immediate and pressing threat, if still a matter of concern in the longer term. Elsewhere, the Spartans did much to re-establish their dominance in the Peloponnese, which was such an important basis for their security. Mantineia returned to the fold, as did other communities, although the situation at Elis is less clear. Athens was not inclined to act against Sparta without allies and shifted attention to restoring its position in the north-east. Both cities decided not to see the active involvement of Athenians on the side of Argos or their presence at Mantineia as sufficient reason to declare the Peace of Nicias at an end. Most of the leading Athenians and Spartans did not want to resume all-out hostilities for the moment, so pretended not to notice the blatant violations of the treaty.[22]

23

LUST FOR GLORY

*The dashing Alcibiades and the Athenian
expedition to Sicily, 418–413 BC*

SPARTA AND ATHENS REMAINED AT PEACE AND PLEDGED TO A defensive alliance. Neither had fulfilled all of its obligations according to the terms of the treaty, and the Athenians were still at Pylos, while the Spartans backed the independence from Athens of Amphipolis and other cities in the area. There was friction between the two states, as well as a good deal of provocation, especially on the part of the Athenians, but so far all of this stayed within limits. Neither side wanted a resumption of all-out war for the moment or felt it would be justified in the eyes of the wider Hellenic world in the current circumstances. At Sparta, the premature attack on Plataea launched by its Theban allies in 431 BC loomed large in memory, and that violation of proper conduct offered an explanation for the overall disappointing outcome of its war effort. There is a strong sense that most Spartan leaders wanted to ensure that any renewal of the struggle with Athens happened only in circumstances where all would agree that Sparta was behaving reasonably and correctly.[1]

In contrast to ever secretive Sparta, Athens seems to have had more debate. Memories of plague and defeats were fading, especially among the younger men who had not been adults during the worst times. Though not perfect in its scope or implementation, the Peace of Nicias at the very least demonstrated Spartan respect for Athens, and Athenian power remained an obvious reality. Athens's citizen population was recovering when it came to numbers, most significantly those of military age, helped by the absence of the plague for the best part of a decade and the promotion in class of poorer citizens granted land as cleruchs in allied territory. Those allies knew their place, because Athenian might was obvious to all and the price of rebellion so terrible. More money came in each year as tribute than in the past, funding naval might, military campaigns, and the active participation in public life permitted by salaried jobs for citizens. Some, perhaps most, Athenians realised that as a consequence of this greater exploitation of the allies, resentment of Athenian leadership had hardened into a deep hatred. Yet Athens was strong, its dominance of the seas giving it immense reach, and its allies were so much weaker that their feelings did not matter too much, at least in the opinion of Athenians. Ultimately the allies had no real choice but to obey or face extinction.[2]

This brutal equation was paraded for all to see in 416 BC, when the Athenians decided that they could no longer allow the island of Melos to remain independent. Their earlier expedition during the war had failed, merely ravaging the land before withdrawing, but resources had been strained then; now the Athenians could devote more of their strength to the task. Athens presented the Melian leaders with a stark ultimatum either to submit or face dire punishment. Thucydides presents the Athenian arguments as entirely cynical. For them, this demand was not about justice or right and wrong, and the Melians should face reality rather than hoping in vain for divine assistance. They were weak, and Athens was so very much stronger that resistance was hopeless. If the Melians chose to fight, then they would lose and must accept whatever punishment the Athenians chose to inflict. The negotiations, uniquely presented by Thucydides as a back-and-forth dialogue, asserted that power alone mattered. In spite of these threats, the Melians refused to give in and fought with stubbornness to defend their homes. It did not matter: Might prevailed, and the Athenians executed all the men and sold the women and children as slaves.[3]

Athens was strong, very strong, and the Athenians saw no reason at all why they should not grow ever stronger and more prosperous. For all the setbacks and suffering, the belief remained very deep that they were special, that their political system was the best possible, and that their power and success were natural and deserved. Equally natural was a desire to expand that power as far as possible and even a sense that they ought to do whatever they could to make Athens more powerful. The hardships of the recent war had diminished only a little the restless ambition of the Athenians and their quickness to plan and act on any opportunity. Some voices, chief among them Nicias, the negotiator of the treaty with Sparta, urged caution and consolidation, at least in the short term. They advocated rebuilding and recovering the lost territories in the Chalcidice and along the Thracian coast rather than seeking new adventures. Others disagreed, impatient for the Athenians to prove their merit by winning fresh successes and adding to their imperial might. The logic was familiar. Security came through power and strength recognised by others, however reluctantly. Caution or hesitation when opportunities beckoned would likely be seen as weakness.

MOST PROMINENT AMONG the speakers advocating boldness in dealing with the wider world was Alcibiades, the same man who three years earlier, as strategos, had encouraged the Athenians to ally with Argos. He had not been elected to the post for the following year and was not at Mantineia, but there is no sign that the ultimate failure of this policy dented his popularity. Alcibiades was very much the aristocrat, with connections to the Alcmaeonids and other important families. When his father was killed serving as a general at Coronea in 447 BC, the young Alcibiades was taken into and raised in the house of Pericles, his close relative by marriage, placing him near the centre of public life from his earliest years. Very much an aristocrat even among other aristocrats, with inherited status, connections, and wealth matched by few and surpassed by none in the Athens of his day, Alcibiades was well placed to play a prominent role in the politics of his city. For all the opportunities open to any citizen in the democracy of Athens, no one who was not wealthy seems ever to have risen to high office and influence, while distinguished ancestry remained a great advantage.[4]

It helped that Alcibiades looked like a hero. Artists in fifth century BC Greece celebrated the human form for its beauty and most of all idealised the young, athletic male form, and Alcibiades was famous for his exceptional good looks. He was handsome, but more than that, though his manner was utterly self-assured, even arrogant, he possessed such style in the way he walked, spoke, and acted that onlookers admired him rather than being offended. Alcibiades charmed people—at least, most people most of the time—so that they excused outbursts of pettiness and cruelty and his flouting of convention in his dress and behaviour. In his gilded youth, he was said to have been pursued by many men eager for his affections. As an adult he consorted openly with courtesans and seduced other men's wives. When his own wife grew weary of this and decided to divorce him, he turned up in the court and simply led her back home—and got away with it. Socrates was very fond of him, and in this case the sources stress that theirs was an entirely intellectual, not physical, relationship.[5]

Alcibiades had the physical beauty, skill with words, and swagger of one of Homer's characters, and if he lacked their exceptional military prowess, his record was certainly decent enough. He had served as a hoplite at Potidaea, where he was wounded and protected by Socrates, although in the aftermath the philosopher led the call to have Alcibiades decorated for his valour rather than the other way around, for such were the realities of politics. At Delium, Alcibiades served as a cavalryman, and during the retreat he stuck with Socrates again, helping the much older man lead out the others who had rallied to him in the face of the Theban pursuit. Then came his term as general and a competent if minor raiding operation in the Peloponnese in 419 BC. Alongside service to the state in war, he added to his own and his city's prestige by competing at the Olympics. At one games, perhaps in 416 BC, or maybe four or just possibly eight years earlier, he entered no fewer than seven chariot teams in the competition, winning first, second, and fourth places. Others drove the chariots, but he was the owner, the man who selected the horses and cars and supervised the training. In a sport dominated in recent decades by the Spartans, his success was on an unprecedented scale. At home, like his father before him, he was lavish whenever he acted as producer for plays at the Dionysia or took part in other festivals.[6]

Yet, for all that Alcibiades reflected very old traditions of what it meant to be a noble and good man, he lived in a democracy, fought alongside his fellow citizens, and was able to lead only when they elected him to office or were persuaded by him in the Assembly. The rich were granted a degree of licence, if rarely as much as someone like Alcibiades, but were still expected to obey the laws and more generally to show respect to the community. Their wealth, often in the form of rural estates, gave them an income and spared them from the need to work, which left them free both for public life and other activities. Well attested in art and on the stage, and archaeologically through the vessels for serving and drinking wine, was the aristocratic drinking club, the *symposium* of at least twelve but never more than twenty members.[7]

Perhaps many Athenians aspired to such entertainment, although only a minority could afford to belong to such clubs, and their exclusiveness was part of the appeal, marking the members out as different from the mass of the population. They assembled at one of their houses, using a room set aside for this purpose, as another sign that only the well off could enjoy such an activity. One, usually the host for that night, took the lead, decreeing how much water to mix with the wine before it was served. Greek wine—like most ancient wines—tended to be strong, so that only barbarians drank it undiluted, which quickly made them drunk and could lead to insanity. The leader also set the tone—of earnest debate, literary recitation, or bawdy exchange, often of competition in insulting each other, or a progression through all of these and more. Respectable women were banned altogether, one reason why such parties were held in a part of the house wholly separate from the women's quarters. On the other hand, female entertainers were often present, playing flutes and other instruments and sometimes providing sexual services, or more expensive professional courtesans might offer wit and conversation as well as sex. Athenian *symposia* were far less regulated than the meetings of Spartan mess mates, even if they fell broadly within the same idea of how well-off Greek men ought to interact with fellow citizens of similar status.[8]

There was no doubt a good deal of variety in the nature of Athenian *symposia*, as there was in the personalities and tastes of those belonging to these clubs. Some were opportunities for excess—in drunkenness, boasting, and insults, or in consumption of luxuries and conspicuously expensive foods, or in sex with women or boys or both—while at the other extreme they were convivial but far more restrained and serious. Plato wrote an account of one heavily idealised gathering, where deep issues were discussed, set in late 416 BC around the time of the brutal punishment of Melos. Part way through, his participants hear the sound of flute players outside and are joined by Alcibiades, already fairly drunk but still able to join in and debate with Socrates. Whether riotous or very serious, these clubs set their members apart not only from the less well off but from their peers, since they bonded the participants together. Associations based on *symposia* extended into every aspect of life, including politics, and though this is hard to trace in any detail, belonging to one club shaped attitudes to those who were members of another, as rivals, friends, or even enemies. Pericles stood apart from all of this by avoiding such celebrations altogether, and others, for instance Nicias, followed the same path. That in turn was a statement of where a man stood, in this case showing that his loyalties lay with the state, in essence the entire community, and not before that with a circle of friends. Though wealthy and, in Pericles's case, from the nobility, they pledged themselves to be men of the city. Other aristocrats showed allegiance to the wider community in other ways, while at the same time setting themselves apart from it. After a *symposium*, the party commonly paraded through the streets, accompanied by torch bearers and musicians. Sometimes they insulted or even physically assaulted passers-by, showing off that they were more powerful and, in essence, better than everyone else—a difficult practice to stop in the unpoliced darkness.[9]

AT THE START of the Peloponnesian War in 431 BC, Pericles had urged the Athenians to concentrate on the struggle with Sparta and not to seek to expand elsewhere, but Pericles was long dead, and for the moment there was a wary peace with the Spartans. In late 416 or early 415 BC envoys came from the city of Segesta in Sicily, asking for help in a dispute with a neighbouring city, in turn backed by Syracuse. The people of Segesta were not considered ethnically Greek, although at some point they claimed descent from Trojan refugees, connecting themselves in this way to that most revered episode of the Hellenic past. Still, Segesta was a city-state very like those of Greece, while Sicily was home to many definitely Greek communities. The Athenians had long shown an interest in the western part of the Hellenic world, in Italy and Sicily. Back in 434/3 BC, the leaders of Corcyra had stressed that their island was well placed for access to these regions, convinced that this would attract the Athenians. Then, during the Archidamian War, expeditions had gone to Sicily, intervening in the rivalries between the cities there. All this was relatively modest in scale, and even if it did not achieve much, the forces sent there had not suffered serious losses before returning home.[10]

Enthusiasm for intervening in Sicily grew rapidly, especially after some Athenians were sent to Segesta, presented with sixty talents of silver to help fund an expedition, and promised far more. Tales spread of the wealth of Sicily, and Plutarch claims that it was common to hear groups of Athenians discussing the island or sketching out rough maps of it in the dirt. Prophecies circulated that were interpreted as promising grand successes, until more and more Athenians fell in love with the idea of sending an expedition to the west. Thucydides described the mood as a form of *eros*—love, passion, even lust—for the strength of the desire and longing. This gave a momentum to what followed as citizens assembled and debated the idea. At first the plans were fairly modest, on much the same scale as the earlier commitment, so that sixty triremes were to go under a single commander.[11]

Not everyone was convinced, and one of the most prominent critics was Nicias, who had proven himself as a general in command of several successful operations during the war with Sparta and had then led the negotiations for peace. Well into middle age or older, he spoke with the authority of his years as well as his past record, although some cynics carped that he had done well militarily because he only ever accepted commands with low risks. Wealthy, because all who were able to influence the Assembly over a long period were rich, Nicias did not hail from the old aristocracy. Most of his income—and presumably that of his father before him—came from hiring out gangs of slaves as labourers in the mines at Laurium. Perhaps through temperament, sincere belief, or political calculation, Nicias was always generous in staging productions or equipping triremes and was known especially for his gifts to shrines and religious festivals—for instance, in the fairly recent redevelopment of the

Temple of Apollo on Delos. In his lifestyle, actions, and age, he was very different from Alcibiades, who had emerged as the most strident voice in favour of backing Segesta and going to Sicily and who was about thirty-five and not noted for his piety.[12]

In the past, Alcibiades had urged his fellow citizens to do all they could to weaken Sparta in the Peloponnese—for instance, by aiding Argos. More generally, he appears to have seen adding to Athens's power as worthwhile for its own sake. Thucydides does not mention him in connection with Melos, although later tradition claimed that he was eager and bought a young slave woman from among the captives and kept her as a concubine. He and Nicias seem often to have clashed during debates, which did not mean that they were always in opposition on every topic. Around this time, the Assembly decided to hold a vote of ostracism for the first time in a couple of decades. Plutarch records a tradition that Nicias and Alcibiades, seeing that they were both at risk, secretly agreed to cooperate, with the result that a rabble-rousing nonentity was expelled instead. This was the last time the process was ever employed.[13]

Alcibiades was keen on the Sicilian expedition and clearly hoped for the command to lead it. Yet sixty ships was not a vast force, suggesting that his ambitions were also on a limited scale at this stage. Nicias was not keen even on this level of commitment and decided to convince his fellow citizens to abandon the idea by stressing the size of Sicily and the strength and resources of its inhabitants. He assured them that sixty ships were far too few to achieve anything worthwhile against such odds and might even lead to a serious defeat. The ploy backfired when other speakers urged him to say how many ships and soldiers a serious intervention in Sicily really needed and, once he had answered, promptly voted to follow his advice. This created an expedition well over double the size of the original plan, with three commanders, Nicias, Alcibiades, and Lamachus, the latter well respected as a commander but less prominent politically. This board of three received considerable licence to act on their own initiative, which made sense given the distances involved and the time it would take for messages to pass to and from Athens to the expedition. Amphipolis was over 200 miles away from Athens, but any practical sailing route from Athens to Syracuse was at least four times longer, and western Sicily was even more distant. The decree ordering the expedition made no explicit mention of Syracuse, even though, as the largest and most powerful state on the island, it was the key to everything and expected to be hostile.[14]

When preparations for the grand expedition were almost complete, an event occurred that even Thucydides felt unable to explain. A herm was a stone pillar topped by a carved head of the god Hermes, usually shown as bearded. There was sometimes an inscription and always a carving of an erect penis on the front. The Pisistratids had set them up in the heart of the city and at midway points on all the roads leading to other communities in Attica, and there were many more outside houses and on other boundaries of one sort or another. One morning, the Athenians woke to find that almost all the herms in Athens itself had been defaced, the carvings broken, which required some effort and a tool like a hammer, for these were not fragile objects. This was a terrible omen, all the more worrying on the brink of the great expedition to Sicily. Talk of drunken aristocrats wandering after a *symposium* and smashing things for no reason faded as the sheer scale of what had been done sank in. Around 100, perhaps more, herms were involved, suggesting that the vandalism was the work of a considerable number of people. If it was not one club of rich men, then perhaps quite a few of these groups had joined together and organised the destruction, the shared desecration binding them together perhaps for an even more sinister purpose. There was talk of a planned revolution to overthrow the democracy, something easy enough to imagine, given the frequency of similar revolutions in other states. If that was the explanation, then a dreadful threat loomed.[15]

Alcibiades, blue-blooded, heroic in his looks and manner, and an Olympic victor, was an obvious candidate as would-be tyrant or leader of an oligarchic coup and soon came under suspicion. His involvement was highly improbable, since the project most likely to be cancelled as a result of the bad omen was the very expedition on which he was so keen. Perhaps another group, opposed to him or to the operation itself, did the deed in the hope that it would be called off, but since no one ever managed to establish the culprits or the motive, it is impossible to say. At the time, rumours spread, and accusations were made, as the mood grew ever more nervous and suspicious. Plenty of people saw this as a chance to hurt a personal or political rival, and informers came forward with all sorts of claims, often unconnected with the desecration of the herms. Alcibiades was one of a number of aristocrats accused of staging in their homes versions of the secret and sacred Mysteries of Eleusis, suggesting arrogant, probably drunken acts of parody, perhaps also meant to bind a group together by involving them all in the same profane secret. Alcibiades demanded the right to a trial before the expedition set out, but enemies in the Assembly blocked this, most likely feeling that he was easier to damage in his absence, when his charisma could not sway a jury. Thus the fleet set out with one of its commanders under deep suspicion of having committed a serious crime that might damage Athens's relationship with the divine powers that had let her grow so strong.[16]

Even so, the departure of the fleet was a spectacular and joyous occasion, the ships decorated and painted to make as good a show as possible and the most enthusiastic captains racing each other as far as the island of Aegina. Athens provided 100 triremes, 40 of them converted into troop transports, and the allies provided another 34 warships. There were 5,100 hoplites, some 2,000 of these Athenian, as well as supporting archers and light infantry, although just a tiny contingent of 30 cavalrymen. The main force travelled around the Peloponnese and along the west coast to Corcyra, where the allies joined them. From there they crossed to Italy, which was still a long haul for the crowded triremes. In the past, smaller Athenian squadrons had found a welcome in many coastal cities, but this time the various Greek and Italiote communities proved wary of such a great armada, off to do who knew what. Rarely were the Athenians allowed into harbours, let alone a city itself, and some communities refused to deal with them at all.[17]

While the main fleet proceeded at a moderate pace down the Italian coast, three ships rushed ahead to make contact with existing and potential allies in Sicily. When these returned, they brought disappointing news, most of all from Segesta, where the authorities had admitted that they did not have the additional money promised to help fund the expedition. The original Athenian envoys had been duped by a ploy worthy of Odysseus, in which all the wealth of the entire community had been piled into the houses of their hosts to create an impression of vast resources. Clearly plans needed to change, most of all over how to fund the expedition, and each of the three commanders had a different opinion. Lamachus urged an immediate attack on Syracuse, trusting to surprise to carry the day, while Alcibiades wanted to send envoys to as many communities as possible to secure allies and only then to attack. Nicias, the most cautious, suggested that they go to Segesta, put on a show of force, hope that this pressured their neighbours to make concessions, and then go back home, having achieved little but lost nothing. Alcibiades got his way, although the results proved modest. A few allies were gained, but most cities were reluctant to commit at this early stage.[18]

While all this was happening, the mood in Athens had turned ever more suspicious, as successive informers came forward, men were arrested, and some blamed others to protect themselves. There were executions, and quite a few of those under suspicion fled abroad to save themselves. Alcibiades and a few others with the expedition were formally charged with profaning the Eleusinian Mysteries, and a trireme was sent to Sicily to arrest them and bring them back for trial. When it arrived, Alcibiades feigned compliance but travelled in his own ship in company with the one sent to arrest him. Part way through the journey, he slipped away. Plutarch claims that when asked why he did not trust his fellow citizens to give him justice, he replied that he would not have trusted his own mother when his very life was at stake. Being charged in this way was a blow to his honour, apart from the real threat to his life, given that others had already fallen victim to this witch hunt. Abandoning his home city, Alcibiades went after a while to Sparta, a nobleman chased into exile by rivals.[19]

This left the expedition with two commanders instead of three and near the end of the summer, they agreed to move on Syracuse. False information fed to the Syracusans by an agent lured their army away, allowing the Athenians to sail to and land outside the city unopposed. For most of them, this was their first real sight of Syracuse, and the prospect was daunting. The city was big, one of the biggest in the Greek world, with a population and resources on a par with those of Athens. By now it was also a democracy, less radical in its involvement of all male citizens in so many aspects of public business than Athens, but still a democracy. Also, unlike Athens, it stood on the coast, with no need for long walls to link it to a port. A smaller harbour formed part of the city itself, while to the south a wide, open bay, only in part closed off by an island, formed the Great Harbour, a natural landing place where the Athenians had arrived. On its return, the Syracusan army had no intention of submitting. Its troops were determined, if lacking recent experience of warfare. The Athenians advanced against them and, after a struggle, put them to flight. This done, they set up a trophy of victory and sailed away because the campaigning season was almost over and they did not feel ready to impose a blockade.[20]

The first year of the expedition to Sicily had achieved little, interrupted by the removal of Alcibiades and also rendered slow and tentative by the deep caution of Nicias. Back in Athens, during the original debate, the latter had emphasised that Sicily, and Syracuse in particular, boasted large numbers of good cavalrymen and that the country lent itself to their use. In spite of this, the Athenians had taken only a handful of their own horsemen with them, and this was already proving a weakness. At the battle outside Syracuse, the Athenian phalanx had broken the Syracusan one, despite its being twice as deep, with sixteen ranks. Yet the victory was limited because the Syracusan horsemen had covered the retreat of their hoplites, so that few were killed or captured. Nicias and Lamachus sent back to Athens asking for more cavalrymen, judging that sealing off Syracuse without them would be very hard.[21]

THIS WAS NOT the only appeal for aid from Greece during the winter months, for the Syracusans requested Spartan assistance. Alcibiades was there and recommended that the Spartan leaders agree to this as in their own best interests. After initial caution, he had won over many leading Spartans, throwing himself into their lifestyle, letting his hair grow long, and apparently revelling in the spare talk and even more basic meals of the communal messes. Now, the Athenian exile told his hosts that they were in danger. As he described it, Syracuse and Sicily were just the beginning of Athenian ambition in the west, and once these were taken, they would seek to overrun Carthage, with its great empire, and mainland Italy as well, at which point they could turn all these resources against Sparta for a final showdown. For their own protection, the Spartans must view the Athenians as enemies and prevent them from growing so strong. He urged them to send a Spartan commander to Syracuse and also to strike at Attica itself, not simply launching a short invasion but establishing a fortified base at Decelea. For the moment, the ephors and council would agree only to the first, and the degree to which Alcibiades influenced them or they came to this conclusion on their own is unclear. For later Greeks, and especially for Athenians like Thucydides, the Athenian turncoat had showed the simple, overcautious Spartans how to do the most damage to Athens.[22]

In 414 BC Nicias and Lamachus were joined by 250 cavalrymen sent from home, albeit in most cases without horses, which were difficult to transport safely. As hoped, purchasing these locally proved possible, and other contingents of cavalry were secured from allies, who were beginning to grow in number. Even so, throughout the rest of the war, the Syracusan cavalry was more numerous and, because of this, far more effective than its counterparts, and this proved a serious disadvantage from the Athenian point of view. In spite of this, they once again arrived outside Syracuse suddenly, surprising the defenders, perhaps in part because they had landed in a different place. The heights of Epipolae overlooked the city and were seen as vital, but in another example of their inexperience, the Syracusans had not secured them, and the troops stationed there were swiftly overwhelmed. Establishing bases on either side of the city, the Athenians began work on a wall to surround it.[23]

The operations that followed were not about large battles in the open but consisted of long days of toil, interspersed with skirmishes, threats, and occasional sudden local attacks. Hoplites still played a part, alongside various lightly equipped and missile-armed troops, as well as the cavalry. The Syracusans built their own wall, designed to cut across the path of the Athenian siege rampart before this had reached that point. If achieved, this would prevent the attackers from cutting off the city by land. Most of the time, the fighting that did develop favoured the Athenians, and they tended to win the sharp encounters fought to take outposts or hinder the work of the rival gangs of wall builders. In one of these little victories, Lamachus, rushing into combat to aid an isolated group of hoplites, was killed. Plutarch reported that he was challenged to single combat by a Syracusan aristocrat on horseback and killed him but sustained a mortal wound in the process. Whether or not this happened, the Athenians now had a single commander in Nicias, the one man who had most opposed the very concept of the expedition at the start.[24]

In contrast, a couple of Corinthian ships had managed to run the dangers of interception and get into the small harbour at Syracuse. With them came Gylippus, the Spartan sent as military advisor. In

Thucydides's account he arrived at a moment when spirits were so low that the Syracusans were on the point of opening negotiations. His immense self-confidence, combined with the Spartan reputation for supreme skill in all military matters, rallied them and even survived an initial setback, when he led them into an attack and was defeated. Gylippus took the blame, explaining that he had fought in a confined area where the cavalry were of little use. He would not repeat the mistake, and afterwards he fought a very skilful war, with plenty of successes and no critical setbacks. Like Brasidas, Gylippus made great use of surprise, deception, and rapid movement—all characteristics supposedly inculcated in Spartan boys at an early age by their education and not generally associated with hoplites and phalanxes. Yet Gylippus was not a true Spartan peer by blood, for even though his father was Spartan, his mother may have been a helot. A wealthy family had sponsored his education, and he was accepted into the community of peers on his merits, and most likely as a reflection of the desperate shortage of citizens following the earthquakes and helot risings. Then, to complicate his life further, his father, a friend of King Pleistonax, was implicated alongside him in taking bribes and similarly exiled. Gylippus had a lot to prove to the wider Spartan community and proceeded to do this to great effect at Syracuse, demonstrating his sound tactical judgement and courage. Unlike Brasidas, he lacked the knack of making the Syracusans love him, but this did not matter because they respected his talents and, for the moment, knew they needed him.[25]

The contrast in leadership between the two sides was stark. It was not that Nicias was incompetent, and his forces did try to press the blockade and did not simply react to enemy activity. Yet he had never commanded an operation on such a large scale and so difficult in its nature, and he may well have been out of his depth. His lack of faith in the whole enterprise appears to have sapped his energy, a problem made worse by his being a sick man with kidney trouble. He did make several major errors—for instance, having his men work on an unimportant section of the siege wall instead of the critical sector so that they lost the race to the Syracusans, who extended their own wall across the path of the Athenian one, rendering the latter next to useless. Alcibiades or Lamachus—or almost anyone else—would most likely have pushed the siege even harder, believing in victory. Even so, the whole project required so much to go right that the prospects had never been all that good.[26]

Nicias was even less sanguine and sent a gloomy letter back to Athens reporting on the state of the campaign. His ships were in a poorer state than the enemy's because he had no chance of drawing them up on land to dry out the hulls. Many of his rowers and other hired men were deserting, leaving to seek better pay elsewhere, while the men who remained were falling sick. The commander of the Athenian expedition clearly wished for orders to withdraw and lead everyone back home, but, as in his earlier speech to the Assembly, pride and concern for his own reputation confused his message and led to the opposite result. Instead of recalling the expedition, the Athenians voted to reinforce it on a grand scale in 413 BC, with more ships, more men, and more money and with Demosthenes, the hero of Pylos, as one of its commanders. The enemy was also gaining fresh support, if in nowhere near the same numbers. Around 1,500 troops came from the Peloponnese, 600 of them helot volunteers like the ones that had served so well under Brasidas, and allies in Sicily also sent contingents.[27]

Gylippus received this boost to his forces first, and quickly set them to work, aggressively pushing back against the Athenians both on land and on sea. His men did not have it all their own way, but they did where it really mattered and seized several key positions. In the restricted waters of the Great Harbour, the Athenians just about held their own, although, even there, they were losing ground for their onshore bases. Around this time, no doubt on the advice of the Corinthians who had come with Gylippus, the Syracusans worked to strengthen the prows of their triremes. This was a Corinthian

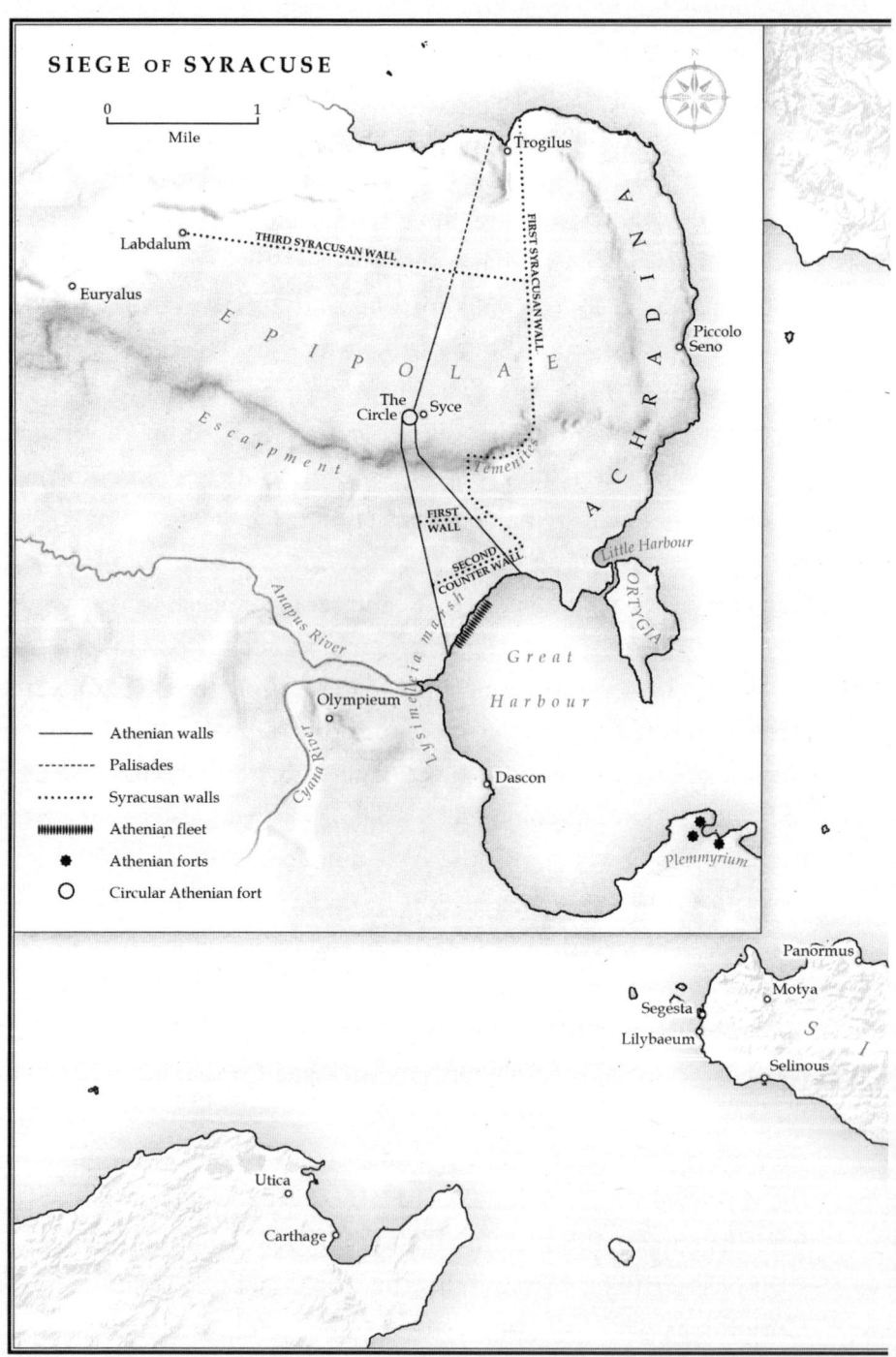

SICILY AND SOUTHERN ITALY

innovation and a recognition of the difficulty of matching the manoeuvrability of the light Athenian ships with their superb crews. Instead, they planned to ram them bow against bow, relying on their stronger build to inflict more damage than they suffered. Learning that Demosthenes was on the way, Gylippus launched more and bigger attacks, and the newly modified triremes did well, for the lack of space in the Great Harbour made it much harder for the Athenian ships to use their normal tactics. The Syracusans did not win the first big encounter, but holding the Athenians to a draw was a considerable achievement in its own right. A lot of Athenian ships were badly damaged, adding to the overall poor condition of Nicias's squadrons. A second battle resulted in a clear Syracusan victory.[28]

Soon after this, Demosthenes arrived with seventy-three triremes and another 5,000 hoplites as well as supporting troops. He also brought a fresh spirit of aggression and very quickly attempted, and failed, to capture the wall built by the defenders. A larger and bolder night attack from a different direction followed. It started well, but Greek hoplites and other troops were not accustomed to fighting at night, and darkness magnified all the confusion of a battle in daylight. Initial success broke down into chaos, then panic, in part because some of the Athenian allies sang the battle chant, the paean, in the same way as their Syracusan enemies and were mistakenly believed to be hostile. The assault failed, leaving an even larger number of Athenians crowded into a poor and rather unhealthy position. Demosthenes was all for withdrawal to consolidate in allied territory on the island. Nicias was against this, assuring his fellow generals that his spies within Syracuse were telling him that the defenders were short of money, low in spirits, and on the brink of surrender. The natural instinct to believe what he most wanted to hear convinced Nicias, who in turn convinced his colleagues, to stay, even though the end of summer was near.[29]

The Syracusans did not surrender, and Gylippus went off and returned, bringing more allies. Eventually Nicias accepted the truth and agreed to abandon what was left of the blockade and retreat to allied territory. Then, before this move commenced, there was a lunar eclipse on the night of 27 August 413 BC. Rational men, of whom there were more than a few among the Athenians, understood that this was a natural event, but many others, including Nicias, interpreted it as a dire warning from the gods. On advice from seers, he ordered the suspension of all plans for three times nine days—effectively, until the next lunar cycle. Thus the Athenians stayed where they were and waited. During this period, the Syracusans made another big attack against the Athenian ships in the Grand Harbour. Coordination was poor between the old fleet and the newer reinforcements, which led to the Athenian formation breaking up and being swept back to shore, losing eighteen out of the eighty-six triremes they had at the start. In the aftermath, they did manage to avoid a fire ship sent against them by the Syracusans but could not prevent the enemy from making a boom of chains and anchored ships to seal off the harbour, effectively cutting them off from supply by sea and escape.[30]

With great effort the Athenians floated and manned 110 triremes, cramming them with troops in an attempt to break through the barrier. Watched and cheered on by the armies on shore and in the city, the Athenians fought a bitter battle as they tried to get through the boom, all the while under attack from Syracusan ships. Losses were heavy on both sides, many from missiles thrown or shot by soldiers on the decks of the rival ships, but eventually the Athenians gave up. That night, Demosthenes and Nicias agreed to try again on the next day, for some sixty ships were still in good-enough shape, and this was more than the Syracusans could muster. Yet, when they gave the orders, the crews refused to embark, such were the depths to which morale had sunk in this part of the once supreme Athenian navy. Simultaneously, the Syracusans were too busy celebrating the victory to give much thought to their enemies.[31]

Two days later the Athenians marched away inland, half the army in the lead under Demosthenes and the other half following under Nicias. Each group formed a square, with hoplites on the outside and the less well armed, as well as the slaves, camp followers, and baggage, sheltered in the centre. Retreat by land was their only option, since they were sealed into the Great Harbour, and they left behind their remaining ships, as well as the sick and wounded incapable of keeping up. Thucydides claimed that the retreating army had 40,000 men, but this figure seems very high, even if half or more were non-combatants. Calculations based on his earlier numbers and the assumption that every trireme not used as transport began with its full complement of men produce a figure on this scale or even larger for the total number sent on the expedition. Casualties from the fighting and the likely heavier toll from disease and desertion cannot be estimated. The odds are that nothing like so many men were left by this last stage of the campaign, but nothing is certain.[32]

Progress was slow for these unwieldy formations and made slower still as the Syracusans began to pay them more and more attention. The Athenians went barely five miles on the first day and less on the second. The aim was to get to allied territory, but nothing was easy. Syracusans occupied a hill in front of them, and successive attacks failed to force them off it, which meant that the columns had to change their route. Even so, the Athenians smashed another force blocking their path, and then Nicias gained some time by leaving fires lit in his camp and setting out at night, but he failed to coordinate this move with the other half of the army. By now the two columns had separated further than was ideal, allowing the Syracusans to close in on and overwhelm Demosthenes. He eventually surrendered on a promise that none of his men would be executed or starved to death. One tradition claimed that Demosthenes himself then tried to commit suicide but succeeded only in giving himself a nasty wound. Shown proof that this defeat and surrender had happened, Nicias tried to make a deal, offering payment to let his force go free. The offer was rejected, and the Athenians staggered on, tired, hungry, and very thirsty. What discipline was left cracked altogether when they reached a river and men stampeded towards it to drink from the muddy water, most of them oblivious to the Syracusans attacking them. Many were slaughtered, barely resisting. Nicias surrendered to Gylippus, and gradually the Spartan managed to stop the killing and take prisoners.[33]

Gylippus wanted to take the two Athenian leaders back to Sparta as trophies and useful hostages, but the Syracusans now had less need of his military expertise and resented his manner and alleged greed. Demosthenes and Nicias were both executed in the first, but not the last, violation of the terms of surrender. The fate of the rest of the captives was often little better, although a high proportion had already been taken off as individuals and groups by the various allied contingents. Around 1,000 were held by the Syracusans in open quarries near the city, crowded and exposed to the sun in the daytime and the increasingly bitter cold at night. Rations were meagre, and sickness quickly spread; those who died were left to decay where they were, adding to the appalling conditions. Some of the survivors were still there eight months later. Others were sold off as slaves, and Thucydides noted that those able to recite passages of Euripides were prized and treated well. Some men were ransomed, and some escaped, so that over time they were able to make their way home, but the vast majority who had set out with such high hopes in 415 BC or in the reinforcement of 413 BC never came back. Altogether some 3,000 Athenian citizens serving as hoplites and many more as rowers and specialists in the fleet were lost.[34]

The Sicilian expedition was a disaster for Athens, appallingly costly in lives for a population only beginning to recover from the dreadful losses inflicted by the plague. At the same time, sending so many ships and men and paying and supplying them during a campaign stretching to three years had been very expensive, devouring the city's annual revenue and eating into its reserves. The lives and the money had both been wasted, for nothing worthwhile was achieved to balance the losses. Athenian expeditions had failed before but never on this scale and at this cost. At the same time, the Athenians, so long the masters of the sea, had been held to draws and then beaten more than once in naval battles. Athenians at the time, and historians thereafter, discussed who was most to blame for the disaster. Thucydides expressed sadness that Nicias had suffered execution, deeming him a man of excellent character and worth who did not deserve such a fate, while at the same time recording all his mistakes.[35]

However decent he was in terms of character, Nicias was without doubt the wrong man to lead this expedition, although that might not have mattered if the Athenians had not recalled Alcibiades and then Lamachus had not fallen in battle. Ultimately, the Athenians willingly embarked on an unnecessary and very risky operation. The Assembly debated and approved its scale and chose its commanders, though its instructions seem to have been fuzzy about precisely what they were to do when they reached Sicily. To fight a war on this scale at such a vast distance was ambitious, verging on the foolhardy. Chance placed Nicias in sole charge, and perhaps a far more aggressive leader like Alcibiades would have achieved more, but the willingness of the Assembly to change its mind robbed the expedition of Alcibiades. At the same time Athenian citizens' tendency to be vindictive against commanders who performed poorly made Nicias hesitate too often and for too long during the campaign, fearing the consequences for being thought to pull out too soon. Ultimately, Nicias was the man on the spot and in charge, and his judgement was poor. Perhaps if the Athenians had withdrawn far earlier, even in those last weeks when he waited for the next moon, then the campaign would have been a failure rather than a catastrophe. As it was, it marked the turning point in the struggle between Athens and Sparta.

Before the final disaster in Sicily, the two cities were already back in a state of open war. Although the Spartans had sent Gylippus to

Syracuse, they remained reluctant to begin hostilities until 414 BC, when Athenian ships raided Spartan territory. This was judged a sufficient violation of the peace treaty to nullify it, and in 413 BC, King Agis of Sparta led an army into Attica. Alcibiades may have accompanied them, and either way his advice was followed, for instead of roving the fields for a few weeks, the invaders built a fort at Decelea, just fifteen miles from Athens. Once the position was secure, a garrison was left behind, and the main army withdrew. From then on, there was always a Spartan-led force in Attica, able to raid and retreat back behind the shelter of its walls. Though fewer in number than a big army, it posed a permanent threat and, in the years that followed, inflicted far more damage to the Athenians economically and also in terms of pride. Thucydides claimed that some 20,000 slaves fled their masters and were given sanctuary at Decelea and then led out of Attica altogether. At the same time, he says the Athenians felt they were under siege and constantly on guard. Simply to defend against a possible attack, larger numbers of Athenians than ever before were required to serve under arms for long periods. What Pylos was to the Spartans, Decelea became to the Athenians, and in most important respects it was worse, for it was right in their heartland rather than on a distant shore. In spite of the short distance, the Athenians judged that they were incapable of capturing the fort before the Spartans could relieve it with an army and challenge them to a battle they could not afford to risk.[36]

Thus Alcibiades had inspired, or at the very least encouraged, another major blow against his home city. Over time his welcome at Sparta began to wear thin. Plutarch claimed that he had seduced the King Agis's wife and was widely believed to be the father of her most recent child, a boy, who would in later life be denied the kingship because of doubts about his paternity. Given the often bitter rivalries surrounding the royal families at Sparta, this slur may or may not have been true, but for whatever reason, Alcibiades gradually came to feel that his welcome might be running out. This was not the end of his story, and he was to play a role as important as it was controversial in the years to come. When he had escaped his Athenian escort and learned that he had been condemned to death in his absence, he was supposed to have said, 'I will show them that I am alive.' It was a promise that he kept.[37]

24

'SHIPS LOST...
DON'T KNOW WHAT TO DO'

*The final phase of the Peloponnesian War and
the great battles at sea, 413–405 BC*

ALTHOUGH ALCIBIADES HAD BEEN ONE OF THE MOST ENTHUsiastic supporters of the expedition to Sicily, his had still been one voice among many. A lot of Athenians had—as Thucydides put it—fallen in love with the idea of victories in this distant, yet still Greek, island. They had voted to send off the expedition on a grand scale, cheering the ships as they set out, and later, when events showed that the task was harder than expected, they had voted to reinforce rather than abandon the enterprise. The ultimate result in Sicily was the utter failure of 413 BC, with the loss of over 100 Athenian triremes and many thousands of citizens dead or captured, apart from the allied losses. Those who did return came slowly, in dribs and drabs, led by any ships and men who, for whatever reason, had not been with the main force in the final stages of the disaster. One tradition claimed that the very first inkling of the calamity came from a foreigner, a traveller who happened to stop at Athens and mentioned it to the barber who was shaving him, having assumed that it was already common knowledge. The barber, probably a slave, rushed to report it to the authorities, who arrested him for spreading false and dispiriting stories, even torturing him to make him recant. He was released as more reports came in.[1]

Reluctantly, naturally hoping that news so sudden and so terrible was not true, the Athenians came to accept the reality. Alongside the dismay, anger flared, as citizens who had voted with such eagerness to support the enterprise now blamed anyone who had spoken in favour of it. Fear stoked the rage, and the fear was reasonable, because the effort devoted to Sicily had drained the city's resources. A high proportion of the best fighters and crews were gone, as were most of the ships, while the treasury had very little left in reserve. Athens was weaker and more vulnerable than it had been in living memory, with enemies all around. In such an emergency it was decided to create an advisory board of ten men to guide both the *Boule* council and the Assembly in their actions. These were not picked by lot but carefully chosen on the basis of age and perceived wisdom. Sophocles the playwright, by this time in his eighties, was among them, and the evidence suggests that others were in their sixties or older. These men were expected to be careful and cautious, providing a check on the sort of reckless ambition that had brought the city to this point.[2]

Some Athenians expected a Syracusan fleet to appear off the Piraeus in a matter of days. In truth there was never any prospect of this, and no Syracusan aid came to assist the Spartans for more than a year. Yet the unavoidable reality was that the Athenian fleet was a shadow of its former self and would take time, money, and considerable effort to rebuild. The Athenians knew this, as did friend and foe in the wider world. Back in 431 BC, at the start of the war, the Spartans had talked of creating a great navy, but nothing had come of this, and its wartime naval operations had proved modest in scale and heavily reliant on the Corinthians and other allies. Now Sparta's leaders felt that at last they could hope to challenge the Athenians at sea and began to construct ships; at the same time, they instructed their allies to build more. They were encouraged as envoys arrived from states within the Athenian empire asking for aid if they rebelled.

At the very least, each revolt of an ally would reduce the tribute going to Athens and distract the Athenians; perhaps this was the moment when the whole edifice of their empire would come crashing down.[3]

The war changed profoundly after the disaster in Sicily. In the years that followed, the Spartans sometimes mustered 'the peers' and hoplites from their Peloponnesian allies to form a field army, but the role of such forces was at best secondary. No large pitched battles were fought on land for the remainder of the war. In itself, this was like most of the earlier fighting, given that Mantineia and Delium were the exceptional events, because the Athenians had consistently refused to risk a land battle in Attica. This did not change, but the Spartan leadership now accepted that its army was no longer the principal means for conducting the war. Decelea as a base in Athenian territory served as much or greater purpose than all the past invasions and ravaging of territory. More often than not, any army mustered reinforced the position at Decelea, mounting raiding expeditions and demonstrations of force from there.

The Spartans planned to win the war by breaking Athenian naval power directly, which led in due course to a succession of large naval battles, seven of them involving fleets of close to or greater than 100 triremes on each side. These were big battles and proved decisive, but of the tens of thousands of men to serve in the Spartan fleets, hardly any were actually Spartans. In each fleet the Corinthians or other coastal allies built or provided the vast majority of ships, so that the formally Spartan vessels were always a minority, rarely amounting to as many as a dozen and usually fewer; even in these, the crews were mostly foreign. Spartan peers did not serve on board ship except as senior officers. There may have been some perioeci, perhaps especially among the marines to fight on deck, but Spartan society could not permit helots to serve as rowers in the numbers required to crew even so few ships. In the campaigns that followed, the Spartans led and directed the war effort, providing the commanders for every fleet, quite a number of whom were killed. Otherwise, the Spartans did not fight or bleed for the cause. Sparta's war effort depended on outsiders, most of them professionals serving for pay.[4]

Building a fleet was very expensive, hence Sparta's reluctance to attempt it in the past, for its territory lacked the natural resources to provide this sort of wealth. The Spartans had no equivalent to the mines at Laurium. Once the ships were made, they required crews, who needed to be fed and paid as long as they were kept in service, with the important consideration that their effectiveness grew the longer they were at sea and training. The Athenians drew on the *thêtes* to provide a significant proportion of their rowers, supplementing these with resident foreigners and slaves, men from the allied communities, and, at least sometimes, some who came from abroad and served purely for pay. The last group probably grew in importance as the war progressed, and losses to plague and fighting eroded the other sources of manpower.[5]

Mercenary service in other states' wars had a very long tradition among the Greeks, although in the past it had mainly involved the hoplite class or its predecessors. Even in normal times, there were always men eager for adventure, and even more exiled from their home cities by political discord and revolution, all willing to fight for pay, and the struggle between Athens and Sparta had greatly added to their numbers. Fleets needed specialist deck crew and vast numbers of rowers, creating an ever-growing demand for anyone prepared to sign up. Such hired crewmen were often experienced, which was an advantage, and did their job well, at least as long as it suited them. Nicias complained that a lot of them serving in Sicily deserted once the campaign bogged down, slipping away in search of better pay and less dangerous work elsewhere. There was a danger that such men would drift to the most generous paymaster, so heavy reliance on this group made supporting a fleet even more expensive.[6]

When Sparta's leaders committed themselves to large-scale warfare at sea, they were fully aware that this was far more expensive than anything they had ever attempted in the past. Athenian weakness after Syracuse presented them with the opportunity, but they could not have taken it if envoys had not arrived at the same time from the Persian Empire. Two satraps governing regions on the Asian coast approached them, apparently independently; both offered financial and other support, and one sent an advance gift of twenty-five talents of silver. From the start, the creation of the Spartan-led Peloponnesian fleet depended on Persian money, fulfilling two Spartan ambitions expressed right at the start of the war of becoming a naval power and getting aid from Persia. For the best part of two decades, negotiations between Sparta and Persia had floundered—for instance, when the Persians complained that just what the Spartans wanted was unclear.[7]

The willingness to give aid now reflected a new situation and not simply the weakness of Athens. When Artaxerxes died after a long reign, a period of confusion followed as different leaders struggled to succeed him. Eventually Darius II—the name was taken on accession—took power and held on to it but faced rebellion in some areas. Tissaphernes, the satrap at Sardis and one of the pair dealing with the Spartans, secured his post by defeating his predecessor, who had rebelled. There are signs that the Athenians gave some support to at least one of these rebellions, a bold, if not necessarily wise, act on their part. The two new appointees were tasked with restoring order and also expected to reassert Darius II's right to take tribute from the Greek cities of Asia, which must have seemed more feasible given Athens's current weakness. Thus the satraps and the Spartans had a common enemy in the Athenians, and even if this did not mean that their wider objectives were the same, cooperation had advantages, at least for the moment.[8]

By 412 BC, a year after the disaster in Sicily, the Athenians faced threats on all sides, and the Spartans had more requests for aid than they could possibly answer. One of the satraps urged them to focus on the Dardanelles, conveniently adjacent to his province and also vital for the food and other resources on which the Athenians depended. At the same time, a group on Euboea, that large island so very close to Attica, asked for assistance if they rebelled, as did a delegation from Chios, the last remaining major ally to provide ships to Athens rather than paying tribute. As always, it is a mistake to speak of the Chians or the citizens of any other community as a simple unit acting with one voice. A faction wanting change believed that breaking away from Athens was beneficial and feasible. Similar groups appeared elsewhere, sometimes gathering enough momentum to seek support if they carried out a coup.

The Spartans decided to back the group on Chios, encouraged in this by Alcibiades. Yet there were delays, not least because the Corinthians insisted on waiting until the Isthmian Games, and the truce associated with them, came to an end. In this case, a Spartan ally proved more scrupulous in respecting a religious festival than the Spartans themselves. An earthquake prompted further delay, until eventually a handful of ships were sent out. Alcibiades went with them, eager to be away from Sparta, where he felt the mood turning against him. Even so, he displayed all his familiar energy and charm, convincing the majority of Chians to back the rebellion, then persuading Miletus on the mainland to join them. Soon he was in direct touch with Tissaphernes, leading the negotiations with him.[9]

At the beginning of the war, the Athenians had voted to set aside 1,000 talents as a reserve in case of crisis, with the death penalty for anyone who urged its use. Now they concluded that the crisis was serious enough to warrant the release of this reserve. Both sides set to building ships and raising crews. The Athenians had the advantage of long experience in doing this and soon took the offensive, sending out forty-eight triremes and an army of 3,500, including 1,000 Athenian hoplites. They crushed stirrings of rebellion on Lesbos and enjoyed a number of other successes, as well as beginning blockades of Chios and Miletus.[10]

The Spartans arrived with fifty-five ships, twenty of them sent by Syracuse, but both sides proved cautious, and there was no battle.

For the Athenians, the risk of losing their only significant fleet currently in existence was too great to justify. At the same time, the Peloponnesians, remembering so many past defeats at sea, were willing to fight only when the numbers seemed overwhelmingly in their favour. Each fleet continued to grow as reinforcements arrived, and the Athenians won some more small victories, although not enough to prevent further rebellions among their allies, for instance on Rhodes. Every revolt deprived the Athenians of tribute from that state and at the same time added to the general uncertainty. Other communities were late in paying or did not pay at all, shrinking the funds available to Athens and simultaneously throwing up more and more challenges, which could only be dealt with by force. With its limited resources, Athens was incapable of sending squadrons of ships to deal with every problem at once. The Spartans were making progress, and the Persians were paying them enough to keep the fleet going, despite bickering over the scale of pay for rowers.[11]

By 411 BC Alcibiades had left the Spartan fleet and was living at Tissaphernes's court. Thucydides states that an order for his execution had come from Sparta, but he had been warned and escaped in time. Presumably suspicion about his reliability was more widespread, and this was not simply the hostility of King Agis. The sources suggest that up until this point, he had served the Spartans well, and only after his flight did he begin to reassess his options and work more actively towards returning to Athens. Plutarch says that he adapted as readily to a Persian lifestyle as he had to a Spartan one, winning over Tissaphernes and warning the satrap that letting Sparta become too powerful might not be in his or Darius II's best interests. An outright victory that established the Spartans as the supreme naval power in the Aegean and along the Ionian coast would only replace an Athenian empire with a Spartan one, which might prove even more hostile. As at Sparta, Alcibiades likely highlighted existing concerns, adding his—very persuasive—voice and energy to thoughts that were already present. From the start the Persians wanted to use the Spartans for their own ends, just as the Spartans wanted to use the Persians. For the satraps and the great king, there was a lot to be said for letting the Greeks squabble and waste their strength fighting each other. A fleet of almost 150 Persian warships assembled on the Phoenician coast, a force that had the ability to prove decisive if it joined either side, giving Tissaphernes a strong bargaining counter. In spite of hints, perhaps even promises, that it could be employed, it never arrived, and in the meantime, as paymaster to the Spartan-led fleet, he had other means of aiding or hindering them.[12]

The Athenians had condemned Alcibiades to death in his absence and confiscated his property, so he needed to be very cautious before trying to return home. He began to make contact with the leaders of the fleet busy suppressing the rising on Samos, hinting that he could sway Tissaphernes to back Athens instead of Sparta, but only if the Athenians changed their constitution away from the radical democracy that had dealt with him so unfairly—at least in his opinion. Events overtook him, for in 411 BC others had come to the conclusion that the fickle mass of citizens voting in the Assembly had caused Athenian failures. The advisory council of ten reflected a mild version of this sentiment and may well have contributed to the cautious strategy followed since their appointment. Yet this was not enough for some and sparked a revolution led by a number of aristocrats, in part working to bring together the members of many of the *symposia*, the drinking clubs. In a way this was an actual conspiracy akin to the one feared at the time of the desecration of the herms. Unlike most upheavals in other states, this one was largely bloodless, with only a little force, and had at the very least a veneer of constitutionality.

Yet the changes were drastic. The *Boule* council of 500, chosen by lot and open to the top three classes established by Solon, was abolished and replaced with an appointed council of 400 members, probably from the two highest classes and chosen to favour the new regime. The Assembly of all citizens was abolished, in theory to be

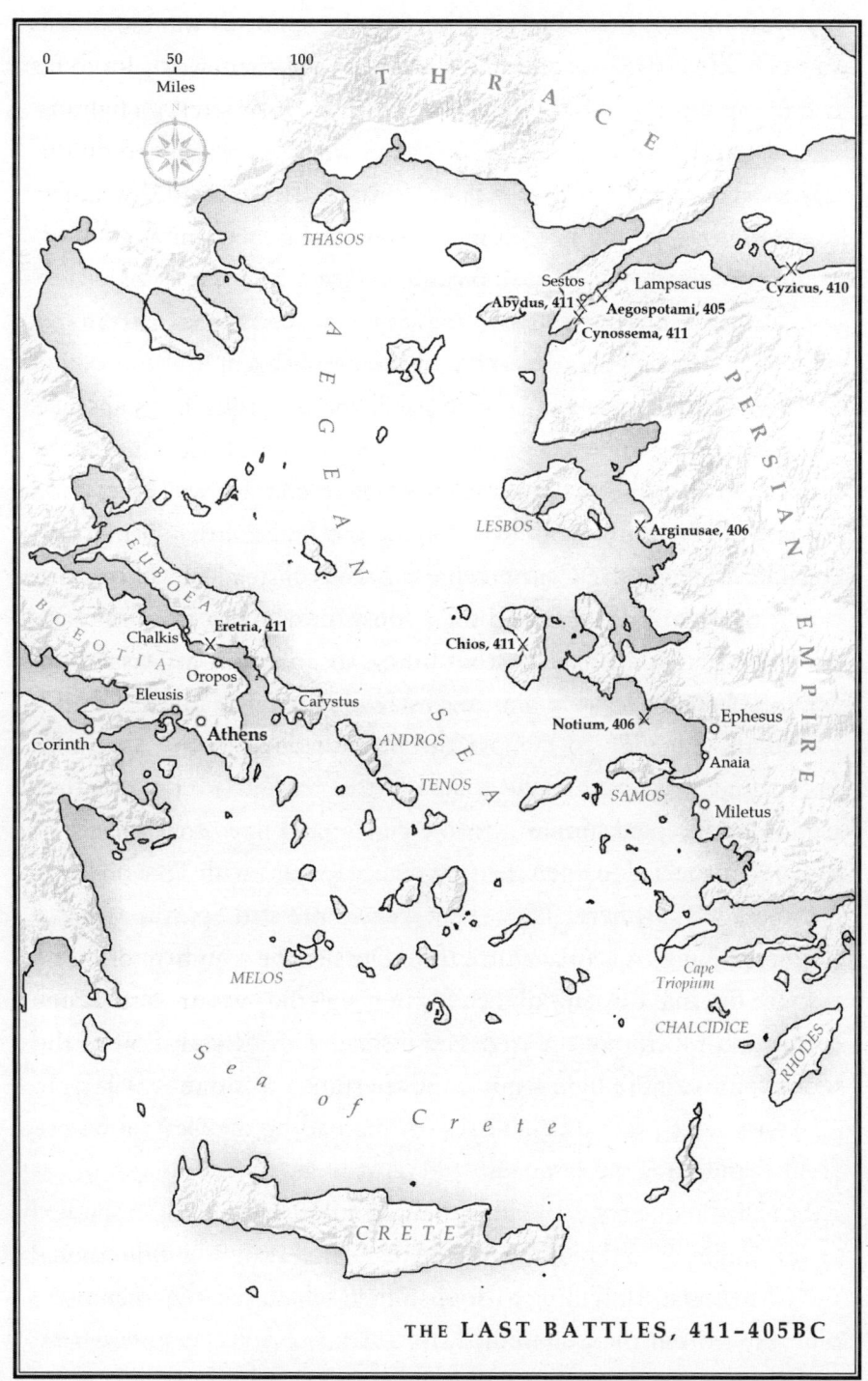

replaced by one described as 'the 5,000', although the two main sources differ over whether this was the maximum or minimum number of members. Either way, this excluded the *thêtes*, the poorest citizens, and perhaps even some of the *zeugitai*, the class traditionally associated with hoplite service. In truth the details did not matter, since the 400 did not show any sign of wanting to convene this reduced Assembly or let it make any decisions. This was an oligarchy, government by a self-selected elite who considered themselves best suited to and most deserving of rule, and at first it was accepted in Athens itself.[13]

The same was not true on Samos, where more than 1,000 of the hoplite class and above, and even more poorer citizens serving as rowers, were risking their lives for the good of Athens. These men considered themselves more representative of the true and traditional Athenian community and, in proper fashion, met, discussed, chose leaders, and voted on what they were to do. There were negotiations, but neither side was at first willing to move, and the 400 lacked the capacity to compel the fleet to obey them. Alcibiades became involved, and in the course of this back-and-forth, the men on Samos accepted him as a fellow citizen and one of their leaders. The 400 also tried to open their own negotiations with Tissaphernes, but these led nowhere. They made peace offers to Sparta, and this prompted King Agis to advance from Decelea with his army, hoping that the internal disputes of the Athenians would encourage a faction to admit his men into the city. Met instead with defended walls and harassing parties of light troops, the Spartans withdrew.[14]

Thucydides praised Alcibiades for dissuading the men on Samos from abandoning the campaign and returning to put down the 400 at Athens. Instead, they demanded that the 5,000 be properly embodied as the Assembly and that the 400 be dismissed and the *Boule* council of 500 restored. Unwilling to abolish themselves, the oligarchs clung onto power, but their continued overtures to Sparta went nowhere, and there were rumours that the Spartans were planning a naval attack on the Piraeus. The main leader of the coup was murdered and another member arrested for a while by the hoplites he was supposed to be commanding. Eretria on Euboea rebelled, and the thirty-six Athenian triremes sent there were badly defeated with the aid of a Spartan squadron, prompting the other communities on the island to join the revolt.

The defeat, so close and in such a sensitive area, stripped the last credibility from the new regime, and after no more than four months of existence, it was overthrown in favour of the 5,000 and a traditional *Boule*. Thucydides believed this new regime was the best Athens ever experienced in his lifetime. It was a moderate democracy, with a substantial demos consisting of men owning at least some property, and in many respects was like the system before the rise in importance of the fleet and the greater role given to the *thêtes*. Yet Athens was still a naval power, and if anything, the navy was even more crucial now that the Spartans were mounting a challenge for control of the sea. Within nine or at most ten months, the rule of the 5,000 also ended, and the system prior to the revolution was restored in every respect, not least because the vast majority of Athenians felt that this was the proper way of doing things.[15]

It helped that the war was going better. In 411 BC a new admiral named Mindarus took charge of the Spartans' main fleet, which by this time was operating in the north, around the Dardanelles. The Spartans favoured a system of appointing a new commander each year, perhaps to share the opportunities and also to ensure that the ephors and ruling council at home retained control of strategy. At this stage, it is hard to see how any Spartans had much experience of controlling large fleets on wide-ranging operations, so presumably these men were guided by the experience of allied subordinates when it came to many practical aspects of operations at sea. Yet several adapted well to their commands, and Mindarus was one of these, out-thinking and outmanoeuvring his Athenian opponents on several occasions. However, a battle fought in the strait near the

Gallipoli Peninsula started well but ended badly when the retreating Athenians rallied and turned on their scattered pursuers, sinking or taking twenty-one ships and only losing fifteen of their own. Even this minor success helped to restore the still fragile Athenian confidence.[16]

A second, even harder-fought battle ended in Athenian victory when Alcibiades appeared over the horizon with reinforcements, hoisting a signal to show who he was. In 410 BC, he led the combined Athenian fleet against Mindarus off Cyzicus, driving the Peloponnesians onto the shore and then continuing the fight on land. The Syracusan contingent burned their ships, but the rest were captured, and many men, including the Spartan admiral, were killed trying to defend them. The remnants were stranded, and the Athenians intercepted a letter sent by Mindarus's subordinate, who had succeeded to the command. It was laconic in style, if not perhaps tone, and read, 'Ships lost. Mindarus dead. Men starving. Don't know what to do.'[17]

Athens was recovering, both in confidence at home and abroad and in actual strength. In 409 BC thirty ships, 1,000 hoplites, and 100 cavalry were sent to cooperate with the main fleet under Alcibiades. His authority was recognised by election in his absence, and later he was granted in addition the same freedom of action as he and his two colleagues had received in 415 BC for the Sicilian expedition. By this time, there was clearly little or no prospect of Persian backing for the Athenians, not least because Tissaphernes now thoroughly distrusted Alcibiades, in a second example of the gifted but slippery Athenian outstaying his welcome. A couple of years later, Alcibiades did negotiate with the other satrap, but the Athenian envoys despatched to the court of Darius II to discuss an alliance never got there. The Persians made sure that they made slow progress until the great king had had time to reach agreement with a Spartan embassy.[18]

Thucydides records three successive agreements between the Spartans and Persians, reflecting a shifting relationship made difficult because it was hard for the Spartans, who had begun proclaiming that they were fighting for the freedom of the Greeks, to agree openly that Ionian and other cities should come back under the control of the great king. In the end, they did accept this, at least for the moment, agreeing that these cities would pay tribute to Darius II but retain local autonomy. The Persians gave the Spartans some support on land, as well as the money to keep up the war at sea, allowing them to replace their naval losses. However, the Persians were unwilling to send and put at risk ships of their own, and the money they provided often fell short of Spartan expectations. One reason was that the satraps had to provide these funds from their own resources and were not able to draw on the immense wealth of the great king, at least not quickly and only when Darius II took a direct interest. As ever, the ruler of the Achaemenid Empire had plenty of other concerns more pressing that the affairs of the Greeks on the fringe of his empire. In addition, controlling the money supply was the best way for the Persians to ensure that their Spartan allies remained dependent on them.[19]

The war continued, and although the main focus and big actions stayed along the Ionian coast, the Dardanelles, and the Bosporus, a good deal of smaller-scale fighting took place elsewhere. Pylos, the tiny fort on the coast of Messenia, was lost when its garrison surrendered to the Spartan besiegers. An Athenian squadron had been on the way to relieve it but was delayed by bad weather until it was too late. Another setback came when Megara recaptured its port of Nisaea, although some honour was regained when a small Athenian army won a victory over a Megarian force aided by a Spartan contingent. Both sides saw successes and failures, without either gaining a clear advantage.[20]

The Athenian fleet did better, gradually taking back the rebellious cities that threatened the security of grain supplies to Athens. Blockades, faction fighting within the communities, the boldness of Alcibiades, and a willingness to grant mild terms as a reward for surrender helped, until only the single city of Abydus remained allied to Sparta and hostile to the Athenians. Following these successes Alcibiades returned to Athens eight years after he had left his home city to embark for Sicily. Plutarch and other sources suggest that he was nervous, since the death sentence remained at least technically in force, and he knew that he had enemies in the city. In the event, an enthusiastic crowd cheered him, and his vindication was complete, as he spoke to the Assembly and was elected to the supreme command in the war. Perhaps to make a point for a man condemned for allegedly profaning sacred rites, that year he led a magnificent escort for the procession walking from Athens to take part in the Mysteries at Eleusis.[21]

By 407 BC, the Spartans had had time to build and man a new fleet, reinforced by remnants of the old. Persian gold paid for this, and Darius II sent one of his sons, a prince named Cyrus, to supervise the war effort from the Ionian coast. He was no more than a teenager and not at this stage considered a likely heir, but this nevertheless signalled the empire's willingness to give more attention and support to the Spartans. A fleet of ninety triremes arrived, under the command for this year of Lysander, who like Gylippus was the son of a Spartan father and a foreign or helot mother. Good connections had furthered his career, and one story claimed that he had been a favourite, perhaps even the older lover, of Archidamus's son Agesilaus. Whatever influence had helped him win selection for this command, Lysander, again like Gylippus, soon proved himself more than capable as an admiral and general, and perhaps even more so as a diplomat. He certainly developed a good working relationship with Cyrus, convincing him to fund an increase in the daily wage given to rowers.[22]

Alcibiades returned to the war at the end of the summer of 407 BC, leading a fleet of 100 triremes. However, his first operation miscarried, and the limited raiding carried on during the winter months showed only modest results. In 406 BC, he led most of the fleet to Notium, close to the Spartans, who were based at Ephesus, before leaving a subordinate in charge while he went in person to assist another general. The acting commander, given strict instructions not to risk a battle with the enemy, for whatever reason ignored these orders and sailed out to attack a small, seemingly vulnerable squadron of enemy ships. In fact, these proved the bait for a trap set by Lysander, and when the rest of the Peloponnesian fleet appeared, the already disordered Athenians panicked and fled back to the shore. Twenty-two Athenian triremes were lost in this embarrassing defeat. The acting commander was among the casualties, but the Athenians still had a strong force, and when Alcibiades returned, he sailed out to challenge Lysander to battle. Unwilling to push his luck, the Spartan commander refused to bring out his fleet to fight, so that Alcibiades was unable to recover lost prestige. One of his colleagues soon began condemning him at Athens and found a receptive audience. Before he had left the city, the ever-exuberant Alcibiades had promised to achieve great things; instead he had allowed this humiliation to occur by not being with the main force at the critical moment. Sensing that formal rebuke and probably worse would follow, he left and went to live on the Thracian coast, where his family owned land and he could control a couple of strongholds. Many aristocrats, like Miltiades and others, had connections and possessions far from their homeland.[23]

Lysander's term as admiral was over, and his replacement quickly soured the relationship with Cyrus, reducing Persian support. In the short term this did not matter, and a sign of the scale of past support came when he was able still to mass a grand fleet of 140 triremes, joined a little later by 30 more. He led these aggressively, capturing several Athenian bases, including one on Chios, and then attacking Lesbos. The Athenian fleet managed to get to Mytilene before the Spartans but was heavily outnumbered and lost thirty ships in fighting outside the harbour. The remainder were bottled up as the Spartans placed the city under blockade, although two Athenian ships managed to sneak through and carry the news to Athens.

Somehow the Athenians put together a fleet in this direst of emergencies. They stripped gold from statues and melted down other dedicated trophies to help pay for the construction and equipping of 110 triremes. Athenians registered as cavalry or hoplites volunteered to row, sitting alongside not only *thêtes* but metics and also a substantial contingent of slaves, who were given—or perhaps promised—not just freedom but citizenship. Aristophanes's near contemporary play *The Frogs* suggests that they got the same rights as the Plataeans, which allowed full political participation and only restricted them from some ritual activities reserved for descendants of specific Athenian family lines. Eight out of the year's ten strategoi were to command, one of them Pericles the Younger, the son of Pericles and Aspasia, who had been made a citizen by special decree after his half-brothers succumbed to the plague.[24]

On the way to Lesbos, another 30 Athenian ships and 10 more from Samos joined the fleet, for a total of 150. Yet these were not the well-trained and superbly handled squadrons of earlier years; nor were the Peloponnesian ships the timidly led and sluggishly manoeuvring vessels of the past. The Corinthian idea of strengthening the bows for head-to-head ramming reduced a ship's handling capacity and was only really suitable for fighting with little sea room, so had been abandoned. In many ways the Spartan-led fleet more resembled the Athenian fleets of the past than the one now facing it. The Peloponnesian crews and captains were experienced, skilful, and confident, following months—in some cases years—of operations. It helped that the difficulties with Cyrus had been resolved and the full flow of money restored, so that everyone was well paid. In this campaign it was the Peloponnesians who wanted to fight a battle of manoeuvre, trusting in their ability to get around behind the enemy ships and ram them in a vulnerable spot rather than trying to board and overwhelm them with numbers. They even seem to have been willing to fight at a numerical disadvantage, in marked contrast to earlier years when they had always wanted numbers on their side.

After some manoeuvring, the rival fleets clashed off the islands of Arginusae in the largest naval battle of the entire conflict. The Athenians formed in two lines, hoping that ships in the second line could deal with enemy ships that slipped through the gaps in the front line and attempted to turn and ram from the rear. They also had one of the islands in the centre of their line, helping them to match the width of the Peloponnesian formation in spite of being two lines deep. As always, the neat formations lasted only for the early stages of the battle, and the fighting eventually came down to each individual ship, the ability and stamina of its crew, and the skill of helmsmen and captain. Xenophon described it as a very hard fight, lasting a long time, and the critical moment seems to have been when the Spartan flagship was sunk and the admiral killed or drowned. Pericles may have achieved this success in his ship, although in the confusion it was surely hard to be certain. Peloponnesian ships began to flee, perhaps some because they had realised what had happened to their commander or because, around the same time, the Athenians' superior numbers were beginning to prevail. One or two ships quitting the action and fleeing could readily make others give in as well, opting to withdraw while they still could. Seventy Peloponnesian ships were sunk or captured, including all save one of the Spartan ships, against twenty-five Athenian vessels. Most of the Athenian fleet pressed the pursuit, but when they regrouped later, almost a third of the remaining vessels were ordered to go to the scene of the battle and search for survivors.[25]

As noted earlier, a trireme was a fairly lightly constructed vessel, Athenian ones in particular designed for speed. In proportion to their size, they carried a very large crew, and the combined weight of the rowers provided most of the ballast for the vessel. When a ship was rammed, water flooded in, but once the crew had abandoned ship, this weight was removed, so that the wreck was likely to float, perhaps turning turtle, as Aeschylus had described the ships at Salamis. This meant that anyone not badly injured in the initial clash could survive by climbing back onto the ship or clinging to other wreckage, which was why, in some battles, the enemy took the trouble to kill them. Friends could go to their rescue, but in this case the weather turned as a storm blew up, so that the ships sent to their aid, along with the rest of the fleet, returned to shelter on the shore, and hundreds, probably thousands, of survivors were left to drown.

The victory at Arginusae broke the blockade of Mytilene and shattered the main Peloponnesian navy. All this had been achieved by a scratched together fleet at a time of terrible crisis, and naturally the news of the triumph was very welcome when it reached Athens. Yet, alongside the euphoria of victory, discontent quickly grew about the failure to save the men in the water. Athenians had often proved ready to punish commanders for perceived failures, hence Demosthenes's decision not to return home after his reverse in Aetolia and Nicias's cautious decisions in Sicily. The eight commanders were recalled to answer for this failure, prompting two to go into exile rather than run this risk. Other factors may have added to the anger against them, including, as some scholars argue, the decision to free the slaves and give them citizen rights in return for serving in this fleet. This was unprecedented, even though slaves had acted as rowers in the past in lesser numbers. Perhaps the owners regretted the decision now that the crisis was safely over, or citizens had had time to resent the dilution of the prized rights of citizenship. Another factor may have been the unusually distinguished composition of the crews, which presumably meant that cavalrymen and hoplites were among those left to drown. For whatever reasons, the Assembly voted to execute the commanders for their dereliction. Pericles the Younger was one of the victims.[26]

If putting together the fleet in this moment of emergency was one of Athenian democracy's most admirable moments, the execution of the successful generals was perhaps its darkest hour. By this stage of the war, so few experienced and gifted leaders remained, so the Athenians could not afford such petty self-indulgence, especially since, as the generals were elected for only a year, there would soon be a less dramatic way of expressing disapproval. Even worse, the example meant that men elected in the future were likely to be even more cautious. In contrast, urged on by Cyrus and their Greek allies alike, the Spartans broke the recent convention of annual commands and reappointed Lysander. At the same time, Persian money paid for the construction of more ships and the hiring of new crews.

The final clash occurred in 405 BC in the Hellespont off a place called Aegospotami (goat's rivers), which the Athenian fleet was using as a base. It was not a good position, for it had no natural or constructed defences to protect the ships and supplies. Alcibiades visited the camp, urging the new commanders to move to somewhere more secure, but they ignored his advice. Perhaps the generals had personal reasons for disliking and distrusting him, or perhaps they did not want to be seen to be in any way influenced by such a controversial figure, a man in self-imposed exile. Days later Lysander struck, catching the fleet unmanned and destroying or taking the moored ships, almost without a fight. From a fleet of some 180 triremes, fewer than 10 escaped. The Peloponnesians took 3,000 prisoners, among them two of the generals. Some, perhaps all, of the Athenians among them were pulled out from the rest and executed.[27]

There was no money to replace the lost ships, even though the bulk of the crews eventually made their way home, and unlike the Spartans, the Athenians had no fount of Persian money to keep rebuilding. In time King Agis led an army into Attica on land, while Lysander sailed up to blockade the Piraeus. The Athenians showed defiance but knew that they could not hope to resist for any length of time, not least because the Dardanelles were in enemy hands, cutting off the grain on which the city relied. Negotiations started, and the Athenians tried to get better terms than those on offer before realising that they had to accept whatever the victorious Spartans imposed on them. Thucydides concluded that the conflict had lasted twenty-seven years, although counting only individual phases of the war lessens the total, whereas considering the conflict to have begun with the clashes in the 450s increases it. Either way, the war between Athens and Sparta was over.[28]

ALCIBIADES DID NOT live long after his last, surely sincere attempt to assist his fellow citizens. If the Athenian commanders at Aegospotami had listened to him, they might well have avoided a disaster; the fleet would have survived and the Athenians been able to fight on. Whether they could indefinitely have kept on beating each new fleet created by the Spartans and funded by the Persians is impossible to say. For Alcibiades, like the rest of the Athenians, the end came suddenly. Shortly after the battle, his house was attacked at night and set on fire; he and the other inhabitants burned to death or were cut down as they tried to escape. No one was ever sure who was responsible; plenty of Persians, Spartans, and Athenians had a sufficient grudge against him to have arranged his assassination. Plutarch, inclined to think that the reason had less to do with grand politics, favoured a story that the gang was led by the brothers of a young woman whom he had taken by force. For a man whose life had resembled that of a hero from an epic poem, such an end was both dramatic and in keeping.[29]

25

TO THE SOUND OF FLUTES AND CELEBRATION

The end of the war and shifting fortunes in the world that took shape afterwards, 405–c. 360 BC

THE ATHENIANS WERE NO LONGER IN CONTROL OF THEIR FATE. They could not afford to replace the lost fleet, and the food supply to the city from the Black Sea was cut. This meant their defeat was total, the enemy's strength impossible to resist. Plenty of Athenians now thought back to times when the roles had been reversed and they had decided on the punishment of whole communities, often ordering mass executions and the enslavement of women and children. The rhetoric Thucydides provided for the debates over such matters emphasised might over justice. The Athenians had possessed overwhelming strength and used it as they wanted, doing whatever they felt brought their community greatest advantage. It is unlikely that he invented this mentality or that many of his fellow citizens had not felt this way to some degree.

Plenty of other people had witnessed and sometimes experienced the cruelty of the Athenians. The population expelled from Aegina remembered the loss of their homeland and yearned for Athenians to feel the same pain. Corinth's leaders had long argued that the rise of Athenian power and the restless and limitless ambition of the

Athenians posed a threat to everyone, most of all the Spartans. They had led calls for war long before the Spartans were willing to act and now felt that the threat of Athens could and should be ended permanently. The Spartan kings, ephors, and other leaders came under great pressure to destroy Athens as a political community, and there were plenty of calls for mass executions and enslavements or deportations. The killing of Athenian prisoners after Aegospotami might well have been taken as a sign of what was to come.

Yet Sparta's allies knew that the Spartans would decide what was to happen and would base this decision on their own best interests, for in this respect they differed little from the Athenians. While they did not interfere in the domestic affairs of their allies as readily as the Athenians, the Spartans' military might and prestige made them the supreme power within their alliance, so their essential worth gave them the right to act as they wanted. It did not matter that in recent years very few Spartans had taken part in the naval campaigns that had ultimately won the war. It was the Spartans who had ordered their allies to build ships and man them, the Spartans who had arranged the successive deals with Persia, which provided the money to do this and to maintain the fleets, and the Spartans who had commanded those fleets. If the later years of the conflict had given no real opportunities for Sparta's famous hoplites to demonstrate their supreme skill in phalanx fighting in actual combat, in a sense the lack of fighting on land confirmed their reputation as the best. The Athenians were simply unwilling to risk an attack on Decelea or to fight en masse outside their walls because they believed that any attempt to face a Spartan army in open battle was doomed to failure. At the same time, the campaigns culminating in Aegospotami, like the Sicilian campaign, proclaimed to the world that Spartan-led alliances tended to win wars.

Victory confirmed the military supremacy of Sparta, and this remained the most important distinction for a state in the wider Greek mindset. Sparta was the most formidable when it came to war fighting, and all the pretension and boasting of Athens had come to nothing, proving that Athens was not Sparta's equal. This in itself was of considerable worth, a confirmation of status that helped determine how others treated the Spartans and also their willingness to accept how the Spartans treated them. Some clearly hoped that the Spartans would make use of this supreme might to destroy Athens. Yet not behaving as the Athenians had done had advantages, for while the severe punishments of several communities had invoked fear, they had not appeared justified to many observers. Talk of fighting for the freedom of the Greeks would appear even more false if the Spartans acted in the same way, rather like the ruthless treatment of the Plataean garrison.[1]

There were also practical considerations. Athens and its territory of Attica were huge by the standards of Greek city-states. This was not a Mytilene, a Melos, a Potidaea, or even an Aegina, and the numbers involved, even after plague and war, meant that massacre, enslavement, or expulsion, if enforced, would be on a wholly unprecedented scale. The Spartans had not added to their own territory for a century or more and had only ever done so with land directly adjacent to their own, when their own population was flourishing. At the end of the fifth century BC, putting aside the difficulty of controlling land separated from the rest of their territory by other states, there were simply not enough Spartans to consider taking Attica and turning its surviving population into a helot labour force. Destroying the Athenian state risked creating a vacuum in the heart of southern Greece, and anyone who took over the land, even allies permitted to do this, would come to enjoy all the resources and advantages that had led to Athens's rise. Whatever happened would represent a major dislocation of the balance of power and wealth in Greece. Given that Sparta had only just confirmed its dominance after an arduous struggle, such change would unlikely be to her benefit and might allow other states to grow in strength and ambition. A humbled Athens, still in existence as a subordinate ally of Sparta, avoided these risks.[2]

The terms eventually imposed reveal what the Spartans deemed most dangerous about Athens. From now on, the Athenian fleet would be reduced to a mere twelve triremes, the sort of force that plenty of relatively small states could afford. In addition, the long walls, those barriers connecting the city to its ports, were to be slighted, as were the defences of the Piraeus harbour itself, so that the Athenians could not avoid battle in Attica and accept the pillaging of the countryside simply because they were able to bring in sufficient food by sea. Significantly, they were not asked to demolish their city walls, that point of contention in the aftermath of the Persian invasion. Athens was not to lie wholly open to any enemy who chose to attack, but Attica was to be vulnerable to a major invasion, which in the foreseeable future meant by a large, Sparta-led army. In essence, the Athenians were required to play by the old rules of warfare, just like everyone else, for the Spartans were confident of success in such circumstances. Once again Sparta and Athens became allies, but this time not as equals. The Athenians pledged to follow where the Spartans led whether on land or sea and to have the same friends and allies, just like the other states of the long-established Spartan alliance. They also agreed to let exiles return, which was a common clause in many peace treaties between Greek states.

When their ambassadors returned with these demands, the Athenians met in their Assembly, but there was never any question of turning them down. On balance, they were mild, albeit a great blow to prestige, since they knew that they had no real choice with Lysander and the fleet nearby. Ironically, the regime on Samos, set up after the rebellion against Athens had been suppressed, continued to hold out for some time until forced to submit by the Spartans. In the meantime, Lysander disembarked many of his crews, and the call went out for anyone who wished to come and help break the long walls. Each wall had more than a mile of its length demolished, enough to make repairing them a major task that could not be done secretly. The mood was festive, with flute girls playing as the men toiled away.

Plenty of people had good reason to enjoy humiliating the Athenians, as well as revelling in the thrill of being on the winning side. Even so, the scale of the task was considerable, and many of the volunteers appear soon to have given up, so that it was a while before the work was completed. The celebratory phase was likely to have been brief and symbolic, with the Athenians left to finish off the rest of the task, which they did slowly.[3]

At first the Spartans did not tell the Athenians to alter their constitution, but before long factions developed within the citizen body, especially among the better off, arguing for change. Debates dissolved into chaos, and after he had subdued Samos, Lysander sailed back to Athens, restored order, and took charge of the situation. A board of thirty was created to frame new laws and govern the city in the meantime, while a Spartan garrison took up residence in the Odeion built by Pericles. Even so, the Thirty struggled to maintain control and to find the money to pay for what it wanted to do. Opponents were exiled, and some unfortunates, both citizens and metics, were executed and their property confiscated. Resentment soon turned into active opposition. In an effort to retain control, the Thirty formally reduced the population of free citizens—or at least the ones eligible to vote—to just 3,000 and expelled many of those stripped of their rights from the city.

One group of opponents took control of the Piraeus and refused to be dislodged. Late in 404 BC, two exiled former generals led a band of followers into Attica from Boeotia and rapidly gained support. The Thirty and the 3,000, along with the Spartan garrison, marched out and tried to terrorise the wider population but only helped fuel opposition. A battle was fought, but although this led to the deposition of the surviving members of the Thirty and their replacement by a board of ten, the result was not decisive. Both sides appealed to Sparta directly, rather than to Lysander, prompting the despatch of an army led by King Pausanias. Divisions among the Spartan leadership worked in favour of the Athenians opposed to the oligarchy, for the king and others had become jealous and suspicious of Lysander's fame. Peace was restored, and only the remaining members of the Thirty and the Ten, plus a few others, were exiled. Pausanias appeared to have little interest in precisely what sort of constitution the Athenians followed, so in less than a year almost all aspects of the previous democracy were once again restored. It would continue with no more than minor modification for most of the next century.[4]

Not everyone in Sparta was impressed by the king's attitude, and on his return home, he was put on trial and acquitted only by a narrow margin. A lot of this may have been to do with personal rivalries, the influence of both the other king and Lysander, and the familiar desire to curb the power of the monarchs. Nothing was done to change the arrangements he had made in Athens, and soon the Spartans had other, far more important priorities. In 402 BC they decided to attack Elis, the state formed from several smaller cities, which had barred them from participation in the Olympic Games back in 420 BC, almost twenty years earlier. This had been simply the highlight of a long pattern of hostility, but before now the Spartans had been too preoccupied to respond. By 400 BC the Spartans had won the war, confiscating territory although not forcing the disunion of the state or making it abandon its moderately democratic system. Not long afterwards, the Spartans also marched on Naupactus, expelling the descendants of the Messenian rebels settled there by the Athenians half a century earlier. The threat of the enemy within, from the subject race of helots denied rights and forced to toil to support the lifestyle of the peers, persisted and was highlighted when a conspiracy to stage a revolution was uncovered. One motivation was that the helots could see how much more numerous they were than their masters.[5]

Yet Sparta was strong and, in the later years of the war with Athens, had become a naval power and intervened in the Dardanelles, and especially in Ionia and the Aegean islands, far more than ever in the past. There was no wish to step away from this imperial role, not least because letting the Athenians take over the leadership in the struggle with Persia back in 478 BC had done so much to fuel the latter's rise. Lysander continued to play a key part in this and had imposed oligarchic councils on many of the communities, including Samos after its defeat. The cities on the Ionian mainland were in most respects given over to the Persians, perhaps with promises that they would retain autonomy in their day-to-day affairs. The Spartans had little real choice about accepting this. Greatly reduced in numbers now that the war with Athens was over, their grand naval power existed only as long as the Persians chose to subsidise it. In the early years, the continued close personal relations between Lysander and Cyrus helped to avoid any real friction. Darius II had died in 404 BC, and although at first willing to accept one of his brothers as great king, in 402 BC Cyrus rebelled, claiming the throne for himself. He asked for Spartan aid, and the ephors and other leaders felt that honour and gratitude meant that they should agree. Unable to commit significant numbers of Spartans, they helped to raise a force of 10,000 mercenary hoplites in the Peloponnese and sent them to Asia. In 401 BC, on the verge of defeating his brother in battle, Cyrus was killed by a javelin and his brother's rule confirmed.* After this, relations between the Persians and Spartans understandably soured, as Tissaphernes, appointed satrap once again, imposed his will on the Ionian cities. The Spartans responded to an appeal for help by sending King Agesilaus with an army composed of small numbers of Spartans and reliant on allied and mercenary manpower.[6]

The Spartans did not have a good reputation for their conduct when active in other lands, and the years after the war with Athens did nothing to improve it. For all the celebration as the long walls were pulled down and for all the hatred of the Athenians, a world dominated by the Spartans soon engendered almost as much

---

* The 10,000 Greek mercenaries were left stranded in the heart of the Persian Empire but fought their way back. Xenophon, a young Athenian aristocrat, had joined the expedition, and his *Anabasis* provides a vivid and detailed account of their adventures.

resentment as the one it had replaced. Athenian decline boosted the status of many communities, especially the bigger cities like Corinth and Thebes, which had suffered a lot during the course of the Peloponnesian War, only to gain little or nothing—not even respect—from the Spartans in its aftermath. Annoyance added to the natural, and very Greek, instinct for the leaders in these places to want to grow even stronger and to assert themselves over as wide an area as possible. The Thebans and Corinthians openly refused to send men or ships to assist the Spartans in their various campaigns in Greece and then to the war in Asia. The limited progress made in the fighting against the Persians further stoked the sense that the Spartans were not so very powerful after all. Lysander was killed when the force expected to rendezvous with him failed to arrive in time. It had been commanded by Pausanias, who this time was condemned and exiled for his conduct, adding another name to the long list of Spartan kings rejected by the ephors and council.[7]

In 395 BC a Theban invasion of Phocis spiralled into a wider war, pitching the Spartans against the Thebans and Corinthians as well as the Argives, once again willing to fight their old enemy. The Athenians also joined them and similarly had refused to contribute to the war in Asia and secretly corresponded with the Persians and sent ships to join them. The Spartans, realising their situation was precarious, recalled King Agesilaus and his army from Asia, judging the threat in Greece to be far more important. Before he arrived, the regent of the other king, who was still no more than a boy, assembled a large army and met the even larger coalition army at the River Nemea, not far from Corinth. All told, something like 40,000 Greek hoplites may have faced each other. Each side's right flank managed to rout the phalanxes facing it, but the unity of the Spartan command and Spartan discipline helped their successful troops to rally and manoeuvre to charge the remaining enemy in the flank. The sources state that there were just eight Spartan fatalities among the 1,100 lost by the army, compared to 2,800 dead on the other side. Even so, the coalition was not willing to seek peace, and the war continued. Still worse, the Persians, aided by an Athenian admiral exiled since the aftermath of Arginusae, had destroyed the Spartan fleet. There was no means of funding a replacement, so this brought the Asian war to an end and allowed the Achaemenid Persians to reassert full control over the Greek cities of Asia.[8]

During the war between the coalition and the Spartans and their allies, the Athenians restored the long walls and the fortifications of the Piraeus and also began to rebuild the navy, if on a far smaller scale than in the past. The Persians had cut off aid to the Spartans and worked with the Athenians at sea and helped to fund them, so there could be no question of challenging the great king or his satrap in Ionia. Eager to regain the advantage that had won them the Peloponnesian War, the Spartans tried to persuade the Persians to switch sides again and back them, making one of the key features of the war the quest to secure and keep Persian backing. The naval fighting was on a far smaller scale than in the past, marked by revolutions within the island communities that led to changes of side and sudden shifts in the balance of power. Fighting spread to Thrace and the Dardanelles, as the Athenians tried to reassert themselves in these regions with access to vital resources. Like the fleets, armies were rarely big, and mercenaries played a growing role. As the raising of the 10,000 had shown, large numbers of Greeks had been left stateless as exiles or become accustomed to fighting for pay and saw no reason to stop. Pitched battles were rare, surprise attacks and raids being the most common form of fighting. At some point all of the major players had their territory ravaged, and the impact on smaller communities tended to be even more severe.

The war went on, neither side—nor any individual state—gaining a decisive advantage as the destruction and death continued. However, although Sparta had been damaged and was a little weaker than in the beginning, the Spartans remained strong enough to continue the war against their array of enemies. Persian money fuelled the fighting, and in the end it was the Persians who brought peace. Approached by Sparta, Artaxerxes II was willing to put pressure on all sides and send envoys to negotiations held at Sparta that led to what became known as the 'King's Peace', concluded in 386 BC. This confirmed Persian control of Ionia but also seems to have included a declaration recognising the territory of each individual state. All swore an oath to abide by the agreement, with the threat of retribution from the great king if they broke this promise. How this would be achieved was not likely specified, and there was no suggestion of a Persian presence, let alone garrisons, in Greece to oversee things. Yet everyone understood the power of Persian gold, and for the moment they were most probably all equally glad to end the wider conflict.[9]

Thus, just over a century since Darius had sent his fleet to invade Greece, all the major Greek cities and plenty of the minor ones accepted a treaty that held the great king as superior to themselves in power and status. That this was largely nominal, not affecting their prestige in relation to each other, did not make it any less significant, and from a Persian perspective it confirmed the majesty and might of the empire and its ruler. Voices had already been raised, and over the next decades would continue to claim that, if only the Greeks could unite, they could easily defeat, even conquer the Persian Empire, but they were always a minority. Most Greeks ignored the Persians or saw them as a potential source of financial aid in the far more important competition with their neighbours. The Spartans remained the strongest military power on the mainland or islands and were content to have this confirmed through Persian intervention. The King's Peace ended the cooperation between the coalition of allies, leaving the Spartans free to reassert themselves in the Peloponnese, punishing states like Mantineia for failing to support them during the war.[10]

The King's Peace meant that the Thebans gained little, which damaged the reputation of those leaders who had been most prominent during the conflict. Inevitably they had rivals, and almost as inevitably, this produced faction fighting, with those hoping for revolution searching for outside support. In 382 BC one group admitted a Spartan force into the city, which seized the Cadmeia, the ancient stronghold and Theban equivalent of the Acropolis. There were arrests, but hundreds of their rivals escaped and took refuge in Athens. In itself this signalled how much attitudes had shifted from the deep hostility to Athens displayed by the majority of Thebans throughout the Peloponnesian War. More than three years later, some of these exiles sneaked back into Thebes, overthrew the current regime, and, with some Athenian assistance, overcame the Spartan garrison.[11]

In 378 BC, the Athenians formed a new alliance, which in time would come to include many of the island and coastal communities that had belonged to the earlier one, with the notable exception of those now under Persian control. The terms of the new treaty emphasised some of the biggest resentments of Athens's first empire, for this time they pledged not to interfere in the internal affairs of their allies, not to place garrisons or governors in them, and not to confiscate land to give to Athenian settlers. In addition, the allies were not to pay any tribute to Athens. War was declared against Sparta, which was accused of having violated the King's Peace. This time the Athenians pledged to force the Spartans to respect the freedom and autonomy of Greek communities—with the exception, of course, of those living under the rule of the great king. This was not the only irony, since, after all, it had been the Spartans who had declared such freedom as their cause in 431 BC, and then the Thebans had eagerly supported them—perhaps too eagerly, given the attack on Plataea before the war had started formally. Now they allied with the Athenians, although, as it turned out, the Thebans would do most of the direct fighting against the Spartans. For much of the time the Athenians concentrated on rebuilding their naval strength and their empire. In due course, they would violate all the pledges they had made to their allies.[12]

By 375 BC all of the main states were willing to renew the King's Peace, and the ending of major conflict seems to have sparked revolutions in a number of cities, including Corinth. In the meantime, the Thebans took the opportunity of building up their power in Boeotia itself, bringing most of the cities into an alliance that they led. Yet friction with Sparta was never far away, and eventually open war broke out once again, although this time the Athenians were not involved. In 371 BC the Thebans and their allies clashed with the Spartans and their allies at Leuctra, a Boeotian community not far from the border with Plataea. This was the largest clash of phalanxes for a long time, although there appear to have been fewer than 10,000 on each side, as far as it is possible to gauge from the vagueness of the sources. King Cleombrotus led the Spartan army, although there were just 700 'peers', who formed on the right in the place of honour as usual. Led by Epaminondas, the Thebans massed their own citizens in a very deep formation and stationed them opposite the Spartans, abandoning the normal convention of putting their best troops on the right of their own army. Details are confused, but he seems to have begun with a cavalry attack to disrupt the enemy and then followed with the deeply ranked phalanx. The result was devastating, leaving Cleombrotus and 400 'peers' dead and the Peloponnesian army in rout. For the first time in over a century and a half, the Spartans had been thrashed in a major battle between phalanxes.[13]

In 362 BC Epaminondas beat them again, this time near Mantineia in the Peloponnese. By this time the Athenians were allied with the Spartans, having become nervous about the growth in Theban power, and sent contingents to join the army. Again, the sources make precision impossible, but all maintain that this was a very large battle, each side fielding some 20,000 or perhaps even more troops. Even so, in spite of the fact that this battle was fought closer to home and was of critical importance, barely 1,000 Spartan peers fought with King Agesilaus. Once again, Epaminondas formed the Thebans exceptionally deep and sent them straight at the enemy's right wing, where the Spartans and the pick of the other troops were placed. He was killed by a spear thrust, but his example and tactics paid off and broke the enemy army. Without him, the Thebans' war effort became less focused, so that they failed to follow up the victory. Yet, at the very least, the second victory showed that the first was not a fluke, even though it proved only a tactical and not a strategic success. The Spartans were not invincible even in phalanx battles fought in the open field, and this revelation did much to diminish Sparta's prestige. At the same time, Epaminondas had weakened the Spartan state in other ways. Eight years earlier in 370 BC, he had marched into the Peloponnese and taken up the cause of the helots. Shielded by the Theban army, a heavily walled city was built, given the name Messene or Megalopolis, and occupied by runaways. For the first time in centuries, there was a free Messenian state in the Peloponnese, one that the Spartans were never able to conquer.[14]

Sparta's decades of supremacy beyond its heartland in the Peloponnese were over. Whatever the cause of the decline, be it earthquake and rebellion or social trends discouraging marriage and the raising of children, the population of 'peers' had dwindled. Loss of a swathe of Messenia and the helot labourers to work the land only meant that this would get worse. Sparta's hoplites were simply too few in number to have any chance of adapting to newer forms of warfare and coping with the higher skills of many opponents. Pre-eminence in the past had come from being the best in war, a claim no one believed anymore. Spartans were still respected, so were not taken lightly as a potential rival or ally, but everyone also now knew that they could be beaten. Over time, Sparta became less and less significant in the wider Greek world.

In contrast, Athens's power was growing. Head of a new alliance, she had naval dockyards, a large fleet, extensive trade, and the long walls to ensure that these advantages were protected and at the city's disposal. Yet she was never again as rich, powerful, or prestigious as she had been in days of Pericles, for there were fewer allies and less revenue. The fleet was smaller and could not regain the lost façade of invincibility it had once possessed. Citizens had to be paid to ensure enough attended meetings of the Assembly. In general, for all the pride in the uniqueness of their city, its people, and their democratic system, there are signs of insecurity and self-doubt. The Athenians had challenged Sparta to be equal leaders of the Greek world and then to claim the highest leadership and, for all their might, had been beaten in the end. Like their fleet, everyone, including the Athenians themselves, knew this. Athens was not invulnerable but could be beaten, just like Sparta. To believe that the Athenians could achieve anything if they set their mind to it was much harder. Culturally, there were achievements in many fields, without reaching the heights of the fifth century BC. Philosophical schools flourished, drawing thinkers from far afield, but Athens was also the city to arrest and condemn Socrates to death in 399 BC. For so many modern observers, his forced suicide remains an even deeper blot on Athens's record than the massacres and mass enslavements of earlier years.

THE STORY OF the decades after the Peloponnesian War is complicated, and this chapter has done no more than brush the surface, greatly simplifying the events and omitting a good deal. Athens lost power and prestige through its defeat. It was not destroyed and would recover but would never again dominate the Greek world in the same way. Sparta won, and for a while became a naval power, willing to intervene in the Aegean and on the shores of Asia and Thrace, as well as in most of the rest of Greece, until its resources were stretched too thin. Spartan society could not adapt to fulfil this greater imperial role, not least because its population continued to shrink.

Strikingly, less than a decade after the Peloponnesian War, Athenians and Spartans were killing each other in the first of a succession of conflicts. Just as 431 BC was not the first outbreak of war between the two cities, 404 BC did not lead to permanent peace between them. Sparta's pre-eminence was confirmed, and Athens's prestige was broken, but neither status was permanent, and the competition for prestige and power went on. Cities like Thebes and Corinth in the past had seen Athens as the great threat to their own position, so had sided with Sparta against the Athenians—and got very little in return. Once Sparta's dominance was clear and no longer challenged by Athenian ambitions, opinion changed, and the Spartans became the biggest threat—and the biggest impediment to these cities growing their own power. Therefore, they allied against Sparta, and the Athenians joined them. Later, when Thebes had become far stronger, the Athenians joined the Spartans to fight against that city. As always, each community wanted to excel and be seen to excel by others—for success continued to require an audience. Each one did what appeared to be in its best interests to achieve this. Every shift in the fortunes of one state and the overall balance of power caused all to reassess their best course. In this sort of system, it is hard to see how stability could have been achieved unless one state gained such overwhelming power that not even a coalition of all the others would dare to challenge it. This never happened and, given the resources of the states involved, was never likely to happen. The rules changed when Philip II united Macedonia and created a state and a military system unlike anything seen before in the Greek world.

Xenophon concluded his history at a point just after the battle of Mantineia, and his tone was deeply pessimistic. He wrote of how both sides set up trophies to claim the victory, but the battle seemed to decide nothing, for the wars went on. When Philip II confirmed his dominance of southern Greece at the Battle of Chaeronea in 338 BC, he smashed an army led by the Thebans and Athenians and including other allies. Yet plenty of Greek cities sent their hoplites to serve under the command of the Macedonian king and fought for him at the battle, while the Spartans remained aloof, not joining either side. Thebes was sacked and—for the moment—eradicated as a political community by Philip's son, Alexander the Great. Neither father nor son chose to punish Athens as severely, another testament to its sheer size and importance. Removing this large state, with its central role in wider trade, its naval power, and the prestige of its fifth century BC history, was no more attractive to them than it had been to the Spartans in 404 BC. Athens was humbled but not destroyed.

Sparta again stayed aloof when Alexander the Great led what he proclaimed as a coalition of all the Greeks to seek vengeance on Persia for Xerxes's invasion and the desecration of Greek temples. After his victory at the River Granicus, a dedication made in the Temple of Athena at Athens pointedly stated that the battle had been won by all the Greeks 'except the Spartans'. In 331 BC, the Spartans and their remaining allies rebelled against Macedonian rule, although their first target was Messene/Megalopolis, the home of the free Messenians. In due course the rebellion was put down by the commander left at home by Alexander, who dismissed the campaign as a mere 'war of mice'. It was a humbling verdict on the once vaunted power of Sparta.[15]

CONCLUSION

THUCYDIDES SUSPECTED THAT A FUTURE VISITOR WHO SAW the remains of Athens with its great monuments and sheer size would conclude that Athens had been far more powerful than it actually was. On the other hand, a visitor to the ruins of Sparta would think that the place had been of little significance. It was a shrewd judgement, and one borne out by archaeology and the simple fact that tourists visiting Athens vastly outnumber those who go to the site of Sparta, where there is far less to see. As Thucydides understood, appearances are not everything, but they are very powerful. The scale and elegance of the Parthenon and its position high on the Acropolis make it one of those instantly recognisable views. In many ways, reinforced by its status as the capital of modern Greece, Athens has come to symbolise the glory of ancient Greece, with all its great culture, beauty, learning, sophistication, and courage in resisting attack from the mighty Persian Empire.[1]

Yet, to repeat a point made at the start and abundantly evident throughout the narrative, there never was an ancient Greece in the sense of a united nation. The monuments of Athens celebrated the might, glory, and sheer worth of the Athenians alone, shouting out the message that this city and its citizens were greater than all the other communities of the Greeks, let alone other peoples of the wider world. Someone from Thebes, Corinth, or Megara, let alone a Spartan, would not have seen the Parthenon or any of the other monuments as in any way belonging to them or as celebrations of a common Greek identity. Instead, they represented a challenge, the Athenians boasting of their own might. Worse, there was a lot of truth to the Athenian claims because, for a long time, they did rule the seas and lead—effectively command—a big alliance, making them both confident and wealthy, although, as it proved, not quite as strong as they had hoped.

The Athenians paraded their achievements, as did other cities to a greater or lesser extent. Monuments were not as important to the Spartans, although they did have their temples and they did erect trophies at Delphi to commemorate their victories. The intent behind these was much the same, honouring the gods and proclaiming their own worth, but they also did this in other ways that left no visible trace. The Spartans were pious, devoting much effort to their many festivals. They were also supreme in war, especially open battle, and confident enough in this never to surround their city with a defensive wall. In this sense, one of Sparta's greatest boasts rested on the absence of anything to see.

The desire for status, to excel and be seen to excel, ran through the shared culture of the Greeks to a pronounced degree. Art celebrated physical beauty in an idealised form, especially of the young, muscular male body, and did not concern itself with the imperfections and individual differences of reality. Instead, a very high standard was set for how a person should look, and the exercises of the gymnasium offered a place to seek such an appearance, something done in public so that comparison could be made with others. That competition assumed an even more obvious form at the games, of which the Olympics were only the most famous, where the winner of each event was held up to public admiration extending well beyond his own city. The plays that survive, remarkable works of art in so many ways, were first written and performed to win a prize, for the desire was to produce a play seen not simply as good but as better than all the others being staged at the same time.

CONCLUSION

So many aspects of this culture reflected the lives of the aristocracy—the 'best men' through wealth, ancestry, and skill with words and arms—and in this way the spirit of Homer's poems remained highly relevant long after other aspects of society had changed. Only those rich enough not to have to labour or supervise a workforce had the time and opportunity to train their bodies to compete at the highest levels in a sport or to hone their minds to write or to probe deep philosophical questions. When artists and sculptors depicted the idealised male, the form was very much that of an aristocrat, body trained to perfection and often displayed nude or semi-nude, and the figures depicted in a contemporary scene looked the same as those in one showing action from the Trojan War or some other myth. Good-looking people—especially men—in the present day were shown as identical to the heroes of the past.

Yet the world had changed as the city-states developed and prospered. In the first place there were far more aristocrats, or families asserting their right to belong to this class, than there had been in the world depicted by Homer. Communities were larger—some far larger. War and battle were no longer dominated by a few, the great men, princes, or kings of the poems, who deserved to be honoured and to lead in peace because of their exceptional skill at arms. Bigger communities fielded bigger armies, and the great warriors of the past now served alongside hundreds or thousands of hoplites. Later, at Athens and to some extent elsewhere, the rise in the importance of naval warfare and the design of the trireme gave an even wider section of the population a critical role in war. No longer did a man need to own heavy equipment, let alone be one of the 'front fighters', to matter. Because more and more men came to play a bigger part in war, they also came to be of more account in peace. One reason for the continuing, perhaps even greater, importance given to athletics and sporting competition, and indeed cultural competition, was that there the aristocracy could still dominate, now that war was no longer so dependent on them. These pursuits offered a glory open only to the richest.

War and politics were intimately linked in ways a modern audience finds unfamiliar—and that some perhaps hope are not universal rules of history. To survive, let alone to grow and excel, a community needed to rely on more than just a few aristocrats and their household warriors—hence the extension, to greater sections of the population, of protection under law and of the rights to vote and to hold office. Sometimes this went in stages. Most cities had got rid of kings before the sixth century BC or, like the Spartans, modified and restricted the institution. There were tyrants, but they relied on support from the wider population, and eventually most were overthrown through internal revolution, often led by aristocrats. Aristocratic government varied considerably, with the trend generally towards including an ever broader and more numerous sector of the city's population. Similarly, democracies varied widely in just who was included among 'the people' and their precise role. Everywhere it became even more important to make clear who belonged to the community and who did not and to define the entitlements and obligations of each. Being a citizen gave rights, but only at the price of involvement in communal life and willingness to fight—and perhaps die—on its behalf.

Sparta's solution created 'the peers', the true citizens who alone possessed political rights and were full members of the community. Freed from the need to work with their own hands by the labour of helots, they lived a life in many ways resembling the Homeric aristocratic ideal. They were expected to train hard, to demonstrate both bravery and skill in war beyond the levels of ordinary men from other cities, and to be serious when they gathered to vote or were chosen by lot to serve as ephor. They were also watchful of each other, judging their fellow peers at all times, and the desire was to produce a race of men not identical in every way but doing their utmost to excel beyond their fellow citizens in showcasing their worth. They displayed their bodies as they trained, their character at all times in their own behaviour and that of their sons, their wit and wisdom in formal debate and conversation at communal meals, and their performance

CONCLUSION

when they went to war—hence the bitterly contested selection of the 300 *hippeis* each year and the bickering between ephors, kings, and the Gerousia council, the most obvious sign of which was the public disgrace of so many Spartan kings.

Spartan peers were not literally equals, although the name conveys some of the sense of this. From the start there were distinctions with those from the established elite owning substantially more land than the majority who had been allocated fields and a helot labour force by the community. Over time, the decline in population concentrated an ever-growing percentage of the estates in the hands of a group who were comparatively few in number. Wealth and ancestry gave advantages at Sparta as they did anywhere else. Only the very wealthy could afford to keep horses, let alone raise and train the chariot teams that for a long time allowed Spartans to dominate the list of winners at the Olympics. Similarly, established influence and connections tended to endure, generation after generation, with every sign that a relatively small number of families provided most leaders. Connections to the two royal families were clearly also of great importance. Thus the Spartan peers were an elite, their privileged lifestyle reliant on others, notably the perioeci and the helots. Yet there were elites within the elite, and merit was only one factor determining this status. In one sense the regime could be seen as an aristocracy, if a broad one, including perhaps 9,000 or even more privileged citizens at the start. On the other hand, so large a group of citizens could be presented as a form of democracy, since the number with the franchise was large, even though the majority of the population was excluded from public life.

The Athenians did not see the Spartans in this way, but their definition of true democracy pushed the idea beyond practices elsewhere. All citizens enjoyed considerable rights. The lowest of the four classes, the *thêtes*, were not eligible for some high offices and roles, but each individual vote they cast counted the same as anyone else's. Since the Athenians gathered to debate and decide all important issues, as well as to elect magistrates and to ostracise the unpopular, this meant a great deal. At Athens the direct participation of citizens in decision-making overshadowed authority delegated to the *Boule* or magistrates. Only on campaign did an elected leader have much freedom of action, and even there he knew that he had to answer to the Assembly on his return. Still, for all this collective responsibility, many Athenians rarely had the time and opportunity to attend the Assembly, while even fewer had the time and freedom to devote themselves to becoming leading figures at its meetings. Thus the leaders were always wealthy and usually from an aristocratic family or had become wealthy and were trying to join the elite. Equal in terms of some of their rights, not least the possession of a vote, Athenians in their democracy were never intended to be equal in every respect. For the politically prominent, ambition meant that men of similar background and wealth were rivals as often or more than they were firm allies.

Within each city, individuals struggled for office and influence. That the leaders were usually well off and well connected meant that they tended to be part of that broader aristocratic world and had personal connections with similar men in other cities. As a consequence, many had somewhere to seek refuge if things went against them and perhaps some people from whom to seek support against their rivals at home. Sparta was spared violent rivalries among the peers during the period covered in this book and was much admired for its internal stability. There were fierce arguments around the conduct of many of its kings and sometimes its magistrates, some leading to exile and death (perhaps verging on execution in the case of Cleomenes and Pausanias), but there was never the descent into civil strife so familiar in many other cities. Yet, in some ways, this is a judgement from a limited perspective. Spartan citizens did not turn on each other using violence, but of course they were a privileged elite, and the threat of the helots, and to a lesser extent the perioeci, was ever present. The peers needed to rely on each other as a defence against this far more numerous and wholly disenfranchised subject population, and most of the time this constant shared threat limited how far they were willing to press rivalries among themselves. That both Cleomenes and Pausanias were accused of inciting helots to some form of resistance was a reminder of this deep-seated—and entirely justified—fear. The privileged lifestyle of the peers was only possible through the subjection of others, and those others would obviously resent this deeply.

Athens saw a succession of bids for tyranny and the eventual success of Pisistratus and his sons, the murder of one of the latter, and the subsequent overthrow of the regime with Spartan assistance. Fear of tyranny remained strong, particularly at the time of the Persian Wars, and at the very least the allegation that they desired it was an insult to hurl at political opponents. Revolution came only in the aftermath of defeat in Sicily and then subsequent disasters. Compared to the factional fighting in other cities, it was at first fairly peaceful. Over time this escalated, although even then the fighting was brief and the return to the established democratic system remarkably quick. After a century of such governance, the majority of Athenians appear deep down to have felt that this was the best and proper way of doing things. Many of them benefited from it, and even if, with the loss of empire and reduction of the fleet, the state could employ fewer citizens, plenty of opportunities were still available. More would come as the Athenians began to assert themselves again in the fourth century BC.

There was some correlation between the benefits of being an Athenian citizen and the ability to gain subordinate allies abroad, and the periods of greatest prosperity at Athens came at the height of its empire. The same was true of its cultural achievements, which coincided with the era of greatest power, wealth, and confidence. While there must always be an element of chance in the appearance of remarkable talent, successful societies can both afford to give such gifted individuals the opportunity to create works of genius and, at the same time, encourage them to do so, celebrating what is and aspiring to even greater things. There is also room for more complex messages—for instance, in depicting the horrors of war, and especially the horrors of losing a war. A good deal came together in fifth century BC Athens to produce such a flourishing of art, architecture, and the written word, but underlying it all was Athenian military and imperial success.

Competition within communities was matched by competition between them—something felt by all citizens, even those with little property and at best a marginal role in the internal affairs of their city. Ultimately citizenship and associated rights were linked to the degree a man contributed to the war effort if and when the community chose to fight against outsiders, so that everyone faced the same Homeric equation: Worth depended on prowess. Greek communities went to war readily, to defend or take land and also for the sake of honour and reputation. They often waged war, but war was not in itself inevitable or essential to support their society and depended a good deal on how others treated them. Those perceived to be strong by other communities received respect, since upsetting or provoking them was seen as dangerous. This was very much an assessment of the moment. Past deeds counted and were remembered, but current perception guided actions.

The Spartans believed that they had taken their land by force and could remember adding to it by further conquests, especially in Messenia, which permitted the fullest development of their society with 'the peers' at its heart. They came to dominate much of the Peloponnese and have an influence further afield because they excelled in war. All of this was well established by the start of the fifth century BC. In contrast the Athenians rose to prominence rather later, turning the potential of their unusually large state and big population into actual power only after the revolution, which led to the establishment of its democratic system. The Persian threat—provoked by the Athenians in particular and to a lesser extent the Spartans—acted as a catalyst,

CONCLUSION

creating Athens's maritime empire at the same time as steadily increasing the democratic element in public life. Both cities rejected Persian demands out of pride and a sense that they were strong enough not to accept the great king as their superior. That same pride in their own worth led to the friction and conflict between them in successive generations. Athenians wanted to be seen at the very least as the Spartans' equals, and the Spartans did not wish to accept this.

The struggles that followed were about power and the perception of power. Athenians' claims rested on their naval supremacy and the array of allies who looked to them for leadership. Allied communities accepted this relationship and sent ships, or more often gave tribute as required by the Athenians, because they deemed association with such a great power to be in their interest. The Athenians offered protection against the Persians or any other potential aggressors—which included the Athenians, at least in the long run. When enthusiasm for the alliance wavered, fear of retribution deterred most of the allies from breaking away, at least most of the time. The wave of defections in the later stages of the Peloponnesian War showed how readily communities broke away from Athens once they judged the Athenians to be weak.

Sparta had a similar relationship with her allies in the Peloponnese. These respected Spartan might but made attempts to break away, especially when the Spartans seemed vulnerable or preoccupied elsewhere. Big cities like Corinth and Thebes worked with the Spartans when doing so seemed useful to them, especially while Athens appeared to represent a greater threat, and then turned against the Spartans when that was no longer true. Neither Athens nor Sparta gave too much concern to the desires and interests of its allies, directing policy and strategy purely in its own interests. This was particularly humiliating for a big community like Corinth, helping to explain the speed with which it repudiated Sparta, but was also true for smaller cities. Athens and Sparta alike felt that they led because of their inherent and proven worth, expressed most of all in their military or naval power. This meant that it was only right and proper for others to follow where they led, and there was no need for constant negotiation to arrive at a mutually agreeable decision. Allies commanded a level of respect based on their own record and worth, which inevitably were seen as significantly less impressive.

The rules of the game were the same for all communities, which meant that these were always watching and judging whether their own status could be protected and perhaps improved. Every community, however small, wanted to excel as far as it could, which meant that ambition was never satisfied, for it was always possible to become greater. The Spartans tended to be cautious in their approach to this, reflecting not only a culture where age and maturity were respected but, even more, the danger within posed by the helots. Taking risks, especially risks that sent large numbers of 'the peers' abroad for any long time, held no real appeal. Although they eventually won the Peloponnesian War by fighting on distant fronts, this was done by other means, sending leaders with or without small forces of non-citizens to Sicily, Ionia, or Thrace and creating navies commanded, but not crewed, by Spartans. This worked, at least for a while, but proved an insufficient basis for lasting empire. Ultimately Spartan society centred on supporting the peers in their unique lifestyle, which in turn required the unrelenting domination of the mass of the population. The Spartans excelled at campaigning en masse for brief periods at comparatively short distances from home, which meant that most of mainland Greece was within their reach. Anything else posed problems and relied heavily on others for the main manpower, while even this core strength became less and less effective as the number of peers dwindled.

In contrast the Athenians were rarely short of citizens, coping even in the aftermath of the plague and the losses in Sicily, the population steadily recovering because conditions were far more favourable than in Sparta. In addition, they faced no threat from within. There were slaves, and they were important for the economy, so that the flight of many to Decelea was damaging, but they were fewer in number than

CONCLUSION

the helots and never likely to form one united community and rebel. At the same time, the democratic system encouraged boldness, not least because in its early days it had survived attacks from all sides and not long afterwards thrown back the Persians. The creation of the navy and its rapid dominance of the Aegean naturally led Athenians to look overseas, giving their military ambitions a far greater reach than was ever possible for the Spartans. Decades of success so reinforced their deep confidence in themselves that the Athenians bounced back from failures such as the expedition to Egypt. If anything, they tended to be too quick to make a decision and too ambitious in their plans, whether it was to intervene in support of the Ionian rebels, the entirety of the Sicilian expedition, or the summary execution of the commanders who had won the Battle of Arginusae. This risk-taking sometimes went badly wrong and at the same time lay behind so many successes. Without it, the Athenians were unlikely to have become so powerful so quickly.

Eventually, Spartan caution paid off, as the Athenians paid the price for overreach and poor decision-making—as well as bad luck. Using Persian money to do what otherwise would have been impossible, the Spartans won the war at sea without having to change their society in any fundamental way. In the longer run, Spartan dominance proved fleeting, not only over its short-lived overseas empire but even in the Peloponnese, while Athens began to recover quickly, and other cities also flourished, so the struggle for pre-eminence went on. It is all too easy to focus on the worst consequences of this Greek longing to excel and be seen as the best, not least because it fostered instability and frequent conflict, where the allies of today readily became the enemies of tomorrow and perhaps the allies of the following week. The same ambition drove them to achieve more and more, from the aspiration of farmers to create an ever-greater surplus, to trade, which had allowed the cities to grow in the first place, to all their later deeds.

Competition drove Greeks in all communities to excel, leading to competition, power struggles, and war. Of all these rivalries, the one between the Spartans and the Athenians led both to the greatest achievements and the worst destruction. Together they saved themselves and the other cities from the Persian threat and later fought a war that drew in the majority of the wider Greek world. The individualism so fundamental to Greek society meant that even when Athens was defeated, the competition soon revived as different states asserted themselves. Centuries later, the Roman historian Justin felt that this played into the hands of the Macedonian King Philip II, who 'watched as if from a high tower' and eventually 'forced victor and defeated alike to submit to his rule'. For him, domination by a larger and united outsider was the natural consequence of rivalries between the leading Greek states.[2]

Yet the Greeks of this era came together to form communities but showed no inclination towards combining these to create a bigger state beyond attempts at leagues and the Athenian imperial experiments. Only in the city did they feel it possible to create effective corporate identity without altogether stifling individual freedom. Thus both the Persians and later the Macedonians dealt with many separate cities rather than a single united opponent. Xerxes lost in spite of this, and the margin of victory for Philip II may well have been less than is often assumed, for the Battle of Chaeronea was not a walkover but a hard-fought, costly victory. Pride inspired the resistance against Xerxes and Philip, the pride of men determined to be seen as worthy as individuals and to belong to a community that also had its share of honour. There was often a tension between the two. Desire to be first, or at least to be ranked among the foremost within a man's city, inspired competition and sometimes revolution, while the quest to maintain and increase a city's prestige led to many wars. At the same time, similar emotion spurred on the great achievements of the Spartans, Athenians, and other Greeks, whether heroism in war or truly magnificent creativity. As with so many aspects of human behaviour, there was good and bad.

CHRONOLOGY

All dates are BC. In many cases the date of an event is uncertain, so these are marked (?), and in some cases an alternative date is also given. For significant periods both the dates of events and their sequence are questionable.

c.1200(?)	Collapse of the Mycenaean palace system.
c.1000	Construction of grand tomb at Lefkandi.
683(?)	Later tradition claims that the archonship was instituted in this year.
636 or 632(?)	Cylon tries to become tyrant at Athens. The bid fails, and his captured followers are killed.
c.594(?)	Solon introduces reforms at Athens. (Other dates are possible.)
582	An archon at Athens refuses to lay down power at the end of his year of office.
c.560/1(?)	Pisistratus's first attempt at making himself tyrant. This proves short-lived. Sometime in the next ten to fifteen years he tries again and is briefly successful.
c.557–5(?)	Pisistratus is installed as tyrant with the aid of Megacles but is later forced to flee.
550	Rise of Cyrus the Great.

c.547	Croesus of Lydia defeated by Cyrus.
546/5	Pisistratus once again becomes tyrant at Athens and this time remains in power.
530	Death of Cyrus the Great.
c.528/7	Death of Pisistratus.
525	Cleisthenes elected archon.
c.524	The Spartans with Corinthian aid attack the tyrant Polycrates on Samos, but the expedition fails.
c.520	Accession of King Cleomenes.
c.519	Plataea allies with Athens.
514	Hipparchus murdered.
511	Spartan-led invasion of Attica defeated by Hippias with assistance from Thessalian allies.
510	The Spartans expel Hippias from Athens.
508	Isagoras becomes archon. Cleisthenes and others exiled.
c.508/7	Reforms of Cleisthenes.
506	Cleomenes organises an invasion of Attica supported by separate attacks by the Thebans and Euboeans. However, Sparta's allies and his fellow king withdraw. The Athenians defeat the other attacks and seize land for settlement on Euboea.
499	Aristagoras appeals to Sparta and then Athens for aid for the Ionian rebels. The Spartans refuse; the Athenians agree. Ionian revolt begins.
494	The Persians defeat the Ionian rebels at the naval Battle of Lade. The Spartans under Cleomenes inflict a very costly defeat on Argos.
493	Miltiades flees to Athens. Themistocles elected archon. Persians expand into Thrace. Mardonius's fleet suffers heavy losses in storm off Mount Athos.

492	Miltiades placed on trial at Athens.
491	Darius sends envoys to demand the submission of the Greek cities. At Athens and Sparta, these men are killed.
490	Darius sends invasion force to Greece. After initial successes, this is defeated at the Battle of Marathon. Possible helot revolt (?).
489	Aristides elected archon. A badly injured Miltiades placed on trial and condemned but dies soon afterwards.
487	Ostracism used for the first time as Hipparchus is sent into exile.
c.487	Lot introduced for the selection of archons at Athens.
486	Megacles ostracised by the Athenians.
486 or 485	Death of Darius; peaceful accession of Xerxes.
c.485	Athens and Aegina at war.
484	Xanthippus ostracised by the Athenians.
484(?)	Persians recover Egypt.
483(?)	Aristides ostracised by the Athenians.
483/2(?)	Encouraged by Themistocles, the Athenians use the profits from new discovery at Laurium to build a large fleet of triremes.
481	The Spartans invite others to a conference and form an alliance to oppose the anticipated Persian invasion.
480	Xerxes leads army and fleet to invade Greece. Leonidas killed in unsuccessful defence of pass at Thermopylae, while the allied fleet manages a draw at the Battle of Artemisium. The Persians sack Athens, but their navy suffers a heavy defeat at the Battle of Salamis. Xerxes returns to Asia

	but leaves Mardonius in charge of a field army in Greece.
479	Pausanias leads a coalition of Greek states to defeat Mardonius at the Battle of Plataea. A Persian fleet is defeated at the Battle of Mycale. Many Ionian communities rebel against the Persians and join the coalition.
478	Pausanias alienates many of the Greeks and is recalled. Athens takes the lead in the seaborne campaigns against Persia. Formation of the Delian League. Most of the Bosphorus and the Thracian coast are cleared of Persians. Athens rebuilds its city walls.
c.478–476(?)	Spartan King Leotychidas campaigns with limited success in Thessaly.
c.477	Pausanias returns to take control of Byzantium.
c.476	Cimon rises to prominence as a leader in the campaigns against the Persians and establishes the power of the Delian League in the Aegean.
c.473–469(?)	The Spartans face opposition in the Peloponnese and win the Battle of Tegea.
c.471/0(?)	Themistocles ostracised by the Athenians. Pausanias recalled by the Spartans from Byzantium.
c.470(?)	Rebellion of Naxos suppressed by the Athenians.
c.469/66(?)	Cimon wins major victory over Persians at Battle of Eurymedon.
468/7(?)	Early peace deal with the Persians (if historical).
c.466(?)	Death of Pausanias. Themistocles flees to Asia.
465	Xerxes murdered. Eventually Artaxerxes becomes king.
465(?)	Athenians attempt to found colony at Ennea Hodoi in Thrace, but it is destroyed. Revolt of Thasos against the Athenians.

465(?)	Argos captures Mycenae.
465/64(?)	Sparta hit by series of big earthquakes. Casualties are heavy, and in the aftermath the helots and at least two communities of perioeci rebel.
463	Thasos surrenders to the Athenians.
c.463(?)	Spartans win Battle of Dipaea against Peloponnesian opponents.
462(?)	The Spartans ask the Athenians for military aid in the war with the helots. Cimon is sent with a significant force. Other cities also send help. Ephialtes carries through some political reforms at Athens. Cimon and the Athenians are told to leave by the Spartans. Athens allies with Megara, Argos, and communities in Thessaly hostile to Sparta.
462(?)	Revolt of Inaros against Persian rule in Egypt.
461	Ostracism of Cimon. Ephialtes murdered in mysterious circumstances.
459(?)	Athenian expedition to Cyprus. This leads to intervention in Egypt in support of Inaros. Fighting in Megara, Aegina, and at sea against the Corinthians. Construction of Athens's long walls commences.
458(?)	Spartans intervene to protect Doris against Phocis. The Athenians oppose the return march of the Spartan army but are defeated at the Battle of Tanagra. Later, another Athenian army wins the Battle of Oenophytra against a Boeotian coalition. For the moment the Athenians dominate Boeotia.
c.457	The archonship at Athens is opened to the third class, the *zeugitai*.
c.456	The Athenians parade their naval strength around the Peloponnese and the west coast of Greece. The rebel Messenian helots surrender in their last stronghold at Mount Ithome and are permitted

	to leave. The Athenians take them to Naupactus, where they are settled.
c.454	Utter defeat of the rebellion in Egypt. The Persians crush the rebels and largely destroy the Athenian forces supporting them. The treasury of the Delian League is permanently moved from Delos to Athens.
c.451	Five-year peace treaty between Sparta and Athens. Thirty-year peace declared between Sparta and Argos. Pericles introduces law restricting Athenian citizenship. Cimon returns from ostracism (assuming he was not recalled earlier, as some believe, c. 454/3).
c.450	Cimon leads expedition to Cyprus and dies before it is over. Some fighting with the Persians in the wider region.
c.449	Peace of Callias concluding hostilities between Persia and the Athenians (if historical).
c.448 or 446(?)	Athenians defeated by Boeotian coalition at the Battle of Coronea, ending their dominance of the area.
c.448	Renewed hostilities between Sparta and Athens at the same time as rebellions against the Athenians in Euboea and elsewhere. Pericles confronts a Spartan invasion of Attica and convinces King Pleistonax to withdraw. The latter is subsequently exiled.
c.447(?)	Pericles invites representatives from the Greek communities to meet at Athens (if historical).
c.446/5	Thirty-year peace declared between Athens and Sparta.
c.443	Foundation of colony at Thurii in Italy with heavy Athenian involvement.
441–440	Revolt of Samos against Athens.
439	Defeat of revolt on Samos.

CHRONOLOGY

c.437	Pericles leads show of force to the Black Sea.
437/6	Athens founds colony at Amphipolis.
435	Corinth clashes with Corcyra over civil strife in Epidamnus.
433	The Athenians ally with Corcyra and take part in the naval Battle of Sybota.
432	Revolt of Potidaea against Athens. Corinth and Athens clash again when the Corinthians aid the rebels. Late in the year, Sparta's allies come to a conference to discuss the situation.
c.432(?)	Megarian Decree prohibits Megara's access to Athenian-controlled trade.
431	Thebans attack Plataea and are defeated, precipitating the wider war. In the summer, King Archidamus leads a very large army into Attica. Inspired by Pericles, the Athenians evacuate their farms and refuse battle. Later in the year the Athenians raid the Peloponnese and launch a large attack on Megara.
430	The Spartans invade Attica for a second time, and again the Athenians refuse to fight. Plague breaks out in crowded Athens. Pericles leads raid on Peloponnese. Troops sent north to Potidaea take the plague with them, leading to heavy losses. Pericles is deposed and fined but soon rehabilitated. Potidaea falls late in the year.
429	Instead of invading Attica, the main Spartan-led effort is against Plataea, which is placed under siege. Death of Pericles. Phormio wins victories at sea.
428	The Spartans invade Attica again with the same result. Mytilene rebels against Athens.
427	Mytilene capitulates, and the Athenians debate what to do with its people, eventually executing 1,000 ringleaders rather than all the male citizens. Some of the garrison of Plataea break out.

CHRONOLOGY

	The rest surrender late in the year and are executed. Corcyra descends into bitter civil war. The Athenians send an expedition to Sicily.
426	Demosthenes campaigns in western Greece, including Aetolia, with mixed fortunes. Nicias raids Melos.
425	The Spartans invade Attica again but withdraw early after news that the Athenians have established a base at Pylos. The Spartans put troops on Sphacteria, but these are isolated once the Athenian fleet arrives. This prompts the Spartans to begin peace negotiations, but these break down, partly because of the arguments of Cleon. He is given charge of the reinforcement to Pylos and with Demosthenes lands on Sphacteria, killing some of the garrison and capturing the rest.
424	The Athenians come up with an ambitious plan for an invasion of Boeotia, but this breaks down, and they suffer a heavy defeat at the hands of a Theban-led army at the Battle of Delium. Brasidas arrives in the north and captures or persuades to defect several cities, including Amphipolis.
423	Spartans and Athenians agree to a one-year armistice, but this is ignored in the north. Cleon is sent there with a force and makes some progress.
422	Cleon's army is routed outside Amphipolis, and both he and Brasidas are killed. The peace talks gather momentum.
421	Peace of Nicias between Athens and Sparta and a fifty-year alliance between the two cities. Neither side fulfils all its obligations, but the broader peace holds. The Athenians retake Scione.
420	The Spartans ally with the Boeotians.
419	Alcibiades is one of a number of Athenians arguing for renewal of hostilities. He is elected

general and given troops, which he takes to the Peloponnese, where they raid in alliance with Argos. A coalition of Peloponnesian states forms to oppose the Spartans.

418   Argos and its allies, including an Athenian contingent, are defeated at the Battle of Mantineia. A new regime at Argos agrees on a fifty-year alliance with Sparta.

417   Revolution at Argos overthrows the pro-Spartan faction. Argos and Athens ally once again.

c.416 Last known ostracism at Athens removes a rival of both Nicias and Alcibiades.

416   The Athenians conquer Melos.

415   Segesta in Sicily appeals for Athenian support against a rival backed by Syracuse. The Athenians vote for a grand expedition to Sicily. The desecration of the herms shocks the city, but the expedition sets out regardless. Later, Alcibiades is ordered back to face charges. He escapes and goes to Sparta. The Athenian expedition wins a small engagement outside Syracuse and then withdraws for the winter.

414   The Athenians begin to blockade Syracuse. Lamachus is killed, leaving Nicias in sole charge of the expedition. The Spartans send Gylippus as military advisor to the Syracusans, and he inspires them to thwart Athenian efforts to enclose the city.

413   The Athenians reinforce the Sicilian expedition, but the situation has already deteriorated before they arrive, and they are unable to reverse this. The Spartans declare war on Athens and establish a fortified base at Decelea. After delays and indecision, the Athenians retreat from Syracuse, but they are pursued and the survivors forced to surrender.

	Nicias and Demosthenes are executed, and many prisoners die of neglect.
412	Many of Athens's allies rebel, including the island of Samos. The Spartans make an alliance with the Persians through two satraps and begin to receive Persian subsidies, which fund the creation of a fleet. Alcibiades takes the negotiations.
411	At Athens, the 400 seize power, restricting voting rights to the 5,000, although these do not appear to meet. The troops and sailors at Samos refuse to accept the revolutionary government. They are joined by Alcibiades, who tries and fails to persuade the Persians to switch sides. The 400 are overthrown and replaced by the 5,000. Aided by Alcibiades, the Athenians win victories in the naval Battles of Cynossema and Abydus.
410	The Athenians win a great victory over the Spartan-led fleet at the Battle of Cyzicus. The 5,000 are replaced, and the traditional system of democracy reinstated. The Spartans ask for peace but are rebuffed by the Athenians.
409–408	Led by Alcibiades, the Athenians regain control of much of the Asian coast and the Dardanelles.
407	Alcibiades returns to Athens. Lysander is placed in command of the rebuilt Spartan fleet, improving relations with the Persians in the person of Cyrus, one of the king's sons. Alcibiades resumes campaigning but achieves little.
406	While Alcibiades is absent, the acting commander of the Athenian fleet ignores orders and is unwisely drawn into battle by Lysander. In the ensuing Battle of Notium, the Athenians suffer a humiliating, although not costly, defeat. Fearing retribution from his fellow citizens, Alcibiades leaves and goes to live on family estates near the Dardanelles. A new Spartan admiral arrives to

replace Lysander and blockades the Athenian fleet. A fresh fleet is formed at Athens, which smashes the Spartans at the Battle of Arginusae. However, the failure to pick up survivors from the water leads the Athenians to condemn the victorious commanders to death. Six are executed, and two more flee into exile.

405	Lysander is appointed to command again. He attacks and destroys the Athenian fleet in the Battle of Aegospotami. Athens is placed under siege.
404	The Athenians surrender to the Spartans. The long walls are slighted, and a tyranny, the Thirty, is established.
403	Restoration of democracy at Athens.
402–1	The Spartans defeat Elis.
401	Cyrus begins campaign to take the Persian throne from his brother but is killed at the Battle of Cunaxa. The 10,000 fight their way back to the coast.
400	Spartans declare war on Persia, mainly targeting one of the satraps who had supported them in the past.
397	Exiled Athenian admiral Conon is appointed to lead a Persian fleet against the Spartans and does so with great success.
396	King Agesilaus campaigns in Asia.
395	Alliance including Corinth, Thebes, and Athens attacks Sparta. Death of Lysander. Agesilaus recalled from Asia.
394	The Spartans win the Battle of Nemea, but the Persians largely drive them from the Asian shore and the Dardanelles.
393	The Athenians begin to restore their long walls.

386	The war continues until the Persian 'King's Peace' is established in Greece.
382	Spartans seize Theban citadel, installing an oligarchy and maintaining a garrison in the city.
379/8	Thebans destroy Spartan garrison.
371	Epaminondas and Pelopidas lead Theban army to victory over the Spartans at the Battle of Leuctra.
362	Tactical defeat of Spartans at Battle of Mantineia proves strategically indecisive, in part because of the death of Epaminondas.

NOTES

INTRODUCTION

1 Cicero, *de Legibus* 1. 5; Plutarch, *de malignitate Herodoti* 1.
2 Thucydides 1. 1.

CHAPTER 1

1 Homer, *Iliad* 1. 1 (Loeb translation, 1924).
2 The literature discussing Homer is too vast to list here. A good starting place for the general reader is R. Lane Fox, *Homer and His Iliad* (2023); see also D. Cairns (ed.), *Oxford Readings in Homer's Iliad* (2001); B. Powell, *Homer* (2003).
3 On an age of heroes, see Hesiod, *Works and Days* 104–200.
4 Thucydides 1.3.
5 Compared to Homer, Hesiod, *Works and Days* 276–280, emphasised the inherent justice of Zeus; criticism of the portrayal of the gods by both authors came in the sixth century BC from Xenophanes *F11* (D-K); for discussion, see B. Lavelle, *Archaic Greece. The Age of New Reckonings* (2020), pp. 76–82, 87–88.
6 J. Bintliff, *The Complete Archaeology of Greece. From Hunter Gatherers to the 20th Century AD* (2012), pp. 28–45 on hunter-gatherers and pp. 46–82 on the rise of the farming communities in Greece.
7 On Uruk, see N. Crüsemann, M. van Hilgert, B. Salje, & T. Potts (eds.), *Uruk: First City of the Ancient World* (2019); for a detailed introduction to Egypt, see A. Lloyd (ed.), *A Companion to Ancient Egypt* (2014), pp. 63–80, esp. 67–70.
8 For a lively and accessible survey of the evidence for Stonehenge and approaches to understanding it, see F. Pryor, *Stonehenge. The Story of a Sacred Landscape* (2016).

9   On the Minoans, see Bintliff (2012), pp. 123–154.
10 Thucydides 1. 4.
11 On the Mycenaeans, see T. Martin, *Ancient Greece. From Prehistoric to Hellenistic Times* (2nd ed., 2012), pp. 23–40; Bintliff (2012), pp. 181–205; A. Knodell, *Societies in Transition in Early Greece. An Archaeological History* (2021), pp. 63–115.
12 On the Ahhiyawa, see I. Morris & B. Powell, *The Greeks. History, Culture, and Society* (2005), p. 67; Bintliff (2012), p. 186, with convincing scepticism in Knodell (2021), pp. 108–111; Pylos Tablet An 657 lists commanders and soldiers guarding a stretch of coastline. The largest group consists of 50 men; the others are smaller; the grand total is 130.
13 For the widespread decline and collapse from the later thirteenth century BC, see Morris & Powell (2005), pp. 67–70; Bintliff (2012), pp. 184–185; J. Hall, *A History of the Archaic Greek World, ca. 1200–479 BCE* (2nd ed., 2014), pp. 41–56; Knodell (2021), pp. 116–119.
14 Knodell (2021), pp. 116–137.
15 Pylos Tablet Tn 316 records sacrifices made to Zeus, Hera, and Poseidon; on language and alphabets, see Hall (2014), pp. 56–59; Martin (2012), pp. 55–56; Knodell (2021), pp. 215–222.

CHAPTER 2

1   J. Bintliff, *The Complete Archaeology of Greece. From Hunter Gatherers to the 20th Century AD* (2012), pp. 213–224.
2   Thucydides 1. 2; in Homer the savage Cyclopes have no knowledge of seafaring, farming, or laws and live apart, *Odyssey* 9. 105–129.
3   T. Martin, *Ancient Greece. From Prehistoric to Hellenistic Times* (2nd ed., 2012), pp. 47–51; A. Knodell, *Societies in Transition in Early Greece. An Archaeological History* (2021), pp. 119–129.
4   On the Dorians and migrations in this era in general, see R. Osborne, *Greece in the Making, 1200–479 BC* (2nd ed., 2009), pp. 47–51; J. Hall, *A History of the Archaic Greek World, ca. 1200–479 BCE* (2nd ed., 2014), pp. 44–56; Knodell (2021), pp.187–191, and N. Kennell, *Spartans. A New History* (2010), pp. 20–31; on the Athenians, the evidence is collected and discussed in V. Rosvlach, 'Autochthony and the Athenians,' *Classical Quarterly* 37. 2 (1987), pp. 294–306.
5   For examples of dubious claims about the past, see the opposing arguments of Demosthenes and Aeschines in fourth-century Athens, in Aeschines, *On the Embassy* 17–20. For a useful discussion of the evidence, see G. Cawkwell, *Philip of Macedon* (1978), pp. 92–95; for the subsequent chronology and background, see I. Worthington, *Philip II of Macedonia* (2008), pp. 86–104; G. Cawkwell, 'Aeschines and the Peace of Philocrates,'

Revue des Études Greques 73 (1960), pp. 416–438; G. Cawkwell, 'The Peace of Philocrates Again,' *Classical Quarterly* 28. 1 (1978), pp. 93–104.

6   Hall (2014), pp. 127–128; Knodell (2021), pp. 73–74.

7   On Homeric society, see Osborne (2009), pp. 140–152; Hall (2014), pp. 126–138.

8   *Iliad* 2. 200–277, 671–675.

9   On landscape and climate, see Bintliff (2012), pp. 11–25; S. Isager & J. Skydsgaard, *Ancient Greek Agriculture. An Introduction* (1992), pp. 9–18.

10   On the Lefkandi and the burials, see Bintliff (2012), pp. 211–212; Knodell (2021), pp. 161–167; Osborne (2009), pp. 5–58, 77.

11   Bintliff (2012), pp. 213–224; Knodell (2021), pp. 194–215.

12   T. Hodos, *The Archaeology of the Mediterranean Iron Age. A Globalising World c. 1100–600 BCE* (2020), pp. 58–64; R. Sallares, *The Ecology of the Ancient Greek World* (1991), pp. 86–90, 122–126; Osborne (2009), pp. 30–31, 66–76.

13   K. Raaflaub, 'Soldiers, Citizens, and the Evolution of the Early Greek polis,' in L. Mitchell & P. Rhodes (eds.), *The Development of the Polis in Archaic Greece* (1997), pp. 49–59, esp. 51–53.

14   For discussion of this type of farm in Homer, see V. Davis Hanson, *The Other Greeks. The Family Farm and the Agrarian Roots of Western Civilization* (1995), pp. 47–88; on the costs of slaves and mules, see T. Gallant, *Risk and Survival in Ancient Greece* (1991), pp. 30–33.

15   Hanson (1995), pp. 33–41.

16   Hanson (1995), pp. 125–176; Isager & Skydsgaard (1992), pp. 19–43, 108–114.

17   Hanson (1995), pp. 179–195; Gallant (1991), pp. 82–87; A. Burford, *Land and Labor in the Greek World* (1993), pp. 67–72, 113–116.

18   Hall (2014), pp. 72–81; Osborne (2009), pp. 75–82.

19   On Al Mina, see T. Hodos, *Local Responses to Colonization in the Iron Age Mediterranean* (2006), pp. 37–40; on Ionian cities, see Osborne (2009), pp. 48–49; Hall (2014), pp. 44–45, 96–97; Knodell (2021), pp. 187–189; on colonization in general, see Hodos (2020), pp. 80–94; G. Tsetskhladze & F. de Angelis (eds.), *The Archaeology of Greek Colonization. Essays Dedicated to Sir John Boardman* (1994).

20   D. Ridgway, 'Phoenicians and Greeks in the West: A View from Pithekoussai,' in Tsetskhladze & de Angelis (1994), pp. 35–46; Hodos (2020), pp. 95–146.

21   J. Coldstream, 'Prospectors or Pioneers: Pithekoussai, Kyme and Central Italy,' in Tsetskhladze & de Angelis (1994), pp. 47–59; Hall (2014), pp. 120–124; Osborne (2009), pp. 110–123; for a useful reminder of the role of violence in the process of colonization, see T. Rihll, 'War, Slavery and

Settlement in Early Greece,' in J. Rich & G. Shipley (eds.), *War and Society in the Greek World* (1993), pp. 77–107.

22 Hanson (1995), pp. 143–146; F. de Angelis, 'The Foundation of Selinous: Overpopulation or Opportunities?' in Tsetskhladze & de Angelis (1994), pp. 87–110.

23 Plato, *Phaedo* 109a-b attributing the words to Socrates; on the alphabet and its adaptation and adoption, see Hodos (2020), pp. 182–208.

CHAPTER 3

1 The research programme undertaken at Copenhagen University is summarised in M. Hansen, *Polis. An Introduction to the Ancient Greek City-State* (2006), esp. pp. 67–100.

2 Arguing in favour of many farms, see V. Davis Hanson, *The Other Greeks. The Family Farm and the Agrarian Roots of Western Civilization* (1995), generally, but esp. pp. 47–88, 125–133, 67–72, with contrasting views in L. Foxhall, 'Farming and Fighting in Ancient Greece,' in J. Rich & G. Shipley (eds.), *War and Society in the Greek World* (1993), pp. 134–145, esp. 136–138; Hansen (2006), pp. 67–72.

3 *Iliad* 18. 497–508.

4 For an insightful, if over sceptical, analysis of the evidence for the Lelantine War, see J. Hall, *A History of the Archaic Greek World, ca. 1200–479 BCE* (2nd ed., 2014), pp. 1–8, with A. Knodell, *Societies in Transition in Early Greece. An Archaeological History* (2021), pp. 205–212.

5 Hesiod, *Works and Days* 248–273, with discussion in R. Osborne, *Greece in the Making, 1200–479 BC* (2nd ed., 2009), pp. 133–140.

6 Osborne (2009), pp. 174–177; for the early law, see C. Fornara (ed. and trans.), *Archaic Times to the End of the Peloponnesian War*. Vol. 1 of *Translated Documents of Greece and Rome* (2nd ed., 1983), p. 11.

7 A handy introduction to the Lyric poets is B. Lavelle, *Archaic Greece. The Age of New Reckonings* (2020), pp. 157–177, with suggestions for further reading; a good collection of translated poetry is M. West (trans.), *Greek Lyric Poetry* (1993).

8 Athenaios 15. 50. 24.

9 See Pausanias 8. 40. 2 for the posthumous victory in the pankration; in general, see Lavelle (2020), pp. 181–201.

10 J. Salmon, 'Lopping Off the Heads? Tyrants, Politics and the *polis*,' in L. Mitchell & P. Rhodes (eds.), *The Development of the Polis in Archaic Greece* (1997), pp. 60–73, esp. 61–62.

11 The sources for Cylon's coup are listed and discussed in P. Rhodes, *A Commentary on the Aristotelian Athenaion Politeia* (1981), pp. 79–84.

12 For the burial, see S. Chryssoulaki, A. Linderholm, A. Kjellström, V. Langerholm & M. Krzewińska, 'Bioarchaeological Field Analysis of Human Remains from the Mass Graves at Phaleron, Greece,' *Opuscula. Annual of the Swedish Institutes at Athens and Rome* 12 (2019).

13 Thucydides 1. 126. 10; Plutarch, *Solon* 12. 1.

14 Thucydides 2. 15. 1–6; Plutarch, *Theseus*, combines various myths and deductions into a biography; mention of Athenians in *Iliad* 2. 546–556, with Knodell (2021), pp. 44–45.

15 Knodell (2021), pp. 9–10, 71–72, 96–98, 118–124; T. Mitchell, *Democracy's Beginning. The Athenian Story* (2015), pp. 25–34; J. Camp, *The Archaeology of Athens* (2001), pp. 14–26.

16 Mitchell (2015), pp. 8–9; in the later fifth century BC, Thucydides 2. 16. 1 claimed that at least half the population lived in the countryside.

17 On wider social indications and burial practices compared with those of Athens, see J. Almeida, *Justice as an Aspect of the Polis Idea in Solon's Political Poems. A Reading of Fragments in Light of the Researches of New Classical Archaeology* (2003), pp. 127–170.

18 Rhodes (1981), pp. 32–34, 98–102.

19 Rhodes (1981), pp. 84–88; R. Osborne, 'Law and Laws. How Do We Join the Dots?' in Mitchell & Rhodes (1997), pp. 74–82, esp. 76–79; Osborne (2009), pp. 176–177, 203.

20 Mitchell (2015), pp. 25–32; Almeida (2003), pp. 1–19, on Solon's career, and pp. 20–26, on the question of dating; Plutarch, *Solon* 1–3. 1, with L. de Blois, 'Plutarch's Solon: A Tissue of Commonplaces or a Historical Account,' in J. Blok & A. Lardinois (eds.), *Solon of Athens. New Historical and Philological Approaches* (2006), pp. 429–440.

21 For Solon's poetry, see in particular A. Lardinois, 'Have We Solon's Verses?' in Blok & Lardinois (2006), pp. 15–35; E. Stehle, 'Solon's Self-Reflective Political Persona and Its Audience,' in Blok & Lardinois (2006), pp. 79–113; F. Blaise, 'Poetics and Politics: Tradition Re-worked in Solon's "Eunomia" (Poem 4),' in Blok & Lardinois (2006), pp. 114–133; on the existence of the laws, see P. Rhodes, 'The Reforms and Laws of Solon: An Optimistic View,' in Blok & Lardinois (2006), pp. 248–260.

22 See Rhodes (1981), pp. 118–179, for sources and discussion, with J. Bintliff, 'Solon's Reforms: An Archaeological Perspective,' in Blok & Lardinois (2006), pp. 321–333; S. Forsdyke, 'Land, Labor and Economy in Solonian Athens: Breaking the Impasse Between Archaeology and History,' in Blok & Lardinois (2006), pp. 334–350.

23 Solon, *Fragments* 36, 37, with discussion in J. Ober, 'Solon and the *horoi*: Facts on the Ground in Archaic Athens,' in Blok & Lardinois (2006), pp. 441–456; on the philosophical aspects of Solon's reforms, see J. Lewis, *Solon the Thinker* (2006), esp. pp. 108–130.

24 L. Foxhall, 'A View from the Top: Evaluating the Solonian Property Classes,' in Mitchell & Rhodes (1997), pp. 113–136; H. van Wees, 'Mass and Elite in Solon's Athens: The Property Classes Revisited,' in Blok & Lardinois (2006), pp. 351–389.

25 Plutarch, *Solon* 25. 4–5.

26 See L. Mitchell, 'New Wine in Old Wineskins. Solon, *arete*, and the *agathos*,' in Mitchell & Rhodes (1997), pp. 137–147, for a discussion of the changing nature of elite influence.

CHAPTER 4

1 Herodotus 1. 65–66; Plutarch, *Lycurgus* 1. 2–5; a good starting place for modern understanding of Lycurgus is M. Nafissi, 'Lykourgos the Spartan "Lawgiver": Ancient Beliefs and Modern Scholarship,' in A. Powell (ed.), *A Companion to Sparta* (Blackwell Companions to the Ancient World) (2017), pp. 93–123.

2 The 'Spartan Mirage', a phrase coined by a French scholar in the 1930s, has been employed by numerous scholars in the late twentieth and early twenty-first centuries to challenge orthodox views of Sparta and its society—for instance, A. Powell & S. Hodkinson (eds.), *Sparta. Beyond the Mirage* (2002); good recent introductions to Sparta, which embrace a range of different approaches, include P. Cartledge, *The Spartans. An Epic History* (rev. ed. 2003); N. Kennell, *Spartans. A New History* (2010); P. Rahe, *The Spartan Regime. Its Character, Origins and Grand Strategy* (2016).

3 See W. Cavanagh, 'An Archaeology of Ancient Sparta with Reference to Laconia and Messenia,' in Powell (2017), pp. 61–92; on Helen and Menelaus, see Cartledge (2003), pp. 46–50.

4 On early history and the coming together of the villages, see Kennell (2010), pp. 20–38; Rahe (2016), pp. 72–80, 90–97.

5 Kennell (2010), pp. 5–9, 39–53; Cartledge (2003), pp. 23–27; Herodotus 1. 66–67.

6 For Tyrtaeus, see C. Calame, 'Pre-Classical Sparta as Song Culture,' in Powell (2017), pp. 177–201; B. Lavelle, *Archaic Greece. The Age of New Reckonings* (2020), pp. 160–161.

7 Tyrtaeus F12. 1–9 for virtues, F11. 29–34 for urge forward; cf. 11. 12, 12. 12, 19. 13 West.

8 Tyrtaeus F10. 1–10, 13–18, 12. 10–44 West.

9 Herodotus 9. 33–34; on differing models for demography, see T. Figueira, 'The Demography of the Spartan Helots,' in N. Luraghi & S. Alcock (eds.), *Helots and Their Masters in Laconia and Messenia. Histories, Ideologies, Structures* (2003), pp. 193–239; W. Scheidel, 'Helot Numbers: A Simplified Model,' in Luraghi & Alcock (2003), pp. 240–247; on Spartan

kingship, see P. Cartledge, 'The Spartan Kingship: Doubly Odd?' in P. Cartledge, *Spartan Reflections* (2001), pp. 55–67; in great detail, E. Millender, 'Kingship: The History, Power and Prerogatives of the Spartans' 'Divine' Dyarchy,' in Powell (2017), pp. 452–479.

10   Plutarch, *Lycurgus* 6. 1–5 (which also quotes Tyrtaeus for confirmation), with discussion in Nafissi (2017), *passim*; Rahe (2017), pp. 98–106; P. Cartledge, 'The Peculiar Position of Sparta in the Development of the Greek City-State,' in Cartledge (2001), pp. 21–38; M. Lipka, 'Notes on the Influence of the Spartan Great Rhetra on Tyrtaeus, Herodotus and Xenophon,' in Powell & Hodkinson (2002), pp. 219–225.

11   Tyrtaeus cited in Aristotle, *Politics* 5. 6. 1–2 [1306b–1307a]; cf. Herodotus 1. 65.

12   J. Ducat, 'The *Perioikoi*,' in Powell (2017), pp. 596–614.

13   A good starting place for this debate is the collection of papers in Luraghi & Alcock (2003), with T. Figueira, 'Helotage and the Spartan Economy,' in Powell (2017), pp. 565–595.

14   S. Hodkinson, 'Spartiates, Helots and the Direction of the Agrarian Economy Towards an Understanding of Helotage in Comparative Perspective,' in Luraghi & Alcock (2003), pp. 248-285.

15   Kennell (2010), pp. 40–53; Rahe (2017), pp. 106–120.

16   Herodotus 1. 65–68.

17   H. van Wees, 'Luxury, Austerity and Equality in Sparta', in Powell (2017), pp. 202–235; P. Davis, 'Equality and Distinction Within the Spartiate Community', in Powell (2017), pp. 480–499; on the wider question of wealth and its implications for equality between Spartans, see S. Hodkinson, *Property and Wealth in Classical Sparta* (2009), *passim*.

18   Plutarch, *Lycurgus* 8. 1–4.

19   Plutarch, *Lycurgus* 16. 1–2; for detailed discussions of the education system, see J. Ducat (trans. E. Stafford, P.-J. Shaw & A. Powell), *Spartan Education. Youth and Society in the Classical Period* (2006); N. Richer, 'Spartan Education in the Classical Period', in Powell (2017), pp. 525–542.

20   A. Eremin, 'Settlements of Spartan *perioikoi*: *poleis* or *komai*?' in Powell & Hodkinson (2002), pp. 267–283; on crafts in earlier Sparta, see P. Cartledge, 'The Mirage or Lykourgan Sparta: Some Brazen Reflections', in Cartledge (2001), pp. 169–184.

21   See T. Figueira, 'The Spartan *hippeis*,' in S. Hodkinson & A. Powell (eds.), *Sparta and War* (2006), pp. 57–84.

22   Calame (2017), pp. 177–201; Cartledge (2003), pp. 153–166; for more detail, see S. Pomeroy, *Spartan Women* (2002).

23   Rahe (2017), pp. 114–120.

24   Herodotus 1. 82–83; on suicide at Sparta, see E. David, 'Suicide in Spartan Society,' in T. Figueira (ed.), *Spartan Society* (2004), pp. 25–46.

25   Tyrtaeus F5. 2–3.

CHAPTER 5

1 Herodotus 5. 22.
2 Plutarch, *Solon* 27. 1–28. 4; Herodotus 1. 30–33.
3 R. Drews, 'The First Tyrants in Greece,' *Historia* 21 (1972), pp. 129–144; G. Cawkwell, 'Early Greek Tyranny and the People,' *Classical Quarterly* 45 (1995), pp. 73–86.
4 See Cawkwell (1995), pp. 73–76, 84–85; R. Osborne, *Greece in the Making. 1200–479 BC* (2nd ed., 2009), pp. 180–185; J. Salmon, 'Lopping off the Heads? Tyrants, Politics and the *polis*,' in L. Mitchell & P. Rhodes (eds.), *The Development of the Polis in Archaic Greece* (1997), pp. 60–73.
5 Plutarch, *Solon* 14. 4–5; Aristotle, *Athenian Constitution* 12. 1–13. 2, with P. Rhodes, *A Commentary on the Aristotelian Athenaion Politeia* (1981), pp. 173–184.
6 Herodotus 1. 59; Aristotle, *Athenian Constitution* 13. 3–5; Plutarch, *Solon* 13. 1–3, with Rhodes (1981), pp. 179–188; on his bodyguard, see H. Singor, 'The Military Side of the Peisistratean Tyranny,' in H. Sancisi-Weerdenburg, *Peisistratos and the Tyranny. A Reappraisal of the Evidence* (2000), pp. 107–129, esp. 119–128.
7 Herodotus 1. 59; Plutarch, *Solon* 30. 1–31. 2; for detailed discussion, see B. Lavelle, *Fame, Money, and Power. The Rise of Peisistratos and 'Democratic' Tyranny at Athens* (2005), esp. pp. 66–98; see also V. Gouščin, 'Pisistratus' Leadership in A. P. 13. 4 and the Establishment of the Tyranny of 561/60 BC,' *Classical Quarterly* 49 (1999), pp. 14–23.
8 Herodotus 1. 60–61; Aristotle, *Athenian Constitution* 14. 2–15. 1, with J. Blok, 'Phye's Procession: Culture, Politics and Peisistratid Rule,' in Sancisi-Weerdenburg (2000), pp. 17–48; B. Lavelle, 'The Compleat Angler: Observations on the Rise of Peisistratos in Herodotos (1. 59–64),' *Classical Quarterly* 41 (1991), pp. 317–324; Lavelle (2005), pp. 98–115.
9 See Herodotus 1. 59 for the omen; for emphasis on the role of Megacles, see G. Anderson, *The Athenian Experiment. Building an Imagined Political Community in Ancient Attica, 508–490 BC* (2003), pp. 67–72.
10 On Pisistratus's war record, see full discussion in Lavelle (2005), pp. 30–65; on Pisistratus and wealth, see B. Lavelle, 'The Pisistratids and the Mines of Thrace,' *Greek, Roman and Byzantine Studies* 33 (1992), pp. 5–23.
11 Herodotus 1. 61–63, with Lavelle (2005), pp. 116–154; on Pisistratus's army, see Singor (2000), pp. 112–119.
12 H. Sancisi-Weerdenburg, 'The Tyranny of Peisistratos,' in Sancisi-Weerdenburg (2000), pp. 1–15; Rhodes (1981), pp. 189–240.
13 Thucydides 6. 54. 5–6; on troops, see Singor (2000), pp. 112–119, contrasting with B. Lavelle, 'Herodotos, Skythian Archers, and the *doryphoroi* of the Peisistratids,' *Klio* 74 (1992), pp. 78–97.

14 Aristotle, *Athenian Constitution* 16. 1–10, with Rhodes (1981), pp. 213–223.

15 S. Slings, 'Literature in Athens, 566–510 BC,' in Sancisi-Weerdenburg (2000), pp. 57–77, esp. 57–61; Lavelle (2005), pp. 306, 311, 325n4.

16 Blok (2000), pp. 20–21; Slings (2000), pp. 67–70; Anderson (2003), pp. 158–177.

17 R. Meiggs & D. Lewis (eds.), *Greek Historical Inscriptions*, (1989) 6 fr. c.

18 Slings (2000), pp. 57–77.

19 J. van der Vin, 'Coins in Athens at the Time of Peisistratos,' in Sancisi-Weerdenburg (2000), pp. 147–153; G. Aperghis, 'Athenian Mines, Coins and Triremes,' *Historia* 62 (2013), pp. 1–24, esp. 14–22.

20 Main ancient sources: Herodotus 5. 55–61, 6. 123; Thucydides 1. 20, 6. 54–59; Aristotle, *Athenian Constitution* 17–18, with comments in Rhodes (1981), pp. 189–190, 228–232.

21 For discussion, see B. Lavelle, 'The Nature of Hipparchos' Insult to Harmodios,' *American Journal of Philology* 107 (1986), pp. 318–331; E. Meyer, 'Thucydides on Harmodius and Aristogeiton, Tyranny, and History,' *Classical Quarterly* 58 (2008), pp. 13–34.

22 Anderson (2003), pp. 197–211; on the thrice Olympic victor Cimon, see Herodotus 6. 103.

23 Herodotus 5. 62–63; Aristotle, *Athenian Constitution* 19. 4, with Rhodes (1981), pp. 236–237; on the nature of exile in this era, see S. Forsdyke, *The Politics of Expulsion in Ancient Greece* (2005), pp. 79–143.

24 Thucydides 3. 68; Herodotus 6. 108.

25 Herodotus 5. 63.

26 Herodotus 5. 63–65; Aristotle, *Athenian Constitution* 19. 5–6, with Rhodes (1981), pp. 237–240.

CHAPTER 6

1 For Spartan attitudes, see P. Rahe, *The Grand Strategy of Classical Sparta. The Persian Challenge* (2015), pp. 92–96.

2 Herodotus 5. 66, 70, 6. 127–128.

3 Herodotus 5. 66, 69; Aristotle, *Athenian Constitution* 20. 1–21. 2, with P. Rhodes, *A Commentary on the Aristotelian Athenaion Politeia* (1981), pp. 240–250.

4 Herodotus 5. 70–72.

5 Herodotus 5. 72–73; Aristotle, *Athenian Constitution* 20. 3–5; J. Ober, 'The Athenians Revolution of 508/7 BC: Violence, Authority and the Origins of Democracy,' in J. Ober, *The Athenian Revolution. Essays on the Ancient Greek Democracy and Political Theory* (1996), pp. 32–52, argues

for spontaneous popular resistance, where others prefer to see more organization and leadership—for instance, G. Anderson, *The Athenian Experiment. Building an Imagined Political Community in Ancient Attica 508–490 BC* (2003), pp. 76–84.

6 Herodotus 5. 73–76, with Rahe (2015), pp. 96–100.

7 Herodotus 5. 77.

8 Rhodes (1981), pp. 240–277, discusses and gathers sources; see also M. Ostwald in *The Cambridge Ancient History* (hereafter *CAH*²) IV (1988), pp. 309–325; B. Develin & M. Kilmer, 'What Kleisthenes Did,' *Historia* 46 (1997), pp. 3–18; E. David, 'A Preliminary Stage of Cleisthenes' Reforms,' *Classical Antiquity* 5 (1986), pp. 1–13; T. Mitchell, *Democracy's Beginning. The Athenian Story* (2015), pp. 39–49.

9 Rhodes (1981), pp. 250–255; Anderson (2003), pp. 34–40.

10 Aristotle, *Athenian Constitution* 21. 4–5, with Rhodes (1981), pp. 251–253.

11 Aristotle, *Athenian Constitution* 21. 6; Anderson (2003), pp. 126–134, 141–142.

12 Anderson (2003), pp. 147–157; F. Frost, 'The Athenian Military Before Cleisthenes,' *Historia* 33 (1984), pp. 283–295.

13 Anderson (2003), pp. 96–97; J. Camp, *The Archaeology of Athens* (2001), pp. 44–45.

14 Rhodes (1981), pp. 267–271; Mitchell (2015), pp. 45–46; C. Robinson, 'Cleisthenes and Ostracism,' *American Journal of Archaeology* 56 (1952), pp. 23–26; N. Doegnes, 'Ostracism and the "Boulai" of Cleisthenes,' *Historia* 45 (1996), pp. 387–404; S. Forsdyke, *The Politics of Expulsion in Ancient Greece* (2005), pp. 79–143, esp. 133–142.

15 Herodotus 5. 78.

CHAPTER 7

1 Herodotus 5. 90–94; Rahe, *The Grand Strategy of Classical Sparta. The Persian Challenge* (2015), pp. 101–103.

2 Herodotus 6. 61–67; P. Cartledge, *The Spartans. An Epic History* (rev. ed., 2003), pp. 94–96.

3 Herodotus 6. 71–84, with Rahe (2015), pp. 187–189; A. Griffiths, 'Was Kleomenes Mad?' in A. Powell (ed.), *Classical Sparta: Techniques Behind Her Success* (1989), pp. 51–78.

4 Plutarch, *Lycurgus* 16. 1–2.

5 For detailed studies of the raising of Spartan children, see J. Ducat (trans. E. Stafford, P.-J. Shaw & A. Powell), *Spartan Education. Youth and Society in the Classical Period* (2006); N. Kennell, *The Gymnasium of Virtue* (1995), pp. 28–48; N. Richer, 'Spartan Education in the Classical Period,' in

Powell (2017), pp. 525–542. Principal sources: Xenophon, *Spartan Constitution* 2. 1–4. 6; Plutarch, *Lycurgus* 16. 3–19. 4; and others.

6   Plutarch, *Lycurgus* 18. 1; Plutarch, *Moralia* 234a–b; Plutarch, *Spartan Sayings* Anon. 35; Xenophon, *Spartan Constitution* 2. 6–9, with discussion in Ducat (2006), pp. 46–48, 80–82, 201–207.

7   P. Cartledge, *Agesilaos and the Crisis of Sparta* (1987), pp. 60–61, discusses the evidence for Xenophon's sons; for a differing view, see N. Humble, 'Xenophon's Sons in Sparta? Perspectives on *xenoi* in the Spartan Upbringing,' in T. Figueira (ed.), *Spartan Society* (2004), pp. 231–250; on the *hippeis*, see T. Figueira, 'The Spartan *hippeis*,' in S. Hodkinson & A. Powell (eds.), *Sparta and War* (2006), pp. 57–84; on the marketplace, see Plutarch, *Lycurgus* 25. 1.

8   Plutarch, *Spartan Sayings* Paidaretos 3; Plutarch, *Moralia* 231b; *Lycurgus* 25. 6; on father repeating punishment of his son, see Xenophon, *Spartan Constitution* 6. 1–2.

9   Plutarch, *Lycurgus* 19. 1–20. 6; Herodotus 7. 226.

10   Xenophon, *Spartan Constitution* 2. 12–14; Plutarch, *Lycurgus* 17. 1, 18. 4, with discussion in Ducat (2006), esp. pp. 11–13, 164–168; P. Cartledge, 'The Politics of Pederasty,' in P. Cartledge, *Spartan Reflections* (2001), pp. 91–105.

11   On education for girls, see Ducat (2006), pp. 223–247; Richer (2017), pp. 537–539; S. Pomeroy, *Spartan Women* (2002), pp. 3–32; on inspection, see Aelian, *Miscellany* 14. 7.

12   Plutarch, *Lycurgus* 16. 6–7; Ducat (2006), pp. 103–104, 124–134.

13   Xenophon, *Spartan Constitution* 2. 1–2; Ducat (2006), pp. 119–124.

14   Plutarch, *Lycurgus* 12. 1–3; for discussion, see H. van Wees, 'The Common Messes,' in Powell (2017), pp. 236–268.

15   On the wealthy paying for boys to go through the education system, see evidence gathered in Ducat (2006), pp. 128–129, 134–135.

16   Plutarch, *Lycurgus* 14. 1–15. 10, with Pomeroy (2002), pp. 37–44; for inheritance of property, see S. Hodkinson, *Property and Wealth in Classical Sparta* (2009), esp. pp. 65–112, 400–409.

17   Plutarch, *Lycurgus* 12. 2–3, 15. 4–5.

18   See van Wees (2017), pp. 238–244, 249–251.

19   P. Rahe, *The Spartan Regime. Its Character, Origins and Grand Strategy* (2016), p. 114, plausibly speculates that there were Spartan garrisons in Messenia and probably Spartan overseers of the helots; for discussion of how helots were supervised, see S. Hodkinson, 'Spartiates, Helots and the Direction of the Agrarian Economy: Towards an Understanding of Helotage in Comparative Perspective,' in N. Luraghi & S. Alcock (eds.), *Helots and Their Masters in Laconia and Messenia. Histories, Ideologies, Structures* (2003), pp. 263–278.

20 Xenophon. *Spartan Constitution* 6. 1–4, with Hodkinson (2009), pp. 199–201.

21 Xenophon, *Spartan Constitution* 9. 4; Plutarch, *Agesilaus* 30. 2; for discussion, see J. Ducat, 'The Spartan "Tremblers",' in Hodkinson & Powell (2006), pp. 1–55.

22 Plutarch, *Lycurgus* 28. 1–7, including the reference to Aristotle; with Ducat (2006), pp. 281–331; Richer (2017), pp. 529–530.

CHAPTER 8

1 H. van Wees, *Greek Warfare. Myths and Realities* (2004), esp. pp. 6–46.

2 J. Lendon, 'Homeric Vengeance and the Outbreak of Greek Wars,' in H. van Wees (ed.), *War and Violence in Ancient Greece* (2000), pp. 1–30.

3 Aristotle, *Politics* 1297b16–18.

4 Herodotus 7. 9. 2. The debate over hoplite warfare has produced an extensive literature, including V. Davis Hanson, *Warfare and Agriculture in Classical Greece* (2nd ed., 1998); V. Davis Hanson, *The Western Way of War* (1989); V. Davis Hanson (ed.), *Hoplites. The Classical Greek Battle Experience* (1991); van Wees (2000); D. Kagan & G. Viggiano (eds.), *Men of Bronze. Hoplite Warfare in Ancient Greece* (2013). W. Pritchett, *The Greek State at War*. 5 vols. (1971–1991), remains fundamental to any examination of Greek warfare.

5 Tyrtaeus II. 17–20; the most detailed descriptions of the phases of campaign and battle remain W. Pritchett, *The Greek State at War*. Vol. 4 (1985), pp. 44–93; Hanson (1989), *passim*; for after the battle, see P. Vaughn, 'The Identification and Retrieval of the Hoplite Battle-Dead,' in Hanson (1991), pp. 38–62; on overview of warfare, see P. Krentz, 'War,' in P. Sabin, H. van Wees & M. Whitby, *The Cambridge History of Greek and Roman Warfare*. Vol. 1 (2007), pp. 146–185.

6 V. Davis Hanson, *The Other Greeks. The Family Farm and the Agrarian Roots of Western Civilization* (1995), pp. 219–318; for a different view, see H. van Wees, 'Farmers and Hoplites: Models of Historical Development,' in Kagan & Viggiano (2013), pp. 222–255; on sieges, see J. Ober, 'Hoplites and Obstacles,' in Hanson (1991), pp. 173–196, esp. 180–188.

7 Hanson (1998), pp. 42–76, 129–173.

8 P. Krentz, 'Casualties in Hoplite Battles,' *Greek Roman and Byzantine Studies* 26 (1985), pp. 13–20.

9 Hanson (1995), pp. 236–286.

10 A. Snodgrass, *Early Greek Armour and Weapons from the End of the Bronze Age to 600 BC* (1964), esp. pp. 3–90; V. Davis Hanson, 'Hoplite Technology in Phalanx Battle,' in Hanson (1991), pp. 63–84; Hanson

(1989), pp. 55–88; G. Viggiano & H. van Wees, 'The Arms, Armor, and Iconography of Early Greek Hoplite Warfare,' in Kagan & Viggiano (2013), pp. 57–75; A. Schwartz, 'Large Weapons, Small Greeks: The Practical Limitations of Hoplite Weapons and Equipment,' in Kagan & Viggiano (2013), pp. 157–175; P. Krentz, 'Hoplite Hell: How Hoplites Fought,' in Kagan & Viggiano (2013), pp. 134–156, esp. 155–157; C. Matthew, *A Storm of Spears. Understanding the Greek Hoplite at War* (2012), pp. 39–59.

11   Herodotus 1. 171. 4, with broader discussion of origins in K. Raaflaub, 'Early Greek Infantry Fighting in a Mediterranean Context,' in Kagan & Viggiano (2013), pp. 95–111; on stance, see Matthew (2012), pp. 39–59, 182–196.

12   Snodgrass (1964), pp. 3–35, 86–90; Hanson (1989), pp. 71–75; Matthew (2012), pp. 96–101, 109–110.

13   J. Anderson, 'Hoplite Weapons and Offensive Arms,' in Hanson (1991), pp. 15–37; Hanson in Hanson (1991), pp. 71–74; Matthew (2012), pp. 1–14, 19–38, 146–164.

14   On reconstructing the hoplite panoply and experiments with it, see W. Dolan & J. Thompson, 'The Charge at Marathon: Herodotus 6. 112,' *Classical Journal* 71 (1976), pp. 339–343; W. Dolan & J. Thompson, 'The Charge at Marathon Again,' *Classical World* 72 (1979), pp. 419–420, with P. Krentz, *The Battle of Marathon* (2010), pp. 45–50; on dedications, see A. Snodgrass, *Archaic Greece: The Age of Experiment* (1980), p. 105.

15   Thucydides 5. 70–71; on spacing, see P. Krentz, 'The Nature of Hoplite Battles,' *Classical Antiquity* 4 (1985), pp. 50–61, esp. 54–55; Asclepiodotus 4. 1–3; Arrian *Tac*. 11; see Aelian *Tac*. 11 for the later Hellenistic spacings; on the depth of the phalanx, see W. Pritchett, *The Greek State at War*. Vol. 1 (1971), pp. 134–143.

16   On 'tearless battle', see Plutarch, *Agesilaus* 33. 3; Xenophon, *Hellenica* 7. 1. 28; in general, see Pritchett (1985), pp. 44–93; Hanson (1989), *passim*; J. Lazenby, 'The Killing Zone,' in Hanson (1991), pp. 87–109; Krentz (2013), pp. 134–156; Matthew (2012), pp. 205–237.

17   On front and rear ranks, see Xenophon, *Memorabilia* 3. 1. 8; cf. *Cyropaedeia* 3. 3. 41–42, 6. 3. 27; on advocates of massed shoving, see Hanson (1989), pp. 68–69, 152–159, 171–184. Other recent advocates of this theory include Pritchett (1985), pp. 65–73; Lazenby, in Hanson (1991), pp. 87–109; R. D. Luginbill, 'Othismos: The Importance of the Mass-Shove in Hoplite Warfare,' *Phoenix* 48. 1 (1994), pp. 51–61.

18   See, for example, W. Forrest, *The Emergence of Greek Democracy, 800 BC–400 BC* (1966); R. Osborne, *Greece in the Making. 1200–479 BC* (2nd ed., 2009), pp. 164–166.

19   van Wees (2004), pp. 45–60, 166–197; Raaflaub (2013), pp. 96–98; for a survey of this and the other associated debates, see D. Kagan & G.

Viggiano, 'The Hoplite Debate,' in Kagan & Viggiano (2013), pp. 1–56; G. Viggiano, 'The Hoplite Revolution and the Rise of the Polis,' in Kagan & Viggiano (2013), pp. 112–133.

20 Pritchett (1985), pp. 7–33; van Wees (2004), pp. 151–165.

21 Viggiano & van Wees (2013), pp. 63–70; H. van Wees, 'The Development of the Hoplite Phalanx. Iconography and Reality in the Seventh Century,' in H. van Wees (ed.), *War and Violence in Ancient Greece* (2000), pp. 125–166.

22 van Wees (2004), pp. 172–174; Anderson (1991), pp. 15–17; Lazenby (1991), pp. 92–95; R. Konijnendijk, *Classical Greek Tactics: A Cultural History* (2019), pp. 72–94.

23 See, for example, A. D. Frazer, 'The Myth of the Hoplite Scrimmage,' *Classical World* 36 (1942), pp. 15–16; G. Cawkwell, *Philip of Macedon* (1978), pp. 150–157; G. Cawkwell, 'Orthodoxy and Hoplites,' *Classical Quarterly* 39 (1989), pp. 375–389; Krentz, 'The Nature of Hoplite Battles' (1985), pp. 50–61; P. Krentz, 'Continuing the Othismos on the Othismos,' *Ancient History Bulletin* 8. 2 (1994), pp. 45–49; A. Goldsworthy, 'The Othismos, Myths and Heresies: The Nature of Hoplite Battle,' *War in History* 4 (1997), pp. 1–26.

24 For differing views, see P. Krentz, 'Deception in Archaic and Classical Greek Warfare,' in van Wees (2000), pp. 167–200; V. Davis Hanson, 'Hoplite Battle as Ancient Greek Warfare: When, Where, and Why?' in van Wees (2000), pp. 201–232; L. Rawlings, 'Alternative Agonies: Hoplite Martial and Combat Experience Beyond the Phalanx,' in van Wees (2000), pp. 233–259.

25 Snodgrass (1964), pp. 58–60.

26 *Iliad* 17. 364–365; cf. 3. 8–9, 14. 368–369, with van Wees (2004), pp. 156–158; Matthew (2012), pp. 182–196.

27 See J. Hale, 'Not Patriots, Not Farmers, Not Amateurs: Greek Soldiers of Fortune and the Origins of Hoplite Warfare,' in Kagan & Viggiano (2013), pp. 176–193, on the role of mercenaries.

28 Caesar, *Gallic Wars* 1. 25, 53.

29 Rawlings (2000), pp. 248–249, cf. Plato, *Laws* 815a; Konijnendijk (2019), pp. 39–71.

CHAPTER 9

1 See E. Frahm, *Assyria. The Rise and Fall of the World's First Empire* (2023), pp. 163–164, 454n16, for the claim that Greek kings were subject to the Assyrian empire and in general for the Assyrians.

2   On the fall of the Assyrians, see Frahm (2023), pp. 323–347; on Lydia, Caria, and the wider region, see Mellink in *CAH*² IV (1988), pp. 211–233.
3   Herodotus 1. 26. 1–33.1, 46. 1–56. 1, 92–94.
4   Herodotus 1. 78. 1–91, with Young in *CAH*² IV (1988), pp. 33–35; L. Llewellyn-Jones, *Persians. The Age of the Great Kings* (2022), pp. 61–63.
5   Llewellyn-Jones (2022), pp. 33–98; Young in *CAH*² IV (1988), pp. 24–46.
6   Herodotus 1. 141.
7   Llewellyn-Jones (2022), pp. 65–67; P. Rahe, *The Grand Strategy of Classical Sparta. The Persian Challenge* (2015), pp. 40–43.
8   Llewellyn-Jones (2022), pp. 127–154, 166–172; Young in *CAH*² IV (1988), pp. 41–46; tyrants in Ionia implied in Herodotus 4. 137.
9   Herodotus 1. 205–216; Llewellyn-Jones (2022), pp. 81–98.
10 Young in *CAH*² IV (1988), pp. 53–63.
11 Llewellyn-Jones (2022), pp. 99–122.
12 Herodotus 1. 136.
13 Herodotus 3. 89, with list of territories and revenue at 3. 89–97.
14 Herodotus 1. 141, 152–153, with Rahe (2015), pp. 37–38.
15 See, for example, Herodotus 1. 164–170.
16 For discussion emphasising Cimon and his family, see D. Stuttard, *Phoenix. A Father, a Son, and the Rise of Athens* (2021), pp. 13–37.
17 Young in *CAH*² IV (1988), pp. 67–70; G. Cawkwell, *The Greek Wars. The Failure of Persia* (2005), pp. 46–53.
18 See Herodotus 3. 130 for spying mission to Italy.
19 Rahe (2015), pp. 43–58.
20 Herodotus 3. 40–57, 120–126; Rahe (2015), pp. 59–62.
21 Rahe (2015), pp. 61–62, 72–73.
22 Herodotus 5. 73.
23 Herodotus 5. 91, 96.
24 Rahe (2015), pp. 85–92, 100–104, 130–140.
25 Herodotus 5. 28–35.
26 Herodotus 5. 35–36.
27 For detailed discussion of the cause and course of the Ionian rebellion, see Cawkwell (2005), pp. 61–80; Rahe (2015), pp. 105–129; R. Evans, *Fields of Battle. Retracing Ancient Battlefields* (2015), pp. 1–39.
28 Herodotus 5. 38–39, 49–51, 55, 97, 99, with Rahe (2015), pp. 73–75.
29 Herodotus 6. 6–17; Cawkwell (2005), pp. 63–65; Rahe (2015), pp. 118–126; Evans (2015), pp. 29–33.
30 Herodotus 6. 18–21.

CHAPTER 10

1 Herodotus 5. 126, 6. 26–30.
2 Herodotus 6. 21.
3 Herodotus 5. 105.
4 Herodotus 6. 48–49, 7. 133; P. Rahe, *The Grand Strategy of Classical Sparta. The Persian Challenge* (2015), pp. 136–140; on Persian campaigns in 493 BC, see Herodotus 6. 42–46.
5 Herodotus 6. 35–41, 104; D. Stuttard, *Phoenix. A Father, a Son, and the Rise of Athens* (2021), pp. 62–69; P. Krentz, *The Battle of Marathon* (2010), pp. 79–81.
6 Herodotus 4. 133–140; Krentz (2010), pp. 81–85.
7 Herodotus 6. 48–49; for preparations for the Persian army, its commanders, and its size, see Krentz (2010), pp. 89–93; G. Cawkwell, *The Greek Wars. The Failure of Persia* (2005), pp. 87–89; R. Billows, *Marathon. How One Battle Changed Western Civilization* (2010), pp. 197–199; J. Lacey, *The First Clash. The Miraculous Greek Victory at Marathon and Its Impact on Western Civilization* (2011), pp. 151–152; J. Lazenby, *The Defence of Greece, 490–479 BC* (1993), pp. 45–47; C. Dionysopoulos, *The Battle of Marathon. An Historical and Topographical Approach* (2015), pp. 39–78; N. Hammond, 'The Campaign and Battle of Marathon,' *Journal of Hellenic Studies* 88 (1968), pp. 13–57, esp. 31–33; N. Doenges, 'The Campaign and Battle of Marathon,' *Historia* 47 (1998), pp. 1–17, esp. 4–6; P. Rhodes, 'The Battle of Marathon and Modern Scholarship,' *Bulletin of the Institute of Classical Studies Supplement* 124 (2013), pp. 3–21, esp. 8–9.
8 Herodotus 6. 94–96, with Rahe (2015), pp. 141–143; Krentz (2010), pp. 94–96.
9 Herodotus 6. 97–98.
10 Herodotus 6. 99–101.
11 Aristotle, *Rhetoric* 1411a9–10; Demosthenes 19. 303; Plutarch, *Moralia* 628E, with Krentz (2010), pp. 101–103.
12 Herodotus 6. 102.
13 On the topography, see Rhodes (2013), pp. 4–8, 12–13; Krentz (2010), pp. 111–136; Dionysopoulos (2015), pp. 133–170; S. Nevin, *The Idea of Marathon. Battle and Culture* (2022), pp. 65–72; on journey time, see Hammond (1968), pp. 34–37.
14 Herodotus 6. 103, 105, with Krentz (2010), pp. 105–108.
15 On Athenian and Plataean numbers, see Lazenby (1993), p. 54; Krentz (2010), pp. 102–103, 190n4; on proportion of hoplites to other troops, P. Krentz, 'Marathon and the Exclusive Hoplite Phalanx,' in C. Carey & M. Edwards (eds.), *Marathon—2,500 Years* (2013), pp. 53–44, esp. 42–43, offers one interpretation.

16 P. Bicknell, 'The Command Structure and Generals of the Marathon Campaign,' *L'Antiquité Classique* 39 (1970), pp. 427–442; on the high levels of experience in the Athenian army, see Lacey (2011), esp. pp. 84–85.

17 Herodotus 6. 105.

18 Herodotus 6. 106; Plato, *Laws* 692d, 698c, with Krentz (2010), pp. 108–110; see Rahe (2015), pp. 147–149, for different interpretations.

19 Herodotus 6. 107–108; Diodorus Siculus 10. 27. 1–3.

20 Herodotus 6. 109–110.

21 For discussion, see N. Whatley, 'On the Possibility of Reconstructing Marathon and Other Ancient Battles,' *Journal of Hellenic Studies* 84 (1964), pp. 119–139; J. Evans, 'Herodotus and the Battle of Marathon,' *Historia* 42 (1993), pp. 279–307; C. Pelling, 'Herodotus' Marathon,' in Carey & Edwards (2013), pp. 23–34; on the afterlife of the battle for the Athenians, see Nevin (2022), pp. 115–154.

22 Lacey (2011), pp. 159–160; Pausanias 1. 32. 3.

23 G. Shrimpton, 'The Persian Cavalry at Marathon,' *Phoenix* 34 (1980), pp. 20–37, surveys the evidence and points out the flaws in the theory.

24 Hammond (1968), pp. 38–41; Krentz (2010), pp. 139–143; Dionysopoulos (2015), pp. 120–121, suggests battle at close to sunset because the cavalry had withdrawn.

25 See Herodotus 6. 111–115, 117, for his account of the battle; Krentz (2010); Billows (2010), pp. 213–227, 142–159; Lacey (2011), pp. 168–174; Dionysopoulos (2015), pp. 199–226; Nevin (2022), pp. 80–86, are among the most recent reconstructions of the actual fighting; P. Fromherz, 'The Battlefield of Marathon: The Tropaion, Herodotus, and E. Curtius,' *Historia* 60 (2011), pp. 383–412, adopts a different approach and reaches different conclusions.

26 Miltiades's shout by scholiast on Aelius Aristides (ed. Dinhoff III 566); on the charge, see Krentz (2010), pp. 143–152, listing the main theories; see Lacey (2011), pp. 181–184, for a very practical analysis; see J. Crowley, *The Psychology of the Athenian Hoplite* (2012), *passim*, for morale in the Athenian military context.

27 'for a long time': Herodotus 6. 113; for discussion of the duration of fighting in hoplite battles, see A. Schwartz, *Reinstating the Hoplite. Arms, Armour and Phalanx Fighting in Archaic and Classical Greece* (2009), pp. 201–225.

28 Lacey (2011), pp. 172–173.

29 Dionysopoulos (2015), pp. 199–238; Nevin (2022), pp. 89–96.

30 Herodotus 6. 115–116, 121–125, with Krentz (2010), pp. 161–166.

31 Krentz (2010), pp. 163–164; Billows (2010), pp. 230–231.

32 Herodotus 6. 120.

CHAPTER 11

1   For discussion of the influence of Marathon, see P. Krentz, *The Battle of Marathon* (2010), pp. 7–11.

2   Herodotus 6. 120.

3   Herodotus 7. 1–7, with G. Cawkwell, *The Greek Wars. The Failure of Persia* (2005), pp. 88–91; P. Rahe, *The Grand Strategy of Classical Sparta. The Persian Challenge* (2015), pp. 161–170; I. MacGregor Morris, 'Xerxes: Ideology and Practice,' in A. Konecny & N. Sekunda (eds.), *The Battle of Plataiai, 479 BC* (2022), pp. 13–69, esp. 39–46.

4   MacGregor Morris (2022), pp. 20–24.

5   Xenophon, *Anabasis* 3. 1. 12; Plutarch, *Moralia* 862B, with discussion and details in Krentz (2010), p. 165, 192n23; Herodotus 6. 105, 117; Pausanias 1. 32. 4–7, 9. 4. 1.

6   Pausanias 1. 32; in general, see J. Camp, *The Archaeology of Athens* (2001), pp. 47–51.

7   Plutarch, *Cimon* 8; for Aeschylus, see *Life of Aeschylus* 11; Pausanias 1. 14. 3.

8   Herodotus 7. 115, 121, with Krentz (2010), pp. 161–163.

9   Herodotus 7. 132–136; Plutarch, *Cimon* 4; Diodorus Siculus 10. 30; Nepos, *Miltiades* 7–8, with D. Stuttard, *Phoenix. A Father, a Son, and the Rise of Athens* (2021), pp. 88–90.

10 Aristotle, *Athenian Constitution* 22. 3–6, with P. Rhodes, *A Commentary on the Aristotelian Athenaion Politeia* (1981), pp. 266–277.

11 For the ostraca and discussion of ostracism, see G. Williams, 'The Kerameikos Ostraka,' *Zeitschrift für Papyrologie und Epigraphik* 31 (1978), pp. 103–113; J. Sickinger, 'New Ostraka from the Athenian Agora,' *Hersperia* 86 (2017), pp. 443–508; J. Kosmin, 'A Phenomenology of Democracy: Ostracism as Political Ritual,' *Classical Antiquity* 34 (2015), pp. 121–162.

12 For wider context of aristocratic competition, see S. Forsdyke, *Exile, Ostracism and Democracy: The Politics of Exclusion in Ancient Greece* (2005).

13 See note 11 for detailed discussion and further references. The most famous story about an ostracism is Plutarch, *Aristides* 7. 5–6.

14 See Plutarch, *Themistocles* 1–3, for Themistocles's early life, even though it is questionable how much accurate information lies behind this. On the development of the Piraeus, see Thucydides 1. 93. 3.

15 For Themistocles's election as general in 490 BC, see Plutarch, *Aristides* 5. 3–4; on Laurium and the shipbuilding programme, see Herodotus 7. 144; Aristotle, *Athenian Constitution* 22. 7; Plutarch, *Themistocles* 4. 1–3.

16 L. Casson, *Ships and Seafaring in Ancient Times* (1994), p. 58; H. Wallinga, *Ships and Sea-Power Before the Great Persian War: The Ancestry of the Ancient Trireme* (1993), esp. pp. 45–53.

17 Thucydides 1. 13; on ship development, see J. Morrison, J. Coates & B. Rankov, *The Athenian Trireme: The History and Reconstruction of an Ancient Greek Warship* (2nd ed., 2000), pp. 25–49.

18 For lessons learned, proposed modifications, and some sceptical voices, see Morrison, Coates & Rankov (2000); B. Rankov (ed.), *Trireme Olympias. The Final Report* (2012). For crew sizes, see B. Jordan, 'The Crews of Athenian Triremes,' *L'Antiquité Classique* 69 (2000), pp. 81–101; but for the argument that many ships were often crewed by fewer than the ideal number, so that estimates for fleet totals may sometimes be too high, see Wallinga (1993), pp. 169–185.

19 C. Haas, 'Athenian Naval Power Before Themistocles,' *Historia* 34 (1985), pp. 29–46; Miltiades in Herodotus 6. 39, cf. 6. 41, where he returned in five triremes; on twenty ships to help Ionian rebels, see Herodotus 5. 97; on purchase from Corinthians, see Herodotus 6. 89, 92.

20 L. Kallet-Marx, *Money, Expense, and Naval Power in Thucydides' History 1–5.24* (1993), pp. 32–39; V. Gabrielsen, *Financing the Athenian Fleet. Public Taxation and Social Relations* (1994), pp. 19–39.

21 Herodotus 7. 144; Thucydides 1. 14. 3.

22 T. Kelly, 'Persian Propaganda—a Neglected Factor in Xerxes' Invasion of Greece and Herodotus,' *Iranica Antiqua* 38 (2003), pp. 173–219.

23 P. Cartledge, *The Spartans: An Epic History* (rev. ed., 2003), pp. 109–114.

24 Herodotus 7. 134–137.

25 Herodotus 7. 239, with Rahe (2015), pp. 192–194.

26 Herodotus 7. 139–145, with Rahe (2015), pp. 192–197; J. Lazenby, *The Defence of Greece, 490–479 BC* (1993), pp. 98–100.

27 Herodotus 7. 145–148, 8. 72–73; Aristotle, *Athenian Constitution* 22. 8; Plutarch, *Themistocles* 11. 1; Plutarch, *Aristides* 8. 1, with Lazenby (1993), pp. 105–109.

28 Herodotus 7. 148–153, 157–169.

CHAPTER 12

1 Herodotus 7. 146–147; see also T. Kelly, 'Persian Propaganda—a Neglected Factor in Xerxes' Invasion of Greece and Herodotus,' *Iranica Antiqua* 38 (2003), pp. 173–219.

2 Herodotus 7. 20–25, with Kelly (2003), pp. 193–196; H. Wallinga, *Xerxes' Greek Adventure—the Naval Perspective* (2005), esp. pp. 38–44; P.

Rahe, *The Grand Strategy of Classical Sparta. The Persian Challenge* (2015), pp. 167–175.

3   Herodotus 7. 25–26, 34–37, 54–100, 184–187.

4   I. MacGregor Morris, 'Xerxes: Ideology and Practice,' in A. Konecny & N. Sekunda (eds.), *The Battle of Plataiai, 479 BC* (2022), pp. 13–69, esp. 44–50.

5   MacGregor Morris (2022), pp. 47–55.

6   Herodotus 7. 40–41.

7   Herodotus 7. 38–40.

8   See, for example, J. Lazenby, *The Defence of Greece, 490–479 BC* (1993), pp. 90–96; Rahe (2015), pp. 175–180; F. Maurice, 'The Size of the Army of Xerxes in the Invasion of Greece, 480 BC,' *Journal of Hellenic Studies* 50 (1930), pp. 210–235.

9   Wallinga (2005), esp. pp. 38–42; B. Strauss, *Salamis. The Greatest Naval Battle of the Ancient World, 480 BC* (2004), esp. pp. 43–44, 51; Lazenby (1993), pp. 94–96; Rahe (2015), pp. 177–179.

10 See Herodotus 7. 55–56, with comments in Maurice (1930), pp. 215–219, 224–226, for the crossing; in general, see Rahe (2015), pp. 202–212.

11 Herodotus 7. 172–173; Diodorus Siculus 11. 2. 5, with C. Matthew, 'Was the Greek Defence of Thermopylae in 480 BC a Suicide Mission?' in C. Matthew & M. Trundle (eds.), *Beyond the Gates of Fire. New Perspectives on the Battle of Thermopylae* (2013), pp. 60–99, esp. 60–63.

12 Herodotus 7. 174, 196–201; on the question of supply during this conflict, see N. Sekunda, 'Greek Logistics at Plataiai and Strategical Planning During the Third Invasion of Greece (480–479 BC),' in Konecny & Sekunda (2022), pp. 153–166.

13 Herodotus 7. 125, 187.

14 Herodotus 7. 175–177, with Lazenby (1993), pp. 117–125; Rahe (2015), pp. 211–216; C. Matthew, 'Towards the Hot Gates: The Events Leading to the Battle of Thermopylae,' in Matthew & Trundle (2013), pp. 22–23; R. Matthews, *The Battle of Thermopylae. A Campaign in Context* (2006), pp. 94–110.

15 Matthew (2013), esp. pp. 65–73, 83–99; Rahe (2015), pp. 220–225; P. Cartledge, *Thermopylae. The Battle That Changed the World* (2006), pp. 123–138, suggests failure was expected.

16 C. Carey, *Thermopylae* (2019), pp. 23–34, with detail in J. Kraft, G. Rapp, G. Szemler, C. Tziavos & E. Kase, 'The Pass at Thermopylae, Greece,' *Journal of Field Archaeology* 14 (1987), pp. 181–198; G. Rapp, 'The Topography of the Pass at Thermopylae Circa 480 BC,' in Matthew & Trundle (2013), pp. 39–59.

17 Herodotus 7. 203, 215–217; for discussion of the Phocians' role in the battle, see E. Meyer, 'The Phocian Debacle at Thermopylae,' *Phoenix* 25 (2021), pp. 84–101.

18 Herodotus 7. 208–209.

19 Herodotus 7. 179–183, 188–196, with Lazenby (1993), pp. 125–129.

20 Herodotus 7. 210–212, 226, with Cartledge (2006), pp. 141–150; Matthews (2006), pp. 123–155; Carey (2019), pp. 79–110.

21 Herodotus 8. 10–12, with Strauss (2004), pp. 24–33; Lazenby (1993), pp. 129–130, 140–141; Rahe (2015), pp. 226–231, on the naval fighting in general.

22 Herodotus 7. 213, 8. 6–9, 12–15.

23 Herodotus 7. 215–218, with Meyer (2021), pp. 86–90.

24 Herodotus 7. 219–222, 229–232.

25 See discussion in Lazenby (1993), pp. 140–147; M. Clarke, 'Spartan *atē* at Thermopylai: Semantics and Ideology at Herodotus, *Histories* 7. 234,' in A. Powell & S. Hodkinson (eds.), *Sparta. Beyond the Mirage* (2002), pp. 63–84.

26 For night attack, see Diodorus Siculus 11. 9. 4–5; Herodotus 7. 223–226 provides a more convincing account.

27 On whipping, see Herodotus 7. 223.

28 Herodotus 7. 225–233, 238, 8.24–25, with MacGregor Morris (2022), pp. 51–53, on Leonidas's corpse.

29 Herodotus 8. 15–23, with Lazenby (1993), pp. 148–150; Strauss (2004), pp. 31–37.

CHAPTER 13

1 Herodotus 7. 227–233; for the context, see J. Ducat, 'The Spartan "Tremblers",' in S. Hodkinson & A. Powell (eds.), *Sparta and War* (2006), pp. 1–56.

2 Herodotus 8. 26–39, with J. Lazenby, *The Defence of Greece, 490–479 BC* (1993), pp. 151–153; P. Rahe, *The Grand Strategy of Classical Sparta. The Persian Challenge* (2015), pp. 244–250.

3 N. Hammond in *CAH*² IV (1988), pp. 558–563; Lazenby (1993), pp. 102–104; Rahe (2015), pp. 198–200, 204–205; R. Garland, *Athens Burning: The Persian Invasion of Greece and the Evacuation of Attica* (2017), pp. 33–60. For the inscription, see C. Fornara (ed.), *Archaic Times to the End of the Peloponnesian War.* Vol. 1 of *Translated Documents of Greece and Rome* (2nd ed., 1983), p. 55.

4 Herodotus 8. 40–41, with Garland (2017), pp. 33–60.

5 Herodotus 8. 51–55, with Garland (2017), pp. 61–86.

6 Herodotus 8. 42–48.

7   Herodotus 8. 49–50, 56–63, with B. Strauss, *Salamis. The Greatest Naval Battle of the Ancient World, 480 BC* (2004), esp. pp. 99–111; Rahe (2015), pp. 255–261.

8   Lazenby (1993), pp. 172–174; Strauss (2004), pp. 43–44, 98–99, 128, 154–165; Hammond in *CAH*² IV (1988), pp. 672–673.

9   Herodotus 8. 65–72, with Strauss (2004), pp. 117–131.

10 Herodotus 8. 75–76; Plutarch, *Themistocles* 12, with Lazenby (1993), pp. 157–158; Strauss (2004), pp. 133–145; Rahe (2015), pp. 262–265.

11 Herodotus 8. 76, 77–82; Plutarch, *Themistocles* 12; Plutarch, *Aristides* 7, 8–9.

12 Herodotus 8. 94; see Strauss (2004), pp. 244–247, on the Corinthians; on triremes, see J. Morrison, J. Coates & B. Rankov, *The Athenian Trireme: The History and Reconstruction of an Ancient Greek Warship* (2nd ed., 2000), esp. pp. 86, 97, 175–178, 256–259.

13 H. Wallinga, *Xerxes' Greek Adventure—the Naval Perspective* (2005), esp. pp. 40–44, noting that if some triremes had skeleton crews of 50 to 60 men, then this meant perhaps 75,000 crew for 1,200 triremes in the Persian fleet.

14 Plutarch, *Cimon* 5.

15 Fornara (1983), p. 55; B. Jordan, 'The Crews of Athenian Triremes,' *L'Antiquité Classique* 69 (2000), pp. 81–101; for the *Olympias* trials, see B. Rankov (ed.), *Trireme Olympias. The Final Report* (2012), *passim*.

16 See, for example, T. Shaw, 'The Performance of Ancient Triremes in Wind and Waves,' in Rankov (2012), pp. 68–75.

17 See Herodotus 8. 83–96 for his account of the battle, with Hammond in *CAH*² IV (1988), pp. 175–180; Lazenby (1993), pp. 163–197; Strauss (2004), pp. 171–253; Rahe (2015), pp. 270–279.

18 Plutarch, *Themistocles* 13, citing the fourth century BC philosopher Phanias of Lesbos as his source; Aeschylus, *Persae* 392–393.

19 See R. Oldfield, 'Collision Damage to Triremes,' in Rankov (2012), pp. 214–224; A. Taylor, 'Battle Manoeuvres for Fast Triremes,' in Rankov (2012), pp. 231–243.

20 Shaw (2012), pp. 68–75.

21 Aeschylus, *Persae* 415–420.

22 Plutarch, *Aristides* 9.

23 Herodotus 8. 88, 92–93.

24 Herodotus 8. 123.

25 For losses, see Diodorus Siculus 11. 19. 3.

26 Herodotus 8. 96–107.

27 Herodotus 8. 113–120; Aeschylus, *Persae* 482–514, 734–736; Justin, *Epitome* 2. 13. 12, with Lazenby (1993), pp. 205–208; Rahe (2015), pp. 279–281.

28 Herodotus 8. 108–112.

CHAPTER 14

1   Herodotus 8. 108, 122, with B. Strauss, *Salamis. The Greatest Naval Battle of the Ancient World, 480 BC* (2004), esp. pp. 277–280, 289–295.
2   Herodotus 8. 111–112, with P. Rahe, *The Grand Strategy of Classical Sparta. The Persian Challenge* (2015), pp. 282–287.
3   Herodotus 8. 123–125; Plutarch, *Themistocles* 16–18.
4   For a full discussion, see N. Sekunda, 'Greek Logistics at Plataiai and Strategical Planning During the Third Invasion of Greece (480–479 BC),' in A. Konecny & N. Sekunda (eds.), *The Battle of Plataiai, 479 BC* (2022), pp. 153–156.
5   Herodotus 9. 1–2, 17; on Mardonius, see J. Wiesehöfer, 'Mardonios,' in Konecny & Sekunda (2022), pp. 71–78.
6   Herodotus 8. 136, 140–144, with Rahe (2015), pp. 287–295.
7   J. Lazenby, *The Defence of Greece, 490–479 BC* (1993), pp. 211–212.
8   Herodotus 9. 4–5.
9   Herodotus 8. 131; for Pausanias, see P. Cartledge, *The Spartans: An Epic History* (2002), pp. 120–127.
10   Herodotus 8. 142, with Rahe (2015), pp. 193–195.
11   R. Garland, *Athens Burning: The Persian Invasion of Greece and the Evacuation of Attica* (2017), pp. 87–104.
12   Herodotus 9. 6–10; Plutarch, *Aristides* 10, with Lazenby (1993), pp. 213–214; Rahe (2015), pp. 297–300.
13   Herodotus 9. 19, 28–30; on army size and the number of helots, see J. Baron in *CAH*² IV (1988), pp. 602–603; Lazenby (1993), pp. 227–228; Sekunda (2022), pp. 153–159; A. Konecny, 'The Battle of Plataiai. Topography and Tactics,' in Konecny & Sekunda (2022), pp. 167–210, esp. 169–170, 189; R. Konijnendijk & P. Bardunias, 'The Face of Battle at Plataiai,' in Konecny & Sekunda (2022), pp. 211–242, esp. 215, 235–237.
14   Herodotus 9. 12–13.
15   See Wiesehöfer (2022), esp. pp. 73–74.
16   I. MacGregor Morris, 'Pausanias, *Best of Men*: Politics, Propaganda, Memory,' in Konecny & Sekunda (2022), pp. 79–132.
17   Herodotus 9. 20–24; Plutarch, *Aristides* 14; Diodorus Siculus 11. 30. 1–4.
18   Herodotus 9. 25–27, 37–40, with Konecny (2022), pp. 167–182.
19   Herodotus 9. 40–47.
20   Herodotus 9. 48–51, with Konecny (2022), pp. 182–185.
21   Herodotus 9. 52–57.
22   Herodotus 9. 72.
23   For the narrative of the battle, see Herodotus 9. 58–74, with Lazenby (1993), pp. 232–247; Rahe (2015), pp. 309–323; Konecny (2022), pp. 185–195; Konijnendijk & Bardunias (2022), pp. 233–237.

24 Herodotus 9. 70, 76, 77–81, 84–85.
25 Herodotus 9. 77, 86–89.
26 Herodotus 9. 90–107; Rahe (2015), pp. 324–326.

CHAPTER 15

1 For differing views of the impact of the Greek expedition on Xerxes, see P. Rahe, *The Grand Strategy of Classical Sparta. The Persian Challenge* (2015), pp. 327–331; I. MacGregor Morris, 'Xerxes: Ideology and Practice,' in A. Konecny & N. Sekunda (eds.), *The Battle of Plataiai, 479 BC* (2022), pp. 13–69, esp. 53–61.

2 Herodotus 9. 108–112.

3 See Herodotus 9. 77 on the men from Mantineia and Elis; Herodotus 7. 168 on Corcyra; Thucydides 2. 71 on Plataea.

4 Herodotus 9. 86–88.

5 Lycurgus, *Against Leocrates* 81; on the archaeology, see J. Camp, *The Archaeology of Athens* (2001), pp. 57–61.

6 Thucydides 1. 90. 1–2; Diodorus Siculus 11. 39. 1–3; Plutarch, *Themistocles* 19; Nepos, *Themistocles* 6. 2–4, with discussion in P. Rahe, *Sparta's First Attic War: The Grand Strategy of Classical Sparta, 478–446 BC* (2019), pp. 28–31.

7 See Camp (2001), pp. 59–60, on archaeological evidence for hastily constructed wall sections using recycled material that has often been associated with this incident.

8 M. McGregor, *The Athenians and Their Empire* (1987), pp. 30–31; see C. Fornara & L. Samons, *Athens from Cleisthenes to Pericles* (1991), pp. 118–125, for scepticism.

9 Thucydides 1. 94. 1; Diodorus Siculus 11. 44. 1–2; Plutarch, *Aristides* 23; Plutarch, *Cimon* 6.

10 Thucydides 1. 94; Diodorus Siculus 11. 44. 13; Nepos, *Pausanias* 2. 1–2; see Herodotus 7. 107 for the suicide of Boges, the Persian commander.

11 Thucydides 1. 95; Herodotus 8. 3. 2; Diodorus Siculus 11. 44. 3–6; Nepos, *Pausanias* 2. 2–6; Plutarch, *Cimon* 6; Plutarch, *Aristides* 23, with Rahe (2019), pp. 33–39; I. MacGregor Morris, 'Pausanias, *Best of Men*: Politics, Propaganda, Memory,' in Konecny & Sekunda (2022), pp. 79–132, esp. 91–102.

12 Thucydides 1. 95; Aristotle, *Athenian Constitution* 23. 1–5; Plutarch, *Aristides* 23–25; Plutarch, *Cimon* 6. 2–3; Diodorus Siculus 11. 46. 6–47; on the creation of the new alliance with Athens, see Fornara & Samons (1991), pp. 80–84; Rahe (2019), pp. 38–43; on Ionians, see Herodotus 9. 106.

13 Thucydides 1. 96, with R. Meiggs, *The Athenian Empire* (1972), pp. 42–67; Fornara & Samons (1991), pp. 76–85.

14   Thucydides 1. 95; Xenophon, *Hellenica* 6. 5. 34; Plutarch, *Aristides* 23; Diodorus Siculus 11. 50; Herodotus 8. 3, with Rahe (2019), pp. 39–42; P. Rhodes in *CAH*² V (1992), pp. 35–37; for Spartan campaign to Thessaly, see Herodotus 6. 72, 7. 6, 130, 9. 58, with Rahe (2019), pp. 49–52.

15   Thucydides 1. 98; Herodotus 7. 107; Plutarch, *Cimon* 7–8, with Rhodes in *CAH*² V (1992), pp. 41–42.

16   Herodotus 7. 183; Thucydides 1. 98; Plutarch, *Themistocles* 31; Plutarch, *Cimon* 8; Pausanias 1. 17. 6.

17   Thucydides 1. 98; Herodotus 9. 105.

18   Thucydides 1. 100; Diodorus Siculus 11. 60. 3–62; Plutarch, *Cimon* 12–14, with Rahe (2019), pp. 73–82.

19   Thucydides 1. 100–101; Herodotus 6. 46, with Meiggs (1972), pp. 83–86; Fornara & Samons (1991), pp. 84–87; Rahe (2019), pp. 89–93.

20   Thucydides 1. 99.

21   See Fornara & Samons (1991), pp. 76–113, depicting the growth of Athenian control as inevitable and largely conscious, in contrast to a more benevolent view, such as Meiggs (1972), *passim*.

22   Thucydides 1. 108.

23   Thucydides 1. 131–135; Diodorus Siculus 11. 44–45; Pausanias 17. 7–9; Nepos, *Pausanias* 3–5, with MacGregor Morris (2022), esp. 86–91, 102–107.

24   Thucydides 1. 135–138; on the Piraeus, see R. Garland, *The Piraeus from the Fifth to the First Century BC* (2nd ed., 2001), pp. 14–22.

25   Plutarch, *Themistocles* 22–32, with Rahe (2019), pp. 106–113.

CHAPTER 16

1   See, in general, M. Flower, 'Spartan Religion,' in A. Powell (ed.), *A Companion to Sparta* (Blackwell Companions to the Ancient World) (2017), pp. 425–451.

2   D. Kagan, *The Outbreak of the Peloponnesian War* (1969), pp. 50–54; A. Powell, *Athens and Sparta. Constructing Greek Political and Social History from 478 BC* (3rd ed., 2016), pp. 111–114; P. Rahe, *Sparta's First Attic War. The Grand Strategy of Classical Sparta, 478–446 BC* (2019), pp. 97–110.

3   See Herodotus 9. 35 for the career of Tisamenos the seer, with discussions in Powell (2016), pp. 111–113; Rahe (2019), pp. 117–122; in the fourth century BC the Athenian orator Isocrates claimed that the Spartans formed in a single rank at the battle.

4   Thucydides 1. 128.

5   Thucydides 1. 101, 128, 2. 27, 3. 54, 4. 56; Diodorus Siculus 11. 63, 15. 66. 4; Pausanias 4. 24; Plutarch, *Cimon* 16; Cicero, *de Divinatione* 1. 112; Pliny, *Natural History* 2. 191.

6   Plutarch, *Cimon* 16; see Herodotus 9. 64, presenting it as 300 men led by a prominent Spartan taking on and being killed by an entire army of Messenian helots.

7   For discussion, see D. Lewis in CAH^2 V (1992), pp. 108–110; S. Hodkinson, *Property and Wealth in Classical Sparta* (2009), pp. 416–423; Powell (2016), pp. 114–115; Rahe (2019), pp. 125–127.

8   S. Hodkinson, 'Marriage, Inheritance and Demography: Perspectives upon the Success and Decline of Classical Sparta,' in A. Powell (ed.), *Classical Sparta: Techniques Behind Her Success* (1989), pp. 79–121, esp. 103–105; J. Lazenby, *The Spartan Army* (1985), pp. 73–81; T. Figueira, 'Population Patterns in Late Archaic and Classical Sparta,' *Transactions of the American Philological Association* 116 (1986), pp. 165–213, esp. 177–179; T. Figueira, 'The Demography of the Spartan Helots,' in N. Luraghi & S. Alcock (eds.), *Helots and Their Masters in Laconia and Messenia. Histories, Ideologies, Structures* (2003), pp. 193–239, esp. 224–227.

9   Hodkinson (2009), pp. 405–432; S. Hodkinson, 'Spartiates, Helots and the Direction of the Agrarian Economy: Towards an Understanding of Helotage in Comparative Perspective,' in Luraghi & Alcock (2003), pp. 248–285; for an alternative view, see N. Birgalias, 'Helotage and Spartan Social Organization,' in A. Powell & S. Hodkinson (eds.), *Sparta. Beyond the Mirage* (2002), pp. 249–266, esp. 255–256.

10 Thucydides 1. 102, 2. 27, 3. 54, 4. 56; Xenophon, *Hellenica* 5. 2. 3; Plutarch, *Cimon* 16–17.

11 Thucydides 1. 102; Plutarch, *Cimon* 16; on Athenian skills and siege warfare, see J. Ober, 'Hoplites and Obstacles,' in V. Davis Hanson (ed.), *Hoplites. The Classical Greek Battle Experience* (1991), pp. 173–196, esp. 187–188.

12 Powell (2016), pp. 37–40, 115; Rahe (2019), pp. 126–134, 138–145.

13 Plutarch, *Cimon* 4–5, 9–10, 17.

14 Thucydides 1. 102; Aristotle, *Athenian Constitution* 25–26, with P. Rhodes, *A Commentary on the Aristotelian Athenaion Politeia* (1981), pp. 309–335.

15 Thucydides 1. 104, with fuller discussions of the campaign in A. Holladay, 'The Hellenic Disaster in Egypt,' *Journal of Hellenic Studies* 109 (1989), pp. 176–182; E. Robinson, 'Thucydidean Sieges, Prosopitis, and the Hellenic Disaster in Egypt,' *Classical Antiquity* 18 (1999), pp. 132–152; D. Kahn, 'Inaros' Rebellion Against Artaxerxes I and the Athenian Disaster in Egypt,' *Classical Quarterly* 58 (2008), pp. 424–440; E. Meyer, 'The Athenian Expedition to Egypt and the Value of Ctesias,' *Phoenix* 72 (2018), pp. 43–61.

16 Thucydides 1. 109.

17 Thucydides 1. 103; Pausanias 1. 15. 1, 2. 20. 5, 10. 10. 3–4, with Rahe (2019), pp. 149–150.

18 Thucydides 1. 103.

19 Thucydides 1. 105–106, with, in general, R. Meiggs, *The Athenian Empire* (1972), pp. 92–102; on the contingent from Aegina fighting alongside the Spartans in Messenia, see Thucydides 2. 27, 4. 56.

20 See IG I³ 1147 for the monument; see Rahe (2019), pp. 159–160, for discussion of this and pp. 152–160 more generally.

21 Thucydides 1. 107.

22 Thucydides 1. 107–108; Herodotus 9. 33–35; Diodorus Siculus 11. 80–82; Plutarch, *Cimon* 17, with Rahe (2019), pp. 163–170.

23 Thucydides 1. 107.

CHAPTER 17

1 Thucydides 1. 109–110, with A. Holladay, 'The Hellenic Disaster in Egypt,' *Journal of Hellenic Studies* 109 (1989), pp. 176–182; E. Robinson, 'Thucydidean Sieges, Prosopitis, and the Hellenic Disaster in Egypt,' *Classical Antiquity* 18 (1999), pp. 132–152; D. Kahn, 'Inaros' Rebellion Against Artaxerxes I and the Athenian Disaster in Egypt,' *Classical Quarterly* 58 (2008), pp. 424–440; E. Meyer, 'The Athenian Expedition to Egypt and the Value of Ctesias,' *Phoenix* 72 (2018), pp. 43–61; R. Meiggs, *The Athenian Empire* (1972), pp. 104–124; P. Rahe, *Sparta's First Attic War. The Grand Strategy of Classical Sparta, 478–446 BC* (2019), esp. pp. 183–190, arguing in favour of very heavy losses.

2 Diodorus Siculus 12. 38. 2; Plutarch, *Pericles* 12. 1; Meiggs (1972), pp. 234–244; Rahe (2019), pp. 188–189; A. Powell, *Athens and Sparta. Constructing Greek Political and Social History from 478 BC* (3rd ed., 2016), pp. 49–52.

3 Plutarch, *Cimon* 17–18; Thucydides 1. 112; Diodorus Siculus 11. 86. 1, with Meiggs (1972), pp. 422–423; C. Fornara & L. Samons, *Athens from Cleisthenes to Pericles* (1991), pp. 138–139; Rahe (2019), pp. 188–194.

4 Plutarch, *Cimon* 18–19; Diodorus Siculus 12. 3–4, with Meiggs (1972), pp. 125–128.

5 Meiggs (1972), pp. 129–151; G. Cawkwell, 'The Peace Between Athens and Persia,' *Phoenix* 51 (1997), pp. 115–130; L. Samons, 'Kimon, Kallias and Peace with Persia,' *Historia* 47 (1998), pp. 129–140; G. Parmeggiani, 'Notes on the Tradition of the Peace of Callias,' *Erga-Logoi* 8 (2020), pp. 7–23.

6 Some scholars argue for earlier negotiations and an agreement around the time of Eurymedon, but there is no consensus. Contrast P.

Stylianou, 'On the Untentability of Peace with Persia in the 460s B.C.,' in Θ. Παπαδόπουλλου (ed.), *Μελέται καὶ Ὑπο μνήματα*, II, Leucosia (1992), pp. 339–371, with Rahe (2019), pp. 86, 113, 141, 155, 199–201; see E. Rung & A. Sapogov, 'The Aftermath of the Peace of Callias,' *Anabasis* 9 (2018), pp. 227–235, on the Persian perspective.

7   Meiggs (1972), pp. 152–174; Powell (2016), pp. 72–77.

8   C. Fornara (ed. and trans.), *Archaic Times to the End of the Peloponnesian War.* Vol. 1 of *Translated Documents of Greece and Rome* (2nd ed., 1983), n. 71, with Meiggs (1972), pp. 112–115, 421–422.

9   IG II² 43. 35–41 for the terms of the second Athenian alliance formed in the fourth century BC, which prohibited Athenians from acquiring a 'house or land in the territories of the allies'.

10 Thucydides 1. 112–114; Plutarch, *Pericles* 23; cf. Aristophanes, *Clouds* 858–859, with Rahe (2019), pp. 217–227; for the memorial for Pythion of Megara, see Fornara (1983), n. 101.

11 See Fornara (1983), n. 103, for Chalkis decree.

12 Plutarch, *Pericles* 17, with discussion of its importance in J. Lendon, 'Athens and Sparta and the Coming of the Peloponnesian War,' in L. Samons (ed.), *The Cambridge Companion to the Age of Pericles* (2007), pp. 258–281, esp. 268.

13 Thucydides 1. 115, 8. 18, with Meiggs (1972), pp. 175–204; Rahe (2019), pp. 228–232.

14 Diodorus Siculus 12. 9–11.

CHAPTER 18

1   Plutarch, *Pericles* 7–18; Thucydides 2. 65; for biographical treatments, see D. Kagan, *Pericles of Athens and the Birth of Democracy* (1991); V. Azoulay (trans. J. Lloyd), *Pericles of Athens* (2010); L. Samons, *Pericles and the Conquest of History. A Political Biography* (2016).

2   Plutarch, *Pericles* 4–6, 24; A. Podlecki, *Pericles and His Circle* (1997), offers the most detailed discussion of the philosophers and others associated with Pericles, with Azoulay (2010), pp. 84–93.

3   Plutarch, *Pericles* 7, with Kagan (1991), pp. 11–64; Azoulay (2010), pp. 40–50; Samons (2016), pp. 53–102.

4   J. Camp, *The Archaeology of Athens* (2001), pp. 63–72; J. Hurwitt, *The Acropolis in the Age of Pericles* (2004), pp. 49–55.

5   Hurwitt (2004), pp. 79–84.

6   Plutarch, *Pericles* 12–13; with Camp (2001), pp. 72–82; Hurwitt (2004), pp. 67–74, 87–154; T. Shear, *Trophies of Victory. Public Buildings in Periklean Athens* (2016), pp. 17–21.

7   Vitruvius, *de Architectura Praef.* 7. *Praef.* 12; Hurwitt (2004), pp. 106–154; Shear (2016), pp. 21–35, 41–135.

8   Plutarch, *Pericles* 12. 2; on the tribute lists, see R. Meiggs, *The Athenian Empire* (1972), pp. 234–254, 524–561; for discussion, see A. Giovannini, 'The Parthenon, the Treasury of Athena and the Tribute of the Allies,' in P. Low (ed.), *The Athenian Empire* (2008), pp. 164–184; L. Kallet-Marx, 'Money Talks: Rhetor, Demos and the Resources of the Athenian Empire,' in Low (2008), pp. 185–210; see B. Meritt, H. Wade-Gerry & M. McGregor (eds.), *The Athenian Tribute Lists.* 4 vols. (1939–1953), for texts and commentaries; for an inventory of the treasures stored in 434/3 BC, see Hurwitt (2004), pp. 113.

9   Plutarch, *Pericles* 13; Camp (2001), pp. 82–92, 100–104; Hurwitt (2004), pp. 99–100, 155–163, 181–191; Shear (2016), pp. 137–160.

10   Plutarch, *Pericles* 12–13, with Hurwitt (2004), pp. 94–105; Shear (2016), pp. 41–78.

11   Plutarch, *Pericles* 12, 14–15; for discussion, see Kagan (1991), pp. 53–60; C. Fornara & L. Samons, *Athens from Cleisthenes to Pericles* (1991), pp. 58–75; Samons (2016), pp. 77–102.

12   L. Kallet, 'The Athenian Economy,' in L. Samons (ed.), *The Cambridge Companion to the Age of Pericles* (2007), pp. 70–95; on Athenian currency, see D. Lewis, 'The Athenian Coinage Decree,' in P. Rhodes (ed.), *Selected Papers in Greek and Near Eastern History* (1997), pp. 116–130.

13   For discussion, see Meiggs (1972), pp. 220–272; P. Rhodes, 'Democracy and Empire,' in Samons (2007), pp. 24–45; H. Mattingly, 'Periclean Imperialism,' in Low (2008), pp. 81–110.

14   See, for example, C. Fornara (ed. and trans.), *Archaic Times to the End of the Peloponnesian War.* Vol. 1 of *Translated Documents of Greece and Rome* (2nd ed., 1983), 71.

15   J. Roberts, *City of Socrates. An Introduction to Classical Athens* (2nd ed., 1998), pp. 128–130; D. Boederer, 'Athenian Religion in the Age of Pericles,' in Samons (2007), pp. 46–69, esp. 53–57.

16   IG II^2 2318 for Pericles as *choregos*; Plutarch, *Cimon* 8; B. Knox in *CAH^2* V (1992), pp. 268–286; Kagan (1991), pp. 36–37; Samons (2016), pp. 66–68.

17   See Samons (2016), pp. 156–166, on the themes of the speeches attributed to Pericles by Thucydides.

18   Plutarch, *Pericles* 8.

19   Plutarch, *Pericles* 24; Azoulay (2010), pp. 85–89, following P. Brulé, *Périclès: L'Apogée d' Athènes* (1994), pp. 115–116, with Podlecki (1997), p. 1–10.

20   Plutarch, *Pericles* 13; Podlecki (1997), pp. 77–100; Azoulay (2010), pp. 94–101.

21   Plutarch, *Pericles* 24; Azoulay (2010), pp. 101–106.
22   Plutarch, *Pericles* 34; Fornara & Samons (1991), pp. 160–161, 165; Podlecki (1997), pp. 31–34, 101–117; Samons (2016), pp. 144–145.

CHAPTER 19

1   Special status for Aegina implied by Thucydides 1. 67, 139.
2   Thucydides 1. 1.
3   Thucydides 1. 23–88, esp. 88. 6; for notable discussions, see D. Kagan, *The Outbreak of the Peloponnesian War* (1969), with E. Meyer, 'The Outbreak of the Peloponnesian War After Twenty-Five Years,' in C. Hamilton & D. Krentz (eds.), *Polis and Polemos. Essays on Politics, War and History in Ancient Greece, in Honor of Donald Kagan* (1997), pp. 23–58.
4   See Thucydides 1. 115–117 for the Samian incident.
5   Plutarch, *Pericles* 16, 24–25.
6   For discussions of the war, see R. Meiggs, *The Athenian Empire* (1972), pp. 188–193; D. Kagan, *Pericles of Athens and the Birth of Democracy* (1991), pp. 130–135; J. Lendon, *Song of Wrath: The Peloponnesian War Begins* (2010), pp. 83–86; P. Rahe, *Sparta's Second Attic War. The Grand Strategy of Classical Sparta, 446–418 BC* (2020), pp. 27–38.
7   Thucydides 1. 40–41.
8   Thucydides 4. 102; Plutarch, *Pericles* 20, with Kagan (1969), pp. 186–189; Rahe (2020), pp. 39–44.
9   Thucydides 1. 24.
10   See Thucydides 1. 24–55 for his detailed account of the escalation of the local dispute; for modern discussions, see Kagan (1969), pp. 203–250; Rahe (2020), pp. 44–49, 54–59.
11   Thucydides 1. 49.
12   See Thucydides 1. 56–67 for narrative, 1. 58 for the Spartan promise to invade Attica, with Kagan (1969), pp. 273–285.
13   See Thucydides 1. 67–87 for the debate at Sparta.
14   Kagan (1969), pp. 251–272; Meiggs (1972), pp. 202–203; for satirical treatment, see Aristophanes, *The Acharnians* 515–539.
15   Thucydides 1. 88, 119–128, 139–146, with Kagan (1969), pp. 193–202, 286–342; L. Samons, *Pericles and the Conquest of History. A Political Biography* (2016), pp. 126–153; Lendon (2010), pp. 101–103; Rahe (2020), pp. 72–82.
16   Thucydides 1. 127–128.
17   Lendon (2010), pp. 99–103.
18   The case for Athens being weaker in 431 BC than in the 450s is convincingly made in Kagan (1969), *passim*. See the additional discussion in Meyer (1997), esp. pp. 39–42, 47–51.

19 On the Spartans, see A. Powell, *Athens and Sparta. Constructing Greek Political and Social History from 478 BC* (3rd ed., 2016), pp. 116–132; Rahe (2020), pp. 72–82.

20 J. Lendon, 'Athens and Sparta and the Coming of the Peloponnesian War,' in L. Samons (ed.), *The Cambridge Companion to the Age of Pericles* (2007), pp. 258–281; Lendon (2010) makes a very good case for the central importance of perceived status.

CHAPTER 20

1 For the army in general and discussion of the manpower, see J. Lazenby, *The Spartan Army* (1985), pp. 51–81, with alternative views in S. Hodkinson, 'Marriage, Inheritance and Demography: Perspectives upon the Success and Decline of Classical Sparta,' in A. Powell (ed.), *Classical Sparta* (1989), pp. 79–121; T. Figueira, 'Population Patterns in Late Archaic and Classical Sparta,' *Transactions of the American Philological Association* 116 (1986), pp. 165–213.

2 Thucydides 2. 10.

3 See Thucydides 7. 28. 3 for the expectation that the war would last no more than three years; on Spartan plans, see D. Kagan, *The Archidamian War* (1974), pp. 17–24; J. Lendon, *Song of Wrath: The Peloponnesian War Begins* (2010), pp. 114–116; P. Rahe, *Sparta's Second Attic War. The Grand Strategy of Classical Sparta, 446–418 BC* (2020), pp. 84–87.

4 Thucydides 2. 7. 2.

5 Thucydides 2. 13. 3; for discussion of Athenian resources and plans, see Kagan (1974), pp. 24–42; Rahe (2020), pp. 78–83; K. Raaflaub, 'Warfare and Athenian Society,' in L. Samons (ed.), *The Cambridge Companion to the Age of Pericles* (2007), pp. 96–124, esp. 96–102.

6 See Thucydides 2. 13. 6–7 for numbers, 2. 8 for unfamiliarity with war.

7 For additional discussion of plans and their implications, see A. Powell, *Athens and Sparta. Constructing Greek Political and Social History from 478 BC* (3rd ed., 2016), pp. 148–157.

8 Thucydides 2. 13. 7–8, 5. 84. 1, 6. 94. 4; on fighting as hoplite more dangerous than serving as cavalryman, see Lysias 14. 7–8, 15. 6; for discussion of cavalry and Pericles's strategy, see R. Gaebel, *Cavalry Operations in the Ancient Greek World* (2002), pp. 90–95; D. Pritchard, *Athenian Democracy at War* (2019), pp. 53–81.

9 See Kagan (1974), pp. 17–42, for discussion of various views and assessment of practicality of the strategies; Lendon (2010), pp. 113–135, emphasises the need to see plans and actions within the context of Greek concepts of honour and status.

10 See Thucydides 2. 2–6 for the full description of the incident, with discussion in Kagan (1974), pp. 43–48; Lendon (2010), pp. 107–113.

11 Thucydides 2. 10–12; see Thucydides 7. 18 on Spartan discomfort at the Thebans attacking before war was declared.

12 Thucydides 2. 14, 16–24, with V. Davis Hanson, *A War like No Other. How the Athenians and the Spartans Fought the Peloponnesian War* (2005), pp. 35–57.

13 Plutarch, *Archidamus* 33.

14 Thucydides 2. 24–27, 30–32.

15 On reserve, see Thucydides 2. 24; on funeral speech, see Thucydides 2. 34–46, with L. Samons, *Pericles and the Conquest of History. A Political Biography* (2016), pp. 154–166; Powell (2016), pp. 157–159; on the balance in the way so far, see Lendon (2010), pp. 132–135.

16 Thucydides 2. 55–57, with J. Lazenby, *The Peloponnesian War. A Military Study* (2004), pp. 38–41; Hanson (2005), pp. 57–64.

17 Thucydides 2. 48–54; Plutarch, *Pericles* 37, with Hanson (2005), pp. 65–88; on a mass grave associated with the epidemic, see comments in R.-M. Bérard & D. Castex, 'Epidemics and Wars: Comparative Archaeology and Anthropology of Ancient Greek Mass Burials,' *Athens Journal of History* 7. 4 (2021), pp. 295–318, https://shs.hal.science/halshs-03334808v1/document. The excavator used dental analyses to suggest an infection related to typhoid, but others contest this conclusion.

18 Thucydides 2. 54–55, 57, 59–65, 70; Plutarch, *Pericles* 35.

19 Thucydides 2. 71–74.

20 Thucydides 2. 75–78, with Hanson (2005), pp. 163–179; Lendon (2010), pp. 148–151; Rahe (2020), pp. 92–93.

21 Thucydides 2. 81–84.

22 Thucydides 2. 85–92.

23 See Thucydides 2. 93–94 for the raid; for contact with Persia, see Thucydides 2. 7. 1, 67, 4. 50.

24 For Spartan killing of sailors and passengers on ships, see Thucydides 2. 67; for the escalating savagery of the war, see Hanson (2005), pp. 93–111.

CHAPTER 21

1 Thucydides 3. 2–6, 8–15, with J. Lendon, *Song of Wrath: The Peloponnesian War Begins* (2010), pp. 171–180.

2 Thucydides 3. 16–19, with D. Kagan, *The Archidamian War* (1974), pp. 132–143; P. Rahe, *Sparta's Second Attic War. The Grand Strategy of Classical Sparta, 446–418 BC* (2020), pp. 117–121.

3   Thucydides 3. 25–31, 35, with J. Lazenby, *The Peloponnesian War. A Military Study* (2004), pp. 49–55.
4   Thucydides 3. 36–50, with Lendon (2010), pp. 196–198; on Cleon, see Thucydides 3. 36, with R. Meiggs, *The Athenian Empire* (1972), pp. 317–319; Kagan (1974), pp. 145–146; Rahe (2020), pp. 170–172; J. Henderson, 'Drama and Democracy,' in L. Samons (ed.), *The Cambridge Companion to the Age of Pericles* (2007), pp. 179–195, esp. 188–191.
5   Thucydides 2. 69; Meiggs (1972), pp. 319–331.
6   Thucydides 3. 70–85, with V. Davis Hanson, *A War like No Other. How the Athenians and the Spartans Fought the Peloponnesian War* (2005), pp. 104–109; Lendon (2010), pp. 203–211.
7   Thucydides 3. 20–24.
8   Thucydides 3. 52–68.
9   Demosthenes 54. 104–106.
10 Thucydides 3. 87–89, 5. 16.
11 Thucydides 3. 91.
12 Thucydides 3. 94–98.
13 Thucydides 3. 100–102, 105–114.
14 Thucydides 3. 104.
15 Thucydides 4. 2–6.
16 Thucydides 4. 8–10, with C. J. Butera & M. Sears, *Battles and Battlefields of Ancient Greece. A Guide to Their History, Topography and Archaeology* (2019), pp. 301–317, for background and the locations today. W. Shepherd, *Pylos and Sphacteria, 425 BC. Sparta's Island of Disaster* (2013), describes the campaign and is splendidly illustrated.
17 Thucydides 4. 11–12.
18 Thucydides 4. 13–15, with Lendon (2010), pp. 249–263.
19 Thucydides 4. 15–22.
20 Thucydides 4. 23, 26–29, with Kagan (1974), pp. 218–245, esp. 239–245.
21 Thucydides 4. 30–41; for Spartan's comment about spindles, see Thucydides 4. 40, with A. Powell, *Athens and Sparta. Constructing Greek Political and Social History from 478 BC* (3rd ed., 2016), pp. 167–171; Rahe (2020), pp. 156–177.
22 Thucydides 4. 42–25.

CHAPTER 22

1   Thucydides 4. 74, 79–80, with contrasting views in A. Paradiso, 'The Logic of Terror: Thucydides, Spartan Duplicity and an Improbable Massacre,' in T. Figueira (ed.), *Spartan Society* (2004), pp. 179–198; D. Harvey,

'The Clandestine Massacre of the Helots (Thucydides 4. 80),' in Figueira (2004), pp. 199–217.

2   Thucydides 4. 55–57.

3   Thucydides 4. 66–74, with J. Lendon, *Song of Wrath: The Peloponnesian War Begins* (2010), pp. 1–6, 295–300.

4   Thucydides 4. 76–77.

5   On the campaign, see Thucydides 4. 89–101, with D. Kagan, *The Archidamian War* (1974), pp. 278–287; J. Lazenby, *The Peloponnesian War. A Military Study* (2004), pp. 87–91.

6   For the battle, the evidence is well presented and discussed in C. J. Butera & M. Sears, *Battles and Battlefields of Ancient Greece. A Guide to Their History, Topography and Archaeology* (2019), pp. 109–123; see also V. Davis Hanson, *A War like No Other. How the Athenians and the Spartans Fought the Peloponnesian War* (2005), pp. 127–132; P. Rahe, *Sparta's Second Attic War. The Grand Strategy of Classical Sparta, 446–418 BC* (2020), pp. 182–186; for Socrates, see Plato, *Symposium* 221; Plato, *Laches* 181b.

7   In general, see P. Vaughn, 'The Identification and Retrieval of the Hoplite Battle-Dead,' in V. Davis Hanson, *Hoplites. The Classical Greek Battle Experience* (1991), pp. 38–62.

8   See Thucydides 4. 78–79 for the journey.

9   Thucydides 4. 81–88, 102–106, with Lendon (2010), pp. 323–337; Rahe (2020), pp. 189–213; see Thucydides 4. 104–108 on his own role and the Athenian reaction.

10   Thucydides 4. 117–119.

11   Thucydides 4. 111–116, 120–132.

12   Thucydides 4.

13   Thucydides 5. 2–3, 6–11, with Kagan (1974), pp. 311–333; Lendon (2010), pp. 354–361; Rahe (2020), pp. 216–225. The hero-shrine to Brasidas may be the site discovered at Amphipolis; see C. Koukouli-Chrysanthaki, 'Amphipolis,' in R. Lane Fox (ed.), *Brill's Companion to Ancient Macedon: Studies in the Archaeology and History of Macedon, 650 BC to 300 AD* (2011), pp. 409–436, esp. 415.

14   Thucydides 5. 14–25.

15   Thucydides 5. 34, with J. Ducat, 'The Spartan "Tremblers",' in S. Hodkinson & A. Powell (eds.), *Sparta and War* (2006), pp. 1–55.

16   Thucydides 5. 24–26, 32.

17   Thucydides 5. 27–32, with D. Kagan, *The Peace of Nicias and the Sicilian Expedition* (1981), pp. 19–59; Rahe (2020), pp. 235–258.

18   Thucydides 5. 36–44.

19   Thucydides 5. 45–56; on Spartans being banned from Olympic Games, see Thucydides 5. 49.

20 Thucydides 5. 57–65; on Agis being told to halt by a call from the ranks, see Thucydides 5. 65.

21 For the battle, see Thucydides 5. 66–74, with Butera & Sears (2019), pp. 319–347; Kagan (1981), pp. 107–134; Lazenby (2004), pp. 120–126; Hanson (2005), pp. 151–161; Rahe (2020), pp. 274–293.

22 Thucydides 5. 74–81, 83–84, with Kagan (1981), pp. 138–155; A. Powell, *Athens and Sparta. Constructing Greek Political and Social History from 478 BC* (3rd ed., 2016), pp. 177–181.

CHAPTER 23

1 Thucydides 6. 105.

2 R. Meiggs, *The Athenian Empire* (1972), pp. 340–348.

3 Thucydides 5. 84–116, with D. Kagan, *The Peace of Nicias and the Sicilian Expedition* (1981), pp. 148–153; V. Davis Hanson, *A War like No Other. How the Athenians and the Spartans Fought the Peloponnesian War* (2005), pp. 186–189; A. Powell, *Athens and Sparta. Constructing Greek Political and Social History from 478 BC* (3rd ed., 2016), pp. 181–183; C. Shaw Hardy, *Athens 415. The City in Crisis* (2020), pp. 25–34.

4 See J. de Romilly (trans. E. Trapnell Rawlings), *The Life of Alcibiades. Dangerous Ambition and the Betrayal of Athens* (2019), esp. pp. 1–14, on background and early life.

5 Plutarch, *Alcibiades* 1–9.

6 Plutarch, *Alcibiades* 10–13, 15; Thucydides 6. 16, with de Romilly (2019), pp. 35–48; P. Rahe, *Sparta's Sicilian Proxy War* (2023), pp. 94–97.

7 H. Shapiro, 'Leagros: An Athenian Life,' in J. Neils & D. Rogers (eds.), *The Cambridge Companion to Ancient Athens* (2021), pp. 7–17, esp. 7–11; Hardy (2020), pp. 35–51; J. Fraser, 'Classical Athens and the Luxury Problem,' in L. Llewellyn-Jones & H. Bishop-Wright (eds.), *Luxury and Power: Greece to Persia* (2023), pp. 90–155.

8 J. Davison, *Courtesans and Fishcakes. The Consuming Passions of Classical Athens* (1997), passim, esp. 43–49, 51–53, 91–97; A. Steiner, 'Eating and Drinking,' in Neils & Rogers (2021), pp. 345–361, esp. 350–352; K. Ormand, 'Sex and the City,' in Neils & Rogers (2021), pp. 362–375, esp. 367.

9 Plato, *Symposium* 212; on political significance, see Thucydides 8. 54. 4; J. Kierstead, 'Associations,' in Neils & Rogers (2021), pp. 379–391, esp. 384–385.

10 Thucydides 1. 36, 6. 1–6.

11 Thucydides 6. 1, 8, 24, 8. 1, with Kagan (1981), pp. 159–191, for scepticism about Thucydides's interpretation.

12 Plutarch, *Nicias* 2–6.

13   Plutarch, *Alcibiades* 13, 16; *Nicias* 6.
14   See Thucydides 6. 9–26 on the debate, with Meiggs (1972), pp. 345–350; P. Matyszak, *Expedition to Disaster. The Athenian Mission to Sicily, 415 BC* (2012), pp. 35–42; Rahe (2023), pp. 94–102.
15   Thucydides 6. 27–29, with Kagan (1981), pp. 193–197; Hardy (2020), pp. 115–131, 138–143; Rahe (2023), pp. 134–141.
16   Plutarch, *Alcibiades* 18–20.
17   Thucydides 6. 30–32, 42–44.
18   Thucydides 6. 46–50.
19   Thucydides 6. 53, 60–61.
20   Thucydides 6. 62–72, with J. Lazenby, *The Peloponnesian War. A Military Study* (2004), pp. 136–144.
21   Rahe (2023), pp. 98–103.
22   Thucydides 6. 72–73, 88–93; Plutarch, *Alcibiades* 23.
23   Thucydides 6. 94, 96–98.
24   Thucydides 6. 99–103; Plutarch, *Nicias* 18.
25   Thucydides 6. 104, 7. 1–5; Aelian, *Various Histories* 12. 43, with Rahe (2023), pp. 49–54.
26   For narratives and analysis of this phase of the campaign, see Kagan (1981), pp. 260–287; Matyszak (2012), pp. 77–107; Lazenby (2004), pp. 146–153; Rahe (2023), pp. 165–188.
27   Thucydides 7. 6–17.
28   Thucydides 7. 21–25, 34, 36, with Rahe (2023), pp. 189–207.
29   Thucydides 7. 31–49, with Kagan (1981), pp. 308–314.
30   Thucydides 7. 50; Plutarch, *Nicias* 23–24.
31   Thucydides 7. 51–55, 59–74.
32   Thucydides 7. 74–75.
33   Thucydides 7. 76–85; Plutarch, *Nicias* 27.
34   Thucydides 7. 86–87; Plutarch, *Nicias* 27–29.
35   Thucydides 7. 86, with Kagan (1981), pp. 359–372; Hanson (2005), pp. 201–235, esp. 229–235.
36   Thucydides 7. 20, 26–30.
37   Plutarch, *Alcibiades* 22, 23; *Agesilaus* 3; Xenophon, *Hellenica* 3. 3. 1–2.

CHAPTER 24

1   Thucydides 8. 1; Plutarch, *Nicias* 30.
2   Thucydides 8. 1. 3; Aristotle, *Politics* 1299b31, 1323a7, with D. Kagan, *The Fall of the Athenian Empire* (1987), pp. 5–7.

3 Thucydides 8. 2–5, with J. Lazenby, *The Peloponnesian War. A Military Study* (2004), pp. 171–173; P. Rahe, *Sparta's Third Attic War: The Grand Strategy of Classical Sparta* (2024), pp. 64–73.

4 V. Davis Hanson, *A War like No Other. How the Athenians and the Spartans Fought the Peloponnesian War* (2005), pp. 235–269, esp. 251–252.

5 D. Pritchard, *Athenian Democracy at War* (2019), pp. 81–104.

6 Thucydides 7. 13–14.

7 Thucydides 8. 5–6.

8 Kagan (1987), pp. 28–33; Rahe (2024), pp. 81–94.

9 Thucydides 8. 7–20.

10 Thucydides 2. 24, 8. 15, with Pritchard (2019), pp. 166–168, on costs at this stage of the war.

11 Kagan (1987), pp. 51–68.

12 Thucydides 8. 45–47, 52, 56, 76–77; Plutarch, *Alcibiades* 23–25, with Rahe (2024), pp. 153–158.

13 Thucydides 8. 48–54, 63–70; Aristotle, *Athenian Politics* 29–33, with P. Rhodes, *A Commentary on the Aristotelian Athenaion Politeia* (1981), pp. 362–415.

14 Thucydides 8. 71–77, 81–83, 86–91, with Kagan (1987), pp. 106–140.

15 Thucydides 8. 92–98, esp. 97, with Kagan (1987), pp. 141–210.

16 Thucydides 8. 99–106.

17 Xenophon, *Hellenica* 1. 1–23; Diodorus Siculus 13. 49–51, with Kagan (1987), pp. 236–245; Lazenby (2004), pp. 202–205; Rahe (2024), pp. 236–263.

18 Xenophon, *Hellenica* 1. 4. 10–20; Plutarch, *Alcibiades* 31–33.

19 Thucydides 8. 18, 37, 58.

20 Diodorus Siculus 13. 64. 5–7; for surveys of the war, see A. Andrews in *CAH*² V (1992), pp. 483–489; Lazenby (2004), pp. 206–218.

21 Xenophon, *Hellenica* 1. 4. 11–20; Plutarch, *Alcibiades* 32–33, with J. de Romilly (trans. E. Trapnell Rawlings), *The Life of Alcibiades. Dangerous Ambition and the Betrayal of Athens* (2019), pp. 141–153.

22 Xenophon, *Hellenica* 1. 5. 1–14; Plutarch, *Lysander* 2–4, with Rahe (2024), pp. 319–322, 328–353.

23 Kagan (1987), pp. 293–324; Lazenby (2004), pp. 217–225; Rahe (2024), pp. 328–335.

24 For the slaves, see P. Hunt, 'The Slaves and the Generals at Arginusae,' *American Journal of Philology* 122 (2001), pp. 359–380, for one interpretation and an introduction to the debate over the question of the freed slaves' status.

25 Xenophon, *Hellenica* 1. 6. 19–37; Diodorus Siculus 13. 98–99; Kagan (1987), pp. 325–353; Lazenby (2004), pp. 230–235; Rahe (2024), pp. 344–364.

26 Xenophon, *Hellenica* 1. 7. 1–35, with Kagan (1987), pp. 354–375; L. Asmonti, 'The Arginusae Trial, the Changing Role of the "Strategoi", and the Relationship Between the "Demos" and Military Leadership in Late Fifth Century Athens,' *Bulletin of the Institute of Classical Studies* 49 (2006), pp. 1–21.

27 Xenophon, *Hellenica* 2. 1–31, with B. Strauss, 'Aegospotami Reexamined,' *American Journal of Philology* 104 (1983), pp. 24–35; Kagan (1987), pp. 376–396; Lazenby (2004), pp. 237–244; Rahe (2024), pp. 364–392.

28 Xenophon, *Hellenica* 2. 2. 1–24.

29 Plutarch, *Alcibiades* 37, 39, with de Romilly (2019), pp. 166–177.

CHAPTER 25

1 Note the view expressed in Xenophon, *Hellenica* 2. 2. 20.

2 See D. Kagan, *The Fall of the Athenian Empire* (1987), pp. 398–412; V. Davis Hanson, *A War like No Other. How the Athenians and the Spartans Fought the Peloponnesian War* (2005), pp. 289–309; P. Rahe, *Sparta's Third Attic War: The Grand Strategy of Classical Sparta* (2024), pp. 392–409; see also A. Powell, 'Why Did Sparta Not Destroy Athens in 404, or 403 BC?,' in S. Hodkinson & A. Powell (eds.), *Sparta and War* (2006), pp. 287–303.

3 Xenophon, *Hellenica* 2. 2. 11–23, esp. 23.

4 Xenophon, *Hellenica* 2. 3. 2–3, 6–4. 4. 43; Aristotle, *Athenian Politics* 34–40, with P. Rhodes, *A Commentary on the Aristotelian Athenaion Politeia* (1981), pp. 415–482.

5 Xenophon, *Hellenica* 3. 2. 21–31; Diodorus Siculus 14. 17. 4–12, 34. 1–2; on conspiracy, see Xenophon, *Hellenica* 3. 3. 4–11.

6 See Xenophon, *Hellenica* 3. 1. 1, for the decision to aid Cyrus.

7 Xenophon, *Hellenica* 3. 5. 1–25; for a more detailed, yet highly accessible history of these decades, see M. Scott, *From Democrats to Kings. The Downfall of Athens to the Epic Rise of Alexander the Great* (2009).

8 For Nemea, see C. J. Butera & M. Sears, *Battles and Battlefields of Ancient Greece. A Guide to Their History, Topography and Archaeology* (2019), pp. 349–359.

9 Xenophon, *Hellenica* 5. 1. 30–36; Diodorus Siculus 14. 110. 3, 15. 5. 1.

10 On calls to unite against Persia, see M. Flower, 'From Simonides to Isocrates: The Fifth Century Origins of Fourth Century Panhellenism,' *Classical Antiquity* 19 (2000), pp. 65–101.

11 Scott (2009), pp. 57–64.

12 For the second Athenian empire, see S. Hornblower, *The Greek World, 479–323 BC* (4th ed., 2011), pp. 240–252.

13 Xenophon, *Hellenica* 6. 4. 1–16, with Butera & Sears (2019), pp. 139–155, for sources and discussion.

14 Xenophon, *Hellenica* 7. 5. 1–26; see Butera & Sears (2019), pp. 332–347; on Messene, see Hornblower (2011), pp. 254–256.

15 Plutarch, *Alexander* 16. 8; *Agesilaus* 15. 4.

CONCLUSION

1 Thucydides 1. 10.
2 Justin, *Epitome* 8. 1.

BIBLIOGRAPHY

J. Almeida, *Justice as an Aspect of the Polis Idea in Solon's Political Poems. A Reading of Fragments in Light of the Researches of New Classical Archaeology* (2003).

G. Anderson, *The Athenian Experiment. Building an Imagined Political Community in Ancient Attica, 508–490 BC* (2003).

J. Anderson, 'Hoplite Weapons and Offensive Arms,' in Hanson (1991), pp. 15–37.

G. Aperghis, 'Athenian Mines, Coins and Triremes,' *Historia* 62 (2013), pp. 1–24.

L. Asmonti, 'The Arginusae Trial, the Changing Role of the "Strategoi", and the Relationship Between the "Demos" and Military Leadership in Late Fifth Century Athens,' *Bulletin of the Institute of Classical Studies* 49 (2006), pp. 1–21.

V. Azoulay (trans. J. Lloyd), *Pericles of Athens* (2010).

R.-M. Bérard & D. Castex, 'Epidemics and Wars: Comparative Archaeology and Anthropology of Ancient Greek Mass Burials,' *Athens Journal of History* 7. 4 (2021), pp. 295–318.

P. Bicknell, 'The Command Structure and Generals of the Marathon Campaign,' *L'Antiquité Classique* 39 (1970), pp. 427–442.

R. Billows, *Marathon. How One Battle Changed Western Civilization* (2010).

J. Bintliff, 'Solon's Reforms: An Archaeological Perspective,' in Blok & Lardinois (2006), pp. 321–333.

J. Bintliff, *The Complete Archaeology of Greece. From Hunter Gatherers to the 20th Century AD* (2012).

N. Birgalias, 'Helotage and Spartan Social Organization,' in Powell & Hodkinson (2002), pp. 249–266.

F. Blaise, 'Poetics and Politics: Tradition Re-worked in Solon's "Eunomia" (Poem 4),' in Blok & Lardinois (2006), pp. 114–133.

J. Blok, 'Phye's Procession: Culture, Politics and Peisistratid Rule,' in Sancisi-Weerdenburg (2000), pp. 17–48.

J. Blok & A. Lardinois (eds.), *Solon of Athens. New Historical and Philological Approaches* (2006).

P. Brulé, *Périclès: L'Apogée d' Athènes* (1994), pp. 115–116.

A. Burford, *Land and Labor in the Greek World* (1993).

C. J. Butera & M. Sears, *Battles and Battlefields of Ancient Greece. A Guide to Their History, Topography and Archaeology* (2019).

D. Cairns (ed.), *Oxford Readings in Homer's Iliad* (2001).

C. Calame, 'Pre-Classical Sparta as Song Culture,' in Powell (2017), pp. 177–201.

J. Camp, *The Archaeology of Athens* (2001).

C. Carey, *Thermopylae* (2019).

C. Carey & M. Edwards (eds.), *Marathon—2,500 Years* (2013).

P. Cartledge, *Agesilaos and the Crisis of Sparta* (1987).

P. Cartledge, 'The Mirage or Lykourgan Sparta: Some Brazen Reflections,' in Cartledge (2001), pp. 169–184.

P. Cartledge, 'The Peculiar Position of Sparta in the Development of the Greek City-State,' in Cartledge (2001), pp. 21–38.

P. Cartledge, 'The Politics of Pederasty,' in Cartledge (2001), pp. 91–105.

P. Cartledge, 'The Spartan Kingship: Doubly Odd?' in Cartledge (2001), pp. 55–67.

P. Cartledge, *Spartan Reflections* (2001).

P. Cartledge, *The Spartans. An Epic History* (rev. ed., 2003).

P. Cartledge, *Thermopylae. The Battle That Changed the World* (2006).

L. Casson, *Ships and Seafaring in Ancient Times* (1994).

W. Cavanagh, 'An Archaeology of Ancient Sparta with Reference to Laconia and Messenia,' in Powell (2017), pp. 61–92.

G. Cawkwell, 'Aeschines and the Peace of Philocrates,' *Revue des Études Grecques* 73 (1960), pp. 416–438.

G. Cawkwell, 'Early Greek Tyranny and the People,' *Classical Quarterly* 45 (1995), pp. 73–86.

G. Cawkwell, *The Greek Wars. The Failure of Persia* (2005).

G. Cawkwell, 'Orthodoxy and Hoplites,' *Classical Quarterly* 39 (1989), pp. 375–389.

G. Cawkwell, 'The Peace Between Athens and Persia,' *Phoenix* 51 (1997), pp. 115–130.

G. Cawkwell, 'The Peace of Philocrates Again,' *Classical Quarterly* 28. 1 (1978), pp. 92–95.

G. Cawkwell, *Philip of Macedon* (1978).

S. Chryssoulaki, A. Linderholm, A. Kjellström, V. Langerholm & M. Krzewińska, 'Bioarchaeological Field Analysis of Human Remains from the Mass Graves at Phaleron, Greece,' *Opuscula. Annual of the Swedish Institutes at Athens and Rome* 12 (2019).

M. Clarke, 'Spartan *atē* at Thermopylai: Semantics and Ideology at Herodotus, *Histories* 7. 234,' in Powell & Hodkinson (2002), pp. 63–84.

J. Coldstream, 'Prospectors or Pioneers: Pithekoussai, Kyme and Central Italy,' in Tsetskhladze & de Angelis (1994), pp. 47–59.

J. Crowley, *The Psychology of the Athenian Hoplite* (2012).

N. Crüsemann, M. van Hilgert, B. Salje, & T. Potts (eds.), *Uruk: First City of the Ancient World* (2019).

E. David, 'A Preliminary Stage of Cleisthenes' Reforms,' *Classical Antiquity* 5 (1986), pp. 1–13.

E. David, 'Suicide in Spartan Society,' in Figueira (2004), pp. 25–46.

P. Davis, 'Equality and Distinction Within the Spartiate Community,' in Powell (2017), pp. 480–499.

J. Davison, *Courtesans and Fishcakes. The Consuming Passions of Classical Athens* (1997).

F. de Angelis, 'The Foundation of Selinous: Overpopulation or Opportunities?' in Tsetskhladze & de Angelis (1994), pp. 87–110.

L. de Blois, 'Plutarch's Solon: A Tissue of Commonplaces or a Historical Account,' in Blok & Lardinois (2006), pp. 429–440.

J. de Romilly (trans. E. Trapnell Rawlings), *The Life of Alcibiades. Dangerous Ambition and the Betrayal of Athens* (2019).

B. Develin & M. Kilmer, 'What Kleisthenes Did,' *Historia* 46 (1997), pp. 3–18.

C. Dionysopoulos, *The Battle of Marathon. An Historical and Topographical Approach* (2015).

N. Doenges, 'The Campaign and Battle of Marathon,' *Historia* 47 (1998), pp. 1–17.

N. Doegnes, 'Ostracism and the "Boulai" of Cleisthenes,' *Historia* 45 (1996), pp. 387–404.

W. Dolan & J. Thompson, 'The Charge at Marathon: Herodotus 6. 112', *Classical Journal* 71 (1976), pp. 339–343.

W. Dolan & J. Thompson, 'The Charge at Marathon Again', *Classical World* 72 (1979), pp. 419–420.

R. Drews, 'The First Tyrants in Greece,' *Historia* 21 (1972), pp. 129–144.

J. Ducat (trans. E. Stafford, P.-J. Shaw & A. Powell), *Spartan Education. Youth and Society in the Classical Period* (2006).

J. Ducat, 'The Spartan "Tremblers",' in Hodkinson & Powell (2006), pp. 1–55.

A. Eremin, 'Settlements of Spartan *perioikoi*: *poleis* or *komai*?' in Powell & Hodkinson (2002), pp. 267–283.

J. Evans, 'Herodotus and the Battle of Marathon,' *Historia* 42 (1993), pp. 279–307.

R. Evans, *Fields of Battle. Retracing Ancient Battlefields* (2015).

T. Figueira, 'The Demography of the Spartan Helots,' in Luraghi & Alcock (2003), pp. 193–239.

T. Figueira, 'Helotage and the Spartan Economy,' in Powell (2017), pp. 565–595.

T. Figueira, 'Population Patterns in Late Archaic and Classical Sparta,' *Transactions of the American Philological Association* 116 (1986), pp. 165–213.

T. Figueira, 'The Spartan *hippeis*,' in Hodkinson & Powell (2006), pp. 57–84.

T. Figueira (ed.), *Spartan Society* (2004).

M. Flower, 'From Simonides to Isocrates: The Fifth Century Origins of Fourth Century Panhellenism,' *Classical Antiquity* 19 (2000), pp. 65–101.

M. Flower, 'Spartan Religion,' in Powell (2017), pp. 425–451.

C. Fornara (ed. and trans.), *Archaic Times to the End of the Peloponnesian War*. Vol. 1 of *Translated Documents of Greece and Rome* (2nd ed., 1983).

C. Fornara & L. Samons, *Athens from Cleisthenes to Pericles* (1991).

W. Forrest, *The Emergence of Greek Democracy, 800 BC–400 BC* (1966).

S. Forsdyke, 'Land, Labor and Economy in Solonian Athens: Breaking the Impasse Between Archaeology and History,' in Blok & Lardinois (2006), pp. 334–350.

S. Forsdyke, *The Politics of Expulsion in Ancient Greece* (2005).

L. Foxhall, 'Farming and Fighting in Ancient Greece,' in Rich & Shipley (1993), pp. 134–145.

L. Foxhall, 'A View from the Top: Evaluating the Solonian Property Classes,' in Mitchell & Rhodes (1997), pp. 113–136.

E. Frahm, *Assyria: The Rise and Fall of the World's First Empire* (2023).

J. Fraser, 'Classical Athens and the Luxury Problem,' in L. Llewellyn-Jones & H. Bishop-Wright (eds.), *Luxury and Power: Greece to Persia* (2023), pp. 90–155.

A. D. Frazer, 'The Myth of the Hoplite Scrimmage,' *Classical World* 36 (1942), pp. 15–16.

P. Fromherz, 'The Battlefield of Marathon: The Tropaion, Herodotus, and E. Curtius,' *Historia* 60 (2011), pp. 383–412.

F. Frost, 'The Athenian Military Before Cleisthenes,' *Historia* 33 (1984), pp. 283–295.

V. Gabrielsen, *Financing the Athenian Fleet. Public Taxation and Social Relations* (1994).

R. Gaebel, *Cavalry Operations in the Ancient Greek World* (2002).

T. Gallant, *Risk and Survival in Ancient Greece* (1991).

R. Garland, *Athens Burning: The Persian Invasion of Greece and the Evacuation of Attica* (2017).

R. Garland, *The Piraeus from the Fifth to the First Century BC* (2nd ed., 2001).

A. Giovannini, 'The Parthenon, the Treasury of Athena and the Tribute of the Allies,' in Low (2008), pp. 164–184.

A. Goldsworthy, 'The Othismos, Myths and Heresies: The Nature of Hoplite Battle,' *War in History* 4 (1997), pp. 1–26.

V. Gouschin, 'Pisistratus' Leadership in A. P. 13. 4 and the Establishment of the Tyranny of 561/60 BC,' *Classical Quarterly* 49 (1999), pp. 14–23.

A. Griffiths, 'Was Kleomenes Mad?' in Powell (1989), pp. 51–78.

C. Haas, 'Athenian Naval Power Before Themistocles,' *Historia* 34 (1985), pp. 29–46.

J. Hale, 'Not Patriots, Not Farmers, Not Amateurs: Greek Soldiers of Fortune and the Origins of Hoplite Warfare,' in Kagan & Viggiano (2013), pp. 176–193.

J. Hall, *A History of the Archaic Greek World, ca. 1200–479 BCE* (2nd ed., 2014).

N. Hammond, 'The Campaign and Battle of Marathon,' *Journal of Hellenic Studies* 88 (1968), pp. 13–57.

M. Hansen, *Polis. An Introduction to the Ancient Greek City-State* (2006).

V. Davis Hanson, 'Hoplite Battle as Ancient Greek Warfare: When, Where, and Why?' in van Wees (2000), pp. 201–232.

V. Davis Hanson, 'Hoplite Technology in Phalanx Battle,' in Hanson (1991), pp. 63–84.

V. Davis Hanson (ed.), *Hoplites. The Classical Greek Battle Experience* (1991).

V. Davis Hanson, *The Other Greeks. The Family Farm and the Agrarian Roots of Western Civilization* (1995).

V. Davis Hanson, *A War like No Other. How the Athenians and the Spartans Fought the Peloponnesian War* (2005).

V. Davis Hanson, *Warfare and Agriculture in Classical Greece* (2nd ed., 1998).

V. Davis Hanson, *The Western Way of War* (1989).

C. Shaw Hardy, *Athens 415. The City in Crisis* (2020).

J. Henderson, 'Drama and Democracy,' in Samons (2007), pp. 179–195.

S. Hodkinson, 'Marriage, Inheritance and Demography: Perspectives upon the Success and Decline of Classical Sparta,' in Powell (1989), pp. 79–121.

S. Hodkinson, *Property and Wealth in Classical Sparta* (2009).

S. Hodkinson, 'Spartiates, Helots and the Direction of the Agrarian Economy: Towards an Understanding of Helotage in Comparative Perspective,' in Luraghi & Alcock (2003), pp. 263–278.

S. Hodkinson & A. Powell (eds.), *Sparta and War* (2006).

T. Hodos, *The Archaeology of the Mediterranean Iron Age. A Globalising World c. 1100–600 BCE* (2020).

T. Hodos, *Local Responses to Colonization in the Iron Age Mediterranean* (2006).

A. Holladay, 'The Hellenic Disaster in Egypt,' *Journal of Hellenic Studies* 109 (1989), pp. 176–182.

S. Hornblower, *The Greek World, 479–323 BC* (4th ed., 2011).

N. Humble, 'Xenophon's Sons in Sparta? Perspectives on *xenoi* in the Spartan Upbringing,' in Figueira (2004), pp. 231–250.

P. Hunt, 'The Slaves and the Generals at Arginusae,' *American Journal of Philology* 122 (2001), pp. 359–380.

J. Hurwitt, *The Acropolis in the Age of Pericles* (2004).

S. Isager & J. Skydsgaard, *Ancient Greek Agriculture. An Introduction* (1992).

B. Jordan, 'The Crews of Athenian Triremes,' *L'Antiquité Classique* 69 (2000), pp. 81–101.

D. Kagan, *The Archidamian War* (1974).

D. Kagan, *The Fall of the Athenian Empire* (1987).

D. Kagan, *The Outbreak of the Peloponnesian War* (1969).

D. Kagan, *The Peace of Nicias and the Sicilian Expedition* (1981).

D. Kagan, *Pericles of Athens and the Birth of Democracy* (1991).

D. Kagan & G. Viggiano, 'The Hoplite Debate,' in Kagan & Viggiano (2013), pp. 1–56.

D. Kagan & G. Viggiano (eds.), *Men of Bronze. Hoplite Warfare in Ancient Greece* (2013).

D. Kahn, 'Inaros' Rebellion Against Artaxerxes I and the Athenian Disaster in Egypt,' *Classical Quarterly* 58 (2008), pp. 424–440.

L. Kallet, 'The Athenian Economy,' in Samons (2007), pp. 70–95.

L. Kallet-Marx, *Money, Expense, and Naval Power in Thucydides' History 1–5.24* (1993).

L. Kallet-Marx, 'Money Talks: Rhetor, Demos and the Resources of the Athenian Empire,' in Low (2008), pp. 185–210.

T. Kelly, 'Persian Propaganda—a Neglected Factor in Xerxes' Invasion of Greece and Herodotus,' *Iranica Antiqua* 38 (2003), pp. 173–219.

N. Kennell, *The Gymnasium of Virtue* (1995).

N. Kennell, *Spartans. A New History* (2010).

J. Kierstead, 'Associations,' in Neils & Rogers (2021), pp. 379–391.

A. Knodell, *Societies in Transition in Early Greece. An Archaeological History* (2021).

A. Konecny, 'The Battle of Plataiai. Topography and Tactics,' in Konecny & Sekunda (2022), pp. 167–210.

A. Konecny & N. Sekunda (eds.), *The Battle of Plataiai, 479 BC* (2022).

R. Konijnendijk, *Classical Greek Tactics: A Cultural History* (2019).

R. Konijnendijk & P. Bardunias, 'The Face of Battle at Plataiai,' in Konecny & Sekunda (2022), pp. 211–242.

J. Kosmin, 'A Phenomenology of Democracy: Ostracism as Political Ritual,' *Classical Antiquity* 34 (2015), pp. 121–162.

C. Koukouli-Chrysanthaki, 'Amphipolis,' in R. Lane Fox (ed.), *Brill's Companion to Ancient Macedon: Studies in the Archaeology and History of Macedon, 650 BC to 300 AD* (2011), pp. 409–436.

J. Kraft, G. Rapp, G. Szemler, C. Tziavos & E. Kase, 'The Pass at Thermopylae, Greece,' *Journal of Field Archaeology* 14 (1987), pp. 181–198.

P. Krentz, *The Battle of Marathon* (2010).

P. Krentz, 'Casualties in Hoplite Battles,' *Greek Roman and Byzantine Studies* 26 (1985), pp. 13–20.

P. Krentz, 'Continuing the Othismos on the Othismos,' *Ancient History Bulletin* 8. 2 (1994), pp. 45–49.

P. Krentz, 'Deception in Archaic and Classical Greek Warfare,' in van Wees (2000), pp. 167–200.

P. Krentz, 'Hoplite Hell: How Hoplites Fought,' in Kagan & Viggiano (2013), pp. 134–156.

P. Krentz, 'Marathon and the Exclusive Hoplite Phalanx,' in Carey & Edwards (2013), pp. 35–44.

P. Krentz, 'The Nature of Hoplite Battles,' *Classical Antiquity* 4 (1985), pp. 50–61.

P. Krentz, 'War,' in P. Sabin, H van Wees & M. Whitby, *The Cambridge History of Greek and Roman Warfare*. Vol. 1 (2007), pp. 146–185.

J. Lacey, *The First Clash. The Miraculous Greek Victory at Marathon and Its Impact on Western Civilization* (2011).

A. Lardinois, 'Have We Solon's Verses?' in Blok & Lardinois (2006), pp. 15–35.

B. Lavelle, *Archaic Greece. The Age of New Reckonings* (2020).

B. Lavelle, 'The Compleat Angler: Observations on the Rise of Peisistratos in Herodotos (1. 59–64),' *Classical Quarterly* 41 (1991), pp. 317–324.

B. Lavelle, *Fame, Money, and Power. The Rise of Peisistratos and 'Democratic' Tyranny at Athens* (2005).

B. Lavelle, 'Herodotos, Skythian Archers, and the *doryphoroi* of the Peisistratids,' *Klio* 74 (1992), pp. 78–97.

B. Lavelle, 'The Nature of Hipparchos' Insult to Harmodios,' *American Journal of Philology* 107 (1986), pp. 318–331.

B. Lavelle, 'The Pisistratids and the Mines of Thrace,' *Greek, Roman and Byzantine Studies* 33 (1992), pp. 5–23.

J. Lazenby, *The Defence of Greece, 490–479 BC* (1993).

J. Lazenby, 'The Killing Zone,' in Hanson (1991), pp. 87–109.

J. Lazenby, *The Spartan Army* (1985).

J. Lendon, 'Athens and Sparta and the Coming of the Peloponnesian War,' in Samons (2007), pp. 258–281.

J. Lendon, 'Homeric Vengeance and the Outbreak of Greek Wars,' in van Wees (2000), pp. 1–30.

J. Lendon, *Song of Wrath: The Peloponnesian War Begins* (2010).

D. Lewis, 'The Athenian Coinage Decree,' in P. Rhodes (ed.), *Selected Papers in Greek and Near Eastern History* (1997): 118–131.

J. Lewis, *Solon the Thinker* (2006).

M. Lipka, 'Notes on the Influence of the Spartan Great Rhetra on Tyrtaeus, Herodotus and Xenophon,' in Powell & Hodkinson (2002), pp. 219–225.

L. Llewellyn-Jones, *Persians. The Age of the Great Kings* (2022).

A. Lloyd (ed.), *A Companion to Ancient Egypt* (2014).

P. Low (ed.), *The Athenian Empire* (2008).

R. D. Luginbill, 'Othismos: The Importance of the Mass-Shove in Hoplite Warfare,' *Phoenix* 48. 1 (1994), pp. 51–61.

N. Luraghi & S. Alcock (eds.), *Helots and Their Masters in Laconia and Messenia. Histories, Ideologies, Structures* (2003).

T. Martin, *Ancient Greece. From Prehistoric to Hellenistic Times* (2nd ed., 2012).

C. Matthew, *A Storm of Spears. Understanding the Greek Hoplite at War* (2012).

C. Matthew, 'Towards the Hot Gates: The Events Leading to the Battle of Thermopylae,' in Matthew & Trundle (2013), pp. 22–23.

C. Matthew, 'Was the Greek Defence of Thermopylae in 480 BC a Suicide Mission?' in C. Matthew & M. Trundle (eds.), *Beyond the Gates of Fire. New Perspectives on the Battle of Thermopylae* (2013), pp. 60–99.

R. Matthews, *The Battle of Thermopylae. A Campaign in Context* (2006).

H. Mattingly, 'Periclean Imperialism,' in Low (2008), pp. 81–110.

P. Matyszak, *Expedition to Disaster. The Athenian Mission to Sicily, 415 BC* (2012).

M. McGregor, *The Athenians and Their Empire* (1987).

R. Meiggs, *The Athenian Empire* (1972).

R. Meiggs & D. Lewis (eds.), *Greek Historical Inscriptions* (1989).

B. Meritt, H. Wade-Gerry & M. McGregor (eds.), *The Athenian Tribute Lists*. 4 vols. (1939–1953).

E. Meyer, 'The Athenian Expedition to Egypt and the Value of Ctesias,' *Phoenix* 72 (2018), pp. 43–61.

E. Meyer, '*The Outbreak of the Peloponnesian War* After Twenty-Five Years,' in C. Hamilton & D. Krentz (eds.), *Polis and Polemos. Essays on Politics, War and History in Ancient Greece, in Honor of Donald Kagan* (1997), pp. 23–58.

E. Meyer, 'The Phocian Debacle at Thermopylae,' *Phoenix* 25 (2021), pp. 84–101.

E. Meyer, 'Thucydides on Harmodius and Aristogeiton, Tyranny, and History,' *Classical Quarterly* 58 (2008), pp. 13–34.

E. Millender, 'Kingship: The History, Power and Prerogatives of the Spartans' 'Divine' Dyarchy,' in Powell (2017), pp. 452–479.

L. Mitchell, 'New Wine in Old Wineskins. Solon, *arete*, and the *agathos*,' in Mitchell & Rhodes (1997), pp. 137–147.

L. Mitchell & P. Rhodes (eds.), *The Development of the Polis in Archaic Greece* (1997).

T. Mitchell, *Democracy's Beginning. The Athenian Story* (2015).

I. Morris & B. Powell, *The Greeks. History, Culture, and Society* (2005).

I. MacGregor Morris, 'Pausanias, *Best of Men*: Politics, Propaganda, Memory,' in Konecny & Sekunda (2022), pp. 79–132.

I. MacGregor Morris, 'Xerxes: Ideology and Practice,' in Konecny & Sekunda (2022), pp. 13–69.

M. Nafissi, 'Lykourgos the Spartan "Lawgiver": Ancient Beliefs and Modern Scholarship,' in Powell (2017), pp. 93–123.

S. Nevin, *The Idea of Marathon. Battle and Culture* (2022).

J. Ober, 'The Athenians Revolution of 508/7 BC: Violence, Authority and the Origins of Democracy,' in J. Ober, *The Athenian Revolution. Essays on the Ancient Greek Democracy and Political Theory* (1996), pp. 32–52.

J. Ober, 'Hoplites and Obstacles,' in Hanson (1991), pp. 173–196.

J. Ober, 'Solon and the *horoi*: Facts on the Ground in Archaic Athens,' in Blok & Lardinois (2006), pp. 441–456.

R. Oldfield, 'Collision Damage to Triremes,' in Rankov (2012), pp. 214–224.

K. Ormand, 'Sex and the City,' in Neils & Rogers (2021), pp. 362–375.

R. Osborne, *Greece in the Making. 1200–479 BC* (2nd ed., 2009).

R. Osborne, 'Law and Laws. How Do We Join the Dots?' in Mitchell & Rhodes (1997), pp. 74–82.

G. Parmeggiani, 'Notes on the Tradition of the Peace of Callias,' *Erga-Logoi* 8 (2020), pp. 7–23.

C. Pelling, 'Herodotus' Marathon,' in Carey & Edwards (2013), 23–34.

A. Podlecki, *Pericles and His Circle* (1997).

S. Pomeroy, *Spartan Women* (2002).

A. Powell, *Athens and Sparta. Constructing Greek Political and Social History from 478 BC* (3rd ed., 2016).

A. Powell (ed.), *Classical Sparta: Techniques Behind Her Success* (1989).

A. Powell (ed.), *A Companion to Sparta* (Blackwell Companions to the Ancient World) (2017).

A. Powell, 'Why Did Sparta Not Destroy Athens in 404, or 403 BC?' in Hodkinson & Powell (2006), pp. 287–303.

A. Powell & S. Hodkinson (eds.), *Sparta. Beyond the Mirage* (2002).

B. Powell, *Homer* (2003).

D. Pritchard, *Athenian Democracy at War* (2019).

W. Pritchett, *The Greek State at War*. 5 vols. (1971–1991).

F. Pryor, *Stonehenge. The Story of a Sacred Landscape* (2016).

K. Raaflaub, 'Early Greek Infantry Fighting in a Mediterranean Context,' in Kagan & Viggiano (2013), pp. 95–111.

K. Raaflaub, 'Soldiers, Citizens, and the Evolution of the Early Greek *polis*,' in Mitchell & Rhodes (1997), pp. 49–59.

K. Raaflaub, 'Warfare and Athenian Society,' in Samons (2007), pp. 96–124.

P. Rahe, *The Grand Strategy of Classical Sparta. The Persian Challenge* (2015).

P. Rahe, *The Spartan Regime. Its Character, Origins and Grand Strategy* (2016).

P. Rahe, *Sparta's First Attic War. The Grand Strategy of Classical Sparta, 478–446 BC* (2019).

P. Rahe, *Sparta's Second Attic War. The Grand Strategy of Classical Sparta, 446–418 BC* (2020).

P. Rahe, *Sparta's Sicilian Proxy War* (2023).

P. Rahe, *Sparta's Third Attic War: The Grand Strategy of Classical Sparta* (2024).

B. Rankov (ed.), *Trireme Olympias. The Final Report* (2012).

G. Rapp, 'The Topography of the Pass at Thermopylae Circa 480 BC,' in Matthew & Trundle (2013), pp. 39–59.

L. Rawlings, 'Alternative Agonies: Hoplite Martial and Combat Experience Beyond the Phalanx,' in van Wees (2000), pp. 233–259.

P. Rhodes, 'The Battle of Marathon and Modern Scholarship,' *Bulletin of the Institute of Classical Studies Supplement* 124 (2013), pp. 3–21.

P. Rhodes, *A Commentary on the Aristotelian Athenaion Politeia* (1981).

P. Rhodes, 'Democracy and Empire,' in Samons (2007), pp. 24–45.

P. Rhodes, 'The Reforms and Laws of Solon: An Optimistic View,' in Blok & Lardinois (2006), pp. 248–260.

J. Rich & G. Shipley (eds.), *War and Society in the Greek World* (1993).

N. Richer, 'Spartan Education in the Classical Period,' in Powell (2017), pp. 525–542.

D. Ridgway, 'Phoenicians and Greeks in the West: A View from Pithekoussai,' in Tsetskhladze & de Angelis (1994), pp. 35–46.

T. Rihll, 'War, Slavery and Settlement in Early Greece,' in Rich & Shipley (1993), pp. 77–107.

J. Roberts, *City of Socrates. An Introduction to Classical Athens* (2nd ed., 1998).

C. Robinson, 'Cleisthenes and Ostracism,' *American Journal of Archaeology* 56 (1952), pp. 23–26.

E. Robinson, 'Thucydidean Sieges, Prosopitis, and the Hellenic Disaster in Egypt,' *Classical Antiquity* 18 (1999), pp. 132–152.

V. Rosvlach, 'Autochthony and the Athenians,' *Classical Quarterly* 37. 2 (1987), pp. 294–306.

E. Rung & A. Sapogov, 'The Aftermath of the Peace of Callias,' *Anabasis* 9 (2018), pp. 227–235.

R. Sallares, *The Ecology of the Ancient Greek World* (1991).

J. Salmon, 'Lopping Off the Heads? Tyrants, Politics and the *polis*,' in Mitchell & Rhodes (1997), pp. 60–73.

L. Samons (ed.), *The Cambridge Companion to the Age of Pericles* (2007).

L. Samons, 'Kimon, Kallias and Peace with Persia,' *Historia* 47 (1998), pp. 129–140.

L. Samons, *Pericles and the Conquest of History. A Political Biography* (2016).

H. Sancisi-Weerdenburg, *Peisistratos and the Tyranny. A Reappraisal of the Evidence* (2000).

H. Sancisi-Weerdenburg, 'The Tyranny of Peisistratos,' in Sancisi-Weerdenburg (2000), pp. 1–15.

W. Scheidel, 'Helot Numbers: A Simplified Model,' in Luraghi & Alcock (2003), pp. 240–247.

A. Schwartz, 'Large Weapons, Small Greeks: The Practical Limitations of Hoplite Weapons and Equipment,' in Kagan & Viggiano (2013), pp. 157–175.

A. Schwartz, *Reinstating the Hoplite. Arms, Armour and Phalanx Fighting in Archaic and Classical Greece* (2009).

M. Scott, *From Democrats to Kings. The Downfall of Athens to the Epic Rise of Alexander the Great* (2009).

N. Sekunda, 'Greek Logistics at Plataiai and Strategical Planning During the Third Invasion of Greece (480–479 BC),' in Konecny & Sekunda (2022), pp. 153–166.

H. Shapiro, 'Leagros: An Athenian Life,' in J. Neils & D. Rogers (eds.), *The Cambridge Companion to Ancient Athens* (2021), pp. 7–17.

T. Shaw, 'The Performance of Ancient Triremes in Wind and Waves,' in Rankov (2012), pp. 68–75.

T. Shear, *Trophies of Victory. Public Buildings in Periklean Athens* (2016).

W. Shepherd, *Pylos and Sphacteria, 425 BC. Sparta's Island of Disaster* (2013).

G. Shrimpton, 'The Persian Cavalry at Marathon,' *Phoenix* 34 (1980), pp. 20–37.

J. Sickinger, 'New Ostraka from the Athenian Agora,' *Hersperia* 86 (2017), pp. 443–508.

H. Singor, 'The Military Side of the Peisistratean Tyranny,' in Sancisi-Weerdenburg (2000), pp. 107–129.

S. Slings, 'Literature in Athens, 566–510 BC,' in Sancisi-Weerdenburg (2000), pp. 57–77.

A. Snodgrass, *Early Greek Armour and Weapons from the End of the Bronze Age to 600 BC* (1964).

E. Stehle, 'Solon's Self-Reflective Political Persona and Its Audience,' in Blok & Lardinois (2006), pp. 79–113.

A. Steiner, 'Eating and Drinking,' in Neils & Rogers (2021), pp. 345–361.

B. Strauss, 'Aegospotami Reexamined,' *American Journal of Philology* 104 (1983), pp. 24–35.

B. Strauss, *Salamis. The Greatest Naval Battle of the Ancient World, 480 BC* (2004).

D. Stuttard, *Phoenix. A Father, a Son, and the Rise of Athens* (2021).

P. Stylianou, 'On the Untentability of Peace with Persia in the 460s B.C.,' in Θ. Παπαδόπουλλου (ed.), Μελέται καὶ Ὑπο μνήματα, II, Leucosia (1992), pp. 339–371.

A. Taylor, 'Battle Manoeuvres for Fast Triremes,' in Rankov (2012), pp. 231–243.

G. Tsetskhladze & F. de Angelis (eds.), *The Archaeology of Greek Colonization. Essays Dedicated to Sir John Boardman* (1994).

J. van der Vin, 'Coins in Athens at the Time of Peisistratos,' in Sancisi-Weerdenburg (2000), pp. 147–153.

H. van Wees, 'The Common Messes,' in Powell (2017), pp. 236–268.

H. van Wees, 'The Development of the Hoplite Phalanx. Iconography and Reality in the Seventh Century,' in van Wees (2000), pp. 125–166.

H. van Wees, 'Farmers and Hoplites: Models of Historical Development,' in Kagan & Viggiano (2013), pp. 222–255.

H. van Wees, *Greek Warfare. Myths and Realities* (2004).

H. van Wees, 'Luxury, Austerity and Equality in Sparta,' in Powell (2017), pp. 202–235.

H. van Wees, 'Mass and Elite in Solon's Athens: The Property Classes Revisited,' in Blok & Lardinois (2006), pp. 351–389.

H. van Wees (ed.), *War and Violence in Ancient Greece* (2000).

P. Vaughn, 'The Identification and Retrieval of the Hoplite Battle-Dead,' in Hanson (1991), pp. 38–62.

G. Viggiano, 'The Hoplite Revolution and the Rise of the Polis,' in Kagan & Viggiano (2013), pp. 112–133.

G. Viggiano & H. van Wees, 'The Arms, Armor, and Iconography of Early Greek Hoplite Warfare,' in Kagan & Viggiano (2013), pp. 57–75.

H. Wallinga, *Ships and Sea-Power Before the Great Persian War: The Ancestry of the Ancient Trireme* (1993).

N. Whatley, 'On the Possibility of Reconstructing Marathon and Other Ancient Battles,' *Journal of Hellenic Studies* 84 (1964), pp. 119–139.

J. Wiesehöfer, 'Mardonios,' in Konecny & Sekunda (2022), pp. 71–78.

G. Williams, 'The Kerameikos Ostraka,' *Zeitschrift für Papyrologie und Epigraphik* 31 (1978), pp. 103–113.

I. Worthington, *Philip II of Macedonia* (2008).

ILLUSTRATION CREDITS

1. Chigi vase with lines of hoplites fighting. DEA/G. NIMATALLAH/Getty Images
2. Nereid Monument. Adrian Goldsworthy
3. Nereid Monument with close-up of shield. Adrian Goldsworthy
4. Nereid Monument, assault on a city. Adrian Goldsworthy
5. Spartan officer cloaked and helmeted. © Boltin Picture Library / Bridgeman Images
6. Athens, view of city, Acropolis and Parthenon in distance. ANGELOS TZORTZINIS/Getty Images
7. View of Sparta today. Zoonar GmbH/Alamy
8. Bronze of Spartan girl running. GRANGER/Historical Picture Archive/Alamy
9. Vase showing Harmodius and Aristogeiton. Wikimedia Commons
10. Athens, Pnyx hill. Sklifas Steven/Alamy
11. Athens, close-up of Parthenon. Make Them All Trips of a Lifetime/Getty Images
12. Parthenon sculptures, horsemen. Adrian Goldsworthy
13. Parthenon sculptures, centaur. Adrian Goldsworthy
14. An Athenian owl coin. Print Collector/Getty Images
15. Relief of seated Darius with Xerxes standing behind his throne. Bettmann/Getty Images

ILLUSTRATION CREDITS

16. Persian soldiers shown on glazed wall panel at Susa. Lanmas/Alamy
17. The Olympias reconstructed trireme. George Atsametakis/Alamy
18. Bust of Themistocles. Wikimedia Commons
19. Bust of Pericles. Art Images/Getty Images
20. Ostraca from Athens marked with names of men chosen for ostracism. DEA/G. DAGLI ORTI/Getty Images
21. View of island of Sphacteria today. Em Campos/Getty Images
22. Corinthian helmet. Sepia Times/Getty Images
23. Spartan shield (at least the bronze covering) captured at Pylos and dedicated at Athens, now in the Agora Museum in Athens. Wikimedia Commons

INDEX

Abydus, 502
Acanthus, 452–453
Acarnania, 434
Achaea and Achaeans, 36, 47–48, 71, 166, 236
Achaemenid Persian Empire
  archers, 219, 268, 275
  armies, 205, 212–213, 246, 248–250
  Battle of Marathon, 17, 208–223, 214(map), 225–227, 307
  Battle of Mycale, 303–304, 305, 313
  Battle of Plataea, 12, 291–304, 307
  Battle of Salamis, 12, 269–284
  Battle of Thermopylae, 2, 11–12, 253–263, 258(map), 265–266
  cavalry and horses, 212, 213, 217, 219, 248, 293–295
  coastal garrisons, 307, 314
  conquests, 180–183, 189
  diplomacy, 192, 201, 207, 241–244, 287–289, 347
  Egyptian rebellion, 356–357
  expansion of, 200–202, 203(map)
  'the Immortals,' 248, 257, 259, 262
  Ionian departure from, 186–187
  kings, 180–186
  military power, 196–197, 247–248, 306
  naval fleet, 250–251, 255, 257, 270–271, 276, 303, 322, 355
  retreat from Greece, 226
  satrapies, 185, 493
  shipbuilding, 245–246
  Spartan alliance, 17–18, 493
  war preparations, 239–240, 241–242, 245
  wealth, 249–250
  See also Persian Wars
Achilles, 23, 27–28, 29, 30, 46, 51, 65, 155, 312
Acropolis, 69–70, 71, 105, 120, 230, 261, 268, 276, 286, 371, 373, 374, 380, 525
Actium, Bay of, 395
Aegean Sea, 15(map), 34, 240, 307
Aegina and Aeginetans, 239, 243, 267, 316, 325, 349, 352–353, 397–398
Aegospotami, 507–508, 510
Aeschylus, 211, 221, 230, 279, 281, 380, 381, 505
Aetolia and Aetolians, 433–434, 441
Agamemnon, 27, 46, 47, 65, 311, 312
agathoi ('good' men), 67, 68, 69, 72, 74–75
Agesilaus, King of Sparta, 502, 515
Agis, King of Sparta, 435–436, 458, 460–461, 487, 507
Agora, 110, 374
agricultural communities, 31–32, 43–44, 51, 56
Agrieliki, Mount, 210
Ahhiyawa, 36
Ahura Mazda, 184, 247, 248
Ajax, 125
Alcibiades, 2, 457–458, 465–467, 471–475, 485–488, 489, 493–495, 500–503, 508
Alcidas, 426–427
Alcmaeonids, 103–104, 111, 114, 119, 129, 133, 340, 370, 399
Alcman, 95–96
Alexander, 101

INDEX

Alexander I of Macedon, 251, 288–289, 296
Alexander the Great, 1, 46, 183, 523–524
alliances
  Athenian, 13, 18, 115, 120, 243–244, 266, 284, 289, 309–310, 330, 348, 355–356, 362–363, 376, 378–379, 388–389, 519, 531, 533
  combined naval fleet, 313–315
  Delian League, 315–316
  Spartan, 13, 17–18, 97, 243–244, 284, 290, 304, 309–311, 330, 348, 349, 385–386, 457, 533
  Spartan-led coalition, 309–312, 316–317
Al-Mina, 55
Ambracia and Ambraciots, 434
Amphictyonic League, 330
Amphipolis, 393, 453–455
Amyclae, 83
anarchia (anarchy), 73, 104
Anatolia, 34, 179
Anshan, 180–181
Aphaia, 372
Apollo, 68, 141, 242, 290, 357, 378, 399, 419, 435, 471
Arcadia, 84
archers, 219, 268, 275, 294–295, 300, 411
Archidamian War, 470
Archidamus, 341, 398, 414–415, 417, 419, 425–426, 435, 502
archons, 69, 72, 104, 111, 128, 435
Areopagus, 128, 346, 375–376
Argeads, 101
Arginusae, Battle of, 406 BC, 505–506
Argos and Argives
  Argive shield, 161
  Athens alliance, 457
  defeated at Mycenae, 339
  hoplite population, 330, 338
  Mardonius warned about Greek army, 292
  massacre by Cleomenes, 134, 338
  opposition to Sparta, 84, 97–98, 136, 243, 244
  peace treaty with Sparta, 456, 462
  tyrants, 102
Aristagoras, 193–195, 199, 206

Aristides the Just, 272, 274
aristocracy, 4–5, 54, 65–66, 89, 103, 106, 118, 125–126, 128–129, 155, 527
Aristogiton, 112–114, 116
Aristophanes, 380, 428
Aristotle
  on Athenian naval power, 315
  on Athenian shipbuilding, 235, 238–239
  on ephors' war on helots, 152, 153
  on ostracisms, 232–233
  on Pisistratus, 104–105
  on political rights, 156
  on tyranny, 103
Artaxerxes, 306–307, 326, 359, 422–423, 493
Artaxerxes II, 518
Artemis, 229
Artemisia of Caria, 281–282
Artemisium, 253, 256, 259, 266, 285, 421
Asia Minor, 55, 58, 69, 102, 177
Aspasia, 382–383, 389, 398, 419
Assembly of the People *(Ecclesia)*, 121, 127–128
Assyrian Empire, 34, 58, 102, 160, 166, 178–179, 180
Athena, 72, 267, 276, 336, 374, 376, 378, 379–380
Athena Nike, 374
Athena Parthenos, 372–373, 383
Athena Promachos, 371–372, 373
Athens and Athenians, 14, 16, 17, 22, 23, 75, 80–81, 118, 125–126, 135–136, 155, 357, 376, 465, 535–536
  alliances, 13, 18, 115, 120, 243–244, 266, 284, 289, 309–310, 330, 355–356, 362–363, 376, 378–379, 388–389, 519, 531, 533
  Battle of Marathon, 17, 208–223, 214(map), 226, 228–231, 277, 312, 324
  Battle of Mycale, 303–304, 305, 313, 325
  Battle of Plataea, 291–304, 325
  Battle of Salamis, 12, 17, 269–284, 273(map), 310–311, 325

INDEX

Battle of Thermopylae, 253, 258(map)
Boule (council), 126–129, 490, 496, 530
coinage, 112, 376
colonization, 187, 318–325, 366–367, 392–393
community identity, 76–77, 80, 125, 130
cruelty of, 509–510
cultural achievements, 531–532
Cylon's attempted coup, 69–70, 72, 79, 102, 103–104
Delian League leadership, 317–325
demes, 122–125, 125(map), 209
democratic system, 3–4, 14, 16, 230–231, 325, 529–530
diplomacy, 242–243
emergence of as a major city, 43
empire, 320–321(map)
evacuation of, 267–268, 277, 290, 414–415
growing power of, 521–522
helot rebellion, 344–346
Herodotus in, 22
historical sources, 20–22, 81
long walls, 335(map), 350–351, 352, 410, 517
monuments, 372–375, 377(map), 525–526
naval power, 14, 17, 135, 235–239, 244, 270, 275, 277, 303, 309, 312, 315, 323, 331, 333, 355, 366, 402, 526, 533, 535
origin stories of, 44, 70–72, 318
plague, 417–419, 423
political system, 64, 69, 72, 121–122, 126–132, 529–532
population growth, 71, 125, 371
prosperity of, 384–386, 408–409, 464–465
re-fortification of, 309–310
ruins of, 371, 525
sacking of, 268–269, 286
shipbuilding, 316, 393
shows of defiance to Persia, 201–202
size of, 511
slavery, 74–75
tyranny, 104–116, 188–189, 204, 531

athletics, 67–68, 139, 526–527
Athos, Mount, 206, 227, 246, 292, 396
Atossa, 228
Attica, 70–71, 79, 107, 108(map), 115, 118, 125(map), 267, 350, 364, 417

Babylonia, 179, 181, 228
'bad' men (*kakoi*), 67, 74–75
barbarians, 30, 101, 135
Bardylis, 183
basileus (king/prince), 46–47, 51–52, 61, 72, 155
Battles. *See specific Battle locations*
bell cuirass, 161, 162, 167
Black Sea, 55, 187, 393
body armor, 161–162, 295
Boeotia and Boeotians, 108(map), 288, 290, 292, 298, 351, 356, 363, 405, 448–452, 457
boule (council), 119, 126–129, 361, 530
bouleuterion (council hall), 127
Brasidas, 415–416, 421, 422, 445–446, 447, 452–455, 461
burial customs, 47, 49–50, 54, 72, 222, 229–230
Byzantium, 314, 325

Cadmeia, 519
calendars, 23–24
Callias, 359
Callimachus, 209, 211, 215–217, 221, 230
Cambyses, 182–183, 185, 190, 227
camels, 246, 252
canals, 246–247, 250–251
Caria and Carians, 58, 102, 161, 179, 196
Carneia festival, 213, 254–255, 269, 462
Carthage, 476
Carystus and Carystians, 207, 319
cavalry (*hippeis*), 95, 138–139, 443, 460
Chaeronea, Battle of, 536
Chalcidice, 396, 452, 465
Chalkis and Chalcidians, 63–64, 120–121, 135, 192, 365
Chigi vase, 167
Chios and Chians, 316, 323, 417, 493

609

INDEX

Cimon
  Battle of Plataea, 276
  capture of Eion, 318
  Cyprus expedition, 358–359, 392
  death, 359
  delegation to Sparta, 290
  as festival judge, 380
  Miltiades's debts paid by, 232
  at Mount Ithome, 345
  opposition to Ephialtes, 344, 345
  ostracism, 345, 352, 357
  Persian naval defeat, 322
  record in warfare, 369
  rumors about, 383
  on Spartans, 317
  squadron fleet command, 313
  stoa construction, 371
  trial, 345
circuit judges, Athenian, 110
cities
  autonomous nature of, 50
  colonization by, 56–57
  community identity, 54–55, 61, 80
  emergence of from palace complexes, 43, 49
  first, 32
  growth in number of, 59–60
  laws, 59, 64
  leadership, 61
  origin stories of, 80
  patron deities, 336
  security, 63
  state formation, 60–61
  variety in sizes of, 60
  walled, 60, 81, 83, 158, 179, 191, 196, 207–208, 231, 309–310, 314, 323, 351, 410
citizens and citizenship
  deme membership and, 123, 129
  entitlements and obligations, 528
  hoplites, 156–165, 230–231, 304
  land ownership, 332, 343
  requirements for, 19, 77, 532
  soldiers, 20, 65, 90, 92, 155–156, 528, 532
  Spartan, 145, 150
  voting rights, 4–5
city-states, 7, 60–61, 71, 527
clans, 103–104, 111
class hierarchies, 65–66, 77, 118

Classical Greece, influence of, 1–2, 14
Cleisthenes
  as archon, 111, 118
  Boule creation, 126–129
  deme system, 122–125, 125(map), 209, 336
  exile, 114, 115, 117–118
  institution of ostracism, 232
  reforms, 121–122, 130–131, 172
Cleombrotus, 520
Cleomenes, 322
  accusations against, 325, 531
  alcoholism, 134, 193
  Argos victory, 134, 338
  Athens intervention, 115, 117
  bribery by Persia, 191
  death, 135, 240, 530
  Demaratus and, 133–134
  erratic behavior, 135, 201
  Ionian request for aid declined, 195
  Isagoras and, 118–120, 136
  plans to attack Athens, 120, 192
  support for Athens against Persia, 193
  surrender and withdrawal from Acropolis, 261
  thwarted by Athens, 154
Cleon, 23, 428–429, 438–439, 441, 443, 454–455
cleruchies, 361, 362, 364, 374, 385
coinage, 76, 112, 376
colonization, 55–57, 79–80, 89, 169, 177–178, 187, 318–325, 366–367, 392–393
community identity, 12–13, 30, 41, 54–55, 61, 76–77, 80, 83, 88–89, 125, 130, 331
competitiveness, 13–14, 54, 532, 535
constitutions, 361–362, 365
Corcyra and Corcyraeans, 270, 307, 393–397, 408, 430–431
Corinth and Corinthians
  Argos alliance, 457–458
  Athens alliance, 18, 355–356, 490
  colonization, 393, 397
  conflict with Athens, 348
  conflict with Sparta, 533
  diplomacy, 192
  dispute with Megara, 348–349
  expedition to Samos, 190

INDEX

Gylippus and, 479
Isthmus of, 48, 251, 269, 289, 291, 309
military power, 13
opposition to tyranny, 120, 133
retreat from Aegina, 349
Sparta alliance, 97, 154, 190, 242–243, 394, 408, 533
trading power, 393
trireme-building, 237, 238, 280
tyrants, 102
war with Corcyra, 393–397, 430–431
Coronea, Battle of, 409, 457, 466
courtesans, 383, 468
Creasey, Edward, 225
Crete, 34–35, 81, 421
Croesus, 102, 179–180
Crypteia ('secret service'), 151
cults, 336, 378, 419
Cyclades, 207
Cyclopean walls, 36
Cylon, 69–70, 72, 79, 102, 103, 187, 340, 399
Cyprus, 178, 190, 196, 244, 313–314, 346, 358–359
Cyrus, 502–504, 507, 515
Cyrus II, 180–183, 185, 186, 190, 227, 228
Cyzicus, 500

Dardanelles, 55, 109, 133, 187, 246–247, 250, 283, 314, 493, 499–500, 507
Darius, 194, 197
  Danube expedition, 189, 204
  death, 228
  Hippias and, 191–193
  invasion of Greece, 189, 203(map), 204–223, 226–227, 243–244
  Mardonius and, 292
  military failures, 226–227
  Miltiades plot against, 204
  murder of Cambyses, 183
  rise to power, 183–185
  satrap system, 199
Darius II, 493, 495, 500–501, 515
Dark Ages, Greek, 38–39
Datis the Mede, 204–205, 206
death penalty, 73

Decelea, 487, 491, 510, 534–535
decision-making, 7–8
Deinomache, 382
Delian League, 394
  Athenian leadership, 317–325
  Byzantium and, 389–390
  capture of Eion, 318–319
  capture of Scyros, 318
  compulsion to join, 319, 325, 353
  formation of, 315–316
  members, 316, 331, 356
  purpose of, 359
  rebellions against, 322–323
  requirements of, 315–316
  shift into Athenian Empire, 365, 390–391
  treasury, 315, 316, 324, 357, 374, 378, 384
Delium, 448–452, 453, 467
Delos, 206, 315, 324, 357, 384, 435, 471
Delphi, 68, 69–70, 81, 90, 102, 114, 133–134, 180, 241–242, 266, 285, 330
Demaratus, 120, 133–134, 241, 255
demes, 122–125, 125(map), 209
democracy (*demokratia*), 5–6, 131
  categories of, 4–5
  emergence of, 2–3
  establishment of, 121, 325
  Marathon victory as vindication of, 230–231
demos ('the people'), 4, 74, 88, 121, 131, 234
Demosthenes, 433–443, 446–448, 479, 482–485, 506
Diodorus Siculus, 22, 341–342, 352
Dionysia festival, 380, 467
Dorian Greek language, 44, 83, 434
Dorian invasions, 44–45, 82, 116
Doris and Dorians, 122, 351
Draco, lawmaker at Athens, 73
drinking parties, 147, 370
Dyrrachium, 393

earth and water offerings, 192–193, 200–201, 207, 240–243
earthquakes, 340–343, 493, 521
Ecclesia (People's Assembly), 121, 127–128

INDEX

education, Spartan, 137–145
Egypt and Egyptians, 32, 33, 34, 37, 40, 58, 179, 190
   Athenian expedition, 348, 350, 356–357, 365, 535
   Greek migration, 177
   invasion by Inaros, 346–347
   naval strength, 196, 282
   Persian rule, 182–183, 228, 356
Eion, 318
Elam and Elamites, 179, 180
Elder Cimon, 188
elected officials, 7
Eleusinian Mysteries, 473, 474
Eleusis, 104, 120, 447
Elis and Elaeans, 68, 307, 338, 416, 457, 458, 514
Epaminondas, 520–521
Ephesus, 55, 502
Ephialtes, 257, 259, 344, 346, 351, 375–376
ephors, 87, 96, 458
Epic of Gilgamesh, 33
Epidamnus, 394–395, 400
Epidaurus, 458
Epipolae, 477
Epirus, 101
Eretria and Eretrians, 63–64, 106, 187, 201, 207, 226–227, 499
Erythrae and Erythraeans, 361–362, 365
Etruscans, 57
Euboea, 259, 493
   Artemisium, 253, 256, 259, 266, 285
   Athenian flocks removed to, 414
   cattle and sheep slaughtered by Athenians, 263
   land allocation by Athens, 123, 211, 361
   Lefkandi, 49–50, 64, 82
   Lelantine War, 63–64
   Persian fleet at, 207
   Persian retreat from, 226–227
   raiding of by Pisistratus, 106
   raid on Athens launched from, 120–121
   rebellion, 499
   size of, 48
eunomia (harmony), 99
eunuchs, 197, 208

Euphrates River, 32
Euripides, 380, 485
Eurotas River, 84
Eurybiades, 253, 269
Eurymedon, Battle of, 322, 372
exile
   of Alcmaeonids, 111, 114, 119, 370, 399
   of Demaratus, 134
   in Draco's law code, 73
   from Euboea, 363, 364
   of Isagoras, 119–120
   ostracism, 127, 232–234, 326, 352
   of Pleistonax, 432
   from Thebes, 519
   of Thucydides, 22

The Fall of Miletus (play), 200
farming
   animal labor, 53
   crop cultivation, 31–32, 52–53
   crop surpluses, 51, 53
   helot workforce, 88–89
   innovation, 52
   irrigation, 32, 33
   land ownership, 63
   loans for, 109–110
   vs. pastoralism, 43–44
   and population growth, 32, 51
   slave workforce, 52, 53
   technology, 51
   uncertainty risks, 332–333
   warfare and, 53–54, 61, 63–64, 156–160, 293, 332
festivals, 67–69, 95–96, 110, 111, 141, 337, 379–381

Gallipoli Peninsula, 188, 202, 500
Gerousia, 87
gods and goddesses, 40, 229–230, 333, 336–337
Gorgo, 240, 241
government and politics
   Athens, 64, 69, 72, 121–122, 126–132, 529–532
   constitutions, 361–362, 365
   democratic system, 2–6, 121, 131, 230–231, 325
   modern sentiments, 5–6

INDEX

Sparta, 86–88, 90, 93, 99, 101–102, 131–132, 133–134, 530–532
Granicus, River, 524
Great Panathenaea, 110, 111, 113, 337, 373, 374, 375, 379–380
greaves, 161–162
Greece
   agricultural communities, 31–32
   burial customs, 47, 49–50
   climate, 48–49
   collective sense of identity, 30, 41
   community identity, 12–13, 30, 41, 54–55, 80
   competitiveness among communities, 13
   continuous human presence in, 31
   Dark Ages, 38–39, 44
   first Persian invasion of, 204–223, 243–244
   geography, 48, 157
   hunter-gatherers, 31, 32
   individualism, 536
   language and dialects, 31, 41, 44, 56, 293
   Minoan era, 34–35
   Mycenaean era, 35–40, 49, 71
   origin stories of, 44–46
   Persian attempts to conquer, 11–12
   Phoenician alphabet, 40–41
   political struggles, 16
   population growth, 32, 51, 333
   second Persian invasion of, 248–263, 265–284, 285–304
   shared culture, 526
   shared language, 12
   warfare, 16
   warrior culture, 18
   writing, 40
Gylippus, 477–479, 482–485, 502
gymnasium, 143, 171, 173, 370, 526

Haleis, 348, 350
Halicarnassus, 22
Harmodius, 112–114, 116
harmony (*eunomia*), 99
Hector, 27–28
Helen, 29, 82
Hellas, 56
Hellenistic era, 84
helmets, 161, 164, 230
Helos, 88
helots, 88–89, 93–94, 96, 148, 151–152, 153–154, 340, 341–346, 347–348, 530–531
Hephaestus, 374
Hephaisteion, 374
Hera, 40, 299
Hercules, 44, 82, 125, 210, 375
Hermes, 472
herms, 110, 472
Herodotus, 81, 84, 87, 156, 172, 200, 201–202, 204, 205, 207
   on Athenian naval power, 315
   on Athenian shipbuilding, 235
   background, 22
   on Battle of Marathon, 208, 211, 212–213, 215–218, 220–223, 226–227, 229, 231
   on Battle of Plataea, 291, 296–301
   on Battle of Salamis, 270, 281–282, 285
   on Battle of Tegea, 339
   on Battle of Thermopylae, 255–256, 260–263
   on Callius, 359
   on Cleisthenes, 131, 135
   on Cleomenes, 135
   on Corinthians fleeing Salamis, 348
   on Croesus, 180
   on Darius, 226–228
   on Demaratus, 241
   on democratic system, 325
   on evacuation of Athens, 268
   on helot revolt, 341
   on Histaeus, 194
   on Persian kings, 185–186
   on Persians, 22, 239, 246
   on the Phocians, 266
   on Pisistratus, 104, 105, 107
   on Polycrates, 191
   on second invasion of Greece, 250–251
   on shield design, 161
   on Xerxes, 245, 248–249, 306
Hesiod, 29, 30, 64, 67, 333
Hestaia, 364
Hipparchus, 110, 111–114, 188, 232
hippeis (cavalry), 75, 95, 138–139, 253, 286, 460, 529

INDEX

Hippias, 111–116, 117, 133, 136, 188, 192–193, 202, 205, 208, 215, 231, 233
Hippocrates, 448–449
Histaeus, 194, 199
Hittite Empire, 34, 36, 37
Homer, 30, 31, 40, 41, 43, 45–47, 144, 155, 333, 345, 373
   Iliad, 27–30, 47–48, 51, 62, 71, 85, 125, 154, 158, 166–167, 236, 311
   Odyssey, 28–29
'Homeric age,' 29, 61–63
homoioi ('peers'), 90, 92, 95, 98–99, 405, 528
hoplites, 210–212, 230–231
   Battle of Delium, 449–450
   equipment, 160–163, 165, 168–170, 230, 294, 300
   farmers as, 156–165, 171, 304
   in naval Battles, 277
   Peloponnesian War, 409–410
   phalanx formation, 156–160, 163–173
Hyacinthia festival, 141, 290
Hyacinthian Way, 148

Iliad (Homer), 27–30, 47–48, 51, 62, 71, 85, 125, 154, 158, 166–167, 170, 236, 311
Illyria, 101
Imbros, 202
'the Immortals,' 248, 257, 259, 262
Inaros, 346–347, 356–357
infant exposure, 137
Ionia and Ionians
   Assyrian Empire and, 178
   Athenian kinship, 195
   Athens alliance, 359
   Lydian alliance, 181
   Peloponnesian War, 534
   request for Sparta to speak to Cyrus on their behalf, 186–187
   request to Sparta for protection, 315
   self-government, 102, 179
   Themistocles's messages to, 263
   tribal system, 122
Ionian Greek language, 44
Ionian Revolt, 193–197, 199
Iron Age, 39–40, 51, 57–58

irrigation, 32, 33
Isagoras, 118–120, 133, 136
Isthmian Games, 68, 251, 493
Isthmus of Corinth, 48, 269, 289, 291, 309
Italy, 57, 89
Ithaca, 28
Ithome, Mount, 344, 345, 347–348

Jewish people, 181
judges, 64, 110
Julius Caesar, 172
juries, 64, 129, 365, 376
Justin, 536

Kadesh, Battle of, 37
kakoi ('bad' men), 67, 74–75
kings, 101–102, 182, 528
King's Peace, 518–520
kinship, 61, 80, 243
Knossos, 34, 35, 36
Kynosoura, 83

Lacedaemonius, 344
Laconia, 83, 341
Lade, 196, 205
Laertes, 46
Lamachus, 471, 474–477
land ownership, 52, 53, 63, 145–146, 149, 172–173, 332, 343
Latins, 57
Laurium, 235, 239, 376, 408, 417
laws and legal systems
   arbitration, 64, 75
   development of, 59, 64
   Draco's code, 73
   juries, 64, 129, 365, 376
   magistrates, 64, 69, 72, 110
   Solon's reforms, 73–77, 104
leadership
   age of heroes, 45–47
   Athens as Delian League leader, 317–325
   basileus (king/prince), 46–47, 51, 61
   burial customs for, 47, 49–50, 72
   in cities, 61
   military, 65
   Sparta as coalition leader, 309–312, 316–317

INDEX

tyrants, 69, 72, 102–103, 187–188, 194
wanax (high king), 37–38, 46
Lefkandi, 49–50, 64, 82
legal system. *See* laws and legal systems
Lelantine War, 63–64, 155
Lemnos, 202, 389
Leon, 255
Leonidas, 290
  army size, 253–254
  ascension to throne, 240
  Battle of Thermopylae, 2, 11–12, 17, 257, 259–263, 265, 287
Leotychidas, 313, 317
Lesbos, 66, 196, 316, 323, 417, 425
Leuctra, 520
Limnai, 83
Linear A language, 34
Linear B language, 35, 36–37, 40
long ships, 236–237
long walls, 335(map), 350–351, 352, 410, 517
Lycia, 430
Lycurgus, 14, 81, 87, 89, 104, 105, 145, 150–151
Lydia and Lydians, 58, 102, 179–180, 190, 359
Lyric poets, 66–67, 74, 85–87
Lysander, 502–503, 507, 512–515

Macedonia and Macedonians, 101, 187, 189, 200, 239, 288
Magnesia, 326
Mantineia and Mantineans, 307, 338, 339, 457, 459–462
Marathon, 107
Marathon, Battle of, 17, 107, 208–223, 214(map), 225–227, 277, 304, 307, 312, 324, 371, 381
Mardonius, 283–284, 287–304, 396, 432
marriage, 146, 240
Media and Medes, 179, 180–181
medimnos (measure), 75
Mediterranean Sea, 57
Megacles, 104, 105–106, 111, 118
Megalopolis, 521
Megara and Megarians
  Athenian control of port, 447–448, 501

  Athens alliance, 348–350, 363, 446
  Battle of Plataea, 294–295
  dispute with Corinth, 348–349
  fortification of, 348, 350–351
  map, 108(map)
  Sparta alliance, 348–349, 364, 405, 447–448
  tyrants, 69, 102, 187
  war with Athens, 74, 106, 155
Megarian Decree, 398–399
Melos and Melians, 433, 464–465
Mende, 453–454
Menelaus, 46, 82
mercenaries, 492, 515n
merchants, 55
Mesoa, 83
Mesopotamia, 32
Messenia and Messenians
  Athens alliance, 355–356
  helot status, 88, 148–149
  land of, 98–99
  rebellion against Sparta, 341–342
  Spartan conquest of, 84, 85, 88–89, 91(map), 98–99
Methone, 416
Miletus and Milesians
  conflict with Samos, 388–392
  creation of as a city, 55
  fall of, 199–200
  Ionian Revolt, 193–194, 196
  Persian rule, 181
Mill, John Stuart, 225
Miltiades, 276, 313
  Athenian citizenship, 188–189, 191, 204
  Battle of Marathon, 208, 209, 215–218, 221, 230
  death, 232
  dedication at Olympia, 230
  elected general, 204, 206
  Paros expedition, 231–232
  return to Athens, 202, 231
  role in Persian Empire, 188, 191–192
  trial, 231
  trireme use, 238
Mindarus, 499–500
mineral resources, 55, 71, 235, 239, 318, 376, 393
Minoans, 34–35, 36–37
Minos, 34, 70

INDEX

monarchy, 4–5, 101–103
Mycale, Battle of, 303–304, 305, 313, 314, 325
Mycenaeans, 35–40, 44, 46, 49, 51, 71, 82
Myrmidons, 51
Mytilene and Mytilenians, 425–429, 506

natural resources, 55, 71, 187, 235, 239, 288, 318, 376, 393
Naupactus, 348, 421, 434, 436, 442, 457, 514
naval fleets
  allied, 313–315
  Athenian, 14, 17, 135, 235–239, 244, 270, 274–278, 303, 309, 312, 315, 323, 331, 333, 355, 366, 526, 533, 535
  Delian League, 315–316
  Persian, 250–251, 255, 257, 270–271, 276, 303, 322
  Spartan, 491–492
naval warfare, 274–278, 285, 527
Navarino, Bay of, 436
Naxos and Naxians, 107, 193–194, 206, 319
Nebuchadrezzar, 181
Nemea, River, 516
Nemean Games, 68
Nicias, 433, 465, 470–471, 474–479, 482–486, 492
Nile River, 32
Nineveh, 179
Nisaea, 501
Notium, 502

Odeion, 375, 379, 513
Odysseus, 28, 46, 47, 105, 154, 236
Odyssey (Homer), 28–29
Oenoe, 414
oligarchy, 4–5, 6, 513
Olympiads, 23
Olympias (reconstructed trireme), 237, 275, 277, 277n, 280
Olympic Games, 12, 14, 23, 41, 54, 67–69, 95, 101, 154, 173, 425–426, 458, 467, 514, 526
Olympus, Mount, 48
oracles, 68, 69–70, 81, 90, 102, 107, 114, 133–134, 180, 241–242, 285

Orchomenus, 363, 449
Orthia, Temple of, 138
ostraca, 233, 234, 235
ostracism, 127, 232–234, 268, 272, 326, 345, 352, 357, 363, 370, 471
'owls' (Athenian coins), 376

Pagondas, 448–449, 451
Painted Stoa, 371
palace complexes
  Dark Ages, 38–39
  Knossos, 34, 35, 36
  Lefkandi, 49–50, 64, 82
  Mycenaean era, 36–38, 40, 49, 51, 71, 82
  re-emergence of as cities, 43, 49
Pan, 213, 229, 336
Panathenaea festival, 110, 111, 113, 337, 373, 374, 375, 379–380
pankration (fighting sport), 67
Paris, 29
Parnon, 84
Paros, 231
Parthenon, 2, 3, 17, 372–374, 525
Pasargadae, 185
Patroclus, 27
Pausanias
  accusations against, 531
  Athenians and, 513–514
  Battle of Plataea, 290–294, 296–302
  capture of Byzantium, 314
  criticism of, 325
  death, 325–326, 338, 399, 530
  naval command, 313–314
  rebuke of hoplites, 307
  unpopularity of, 314
Peace of Callias, 359–360, 391
Peace of Nicias, 455–456
'peers' (*homoioi*), 90, 92, 95, 98–99, 405, 528
Peloponnese and Peloponnesians, 48, 82, 133, 268, 269, 288, 312, 316, 334–335(map)
Peloponnesian War, 13, 22, 330, 388, 410–411, 425, 469, 507–508
  Athenian defeat, 509–513
  Athenian preparations, 408–412, 416
  Battle of Pylos, 435–444
  events leading to, 14, 18, 400–403

INDEX

hoplites, 409–410
last battles, 497(map)
Mytilene rebellion, 425–429
Sparta and its Peloponnesian allies, 334–335(map)
Spartan preparations, 405–408, 411–412, 416
Spartan victory, 509–513, 534, 535
Penelope, 46
pentakosiomedimnoi ('500 measures men'), 75, 76
pentaconters, 236–237, 238, 270, 275
People's Assembly (*Ecclesia*), 121, 127–128
Perdiccas, 397, 452, 454
Pericles
  adversaries, 369–370
  affairs, 382–383, 388–389
  Alcibiades and, 457, 466
  anglicization of name, 23
  argument for war with Sparta, 399–400, 422
  aristocratic background, 370–371, 383, 469
  Athenian heralds turned away, 414
  Black Sea voyage, 393
  conference of Greek states, 378
  death, 469
  elected general, 369, 419
  expedition to Samos, 389–390
  family life, 382
  festivals, 379
  jokes about, 398
  Megara invasion, 416
  monument-building program, 372, 374–375, 384, 513
  oration to honour war dead, 417
  Peloponnesian War, 410
  plague losses, 419
  recalled from Euboea, 363
  resemblance to Pisistratus, 370
  responsibility of for Peloponnesian war, 401
  stories about, 381–384
  support for Ephialtes, 376
  wiliness, 364
perioeci ('neighbors'), 87–88, 90, 92, 94, 96, 148, 341, 351
The Persae (Aeschylus), 279
Persepolis, 185

Persian Empire. *See* Achaemenid Persian Empire; Persian Wars
Persian Wars, 18
  Battle of Marathon, 17, 107, 208–223, 214(map), 225–227
  Battle of Plataea, 12, 17, 291–304
  Battle of Salamis, 12, 17, 269–284, 273(map), 285–287
  Battle of Thermopylae, 2, 11–12, 253–263, 258(map)
  first invasion of Greece, 204–223, 243–244
  Ionian Revolt, 193–197, 199
  second invasion of Greece, 248–263, 265–284, 285–304
phalanx formation, 156–160, 163–173
Phaleron, 235
Pheidas, 372–373, 383–384
Philipiddes, 209, 213, 229
Philip II of Macedon, 1, 523–524, 536
philosophy, 333, 370, 522
Phocis and Phocians, 254–255, 259, 262, 266–267, 288, 351, 363, 516
Phoenicia and Phoenicians, 40–41, 48, 50, 55, 57, 190, 196, 237, 282
Phormio, 421
piracy, 35, 106, 171, 189–190, 236, 318
Piraeus, 235, 276, 326, 350, 410, 490, 499, 507, 517
Pisistratus
  death, 110, 111
  expulsion, 105, 106–107
  faked attack on self, 105
  festivals created, 379
  life abroad, 106–107, 187
  Pericles's resemblance to, 370
  purification of Delos, 435
  reforms, 109–110
  relationship with Spartans, 114, 117
  stories about, 106
  supporters of, 104–105, 111
  as tyrant, 105, 107–111, 208, 233
  war-making, 126, 155
Pitane, 83
plague, 417–419, 423, 430, 435, 446, 485
Plataea, Battle of, 12, 17, 291–304, 307, 325, 330, 338, 339, 342, 371

617

INDEX

Plataea and Plataeans
  Athens alliance, 266
  Battle of Marathon, 210, 226, 324
  conflict with Thebes, 115, 308, 412–414
  evacuation of, 419–420
  rejection of Persian appeal, 201
  restored to homeland, 307–309
  siege of, 420, 425, 431–432
  as Spartan prisoners of war, 432
  Theban occupation of, 432, 463
Plato, 57, 213, 468
plays and playwrights, 200, 279, 380–381, 428
Pleistonax, 364, 410, 432–433, 478
Plutarch, 22, 87, 137, 340, 365, 477
  on Alcibiades, 475, 487, 495, 508
  on Battle of Plataea, 295
  on Cimon, 352
  on helot rebellion, 340, 341, 344
  Lycurgus biography, 81, 150–151
  on Nicias and Alcibiades potential ostracism, 471
  on Pericles, 370, 375, 376, 383
  on Sicily, 470
  Solon biography, 74
  on Spartan child rearing, 138
  on Spartan marriage, 146
  on Themistocles, 235
poets, 66–67, 74, 85–87, 95–96, 111
polemarch, 72, 209, 215
Polycrates, 189–191
population growth, 32, 51, 71, 89–90, 118, 333, 371
Poseidon, 40, 340, 399
Potidaea, 396–397, 399–400, 405, 410, 416, 418, 419
Priam, 27–28
Priene, 388
Procles, 433–434
Propylaea, 374–375, 379
prytany (delegation), 127–128
Psytalleia, 278
Pylos, 435–444, 440(map), 456, 479, 501
Pyrrhic dance, 173
Pythia, 114
Pythian Games, 68
Python, 364

raiding, 171, 172
religious beliefs and practices
  Carneia festival, 213, 254–255, 269, 462
  central role of, 68–70, 336
  cults, 336, 378, 419
  earth and water offerings, 192–193, 200–201, 207, 240–243
  gods and goddesses, 40, 229–230, 333, 336–337
  gods honored after success in Battle, 229–230
  Hyacinthia festival, 141, 290
  priestly class, 33
  ritual punishment, 247
  sacrifices, 33, 49, 68–69, 72, 109, 122, 158, 209, 229, 255, 263, 279, 299
  temples, 336–337
  Zoroastrianism, 184
round ships, 236

sacrifices, 33, 49, 68–69, 72, 109, 122, 158, 209, 229, 255, 263, 279, 299
Saka, 218
Salamis, 74, 104, 123, 125, 155, 242, 267, 290, 304, 348
Salamis, Battle of, 12, 17, 269–284, 273(map), 285–287, 311, 314
Samos and Samians, 206
  acceptance of Alcibiades, 498
  blockade, 390
  Byzantium alliance, 389–390
  conflict with Miletus, 388–392
  Delian League, 316, 323
  made a democracy, 389
  Persian fleet at, 290, 303
  Persian support of, 389–391
  Polycrates rule, 189–191
  Spartan siege, 190–191
Sappho, 66
Sardis, 180, 200, 227, 248, 493
Saronic Gulf, 267, 271–272, 274, 278
satraps, 185, 191, 199, 493
Schliemann, Heinrich, 35
Sciathos, 255
Scione, 453–454
Sciritae, 460–461
Scyros, 318

INDEX

Scythia and Scythians, 134–135, 189, 202
sea peoples, 38
Segesta, 469–470, 474
Seven Sages, 73
shields, 160–161, 165, 169–170, 230, 436
shipbuilding, 235–239, 245–246, 288, 393
Sicily, 57, 125, 244, 469–485, 480–481(map), 489–491, 531, 534
siege warfare, 29, 116, 169, 179, 190–191, 194, 196, 207–208, 231, 414
slaves and slavery
  acceptance of, 4
  as a consequence of debt, 74–75
  exclusion of from civic life, 65
  farming workforce, 52, 53
  as fighters during invasions, 209, 230
  flight to Decelea, 534–535
  helots, 88–89, 93–94
  treatment of, 52
  war captives, 52, 90
Socrates, 16, 451, 466–467
Sollium, 416
Solon, 14, 73–77, 85, 102, 104, 105, 109, 118, 155, 496
Sophocles, 380, 381, 382, 389
Sparta and Spartans
  alliances, 13, 17–18, 97, 243–244, 284, 290, 304, 309–311, 330, 334–335(map), 343–344, 385–386, 457, 533
  aristocracy, 89, 528–529
  Battle of Marathon, 223, 226, 337
  Battle of Mycale, 303–304, 305, 313
  Battle of Plataea, 17, 291–304
  Battle of Salamis, 269–284, 273(map)
  Battle of Thermopylae, 2, 11–12, 253–263, 258(map), 265–266, 301, 337
  Carneia festival, 213, 254–255, 269, 462
  child rearing and education, 137–145
  citizenship, 145, 150
  class hierarchies, 93–95, 98
  coalition leadership role, 309–312, 316–317
  colonization, 89
  community identity, 83
  conquests, 84, 89–90, 91(map), 92, 96–97, 153, 532
  Crypteia ('secret service'), 151
  daily life, 149–151
  decline of, 521
  diplomacy, 186–187, 190, 240–241, 242–243
  earthquakes, 340–343
  espionage, 245
  helots, 88–89, 93–94, 96, 148, 151–152, 153–154, 340, 341–346, 347–348, 530–531
  historical sources, 20–22, 81–82, 136–137
  homoioi ('peers'), 90, 92, 95, 98–99, 405, 528–529
  Hyacinthia festival, 141, 290
  laconic personality of, 139–141
  land ownership, 145–146, 149, 172–173, 343
  Lycurgus's reforms, 81
  military power, 98, 135–136, 154, 173–174, 213, 317, 331, 337–338, 347, 404–405, 510–511, 526
  military training, 93, 95, 138–139, 144, 149, 173, 206, 297
  naval fleet, 491–492
  origin stories of, 44–46, 82–83
  Peloponnese dominance, 339–340
  perioeci, 87–88, 90, 92, 94, 96, 148, 341
  phalanx formation, 163, 167, 173–174
  political system, 86–88, 90, 93, 99, 101–102, 131–132, 133–134, 530–532
  population growth, 89–92, 404–405
  religious beliefs and practices, 337–338, 526
  rivalry with Athens, 17, 535–536
  secrecy of, 20, 81, 150
  security, 83–84, 402
  shows of defiance to Persia, 201–202, 240
  slavery, 88, 90, 93
  territory growth, 83–84
  the 300, 2, 11–12, 253–254, 259, 265, 300, 337

INDEX

Sparta and Spartans (*continued*)
  trade, 177
  truce with Athens, 357
  villages, 140(map)
  women's freedom and independence, 95, 145–146, 240
spears, 162, 164, 167, 230
Sphacteria, 436–444, 440(map), 455
spoils of war, 97, 162, 319, 372
states, 60–61
Strymon, River, 318, 392–393
Sumer and Sumerians, 32, 33
Susa, 185
symposia (drinking clubs), 467–469, 472, 496
Syracuse and Syracusans, 125, 244, 408, 469, 472, 475–477, 480(map), 482–485, 490

Talents, weight, 231n
Tanagra, 352, 353, 448, 449
Tarentum, 89
taxation, 76, 110, 182, 185, 194, 430
Taygetus, 84
Tegea and Tegeans, 84, 90, 97–98, 154, 298–300, 339, 458–460
Telemachus, 46
Tempe, 253
temples, 336–337
The Ten, 514
Thasos and Thasians, 322–323, 343, 345–346
Thebes and Thebans
  alliance with Mardonius, 292
  Athens alliance, 18, 519
  Battle of Delium, 449–450
  Battle of Thermopylae, 262–263
  conflict with Athens, 18, 298
  conflict with Sparta, 18, 308
  defeat by Plataea, 115
  invasion of Athens, 120, 135, 192
  invasion of Plataea, 412–414
  as a major city, 43
  military strength, 330
  Sparta alliance, 414, 533
Themistocles, 339
  Battle of Marathon, 235
  Battle of Salamis, 269–272, 274–275, 281–283, 286
  Battle of Thermopylae, 253, 257

  delegation to Sparta, 309–310
  extortion accusations, 286
  fortification of Piraeus, 326, 350
  hoplite service, 287
  invasion of Phocis, 516
  naval fleet expansion, 235, 238–239, 246, 376
  ostracism of Pericles, 363
  ostracism votes against, 234–235, 326
  Persian ruse, 271–272, 274–275, 289
  popularity of, 286, 326
  sacrifices, 279
Thermopylae, Battle of, 2, 11–12, 253–263, 258(map), 265–266, 287, 301
Thersites, 47
Theseus, 70–71, 125, 318, 375
Thespiae, 449
Thessaly, 94, 251–252, 287, 292, 352
thêtes ('hired men'), 75–76, 118, 129, 130, 230, 492, 498, 499, 504, 529
the Thirty, 513–514
Thirty Years' Peace, 387, 398, 405
Thrace and Thracians, 101, 106–107, 187, 189, 200, 206, 292, 314, 322, 534
Thucydides, 24, 35, 40, 312–313, 359, 365–366
  on Alcibiades, 495
  on Athenian hoplites, 409
  on Athenian shipbuilding, 315
  background, 22
  on Corinth's war with Corcyra, 395, 396, 430–431
  on Delian League, 316, 319, 323
  on early Greek inhabitants, 43
  on earthquake in Sparta, 341, 343
  on Egyptian rebellion, 356
  exile, 22
  on future visitors to Athens and Sparta, 525
  on helot rebellion, 345
  on Homer's use of Hellene, 30
  on the Megarian Decree, 398–399
  oratory skills, 369
  on Peloponnesian War, 22, 388, 400–401, 403, 423, 427, 434, 435, 442, 445–446, 451, 453, 455, 457, 460, 464–465, 500–501, 507–508

on Pericles, 369, 380–381, 417
on Persian fleet, 322
on phalanx formation, 163, 167
on Pisistratus, 109
on plague, 417
on Samos-Miletus conflict, 392
on Sicilian expedition, 470, 478, 484, 485, 489
on Sparta's opposition to Athenian fortification, 309
on Themistocles, 239
on tyranny, 103
Thurii, 366–367
Tigris River, 32
Tissaphernes, 493–496, 498, 500
Torone, 454
trade, 50, 53, 55–56, 58, 177, 236, 333, 376
treaties, 97, 159, 346, 359–360, 366, 387, 391, 398, 405, 519
'tremblers,' 150, 456
triaconters, 236
trials, 109, 110
tribal system, 122–125, 336
tribute, 58, 178, 179, 182, 324, 374, 378–379, 430, 501
triremes, 205, 235, 237–238, 246, 250, 253, 255, 257, 270, 274–278, 280–281, 322
Troezen, 267
Trojans, 166
Trojan War, 27–28, 29, 44, 71, 373, 527
Troy, 27–28, 312
truces, 68, 134, 154, 352, 358, 366, 387, 425, 426, 438, 458, 494
Turkey, 55
tyrants, 69, 72, 102–103, 187–188, 194, 528
Tyrtaeus, 85–89, 95, 96, 98, 144, 157, 167–168, 173, 460

Uruk, 32, 33

wanax (high king), 37–38, 46
warfare
 archers, 219, 268, 275, 294–295, 300, 410
 army composition, 211–212
 Assyrian Empire, 178–179
 Athenian, 125–126
 basileus leadership, 51
 body armor, 161–162, 295
 burial customs, 221–222, 229–230
 casualties, 97, 156, 222, 226, 227, 257, 276, 293, 350, 461
 citizen soldiers, 20, 65, 90, 92, 171–172, 532
 farming and, 53–54, 61, 63–64, 156–160, 293, 332
 gods honored after success in Battle, 229–230
 in Greek art and literature, 154–155, 166–169
 helmets, 161, 164
 hoplites, 156–171, 210–212, 409–410
 in the *Iliad*, 166–167, 170, 311
 Mycenaean era, 36
 naval, 274–278, 285
 phalanx formation, 156–160, 163–173
 poems about, 66–67
 rules of, 160, 415
 shields, 160–161, 165, 169–170, 230, 436
 siege, 29, 116, 169, 179, 190–191, 194, 196, 207–208, 231, 344, 414
 spears, 164, 167, 230
 spoils, 97, 162, 319, 371–372
 truces, 68, 134, 154, 352, 358, 366, 387, 425, 426, 438, 458, 494
 weapons, 162
warrior culture, 18, 85
warships, 205, 235–239, 285. *See also* triremes
wealth, 65–66, 77
weapons, 162, 164, 167, 230
women, 5, 65, 66, 68, 95, 145–146, 240, 267, 337, 382, 383, 468,
wrestling, 370
writing, development of, 33, 40

Xanthippus, 232, 363
Xenophon, 22, 505, 523
 on lover-beloved relationships, 141–142
 on Spartan child rearing and education, 138, 144

INDEX

Xerxes, 239, 248–249, 263, 267, 536
  accession to throne, 228
  assassination, 306
  Battle of Salamis, 12
  Battle of Thermopylae, 11–12, 253–263, 265–266
  diplomacy, 240–241
  invasion of Greece, 248–263, 305–306, 329, 343
  Mardonius and, 292, 294
  reputation damage, 305–307
  tent of, 375
  war preparations, 244, 245, 355

'yoked men' (*zeugitai*), 75, 76, 118–119, 121, 126, 498

Zakynthos, 416
zeugitai ('yoked men'), 75, 76, 118–119, 121, 126, 498
Zeus, 40, 68, 69, 347–348, 384
Zoroastrianism, 184